CANADIAN HISTO
BEFORE CONFEDERATION

Essays and Interpretations

CANADIAN HISTORY BEFORE CONFEDERATION

Essays and Interpretations

Edited by

J. M. BUMSTED
Simon Fraser University

Second Edition

1979

IRWIN-DORSEY LIMITED
Georgetown, Ontario   L7G 4B3

© IRWIN-DORSEY LIMITED, 1972 and 1979

ISBN 0-256-02136-8

Printed in the United States of America

1 2 3 4 5 6 7 8 9 0 ML 6 5 4 3 2 1 0 9

PREFACE

The purpose of this revised collection of readings is to offer to teachers and students of pre-Confederation Canada a convenient sampling of some of the best articles—most of them comparatively recent—written on a complex period. The basic criteria that have been employed in first compiling and then revising this collection are many. I have attempted to provide some sort of comprehensive regional and chronological coverage, although obviously perfection is impossible. This Second Edition contains more material on French Canada, including several articles appearing for the first time in English. In general, articles which have been selected are highly interpretive and stimulating because of interesting methodological or conceptual frameworks; many offer revisionist views of longstanding interpretations. The reader will also note a continued preference for material outside the traditional political and constitutional history. Such emphasis more than ever reflects recent broad trends in the historiography of the pre-Confederation period, providing a useful supplement to textbooks and other teaching aids which have emphasized political and constitutional developments. It must be added that I have purposely kept the structural organization of the selections which follow to a minimum, in an attempt to permit maximum flexibility for those who use this work in the classroom situation.

March 1979   J. M. BUMSTED

PREFACE

CONTENTS

part one

Discovery, Exploration, and Early Colonization to 1645

1

NEW LIGHT ON VINLAND FROM THE SAGAS*

Haraldur Bessason

Who first discovered America? This is a question which has been hotly debated for a very long period of time, with any number of alternatives to the popularly accepted Christopher Columbus being advanced. Suggestions have ranged from the Phoenicians of classical antiquity to Irish monks in the first centuries after Christ to Portuguese mariners in the 14th century. In such cases very scanty evidence—perhaps only a line or two in a manuscript stating the sighting of "land across the seas"—has been combined with assumption and imagination to produce another challenger for Columbus.

Of all the pre-Columbian candidates, the strongest case can be made out for the Vikings, those great Scandinavian warriors and mariners of the Middle Ages. It is indisputable that the Vikings settled Iceland and Greenland in the North Atlantic before A.D. 1000, and evidence from a variety of sources supports Viking literary remains which tell of the discovery of a new land to the west of Greenland. Recent archaeological excavations in Newfoundland and a manuscript map which has been dated as being from the mid-15th century would seem to indicate that the Vikings not only made a landfall but even attempted a settlement in North America. Nevertheless, as Professor Haraldur Bessason suggests in the following article, the basis of our knowledge of Viking activities in North America comes principally from Icelandic prose epics of a somewhat later date than the events they chronicle. As with other such sources—the *Iliad*, for example—it is difficult to distinguish demonstra-

*Mosaic, 1 (1967), 52-65.

ble fact from poetic license. Professor Bessason attempts to make this separation by comparing the sources with the known historical and archaeological evidence. How does he go about doing this? Can his techniques be applied to other nonhistorical literary evidence in other times? What limitations do his efforts and the whole body of evidence for Viking exploration have? Are his arguments convincing?

SUGGESTIONS FOR FURTHER READING

Gwyn Jones, *The Norse Atlantic Saga* (London: Oxford University Press, 1963).

T. J. Oleson, *Early Voyages and Northern Approaches, 1000–1632* (Toronto: McClelland and Stewart, 1963).

R. A. Skelton, et al., *The Vinland Map and the Tartar Relation* (New Haven: Yale University Press, 1965).

J.M.B.

In 1964 Helge Ingstad claimed to have uncovered proof of a pre-Columbian Viking settlement in northern Newfoundland. Mr. Ingstad's announcement of his discovery, and the subsequent publication by Yale University in 1965 of a formerly unknown pre-Columbian geographic map showing Vinland, have intensified scholarly interest in the Old Icelandic sources on Vinland.[1] It is safe to say that if Old Icelandic records of the early voyages to the Western Hemisphere had not been preserved, these two events would have had little significance.

The two Icelandic sagas which deal with the voyages to Vinland about A.D. 1000 fall into the category of Family Sagas, prose narratives which are regarded primarily as literature. A comparison between the Family Sagas and historical works from the era in question (cf. for instance, *Landnámabók (The Book of Settlements)*, from about 1140 which contains a list of settlers in Iceland between 874 and 930) has convinced scholars that in numerous details the authors of the Family Sagas digressed from historical fact. It is therefore safe to state that the chief merit of the Family Sagas lies in their stylistic qualities and the way in which they depict a heathen heritage in a newly Christianized society. However, it is also correct that in varying degrees the Family Sagas are based upon an historical foundation.

In the present article special emphasis has been placed upon a recent

---

[1]The following works are cited throughout the article: Helge Ingstad, *Vesterveg til Vinland*, vol. 9 (Oslo: Gyldendal Norsk Forlag, 1965), pp. 245–53; *The Vinland Map and the Tartar Relation* (New Haven: Yale U.P., 1965) [abbreviated VM in subsequent references]; Jón Jóhannesson, *Íslendinga saga*, (Reykjavík, 1956); *Íslendingabók*, ed. H. Hermannsson, issued by Cornell University Library as *Islandica*, 20 (Ithaca, N.Y., 1930); G. Turville-Petre, *Origins of Icelandic Literature*, (Oxford U.P., 1953); for a detailed discussion of the historical and imaginative components of the sagas, see Sigurður Nordal, "Sagalitteraturen," *Nordisk Kultur*, vol. 8, B, especially pp. 270–73; Sven B. F. Jansson, *Sagorna om Vinland*, vol. 1 (Lund, 1944), pp. 259–60; Vilhjálmur Stefánsson, *Iceland*, (New York, 1939); T. J. Oleson, *Early Voyages and Northern Approaches* (Toronto: McClelland & Stewart, 1963).

but frequently overlooked theory (cf. the works by Nordal and Jóhannesson referred to below) which claims that one of the two Sagas about Vinland, i.e., *Groenlendingasaga*, contains a particularly strong element of fact. This theory has been slightly expanded below. In their attempts to determine the relative strength of the historical foundation in the sagas about Vinland, scholars have naturally made a detailed comparison of them. In most instances (Jóhannesson's work quoted below is excepted) this has been a futile effort, because of many difficult problems regarding both the origin and dating of the two sagas. It will be shown here that the newly discovered cartographical evidence of the Vinland Map tends to confirm the historical element in the literary sources.

This article will also suggest that, in addition to a reasonably accurate account of the discovery of the Western Hemisphere, the author of *Groenlendingasaga* may have wished to endow his book with certain moral-social overtones. This point is intended merely as a suggestion of a new approach to one of the literary aspects of the sagas about Vinland.

I

The Icelanders established their ancient Republic in A.D. 930. At that time the art of writing still had not been introduced; thus the code of laws announced by the speaker of the legislative assembly could not be recorded. This long and detailed code grew even longer over the years with the addition of amendments. In the early years of the Icelandic National Assembly *(Althing)*, it became standard procedure for its Speaker *(Lögsögumaður)* to proclaim, from memory, one third of the law code every year. Thus, through three consecutive sessions of *Althing*, the recital of the entire (unwritten) code was carefully checked by those in attendance who were competent in law. This surely arduous feat of memorization probably contributed, early in the 12th century, to the use of writing: according to ancient sources, a portion of the Old Icelandic law code is the first recorded item in Icelandic, and dates from the winter of 1117–1118.

One may imagine that nostalgia for Norway provided early generations of newcomers to Iceland with a sharper awareness of their heritage than was the case with those relatives who had never left their native valleys of Norway. Later on, in 12th and 13th century literary works, this awareness manifested itself as a preoccupation with Iceland's heroic past. The first settlers reached Iceland about A.D. 870; 60 years later the Icelandic *Althing* was founded. These events and the subsequent introduction of Christianity in the year 1000 provided the Icelanders with enough material for their books when they were prepared, finally, to begin writing in the vernacular.

The first historical work to be written in Icelandic was *Íslendingabók (The Book of the Icelanders)*, composed and committed to parchment shortly after 1122 by Ari Thorgilsson the Learned, whom Turville-Petre called "the father of Icelandic history." Of the original two versions of *Íslendingabók*, only one has survived covering the history of Iceland from the beginning of the settlement in 874 up to the period when the book was written. Though consisting of a mere summary of major events, *Íslendingabók* is the most valuable Icelandic historical source, the more so because of the author's meticulous care in recording only such information as he was able to prove to be correct. However, this modest scholar reminded his readers that "it will be our duty to correct misstatements, if any, which occur in this history" (*Islandica,* vol. 20, p. 47).

Íslendingabók contains the earliest reference in Icelandic to both Greenland and Vinland. It reads as follows:

> The country which is called Greenland was discovered and settled from Iceland. Erik the Red was the name of a man from Breidafjord who went from here thither and took possession of land at the place which since has been called Eriksfjord. He gave a name to the country and called it Green-land, and said that the people would desire to go thither, if the country had a good name. Both east and west in the country they found human habita-tions, fragments of skin boats and stone implements from which it was evident that the same people had been there as inhabited Wineland and whom the Greenlanders called Skrellings. He began colonizing the country fourteen or fifteen winters before Christianity came to Iceland [985 or 986] according to what a man who himself had gone thither with Erik the Red told Thorkel Gellisson in Greenland.[2]

Even though this chapter does no more than mention Vinland, its careful documentation makes it our most important historical evidence about the discovery of North America prior to Columbus. Ari the Learned selected his informants with extreme caution; the people he quoted were "learned in many things and trustworthy." Among these people was Ari's paternal uncle, Thorkell Gellisson "who remembered far back," and who not only had been to Greenland himself, but had learned about its early history and about Vinland from a man in Greenland "who himself had gone thither with Erik the Red" (*Islandica,* vol. 20, p. 60).

In the author's own time the Icelanders seem to have formed so defi-nite a concept of the land discovered named Vinland that references to it required no explanation. Its native population were referred to as Skraelings (meaning "weaklings") which, as Ari the Learned states, was a term later applied to the indigenous people of Greenland by settlers from Iceland. However, it was upon the cultural evidence of certain artifacts—not physical resemblance—that the settlers of Greenland con-cluded that the people who inhabited that country must be the same as the Skraelings of Vinland (*Islandica,* vol. 20, p. 64).

---

[2]*Islandica,* 20 (1929), 64, Halldór Hermannsson's translation is used here; his spelling of proper names has not been changed, even though the same names are spelled differently elsewhere in this article; Eiríkr the Red is usually considered to have been born in Norway; recently the present writer tried to prove that Eiríkr must have been born in Iceland, see *The Icelandic Canadian* (Winnipeg), Winter 1965, 13-15. An Icelandic author, Árni Óla, has maintained the same theory about Eiríkr's birthplace, see *Lesbók Morgunblaðsins* (Reyk-javík, December 25, 1965). This problem concerns the chronology of 10th-century events, and a correct solution is therefore important.

II

Ari the Learned's scholarly influence on Old Icelandic writings prevailed through both the 12th and 13th centuries. During the latter half of that period, the saga authors' concern for historical correctness and their steadily evolving literary technique may be said to have achieved a good balance in both the Sagas of the Kings (*Konungasögur*) and the Family Sagas (*Íslendingasögur*). The authors of these works were prepared to restrain their imaginations and to avoid writing about subjects which had little or no foundation in reality. Every Family Saga contains a literary component in addition to a factual-historical one. These two elements can be evaluated only by placing each saga in its proper relation to other Family Sagas and by comparing its accounts with the relatively few historical works such as *Íslendingabók* and *Landnámabók*, both from the 12th century. The two sagas about Vinland—The Saga of the Greenlanders (*Groenlendingasaga*), Greenlanders signifying Icelandic settlers there, and The Saga of Eiríkr the Red (*Eiríks saga*)—belong to the group of Family Sagas.

In content the Family Sagas are not entirely restricted to Icelandic themes. Pre-Christian Iceland is, to be sure, the main theme in most of them, but every saga contains description of places outside Iceland, some as remote as Constantinople or Vinland. As far as their origins go, translations of clerical writings exercised some influence on their form. G. Turville-Petre pointed out that among the religious writings which found their way into Iceland were the first written biographies; this type of literature "did not teach the Icelanders what to think or what to say, but it taught them how to say it" (*Origins of Icelandic Literature*, p. 142).

Long before the first Family Sagas, orally preserved legends about ancient Scandinavian or ancient Germanic heroes were popular in Iceland. Leading laymen and learned church officials of the 12th and 13th centuries did not consider it worth their while to record such stories, because of their disproportionate supernatural element, even though they were valued as entertainment (for the early existence of these stories, cf. *Sturtunga saga* [Reykjavík, 1946], p. 27).

Although Old Icelandic legends are not to be regarded as historical sources, the authors of the Family Sagas were well aware that if their own books were to meet with approval—as these were circulated in a few manuscripts, probably among chieftains, and read out aloud at public gatherings—they must incorporate some of the features which had made the heroic legends popular. This explains in part why a certain portion of a Family Saga must be discarded, in order to reveal those elements which are historically relevant.

There was an interval, between the events (often dealing with pre-Christian Iceland) related in the sagas and the time they were written down, of up to three centuries. Probably a Family Saga could never have been preserved in oral tradition in its entirety. It seems that every saga was simultaneously created and written down by an individual author who deliberately added his own literary touch to subject matter gathered from both oral and written sources. Of the oral sources, Old Norwegian and Icelandic poetry dealing with the most ancient events is of particular significance. Because of its rhyme and metre this poetry could be memorized and preserved intact, from the time of its composition in either the 9th or the 10th century, until it was written down and used as historical evidence by saga authors some centuries later.

Groenlendingasaga, which, according to recent scholarly findings, is the older of the two sagas about Vinland, draws quite heavily on oral accounts. Indeed it is stated at the end of the saga that some of its accounts originated with Thorfinnr Karlsefni, the man who made the most determined attempt to settle in Vinland before he moved back to Iceland early in the 11th century. *Eiríks saga,* which has been assigned to a later date than *Groenlendingasaga,*[3] may have been largely based on written sources and even on the *Groenlendingasaga.*

The attitude of the Icelanders towards their own literature underwent certain changes during the Family Saga period, 1200 to 1300. One notices gradually increasing use of such conventional devices as dreams, forebodings, and predictions, bearing upon the future of the characters concerned. At the same time, earlier scholarly precision gradually yielded to a steadily growing demand for dramatic presentation.

A few works written by members of the Benedictine Order at Thingeyrar in northern Iceland, c. 1200, did not follow the main trends in Old Icelandic literature at that time, being designed to glorify the founders of Christianity in Scandinavia, especially the two Christian champions of Norway, King Olafr Tryggvason and King Olafr Haraldsson (St. Olaf). It may be suggested that the clerics at Thingeyrar felt that "the end justifies the means," for they did not hesitate to exchange uninteresting fact for exciting fable if such an exchange would enhance the reputation of their Christian heroes. There is at least one instance where this unscholarly attitude may have subsequently confused the author of *Eiríks saga,* in his account of Leifr Eiríksson's discovery of North America (Nordal, pp. 248–49).

III

There is only one manuscript in which *Groenlendingasaga* has been preserved in its entirety, the *Flateyjarbók* from the late 14th century; two similar versions of *Eiríks saga* have been preserved, the *Hauksbók* from the early 14th century, and a 15th century manuscript called *Skálholtsbók.* Even though the manuscripts of the two sagas about Vinland date back only to the 14th and the 15th centuries, they are copies of transcripts of older books which were lost before book collectors were able to get hold of them. Nevertheless, there is every reason to believe that these extant vellum manuscripts are close to their 12th and 13th

---

[3]*Islenzk fornrit,* vol. 4 (Reykjavik, 1935); *Groenlendingasaga,* p. 269; Jón Jóhannesson, "Aldur Graenlendinga sögu," *Nordaela* (Reykjavík 1956) pp. 150–57; for an English translation, see *Saga-Book,* vol. 26, pt. i (London: Viking Society for Northern Research, 1963).

century originals.[4] What the sagas have to say about Vinland is briefly summarized below.

Groenlendingasaga tells about six voyages from Iceland and Greenland in the direction of the Western Hemisphere shortly before and after 1000 (*Íslenzk fornrit*, vol. 4, pp. 246–268). The first voyage was that of Byarni Herjólfsson who in 986 undertook a voyage from Iceland to Greenland, but was driven off course to the eastern shores of North America. According to the saga, Bjarni never stepped ashore in the three lands or regions which he discovered as he sailed northward along the eastern seaboard. The first land which Bjarni sighted was heavily treed and hilly, the second was wooded and level, the third was a mountainous land with glaciers. The second voyage in *Groenlendingasaga* is that of Leifr, who, having learned about the lands to the westward from Bjarni Herjólfsson, decided to buy Bjarni's ship and sailed from Greenland with 35 men, until he reached the land which Bjarni had sighted last. Having explored this land, Leifr named it Helluland (Flatstoneland). From Helluland Leifr and his men sailed southward, until they reached a level and wooded land to which Leifr gave the name Markland (Woodland). Two days' sailing from Markland, Leifr and his men came to the third land, north of which lay an island. This was the land of plenty to which Leifr gave the name Vinland (Wineland) after having wintered there. The third voyage in the direction of Vinland was made by Thorvaldr, Leifr's brother, who was slain. The fourth voyage under the direction of Thorsteinn Eiríksson, Leifr's brother, and his wife Gudridr Thorbjarnardottir, was unsuccessful. Their ship ran into foul weather and was driven back to Greenland, where Thorsteinn soon died. The fifth voyage described in our saga was made by Thorfinnr Karlsefni Thordarson, Gudridr Thorbjarnardottir's second husband. Thorfinnr and Gudridr went to Vinland with 60 men and 5 women and had every intention of settling there. However, these people met with violent opposition from the native population of Vinland, and returned to Greenland. Later man and wife moved to Iceland. During her stay in Vinland Gudridr gave birth to a son who was named Snorri Thorfinnsson, who thus appears to have been the first white child to be born in North America. The sixth voyage described was eventually dominated by the somewhat notorious sister of Leifr Eiríksson, Freydís, who after an eventful stay in Vinland took her party back to Greenland.

Now we turn to the second saga, *Eiríks saga*, which contains accounts of only three voyages (*Sagorna om Vinland*, vol. 1, pp. 48–77). The first voyage is that of Leifr Eiríksson who was commissioned by King Olafr Tryggvason of Norway to bring Christianity to his father's (Eiríkr the Red's) settlement in Greenland in the year 1000. Our source has it that on his way from Norway to Greenland Leifr was blown off course to the shores of a land of which he had no previous knowledge. The land which Leifr discovered is not mentioned by name, but later on in the saga it is referred to as Vinland. The second voyage was made from Greenland

---

[4]This matter has been carefully analyzed by S. B. F. Jansson, *Sagorna om Vinland*, vol. 1, (Lund, 1944).

with either Thorsteinn Eiríksson or his father, Eiríkr the Red, at the helm. The saga states that these men headed for the land which Leifr had discovered, but, having failed to reach it, they managed to get back to Greenland. The third voyage in *Eiríks saga* is that of Thorfinnr Karlsefni whose party is said to have sailed to Vinland on three ships carrying 160 men and women as well as livestock. Karlsefni's stay in Vinland and his attempt to settle there is recorded in detail.

Neither *Groenlendingasaga* nor *Eiríks saga* claims to have recorded all the voyages that had been made to the Western Hemisphere up to the time of writing. Therefore discussion of the total number of voyages will not be attempted. Rather, our primary problem here is to note the way in which the two sagas about Vinland overlap in their accounts and the obvious discrepancies which exist between them.

IV

The theory that *Groenlendingasaga* is older than *Eiríks saga* is well established, if fairly recent; yet this question of dating has been unduly overlooked, even by such notable scholars as the editors of the Vinland Map which was published in 1965. The correct dating of the two sagas about Vinland is of great importance, because it concerns their relative merits as historical documents. Until recently, *Eiríks saga* was considered to be older and historically more reliable than *Groenlendingasaga* (*Íslenzk fornrit,* vol. 4, pp. lxxxv and xci). This concept has still not been completely abandoned, though scholars have attained a high degree of accuracy in determining the dates of composition of the two sagas.

In his survey of 1953, Sigurður Nordal argued that possibly an Icelandic monk, Gunnlaugr Leifsson (d. 1219), was responsible for creating the story which claims that Leifr Eiríksson accidentally came upon the shores of North America while on a Christian mission from Norway to Greenland, and that the author of *Eiríks saga* subsequently incorporated this story in his saga ("Sagalitteraturen," pp. 248-9). Gunnlaugr Leifsson was a member of the Benedictine House of Thingeyrar in the north of Iceland, and he wrote this story as a part of a saga which he composed in order to glorify the somewhat notorious Christian champion, King Olafr Tryggvason of Norway, who, during his reign of five years (995-1000), was reputed to have christianized no fewer than five countries. The oldest sources describe these countries as the Orkney Islands, the Faroe Islands, Shetland, Iceland, and Norway. Other ancient sources, in place of the Faroe Islands, substitute Greenland—one source inadvertently citing all six.

However, there is a body of evidence that makes it more likely that Christianity was brought to Greenland, not from Norway, but from Iceland. Perhaps the monk, Gunnlaugr Leifsson, had followed one of the above sources which wrongly included Greenland. Compounding this error, the unscholarly monk of Thingeyrar took a further liberty in purporting to explain just how King Olafr Tryggvason managed to bring the Christian faith to the Greenlanders. This could not be done in a more impressive way than to claim that it was Leifr Eiríksson, Greenland's most illustrious citizen, who accepted the assignment from King Olafr to convert the pagans there. Then, to make Leifr's mission more memorable, Gunnlaugr Leifsson decided to combine it with the discovery of Vinland! Gunnlaugr Leifsson's fictitious story was accepted until about a decade ago, and found its way into several historical works of both the 13th and 14th centuries: *Eiríks saga* was one of these, and even the great Snorri Sturluson incorporated it in his *Heimskringla* (*c.* 1235).

As has been mentioned, the author of *Groenlendingasaga* does not refer to any accounts of Leifr's voyage from Norway in the year 1000, indicating that it may have been written before Gunnlaugr Leifsson concocted his story. Research on the genealogies contained in the sagas about Vinland further supports this thesis (see Jóhannesson's article cited above). For the genealogies imply that *Groenlendingasaga* must have been composed about the end of the 12th century, while *Eiríks saga* could not have been written until after 1264.

Whether the author of *Eiríks saga* based his work directly on *Groenlendingasaga* or not, it seems obvious that he deliberately digressed from it in places. Nowhere is this more obvious than in the part dealing with Leifr Eiríksson's voyage from Norway. The inclusion of this episode in *Eiríks saga* left its author no choice but to dismiss *Groenlendingasaga's* accounts of Bjarni Herjólfsson's discovery of the Western Hemisphere and Leifr's exploratory voyage from Greenland to Vinland. It would seem that the author of *Eiríks saga* did not make this digression without subsequent feelings of remorse. Realizing that he had elevated Leifr at the expense of Bjarni, he decided, apparently for the sake of fairness, to deprive Leifr of the honour of having been the first man to assign topographic names to the various regions in the New World. Thus the author has Leifr leave the land as nameless as it had been before his arrival; and later on when the name Vinland crops up without explanation, the author attributes the geographic names of the western lands to Thorfinnr Karlsefni and his party. One must say that it would indeed have been contrary to ancient custom had North America's first explorer in fact refrained from coining suitable names for some of the regions he discovered, and decided instead to leave that task to his successors. Leifr Eiríksson was a man of many virtues, but it is doubtful if excessive humility was one of them.

It does not escape one's attention that the *Groenlendingasaga's* account of Bjarni Herjólfsson's voyage from Iceland in 986, during which he was driven to the eastern seaboard of the continent, may well have influenced the *Eiríks saga's* account of Leifr Eiríksson's voyage from Norway in 1000, for the two have many important features in common. The later *Eiríks saga's* description of the preparations for a second voyage to the newly discovered lands to the westward resembles *Groenlendingasaga's* account of Leifr Eiríksson's unsuccessful attempts to persuade his father, Eiríkr the Red, to head an expedition to the lands found by Bjarni Herjólfsson (Jóhannesson, 156). The second voyage in the later saga has other elements resembling the *Groenlendingasaga's* fourth voyage, while its third voyage has features in common with the earlier saga's descriptions of the voyages in which neither Bjarni Herjólfsson nor Leifr Eiríksson took part.

A comparison of the references to Vinland in the two sagas indicates that the portion of *Eiriks saga* which deals with the voyages to Vinland is an inaccurate version of the corresponding section in the earlier *Groenlendingasaga*.[5] Apart from questions of dating and derivation, the description in *Groenlendingasaga* of the discovery of the Western Hemisphere conveys much the stronger impression of authenticity. Of special interest is its description of the eastern seaboard, which has enabled scholars to reach partial agreement about the location of such places as Helluland and Markland. But one of the compelling reasons for preferring the *Groenlendingasaga* as historically the more correct is simply that it is, by at least 60 or 70 years, closer to the events described in both these sagas. Also *Groenlendingasaga* belongs to the early part of the Family Saga period when Ari the Learned's insistence on historical accuracy still exercised a stronger influence on the authors of Family Sagas than was to be the case half a century later when *Eiriks saga* was written.

If *Groenlendingasaga*'s account of the discovery is accepted, it provides us with a very realistic description of Leifr Eiríksson's exploratory voyage. Far from implying that there was anything accidental about this voyage, it gives the impression that Leifr Eiríksson was a serious explorer and that he made suitable preparations before embarking upon his historic journey to the Western Hemisphere.

V

Until recently there was only one known medieval source from outside Iceland in which mention was made of Vinland. This is a brief description in the late 11th century history of the Archbishops of Hamburg and Bremen *(Gesta Hammaburgensis ecclesiae pontificum)*, written in Latin by a teacher and a member of a holy brotherhood, Adam of Bremen. Adam's book preceded Ari the Learned's *Islendingabók* by some 50 years. It represents therefore the oldest written source on Vinland. Adam of Bremen has this to say about information he obtained from Sveinn Úlfsson, King of Denmark:

> He told me that there was still another island, discovered by many in that ocean, and that it is called Vinland, because vines grow there of their own accord and produce the most excellent wine. That there is abundance of self-sown grain there we have learned not from fabulous conjecture but from the reliable reports of the Danes *(Grönlands historiske Mindesmaerker,* vol. 3, p. 404).

Even though Adam of Bremen may not have been a man of scholarly precision, his mention of Vinland indicates that the early explorations

---

[5] Scholars are not in complete agreement about the connection between the Vinland sagas: Einar Ol. Sveinsson, *Ritunartımi Íslendingasagna* (Reykjavík, 1965), p. 50.

from Iceland and Greenland became known in Europe at an early date. This explains in part why scholars have not regarded the Vinland voyages as an historically isolated incident. Some historians, including the famous Vilhjálmur Stefánsson in his book *Iceland* (pp. xv–xvi), have even been inclined to believe that Columbus himself may have been fully aware of his distant predecessors. Then, it has been suggested that knowledge about Greenland and the North American continent was obtained from Iceland by English merchants from Bristol who as early as 1412 had included Iceland within the sphere of their operations. It is also worthy of note that the phrase "by way of Iceland" was used by a 15th century historian, Francesco Lopez Gomara, when he was describing a voyage to the North American continent (in Oleson, pp. 115–6, 134). To this one may add that competent historians have vigorously maintained that Greenland was in fact the gateway between Europe and North America in the Middle Ages.[6]

The most publicized source on Vinland is, without question, the previously mentioned Vinland Map published in the United States in 1965. Scholars have reached the conclusion that this map dates from *c.* 1440 (*VM*, pp. 228–230). The Vinland Map shows a sketch of Greenland which, even in detail, is remarkably close to the correct geographic image of that country. Vinland itself is, on the other hand, rather primitive in appearance, even though the map appears to accord with a prototype showing the three countries of the sagas, i.e., Helluland, Markland, and Vinland. However, the first two are not identified by name on the Vinland Map. Just above the sketch of Vinland is the following comment in Latin: "Island of Vinland, discovered by Bjarni and Leifr in company" (*VM*, p. 138). Further up on the map there is a longer sentence, also in Latin, the first part of which reads:

> By God's will, after a long voyage from the island of Greenland to the south toward the most distant remaining parts of the western ocean sea, sailing southward amidst the ice, the companions Bjarni and Leifr Eiríksson discovered a new land, extremely fertile and even having vines, the which land they named Vinland (*VM*, p. 140).

Both the Vinland Map itself and its accompanying explanatory notes are of great interest. One can say that by mentioning Bjarni Herjólfsson, if only by Christian name, the author of the Vinland Map has lent support to the *Groenlendingasaga*'s version of the voyages to Vinland. Further, the Vinland Map is in agreement with Adam of Bremen's reference to Vinland as an island. It is noteworthy that in the two sources on Vinland found outside Iceland, the name Vinland appears to have been adopted as an "onomastic generalization" to the exclusion of other names.[7] However, in Iceland people retained some of the other names of the sagas about Vinland, as is borne out by the following entry in the Icelandic Annals for the year 1347:

---

[6]Jón Dúason, *Landkönnum og landnám Íslendinga í Vesturheimi* (Reykjavík, 1941–1947); also T. J. Oleson, op. cit., 51–127.

[7]*Scandinavian Studies*, 39, no. 2 (1967) 185.

> There came also a ship from Greenland, smaller in size than small Icelandic boats; she came into the outer Straumfjöðr (near Búðir on Snaefellsnes) and had no anchor. There were seventeen men on board. They had made a voyage to Markland, but were afterwards stormdriven here [i.e., to Snaefellsnes in Iceland.[8]]

Markland is here spoken of as a well-known and well-defined region. In the words of Vilhjâlmur Stefánsson, "the scribe would have entered something about this voyage having been extraordinary had it been extraordinary" (*Iceland*, p. xxxvii).

Helluland, Markland, and "Promontorium Winlandiæ" (Vinland) are shown on an Icelandic geographic map, originally prepared in the last quarter of the 16th century by Sigurður Stefánsson. The Stefánsson Map is in all probability a copy of a pre-Columbian map (Jones, pp. 79–80, and *VM*, p. 262). It is particularly interesting to note that "Promontorium Winlandiæ" on this map coincides with what later became known as Newfoundland.

The Stefánsson Map takes us back to Helge Ingstad's discovery in 1964 of Norse artifacts at L'Ance-aux-Meadows in Newfoundland. This discovery proves that voyages were made to the eastern seaboard of the continent by people of a Scandinavian background about the year 1000. Did some of the people of the two sagas about Vinland build their homes at L'ance-aux-Meadows? This question will have to go unanswered, but, having established that, in all probability, voyages were made to Vinland, we are justified in asking another question more penetrating than the first one: Did the main characters of the Vinland Sagas ever exist?

Ari the Learned's *Íslendingabók* appears to be sufficient proof that Eiríkr the Red settled Greenland. Eiríkr's son, Leifr, is discussed in so many sources that his having existed is beyond question. Scholars have for a long time had difficulty in accepting Bjarni Herjólfsson as an authentic explorer.[9] But it is safe to say that the previously discussed re-evaluation of the element of fact in *Groenlendingasaga* and the publication of the Vinland Map with Bjarni's name on it have finally provided him with a firm foundation in history.

It is of interest that many of the pioneers in Greenland and Vinland became later firmly rooted in the history of Iceland through their descendants. This is particularly true in the instance of Eiríkr the Red, Thorfinnr Karlsefni, and Gudridr Thorbjarnardottir. Four of the bishops who held office in Iceland in both the 12th and the 13th centuries were descended from Gudridr Thorbjarnardottir. Two of these were also descended from Eiríkr the Red. To give one important illustration, Bishop Thorlakr Runólfsson (1118–1133) was the great-grandson of Thorsteinn Eiríksson, Eiríkr the Red's son. According to Ari the Learned's testimony, Bishop Thorlakr was one of the three men who supervised the writing of

---

[8]Gustav Storm, ed., *Islandske Annaler indtil 1578* (Christiania, 1888), p. 213; *Annalbrudstykke fra Skálholt* (1328–1372); see also Gwyn Jones, *The Norse Atlantic Saga* (Oxford U.P., 1964), p. 96.

[9]For instance, Halldór Hermannsson, "The Problem of Wineland," *Islandica*, 25 (Ithaca, N.Y., 1936) 36.

Íslendingabók, the book which contains the most carefully documented evidence about the discovery of both Greenland and Vinland.[10]

A considerable portion in both the sagas about Vinland presents a gradually unfolding prediction about Gudridr Thorbjarnardottir's future. One must avoid accepting a superstition by stating that this particular prediction must have succeeded the very events it forecast by about 200 years. A prediction is, as has been stated earlier, a common literary device in the Old Icelandic saga literature. It seems, however, that in the sagas about Vinland the prediction about Gudridr's future was not only included as a useful literary device, but as an element of deeper significance.

Groenlendingasaga's version of the prophecy is that Gudridr Thorbjarnardottir's descendants in Iceland were supposed to become "endowed with strength" and to be looked upon as "bright and noble" and "sweet and fragrant" (*Íslenzk fornrit,* vol. 4, p. 260). The clerical overtones of the latter part of this statement, along with other features, may well indicate that one of the leaders of the Icelandic Church played a part in giving the saga its original shape. Furthermore, the author seems to have been close to Bishop Brandr Sæmundsson (1163–1201), one of Gudridr Thorbjarnardottir's great-grandsons, if the Bishop himself was not indeed the author.

Assuming that the above conjecture cannot be easily dismissed, the question arises whether the authors of the sagas about Vinland felt that the voyages to Greenland and Vinland in themselves justified their inclusion. Doubtless, the discovery of new lands must have been considered to be a major accomplishment. Nonetheless, one wonders whether the commemoration of the explorer's noble descendants—the authors of the sagas about Vinland probably included—did not rather constitute the chief motivation for the writing of our two sagas.

The Old Icelandic Family Sagas represent, it has been said, a "unique blend of pagan inheritance and Christian acquisition."[11] This distinctive blend is clearly discernible in both the sagas about Vinland, and, among other things, it reveals itself in a certain measure of tolerance on the part of the Christian authors as they present their heathen forefathers. As a rule, the saga authors displayed objectivity in their writings and refrained from passing judgements on those they were writing about. On the other hand, one sometimes comes across a judgement, as in the *Groenlendingasaga's* description of Leifr Eiríksson: "Leifr was big and strong, of striking appearance, shrewd, and in every respect a temperate, fair-dealing man" (*Íslenzk fornrit,* vol. 4, p. 252). Later on the saga implies that Leifr earned his nickname "the Lucky" through an act of mercy when he found a group of shipwrecked mariners on his voyage from Vinland to Greenland.

In a subsequent chapter of *Groenlendingasaga* dealing with the voyage to Vinland of Leifr's brother, Thorvaldr Eiríksson, we are informed

---

[10]*Islandica,* 20 (1929) 60; also the genealogical tables in *Íslenzk fornrit,* vol. 4.

[11]Peter Foote, "An Essay on the Saga of Gisli and its Icelandic Background," appended to *The Saga of Gisli* (University of Toronto Press, 1963), p. 98.

that at a certain place in Vinland Thorvaldr went ashore with his men, and, having looked around, decided that he had discovered a place attractive enough in which to make his home. Having expressed himself on the qualities of the new land, Thorvaldr came upon three skin boats and noticed that each boat sheltered three men who were natives of Vinland. Thorvaldr and his men captured eight of these men and without any apparent reason killed them. However, the one who managed to escape came back with reinforcements and in the battle which ensued, Thorvaldr Eiríksson was slain. In the saga the slaying of Thorvaldr is all the more dramatic as it occurred only a short while after he had expressed his favourable opinion of Vinland (*Íslenzk fornrit*, vol. 4, p. 256). The author does not refer to Thorvaldr Eiríksson's treatment of the natives as having been an evil act. Nonetheless, one is tempted to conclude that, in the eyes of the author, the examples of the two brothers, Leifr and Thorvaldr, constituted a significant point. The Christian author of *Groenlendingasaga* does not imply that Thorvaldr Eiríksson's misfortune could be put down to pagan outlook or behaviour, or that Leifr's good luck stemmed from his Christian way of life. The saga does not deal with a conflict between two religions, even though the episodes about the two brothers may well have been presented in *Groenlendingasaga* as a lecture on desirable human relations. It is not unlikely that the author himself may have attached greater importance to the content of that lecture than has yet been recognized by his readers.

2

THE ARGUMENT FOR THE ENGLISH DISCOVERY OF AMERICA BETWEEN 1480 AND 1494*†

David B. Quinn

In 1492 Christopher Columbus crossed the Atlantic and made a landfall in the West Indies. Of this historians are certain. But beyond Columbus, the details of the early discovery and exploration of the New World are shrouded in a mist of doubt. Aside from the whole question of Viking activities, the demonstrable achievements of a variety of European mariners contemporary with Columbus have been the subject of great historical debate. A number of scholars have argued that Columbus was not the first European to discover—or rediscover—America at the end of the 15th century. Claims have been advanced for a number of other intrepid sailors, most of them Portuguese, with varying degrees of plausibility. Even the case of John Cabot is hardly clear, for disagreement exists as to where Cabot actually made his landfall in 1497, although most experts agree it was probably somewhere in Newfoundland. The fundamental reason for all the uncertainty is the relative lack of clear-cut documentary evidence and the difficulty of interpreting the scattered records which do exist. In studying an age of primitive navigation, when even the most level-headed mariner could intertwine fact and fancy in his own mind and in his accounts of his accomplishments, and where corroborating evidence simply does not survive, differences of interpretation are to be expected. This is particularly true when questions of chronology, timing, influence, and geographical location become as

---

*Geographical Journal, 127 (1961), 277-85, with references updated by the author to August 1968.

†A further brief article, "John Day and Columbus" (ibid., 133 [1967], 205-9) examined some of the reasons which may have brought Day into contact with Columbus in 1497-8.

critical as they are in attempting to assess the accomplishments of the early explorers. Professor David B. Quinn deals with most of these problems in the following article. What is the nature of the historical evidence with which he is working? What sorts of assumptions does he make? How much of his argument is based on incontrovertible fact, how much on informed deduction, and how much on speculation? Can historians be dogmatic about the "facts" of early exploration and discovery?

SUGGESTIONS FOR FURTHER READING

H. P. Biggar, *The Precursors of Jacques Cartier* (Ottawa: Government Printing Bureau, 1911).

David B. Quinn, *England and the Discovery of America, 1481-1620* (New York: Knopf, 1974).

J. A. Williamson, ed., *The Cabot Voyages and Bristol Discovery under Henry VII* (Cambridge, England: University Press, Hakluyt Society, 1962).

J.M.B.

I

In 1956 Professor Louis André Vigneras published a letter which he had found in the archives at Simancas[1] which has greatly affected and will continue to affect consideration of the circumstances of the discovery of America. In Spanish and undated, the letter was addressed by John (Johan) Day, an Englishman, to a Spanish official "el Senor Almyrante mayor." This could either have been Fadríque Enriquez, Marqués de Tarifa, Grand Admiral of Castile, or Christopher Columbus, whose title of Admiral of the Ocean Sea ("Almirante del Mar Oceano") was frequently generalised to "El Almirante Mayor," while he signed himself, on occasion, as "El Almirante." Fadríque is considered the less likely candidate by Dr Vigneras, and, indeed, the contents of the letter make the identification with Columbus the more probable since no interest in or special knowledge of the overseas discoveries on the part of Enriquez has so far been demonstrated. More recently, Dr A. A. Ruddock has demonstrated[2] that the name of John Day conceals that of another

---

[1]"New light on the 1497 Cabot Voyage to America," *Hispanic American Historical Review*, 36 (1956), 503-9 (from A. G. S., Estado de Castilla, legajo 2, folio 6); "The Cape Breton Landfall: 1494 or 1497. Note on a Letter from John Day," *Canadian Historical Review*, 38 (1957), 219-28 (with the first English translation); "État présent des études sur Jean Cabot," *Congresso Internacional de História dos Discobrimentos, Actas*, vol. 3 (Lisbon, 1961), pp. 657-68 (with a revised Spanish text). Dr Vigneras's views on the letter developed over the period covered by these three papers. Additional discussions of the letter relevant to this paper include R. Almagiá, "Sulle navigazioni di Giovanni Caboto," *Rivista geografica italiana*, 67 (1960), 1-12; M. Mahn-Lot, "Colomb, Bristol et l'Atlantique Nord," *Annales*, vol. 19 (Paris, 1964), pp. 522-30. Dr J. A. Williamson, in the introduction to *The Cabot Voyages and Bristol Discovery under Henry VII* (Cambridge, 1962), devoted much space to the letter, his conclusions being, broadly, similar to those in this article. An attempt to fit the letter into a more general perspective is made in D. B. Quinn, "État présent des études sur la redécouverte de l'Amérique au XVᵉ siècle," *Journal de la Societé des Américanistes*, 55 (1966), 343-82.

[2]"John Day of Bristol and the English Voyages across the Atlantic before 1497," *The Geographical Journal*, 132 (1966), 222-33.

Englishman, Hugh Say, a member of a cultivated London merchant family, who for reasons of his own was trading as John Day of Bristol.

The letter is the work of a man of some learning, familiar with the geographical knowledge of the time, who has been carrying on a correspondence with the Grand Admiral, exchanging books with him, and sending him information on English voyages on at least one earlier occasion. Where its information can be checked against other evidence it is correct, which suggests that its unsupported statements are serious and probably authoritative ones. The letter is mainly concerned with reporting a successful voyage from Bristol by an unnamed explorer which has found across the ocean a land which Day identifies with "the Island of the Seven Cities." Both by its general character and by specific details—the grant, for example (on December 13, 1497) of a pension of 20 pounds by the king to the explorer on his return—this voyage can be clearly and unambiguously identified as that made by John Cabot in 1497 during which he coasted a substantial part of the Newfoundland and mainland shores across the Atlantic.[3] The letter, moreover, states that the explorer had earlier made an unsuccessful voyage from Bristol, thus adding a piece of hitherto unknown information on John Cabot, while it also gives some details of the preparation for a further voyage which Cabot was making to follow up his discovery. From this last information it is possible to tie down the composition of the letter to the latter part of December 1497 or the opening month or so of 1498. For the Cabot voyages the letter is an important source, the most important, indeed, to be published in the present century, while the details it gives of the 1497 discoveries will continue to provide material for interpretation and controversy. One passage in it goes beyond the Cabot voyages themselves and raises the question of the priority of the discovery of America in a novel form. Its interest is such that it is worth segregating it from the Cabot material and considering what its implications may be if it is taken literally as a statement of fact.

The text reads, in translation: "It is considered certain that the cape of the said land [that found by Cabot in the 1497 voyage] was found and discovered in other times by the men of Bristol who found 'Brasil' as your Lordship knows. It was called the Ysle of Brasil and it is assumed and believed to be the mainland that the Bristol men found." (The Spanish being: "Se presume cierto averse fallado e descubierto en otros tiempos el cabo de la dicha tierra por los de Bristol que fallaron el Brasil como dello tiene noticia Vra Sᵃ la qual se dezia la Ysle de Brasil e presumese e creese ser tierra firme la que fallaron los de Bristol.") (Archivo General de Simancas, Estado de Castilla, leg. 2, fo. 6.) The Spanish of the letter shows few signs of being written by a foreigner, but Dr Vigneras has found that John Day, its author, as an English merchant, appears also in a Spanish document of 1500.[4] The literal meaning is clear enough. The land, or part of the land, which Cabot found in 1497 is equated with "Brasil" or the "Isle of Brasil," which the Bristol men had found already

---

[3] Williamson, ed., *Cabot Voyages* (1962), p. 217.

[4] C.I.H.D., *Actas*, vol. 3, pp. 660-61, 668-69 (from A.G.S., Cédulas de la Cámera, libro 4, folio 252ʳ).

some time before. Cabot's discovery, although the possibility of a redis-
covery of land found and lost again is not ruled out, had not, Day is
asserting, any claim to absolute priority. When, then, could this first
discovery have taken place? Or between what limits can we place it? The
major ambiguity lies in the words, "en otros tiempos," with which Dr
Vigneras has already wrestled.⁵ The expression is a vague one, "in times
past," rather than "in past times," having only the implication that the
"times" were not very recently passed, but even that not very clearly.
Certain dates, 1480, 1481, 1490 give us a framework of known facts in
which to insert a series of questions and an argument on the implications
of the statement.

1. Could the discovery have taken place before 1480? Clearly it could
have done so, but no evidence whatever of specific English voyages of
discovery into the Atlantic before that date has yet come to light. That
being so, nothing useful can be said except that the first positive evidence we have, that for 1480, which follows, is slightly weighted against
a discovery before that date, and that for 1481 more heavily.

2. On July 15, 1480, a ship, partly owned by John Jay the younger
and with "Thloyde" (identified as John Lloyd with some probability,
though it could be Thomas Lloyd) as master, left Bristol for the Island of
Brasil, west of Ireland, and returned by September 18 following, having
through bad weather failed to find the island. The Latin of William Worcester on its objective reads: "usque ad insulam de Brasylle in occiden-
tali parte Hibernie" (Itinerarium of William Worcester, Corpus Christi
College, Cambridge, MS 210, p. 195).⁶ Since the Island of Brasil appeared on many maps, in many different locations, from 1325 onwards,
without apparently having been discovered in practice, this would appear on our present information to have been an unsuccessful voyage of
discovery to an island known only in theory. Nevertheless, the alternative, that it was an unsuccessful voyage to an island or land already
known and discovered before 1480, cannot be entirely ruled out. At least,
however, the discovery did not take place in 1480 as the result of this
expedition.

3. On, or shortly after, July 6, 1481, two ships, the George and the
Trinity of Bristol, partly owned and victualled by Thomas Croft, one of
the collectors of custom for Bristol, left the port "to serch & fynde a
certain Isle called the Isle of Brasile."⁷ The terms of their objective
would, more strongly than the document of 1480, indicate that the Isle of
Brasil had not been located and that this was another voyage of discovery. Moreover, on June 18, 1480, probably too late to be connected with
the 1480 voyage, a licence was given to Croft and three Bristol mer-

---

⁵C.H.R., vol. 49, pp. 224–25.

⁶The Overseas Trade of Bristol in the Later Middle Ages, ed. E. M. Carus-Wilson (Bristol
Record Society Publications, 1937), vol. 7, pp. 157–58; Williamson, Cabot Voyages (1962), pp.
187–88.

⁷Three versions (all containing the same phrases relating to the purpose of the voyage, the
names of the ships and the nature of Croft's participation) survive in the Public Record Office
(Exch. K.R. Customs Accounts, 19/16; Exch. K.R., Memoranda Rolls, 22 Edw. IV, Hilary, m.
30; Exch. L.T.R., Memoranda Rolls, 22 Edw. IV, Hilary, m. 10). Carus-Wilson, Bristol Trade,
pp. 161–65; Williamson, Cabot Voyages (1962), pp. 188–89.

chants, William Spenser, Robert Straunge and William de la Fount, to trade for three years to any parts, with any goods except staple goods, despite any statute to the contrary, with two or three ships, each of 60 tons or less.[8] Since Croft was precluded by his office from engaging in trade and was questioned on September 24, 1481, about shipping 40 bushels of salt in the *George* and *Trinity* on July 6, 1481, it would appear that this licence was for exploration, not commerce, while Croft's excuse that the two ships which he had helped to victual were intended not for commerce but for the search for the Isle of Brasil, was accepted. The 1481 voyage, of the failure of which there is no record, and of the return of which the proceedings against Croft are probably circumstantial evidence, is one which could have resulted in the English discovery of America. A discovery by this expedition would fit, without straining, the requirements of John Day's letter. Moreover, it is the earliest known voyage which could have so succeeded. 1481 is therefore the earlier limit on our present information for a successful discovery and could be the year of the discovery itself.

4. If the discovery did not take place in 1481, Croft and his partners, provided the licence of 1480 was for the purpose which has been presumed, had still authority to set out ships in 1482 and in 1483 up to June 17. Evidence is still entirely lacking that any such further voyages were made or, if made, that they had any results, but it is within the years of the currency of the licence that the English discovery of America is least unlikely to lie.

5. The years between 1483 and 1490 are as blank of even the suggestion of evidence for a voyage as those before 1480, but they are still within the period of discovery appropriate to the Day letter.

6. One of the Spanish representatives in England provides a well-known piece of evidence about English western voyages which reaches back, perhaps, to 1490. Pedro de Ayala wrote from London to Ferdinand and Isabella on July 25, 1498, to report on Cabot's discoveries in 1497 and on the progress, so far, of his 1498 expedition. He added: "Los de Bristol ha siete años que cada año an armado dos, tres, quatro caravelas para ir a buscar la isla del Brasil, i la Siete Ciudades con la fantasia deste Ginoves," which has, since 1862, been invariably translated: "For the last seven years the people of Bristol have equipped two, three, four caravels to go in search of the island of Brazil and the Seven Cities according to the fancy of this Genoese."[9] It is not certain which years are meant. Is Ayala writing of seven years before Cabot's voyage of 1497 or of seven years before his letter? The range is either 1490 to 1496 or 1491

---

[8]Calendared from P.R.O. Treaty Rolls, 164, m. 10 (in Carus-Wilson, *Bristol Trade*, p. 157). Professor Carus-Wilson thought that the men named in it "were perhaps responsible for the venture in the following month, as well as for that of 1481" (p. 204). Evidence for this is still to seek, but it is at least unlikely that the 1480 expedition depended on this grant for authorization, since preparations would have been too far advanced to make it possible to bring them to fruition so soon. What it does prove is that an outbreak of activity in overseas voyaging occurred at Bristol in 1480-81, the precise stimulant to which has not been discovered.

[9]*Calendar of State Papers, Spanish, 1485-1509* (1862), p. 177; H. P. Biggar, *The Precursors of Jacques Cartier* (Ottawa, 1913), pp. 27-29; Williamson, *Cabot Voyages* (1962), pp. 288-89. Biggar gives the Spanish as well as an English translation.

to 1497, and choice between the alternatives is not easy to make; both must be regarded as possible. How far Ayala was speaking precisely, and authoritatively it is also impossible to say, but it is reasonable to take his statement at its face value that a series of Bristol voyages began in 1490 or 1491 and was continued in, perhaps, each of the six years following.

To determine how much or how little John Cabot had to do with these voyages is a delicate matter. "According to the fancy of this Genoese" has been taken, almost invariably, to mean that John Cabot, Genoese by origin though Venetian by adoption, inspired this series of Bristol voyages and proposed their objectives to those who took part in them. This does not necessarily follow. The phrase as it stands can mean simply that in Cabot's "fancy" the objectives of the Bristol voyages were the Isle of Brasil and the Seven Cities. He would stand outside the voyages entirely and his comment would be that of an observer only, made to Ayala's informant near to the time of writing in 1498. An alternative translation of the passage could read: "The Bristol men for seven years have fitted out yearly two, three, or four small ships to go in search, as this Genoese fancies, of the Isle of Brasil or the Seven Cities." Which interpretation is correct must remain a matter for argument. Each appears to be legitimate.[10]

The alternative interpretation fits usefully into a pattern formed by the newer documents. It is in line with the evidence already used on the 1480 and 1481 voyages. The English are continuing in the 'nineties their westward voyages from Bristol, only now they are using as many as three or four little ships instead of one or two; they are said to be looking for the Seven Cities in addition to their old objective the Isle of Brasil. Moreover, the evidence found by Professor M. Ballesteros Gabrois in the Aragonese archives, if it is to be accepted, puts John Cabot in Valencia between the middle of 1490 and the end of February 1493 at least, and so rules him out from influencing some of the earlier voyages of the series. This involves identifying the Juan Caboto Montecalunya, a Venetian engaged on harbour works at Valencia with the "English" John Cabot. While this is not certain it is highly probable.[11] The discoveries of R. Gallo[12] on the "English" John Cabot's activities in Venice between 1476 and 1485 make it unlikely that there was a second John Cabot with Venetian nationality, though the cognomen "Montecalunya" remains mysterious. The consequence of accepting this identification would be that the voyages of 1490 (if there was one), 1491, 1492 and 1493 (probably), of the

---

[10]Dr Sloman (in 1960, Head of the School of Hispanic Studies, University of Liverpool) and other members of the School, helped greatly with advice on the word *fantasia*, normally understood as fantasy, fancy, or imagination. It can also carry a nautical meaning, reckoning, or estimation (of direction or distances). See A. Jal, *Glossaire nautique* (Paris, 1848), s.vv. *Fantasia, Estime*. Dr Vigneras kindly pointed out to me a passage in Pedro de Medina, *Arte de Navegar* (1545), fols. xxxii^v–xxxiii^r, which illustrates this use:—*Este aviso se terma quando se echa punto por el quadria o fantasia, que es contando las singladures que el navio a hecho y arbitrar quanto pundo ser el camino.*

[11]Ballesteros-Gabrois, "Juan Caboto en España," *Revista de Indias*, vol. 4 (1943), pp. 607-27, "La clave de los descubrimientos de Juan Caboto," *Studi Columbiana*, vol. 2 (Genoa, 1952) pp. 553-60.

[12]R. Gallo, "Intorno a Giovanni Caboto," Accemia dei Lincei, *Rendiconti della Classe di Scienza morali, storiche e filologiche*, 8th ser., vol. 3 (1948), pp. 209-20.

series were purely English expeditions, and so they could be considered as coming within the range of the independent English discovery described by John Day. Dates as late as 1490 and 1491 could be covered by his "en otros tiempos"; later dates, 1492, six years, and 1493, five years, before the Day letter, seem too near, or at least to be at the outer limit of credibility: 1494, if worth considering, would be rather absurd. We are entitled to say, remembering that we have selected one meaning of two from the Ayala letter and have accepted the Valencia material, that 1490 and 1491 come within the probable range of the independent English discovery of America, and 1492 and 1493 within the possible limits.

7. Robert Thorne the younger, in 1527, claimed that his father, Robert Thorne the elder, and Hugh Eliot, merchants of Bristol, were "discoverers of the New Found Landes."[13] The claim appears to have been made in good faith and, accepting Day's statement of a pre-Cabotan English discovery, it seems not unlikely to be true, or at least to indicate that these men had something to do with a voyage to the Isle of Brasil before Cabot came on the scene. No date is associated with the claim, but John Dee in 1580[14] adopted it and associated it with the date 1494, doing so only tentatively, placing it "Circa An. 1494," and leaving no evidence to show whether or not he had specific reasons for the choice of date. "1494" therefore has no special authority: a Thorne-Eliot voyage before 1494 which had a successful outcome is as possible as one in that year if not more so. 1494 can, however, be dragged in as the furthest forward limit of the discovery recorded by John Day and, as already indicated, it is already so late that it can legitimately be thought of as beyond the limit.

8. John Cabot, if he still had unfinished business at Valencia at the end of February 1493, is unlikely to have come to England in time to take part in westward voyages from Bristol before the end of the sailing season (September) in that year. 1494 is therefore the first year in which he, if the Valencia evidence be accepted, is likely to have been available to make a voyage from Bristol. John Day records that he did make one unsuccessful voyage before 1497. On the arguments advanced so far this would leave 1494, 1495 and 1496 open to him for it. It is difficult to say with any confidence that one year is much more probable than another. The first is still a possible Thorne-Eliot year and is therefore a shade less likely for a Cabot voyage. Dr Vigneras argues that Cabot would not have made a voyage until he had got a royal licence to do so and so could not have made his first, unsuccessful voyage until 1496.[15] This is reasonable but it does not exclude alternative suppositions. If Cabot intruded himself at Bristol he may have found himself handicapped by secrecy and obstruction so that his first venture had little chance of success and he may therefore have sought a royal licence so that he could overcome it. This is pure speculation, but it is made to show that Cabot could have made his first voyage in, for example, 1495. If 1496 is regarded as more

---

[13]Williamson, *Cabot Voyages* (1962), p. 202.

[14]Ibid., p. 201.

[15]*C.H.R.*, vol. 38, p. 222.

likely, however, following on Cabot's petition to Henry VII and the issue
of a patent on March 5 granting him powers to occupy and govern lands
found, and to trade with them through the port of Bristol[16] a further point
remains. In that case Bristol voyages made in 1495 as well as in 1494, in
Ayala's series, would have been purely English voyages. The limiting
date of an English discovery could therefore be pushed up to the very eve
of the Cabot grant but, if it is, John Day's "in other times" must be called
in question because if 1494 is an absurd date to associate with it, 1495 is
impossible. A run of annual Bristol voyages, beginning about 1490 and
continuing to include 1495, though not including a discovery in the later
years, seems credible. The series would then be continued or paralleled
by an unsuccessful Cabot voyage in 1496.

9. In summary, then, since, according to John Day, the English discovered America before 1497 they must have done so either before 1480
or between 1481 and, at the furthest limit forward, 1494. 1481 or a date
near it would best fit the phraseology of the Day letter on the information
now available. A date of 1490 or 1491 is still possible though less likely,
but it seems desirable to bring in at least one of the years covered by
Ayala's evidence. A date between 1492 and 1494 appears progressively
less acceptable and 1495 unacceptable (though of course the drawing of
a line in this case must be at least partly subjective). Allowing ourselves
room for speculation on years both before and after, we can say that an
argument on the present basis indicates that the English discovery could
reasonably have taken place between 1481 and 1491, with the initial
date, 1481, and the concluding one, 1491 (if it is the first of Ayala's
series), as slightly less unlikely than the others, though with the chances
otherwise in favour of a year in the early part of the series rather than the
later. Further than this it would seem undesirable to go until something
fresh can be adduced. The sequence of information is so fragile and
incomplete that any single scrap of new evidence can upset it. It does not
provide a basis for any dogmatic statement other than that made by John
Day himself. Nevertheless, with all its limitations, it does provide a rational case for placing the English discovery of America in the decade
before Columbus sailed in 1492, and possibly as early as 1481.

II

In what was said above, the possible implications of one statement
only in the Day letter was followed. But with that done it may be worth
considering what kind of speculation may seem appropriate to the information which can be squeezed out of this statement. The main and obvious point is that we should ask what kind of a discovery was it that
remained so little remarked before Cabot's patent brought the search for
land in the west into the open. The descriptions in the documents of 1480
and 1481, in the Day letter and in Ayala's, mention the insular character
of Brasil and the last two of them of the Seven Cities as well, though John
Day also indicates each island, after the Cabot voyage of 1497, as a

---

[16]Williamson, *Cabot Voyages* (1962), pp. 203-5.

mainland ("tierra firma") as well. The insular nomenclature is in accordance with the appearance of these names as denoting islands in the cartographic record, into which it is not proposed to enter, except to emphasize that charts of the 14th and 15th centuries do not give stable locations for Brasil and seldom specify the Seven Cities as such,[17] and so cannot be convincingly tied to discoveries. But whatever the English discovery was, in fact, the old insular name (or names) was applied to it. A discovery of the Isle of Brasil by the English between 1481 and 1491 would lead us to expect some publicity, or else some attempt to exploit the discovery by further voyages of exploration, but until 1956 no unambiguous statement of even an initial discovery had come to light. The implications of this appear to be twofold; either there was a discovery, which was quickly lost sight of and which subsequent searchers failed to disclose until 1497, or the discovery, when made, was valued only as incidental to some other purpose or objective. The first is possible; navigation in northern waters at this time was anything but accurate. Yet Day's statement does not easily admit of such an interpretation. The alternative seems rather more attractive in view of the later history of the waters between lat. 45° and 50° N. off the North American continent. Fishing was contemplated in 1481, as can be clearly seen from the amount of salt shipped;[18] the discovery of land, believed to be an island, at Newfoundland or even Cape Breton, would attract attention and interest primarily as a landmark for fishermen intending to operate on the Banks nearby. The history of the Newfoundland fishery, from the time it emerges in the early 16th century, demonstrates how incidental and casual was the attention of the fishermen of four nations to the land which bordered the fishing grounds. Speculation about the English-found Isle of Brasil which regards it as likely to be a territorial key to a fishery on the Banks and valued primarily as such, may well be fruitful. This could explain the lack of publicity about the land, if it was not thought to be of great importance in itself. Moreover, the silence about the fishery, the lack of publicity about the discovery of new and extremely rich grounds, would be entirely intelligible and could be supported by analogies from the 16th century. Bristol merchants and fishermen would not wish to have even their countrymen, let alone foreigners, as their competitors. But, given this possibility, the yearly expeditions of "discovery" mentioned by Ayala from 1490 (or 1491) would look, instead, like annual fishing fleets on their way to and from Newfoundland waters. If the English discovery can be pushed back into the period 1481-91, as it can if the argument above is reasonable, then so, it is likely, can the history of the English Newfoundland fishery, always supposing that the Isle of Brasil was not found and lost again, but was used mainly, perhaps solely, as a landmark for the fishing grounds.

The intrusion of John Cabot into the sequence of westward English voyages becomes more difficult to explain now that the Day letter gives a

---

[17]Armando Cortesäo, *The National Chart of 1424* (Coimbra, 1954), pp. 68–74.

[18]Forty bushels (320 gallons). Carus-Wilson, *Bristol Trade*, p. 164; Williamson, *Cabot Voyages* (1962), p. 189.

clear statement that there was an earlier English discovery. Before it appeared John Cabot could be seen as the expert Italian navigator who came to Bristol to teach the local seamen how to cross the Atlantic and succeeded in doing so after they themselves had failed. But if they had already succeeded why should they permit him to intervene, or, when the patent had been issued giving him rights to rule lands found, associate themselves with him? The answer, if the land first found had been rapidly lost again, might well remain the traditional one, but if the Isle of Brasil continued to be known and to be used to mark a fishery the difficulty is a real one. Cabot is unlikely to have got his patent or to have been able to operate from Bristol from 1496 onwards without having something new to offer.

In trying to answer what John Cabot may have had to offer, speculation can, at least, state probabilities rather than possibilities. Cabot, like Columbus, Ayala said in 1498, had been in Lisbon and in Seville seeking support for his plans for exploration. This would have been either before 1490, probably after his journey to Mecca of which Soncino wrote in 1497,[19] or in intervals during the period when he was mainly engaged in Valencia in planning harbour works, if he is indeed Juan Caboto Montecalunya, from 1490 to 1493. It is less likely that he should have begun to press for support in either Spain or Portugal for his own plans after Columbus had returned, as he would know in 1493, triumphant in his belief that his island discoveries lay just off the shores of Asia. For the nature of these plans we have no documentary evidence prior to the 1497 voyage, but it is highly probable that they were similar to those of Columbus, a westward passage to Cathay and the rest of Asia on a sea route thought to be shorter than it actually was. The reports of Cabot's discoveries in 1497,[20] leave little doubt that he believed he had found a way to Asia. His departure from the Iberian peninsula in 1493 or 1494 for England in pursuit of his plans would therefore fit in with a belief that he could still compete with Columbus in the exploitation of his route to Asia by an approach from a somewhat different direction.

To pursue this film of speculation it is now necessary to presume the leakage of news of a Bristol discovery of the Isle of Brasil to either Portugal or Spain. Trading contacts make it possible. The need for Cabot to have some specific incentive to come to England makes it, perhaps, probable. We have John Day's statement to the Grand Admiral, who is likely to be Columbus himself, that the English had discovered the land found by Cabot in times past "as your Lordship knows." This could mean recent knowledge on Columbus's part, imparted to him perhaps by Day not long before the surviving letter, but it could also mean knowledge which had been in his possession for some years, conceivably at the same time as John Cabot could have obtained it. If it was circulating as a story in Lisbon or Seville it is as likely that one would have heard it as another. All that is necessary here is to permit the inclusion of a leakage about the

[19]Williamson, Cabot Voyages (1962), pp. 209-10.
[20]Ibid., pp. 207-11.

English discovery into the possible sequence which brought Cabot to England.

With this kind of background, John Cabot's appearance at Bristol would seem logical. He would be able to point to the success of the Columbus voyage of 1492, although he could well have expressed some scepticism as to whether the islands found were so near the Asiatic mainland as Columbus claimed; he could propose to use the Isle of Brasil as a half-way house to a more northerly part of the Asiatic coast, with a still shorter sea passage than that followed by Columbus, so as to tap the commerce of Cathay and the Spice Islands. It could have taken him several years to establish himself in Bristol and the suggestions already made that he might have had to overcome secrecy and even obstruction in his plans and in his initial voyage would remain relevant, but his success in getting the backing of Bristol merchants and of Henry VII would rest on convincing them that he could exploit the earlier discovery as a major trading route across the ocean, thus overlaying fishing by commerce. He came back from the 1497 voyage convinced that he had found the land of the Great Khan and that a further penetration down the coast of Asia would bring him to Marco Polo's Cipango.[21] He also revealed the existence of vast quantities of fish in the American waters through which he sailed, thus publicizing perhaps, rather than discovering, the Banks. It should be remarked that his patent of 1496 gave him rights over lands hitherto unknown to Christian people.[22] This would not strictly give him any rights over the Isle of Brasil as previously found; that would still, if the speculations above prove to have any foundation, remain in the charge of its discoverers if they cared to assert rights to it or continued to use it to mark the approach to a fishery or as a shore base of any sort. The patent of 1496 (and indeed those of 1501 and 1502 to other grantees which followed[23]) made no mention whatever of a fishery. If it had been established before 1497, on the basis of the discovery of the Isle of Brasil, it presumably would continue as before, separate from and independent of, the expeditions to search for a route to Asia or for other lands along that route, such as the island and mainland of the Seven Cities which Day thought Cabot had found. A prior English discovery of land to the west, which was not publicized before or after 1497, though information about it could have leaked out at some stage before 1497, would provide the basis for an English claim to a footing across the Atlantic anterior to and separate from Cabot's discoveries. Finally, if the leakage by which it is suggested John Cabot learnt of the English discovery of the Isle of Brasil reached Christopher Columbus before he sailed to America in 1492, and he was well aware of it, in John Day's terms, so long before the Day letter was written, then the English discovery could have been one of the more significant pieces of information which led Columbus across the Atlantic with the conviction that there was land to

---

[21]Ibid., pp. 208–9.
[22]Ibid., p. 204.
[23]Ibid., pp. 204–5, 226–27, 236–37, 250–61.

be found within the range of distances which he anticipated. The Isle of Brasil as found by the English can therefore join the tales by the Unknown Pilot and the traditions of the Vinland voyages amongst the data which Columbus could have had at his departure.[24] Though the Day reference is suggestive, rather than conclusive, it is more specific than other indications of knowledge of pre-Columbian voyages at the disposal of the discoverer in 1492 and may therefore find a place in the Columbus story.

III

It should, in conclusion, be emphasized that the two parts of this short paper ought to be sharply differentiated. The first part is merely a common sense attempt to see where an argument from known evidence can lead. The second is a purely speculative reconstruction, novel only in its attempt to include the Day evidence of an earlier English discovery of America inside a larger perspective, but claims no objective validity. It may be useful, however, as indicating one new perspective which the Day letter has made possible. There will, no doubt, be many others.

Acknowledgement.   My thanks are due to Professor A. E. Sloman and members of the School of Hispanic Studies, University of Liverpool, for having checked Dr Vigneras's transcription and translation of the Day letter.

[24]M. G. P. B. Naish pointed out to me that I have almost returned to the position reached by Bacon when he published *The history of the reign of King Henrie the Seventh* in 1622: "And there had beene before that time [1492] a discouerie of some *Lands,* which they tooke to bee *Islands,* and were indeed the *Continent of America,* towards the *Northwest.* And it may be that some Relation of this nature comming afterwards to the knowledge of COLUMBUS, and by him suppressed, (desirous rather to make his Enterprise the *Child* of his *Science* and *Fortune,* then the *Follower* of a former *Discourie*) did giue him better assurance, that all was not at *Sea,* from the *west* of *Europe* and *Africke* vnto *Asia*" (1st ed., 1622, p. 188).

3

THE GLORIOUS KINGDOM
OF SAGUENAY*

J. E. King

Following the American landfalls of Christopher Columbus and John Cabot, Europeans in the 16th century began to search further and expand their knowledge of the New World. It quickly became clear that these were new land areas between Europe and Asia, and the Spanish, moving out from the Caribbean islands discovered by Columbus, found in Central and South America a series of relatively advanced Indian civilizations which had access to vast quantities of precious minerals. Soon gold and silver were being shipped off to Spain, to the envy of other European nations. The countries of northern Europe, recognizing the superior position of Spain (and to some extent Portugal) in the southern regions, undertook most of their exploratory voyages on the Atlantic coast of North America. The hope behind these activities was twofold: first, to uncover a water route to Asia through the newly found landmass (the Northwest Passage), and second, to find northern equivalents of the rich Indian kingdoms of Central and South America. Despite the Cabot voyages, England was not particularly active in such quests until the second half of the century; Henry VIII and his successors were too busy with the English Reformation. So the mantle of discovery fell to Francis I of France. France had been engaged in warfare with Spain over Italy, in the course of which Francis had been humiliatingly captured by the Spanish. Seeking some measure of revenge, Francis pinned his New World hopes on the efforts of Jacques Cartier, about whose early life very little is known. He apparently had some experience in voyages of explo-

*Canadian Historical Review, 31 (1950), 390–400. Reprinted by permission of the author and University of Toronto Press.

ration prior to receiving a commission from Francis in 1534 "to discover certain islands and lands where it is said that a great quantity of gold, and other precious things, are to be found." Cartier has been lionized as a great explorer, although as J. E. King points out in the following article, his positive achievements were inextricably interwoven with false hopes, erroneous information, and credulity. What was it which excited the French and Cartier? Who was responsible for the false image they had of the Saguenay? Are Cartier and the French to be criticized for acting on the information they received? Does the "myth of Saguenay" detract from Cartier's stature as an explorer?

SUGGESTIONS FOR FURTHER READING

H. P. Biggar, *The Early Trading Companies of New France* (Toronto: University of Toronto Press, 1901).

John B. Brebner, *The Explorers of North America, 1492-1806* (Cleveland: World Publishing Company, 1964).

J. H. Parry, *The Age of Reconnaissance* (New York: New American Library, 1963).

Marcel Trudel, ed., *Jacques Cartier. Textes, Choisis et Presentes par Marcel Trudel.* (Montreal: Fides, 1968).

J.M.B.

Т he glorious kingdom of Saguenay had no more existence than Olympus of the Gods. But, like Olympus, Saguenay was thought to exist, and the men who had this thought found it a powerful driving force to action. Very often, in the lives of men, not the truth, but what they feel to be the truth, is important, and must be sought out with care and precision. For what men have believed to be facts has always been the dynamic fact of history.

When Jacques Cartier, the Captain and Pilot to the King of France, dropped anchor in St. Malo Bay, on the Brittany coast, early in September 1534, his outlook was far from one of complete satisfaction.[1] He had returned from a voyage whose purpose had been to uncover a source of wealth and gold in the New World.[2] He brought back no great treasures, but he was able to lead ashore, onto the streets of the ancient seaport, two Canadian Indians, Taignoagny and Dom Agaya.[3] These col-

---

[1] H. P. Biggar, ed., "The Voyages of Jacques Cartier" (*Publications of the Public Archives of Canada*, no. 11 [1924], 79). Cartier arrived in France on September 5, 1534.

[2] H. P. Biggar, ed., "A Collection of Documents Relating to Jacques Cartier and the Sieur de Roberval" (*Publications of the Public Archives of Canada*, no. 14 [1930], 42, Grant to Cartier, March 18, 1533-4).

[3] The material results of the first voyage were furs and a few trinkets which the Indians traded for knives and bits of cloth (Biggar, "Voyages of Cartier," pp. 52-3, 56). The father of the two Indians granted permission to the French to take his sons across the water (ibid., pp. 66-7). This was on July 24, 1534, on the Gaspé Peninsula (ibid., p. 64). The names of the natives are not mentioned until after the second voyage had started (ibid., p. 120).

ourful characters, no doubt, served to arouse and maintain official interest in another voyage to the western waters.

The following spring, the captain-pilot embarked once again in quest of treasures, and the two Indians sailed with him.[4] His little flotilla crossed the North Atlantic, and, as it worked westward past Anticosti Island into the St. Lawrence, the homecoming aborigines, claiming to recognize the landmarks, announced that only two days' journey to the west began the limits of the Kingdom of the Saguenay.[5] In this manner, on Friday, August 13, 1535, the fabulous domain of Saguenay came into the white man's ken. For a decade this was "to be an *ignis fatuus* for French explorers."[6]

The Canadian tribe of Indians,[7] kinsmen of the pair who had been to France, made only occasional and fleeting references to Saguenay,[8] and it was not until October that the French learned more about it. Cartier and a few of his companions travelled up the St. Lawrence to Hochelaga, where the characteristics of Saguenay were revealed in a more liberal fashion.[9] Pointing to the gold and silver insignia of the explorers, the Indians—by signs and gestures—made it known that these metals came from the north-west, where bellicose tribes carried on incessant warfare.[10] As if to test his informers, Cartier held a copper object before them, but the natives only pointed south, indicating that no copper was to be found in Saguenay.

Leaving Hochelaga, the Frenchmen returned to their anchorage near the Canadian village of Stadacona.[11] During the harsh and tedious winter that followed, the conversation turned occasionally to the mysterious Saguenais.[12] The French were informed that they dwelt in a land wherein lay large supplies of gold and copper.[13] They were a numerous

[4]Biggar, "Voyages of Cartier," pp. 90-1; they set sail on May 19, 1535, and made their landfall on July 7, off Newfoundland (ibid., pp. 93-4).

[5]Ibid., pp. 102-103.

[6]Arthur G. Doughty, "The Beginnings of Canada" (*Canada and Its Provinces*, vol. 1, Adam Shortt, Arthur G. Doughty, eds., [Toronto, 1914-17] p. 34), gives this apt and pithy phrase for the Kingdom of Saguenay. The literature on the Kingdom of Saguenay is not plentiful; it is generally referred to only in passing. The *Canadian Historical Review*, for example, in its quarter-century of existence, has no article about it; the *Bulletin des recherches historiques*, published since 1895, has had only one comment, and that was at the primer stage of history: "En parlant du Saguenay on dit souvent 'le royaume de Saguenay'. Qui s'est servi le premier de cette appellation? C'est Jacques Cartier. . . ." (13[1907], 30).

[7]According to Cartier's informers, there were three nations of Indians living in the general vicinity of the St. Lawrence River: (1) the Canadians, who dwelt about Quebec (Biggar, "Voyages of Cartier," pp. 119, 227); (2) the Hochelaga tribe, which lived about Montreal (ibid., pp. 154-5); and (3) the Saguenais, who inhabited the lands to the north-west (see Map 1).

[8]Biggar, "Voyages of Cartier," pp. 105-106, 113-14, 116, 161.

[9]Ibid., pp. 141-51.

[10]Ibid., pp. 170-1. There were no interpreters, Taignoagny and Dom Agaya having refused to accompany the French (ibid., p. 140).

[11]Ibid., p. 172. Stadacona was the Canadian village located about where the city of Quebec is now; cf. W. F. Ganong, "Crucial Maps in the Early Cartography and Place-nomenclature of the Atlantic Coast of Canada": vol. 6, "The Voyages of Jacques Cartier" (*Transactions of the Royal Society of Canada*, 3rd series, vol. 28, sec. 2 [1934], p. 206).

[12]Biggar, "Voyages of Cartier," p. 210, describes the extreme severity of that winter.

[13]Ibid., pp. 200-201. This was probably mentioned shortly after the trip west.

MAP 1
Southeastern Canada

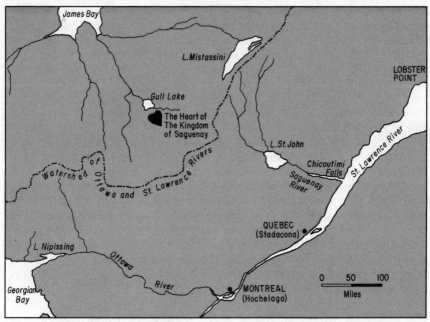

people, they were wealthy and law abiding, and dressed in clothing similar to that worn by the white men. Later this story was enlarged upon by Donnacona, the chief, who told them that there were, not only gold, but also rubies and other materials of great value.[14] Not only did the inhabitants dress like Europeans, but their skin was every bit as white!

It is not hard to picture the old chieftain, sitting before a fire on the long cold winter nights, becoming more and more intrigued with the interest of the French and with their amazing credulity. Even in the light of such anatomical knowledge as the 16th century possessed, it is hard to understand why Cartier was not warned by some of Donnacona's preposterous tales. "He told us also," Cartier wrote, "that he had visited another region where the people, possessing no anus, never eat nor digest, but simply make water through the penis. He told us furthermore that he had been . . . to another country whose inhabitants have only one leg, and other marvels too long to relate."[15]

When the winter was over and gone, Cartier, in preparing to return home, decided that it would be a fine thing to fetch Donnacona along and let the king of France hear these wonders from the mouth of one who claimed to know.[16] The promise of a present was the only inducement

[14]Ibid., p. 221.
[15]Ibid., pp. 221-2.
[16]Ibid., p. 221.

needed, and the loquacious chief set sail to drink in more of the world's prodigies.[17] To assume that because Chief Donnacona had deceived Captain Cartier, he would also deceive the King, is hardly logical, yet that is exactly what happened. If anything, the sophisticated and cultured Francis put even greater faith and belief in the Canadian savage.[18]

Sometime in 1537 or 1538, the two rulers faced each other, the one spinning his marvellous tales out of whole cloth, the other wrapping himself in them.[19] A third expedition to the west was being readied and the Most Christian King desired it to sail to Canada and thence up a river 800 leagues in length, at the end of which lay the great city of Saguenay.[20] Here there were numerous gold mines and silver mines. The winters were long and exceedingly cold, yet huge crops of clove, nutmeg, and other spices came to maturity! The pelts of the Saguenay animals were very fine and valuable. Some of the inhabitants of this strange land resembled the French, they looked like them and dressed like them; yet other men living there could fly like bats! Not far, pointed out the King to one who repeated his conversation, only from one tree to the next, but fly they could! The King explained to a Portuguese adviser why he believed such tales so implicitly. Chief Donnacona had never been found in error; and if any listener justifiably evinced a little scepticism in the royal presence, the ruler announced that all this had been uttered before a notary.[21] This was the bright noontime of the Kingdom of Saguenay; the *ignis fatuus* was a roaring conflagration.

In 1542 a huge expedition was fitted out, under the command of the Sieur de Roberval, a nobleman whose rank justified his appointment to the dignity of Viceroy of Saguenay.[22] Cartier, who sailed as pilot,[23] and the Viceroy himself, when they had reached Canada, set out to find this weird and fabulous domain. Only a few fragments of their reports are extant.[24] The results, of course, were entirely fruitless and sterile.[25] The *ignis fatuus* was burning itself out; the glare of discovery cut through the nebulous kingdom, and after the middle of the 16th century its name

---

[17]Ibid., pp. 227-9, 233.

[18]It will be noted in the passage cited above that Cartier merely sets down these wonders as statements of the chief. The King is not as cautious—he asserts them as facts.

[19]The voyagers returned to St. Malo on July 16, 1536 (ibid., p. 240). It is probable that some time was occupied in straightening out affairs at the seaport before Cartier was able to set out for the royal court.

[20]Biggar, "Cartier and Roberval," pp. 76-9, Lagarto to the King of Portugal, January 22, 1539(?). Lagarto was a Portuguese navigator in the employ of Francis I (ibid., p. 76).

[21]The King pointed out that his reason for so implicit belief in the Indian was that the story had been told many times without any variation (ibid., pp. 79-80).

[22]Biggar, "Cartier and Roberval," p. 179, Roberval's Commission, January 15, 1540-1.

[23]Ibid., p. 128, Cartier's Commission, October 17, 1540.

[24]The account of Cartier's third voyage takes the reader as far as Hochelaga, on the way to Saguenay, then it ends abruptly (Biggar, "Voyages of Cartier," pp. 249-59). The expedition started in May 1541 (ibid., p. 251 n.). Roberval started in April 1542, and the account leaves him as he has departed to the Saguenay country (ibid., pp. 263-70).

[25]The assumption that they found nothing is incontrovertible, for both men returned to France and neither made any statement startling enough to warrant notice. See Biggar, "Cartier and Roberval," pp. 486-87, for proof of their presence in France by 1545.

came to be used only in reference to the river which was once believed to wind through its borders.[26]

II

The rise and fall of the Glorious Kingdom of Saguenay, in common with the rise and fall of other great kingdoms—real and imaginary— have numerous aspects. The historical one has already been delineated. The geographical phases will now be examined.

It will be recalled from what has already been said, that, while coasting westward in the Gulf of St. Lawrence, just above Anticosti Island, Jacques Cartier was informed during August 1535, that the Kingdom of Saguenay lay two days' journey ahead. Accordingly, two days after this announcement, his young Indians shouted that the border of Saguenay was to starboard, on the north shore of the Gulf.[27] An analysis of these two bits of information apparently induced the French to pay very little attention to them. The little flotilla had covered about 100 miles in those two days, an average of 50 miles a day. It is highly improbable that any Indian of that period would conceive a day's journey as being 50 miles. More probably, the Indians, at the end of two days, made an announcement to corroborate their earlier assertion, and would have made such a statement even if the ships had been becalmed.

Two weeks after this, as they slid past the mouth of the Saguenay River, the Indian guides pointed it out as the route to the Kingdom.[28] This statement was later substantiated by their father, the chief, and the French acted on it some years later when the Sieur de Roberval undertook to reach Saguenay by this route.[29]

Late in September, the Frenchmen travelled up the St. Lawrence to Hochelaga, the site of Montreal. The Indians in that vicinity pointed out a tributary of the larger stream, one which emptied into it a short distance from where they stood.[30] The smaller river, the Ottawa, was the direct approach, they said, to a kingdom of gold. Cartier assumed this to be the Kingdom of Saguenay.

Had the young guides been given credence, Saguenay would have assumed more fantastic characteristics than ever. They were now 550 miles west of the outpost of Saguenay, which Taignoagny and his brother

---

[26]One authority claims that Saguenay is an Indian word, meaning "water which issues forth" (C.-H. Laverdière, ed., *Œuvres de Champlain*, vol. 2 [Québec, 1870], 4 n.). I am inclined to agree with Ganong ("Crucial Maps," p. 216), when he states that one can find just what is sought if the search is long and uncritical enough. That interest in the mythical realm died down by the latter part of the century is evident from a perusal of some of the Royal Proclamations regarding America; H. Michelant and Alfred Rame, eds., *Voyage de Jacques Cartier au Canada* (Paris, 1865), app., pp. 32-34, Proclamation of Henry III, August 29, 1575; 34-38, Proclamation of Henry III, March 11, 1588; pp. 48-51, Proclamation of Henry III, July 9, 1588. The argument from silence is always a dangerous one, but I feel that in a case like this, where great marvels would have evoked greater comment, silence is proof conclusive that Saguenay had departed into the northern fog.

[27]Biggar, "Voyages of Cartier," pp. 104-6. They were probably passing Lobster Point, about 100 miles west of their position two days earlier (ibid., p. 105).

[28]Ibid., p. 113. This occurred on September 1, 1535.

[29]Ibid., pp. 269-70.

[30]Ibid.

pointed to in mid-August. But, although deep in their territory, not one Saguenais had accosted them; this quality of invisibility, of course, was too unbelievable, and, as has been pointed out, the statements of the two young men were not accepted.

Upon his return to Stadacona, Cartier learned from the chief that the Kingdom of Saguenay was indeed a month's journey from Hochelaga up the Ottawa River, and that beyond it lay a great fresh water sea. A secondary route was also available, Donnacona related. This alternate route ran up the Saguenay River, which was navigable for the first eight or nine days in the large boats, and thereafter the smaller boats could be utilized.[31]

Apparently the chief was referring to Chicoutimi Falls as the limit beyond which the big vessels could not go.[32] Thus he estimated a day's journey as 10 miles, for the falls are about 80 miles above the confluence of the Saguenay and the St. Lawrence. On this basis, the Kingdom of Saguenay, at least the core of this domain, may be placed near Gull Lake, 50° north latitude and 77° west longitude. It extended out from there, and in one direction reached down toward Georgian Bay, an inlet of Lake Huron, the "fresh water sea." But the heart of the realm was not directly accessible by water from the St. Lawrence, for a glance at the map will show that it lay beyond the watershed of that great stream.[33]

Geographically, it must be granted that Donnacona was correct, in a vague sort of way, about certain points of the physical structure of Canada. His errors can be attributed to the fact that he was repeating hearsay, and, in the case of Donnacona, that was an irresistible temptation to violate the truth. The subsequent lengthening of the voyage to Saguenay from 300 miles to 2,000 as King Francis believed, will be dealt with later.

Contemporary maps and charts buttress the assertion that Saguenay came into the world in the fourth decade of the sixteenth century and ceased to exist shortly thereafter. At the start of the century, an anonymous Portuguese chartmaker depicted Newfoundland as an island.[34] But this island—the land of Cortereal, as he called it—was one of indeterminate size, and there is no trace of the American mainland or of shining Saguenay to the west. A quarter of a century later, an Italian cartographer sketched the eastern American coastline in a recognizable way, but the area about the southern approach to the St. Lawrence is outlined in rudimentary fashion; no bold cleavage exists between Cape Breton Island and Cape Race.[35] There is no trace of Canada, and mysterious Saguenay is still wrapped in mystery.

---

[31] Ibid., pp. 200-1.

[32] See Map 1.

[33] Ibid.

[34] Konrad Kretchmer, *Die Entdeckung Americas* (Berlin, 1892), table 8, no. 2 (Karte eines Anonymous, nach 1502).

[35] Ibid., table 14, no. 7 (Karte des Visconte Maggiolo, 1527). Maggiolo calls what is now the eastern part of the United States "Francesca," as a result of the voyage of Giovanni da Verrazano to that part of the world in 1524 under the auspices of the French king; cf. Giovanni da Verrazano, "Voyage de Giovanni da Verrazano a la 'Francesca'" (*Les Français en Amérique,* Ch.-A. Julien et al., eds., [Paris, 1946], pp. 53-76).

One of Roberval's pilots has furnished a sketch that is both valuable and disappointing. It was made, presumably, during or shortly after the attempt to discover Saguenay by passing up the river of that name.[36] The east bank of the Saguenay River, according to this sketch, is one of the frontiers of the kingdom, which appears as a peninsula; some distance upstream there is shown "La Mer du Saguenay," a huge body of water bending toward the west. Here the artist has confused his sources of information—he had heard of the freshwater sea and of the lake above Chicoutimi Falls, and it was common knowledge that one aim of the expedition was a sea route to Cathay or the Orient.[37] The attempt to reconcile all this information is disappointing from a cartographical point of view, yet from an historical outlook I feel that the chart clearly demonstrates that Roberval did not go as far as the Chicoutimi Falls.

Of the early maps showing the area perhaps the most ornate is one by Desceliers, published in 1546.[38] Saguenay, or "Sagne," as it is here named, is put somewhat south of the location I have plotted, but otherwise the map appears to be close to the facts that were available in Cartier's accounts of his voyages.

Mapmakers being conservative by nature, the geographical heyday of Saguenay followed its historical one by a few years.[39] By the last years of the century, however, even these men had become firmly convinced that Saguenay was a myth, and it disappeared from maps as it had disappeared from the minds of men.[40] It lingered on only in the name of the gloomy river that was supposed to lead to the great empire.

III

What were the faggots that fed this *ignis fatuus*? Who heaped them on the blaze? Was that which launched a score of ships the hallucination of some aborigine along the St. Lawrence's shores, or was it a vicious circle, in which the wild dreams of the French drove them on to heroic actions to find those same wild dreams? At this point an analysis of the parentage of Saguenay will be attempted; was it French or Indian or half-breed?

The obvious sources are Indian and French. To make the analysis clearer each will be scrutinized separately. When the Indians told Cartier

---

[36]See Map 2. This is an enlarged sketch from Justin Winsor, *Cartier to Frontenac* (Boston, 1894), p. 43, showing the Saint Lawrence and the Saguenay as sketched by Allefonsce. Allefonsce, or Alphonse, wrote a treatise on the geography of his voyage with Roberval (cf. James Phinney Baxter, *A Memoir of Jacques Cartier* [New York, 1906], pp. 245–60); for his remarks on the Saguenay, see pp. 253–4.

[37]The King states that he is sending Cartier to the ". . . grand pays des terres de Canada et Ochelaga, faisant un bout de l'Asie du coste de l'occident . . ." Biggar, "Cartier and Roberval," p. 128, Cartier's Commission, October 17, 1540.

[38]A. E. Norderskiold, *Periplus* (Stockholm, 1897), plate 51 (Desceliers, 1546): north-west of Le Sagne Desceliers has put down "Terre Incogneve," which, judging from the shape of Canada, might be a good name for the whole map.

[39]For an opinion on the conservatism of mapmakers, cf. Ganong, "Crucial Maps," pp. 153–4.

[40]Kretchmer, *Entdeckung*, table 19, no. 5 (Karte des Cornelius de Judaeis, 1593).

MAP 2
A Sketch by Allefonsce, Roberval's Pilot, 1542

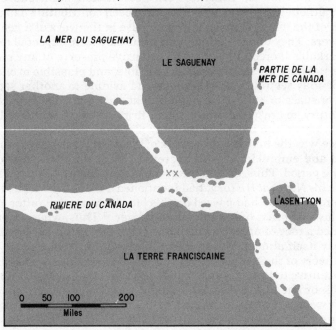

about Saguenay, were they merely relating to him the ancient mythology of the forest? This seems highly improbable. Mythology and tradition tend to assume a very definite and concrete form, and while the discrepancies between the Canadian and the Hochelaga tribesmen, relative to Saguenay, might be dismissed as mere accidental differences, to be expected where the two groups lived so far apart, this does not explain the difference which existed in the statements of Donnacona on the one hand and his sons on the other.[41] Differences about so basic a thing as the territorial limits of Saguenay, existing within a family, clearly denote that the tradition was not ancient or firmly established. Investigations by experts in this field reveal that Saguenay occupied no place in the mythology of the Indians dwelling in eastern Canada.[42]

Since tradition based on myth or legend did not exist, *a fortiori* it did not exist based on fact. The presence of Norsemen or other Europeans is not to be accepted by any save those who feel that it is connected with the

---

[41]"The oral tradition of illiterate groups enjoys a double advantage over that of literate peoples; it is carried along by means of an exceptionally developed power of memory, and in a set form of words." Cf. Gilbert J. Garraghan, *A Guide to Historical Method* (New York, 1946), p. 262. The tradition about Saguenay was obviously too fluid and flexible to conform to this criterion.

[42]In Louis Herbert Gray et al., eds., *The Mythology of All Races* (Boston, 1914-32), there is no mention of Saguenay in the treatment of the American Indians.

Norse who allegedly carved the Kensington Rune Stone.[43] The evidence clearly shows that the Indians were not the activating cause of Saguenay, although they very well may have been contributing causes. The children of the forest very soon became wise in the ways of a generation of explorers. They told the white men what they were expected to tell.[44]

Remarkable incredulity is not the exclusive preserve of any race or of any age.[45] What may seem possible, probable, and plausible to one group of people may seem utterly ridiculous and asinine to another separated by time or space or both. To understand the background of France in the 16th century, to grasp the time element firmly, while it will not alter any fact, may cast some light on this foggy problem.

France was the heir to a great bulk of classical learning in every field, adorned and embroidered with accretions from the not-so-classical intervening period. Thus, during the great days of imperial Rome, Pliny the Elder, in his *Natural History*, had mentioned a race of one-legged men.[46] St. Isidore of Seville had passed on this bit of information, after clothing it with his authority, half a millennium later.[47] Thus, when Donnacona mentioned a race of unipeds which lived near Saguenay, his words about Saguenay itself almost took on the authority of St. Isidore.

The theory of the antipodes, expounded by Macrobius, certainly acted as an incentive to French exploration, and if the king did not originate it, Roberval, or one of his associates, could very well have intimated that Spanish wealth in the south must be balanced by wealth in the north, and Portuguese spices in the east must be balanced by spices in the west.[48] This was consoling and *ex parte* reasoning, but modern governments have argued themselves into expensive projects, the results of which have been less productive and more costly than the explorations of Cartier and Roberval.

If this were not enough to convince the French, there was the belief that Asia jutted right down to the St. Lawrence, and that the Saguenay flowed 2,000 miles to the north and west, that it was the short Northwest

---

[43]"But the people said to live in that wild region of Saguenay must be wholly mythical, with a basis in rumors of Indian tribes in the far west, unless, indeed, the woolen clothes and the white skins (in the light of the Kensington stone?) may reflect ancient tradition of Norsemen in Hudson Bay" (Ganong, "Crucial Maps," p. 231). I feel Ganong has erred in not analysing that tradition and applying strict standards to it. Unless, of course, he is merely throwing out this thought for speculation.

[44]As one writer on the age of discovery put it, "and the Indians, ever eager to please, cheerfully agreed to everything [Columbus] said." Cf. Samuel Eliot Morison, *Admiral of the Ocean Sea*, vol. 2 (Boston, 1942), pp. 133 and 145 n.

[45]Witness in our own day the hysteria created by the so-called Martian Attack, broadcast as a play by Orson Welles, and now recently by reports about flying saucers.

[46]E. E. Sikes, "Latin Literature of the Silver Age" (*Cambridge Ancient History*, vol. 11 [Cambridge, 1923–39], p. 732).

[47]Dr. Rafael Altamira, "Spain under the Visigoths" (*Cambridge Medieval History*, vol. 2 [Cambridge, 1911–36], pp. 192–3), remarks on the great popularity of St. Isidore's works. "In Spain, France and other European countries, there was scarcely a single library belonging to a chapter-house or an abbey, whose catalogue could not boast of a copy of St. Isidore's work."

[48]For a brief discussion of the theory of the antipodes, see William H. Tillinghast, "The Geographical Knowledge of the Ancients Considered in Relation to the Discovery of America" (Justin Winsor, ed., *Narrative and Critical History of America*, vol. 1 [Boston, 1884–89], p. 31).

Passage to the Orient.[49] This required the sevenfold increase of Don-nacona's assertion that the river was 300 miles long, but, as the Indian measured distances by moons, or months, rather than by miles, the sub-stitution of 70 miles a day for 10 was effected with no violence what-soever. Seamen were accustomed to sailing at least that distance within the course of 24 hours. Thus the moon's journey up the Saguenay was stretched to put its terminal in the hidden East. As far as objective truth was concerned, then, the Indians and the French were working at cross purposes. The red men told, as has been stated, what they were expected to tell; the white men believed what they wanted to believe.

Within a few years the untruth of all these premises was ascertained. Among professionals, that is to say, among chartmakers and explorers, the river contracted to its proper length, and the Kingdom of Saguenay disappeared from maps. Yet so firmly had these things been held, that among those with only a casual interest in farflung geography or among those moved by sheer adventure, the river shrank only little by little.[50]

---

[49]Cf. above, n. 37; the distance of a French league has been computed at 2½ miles (cf. Samuel Edward Dawson, *The Saint Lawrence, Its Basin and Border-Lands* [New York, 1905], p. 123).

[50]Reuben Gold Thwaites, ed., *Travels and Explorations of the Jesuit Missionaries in New France 1610-1791*, vol. 2 (Cleveland, 1896-1901), Relation of 1613-14, p. 205: "These rivers are open for navigation far Northward—the Saguenay five hundred leagues, . . ." Shrinkage was slow among the Jesuits who were not concerned with going to the East. A few years later, however, they advised an English adventurer not to try to find a passage to the Pacific by way of the Saguenay. "This poor man would have lost fifty lives, if he had had so many, before reaching this North sea by the way he had described; and if he had found this sea, he would have discovered nothing new, nor found any passage to new Mexico. One need not be a great Geographer to recognize this fact." Ibid., vol. 18, Relation of 1640, p. 237.

4

PROBLEMS OF ASSIMILATION IN NEW FRANCE, 1603–1645*

Cornelius J. Jaenen

The Europeans who discovered and first settled on the mainland of North America did not find the continent devoid of human habitation, however frequently they have spoken of it as a howling wilderness. North America had a native population—usually labelled Indians—and how to deal with these peoples was one of the critical problems of the early years of European penetration. The Spanish in their territories of South and Central America had found a native population which was relatively advanced in terms of culture and civilization, and they simply substituted themselves for the Indians' former Inca, Maya, or Aztec masters. But the Indian tribes of North America could not be dealt with in this way. They were seminomadic hunters and farmers, and their culture, usually called "primitive" by the Europeans (although anthropologists frequently find great complexities in primitive cultures), was certainly one that was unfamiliar to the early explorers, missionaries, and fur traders. Political organization among the natives was far less stable and hierarchic than in Europe; Indian culture was preliterate and native mores quite different from those of the white man. The Indians were not, of course, Christians, and this provided one of the major motivating forces behind much of the European presence in the early years. But the missionaries, too, frequently fell into the trap of attempting to judge the natives by European standards. Unable to transcend European assumptions, the white man had great difficulty in understanding the Indians; learning the native languages was hardly

*French Historical Studies, 4 (1966), 265–89.

enough. As Professor Cornelius Jaenen points out in the following article, some of the early French missionaries proposed a typically European
solution to the problem: assimilate the Indians into the white man's
society. Was this a reasonable solution to the problem of the clash of
alien—and to some extent unequal—cultures? Did the Indians resist
this? Why? Why did the missionary policy of assimilation fail? Was the
French record with their natives an "enlightened" one in terms of the
times?

SUGGESTIONS FOR FURTHER READING

Cornelius J. Jaenen, *Friend and Foe: Aspects of French-Amerindian Cultural
Contact in the Sixteenth and Seventeenth Centuries* (Toronto: McClelland and Stewart, 1976).

F. Parkman, *The Jesuits in North America* (many editions).

Marcel Trudel, *The Beginnings of New France 1524-1663* (Toronto: McClelland and Stewart, 1973).

J.M.B.

T he purpose of this paper is to examine briefly the problems raised
by the initial cultural contacts between French and Amérindians
from the granting of a commercial monopoly to Huguenot merchants in 1603 to the creation of a Canadian-based trading company, the
Community of Habitants, in 1645. Such an approach will of necessity
indicate only the direction and trends; nevertheless, it can be effective in
supplying a unified critique of the evolution of assimilation theories and
the effects of the cultural confrontation on Indian society.

The mandate to evangelize the Amérindians of New France and to
assimilate them into French life dates from the foundations of the colony. Henry IV's commission to Pierre du Gua, Sieur de Monts, a Huguenot, in 1603 instructed him to "provoke and rouse them [Indians] to
the knowledge of God and to the light of the Christian faith and religion,"
as well as safeguard and educate any Europeans who might come to the
colony.[1] The Vice-Regent, the Duke of Montmorency, amplified the
king's instructions:

> . . . to seek to lead the natives thereof to the profession of the Christian
> faith, to civilization of manners, an ordered life, practice, and intercourse
> with the French for the gain of their commerce; and finally their recognition
> and submission to the authority and domination of the crown of France.[2]

Verbally, at least, the French government recognized, even at this early
date, that religious conversion alone would not suffice. In order to gain

---

[1]W. L. Grant, ed., *Marc Lescarbot: The History of New France*, vol. 2 (Toronto, 1914), p. 22.

[2]Ibid., vol. 1, p. 217.

both economic advantage and political sway over the Amérindians, they saw that a certain degree of "civilization" or "Frenchification" and, from thence, assimilation, would be necessary. In practice, of course, no such easy distinction between conversion and cultural assimilation could be maintained as the experiences of the first missionaries between 1603 and 1645 clearly demonstrate. Nor, for that matter, could certain conflicts between the two be easily resolved. The Christianizing of the Indians, however, remained the primary goal of most missionaries of the period, a fact which suggests reasons for some of the failures and some of the successes of these earliest purveyors of European culture on the American continent.

The administration of the North American region was ceded to companies of entrepreneurs, usually Huguenot merchants from Dieppe and Rouen,[3] who promised to settle the new found lands in return for enjoyment of the benefits of a trade monopoly. But the wealthier nobles and merchant capitalists, hungry for the protected profit which monopoly promised, kept up political pressures and court intrigues to have charters cancelled and new ones granted. Any group which had an interest in the New World sought to obtain concessions whenever the royal monopolies were revised. Thus, when de Mont's seigneurial rights over Port Royal were transferred to the Baron Jean de Poutrincourt, a former Huguenot pastor and a companion in arms of de Monts in the religious wars, and this transaction came up before Henry IV for ratification, the royal confessor, Father Coton, persuaded the monarch to send some Jesuit missionaries to New France. Although the king agreed, there were delays in implementing the proposal because of the opposition of certain Huguenot merchants to the scheme. In order to forestall Father Coton's plan the Huguenot merchants took a secular priest, the Abbé Jessé Fléché of Langres, with them to the colony in 1610. After only three weeks of missionary work among the Micmacs this priest baptized 21 of the Indians. The following year, the Huguenot seamen agreed to transport the Jesuit missionaries only if they paid the entire costs of the expedition. The Marquise de Guerchville, wife of the Duke de la Rochefoucauld-Liancourt, raised the necessary funds among her friends at Court to satisfy this stipulation.[4] When Fathers Pierre Biard and Ennemond Massé did reach the colony, in 1611, they resolved to commence learning as many Indian languages as possible so they could baptize many converts. They had resolved not to imitate Fléché and "not to baptize any adults unless they were previously well catechized."[5] The pres-

---

[3]There was a very active colony of Dutch, Flemish and German Protestant merchants in Rouen at the beginning of the 17th century. Some of these foreign Protestants entered into partnerships in the Acadian trade and in this way Dutch interest in a New Netherland was aroused. Simon Hart, *Voorgeschiedanis van Nieuw Nederland* (Amsterdam, 1959), pp. 44, 68.

[4]Auguste Carayon, *Première Mission des Jésuites au Canada: Lettres et Documents Inédits* (Paris, 1814), Biard to Claude Aquiaviva, January 21, 1611, pp. 6–7; also Pierre Biard, *Relation de la Nouvelle-France* (Lyon, 1616), p. 134.

[5]R. G. Thwaites, ed., *The Jesuit Relations and Allied Documents,* vol. 1 (Cleveland, Ohio, 1896–1901), pp. 9, 53 [henceforth *Jesuit Relations*].

ence of Huguenots, including some pastors, in Acadia may have had some bearing on the decision.[6]

It was not long before Biard recognized the inadequacies of the Indian languages as vehicles for expressing the mysteries of the Catholic religion. He wrote:

> . . . where words, the messengers and dispensers of thought and speech, remain totally rude, poor and confused, it is impossible that the mind and reason be greatly refined, rich and disciplined.[7]

He and his companions emphasized drill in catechism and rote mimicry of ritual. He seems to have entertained no misgivings about the pedagogical soundness, not to speak of the religious quality, of such an approach:

> It comforts me to see these little savages, though not yet Christians, yet willing, when they are here, carrying the candles, bells, holy water, and other things in the processions, and the funerals which occur here. Thus they become accustomed to act as Christians, and will become so in His time.[8]

An observation that he made on several occasions was that the Indians craved alcoholic beverages to greater excess than did Europeans.[9] Learning the Micmac language and gaining the confidence of the aborigines by living among them were missionary activities that were cut short by the destructive raids of Samuel Argall of Virginia. The Jesuits had succeeded in baptizing only 20 children before the French establishments were razed.

The second venture in building an Indian Christian state was launched on the St. Lawrence entrance to the continent. There, Samuel de Champlain, commandant of New France from 1612 to 1627, a man of many talents who had also fought under Henry of Navarre in the wars of religion, commented on the responsibility of both church and state for evangelizing the Amérindians:

> It is a great wrong to let so many men be lost and see them perish at our door, without rendering them the succour . . . which can only be given

---

[6]R. P. Duclos, *Histoire du Protestantisme français au Canada et aux États-Unis* (Montreal, 1913), p. 17.

[7]Thwaites, *Jesuit Relations*, vol. 1, p. 9.

[8]Ibid., vol. 2, p. 13.

[9]P. Biard, *Relation de la Nouvelle-France* (Lyon, 1616), pp. 14, 31, 69. A widely accepted thesis is that the Indians became easy victims to alcohol because, with the exception of several Central American tribes, none of them knew how to brew. Therefore, they were very susceptible to alcohol addiction. Cf. J. F. Lafitau, *Mœurs des Sauvages*, vol. 3 (Amsterdam, 1732), pp. 101, 103. The Recollet missionary Sagard-Théodat records, however, that some of the Hurons allowed maize to ferment in pools of stagnant water and greatly prized the potent drink derived therefrom. Another explanation is that chronic fasting was already a part of Indian culture and so excessive consumption of intoxicants found ready acceptance. Some medical authorities suggested that the absence of salt in Indian diet reduced resistance to alcohol. This author's conclusion is that, while the aforementioned explanations are valid in elucidating contributory and reinforcing factors, the major factor was the desire to experience spirit possession. The experience of intoxication was related to the very coveted state of spirit possession in Indian culture. This explains, also, the repeated emphasis in European literature and correspondence of the period on the Indian desire to imbibe only if a state of complete inebriation could be attained.

through the help of princes and ecclesiastics, who alone have the power to do this. . . .[10]

In 1617, Pope Paul V granted the request of the Superior of the Recollets (a branch of the Franciscan Friars Minor, sometimes called Greyfriars) of the Province of Aquitaine, who had reached an agreement with Champlain and Louis Houel, controller of the salt works at Brouage, to entrust the task of converting and civilizing the Amérindians to the "begging friars of Brouage."[11] During the meeting of the Estates-General in 1614, Champlain, Houel and the Recollets were able to obtain the approval of the Prince of Condé of their project. They also raised money to underwrite the venture. In February 1615, Champlain went to Rouen to obtain from the associated merchants interested in the Canadian fur trade a promise of transportation and protection.[12]

Although the four Recollet missionaries assigned to Canada arrived in June 1615, it was not until June 1620, that they opened their monastery at Notre Dame des Anges, half a league from the palisaded town of Quebec.[13] The problem that faced them in the New World arose out of the great cultural differences between the primitive hunting economies of seminomadic Amérindians and the commercial capitalism of Europeans, both Calvinists and Catholics. The Recollets soon concluded that the success of evangelization depended, in good measure, on the success of efforts by both church and state to induce the Indians to adopt a sedentary way of life. They decided to found agricultural mission stations and to invite the Indians to settle around these *bourgs*. They planned, also, to intersperse French families of virtuous Catholic background in these settlements. In 1616 the Recollets met with Champlain and some pious laymen to discuss these plans. It was unanimously decided that it was necessary "to render the Indians sedentary and to bring them up in our manners and laws."[14]

The Recollets demonstrated considerable insight into the problems of Indian missions. Father Denis Jamet, later the superior of the friary at Quebec, as early as 1615, held little hope of a rapid conversion of the Amérindians because of their cultural difference from Europeans. The nomadic way of life of the Algonquins and Montagnais he believed to be an insurmountable obstacle to assimilation; of the Hurons who were settled in villages he was more hopeful.[15] Jamet also saw some difficulty

[10]W. L. Grant, ed., *Voyages of Samuel de Champlain, 1604–1618*, vol. 1 (New York, 1907), p. 323.

[11]*A.A.Q., Eglise du Canada VII*, Provincial of Recollets to Paul V, November 7, 1617, p. 97. [The following abbreviations are employed hereafter in footnoting: *P.A.C.* for Public Archives of Canada; *A.S.Q.* for Archives du Séminaire de Québec; *A.A.Q.* for Archives de l'Archevêché de Québec; *A.C.* for Archives des Colonies; *B.R.H.* for Bulletin de Recherches Historiques.]

[12]E. Réveillaud, ed., *Histoire chronologique de la Nouvelle-France ou Canada* (Paris, 1888), pp. 89–90.

[13]*A.S.Q., Polygraphie VII*, no. 83, which includes a copy of the royal letters-patent of June 14, 1618.

[14]J. G. Shea, ed., *Chrestien Le Clercq. First Establishment of the Faith in New France*, vol. 1 (New York, 1881), p. 56.

[15]*P.A.C., 500 de Colbert*, 483, Jamet to Cardinal de Joyeuse, July 15, 1615, fols. 581-2.

arising out of the presence of Frenchmen, particularly traders itinerating in the hinterland, who, in his words, were "great swearers of the holy name of God."[16] He was becoming aware that the competitive and individualistic mores of the French would be a danger to the collective ownership which characterized the Algonquin mode of life and gave it stability. Traditional institutions and patterns of living were shattered before the missionaries, or other cultural ambassadors, could replace the former culture with the more substantial values and attributes of Western European culture. Many of the nomadic peoples were estranged from their nativistic ways before they could assimilate into European ways of life. This condition was to become characteristic of many bands of Amérindians.

Jamet's awareness of the threat posed by European culture to Indian folkways and mores stand in sharp contrast to the attitudes of Champlain, Biard and Massé. It is significant that the first cultural confrontation of European and Amérindian led him to such pessimistic observations. The view that the fur trade was the decisive factor in the disruption of the traditional Indian way of life is challenged, on the other hand, by the contention that in the case of semisedentary peoples, such as the Hurons, the commerce of the French provided the missionaries with an important ally in establishing missions. There is archaeological evidence that the development of the fur trade induced a greater concentration of Indian population in the productive areas close to the Canadian Shield and the waters of Georgian Bay than did either intertribal wars or fear of Iroquois attack.[17] By encouraging a more settled existence the fur trade aided the missions in the task of evangelization, but not of Frenchification because of the absence of any numerically significant French population besides missionaries, *donnés* and *coureurs de bois*. The Recollets demonstrated their understanding of the situation when they chose Huronia as the site of their evangelical labours. The Jesuits later succeeded to this mission, but their efforts were brought to nought by the Iroquois invasion of 1648–49.

Whatever the long range effects of these cultural contacts between Amérindian and European, the immediate aboriginal reaction to the French was favourable. The stereotype of the Frenchman was a trader who came not to dispossess the Indian but to furnish him with some of the coveted utensils, arms and blankets every European possessed. In these circumstances it was reasonable for the Recollets to believe that the education of Indian children was a logical approach to missionary activity. Education would lead to both Christianization and Frenchification. The Recollets, accordingly, founded a seminary (as they preferred to call their school because of their hope of training a native clergy for the colony) and hoped through this institution to rear young Christians who would assist in the conversion of their elders.[18] Champlain encouraged

---

[16]Ibid., fol. 582.

[17]B. G. Trigger, "Settlement as an Aspect of Iroquoian Adaptation at the Time of Contact," *American Anthropologist*, 65 (1963), 92–93.

[18]Shea, *Chrestien Le Clercq*, vol. 1, pp. 112, 144.

them and expressed the idea that close associations between Europeans and Amérindians in this seminary, and eventually in integrated agricultural settlements, would produce mutually beneficial results:

> You will perceive that they [the Indians] are not savages to such an extent that they could not, in the course of time and through association with others . . . become civilized . . . with the French language they may also acquire a French heart and spirit.[19]

It is clear that Champlain, like most of his contemporaries, did not perceive any difference between Christianity and European culture. Christianize and Frenchify, or convert and assimilate, were regarded as synonymous. Amérindians who converted to Christianity were expected to adopt the manners of Europeans: An assimilated Indian was one who became a practicing Catholic.

The scheme for evangelization and assimilation of the Amérindians required financial resources which the Recollets did not possess; one of the missionaries, therefore, was sent to France to solicit funds for the seminary for Indian children. Champlain personally petitioned Louis XIII for assistance:

> That it may please Your Majesty to found, and endow for six years only, a seminary for fifty Indian children, after which period they can be supported in consequence of the increased return of the lands which will by that time be cultivated. The children are daily offered by their parents to your petitioners to be instructed and brought up in the Christian religion.[20]

Champlain represented the situation as one which required enormous expenditures because of the Indian interest in the education of their children. The truth of the matter, however, was that substantial subsidies were required to induce them to part with their children, especially sons, even for short periods.

The seminary for Indian children was the Recollets' principal means of laying the foundations of Catholicism among the Amérindians. Three French boys and eventually six Indian boys lodged in the seminary and received basic instruction in catechism, reading and writing. By 1626 only three or four Indian families had been induced to settle near Notre Dame des Anges and take up agriculture. The efforts to evangelize and assimilate were equally disappointing in their results. The seminary closed when both pupils and funds were lacking.[21] Numerous provisions in the royal edict of 1627 establishing the Company of New France (One Hundred Associates) were designed to encourage the missionaries—for example, exclusion of all Huguenots from the colony, and the provision of a common citizenship for natural-born Frenchmen and converted-assimilated Indians.[22] The edict of 1627 also required the associated mer-

---

[19]Grant, *Voyages of Samuel de Champlain*, vol. 1, p. 264.

[20]Shea, *Chrestien Le Clercq*, vol. 1, pp. 164–65.

[21]Ibid., vol. 1, pp. 144, 251.

[22]The citizenship clause gave formal and official recognition to the assimilationist views of Champlain. Assimilated Indians came not only under the protection of the French Crown but also became subject to the laws of France. In practice, this made little or no difference before

chants who received the seigneury and property of the colony, as well as a trade monopoly, to colonize and provide three resident priests for each *habitation* or settlement. The Recollets did not reap any benefits from these provisions because the new company's supply fleet, with colonists and provisions, was captured in 1628. The following year, Quebec itself was captured by the English. This terminated the unsuccessful Recollet experiment in Frenchification of the Indians.

But the Recollets had realized before the conquest of 1629 that the task they had undertaken was too formidable for their limited resources of manpower and money. In 1624, Father Irenée de Piat, on his return to France, asked the Society of Jesus to join the Recollets in the work of evangelizing the Amérindians. At first, he did not have the support of his own order but eventually his view prevailed. A Recollet memorandum of 1637 gives the following account:

> . . . then afterwards, having proposed the matter, he had it agreed to by the superiors of the Recollectz, who even solicited on their (i.e., Jesuit) behalf among the merchants who did not want them, and the Recollectz managed this business so well, that the Jesuit Fathers and they crossed over on the first sailing.[23]

Recollets and Jesuits co-operated "contrary to the will of the merchants"[24] for a period of two years. The Recollets came to believe that the Jesuits were intent upon undermining their work:

> . . . the Society of Jesus prefers for its own temporal interests to see an infinity of savage nations remain in spiritual darkness and be miserably lost rather than allow the Recollets, who seek only the salvation of souls, to become involved.[25]

This growing rivalry was terminated temporarily by the English occupation of Quebec.

Recollet pioneer work was very important despite the recognition of weaknesses. They had expended much energy in the teaching of Indian youth and preaching to the adults; they compiled Indian dictionaries and grammars; and they founded a school or seminary, and four mission

---

1663. *Edict du Roy pour l'Establissement de la Compagnie de la Nouvelle-France* (Paris, 1657), articles ii, iii, xvii, pp. 5, 6, 13; also found in *A.S.Q., Polygraphie III,* no. 2. As early as 1621, the Recollets had started agitating for the expulsion of Huguenots and to that end had called an assembly at Quebec. Cf. *A.P.Q., Manuscrits II,* I, 37. In 1624 they successfully petitioned the Viceroy to prohibit Huguenots practicing their cult aboard ship because their hymn singing and preaching attracted Indians to the wharves during such religious services. Réveillaud, *Histoire chronologique . . . ,* p. 121. Pressure was brought to bear on the numerous Huguenots at Quebec and Trois Rivières from 1646 onwards, for we read of numerous conversions. *Journal des Jésuites,* pp. 46, 74, 208, 334, 336; Dollier de Casson, *Histoire du Montréal, 1640-1672* (Montreal, 1871), p. 80; *A.S.Q., Polygraphie VIII,* no. 66, Petit cahier de l'abbé Antoine Parant.

[23]P. Margry, *Découvertes et Etablissements des Français dans l'ouest et dans le sud de l'Amérique septentrionale,* vol. 1 (Paris, 1879), p. 8 [henceforth *Découvertes*]; also Réveillaud, op. cit., p. 125.

[24]*A.S.Q., Polygraphie III,* no. 74; also Réveillaud, op. cit., p. 126.

[25]Réveillaud, *Histoire chronologique . . . ,* p. 137. Among the Recollets' complaints was an objection to the Jesuits having made a pompous and ostentatious ceremony of the baptism of an Indian converted and sent to France by the Recollets.

stations. Their work could not be measured only in terms of evangelization:

> In the year 1618 they had two savages who were educated, and one of these, brought to France, baptized and put in boarding at the college of Calleville, was very well educated. They raised others too and baptized several. . . .[26]

Their objective was a bi-racial colony of Europeans and assimilated Indians. The means of attaining this objective were defined in these terms:

> It must be hoped that as the Colony is peopled, we shall civilize the Indians. This is necessary first; their minds will open and their good sense, of which they have the base. They will be regulated by French laws and modes of living, in order to render them capable of understanding such profound mysteries; for all that concerns human and civil life is a mystery for our Indians in their present state, and it will require more expense and toil to render them men than it has required to make whole nations Christian.[27]

The Recollets, in other words, had come to believe that assimilation would have to precede mass conversion. They had also come to believe that assimilation would be achieved only over a long period of time and with many attendant difficulties.

When Quebec was restored to France in 1632, Cardinal Richelieu, who had at first decided to assign the Canadian mission to the Capuchins,[28] was prevailed on by Jean de Lauzon, president of the Company of New France, and other friends of the Jesuits, to restrict the mission field of Canada to the Jesuits.[29] The latter were aware of the Recollets' conclusions; nevertheless, as shall be demonstrated, they made several errors of judgment. They appeared to have a better chance of success than the Recollets because of their superior financial resources, their unequalled missionary fervour, their influence at Court, and their effective propaganda through the edited journals of their missionaries under the title of *Relations*. The first step in Jesuit mission work was, as always, learning the native languages. They employed what would be called the direct method of language study; they took up residence in the native encampments, painstakingly began learning the dialects (which bore no resemblance to European vernacular or classical tongues in vocabulary forms, syntax, sentence structure and expression of abstract ideas), and reduced their knowledge to vocabularies and grammars, and eventually catechisms and hymnaries. One missionary explained:

> Those who know what languages are will rightly consider that to learn one without books and almost without an interpreter, among wandering people, and in the midst of several other occupations, is not the work of a day.[30]

---

[26]Margry, *Découvertes*, vol. 1, pp. 5-6.

[27]Shea, *Chrestien Le Clercq*, vol. 1, p. 214.

[28]F. Martin, ed., *F. J. Bressani: Relation Abrégée de Quelques Missions des Pères de la Compagnie de Jésus dans la Nouvelle-France* (Montreal, 1852), Appendix C, p. 295.

[29]Margry, *Découvertes*, vol. 1, p. 11; M. Eastman, *Church and State in Early Canada* (Edinburgh, 1915), pp. 11-15; H. P. Biggar, *The Early Trading Companies of New France* (Toronto, 1901), p. 279.

[30]Thwaites, op. cit., *Jesuit Relations*, vol. 9, pp. 87-88.

These élite warriors of the church had been carefully selected for the warfare against ignorance, and had been ruthlessly purged of the unfit and unwilling, with close scrutinization of health, intelligence, good judgment, family background, appearance, education, teaching experience and absolute devotion for and obedience to their superiors.[31] Once the missionaries had acquired one or more native languages they became extremely valuable to the state as interpreters and political agents.[32] Their stated objective and purpose remained religious, as defined in the papal letter of approbation in 1540, namely, to promote "the good of souls and the propagation of the faith by means of public preaching, the ministry of the word of God, spiritual exercises and works of charity, but in particular through the instruction of children and the ignorant in the Christian doctrine."[33] Subsequent developments indicated, in some measure, how these objectives accorded with colonial conditions and attitudes.

The Jesuit mission began in earnest in New France with the arrival of Father Paul Le Jeune as Superior in July, 1632. The Company of New France gave them the monastery at Notre Dame des Anges, which had belonged to the Recollets, for their Indian work. Le Jeune decided to adopt the Recollet policy of operating a seminary for Indian children, so appealed in France to readers of the *Relations* for financial assistance.[34] The Marquis de Gamache, a *dévot* whose son had entered the Society of Jesus, provided most of the money required.[35] Le Jeune sent a few select pupils to France,[36] but preferred, in general, to attract Indian children to schools where they could be brought into close contact with the children of the colonists. He was convinced that "if animals are capable of discipline, the young savage children are much more so," and intellectually he regarded them equal to Europeans.[37] No concessions were made for

[31]Only Fathers de Noue and Chabanel lacked superior ability in linguistics. Thwaites, *Jesuit Relations*, vol. 29, p. 26; vol. 25, p. 150. There is record of only one priest, Jean François Élie, being forced to leave the order and the colony in disgrace. *Journal des Jésuites*, p. 357.

[32]It was Father Isaac Jogues, for example, who warned Governor Montmagny in 1643 that the Iroquois objective was the annihilation of the Huron middlemen in the fur trade. *B.R.H.*, vol. 36, no. 1 (January 1930), Jogues to Montmagny, June 30, 1643, pp. 48–49. Similarly, it was Father Druillettes who visited the English colonies in 1650 to secure an intercolonial nonaggression pact, and this at a time when Jesuits were neither safe nor welcome on English soil. *Collection de Manuscrits*, vol. 1 (Quebec, 1883), p. 127.

[33]A. P. Farrall, *The Jesuit Code of Liberal Education, Development and Scope of the Ratio Studiorum* (Milwaukee, Wis., 1938), p. 8.

[34]Thwaites, *Jesuit Relations*, vol. 5, p. 196; vol. 6, pp. 150–2; vol. 7, p. 265.

[35]Thwaites, *Jesuit Relations*, vol. 6, pp. 85–9, 153–5, 327, no. 9; vol. 8, pp. 227, 237. The appeal was directed especially to the devout men and women who were organized into a semisecret spiritual fellowship, the Company of the Holy Sacrament. Many of the pious founders and supporters of the Canadian colony belonged to this puritanical élite which grew out of the Catholic revival of the early 17th century in France. The first five members of the Society of Jesus to come to New France had come as individual missionaries, not as a religious community, therefore, according to article 277 of the Custom of Paris and article 131 of the Ordinance of 1539 they were forbidden to solicit or accept monetary gifts. *A.S.Q.*, *Polygraphie VIII*, no. 60.

[36]Thwaites, *Jesuit Relations*, vol. 11, p. 94. The successful scholar the Recollets had sent to France reverted to barbarism in Canada. Cf. H. Harrisse, *Notes pour Servir à l'Histoire, à la bibliographie et à la cartographie de la Nouvelle-France et des Pays adjacents, 1545–1700* (Paris, 1872), p. 71.

[37]Thwaites, *Jesuit Relations*, vol. 16, pp. 179–181.

the cultural background of the Indian children. Jesuit education in New France demonstrated the application of the classroom techniques, discipline and curriculum prescribed in the *Ratio Studiorium*.[38] There were, therefore, many exhibitions of student achievement; public awards and public exhibits were employed to create incentive and foster competition; academic awards were much emphasized; and in the classroom, memory recitation, repetitions, concertations, and examinations were the usual fare. Father Jean de Brébeuf wrote about "weekly reviews," "awarding prizes of merit," "the stimulation of learning through awards," and "holding public exercises for children before both French and adult Indians."[39]

Another aspect of the rationale underpinning missionary work, as revealed in the correspondence and official reports of the period, was the belief that devotion and self-sacrifice on the part of dedicated missionaries, some zealous to the point of welcoming martyrdom, would prepare Indian hearts and minds to receive their gospel. The statements that eventually came from the plumes of these dedicated, perhaps desperate, proselytizers indicate, on the contrary, that the emotional appeal of self-sacrifice meant little to the Amérindians. One such statement was:

> If you love the French people as you say you do, then love them, and they will teach you the way to heaven. This is what makes them leave their friends, their country and their comforts to instruct you and especially to teach your children a knowledge so necessary.[40]

The Indian, on his part, saw little love or self-sacrifice among the French traders. In addition, the European-type education the missionary wanted to subject Indian children to had little meaning in the wilderness. Moreover, the missionary himself remained an enigma; his presence and his mission were never understood by the tribesmen.

There were several innovations arising out of the Canadian environment. In France the Jesuits did not concern themselves with elementary education, but in New France they found it necessary to do so. Moreover, contrary to their European practice, they came to concern themselves with the education of girls. They even experimented with co-education in their school for Indians. Le Jeune, in drawing up a long-range plan for the Canadian missions, decided on separate seminaries for each of the Indian tribes and the encouragement of the construction of permanent houses and the adoption of sedentary agriculture by all the Indians near mission stations. In these ways the environment had imposed modifications of preconceived European ideas concerning schooling.

In 1635 the Jesuits began teaching elementary subjects at Notre Dame des Anges. At first, the French and Indian children were segre-

---

[38]A succinct summary of Jesuit educational principles is given in J. V. Jacobsen, *Educational Foundations of the Jesuits in Sixteenth Century New Spain* (Berkeley, 1938). A. P. Farrall, *The Jesuit Code of Liberal Education, Development and Scope of the Ratio Studiorium* (Milwaukee, 1938), is useful, too.

[39]Thwaites, *Jesuit Relations*, vol. 11, p. 225.

[40]Ibid., vol. 5, p. 251.

gated and a different teacher taught each group. Soon the two classes were integrated because only six Indian children had come to receive instruction and these had arrived frightened, homesick, undernourished, and practically naked. Indian parents were loathe to part with their children but they did believe the French would feed and clothe them well. Very soon the Indian children found the routine of school too much for them and they began to act like "wild asses' colts." The cultural conflict was too great to bear and before the year was completed all these children had left.[41] The *Relations* indicate the extent of this cultural conflict:

> . . . these new guests, giving themselves up . . . to thieving, gourmandizing, gaming, idleness, lying and similar irregularities, could not endure the paternal admonitions given them to change their mode of life, and above all the tacit reproofs, conveyed by the example of their companions, who showed as much restraint as they did of lawlessness and immoderation.[42]

The permissiveness of Indian upbringing clashed seriously with the strict regimen of Jesuit pedagogy.

Le Jeune decided that in the absence of large numbers of French children at Notre Dame des Anges, located half a league from Quebec and therefore more suitable for a monastery than a school,[43] it was necessary to find another location because, in his words, "experience has shown us that it must be established where the bulk of the French population is, to attract the little savages by the French children."[44] This lesson ought to have been learnt from the Recollets. Le Jeune was becoming aware of the fact that assimilation could occur only if one group were a large majority of a very superior culture and the minority group were dispersed throughout the majoritarian community. Nevertheless, he was an inveterate optimist. He saw two factors in particular standing in favour of the absorption of the Amérindians into a French way of life. First, all the Indians appeared to be intelligent, educable, and amenable to assimilation if rendered sedentary: "It seems to me that the tribes who have stationary homes could easily be converted. It is only necessary to know the language."[45] Secondly, the hardships of a seminomadic or temporary village type of life encouraged adoption of a settled existence: "In New France there are some among them who have begun to cultivate the soil and plant Indian corn, having become weary of their difficult and miserable way of life."[46]

During his missionary tour among the northern Indians in 1633-34, Le Jeune became convinced that empty stomachs rendered Indian ears dull of hearing for the gospel. He was certain that a sedentary way of life

[41]*A.S.Q., Fonds Verreau XIII*, no. 27c; also Thwaites, *Jesuit Relations*, vol. 6, p. 242; vol. 8, p. 226; vol. 9, p. 284; vol. 12, pp. 44, 48.

[42]Thwaites, *Jesuit Relations*, vol. 14, p. 233.

[43]Sacra Rituum Congregatio, Sectio Historica, *Quebecen. Beatificationis et Canonizationis Ven. Servi Dei Francisci de Montmorency Laval* (Rome, 1961), Document 43, no. 17, Memorandum of 1684, p. 314.

[44]Thwaites, *Jesuit Relations*, vol. 9, p. 707.

[45]Ibid., vol. 5, p. 33.

[46]Ibid., vol. 5, p. 33.

was more conducive to missionary success than a seminomadic existence. Since the efforts to convert young Indians at a seminary had
proved unsuccessful, he resolved to attempt to resettle Indian families at
Sillery and Trois Rivières where they would be isolated cells, the nucleus
of a new Israel. Noel Brulart de Sillery, a friend of François de Sales and
Vincent de Paul and an active member of the Company of the Holy Sacrament,[47] who at the age of 54 had retired from a successful public life
and devoted himself to religious activities, donated 32,000 *livres* to
launch the program and establish two Indian families at Sillery, near
Quebec.[48] This settlement was first called a *réserve* in an ordinance
issued by Pierre Boucher of Trois Rivières in 1653 forbidding soldiers and
settlers to trade with domiciled Indians.[49]

The Indian reservation created in 1637 would provide isolation and
insulation from the evil influences of both the Indian encampments and
the French trading posts. Segregated communities of this kind had been
created first in Mexico and Paraguay under the name of *reducciones*. Le
Jeune acknowledged that the Jesuit experience in Spanish America had
been his source of inspiration.[50] Both Algonquins and Hurons were attracted to Sillery. A number of children presented themselves for
schooling but the final outcome was the same as before. All had run off
by the following spring.[51] More children came the next year but disease
severely thinned their ranks.[52] One of the unfortunate consequences of
proximity to the French settlements was exposure to European diseases,
to which the aborigines were extremely susceptible. In the early flush of
enthusiasm, Le Jeune had written about the dry rot of the "old stumps"
and had maintained that the future of the Church depended on the
youth. By 1638, he began to write about the power of God to renew life in
the "old wild trunks."[53] This indicated his decision to shift emphasis to
preaching to adults. By 1645 there were no less than 167 Christianized
Indians at Sillery.[54]

The introduction of the reservation system made possible another innovation in missionary work. The Canadian mission encouraged the
participation of women in the task of evangelization. The reservation
system made it possible for the teaching and nursing orders to serve in
the front ranks of the cultural assault on forest folkways. It was out of the
question to ask the nuns to serve in the Indian encampments but their
role in sedentary settlements of Indians might be vital. In 1636 several

---

[47]For the role of the Company of the Holy Sacrament in early Canada see R. Allier, *La
Compagnie du Très Saint-Sacrement de l'Autel: La Cabale de Dévots, 1627-1666* (Paris,
1902), pp. 10-17; E. R. Adair, "France and the Beginnings of New France," *Canadian Historical Review*, 25, no. 3 (September 1944), 246-78.

[48]*A.S.Q., Fonds Verreau XIII*, nos. 8, 28b; also Thwaites, *Jesuit Relations*, vol. 14, pp.
124-6.

[49]*B.R.H.*, 32, no. 3 (March 1926), p. 188.

[50]Thwaites, *Jesuit Relations*, vol. 12, p. 221.

[51]Ibid., vol. 12, p. 42.

[52]Ibid., vol. 14, p. 242; vol. 16, p. 167.

[53]Ibid., vol. 15, p. 108.

[54]*Journal des Jésuites*, p. 24.

Indian families had given their daughters to be raised with French families at Quebec.[55] This proved unsatisfactory to both parties to the agreement. With the arrival, in 1639, of the Ursulines[56] from Tours, in the company of their benefactress, Madeleine de Chauvigny (better known as Mme. de la Peltrie), the Jesuits turned over the education of Indian girls to the nuns.[57] The nuns were not well impressed by the progress made by their first students. Mother Marie de l'Incarnation, the first superior of the Ursulines in New France, left the following description:

> When they give them to us they are as naked as a worm, and it is necessary to wash them from head to foot, because of the grease with which their parents anoint them over their entire body; and whatever care we take, and although we change their linen and clothes often, it is a long time before we can rid them of vermin because of the abundance of this grease. One sister spends part of the day at this. It is a task which one desires ardently.[58]

The Ursulines spent their first few months in Quebec in a two-roomed house overlooking the harbour but within a year they were operating a small *hospice* at the Jesuit reservation at Sillery.[59] Before long, they abandoned this unrewarding venture for the kind of educational work associated with their convents in France. They opened in the upper town of Quebec an elementary day and boarding school for the children of the French economic élite of the colony.[60] The Jesuits were very disappointed in the Ursulines and did not refrain from saying so.[61]

In 1639 three members of the Congrégation des Hospitalières de la Miséricorde de Jésus, commonly known as the Hospital Nuns from Dieppe, also landed at Quebec.[62] They provided nursing services for the Indians at the Sillery reservation from 1640 to 1645. They complained of the high costs of clearing land and of building on the reservation. Within a period of a few months they began to wonder if their chief responsibility was not to the European community. In 1646 they established their Hôtel Dieu in the town of Quebec, a move which was welcomed by the townspeople but which was much regretted by the Jesuits as another

---

[55]Thwaites, *Jesuit Relations*, vol. 9, p. 102.

[56]The Religieuses de Ste. Ursule of Bordeaux were founded in 1606 by the famous teacher, Mother Françoise de la Croix. The three nuns who came to Canada in 1639 were from Tours. Others came later from Paris. The Quebec convent was the 42nd daughter house of the order. A.S.Q., *Polygraphie III*, no. 37.

[57]A.S.Q., *Fonds Verreau XIII*, no. 65, June 1, 1639.

[58]André Rayez, "Marie de l'Incarnation et le Climat spirituel de la Nouvelle-France," *Revue d'Histoire de l'Amérique française*, 16, no. 1 (June 1962), 15.

[59]H. Cahingt, ed., *Documents sur le Canada, 1639–1660* (Rouen, 1913), doc. xii, Le Jeune to Mother Elizabeth, September 2, 1640, p. 21.

[60]F. Du Creux, *The History of Canada, or New France*, vol. 1 (Toronto, 1951-52), p. 268.

[61]A.S.Q., *Polygraphie XXII*, no. 57, Vimont to Superior of Hospital of Dieppe, September 1, 1640; *Journal des Jésuites*, pp. 94, 116.

[62]A.A.Q., *Registre A*, No. 363, pp. 387-92; A.A.Q., *Registre B*, pp. 13-19; A.C., *series F3*, III, fols. 137-147, 192, 202-8. The Hospital Nuns were financially supported by Mme. Claude de Bullion, a niece of Sillery, and Marie de Wignerod, Duchess d'Aiguillon, a niece of Cardinal Richelieu. The Duchess d'Aiguillon had raised an Iroquois girl in her home and had acted as godmother to a little Montagnais girl sent to France to be educated.

reverse in their efforts to convert and assimilate the Indians.[63] Both communities of women had seen little prospect of success by concentrating their educational and charitable efforts among the Indians.

Is it possible that the French adopted the policy of segregation for quite different reasons than those stated? Is there any evidence of discriminatory practices directed against the Indians in this period? It is evident from the *Journal des Jésuites* that the Indians did not participate in many of the sacramentals of the church, and that when they participated in religious processions they did so as a separate group.[64] When Bishop Laval administered the sacrament of confirmation to some Indians before Europeans it was an occasion for comment that this was a reversal of the colonial rules of precedence.[65] The tolling of church bells during the funeral of an Indian girl drew the comment from the Jesuit superior that this was not "ordinarily done for the death of savages."[66] The fact that horses were not given or sold to the Indians, although there was an abundance of these animals in the colony by 1670, may indicate some form of discrimination.[67] References to the Governor and Bishop having to approve interracial marriages after the establishment of Royal Government in 1663 suggest the unusual nature of such alliances and confirm the belief that they had been uncommon in previous decades.[68] If these matters reflect discriminatory practices it must be acknowledged, nevertheless, that the basis of any discrimination that might have existed was cultural and not racial.

There is evidence that the French were favorably disposed to miscegenation. Champlain told the Hurons that if they accepted the Catholic religion brought by the Recollets the French would go to live among them, marry their daughters, and teach their relatives their arts and trades.[69] In 1635, the commissioner-general of the Company of New France reproached the Indians in the vicinity of Trois Rivières for marrying only within their own tribe and for avoiding marriage alliances with Frenchmen.[70] There has been some suggestion that intermarriage deprived the Indians of their potential mates, especially in areas where cross-cousin marriage prevailed. Also, it is sometimes alleged, deprivation resulted from the segregation of Christian Indian girls in convents and French homes. There is no evidence to sustain the allegation that intermarriage contributed to that state of *tedium vitae* resulting from

---

[63]*A.S.Q., Documents Faribault*, no. 163, September 20, 1649; no. 164, December 28, 1651.

[64]*Journal des Jésuites*, pp. 17-18, 20, 31, 102-3, 122, 126, 139-40. This is the daily journal of the Superior at Quebec and was never intended for publication. The candid comments are very revealing of attitudes and aspirations in this period.

[65]*S.R.C.*, doc. 18, Relation of September 12, 1659, pp. 37-39.

[66]Thwaites, *Jesuit Relations*, vol. 52, p. 244.

[67]The law of New York in 1670 forbade the selling of horses to Indians. *Second Annual Report of the State Historian of the State of New York* (Albany, 1897), p. 166. Practice may have accomplished the same ends in New France as legal enactment attempted in New York.

[68]Thwaites, *Jesuit Relations*, vol. 45, p. 148; *Journal des Jésuites*, pp. 281, 312.

[69]Thwaites, *Jesuit Relations*, vol. 10, p. 26.

[70]Ibid., vol. 9, p. 216-18.

contact with the French, or the allegation that sexual irregularity was thereby encouraged. Intermarriage was sufficiently rare not to be a major contributing factor to the social crisis arising out of the contact of the two cultures. The missionaries and traders had found sexual "irregularities" to be part of Indian mores. Furthermore, the most frequent unions between French traders and Indian women were of an "irregular" nature and not sacramental marriages.

The Indian approach to the reservation system needs to be considered as well as the French approach. The motives for Indian adoption of a sedentary life are no clearer than French motives for encouraging it. It is known that those who settled at Sillery did not always do so in order to take up farming because some continued their seminomadic ways.[71] Others found it much easier to obtain brandy on the reservations than in the upper country. By the 1660s alcohol addiction became the chief social problem of the colony. The Indians seemed to seek inebriation as a state of spirit possession. Pierre Boucher wrote on this subject:

> All the Indians who reside near the Europeans become drunkards and that does a lot of harm to our Indians, for, of those who were very good Christians, many have relapsed. The Jesuit fathers have done what they could to prevent this evil. The Indians drink only to get drunk, and when they have begun they will give everything they own for a bottle of brandy in order to drink to oblivion.[72]

Close relations with the French community made the Indians aware of the weaknesses in the European character, too. The Algonquins at Sillery, while willing to submit to rigorous penance for their frequent bouts of drunkenness, were most indignant that the clergy were less exacting when Frenchmen became drunk and abusive.[73] Sometimes the motive for settling on a reservation caused the Indians to join themselves to a charitable institution. In October 1645, for example, there was great concern because some Hurons came to reside at the hospital in Quebec, where they received rations of wheat and eels (equivalents of "loaves and fishes"), and took up the places required for the sick and infirm.[74] In short, the reservation system and association with the French did not solve the problems of assimilation nor did they aid in the evangelization of the tribes.

Did the reservation system hold the converts to their religion? Many of the domiciled or reservation Indians were very religious. Nondomiciled Indians referred to the families at Sillery as the "true believers." It is difficult to evaluate the effects of segregation. In the matter of drunkenness, it has been said, there was no appreciable improvement when In-

---

[71]*Journal des Jésuites*, pp. 36, 42–44, 131. During the winter of 1646 only two Europeans remained at Sillery, all the Indians having taken to the woods to hunt. This may have been out of economic necessity because there is mounting evidence that the supply of game in the immediate area was scarce.

[72]Pierre Boucher, *Histoire véritable et naturelle des mœurs et productions du pays de la Nouvelle-France* (Montreal, 1882), pp. 118–19.

[73]*Journal des Jésuites*, p. 14.

[74]Ibid., p. 10.

dians moved to a reservation—indeed, sometimes the situation was aggravated by the proximity of Europeans. While this may not have reflected well on the sincerity of Indian conversion it did indicate one area of behaviour where the Indian had assimilated European standards. In the matter of religious observance, it is difficult to establish any significant difference between converts who lived on reservations and those who did not. Thus, at Tadoussac, in 1645, the missionaries had to intervene to terminate scenes of spontaneous public penance accompanied by bloody self-flagellation, and some years later the converts at the reservation of Lorette wanted to mingle their blood with their tears during the observances of Holy Week, particularly on Good Friday.[75] At Sillery the Jesuits introduced the principle of elective chieftains, two of whom were directed specifically "to keep the young people in their duties."[76] One of the unexpected results was the intolerance of the converted Indians who wished to exclude all pagans from the settlement. There is no doubt that many of the converted Indians lived very moral lives, by colonial standards. But this did not solve the economic and social problems attendant upon French competitive pressures, the inroads of drunkenness and disease, the importation of European trade goods and implements, and the changing pattern and standard of living. The fact that some Indians became devout Catholics in no way reduced the intensity of the cultural conflict which engulfed their whole society.

The Jesuits continued to expound their theory of conversion and assimilation:

> Now, I must state, in passing, that here are four great works bound together by a single tie—the settlement of the savages, the Hospital, the seminary for little savage boys, and the seminary for little savage girls. These last three depend on the first. Let these barbarians remain always nomads—then their sick will die in the woods and their children will never enter the Seminary. Render them sedentary and you will fill these three institutions, which all need to be vigorously aided.[77]

Missionaries who deplored the unruliness and immorality of Indian youth continued to call for the conversion of whole families so that the young might be raised to know discipline and the teaching of Christian parents.[78] It was admitted that "one saw no notable fruit among the savages, beginning the instruction of a people by the children."[79] Finally, came the admission that "God has confounded our thoughts and upset the foundations."[80] In the outlying missions most of the converts were made on death-beds so that the missionaries had very few living witnesses for the religion they propagated. One missionary estimated that

---

[75] Thwaites, Jesuit Relations, vol. 18, p. 198, vol. 55, p. 276.
[76] Ibid., vol. 18, pp. 100, 102.
[77] Ibid., vol. 16, p. 33.
[78] Ibid., vol. 16, p. 250.
[79] Ibid., vol. 24, p. 102.
[80] Ibid., vol. 29, p. 192.

about 10,600 converts were made in a 40-year period.[81] Numerous death-bed baptisms not only robbed the church of an effective witness, but also gave rise to the superstition that the rite was the cause of death. The missionaries had demonstrated in practice that they were interested in evangelization rather than assimilation of the Amérindians.

The meeting of European and Amérindian cultures resulted in a breakdown in certain vital areas of Indian society. That is not to say that French culture was not profoundly affected, too, by the contact with Amérindians in their environment. Indeed, the story of the development of New France, of European adjustment to the North American environment, is a tale of progressive "barbarization" of French culture. For the Amérindians the effects were more traumatic than for the French. Even the seminomadic tribesmen who came to settle on reservations found it difficult to accustom themselves to confined conditions and steady labour. Their whole way of life, not just their religion, was altered. Even in religion, the changes expected were frightening. They were asked to accept the idea of individual salvation, a concept completely lacking in their culture; they often continued to hold to their own concept of the kinship group's sharing an idealized hereafter. In technology, the French were so superior that they were able to impose their social forms. Economically, the whole Indian way of life in communities having contact with the French commercial enterprise on the St. Lawrence was transformed or disrupted. The highly competitive and individualistic fur trade struck at the roots of collective ownership. The sense of group solidarity which Indian bands had possessed was disrupted by a competitive individualism which forced upon the Amérindians some new and very bewildering standards of behaviour. Political and military alliance with the French was accompanied by the brandy traffic and Iroquoian hostility. The Indian sense of security was badly shaken.

> Moreover, just at a time when he needed all the self-confidence that he could muster, the Indian's reliance upon many of his own technical skills vanished as his stone, wood, bark, and bone materials were swept into the discard by the implements and utensils of European manufacture. Pride in craftsmanship could no longer be entertained and dependence upon an external source for essential materials was a blow to self-esteem, since the Indian inevitably came to feel himself as inferior to the purveyors of such technical marvels as fire-arms, iron axe-heads, and copper kettles.[82]

This breakdown in Indian society, it might be argued, should have prepared the Amérindians for absorption into French culture. Assimilation did not follow because New France was an extremely small community, a frontier community struggling for survival in an inhospitable

---

[81] N. Pouliot, *Étude sur les Relations des Jésuites de la Nouvelle-France* (Montreal, 1940), p. 233 indicates there were 16,014 converts made between 1632 and 1672. The most successful years were 1649, 1650. Of the total, 1,948 converts are known to have died immediately following receipt of baptism.

[82] A. G. Bailey, "The Indian Problem in Early Canada," *America Indigena*, 2, no. 3 (July 1942), p. 37.

virgin land, a pioneer community of a handful of men and fewer women deeply divided among themselves over materialistic and spiritual values. If Amérindian society was seriously disrupted it was also not given the opportunity of a rebirth into the French social and economic order.

French citizenship and racial equality were the basis of French colonization. Throughout the French régime the ideal of one people, one religion, one law and one king would remain. But, the moot question remained whether the ideal was practical. The missionaries who had given lip service to the ideal worked for conversion rather than Frenchification of the aborigines. The assimilated Indian was to have his place in the Empire. The French had an initial advantage in not appearing to dispossess the native of his land. While the French may not have recognized any Indian proprietary rights, as did the English colonists to the south, because the Indians were not classified as members of the "family of nations" receiving diplomatic recognition, they never regarded them as savages reserved for liquidation. One English colonial Governor went so far as to suggest that since the humanity of Anglo-Saxons forbade them to slaughter the Indians, as did the Spaniards, Divine Providence had intervened to wipe out the savages with measles, smallpox, and chicken pox.[83] The French, for their part, regarded the Amérindians as proper subjects for assimilation, absorption and civilization. There is some truth in Parkman's dictum: "Spanish civilization crushed the Indian; English civilization scorned and neglected him; French civilization embraced and cherished him."[84] Although the French sought to civilize and assimilate the Amérindians they failed as miserably as did the English and Spaniards.

---

[83] William T. Hagan, *The Indian in American History* (New York, 1963), p. 7.

[84] F. Parkman, *The Jesuits in North America in the Seventeenth Century* vol. 1 (Toronto, 1899), p. 131.

part two

French Domination and Anglo-French Rivalry, 1645–1760

5

JANSENISM, GALLICANISM, ULTRAMONTANISM: THE CASE OF FRANÇOIS DE LAVAL*

Pierre Hurtubise

The role of the Church in New France is a subject which has fascinated students of the colony for centuries. Probably the most famous leader of the Church during the French Regime was François de Montmorency-Laval, its first bishop. Inextricably interwoven with Laval's career (and with appraisals of the Church) are the terms *Jansenism, Gallicanism,* and *Ultramontanism,* which the reader will find employed elsewhere in the articles of this collection. In the following selection, Pierre Hurtubise attempts to relate Laval to these three terms in the context of his own time.

The historical interpretation of the Church in early Canada has been markedly affected by developments in the period after the Conquest, particularly in those days when the clergy represented an intellectual elite in Quebec and saw themselves as the custodians of French Canada's past and traditions. Not surprisingly, the clerical view of the history of New France emphasized the centrality of the Church and Roman Catholicism for the colony, often at the expense of other factors. Equally unsurprisingly, the clergy's appraisal of its own past, particularly in the latter years of the 19th and the early years of the 20th century, emphasized certain aspects of religion which seemed important at the time the histories were being written. Professor Hurtubise does not deal with the question of the relative importance of the Church and religion for early French-Canadian society, but he is concerned to free Laval from the dead hand of the past. His study is based on two related points. First,

*Originally published as "Ni Janséniste, Ni Gallican, Ni Ultramontain: François de Laval," *Revue d'Histoire de L'Amerique Francaise,* 28 (1974), 3-26. Translated into English by Dr. Robert Perin.

that Laval must be understood in the context of the society and culture of his own time, and not in the light of subsequent developments and controversies within the Church. Second, that Laval must be studied in the light of a full appreciation of modern reappraisals (done mainly in France) of the history of the French Church in the 17th century. Although Hurtubise is quite direct about the first point, he is less explicit about the second. Nevertheless, the historical interpretation in France of the Church of Louis XIV has clearly undergone a great transformation in recent years, and Professor Hurtubise is attempting to understand New France in light of those changes. One of the great dangers of Canadian historiography—whether of French or English-speaking Canada—is that in concentrating on the *Canadian* aspects the historian can fail to benefit from relevant scholarship dealing with matters outside the direct Canadian experience. The Church in New France, Hurtubise argues, cannot be understood except in terms of French developments of the time, and those developments must be viewed in terms of recent scholarship.

Do the terms Jansenism, Gallicanism, and Ultramontanism as defined and explained here differ in their meaning from other readings in this collection? Does their reinterpretation significantly alter our view of the Church in New France? Is Hurtubise convincing in his reappraisal of the relationship between Gallicanism and Ultramontanism? Why does he play down theological divisions?

SUGGESTIONS FOR FURTHER READING

Mack Eastman, *Church and State in Early Canada* (Edinburgh, 1911).

A Gosselin, *L'Église du Canada depuis Mgr de Laval jusqu'à la conquête.* 3 vols. (Quebec: Laflamme et Proulx, 1914–1917).

Cornelius J. Jaenen, *The Role of the Church in New France* (Toronto: McGraw-Hill Ryerson, 1976).

J.M.B.

FRANÇOIS DE LAVAL

When, on February 10, 1673, Louis XIV published his declaration extending the *régale*, François de Laval, Bishop of Petrea, was already in Paris where for several months he had been trying to get the pope to create an episcopal see for him at Québec. Rome did not immediately react to the king's statement, but the long and complicated negotiations over the Québec diocese, carried on at least since 1662, showed clearly enough how difficult relations between the Court and the Holy See could be.

The details of these confrontations are of little interest to us here. We know that they existed. We know of their profound impact on religious life, indeed on all life in France in the second half of the 17th century.

Was New France similarly affected? If so, how did these conflicts take shape and how were they perceived? What were the reactions and positions of those concerned? The man most immediately involved in these events and most vulnerable to the consequences, François de Montmorency-Laval, Vicar Apostolic of New France and first Bishop of Québec could provide us with some answers.

The Man

François de Laval was born in Montigny-sur-Avre, Perche, in 1623 and belonged, like most French prelates of his day, to the nobility. His father, Hugues de Laval, a member of the *noblesse d'épée*, descended from a cadet branch of the famous Montmorency family. His mother, Michelle Péricard, the daughter and granddaughter of Rouen judges, belonged to the *noblesse de robe*.

His whole life was to be marked by this family background. Contemporaries unanimously testify to his zeal, his piety, his self-sacrifice. Yet these virtues never obscure his obstinacy. Marie de l'Incarnation calls it "inflexibility." François de la Colombière, his panegyrist, refers to it as "courage." Both attribute it to his episcopal zeal. But it was more likely the negative expression of his aristocratic convictions. In 1654, he will suppress popular demonstrations in his native seigneure de Montigny on the feast of St. John Baptist just as rigidly as later he will carry out his episcopal functions in Québec. It is perhaps the only personality trait linking him to his family background. Everything else will be moulded by other influences. Yet it remains an important psychological trait which will colour his whole personality and therefore deserves our special attention.

In 1631, at the age of eight, François de Laval left Montigny to study the humanities at La Flèche. This was the beginning of a long intellectual and spiritual journey which was to lead him from La Flèche to Paris and then to Caen. He came into contact with men totally committed to the mystical and moral regeneration of the kingdom. They made him into a *dévot*. Two figures in particular were highly influential during this phase of his life: the Jesuit, Jean Bagot, director of the Marian Congregation at the Collège de La Flèche, founder of the AA (Societe des Bons Amis) of Paris; and the layman, Jean de Bernières, a committed mystic who established the *Ermitage* in Caen. The former became François de Laval's spiritual father and introduced him to a life of contemplation and proselytism through the two pious confraternities which he directed. The latter would become a model of the future bishop of Québec. Under his guidance, Laval would learn to divest himself of all worldly attachments.

Throughout his life, François de Laval would keep vivid the memory of these two men, and remain unflinchingly loyal to their ideals and institutions. Mindful of this, his former Jesuit masters tried, as early as 1653, to have him nominated Vicar Apostolic of Tonkin. Five years later, they successfully got him appointed Vicar Apostolic of New-France. Former AA associates, such men as Pierre Lambert de la Motte, Vincent De Meur, and François Pallu, to name a few, were also aware of his attachments. When in 1658 a number of them laid the groundwork for

the Foreign Missions Seminary, they were careful to include him in their
enterprise and to develop lasting material and spiritual bonds with him.
Equally mindful of his loyalties, former colleagues of the *Compagnie du
Saint Sacrement* (to which he belonged as a member of the *Ermitage*)
took a particular interest from the very beginning in his missionary activities in New France.

These various commitments help us to delimit the spiritual borders of
François de Laval's world. The future bishop of Quebec was above all a
dévot, haunted by the idea of converting the heathen, which explains his
departure for New France. But, as well, he was profoundly affected by
the rigourism of his age and by the myth of a restored Christian society.
This explains the intransigence of some of his episcopal interventions,
which, even then, were considered by some to be outside his competence.

In this he differed little from a good many of his colleagues. In the
second half of the 17th century, the Tridentine reform movement was
beginning to take root in France. Despite the prevailing system of benefices, which made episcopal nomination very often a matter of chance
and good timing, there existed in the kingdom a number of zealous prelates who might not have had François de Laval's spiritual dynamism but
shared with him certain expectations about the "re-establishment" of
religion in France.

The Episcopal Context

Pierre Blet (author of *Les Assemblées de clergé*) has drawn an accurate and very detailed picture of this group of bishops, the outlines of
which will help us to put Laval in the right social and ideological context.

The most striking thing about these bishops was their acute awareness of their rights and privileges. They were convinced that they should
play a pre-eminent role within the kingdom. They were of course subjects of the king, but answerable to him alone. In their eyes, all of the
"Prince's officials" had to yield to the "ministers of the Lord." The
bishops wanted to apply these principles at every possible opportunity—
"down to the details of funeral ceremonies." There occurred numerous
quarrels over precedence, and there were frequent run-ins with civil
authorities which they themselves initiated or in which they were of
necessity implicated. François de Laval could almost be considered an
archetype in this instance.

How these noblemen-prelates perceived themselves and their rank
was influenced by a pride they all shared in their family's history and
present social status. They were very much aware that their "ancestors
governed counties and duchies" and that their brothers and cousins
"commanded the king's regiments." But, as well, they genuinely wanted
to fulfill their function as successors of the Apostles.

Their great concern in the 17th century was the Catholic faith—a
faith which they wished to restore in unity and truth, against enemies
from without as well as from within. In this struggle for orthodoxy, they
felt solidarity with the bishop of Rome. As P. Blet has emphasized so
rightly,

it is really a Roman Catholic unity which the king and the bishops wanted to restore. Such men as Boussuet, Harlay, Le Tellier recognized the bishop of Rome as the centre of unity, the supreme guardian of faith and discipline, the successor of the prince of the Apostles, the Vicar of Christ, par excellence. They did not deny the right of every bishop to go all the way to Rome with his case or his complaint, for they knew that the pope's authority was a guarantee of their own. They considered the Apostolic See the fortress of ecclesiastical liberty.

On the other hand, they frankly admitted that self-interest as much as duty motivated them to preserve this liberty.

Of course, the bishops did not always agree with Rome about their respective powers and the nature of their relations. Conflicts between members of the episcopate and the Holy See occurred throughout the 17th century. Despite these manifestations of autonomy, they proclaimed loudly and often their respect for "the august and . . . sacred authority which Jesus Christ granted to his vicars on earth." Similarly, their protests to the king, which in some instances were as daring as those addressed to the pope, did not imply that they rejected monarchy or challenged royal prerogatives.

In spite of their audacity and sensibilities, Gallican bishops showed the same respect and veneration for the two powers. The bishop of Rome was their spiritual ruler, the king their temporal ruler. The first was Vicar of Christ in spiritual matters; the other, Vicar of God in temporal matters. "Their faces both reflected divine majesty." The two were seen as holding dominion not oppressively, but in a way which was both protective and complementary to their own authority.

Inevitably, conflicts arose, hostilities erupted, which, momentarily at least, broke the harmony between the two powers. The prelates had to take sides and, every time they did, it was usually in the king's favour. Were they then acting out of self-interest or servile fear as the papal bull *Paternae Charitati* charged in 1682? Things, it seems, were not that simple.

The many addresses of praise which the clergy presented to the king, particularly at their Assemblies, may be labelled obsequious; the bishops may be accused of moral weakness for not standing up to a master who besides being their king was the patron of all the rich benefices in the kingdom. And yet it seems that Cardinal de Bouillon was closer to the truth when in 1682 he explained to Cardinal Cibo:

> "those who attended the Assembly did not have the courage to oppose what the majority knew in their hearts to be wrong—the declaration on the *régale*—partly because of their submission to the king's will and partly because they wanted to please a Prince whose qualities the whole world should worship, if it were possible to worship something on earth."

The bishops respected and venerated the man who was in their eyes the living image of divinity. They believed that he had an almost priestly power over his subjects. They were also convinced that the Church of France was greatly indebted to him.

Obviously neither the king nor the bishops contemplated even a slight break with Rome. In fact, while the bishops supported their king, they usually sought accommodations between the pope and him behind the scenes. Similarly, the king az various times adopted the role of "conciliator and arbiter between the pope and the bishops."

This Gallican episcopate so often termed either fawning or rebellious depending on the school of thought was in fact neither. The bishops insisted on their rank and prerogatives and defended them jealously at every opportunity. But they knew how closely their own authority was tied to that of the pope and the king. They could not break with either of them without jeopardizing their own prerogatives and indeed their existence. Harlay de Champvallon, Archbishop of Paris, understood this well. In 1681 he reminded his colleagues that "the French clergy had always shown a deep respect for the Holy See, an inviolable loyalty to the king, and an unshakable resolve in preserving the rights and freedoms of the Gallican Church. This spirit, which made the Church of France such an eminent body, had to endure."

This is the picture which seems to emerge from studies of the French episcopate in the 17th century. To what extent does François de Laval conform to this image? Does he differ from it to any degree? This is the question now to be considered.

Indications and Circumstances

The task is not an easy one. Part of the problem lies in Laval's personality. He did not have a theoretical or speculative bent. His concerns were of an altogether different nature. He left little written material behind and few commentaries on the important issues of the day: nothing on Jansenism, little on Gallicanism, and not much more on Ultramontanism.

Another aspect of the problem is that, by some strange twist of fate, François de Laval avoided the various tests of orthodoxy to which the Gallican clergy were subjected in the second half of the 17th century. The anti-Jansenist declaration was published in 1657 when he was at the *Ermitage* in Caen. Fully one year passed before it was promulgated in the diocese of Bayeux. By that time he had left the *Ermitage* to become Vicar Apostolic of New France. With this new office, François de Laval became directly responsible to Rome, and thereby eluded the declaration of 1661 addressed to every clergyman, tutor, teacher, member of a religious order, and to all those who held a benefice in the kingdom. He was also exempted from the papal bull with its appended statement of 1665. He was not asked to subscribe to the Edict on the *régale* (1673, 1675) nor to the four famous Gallican Articles (1682) because the king failed to have these ordinances registered with the Sovereign Council (of Québec).

Apart from the 1657 declaration, all the other exceptions are due to New France's special position vis-à-vis the metropolis. The colony was subject to the king's direct authority, even prior to 1663, and although both the structure and the functioning of the administration resembled those of a French province, notable exceptions existed. These were due in large measure to particular circumstances, such as the size of the colony and its distance from the metropolis. A number of royal edicts, ordinances, and declarations were not registered in New France; some were not thought to apply to conditions in the colony; others were not considered useful or necessary to its good government.

New France was a special case. The proof is that in 1687 the Court did not hesitate to ask the Holy See for letters making Mgr. de Saint Vallier the new Bishop of Québec, notwithstanding the fact that five years earlier on Cardinal D'Estrée's advice the king had resolved not to present episcopal candidates to Rome as long as the pope maintained his veto against prelates who attended the 1682 Assembly. With the exception of Québec, the Court adhered to this decision until 1692, the year that Paris and Rome reached an accord on the question.

François de Laval's legal status as Vicar Apostolic from 1658 to 1682, and then as bishop of Québec, also differed from that of the French episcopate. He was, as were they, appointed by the Court. On this point, Rome was willing to abide by the Concordat. He took, as did his colleagues, an oath of allegiance to the Crown. But neither in 1658 nor in 1682 was he part of the structure of the Gallican Church. We have seen that, as Vicar Apostolic, he was subject directly to the Holy See. As Bishop of Québec, he found himself in an ecclesiastical no-man's land since Rome obtained that Québec not be attached to any French see.

François de Laval was a member of the Gallican episcopate. By interest and friendship, he was tied to a number of French prelates. Yet he could not participate in any of the activities of the Gallican Church. He could not sit in nor could he appoint a delegate to the Assemblies of the clergy and therefore was cut off from the important debates and controversies of the period. This explains the little interest which these events raised in New France and the almost total silence with which François de Laval greeted them before and after 1674.

Since direct commentaries are lacking, we must rely on more circumstantial evidence. We must look to indications suggested by the people and places whom François de Laval frequented in his formative years and in his later life. Biographers of the first bishop of Québec have concluded, on the basis of the old saying, "birds of a feather flock together," that François de Laval, reflecting the ideas of his teachers and their surroundings, was a sworn enemy of Jansenism and an unqualified ally of Rome. In general, this has been the accepted version. Even today we would be tempted to subscribe to it were we not increasingly aware of the fragile bases on which it rests.

A few years ago, Father Blet refuted the rather simplistic notion of a French Jesuit regiment which unanimously endorsed Ultramontanism as expounded in Rome (in the 17th century). The Jesuits met with considerable trouble in the 16th century because of suspicions that they taught and upheld the theory of regicide. They became extremely cautious on these matters in the 17th century and carefully avoided anything which might give the king or the courts cause to suspect them. When François de Laval was studying theology at Clermont, for example, professors there were forbidden to discuss or even to bring up such "delicate" matters before their students. In fact, many Jesuits accepted the views of Father de La Chaize, Louis XIV's confessor, on the doctrine of the king's absolute independence in the temporal sphere, as expounded in the first of the Four Gallican Articles. In this, they were in agreement with the whole of the French clergy and society, from which historians have too often tried to separate them. They, too, were good Frenchmen who were determined to delimit the temporal and spiritual realms and thereby give the king and the civil power their due.

The Jesuits were anti-Jansenist in the sense that they openly fought against that party and a number of Jansenist ideas. Father Jean Bagot, referred to above, was in 1650 one of the most active Jesuits in this field. His main anti-Jansenist campaign involved his defending the privileges of religious orders, which Saint Cyran had attacked on the grounds that episcopal rights should take precedence. Judging by this incident it is obvious that several kinds of anti-Jansenism existed within the Jesuit Order, some of which had little to do with Jansenism itself. In the controversy between Jean Bagot and Saint Cyran, we would expect François de Laval, the nephew of a bishop and himself a future bishop, to lean more towards the "Jansenists" than the "Jesuits."

Jean de Bernières was also depicted as an avowed enemy of the Jansenists. They attacked him violently, and he in turn had harsh words for them. But in what way was he hostile to them? Here again, conflicts rarely involved doctrine. Rather, they revolved around struggles for influence. The aim of these intrigues was often to get spiritual control of a group, a congregation, or a convent. One wonders whether, in most cases, these problems were not related more to factions than to faith.

Ideologies and People

This brings us to a fundamental problem which we can no longer avoid if we wish to relate François de Laval to the people and the ideas of his time. What do words like Gallicanism, Jansenism, Ultramontanism mean when applied to real events in the 17th century?

These new terms were convenient categories invented in the 19th century in the case of Ultramontanism and Gallicanism, and in 1650 in the case of Jansenism. They have undergone various transformations at the hands of theologians, historians, polemicists. To what extent do these terms correspond to 17th-century reality? To what extent do they betray it? This is the question which we now must answer.

Canon Martimort (in *Le gallicanisme de Bossuet*) rightly observed that the 19th century understood Gallicanism to mean the doctrine contained in the Declaration of the Clergy of 1682 judged in the light of all the subsequent events of the 18th century and the polemical atmosphere of the first Vatican Council.

It is this definition that François de Laval's biographers generally have in mind when they try to acquit their subject of Gallicanism. In the 17th century, the word did not exist. The ideas and practices later labelled "gallican," did not constitute a distinct whole, a coherent and homogeneous body of doctrine. There were several currents of opposition to the Holy See, each having a distinct origin and a different development.

Victor Martin (in *Les origines du gallicanisme*) has tried to give this diversity a common denominator. He described Gallicanism as an understanding between the king and the clergy to govern the French Church by restraining the intervention of the Holy See. This definition is not without merit, but it ignores too many elements which make up the many facets of Gallicanism in 17th-century France.

Some commentators have tried to differentiate political and ecclesiastical Gallicanism. The first is seen as an attempt to secure the Crown's total independence from the spiritual authority of the papacy and to achieve full power over the everyday life of the Church. The second is defined as a doctrine which strives to protect the rights of the clergy against royal and papal interference while accepting the consequences of a kind of royal "absolutism." Other commentators have identified two different types of political Gallicanism: the first, termed "parliamentary," is seen as more theoretical and, therefore, rigid; the other, "royal," is considered to be more practical and flexible.

For the period under consideration, it would be easier to speak of two main categories of Gallicanism: ideological and pragmatic. The first is represented by theologians and judges—the "thinkers" who in their own way theorized about "Gallican" rights. The other is typified by the king, his ministers, and the episcopate—the "doers" who put these "rights" into practice insofar as their interests, particularly their jurisdictional interests, were involved. Of course, the "doers" often used the "thinkers'" arguments, not because of their intrinsic value, but for tactical reasons if not for expediency.

The *régale* controversy illustrates this point well. Louis XIV wanted to follow the advice of his councillors and judges on this question. But, while they made it into a matter of principle, the king was really interested only in the political capital which he could draw from it. In the face of papal opposition he was even ready to accept an indult from Rome granting him the power of *régale*. This clearly would negate the parliamentary theory of *régale* defined as an innate and inalienable prerogative of the Crown. At the same time he made a series of concessions to the bishops who stated their opposition to the very idea of *régale*. The king was so successful in calming their fears that they all rallied round him. They, too, foresook principles when their interests and those of the Gallican Church were at stake.

Unfortunately for them, Innocent XI was not as understanding. His obstinate refusal provoked the special meeting of 1681-82 and eventually the formulation of the Four Articles. It might be thought that by publishing the Articles the king and the bishops had finally come round to the Gallican theorists' point of view. Nothing could be further from the truth. Hindsight has shown that rumours of an imminent papal censure convinced Louis XIV to speed up the discussion and publication of the Four Articles. Apparently his intention was to use the document for tactical purposes or, simpler still, to provoke panic. The incident has prompted Father Blet to observe: "Once the false alarm was over, Louis

XIV no longer appeared a very convinced defender of the Four Articles."
First, he sent the bishops back to their dioceses. Then he expressed his
willingness to relegate the Articles to oblivion, although he was opposed
to a simple retraction of the doctrine. (Rome, of course, never requested
this, as was made clear in 1692.) Louis XIV wrote in 1689 to his ambas-
sador in Rome:

> I can alter nothing of what was done at the Assembly of the clergy of my
> kingdom nor can I deviate from my subsequent Declaration. Though my
> authority in this kingdom be absolute, Rome cannot expect me to do what it
> wishes.

He was referring here to a retraction. But he hastened to add that the
Declaration, which was believed to be imperative a few years earlier,
was no longer so and that consequently "all this toil must be seen as
nothing more than an earthen rampart which easily will collapse and
soon level out if both sides disregard it. The Holy See must no more think
of attacking it than I of defending it when good relations are re-estab-
lished between us."

This was not considered sufficient. Louis XIV agreed in 1693 to what
Rome demanded from the start—the cancellation of the 1682 Declaration. It is significant that the bishops obligingly signed a retraction, the
text of which was prepared by the courts of Paris and Rome.

The complexity of these manoeuvres underline Blet's observation
about

> all the flaws which a term such as Gallicanism can have, when applied
> equally to the statism of the magistrates and to the French prelates' desire
> for autonomy. Even by distinguishing between a parliamentary, episcopal
> and royal Gallicanism, we run the risk of using one term to describe con-
> tradictory phenomena.

Ultimately, the king and the bishops placed little importance on the
speculations of jurists and theologians. They wanted above all to preserve their rights in the face of Ultramontane pretentions. Colbert delighted in saying: "When the pope is our friend, he is infallible; but when
he is not, he is a heretic." This little witticism reflected quite accurately
the feeling at the Court.

The bishops knew that they and the king had a common cause in this
instance. They therefore gave him their support. But they also had
reasons of their own to behave as they did. They could not possibly accept
an extreme interpretation of the powers of the bishop of Rome, which
apparently threatened their own prerogatives. They were jealous of their
rights and had no intention of becoming "mere vicars of the pope, re-
movable at will." On the contrary, they wished to preserve the episcopate
in all its grandeur and dignity. The Assembly of the clergy proclaimed in
1655:

> Each bishop alone is the vicar of Christ in his diocese, he alone is the head of
> his Church, he is the first pastor of that part of Christ's flock and finally he is
> the husband of his see . . . He cannot be divested of the authority which by
> divine right he holds over his flock.

To acknowledge this, said Bossuet in 1681, "does not diminish the fullness of apostolic power. There are limits even to the Ocean's vastness and if it should overstep them to any extent, its vastness would become a deluge which would ravage the universe."

It is doubtful that François de Laval would have disclaimed such talk or that he would have opposed this concept of episcopal dignity. Like his colleagues in France, he had a very high opinion of his office as judge and pastor. Like them, he was extremely devoted to the king and to the interests of the Crown. He was a good Frenchman who was just as wary as they in defending and preserving "Gallican prerogatives."

In 1674 he bitterly reprimanded his friend Gazil for having neglected "the privileges of the Gallican Church" in the text of the bulls which (in Laval's name) he submitted to Rome. Gazil's reply deserves to be cited in full; it speaks volumes on the Gallicanism of François de Laval's milieu and on its conception of Gallican prerogatives.

> We do not claim to have privileges in the Gallican Church. Such a term is odious and has been censured in a Faculty thesis by the Advocate General among others. The reason is that if we maintain that these rights are privileges, the papacy conceivably could thwart them and we then would hold them simply by the grace of the Holy See. We believe on the contrary that these prerogatives belong to us by common law to which the Church of France has remained steadfast against the manoeuvres of the Court of Rome which always tries to increase its power and as much as possible to advance it (imperceptibly) by stages. We have done nothing in this Quebec matter which inhibits the Canadian Church from remaining true to the common law of the Gallican Church. The Quebec Church no more will be subject to the special provisions of the Court of Rome than any of our metropolitan sees in France whose authority comes directly from Rome, such as Lyon, Rouen, Bourges. Their appeals go directly to Rome and by virtue of the Concordats, the pope names the judges *in partibus*. That is our custom and so shall it be for Canada.

Gazil's opinions were not those of a theoretician. Far from it. He was expressing an attitude which was commonplace in the kingdom at this time: the idea of an ecclesiastical tradition indigenous to France, which had to be safeguarded for the greater good of religion. If this should be termed Gallicanism, why should François de Laval not be called a Gallican, provided, of course, the term not have the narrow meaning given to it in the 19th century? It should rather have a broader connotation, and one more in keeping, we believe, with the realities of the 17th century. It should be seen as a profound, almost instinctive, attachment to an idea and to an ecclesiastical practice rooted in a respect for the past and on a firm resolve to shield this past from the powers of centralization.

Certainly there were in the 17th century a number of prelates who advocated in varying degrees the ideas of Gallican theoreticians, men such as Maurice Le Tellier, Gilbert de Choiseul, Jacques Bossuet, to name the most important among them. However, the French episcopate as a whole would appear to adhere to a much more visceral, more practical, Gallicanism. It was less the expression "of an undeniable and universally accepted doctrine" than an instinctive suspicion of anything which threatened their prerogatives and the traditions of their Church. It is to this body which François de Laval belonged.

JANSENISM

As we noted above, the word "Jansenism" came into use in the middle of the 17th century. At the time, it simply meant the "doctrine of Jansenius," that is, "the theological theory of Jansenius, Bishop of Ypres, on grace and predestination." A century later, the *Encyclopédie* defined it as a "controversy about grace and various other points of Christian doctrine sparked by a work of Cornelius Jansenius." The expression was already broader, but it still was short of the modern meaning. In the 19th century, the term became so elastic that it was almost impossible to give it "a precise intellectual content."

> There is an enormous difference between Jansenius' rigid and old-fashioned Augustinianism; St. Cyran's practical spirituality, closer to that of Berulle than to St. Augustine; the subtle ideas of Arnaud and Nicole steeped in Thomism, although Father Quesnel portrayed them in strong Gallican and Richerian tones; and finally the political and partisan obstinacy of the *appellants*. Only the movement of history can hide these dissimilarities. (L. Cognet, *Le Jansénisme.*)

Louis Cognet, a specialist on this question, believes that the various currents of this movement have two things in common. First, Jansenists held to "the concept of an extremely demanding Christianity which does not make concessions or compromises." Second, they all had an "intense awareness of individual rights, especially of individual conscience, in the face of absolute power, be it civil or spiritual". Obviously, in the 17th and 18th centuries the Holy See condemned particular doctrines and took great pains to identify the authors and the well-known works from which they were drawn. But when people at the time attacked the Jansenist party, they had certain stereotypes in mind that were not necessarily those anathematized by the papacy.

Let us leave aside contemporary scholarly treatises on grace and freedom, which only an elite read and understood, and look instead at what public opinion thought of Jansenism. For some, generally those who sided with authority, Jansenists were rebellious and ill-intentioned spirits who had to be brought to reason. For others, they were crafty logicians who, for good or ill, denounced the changes which the Christian message underwent in past centuries. For still others, they were ascetic, austere men and, for this reason, were declared enemies of the Jesuits who they believed were taking the Church down the slippery slope of latitudinarianism. Antonio Favoriti, Innocent XI's intimate collaborator, depicted them as "Men of eminent virtue and piety who were not fond of the Jesuits."

Some of these opinions are too simplistic, if not too "trivial," to serve as barometers of orthodoxy for the period. Favoriti's definition for example, could seem to suggest that Jean de Bernières and his disciple, François de Laval, were not Jansenists simply because of their friendship with the Jesuits. This would be a paradoxical conclusion indeed. But the very simplicity of these definitions—betraying, as it does, an element of truth—reveals the typical concerns of the 17th century. It helps us to explain how Jansenism was perceived and what reactions it provoked.

To limit ourselves to representative circles of the episcopate and the clergy in the 17th century, those to which François de Laval belonged, nothing is more revealing than the attitude of François Pallu, a man who studied with François de Laval, was one of his closest friends, and whose career offers a striking parallel to that of the bishop of Quebec.

Accused in 1680 of Jansenism, Pallu defended himself with vigour. He insisted that he "always had shown himself to be far removed from Jansenism, that he still believed himself to be so, and that he avoided all persons suspected of the error." But shortly before that statement he had written a letter to the directors of the Foreign Missions Seminary in which he acknowledged that his ethics were very austere, adding that what prevented him from being a Jansenist was his complete submission to the decisions of the Holy See.

This testimony is significant and reflects the reaction of the vast majority of the clergy to Jansenism. They did not so much object to Jansenist tenets, many of which they probably accepted. It was rather that for the sake of these tenets Jansenists seemed prepared to subvert the established order. That was their main fault. At stake was a whole conception of society, which François Pallu and François de Laval shared with the higher clergy.

To understand that conception, we must refer to the famous debate which took place at the Council of Trent over the nature and extent of powers related to order and to authority in the Church. Two theories confronted each other: the first, termed "hierarchical," wanted to go back to a fundamentally episcopal Church structure; the second, called "missionary," elaborated particularly by Lainez, the general of the Jesuits, sought to diminish episcopal power and to increase that of the pope. It sought to give the Church greater flexibility to adapt more readily to an expanding and increasingly changing world. The Council refused to decide the matter. But due to the influence of Charles Borromeo, a champion and model of the Counter Reformation in Europe, the first thesis triumphed. This meant that in the 17th and 18th centuries, churches generally were oriented more to the past than to the future. They were less interested in adapting to new problems than to maintaining or restoring a pre-established order, which of course was the order prevailing in contemporary European society. The Church was part and parcel of that order. Each of its members had an assigned place, a role, a function within it. The civil and ecclesiastical hierarchy were considered to be pillars of this immutable and sacred system.

The king and the Gallican episcopate viewed any challenge to this structure as a threat to society. The Jansenist party was therefore dealt with severely. Oddly enough, the bishops and the Jansenists fundamentally agreed with the ecclesiastical idea outlined by Charles Borromeo. We have seen that on this point Saint Cyran and his disciples allied themselves with the hierarchy against the pretensions of the religious orders. But when the Jansenists refused to submit to established authority, the bishops had no choice but to turn against them.

Just like his colleague Pallu, François de Laval entirely accepted this conception of the Church and society. The way in which he dealt with the Récollets in New France between 1670 and 1685 points this up well. Had it not been for his friendship with the Jesuits, he might have had similar conflicts of jurisdiction with them. The example of François Pallu in Indochina illustrates that relations between missionary bishops, drawn from the secular clergy, and their Jesuit collaborators were far from easy during this period.

In the second half of the 17th century, the Gallican episcopate seemed to be suspicious of the Jansenist party more because of the latter's insubordination than because of its ideals. Souriau (author of *Le mysticisme en Normandie au XVlle siècle*) has shown great interest in the *Ermitage* in Caen as an institution and believes that the bishop of Quebec while perhaps hostile to Jansenism was not an opponent of the Jansenists. He tells us that the prelate considered giving the Abbey of Estrée over to a group of Bernardine nuns and had been in correspondence on the matter with the Abbess at Port-Royal des Champs. François de Laval was probably sympathetic to the moral ideal put forward by the Jansenists. He himself was a prelate of unusual self-effacement and was well known for his austerity. It is likely, however, that he had little interest, indeed that he might have felt repugnance, for their theological speculations. In this he agreed with St. Francis de Sales and a good many other *dévots* who said "it was far better to strive to make good use of grace than to quarrel about it."

ULTRAMONTANISM

If we may say of François de Laval that he was in some way Gallican, if we may acknowledge that he was not a systematic anti-Jansenist, may we then still call him an Ultramontane as his biographers have done?

Before answering this question, it would help to know what these biographers understood by "Ultramontanism." The term, as we have seen, was created in the 19th century. Littre defines it as the "doctrine of papal infallibility." This is the meaning most often used at the time of the first Vatican Council. Roger Aubert's definition is more detailed and complete. For him, the term covers a body of doctrine which on the one hand, involves the rights and special privileges of the pope, notably the primacy of his authority over the entire Church and his personal infallibility; on the other, the rights of the Church in relation to the State—that is, the Church's total independence from the State in spiritual matters and the State's indirect dependence on the Church in questions of mixed jurisdiction.

In the 17th century, the word, used as an adjective or a substantive, designated those who "were forever seeking to exalt the greatness of the Holy See" and who followed on these matters the opinions of Italian canon lawyers. It was used so often by Jansenists and Regalists in the 17th century and by Josephists and Febronianists in the 18th as a label for their opponents that "Ultramontane" regularly ended up meaning a person favourable to the Holy See.

François de Laval's biographers thought that they had good reasons for considering him an Ultramontane, because of his deep attachment to the pope and his great respect for the rights and prerogatives of the Holy See.

They are very insistent on the fact that he corresponded frequently with the Court of Rome. This is true for the period when he was Vicar Apostolic, because New France was then a mission territory, dependent directly on the Holy See. It is no longer true after 1674, when Québec becomes a "full-fledged Church" and "henceforth communicates with Rome through the usual channels." From that time on, most questions are "definitely settled in France and those which go to Rome do not necessarily go through the Propaganda." They are instead "given over to the various Roman Congregations according to their respective jurisdictions." During these same years, a number of French bishops correspond often with Rome without considering themselves or being considered Ultramontane. Quite the contrary.

Intent on proving their thesis, François de Laval's biographers exploit the fact that the bishop of Québec regularly requested special jurisdictional powers from Rome. These were called "missionary" faculties granted by the Congregation of the Propaganda to those working with infidels, heretics, or schismatics. Bernard Jacquelines, a scholar greatly interested in this aspect of the Propaganda's work, has shown that Gallican bishops, by the dozens, requested these same powers from Rome. Should we then consider them "Ultramontane?"

François de Laval's biographers also emphasise that the bishop of Québec was responsible for introducing the Roman liturgy in New France. But here again, he was following a practice which existed in the vast majority of French dioceses in that era. Neo-Gallican liturgies only began to appear at the end of the 17th century and during the course of the 18th, until they gradually became entrenched in every part of France.

Finally, August Gosselin, basing himself on François de Laval's correspondence, boldly proclaims that his hero had extraordinarily strong feelings of respect, affection, and devotion for the Court of Rome. He adds: "This was a time when the bishops of France almost all were imbued with Gallican ideas of one kind or another. We can only admire the sentiments of devotion to the Holy See and respect for the Supreme Pontiff which his letters exude." But these feelings of respect and deference were common to most French prelates, indeed to the most Gallican of them. The works of Pierre Blet on the Assemblies of the clergy in the 17th century bear this out. If François de Laval was an "Ultramontane," we would have to include all those bishops "imbued with Gallican ideas of one kind or another" of which Gosselin spoke. Would that make any sense?

*   *   *   *   *

One way of dealing with this dilemma is to admit that François de Laval, like most contemporary prelates, does not fit into the convenient categories created by 19th-century historians. These categories, as we have noticed, are alien to the 17th century in all its living and moving reality. They are too closely tied to the self-interest and preoccupations of those who invented them in the 19th century. They are too ethereal to be applied with discernment to an infinite variety of ideas and passions existing in 17th-century France.

To correct the rather simplistic image of François de Laval left to us by his biographers, we could perhaps say that he was less anti-Jansenist, less Ultramontane, and more Gallican than they contended. But in doing so, would we not be falling into the trap which, consciously or not, they have set for us? Should we not simply recognize that François de Laval escapes categorization? We forget all too easily that the majority of the French prelates of that era were neither professional theologians nor canonists. Indeed, they feared the subtleties of the former and the intransigence of the latter. Following their example, François de Laval had one aspiration: to exercise freely his duties of pastor and judge within the boundaries of his diocese under the double protection of Pope and King, each of whom was equally respected. And this he endeavoured to do in conformity with the traditions of the Gallican Church and respecting Tridentine norms and ideals. All else is pure speculation.

6

AN EXPERIMENT IN "FEUDALISM": FRENCH CANADA IN THE 17TH CENTURY*

Sigmund Diamond

The outlines of the familiar picture of New France were formulated in the 18th century and found classic expression in the writings of the 19th-century American historian, Francis Parkman, in his multivolumed study of the struggle between France and England for mastery of the North American continent. It would be much too simple to say that Parkman lauded the British and condemned the French; he found a good deal to admire in French Canada. But Parkman did see the great conflict as a clash between two very different societies. English America emphasized individualism, political liberty, and material advancement; New France stressed stability, order, and tight political-religious controls. In short, English America was a modern society in the process of formation, while New France was the European feudal order transplanted to the New World. This picture not only suited Parkman's own preconceptions and made for epic history, but it also agreed with most historians within Canada who had written about the early period. For this reason, it is probably inaccurate to see Parkman as responsible for the perpetuation of this view of Canada's early historical development and conflicts; he simply painted the picture with a greater art. Only within recent years have historians begun to question the validity of the traditional interpretation of New France. One of the best statements of the new viewpoint has been made by an American sociologist, Professor Sigmund Diamond. Like Parkman, Diamond has been interested in comparing and contrasting New France with the English colonies, but his assumptions are considerably different. What does Diamond see as

---

*The William and Mary Quarterly, 3d ser., 18 (1961), 3-34.

the important questions to ask when examining the development of New France? Is he able to explain away or refute the older point of view? What problems does he see facing New France? What factors explain French successes and failures in the New World? Are these factors different from those in operation elsewhere in North America?

SUGGESTIONS FOR FURTHER READING

W. J. Eccles, *Canada under Louis XIV* (Toronto: McClelland and Stewart, 1964).

R. Cole Harris, *The Seigneurial System in Early Canada* (Madison: University of Wisconsin Press, 1966).

Francis Parkman, *The Old Regime in Canada* (Boston: Little, Brown and Company, 1874).

J.M.B.

I

The history of 16th- and 17th-century colonization provides an almost unique opportunity for the study of certain problems in social organization. The very requirement, as in the case of the British and French in North America, to establish settlements "where none before hath stood," or, as in the case of the Spanish in Central and South America, to devise a mode of accommodation with pre-existing societies, imposed the necessity of considering problems of social organization with a clarity and directness rarely before achieved. Nor was this entirely a matter of necessity. The creation of new societies raised thought about appropriate forms of organization to a new level of consciousness, not only because the situation created the need, but also because it created the opportunity. Man had now the possibility, so at least it seemed, of making a fresh beginning. Was it really necessary that he be forever burdened with the residue of the iniquity and folly of past history? Was it not possible to devise a new form of social organization in which at least some of the less desirable characteristics of the old would be eliminated? From consciousness of both necessity and opportunity came the impetus to create forms of social organization appropriate to achieve the ends held by the leaders of colonization ventures—whether corporations, private individuals invested with almost regal authority, or the crown.

How were the members of the new societies to be recruited? How were they to be motivated to accept the obligations attached to their positions in these new societies? How was order to be maintained between persons of different statuses? What should be the proper balance among ethic, reward, and sanction in getting persons to behave in the proper fashion? Would the family detach persons from their loyalty to the colonizing organization, or would it increase their satisfaction with their lot in the New World? What special features of social organization would have to be created to accommodate the new societies to sponsorship by joint-stock companies, and how might these be different in colonies undertaken by individuals or by government?

Simply to state these questions is to suggest that implicit in the history of early modern colonization is the problem of planned social action, and that this history may be re-examined with the view in mind of analyzing the discrepancy between the plan for the new society and the actual outcome of the effort to apply the plan. If, as appears to be the case, the effort to plan certain aspects of a social system may have unanticipated effects elsewhere in the system—effects that may negate the very purposes of the planners—an examination of the sources of these unanticipated effects may reveal to us more than we now know of the ways in which the different parts of a society are related, and how that society worked.

II

In New France, as in Virginia,[1] the first persistent instrument used to achieve the purposes of colonization was the chartered commercial company. Society was brought to both Jamestown and Quebec in the ships of a commercial company, in both cases for the same reasons and with much the same consequences. The form of organization devised by the company proved incapable not only of balancing the somewhat contradictory objectives of the merchants—and others—who invested and the government which patronized, but even of solving the strictly business problem of recruiting the supplies of capital and labor necessary for the survival of the company. To take but one example, the great Company of One Hundred Associates, the most prominent of several that failed in New France before 1663, undertook by the terms of its charter to transport 4,000 settlers between 1627 and 1642. It was, however, unable to devise a form of social organization that could reconcile its own interests in deploying its labor force into the most profitable economic pursuits with the interests of the government in fixing immigrants to the land and in establishing a polity, and with the interests of the population in receiving as many as possible of the rewards for undertaking the hazardous task of bringing society to a wilderness. Colonization under commercial auspices was considered a failure, and with the demise of the company in 1663, it devolved upon the government in France, as it had upon the government in England in the case of the Virginia Company in 1624, to create a more adequate form of social organization. The cost of recruiting a population, of supplying it, of motivating it to work, of

---

[1] Sigmund Diamond, "From Organization to Society: Virginia in the Seventeenth Century," *American Journal of Sociology*, 63 (1957-58), 457-75. The Virginia Company attempted to establish a form of social organization in which the behavior of the members would be determined entirely by their positions within the organization. It was necessary, however, to offer concessions to recruit a voluntary labor force and once these concessions—land, marriage, political rights—were offered, social relations could no longer be determined exclusively by the positions persons held within a single system, the organization of the company. Each concession created a new status, each new status involved the person in a new relationship imposing its own necessities, and behavior was determined not by a single position within a single relationship, but by all the positions each person held in a network of sometimes complementary, sometimes contradictory relationships.

defending it against its enemies became a charge upon government and not upon private business.[2]

What followed was a remarkable experiment in creating a society according to plan, an attempt to utilize existing institutions—religion, family, land tenure, law—and to adapt them, under government auspices, to the objectives of the planners and the needs of an immigrant population under frontier conditions. The administrative demands entailed in such an effort were staggering. Hundreds of manuscript volumes of home and colonial decrees and an even larger mass of correspondence, court decisions, and other official documents stand today as mute testimony to the scope of the attempt. What, above all, characterizes the plan is that it bore so clearly the stamp of that passion for rationality—the desire to achieve order, symmetry, and harmony—which is the hallmark of bureaucratic endeavor. It would be anachronistic and yet truthful to describe the objective of the French authorities in Canada after 1663, not as the creation of a society to be governed by political means, but as the creation of an administrative system in which persons would have fixed positions in a table of organization, would behave in the way deemed appropriate for those positions, and would be manipulated, deployed, and disciplined by measures more compatible with the requirements of a formal organization than of a society.

To a degree, of course, this desire to rationalize the operations of the system of governance was already highly developed in France. The attempt of the seigniors of the *ancien régime* to bring order into their own economic activities and into their relations with tenants is by now well known;[3] even better known is the celebrated effort of the monarchy under Louis XIV and his successors to reform the system of administra-

[2] For the early history of colonization under commercial auspices, see H. P. Biggar, *The Early Trading Companies of New France* (Toronto, 1901), passim; George M. Wrong, *The Rise and Fall of New France*, vol. 1 (New York, 1928), pp. 242–48, 253–55, 361–84; Dorothy A. Heneker, *The Seigniorial Regime in Canada* (n. p., 1927), pp. 49–63; J. M. S. Careless, *Canada: A Story of Challenge* (Cambridge, Eng., 1953), chap. 3; Henri Blet, *Histoire de la colonisation française* (Paris and Grenoble, 1946), pp. 20–26; William B. Munro, *The Seigniorial System in Canada* (New York, London, and Bombay, 1907), pp. 17–22. For a discussion of the relationship between the form of social organization and the objectives of colonization, see Georges Hardy, *Histoire sociale de la colonisation française* (Paris, 1953), p. 16; S. D. Clark, *The Social Development of Canada* (Toronto, 1942), pp. 1–14; W. T. Easterbrook and Hugh G. J. Aitken, *Canadian Economic History* (Toronto, 1956), pp. 47–48. On devices calculated to increase labor productivity by providing incentives, see Paul-Émile Renaud, *Les Origines économiques du Canada* (Mamers, 1928), pp. 306–9; Compagnie des Iles d'Amérique, Mémoire sur le Canada," 1666, Archives du Ministère de la France d'Outre-Mer, ser. F²A, Carton 15, Archives Nationales, Paris. Archives du Ministère de la France d'Outre-Mer is hereafter cited FOM.

[3] Marc Bloch, *Les Caractères originaux de l'histoire rurale française*, vol. 2 (Paris, 1955), pp. 170, 197–200. In the colonization of German lands beyond the Elbe, the same opportunity to build a society virtually *de novo* provided an added incentive, as in New France, to rationalize the processes of administration. "The eastern colonial lands were thus particularly well suited, economically and socially for that attempt to construct a more modern form of territorial government, untrammelled by early medieval theories and practices, which was one of the main objects of all rulers, great and small, after the Investiture Contest. . . . Above all else there was the opportunity of introducing, under the most favourable conditions, a systematic quasi-modern administration, organized on rational territorial principles, manned by *ministeriales* and run on bureaucratic, non-feudal lines." Geoffry Barraclough, *The Ori-*

tion. What permitted the same effort to be carried even further in Canada was the possibility of beginning at the beginning. Where a society did not already exist, there was no necessity to make the best of a bad situation, to compromise the goal of rationality by having to reckon with the need to adjust to established institutions and traditions.

Instructing the Dauphin in the desirability of recruiting only persons of moderate social position into the civil service, Louis XIV wrote: "It was not to my interest to select subjects of higher degree. It was important that they should not conceive hopes any higher than it pleased me to grant them, something which is difficult among persons of high birth."[4] The tendency betrayed by the King's instructions to regard his civil servants as instruments to aid him in achieving his own purposes had an even wider extension in Canada, for there everyone was looked upon as the King viewed his civil servant, as an agent of the state. The letter of Jean Baptiste Colbert to Marquis Prouville de Tracy upon the latter's assumption of the governorship is exceptional only because Tracy's position in the administration imposed the necessity of greater explicitness. "The first thing that I must insist upon," wrote Colbert, "is that, since the king takes note of all of his affairs, you must address yourself directly to him in making reports and receiving his orders. It would be well for you to observe this in the future, for although I inform him of everything written to me, those, like you, who hold positions of trust ought to have it as a maxim to have their main relationship with His Majesty."[5]

Relying upon the loyalty of their direct subordinates and the self-discipline of the population, the metropolitan authorities aimed at the creation of a society in Canada in which the vast majority of persons would be firmly fixed to the land, would live peaceably in their villages, and would respond obediently to the commands of their superiors. The reins of legitimate power were held firmly in the hands of the administrative authorities and their designated surrogates, and any tendency toward the development of competing authority, even when it conformed to practices already established in France, was rigorously suppressed.[6]

---

gins of Modern Germany (Oxford, 1949), pp. 278-79. Indeed, Barraclough goes so far as to describe the society established in the eastern territories in terms of conscious planning; ibid., pp. 274-75. See also James Westfall Thompson "East German Colonization in the Middle Ages," American Historical Association, Annual Report . . . 1915 (Washington, 1917), 140, 143, 147.

[4]Quoted in John Lough, An Introduction to Seventeenth-Century France (London, New York, and Toronto, 1957), p. 49.

[5]Quoted in Émile Salone, La Colonisation de la Nouvelle France, 2d ed. (Paris, n. d.), p. 145n.

[6]Renaud, Origines économiques, p. 93; Blet, Colonisation, pp. 126-27; Mason Wade, The French Canadians, 1760-1945 (New York, 1955), pp. 18-19; Gérard Filteau, La Naissance d'une nation, vol. 1 (Montreal, n.d.), pp. 79-81. ". . . it is to be feared that as a result of engaging in trade the inhabitants will live a good part of the year in idleness, whereas if they had no such freedom to engage in trade it would be necessary for them to apply themselves in cultivating their lands." Colbert to Talon, April 1, 1666, FOM, ser. C11A, II, fol. 200. As late as the eve of the final struggle with the British for the mastery of Canada, the King of France was still exhorting his officials to make the progress of agriculture their first concern; see, for example, the extracts from the royal correspondence in Report Concerning Canadian Archives for the Year 1905, vol. 1 (Ottawa, 1906), pp. 73, 165, 202.

Every aspect of life in Canada was subject to rational calculation and was alterable by purposeful action. Political institutions, the family, Indian affairs, the range of permissible trades and occupations, the amount of prestige and honor to be associated with each status in the society were all carefully regulated. The behavior of each major segment of the population was prescribed in the minutest detail, even to the point of regulating the order of precedence in religious and secular ceremonies, the appropriate forms of address, and the types of weapons that each might bear.[7] The total corpus of these regulations betrays the assumption, central to the conception of the administrator, that each person is essentially the occupant of a position in an organization and that his behavior can be made to conform to the needs of the system for order and stability.

Precautions were taken that nothing should interfere with the flow of authority in the established chain of command. Though occasional meetings of the population were held to discuss problems and to hear proposed programs, never did these assume the character of representative assemblies; they were *ad hoc* bodies, summoned to listen and not to argue. When, elated by his own cleverness, Governor Louis de Buade, Comte de Frontenac, informed Colbert in 1672 that he had administered an oath of loyalty to the seigniors and, for convenience, to a group of habitants acting on behalf of all, he received a blistering reply. "Since our Kings have long regarded it as good for their service not to convoke the Estates-General of the Kingdom in order perhaps to abolish insensibly this ancient usage, you, on your part, should very rarely, or, to speak correctly, never, give a corporate form to the inhabitants of Canada. You should even, as the colony strengthens, suppress gradually the office of Syndic, who presents petitions in the name of the inhabitants, for it is well that each should speak for himself and no one for all."[8]

Nothing was permitted to escape the hawklike eyes of those responsible for seeing that the colonists behaved according to plan, and no problem was too small to be taken to the highest official. Jérôme de Pontchartrain himself, the minister of colonies in Paris, was called upon to decide disputes involving a cow strayed into someone's garden, a brawl at a church door, the virtue of a certain lady. Colbert had to be informed, as evidence of the degree to which prescriptions for proper behavior were observed, that two captains had been married, one lieutenant engaged, and "four ensigns are in treaty with their mistresses, and are already half

---

[7] Ordinance regulating forms of address, April 10, 1684, FOM, ser. F³, VI, fol. 104; FOM, ser. C¹¹A, CXX, fol. 406; "Honneur dans les églises en Canada," April 28, 1716, FOM, ser. C¹¹A, CVI, fols. 390-91; Guy Frégault, *La Civilisation de la Nouvelle France (1713-1744)* (Montreal, 1944), pp. 171-72; *Supplement to . . . Report on Canadian Archives for the Year 1899* (Ottawa, 1901), 68, 83, 85-86, 536; Pierre-Georges Roy, ed., *Ordonnances, commissions, etc., etc., des gouverneurs et intendants de la Nouvelle-France, 1639-1706*, vol. 1(Beauceville, 1924), p. 179, vol. 2, pp. 83-84, 98-101.

[8] Frontenac to Colbert, November 2, 1672, FOM, ser. C¹¹A, III, fols. 270-71; Allana G. Reid, "Representative Assemblies in New France," *Canadian Historical Review*, 27 (1946), 20-23; Morden H. Long, *A History of the Canadian People*, vol. 1 (Toronto, 1942), p. 277; Salone, *Colonisation*, p. 269; *Collection de manuscrits contenant lettres, mémoires, et autres documents historiques relatifs à la Nouvelle France*, vol. 1 (Quebec, 1883), pp. 225-27.

engaged."[9] Jean Talon, struck with the thought that population increase might be achieved by the intermarriage of Indians and French, studied the reproductive capacity of Indian women and reported that it was impaired by their nursing children longer than necessary; but, he added, "this obstacle to the speedy building up of the colony can be overcome by a police regulation."[10]

In short, what was planned was a society in which all persons would be under a jurisdiction and patronage that were at once French, royal, and orthodox. Stability would be guaranteed by each person's having a precise place and acting in accordance with the behavior defined as appropriate to that place. The elements of this society were, of course, diverse—government regulation of economic activity, a special system of land tenure, an elaborate code of law, an established church, royal patronage of the institution of the family—and every effort was made to weld them together into an organization in which discipline would be achieved because each man would remain loyal to the institutions to which he was attached.

The fur trade, which had been at once a blessing and a curse to the colony, was the subject of endless consideration by government officials. Although the form of regulation varied, the trade was controlled at virtually all times so as to restrict the number and influence of persons engaged in it. The privileged few were thus to be attached to the government with the ties of gratitude that flow from profit, while the mass of the population would not be diverted from the performance of necessary agricultural tasks.[11] The *coureurs de bois* were to be quarantined so that their lawlessness could not contaminate what was hoped would be an obedient agricultural society. Men who desert the land to enter the forests, said Talon, are men, "without Christianity, without sacraments, without religion, without priests, without laws, without magistrates, sole masters of their own actions and of the application of their wills. . . ."[12]

Population growth, recognized by government officials as indispensable to increasing agricultural production and, at least indirectly, to reducing the overhead costs of administering the colony, was promoted through immigration, encouragement of marriage, family subsidies, and attempts to mobilize the Indians into the labor force. The policy of "Francisation," which included conversion, domiciliation, intermarriage, and education of the Indians in the ways of the white man, was undertaken in the hope that, made tractable by their re-education, they

---

[9]Wrong, *New France,* vol. 2, p. 566; Talon to Colbert, October 20, 1667, FOM, ser. C[11]A, II, fol. 307.

[10]Talon, "Mémoire sur l'éstat present du Canada," FOM, ser. C[11]A, II, fol. 355.

[11]For an excellent summary view of the Canadian fur trade, see Easterbrook and Aitken, *Economic History,* pp. 39–45, 76–78, 87–89, 112–24. See also, R. M. Saunders, "Coureur de Bois: A Definition," *Can. Hist. Rev.,* 21 (1940), 123–31; Salone, *Colonisation,* pp. 250–61; Clark, *Social Development,* 25–43; Wrong, *New France,* vol. 2, pp. 541–42; Charles A. Julian, *Les Français en Amérique,* Centre de Documentation Universitaire, vol. 2 (Paris, n.d.), pp. 26–28.

[12]Quoted in Roy, ed., *Ordonnances,* vol. 1, pp. 107–9; Donald Creighton, *A History of Canada* (Boston, 1958), p. 79; M. Patoulet to Colbert, January 25, 1672, FOM, ser. C[11]A, III, fol. 274.

would swell the labor force. It quickly became evident that the policy had failed, and that population growth would have to come about through immigration and natural increase.[13]

In 1668 Colbert suggested to Talon that those "who may seem to have absolutely renounced marriage should be made to have additional burdens, and be excluded from all honors; it would be well even to add some marks of infamy." The Intendant was quick to take the hint; bachelors were barred from the right to hunt, fish, trade with the Indians, and even to enter the woods. By act of the Sovereign Council of Canada, "any inhabitant having in legitimate marriage ten living children, not priests, *religieux* or *religieuses* shall be paid three hundred livres a year, and those who have twelve shall be paid four hundred livres a year." Young men who married before the age of 20 were given a bonus. Fathers whose sons were not married by the age of 20 or whose daughters were still vestals at the age of 16 were to be fined and summoned to the court every six months.[14]

But to encourage marriage the government would have to take the initiative in providing women, unless it were willing—which it was not—to tolerate "a thousand disorders in the settlements . . . where the women are very glad to have several husbands and where the men cannot get even one wife." Marriage, it was anticipated, would not only increase the birth rate but would lead to a more settled and orderly life.[15] As in Virginia, therefore, the government assumed the responsibility of shipping from France "demoiselles" for the military officers and what pious Mother Marie de l'Incarnation called "une marchandise mêlée"—mixed goods—for the ordinary settlers, something more than a thousand altogether.[16]

---

[13]Renaud, *Origines économiques*, pp. 226-29; Salone, *Colonisation*, pp. 115-16; R. Mousnier, *Les Européens hors de l'Europe de 1492 jusqu'à la fin du xviie siècle*, vol. 1 (Paris, n.d.), pp. 129-30.

[14]Colbert quoted in Francis Parkman, *The Old Regime in Canada* (Boston, 1922), pp. 287-88. The Council's act is in Arrêt of April 13, 1669, FOM, ser. C¹¹A, III, fols. 26-29. That Colbert's decree was not entirely a dead letter may be seen from the verdict in the case of François le Noir, of La Chine, summoned before the court on the charge that, though unmarried, he had traded with the Indians. Le Noir confessed, but was released on his promise to marry within three weeks of the arrival of the next ship bringing women from France or payment of a financial forfeit to the church and hospital at Montreal. He lived up to his promise and married Marie Charbonnier of Paris. Parkman, *Old Regime*, pp. 287-88.

[15]Frontenac to Colbert, November 2, 1672, FOM, ser. C¹¹A, III, fol. 257; Talon to Colbert, October 20, 1667, ibid., II, fol. 316; Wrong, *New France*, vol. 1, pp. 394-96.

[16]Quoted in Parkman, *Old Regime*, p. 284. See also Isabel Foulché-Delbosc, "Women of New France," *Can. Hist. Rev.*, 21 (1940), 132-49; Clark, *Social Development*, p. 52; Munro, *Seigniorial System*, pp. 70-71. For an account of the shipment of these women as it was in historical reality and in the minds of men, see Gustave Lanctot, *Filles de joie ou filles de roi . . .* (Montreal, 1952). Immigration to French Canada 1608-1760 amounted to just over 10,000, while total population reached the 65,000 mark in 1763; *Censuses of Canada, 1665 to 1871*, vol. 4 (Ottawa, 1876), pp. 2-67; see also, Georges Langlois, *Histoire de la population canadienne-française* (Montreal, 1934), pp. 59-60; Ivanhoe Caron, *La Colonisation du Canada sous la domination française* (Quebec, 1916), pp. 56-57; Paul Veyret, *La Population du Canada* (Paris, 1953), pp. 10-12. Recent studies indicate that women in Canada did not enter the marriage market much before their sisters in France, but they performed well, once in it. At no time between 1660 and 1770 did the birth rate by decade fall below 47.3 per 1,000, and twice it exceeded 60 per 1,000; Jacques Henripin, *La Population canadienne au debut du xviiie siècle*, Institut National d'Etudes Démographiques, Cahier no. 22 (Paris, 1954), pp. 39, 96-101. See also Sr. Pastoulet to Minister Pontchartrain, November 11, 1699, FOM, ser. C¹¹A, III, fols. 64-65.

Still, French Canada's population growth, dependent overwhelmingly upon natural increase and very little upon immigration, lagged far behind that of the British North American colonies and even behind Canadian requirements. As late as 1710 Governor Philippe de Rigaud, Marquis de Vaudreuil, complained that there was not enough labor for the seigniors to cultivate even half their estates; six years later he was recommending that condemned salt-smugglers in France be shipped as indentured servants at the expense of the farmers-general. In 1733 Governor Charles de la Boische, Marquis de Beauharnois, and Intendant Gilles Hocquart echoed the complaint: "The scarcity of men, and the high wages of both agricultural and urban labor, considerably diminishes the revenues of landlords and merchants." Despite every effort of a government that exhorted and a people that produced, the population of French Canada amounted to only about 5 percent of the population south of the St. Lawrence River by the middle of the 18th century.[17]

But neither government regulation nor family attachments were, in the view of the French authorities, sufficient to maintain social discipline; religion, too, was counted on to disseminate an ethic calculated to remind each man to keep to his allotted place. From the beginning of New France, the Roman Catholic Church was given major responsibility for enforcing the ban on Protestants in Canada, and the zealousness with which it responded to the task of rooting out unorthodoxy in both its Jansenist and Protestant forms revealed that secular as well as religious discipline was its proper concern. The importance of orthodoxy from the religious viewpoint was self-evident. "On the side of the state," wrote Bishop François Xavier de Laval, "it appears to be no less important. Everyone knows that Protestants in general are not so attached to His Majesty as Catholics. . . . To multiply the number of Protestants in Canada would be to give occasion for the outbreak of revolutions."[18]

Doctrinal conflict was minimized, therefore, by screening prospective immigrants, but the church played a no less significant role in disciplining colonists once they had arrived. The keynote was sounded in a letter from Louis XIV to Bishop Laval: "As I have been informed of your continued care to hold the people in their duty towards God and towards me by the good education you give or cause to be given to the young, I write this letter to express my satisfaction with conduct so salutary, and to exhort you to persevere in it." The nature of this education may be inferred from the list of virtues commended to boys, drawn from the rulebook of the Petit Séminaire in Quebec: "humility, obedience, purity,

[17] H. A. Innis, *Select Documents in Canadian Economic History, 1497-1783* (Toronto, 1929), pp. 302, 360; "Pour Peupler et défricher le païs," FOM, ser. C¹¹A, II, fols. 45ff; William B. Munro, *Documents Relating to the Seigniorial Tenure in Canada, 1598-1854* (Champlain Society, *Publications*, 3 [Toronto, 1908]), 151-52; Maurepas to Beauharnois and Claude Dupuy, May 27, 1728, FOM, ser. D²D, I; Wade, *French Canadians*, p. 20; Frégault, *Civilisation*, p. 39. The farmers-general were private contractors to whom the king leased the right to collect taxes in return for a fixed payment to the state.

[18] Mémoire of the Bishop of Quebec, 1670, *Collection de manuscrits*, vol. 1, pp. 204-5. See also *Report Concerning Canadian Archives for 1905*, vol. 1, p. 192; Wade, *French Canadians*, p. 13; Filteau, *Naissance d'une nation*, pp. 169-70; Walter Alexander Riddell, *The Rise of Ecclesiastical Control in Quebec* (Columbia University, *Studies in History, Economics, and Public Law*, 74 [New York, 1916]), pp. 44-45, 73-75.

meekness, modesty, simplicity, chastity, charity, and an ardent love of Jesus and his Holy Mother." All schools but one were under control of the church, and that single exception—the School of Mathematics and Hydrography—passed under its influence early in the 18th century.[19]

In its role as custodian of morals and, though its pretensions in this area were disputed, of law,[20] the church went even further. It regulated the style of clothing; it censored books; it established with meticulous accuracy the order of priority of both religious and secular officials on ceremonial occasions; it attacked usury and supported its attack by refusing confession to usurers; it shipped back to France immoral men, including those who were so unmindful of their situation in life as to fall in love with more highly placed girls; and it attempted to cultivate an ethic of obligation and obedience, of simplicity and austerity.[21]

Most important of all, however, it threw the weight of ecclesiastical discipline behind the effort to fix the population into assigned positions; the sanction of excommunication itself was invoked against those who left the land without permission and traded illegally for furs with the Indians. Although there were disputes between secular and religious officials when either tried to exercise authority that pinched the other, they were as one in recognizing the importance of the church in disciplining the inferiors of both, in urging upon them acceptance of a code of beliefs that would confine their behavior within the limits desired by higher authority.[22] We must "multiply the number of parishes and . . . render them fixed . . . ," wrote Governor Jacques-René de Brissay, Marquis de Denonville, to Colbert in 1685. "This undertaking . . . would be a sure means of establishing schools, with which the *curés* would occupy themselves and thus accustom the children at an early hour to control themselves and become useful."[23] Finally, in its capacity as landowner, the church assumed the role of model seignior, and attempted by the force of its own example to influence the behavior of other landlords. By 1750 the church held over two million arpents of land, more than one-third of all the grants that had been made.[24]

---

[19]Quoted in Parkman, *Old Regime*, pp. 426–27; Riddell, *Ecclesiastical Authority*, pp. 83–84.

[20]For a discussion of church-state controversies over such matters as the liquor trade with the Indians, the right of precedence in civil and religious ceremonies, and the like, see, for example, Wrong, *New France*, vol. 1, pp. 347–51; Jean Delanglez, *Frontenac and the Jesuits* (Chicago, 1939), passim; Parkman, *Old Regime*, pp. 166–68; and the royal instructions to administrators in Canada, *Supplement to Report on Canadian Archives for 1899*, pp. 92, 245, 248.

[21]H. Têtu and C. O. Gagnon, *Mandements, lettres pastorales, et circulaires des évêques de Québec*, vol. 1 (Quebec, 1887), pp. 106–8, 114–15, 167–74, 275–81, 318, 330–31, 334–35, 363–65, 382–84; Roy, ed., *Ordonnances*, vol. 2, pp. 328–30; Salone, *Colonisation*, pp. 134–35; Wrong, *New France*, vol. 2, pp. 531–32, 538–40.

[22]Têtu and Gagnon, *Mandements*, vol. 1, pp. 30–31, 267–70; Munro, *Seigniorial System*, pp. 178–79; Renaud, *Origines économiques*, pp. 341–42; Heneker, *Seigniorial Regime*, pp. 199–203.

[23]Quoted in Clark, *Social Development*, p. 73.

[24]Munro, *Seigniorial System*, pp. 180–81; Salone, *Colonisation*, pp. 314–16; Heneker, *Seigniorial Regime*, pp. 197–200. One "arpent de Paris" is equivalent to approximately five-sixths of an English acre.

But the most characteristic institution of the old regime in Canada—the one that gave tone to the entire society—was the seigniorial system. There was much in it that was reminiscent of medieval feudalism, but only reminiscent. Feudalism in France was an organic growth; in Canada it was a transplanted institution, and the French administration saw to it that in the transplanting it was pruned of less desirable characteristics. The French monarchy had established itself in the teeth of feudal opposition and was in no mood now to offer the seigniors sufficient independence and power so as to require repetition of the experience. When Governor Tracy and Intendant Talon drew up their "Projet de Règlement" in 1667, they warned that since "obedience and fidelity [two words obscured] are most likely to suffer attenuation in distant provinces of the state than in the neighbors of the Sovereign Authority, which resides mainly in the person of the prince and has more force and virtue there than in any other person, it is the part of prudence to prevent in the establishment of the growing state of Canada all those vexations revolutions which might render it monarchical, aristocratic, or democratic, or even—by a balanced power and authority between subjects—divide it into parts and give rise to such a dismemberment as France suffered by the creation of such sovereignties within the kingdom as Soissons, Orleans, Champagne, and others."[25] In their concern lies the clue to the essential difference between French and Canadian feudalism. The landed seignior in Canada was entitled to many of the rights possessed by his counterpart in France—potential membership in the nobility; ceremonial rights like fealty and homage; judicial rights like holding private courts; and more lucrative rights such as the collection of rents and mutation fines, the imposition of labor services, and the monopoly of all milling—and the enforcement of these rights was presumably guaranteed by the extension to Canada of the law code known as the Custom of Paris and the beneficent protection of the royal authority. Nevertheless, the position of the Canadian seignior was far different from that of the French.

The right to have a private court was his, but the use of the terms *haute, moyenne, et basse justice* in Canada must not delude us into thinking that it held the same meaning as in France. The existence of the competing royal court eventually limited private jurisdiction to relatively simple cases about seigniorial dues and obligations, and even in these the habitant had free right of appeal to the royal court. Nor were the profits of justice as lucrative in Canada as in France; where population was sparse, the opportunity to squeeze income from it in the courts was limited by the small number of cases and by the fear that too much repression would cause the seignior's labor force to move to the lands of a less exacting landlord. "I will not say that the Goddess of Justice is more chaste and impartial here than in France," wrote Baron Louis Armand

---

[25] "Projet de règlement fait par M[ess]rs. de Tracy et Talon pour la justice et la distribution des terres du Canada," January 24, 1667, Nouvelles Acquisitions Français, 9271, fols. 60V°-61R°, Bibliothèque Nationale, Paris. [This collection is hereafter cited as NAF.]

de la Hontan, "but at any rate, if she is sold, she is sold more cheaply."[26] In Canada the problem was not so much to check the encroachments of the seigniorial courts as to force the reluctant seigniors to accept the profitless and limited jurisdiction the Crown imposed on them.

So, too, the seigniors of Canada had the rights of *banalité* and *corvée*. Under conditions of severely limited population, however, these were drained of most of their significance. The intendants of Canada, conscious of the fact that onerous obligations on the peasantry would hamper immigration, restricted the size of the payments to the seigniors and forced them to improve their mills. So profitless were these rights that, as with private courts, the problem was not so much to control their abuse as to get the seigniors to exercise them at all. In 1686 a royal decree was issued requiring the seigniors to build mills on their land grants on penalty of losing their monopoly, but for 20 years the seigniors sabotaged enforcement of the decree by not promulgating it.[27] What under other circumstances would have been a profitable privilege was for the Canadian seignior a burdensome cost.

Even the conditions under which he held land and could legitimately demand payments from his sub-infeudees were different from those in France. Squirm though he might, never could the seignior wholly evade the scrutiny of the intendants, who were determined to prevent the payments owed by the *censitaires,* the peasants, from becoming too burdensome. Even more, his power to dispose of his own domain was limited in such a way as to reduce his maneuverability and to make him essentially an agent of the Crown in the achievement of its purposes. After several preliminary gestures, the King, through the Arrêts of Marly in 1711, decreed that all seigniorial grants not settled and developed through sub-infeudation would revert to the Crown, and that the payments to seigniors from sub-infeudated lands must be uniform and limited. In the minds of the administrators, the seigniors were less proprietors than trustees, entitled to occupy the land only if they performed the essential tasks required of them.[28]

Though the Canadian seignior was sometimes able to evade some of the restrictions imposed upon him, there can be little doubt that his rights were more limited than were those of the French. Still, they were believed sufficient to get him to assume the tasks for which the Crown held him responsible—to clear the land, to settle it with farmers, to support the church and the state, and to keep his subordinates in their places. For those who did their tasks well, there was the added incentive of possible ennoblement: We must grant titles, Talon told Colbert in 1670, to "fill the officers and richer seigniors with a new zeal for the

---

[26] Quoted in Munro, *Seigniorial System,* pp. 156-57. *Report Concerning Canadian Archives for the Year 1904* (Ottawa, 1905), app. K, p. 195; Filteau, *Naissance d'une nation,* vol. 1, pp. 106-7.

[27] Munro, *Seigniorial System,* pp. 101-44; Heneker, *Seigniorial Regime,* pp. 126-35.

[28] The most complete descriptive accounts of the seigniorial system are in Munro, *Seigniorial System,* and Heneker, *Seigniorial Regime.* But see also, Munro, *Documents,* pp. xv-cxvi; Rodolphe Lemieux, "La Régime seigneuriale au Canada," Royal Society of Canada, *Transactions,* 3d ser., 7 (Ottawa, 1913), sec. 1, pp. 151-68; Hardy, *Colonisation,* pp. 21-22.

settlement of their lands in hope of being recompensed with titles as well."[29] Having deprived the seignior of many of the attributes that permitted him to be a seignior, the King's administrators yet hoped he would act like one.

As with the seigniors, so with the *censitaires*. They, too, had rights and obligations differing somewhat from their brothers' in France. They had to clear the land lest it revert to the seignior; they owed him rent and mutation fines; they worked for him and gave him part of their catch of fish; they paid him deference; they were not allowed to engage in the fur trade. Yet, their duties were less onerous than in France, and they were protected from excessive exploitation by a solicitous officialdom. Besides, the prospect of improvement was such, so it was anticipated, as to induce them willingly to accept their position. "There are so many strong and robust peasants in France," wrote Father Paul le Jeune, "who have no bread to put in their mouths; is it possible they are so afraid of losing sight of the village steeple, as they say, that they would rather languish in their misery and poverty, than to place themselves some day at their ease among the inhabitants of New France, where with the blessings of earth they will more easily find those of heaven and of the soul?"[30] In short, the seigniorial system in Canada was transformed by the authorities into an agency of land settlement, an instrument for peopling the country, and a mechanism for insuring social stability.[31]

III

How did the system actually work? If long-term stability and social discipline were the objectives desired by the authorities, they were not the objectives attained.

The *sine qua non* of successful colonization was the mobilization of an adequate labor force. In Canada, as in British North America, experiments in the use of forced labor and of the local Indians failed, and it soon became necessary to recruit labor by voluntary means.[32] To do so, however, such substantial concessions had to be made that the real position occupied by the labor force in the new society was utterly different not only from its position in Old World society but even from what the planners of the system had intended.

---

[29] Quoted in Munro, *Seigniorial System*, p. 163. See also, Talon to Colbert, October 20, 1667, FOM, ser. C¹¹A, II, fol. 320; Filteau, *Naissance d'une nation*, vol. 1, pp. 122–23; Wrong, *New France*, vol. 1, pp. 412–14; Heneker, *Seigniorial Regime*, pp. 227–40; Benjamin Sulte, "La Noblesse au Canada avant 1760," Royal Soc. of Canada, *Trans.*, 3d ser., 8 (1914), sec. 1, pp. 103–5. "This manner of compensation is more economical and often more powerful than any other," Talon told Colbert on November 10, 1670, FOM. ser. C¹¹A, III, fol. 90.

[30] Quoted in Innis, *Select Documents*, pp. 283–84.

[31] Munro, *Seigniorial System*, passim; Heneker, *Seigniorial Regime*, pp. 142–50; Munro, *Documents*, pp. lxxvii–cxii.

[32] H. P. Biggar, comp., *A Collection of Documents Relating to Jacques Cartier and the Sieur de Roberval* (Public Archives of Canada, *Publications*, 28, no. 14 [Ottawa, 1930]); R. M. Saunders, "The First Introduction of European Plants and Animals into Canada," *Can. Hist. Rev.*, 16 (1935), 394–95; Leon Vignols, "La Mise en valeur du Canada à l'époque française," *Revue d'histoire économique et sociale*, 16 (1928), 732.

The companies before 1663 recognized the necessity of offering incentives, but sought to minimize them in an effort to keep costs low. Louis Hébert, the Paris apothecary who became the first settler at Quebec, had been offered full support for himself and his family for a period of two years plus 200 crowns per year for three years as inducement to emigrate. After he arrived, however, the company imposed harsher terms: he was given only 100 crowns per year; his entire family and his servant were required to work for the company for three years, after which time he was required to sell all his produce to the company at prices current in France; he could work on clearing his land and building his house only when the chief factor did not need his services; he was not to engage in the fur trade; and he was to offer his professional services free of charge to the company.[33]

Samuel de Champlain had been quick to see that the terms were not sufficiently attractive to encourage immigrants. "The Companies having refused to give them the means of cultivating the land," he wrote, "had thus taken away all reason for them to become settlers. At the same time, these Companies gave out that there were numerous families in the country; the truth is that, being entirely useless, they served only to count, and burdened the settlement more than they helped it. . . . That was not the way to create a great desire on the part of anyone to go and people a country, when a man cannot have any free enjoyment of its returns. . . ."[34]

Men who knew the country best, like Father le Jeune, could not agree with him. Those who emigrate for regular wages, he argued, do not provide the most efficient labor force; they "try to be like some of our neighbors, who, having scarcely passed the line of the Equator, all begin to call themselves Gentlemen, and no longer care to work; if they felt constrained to do it for themselves, they would not sleep over it." The right of ownership, even if limited, was his solution. He explained that immigrants ought to "engage themselves to some family for five or six years on the following conditions."

> That they should be boarded during all this time without receiving any wages, but also that they should possess entirely and in their own right one-half of all the land they clear. And, as they will need something for their own support, the contract should provide that all they get every year, from the lands they have already cleared, should be shared by half; this half, with the little profits they can make in the Country, would be enough to keep them, and to pay after the first or second year for half the tools which they will use in clearing and tilling the land. Now if four men could clear eight arpents of land a year, doing nothing else, winter or summer, in six years forty-eight arpents would be cleared, of which twenty-four would belong to them. With these twenty-four arpents they could support thirty-six persons,

---

[33]Biggar, *Early Trading Companies*, p. 105. On early company colonization, see also Wrong, *New France*, vol. 1, pp. 242–48; Munro, *Seigniorial System*, pp. 22–27; Salone, *Colonisation*, pp. 55–61.

[34]H. P. Biggar, ed., *The Works of Samuel de Champlain*, vol. 5 (Champlain Soc., *Pubs.* [Toronto, 1933]), pp. 326–27.

or even forty-eight, if the land is good. Is this not a way of being rich in a little while?[35]

Throughout the long history of New France, the concessions offered to immigrants assumed many different forms, but in the final analysis they amounted to the same thing—the promise, even the guarantee, of social mobility.[36]

Those who came at their own expense had the promise of land and even, if they performed "notable service" in the interests of the authorities, of titles and patents of nobility.[37] If, as now appears to be the case, most of the *engagés* did not have the promise of land at the time they agreed to their contracts of engagement, many did receive land after completion of their term of service; and, in any case, the wages they could expect in Canada allowed them a substantial increase in living standards.

To induce soldiers to remain in Canada after the period of their enlistment, land and financial subsidies were promised according to rank. Nearly 1,500 remained, "finding there land that they could not perhaps have had in their own country."[38] For skilled artisans there was not only the guarantee of high wages but, significantly, the promise that they would not forever be tied to the same position. Throughout the entire French occupation of Canada, ordinary craft restrictions on the achievement of mastership were loosened, and the opportunity to return to France in the higher status was freely granted.[39] To be sure, the lure of the carrot was not the only means used; there was also the stick. Servants were forbidden to leave their masters and others to hide them on pain of severe punishment; marriage without consent of the master was banned; artisans were forced to do whatever their masters required, even when that meant working outside their trades; wages of unskilled workers were regulated.[40]

The net effect of the administration's policy was to introduce slackness rather than rigidity into the society, even to the point of seriously compromising its own ability to obtain revenue. The state *corvée* had to be curtailed, eventually suppressed, for fear that word of its existence would restrict emigration from France and would antagonize the labor force, which, in another capacity, was counted on to provide militia

---

[35] Reuben Gold Thwaites, ed., *The Jesuit Relations and Allied Documents*, vol. 9 (Cleveland, 1897), pp. 184-91.

[36] Blet, *Colonisation*, p. 136; Hardy, *Colonisation*, pp. 18-20; for colonization under Talon, see Salone, *Colonisation*, pp. 156-69.

[37] Vignols, "Mise en valeur," p. 732; Renaud, *Origines économiques*, pp. 221-22; Salone, *Colonisation*, pp. 41-43.

[38] G. Debien, "Engagés pour la Canada au xviiᵉ siècle vus de La Rochelle," *Revue d'histoire de l'Amérique française*, 6 (1952-53), 211-13; Benjamin Sulte, "Le Régiment de Carignan," *Mélanges historiques*, 8 (Montreal, 1922), 61; Parkman, *Old Regime*, pp. 276-79; Salone, *Colonisation*, pp. 342-46.

[39] *Supplement to Report on Canadian Archives for 1899*, p. 279; Renaud, *Origines économiques*, pp. 385-86; Salone, *Colonisation*, pp. 196-97.

[40] Talon to Colbert, May 21, 1664, FOM, ser. C¹¹A, II, fols. 137-38; Clark, *Social Development*, p. 47; Roy, ed., *Ordonnances*, vol. 1, pp. 258-59; Vignols, "Mise en valeur," p. 732.

service. The billeting of soldiers, always a source of complaint, was progressively limited until in 1683 it was entirely abolished and became a regular fixed charge upon the state. Direct payments in the form of seigniorial rents and ecclesiastical tithes were reduced considerably below the level prevailing in France.[41] Indeed, *liberté* and *tranquilité*—eventually the major objectives of colonial policy—were seen as attainable only by offering concessions to induce a labor force to migrate and increase its productivity. "Such are the means of attracting colonists and keeping them," wrote M. Petit in his treatise on colonization. "But the most important of all is gentleness and moderation in the government, in extending its hand so that the colonists find, at least in the legitimate use of authority, compensations for the harshness of their labor and the sacrifice of their health in establishments recognized as so useful to the state."[42]

Despite all inducements, the population of Canada never reached the desired quantity and quality. From beginning to end, the reports to the authorities bemoaned the scarcity of labor and its lack of discipline. "Sixty indentured servants have been sent to this country again this year with the notion that they would be immediately useful," Intendant Jacques de Meulles wrote to the Marquis de Seignelay, Colbert's son, in 1684. "The oldest is not seventeen, and . . . I believe that those who sent them are making a mockery of us, there being no one of an age to render service."[43] Send us no more gentlemen, Governor Denonville pleaded in 1686, only "sturdy peasants . . . used to hatchet and pickaxe."[44] "We entreat, you, Monseigneur," wrote Beauharnois and Hocquart to Minister Jean-Frédéric Phélypeaux, Marquis de Maurepas, in 1730, "to stop sending libertines to the colony. There is already a very great number, and it is more difficult to restrain them in this country than anywhere else because of the facility they have for escaping and the difficulty of convicting them."[45] By 1712 the seigniory of Isle Perrot, granted in 1672, had only one inhabitant; those of Chicouanne and Boisseau, granted that same year, had none; Pointe du Lac, granted early in the 17th century, had one settler; Lussaudière, granted in 1672, had none; the seigniory of Jacques Cartier, granted in 1649, had only one inhabitant—he fished for eels—and dozens more were so sparsely inhabited as to be profitless to their owners and to the state.[46] The problem of maintaining an adequate labor force was made even more difficult by the flight into the wilderness of those who were expected to remain fixed to the land. Throughout the

[41] Vignols, "Mise en valeur," pp. 780–82.

[42] M. Petit, *Mémoires sur l'administration des colonies françaises en Amérique et projets de legislation pour les d. Colonies*, Manuscrits Français, 12081, fols. 314–15, Bibliothèque Nationale, Paris. The reason for the government's ban on the arbitrary arrest of habitants was its recognition that the practice was "wholly contrary to the wealth and augmentation of the colonies. . . ." Ordinance of May 7, 1679, FOM, ser. C¹¹A, V, fol. 99.

[43] Quoted in Clark, *Social Development*, p. 45.

[44] Quoted in François Xavier Garneau, *History of Canada*, vol. 1, trans. Andrew Bell, 3d ed. (Montreal, 1866), pp. 181–82.

[45] Quoted in Clark, *Social Development*, p. 61.

[46] The figures may be found in the survey of Gédéon de Catalogne, in Munro, *Documents*, pp. lix–lxxvi. See also, Heneker, *Seigniorial Regime*, pp. 157–76.

18th century, when the population of able-bodied adult males was always pathetically small, an average of 300 men were absent each year, won over to the freedom of forest life, deserters to the English, or seekers after their fortune in Louisiana.[47] Above all, however, the problem of disciplining labor and raising its productivity was exacerbated by the refusal of the population to behave in the expected manner.

The continued loyalty of the seignior to the system depended on his ability to profit from his privileges, and his privileges were such as to require a large and expanding population. But in Canada, unlike France, land was plentiful and people scarce; and the competition was among seigniors for tenants and not among tenants for land. And even the land system itself conspired against the desire of the authorities to fix people to the land and against the ability of the seigniors to make their living from it. The estates, laid out in parallelograms with the short side fronting on the St. Lawrence River, became split up into ever-narrowing ribbons of farms as, with the passage of time, they were divided among heirs; and agricultural productivity suffered accordingly. Instead of wealth and the grandeur of privileged status, poverty was the lot of most seigniors. "It is necessary to help them," wrote Denonville to Seignelay, "by giving them the means of . . . livelihood for, in truth, without that there is great fear that the children of our nobility . . . will become bandits because of having nothing by which to live."[48]

What was a bad situation to begin with was worsened by the propensity of many seigniors to adopt a style of life better in accord with their expectations than with realities. "The Gentlemen that have a Charge of Children, especially Daughters," wrote Baron La Hontan, "are oblig'd to be good Husbands, in order to bear the Expence of the magnificent Cloaths with which they are set off; for Pride, Vanity, and Luxury, reign as much in *New France* as in *Old France*."[49] "One finds here no rich persons whatever," Father Pierre F. X. de Charlevoix wrote. "In New England and the other British colonies there reigns an opulence by which the people seem not to know how to profit; while in New France poverty is hidden under an air of ease which appears entirely natural. The English colonist keeps as much and spends as little as possible; the French colonist enjoys what he has got, and often makes a display of what he has not got."[50]

To persist in behaving in New France in ways that were appropriate to Old France was to fly in the face of reality. When the Sieur de Frédéric, captain in the Carignan-Salières regiment and nephew of its colonel, punished a habitant for complaining to the intendant about injury done to his crops when Frédéric rode over his land, he doubtless felt that the propriety of his behavior could not be impeached. He was, however, re-

[47] Filteau, *Naissance d'une nation*, vol. 2, pp. 192-93. For the complaints of the seigniors that the absence of able-bodied men was intensifying the labor shortage, see Duchesneau to Colbert, November 13, 1681, FOM, ser. C^{11}A, V, fol. 298.

[48] Quoted in Clark, *Social Development*, p. 72.

[49] Quoted in ibid., p. 71.

[50] Quoted in Parkman, *Old Regime*, pp. 459-60.

turned to France by Intendant Talon.[51] In France, conscience required that sympathy be extended to peasants whose fields were trampled by seigniors. In Canada, the reverse was true: "divers persons so [abuse] the goodness of the seigneurs of this island [Montreal], who allow them such freedom, that they hunt and fish everywhere on the superior's private domain . . . where they kill the pigeons on pretence of their being other game, and break down all the fences, even threatening the overseer, a most worthy man placed there by the seigneur."[52] So widespread was the abuse that the seigniors had to beg the protection of the authorities.[53]

The protection to the ego offered by keeping up appearances at all costs rather quickly reached its limits. Louis Hamelin, the seignior of Grondines, was himself reduced to working his own mill when his miller was called to military service.[54] Even such notable families as Saint-Ours, Verchères, Repentigny, and Aubert de la Chesnaye were impoverished and forced to besiege the King with petitions for military commands, judicial posts, licenses to trade in furs, pensions—anything that might provide income. Others gave up entirely and returned to France.[55] When the owners of the seigniory of Monts-Pelées donated it to the Dames Religieuses de la Miséricorde de Jesus, they wrote wistfully and pathetically: "the present donation is made because the donors find themselves at a very advanced age which does not permit them to work to gain their livelihood and because the little property they have is not sufficient to produce enough income to support them in sickness or in health for the rest of their days; they are, moreover, abandoned by all their relatives and friends."[56] In the circumstances, the seigniors began to behave not as their role prescribed, but as conditions seemed to require.

They violated their obligations to their tenants, attempting to exact from them rights to which they were not entitled. They "grant to their habitants leave to cut timber on the ungranted lands, on condition that they pay 10 percent of the value of the boards obtained therefrom," Intendant Michel Bégon wrote Victor Marie d'Estrées, president of the Conseil de Marine, in 1716. "When they concede woodlands they reserve for themselves all the oak and pine timber thereon without compensation to the habitants, and they are able to exact any price they please for this

---

[51] Talon to Colbert, October 20, 1667, FOM, ser. C^{11}A, II, fols. 318-19. "On the judgment that the King will pass on the conduct of this officer depends the security and tranquillity of the colonists of Canada," Talon added.

[52] Dollier de Casson, A History of Montreal, 1640-1672, trans. Ralph Flenley (London, Toronto, and New York, 1928), p. 29.

[53] Roy, ed., Ordonnances, vol. 1, pp. 183-84, 224-26; Arrêt of July 6, 1670, FOM, ser. C^{11}A, IV, fols. 148-49. For the effect of the poverty of the Canadian seigniors in weakening their position against the church, as compared with the French seigniors, see E. R. Adair, "The French-Canadian Seigneury," Can. Hist. Rev., 35 (1954), 201-4.

[54] Heneker, Seigniorial Regime, p. 192.

[55] "Demands des officiers, 1696," FOM, ser. D^{2}C, XLIX, fols. 33-38; List of petitions, FOM, ser. D^{2}D; I, fols. 18-19; List of petitions, 1694 et seq., FOM, ser. C^{11}A, CXX, fols. 1-200; Salone, Colonisation, pp. 233-34, 236-37, 310-13.

[56] Pierre-Georges Roy, ed., Inventaire des concessions en fief et seigneurie . . . , vol. 3 (Archives de la Province de Québec, Quebec, 1927-29), p. 158.

wood. . . . ."[57] They attempted to squeeze more labor through the *corvée* than they were entitled to, made attractive verbal promises to the habitants and then stiffened the terms in writing, induced tenants to clear land for pasture which they later sold, and extorted illegal payments.[58]

Instead of using land for agriculture and settlement, they used it for speculation. Without themselves making any improvements or insisting that their tenants do so, the seigniors, so the local authorities reported to Paris, encouraged the habitants to buy and sell land so that they might collect the mutation fine that went with every change in ownership.[59] "There will always be some people," Intendant Jean Bochart de Champigny informed Minister Louis de Phélypeaux, Comte de Pontchartrain, in 1691, "who will seek land concessions in distant places . . . for the sole purpose of going there to trade . . . without thought of settling."[60]

Instead of doing their duty in the preservation of law and order, the seigniors connived with lawbreakers. Fearful in Canada as in the Antilles that the establishment of too many taverns would distract workmen and increase delinquency, the authorities sought to use the seigniors as direct agents of social control. "The trade of tavern-keeper has attracted all the rogues and lazy people who never think of cultivating the land," Denonville wrote Seignelay in 1685; "far from that, they deter and ruin the other inhabitants. I believe, Monseigneur, that in the villages, the Seigneur should hire and dismiss the tavern-keeper according to his good and bad conduct, and the Seigneur would be responsible for him. I know of seigneuries where there are only 20 houses and more than half are taverns. . . ."[61] But instead of upholding the law against tavern-keepers, they helped them to break it; as, indeed, they helped others also to break the law. "I must not conceal from you," Intendant Jacques Duchesneau wrote Colbert, "that the disobedience of the *coureurs de bois* has reached such a point that everybody boldly contravenes the King's interdictions. . . . I have enacted ordinances against the *coureurs de bois;* . . . against the gentlemen . . . who harbor them; and even against those who have any knowledge of them, and will not inform the local judges. All has been in vain; inasmuch as some of the most considerable families are interested with them. . . ."[62]

The seigniors broke the law themselves, especially when the authorities put them in such a position that to act in accordance with their status as loyal servant of the state seemed to conflict with the pressures on behavior that followed from their position as seignior. On October 21, 1686, a royal edict ordered all seigniors to establish mills on their prop-

[57] Quoted in Munro, *Seigniorial System*, p. 135.

[58] Vignols, "Mise en valeur," pp. 745–47; Munro, *Documents*, pp. 153–56, lxxvii–lxxix; Salone, *Colonisation*, pp. 360–61; Heneker, *Seigniorial Regime*, pp. 425–30.

[59] Munro, *Documents*, pp. 169–74, liv–lix, lxxix–lxxxii; Heneker, *Seigniorial Regime*, pp. 186–88.

[60] Quoted in Clark, *Social Development*, p. 66.

[61] Quoted in ibid., p. 60. See also Leon Vignols, "Les Antilles françaises sous l'ancien régime: les cabarets et leurs grands protecteurs," *Revue d'histoire économique et sociale*, 15 (1927), 359–65; Roy, ed., *Ordonnances*, vol. 1, pp. 86–88, 200–201.

[62] November 2, 1679, FOM, ser. C¹¹A, V, fol. 38.

erty, but for 20 years the law remained a dead letter because, contrary to orders, it was not promulgated by the Superior Council in Quebec.[63]

Above all, the seigniors failed in their obligation to support the social system that they, more than anyone else, were counted on to uphold. In making use of the major opportunity that existed to escape the discipline of the system—participation in the fur trade—they provided an example that others were quick to follow. "These disorders," wrote Denonville, "are much greater in the families of those who are gentlemen or who want to be so, either because of indolence or vanity. Having no other means of subsistence but the forest, because they are not accustomed to hold the plow, the pick, or the ax, their only resource being the musket, they must spend their lives in the woods, where there are no priests to restrain them, nor fathers, nor governors to control them. . . . I do not know, Monseigneur, how to describe to you the attraction that all the young men feel for the life of the savage, which is to do nothing, to be utterly free of constraint, to follow all the customs of the savages, and to place oneself beyond the possibility of correction."[64]

At times even the authorities recognized that a vast discrepancy had developed between the real position of the Canadian seignior and the one he had been given, and that the pressure of new necessities was a more powerful influence on behavior than the designs of the administrators. Contrasting the behavior of the Canadians with that of the young men in the Antilles, Beauharnois and Hacquart reported to the King that most Canadians "prefer voyages and trade, which give them the means of livelihood. It is not surprising that the young men of the Islands seek to fill vacancies for the position of councilor, because not only are their customs different from those of the Canadians, but, having been born with money, they are ambitious only for honors. Poverty reigns in Canada; men seek to escape from it and obtain a little comfort."[65]

Conditions that were poison for the seigniors were meat for the *censitaires,* though they, too, disrupted the social organization by refusing to behave in accordance with expectations or even frequently as custom and law dictated. In the design of the administrators, the *censitaires* were intended as a docile and obedient labor force. The very concessions, however, that were offered to entice them into the labor force—concessions that took the form both of direct incentives and limitations on the authority of their seigniorial masters—made it impossible to keep them in their assigned position or to fix their behavior in the desired mold. Their situation in the New World was a very decided improvement over their situation in the Old World, and they acted less in response to old prescriptions than to new imperatives.

In classic feudalism, institutions and rules existed which empowered the seigniors to compel obedience. Marc Bloch has observed:

---

[63] Munro, *Documents*, pp. 77–78.

[64] September 13, 1685, NAF, 9272, fols. 81V°–82R°. See also, Creighton, *Canada*, pp. 80–81; Leon Gérin, *Aux Sources de notre histoire* (Montreal, 1946), p. 214.

[65] Quoted in Frégault, *Civilisation*, pp. 219–20. See also, *Report Concerning Canadian Archives for 1904*, app. K, pp. 262–63.

Now, in the hands of the seigniors the almost unrestricted exercise of the rights of justice place an infinitely powerful weapon of economic exploitation. It reinforced their power of command, which in the language of the time . . . was called their "ban.""You can compel us to observe these rules" (those relating to the oven), the inhabitants of a village in Roussillon tell the Templars, masters of the place, in 1246, "even as a seignior can and ought to compel his subjects." . . . Among the multiple applications of this discipline, one of the most significant and, in practice, the most important, was the formation of seigniorial monopolies. . . . With very sure instinct, the jurists, when they began in the 13th century to create a theory of society, found themselves in agreement in linking the *banalités* with the organization of justice. The right to judge had been the strongest prop of the right to command.[66]

These were the rules and institutions that permitted the seigniors to maintain distance between themselves and the *censitaires* and that compelled the latter to accept the discipline imposed on them. In Canada, these institutions did not exist—or, at least, they existed in a most attenuated form—and it proved impossible to subject the *censitaires* to a discipline that implied a far wider distance between themselves and their superiors than in fact was the case. Not only were the seigniors' traditional monopolies emptied of meaning and their authority curbed by the administration, but the *censitaires* now competed directly with them in areas that had once been their private preserve. It was the *censitaires*, not the seigniors, who were appointed to the position of *capitaine des milices*, a post that involved the exercise of civil as well as military authority; and the complaints of the seigniors, faced with declining prestige, were to no avail. "You should," wrote Minister Jérôme de Pontchartrain to Governor François de Galiffet of Three Rivers, "make the seigniors of the parishes in your jurisdiction understand that the *capitaines des milices* must not communicate to them the orders that they receive from the governors and intendants before executing them; that is not due to them and they have no right to demand it of the *capitaines*, who might do so as a matter of courtesy, however, when it is of no interest to the service."[67]

The *censitaires* hunted and fished almost at will, they were occasionally called in to offer advice on government policy, and they were urged to report all "torts, exces, violances" committed by the seigniors.[68] Small wonder, then, they responded to their new situation by surrounding themselves with some of the trappings of the status that had so long been denied them. Though the government appealed to their own self-interest in urging them to concentrate on the production of cattle, pigs, and sheep, and though it imposed ban after ban on the raising of horses, they

---

[66] Bloch, *Caractères originaux*, vol. 1, pp. 82–84.

[67] Quoted in Frégault, *Civilisation*, pp. 176–77. See also, *Report Concerning Canadian Archives for 1904*, app. K, p. 59; Filteau, *Naissance d'une nation*, vol. 1, pp. 89–90; Benjamin Sulte, "The Captains of Militia," *Can. Hist. Rev.*, 1 (1920), 241–45.

[68] Roy, ed., *Ordonnances*, vol. 1, pp. 83–84; Wrong, *New France*, vol. 2, pp. 646–51; *Supplement to Report on Canadian Archives for 1899*, p. 71; Ordinance banning arbitrary arrest of habitants, May 7, 1679, FOM, ser. F³, V, fols. 234–35.

continued to breed horses and to ride through the countryside, as if in unconscious remembrance of the age-old connection between *cheval* and *chevallerie*.[69]

Even in the area of landownership, they reduced the distance between themselves and the seigniors. In 1712 Gédéon de Catalogne, a military engineer, made a survey of the more than 90 seigniories that then existed in Canada. Excluding those granted to religious orders, it is possible—by comparing the secular owners in 1712 with the original owners—to arrive at some estimate of the degree to which the barriers of privilege and aristocracy were melting away. Of the 76 secular grants for which it is possible to find the names both of the persons to whom they were originally granted and who held them in 1712, only 45, or 59 percent, were in the hands of the same families. Of the seigniories issued from 1670 to 1710, 62 percent remained in the original families. Clearly, time was on the side of mobility. And equally significant, Catalogne's report shows that of the 76 secular seigniories in 1712, at least 22 were owned by families of bourgeois or lower origin.[70]

Though the intention of the administration and the wish of the seigniors was that the *censitaire* should behave with the oxlike placidity of the peasant, he refused to do so because he was not, in truth, a peasant. As Baron La Hontan wrote: "The peasants there are at their ease. What, did I say peasant? Honorable apologies to these gentlemen! That term, taken in its usual meaning, would put our Canadians into the fields. A Spaniard, if he should be called a rustic, would not wince, nor twirl his mustache more proudly. These people are not wrong after all; they do not pay the salt tax nor the poll tax; they hunt and fish freely; in a word they are rich. Then how can you compare them with our wretched peasants? How many nobles and gentlemen would throw their old parchments into the fire at that price."[71]

That the Canadian *censitaire* had ceased to be a French peasant received stunning confirmation in the 18th century, but by then time had run out on the French government. Taking pity on those displaced Acadians who had managed to return to France, the government devised a variety of plans to attach them "à la glebe de France," all of which involved tenurial terms far superior to those of the generality of peasants and at least one of which was drawn up on the basis of the most advanced physiocratic theory. Each attempt to place the Acadians on the land proved a fiasco, for the way in which they had assimilated their own history made them unfit to assume the status of peasant. "I think, really, that the Acadians are mad," wrote the Commissaire Général in 1772. "Do they imagine that we wish to make seigniors of them? The intention of the government is to put them on the level of the cultivators in the

---

[69] "Extrait du mémoire au Beauharnois et Hocquart," April 22, 1732, FOM, ser. F³, XII, fol. 15; Vignols, "Mise en valeur," p. 758.

[70] The figures are computed from Catalogne's report, Munro, *Documents*, pp. 94-150.

[71] Quoted in Salone, *Colonisation*, p. 240. See also Munro, *Documents*, pp. 185-87; Innis, *Select Documents*, p. 351; Wade, *French Canadians*, p. 35.

provinces where they might be established, giving them the means to subsist by their labor. They seem offended by the fact that we wish to treat them like our peasants."[72]

Not all *censitaires*, of course, did well in Canada. But, whether the peasant profited under the system or suffered under it, how was it possible to retain him in the same subordinate position he had held in France? Indeed, he rejected the very title of *censitaire* because of its connotation of servility and succeeded in having himself referred to even in official documents simply as "habitant."[73] Corresponding to this change in title was a change in his behavior.

Instead of obedience to the seignior, there were "mutinerie et l'indépendence." The state, too, on occasion felt the wrath of its citizens,[74] and even the church, though protected by the loyalty of the people to Catholicism, became the target of popular hostility. When Bishop Laval introduced the French tithe into Canada in 1663, the resistance was so widespread that he was quickly forced to offer concession after concession—reduction from one-13th to one-20th and finally to one-26th; exemption of fish, eggs, timber, and livestock; and a five-year exemption on newly cultivated land. For more than 50 years the conflict raged between church and inhabitants, and not even the refusal to grant absolution to those who withheld the tithe or who paid in spoiled wheat could quell the "great murmuring at the door of the church." "Many individuals," wrote Duchesneau in 1677, "through plain disobedience . . . and scorn of the church not only refuse to pay the tithes, but are even carried away to the point of violence." As late as 1727 the inhabitants of the parish of St. Antoine-de-Tilly had to be *ordered* by the intendant to pay their tithes to the curé.[75]

Worst of all, their disobedience took the form of wholesale desertion of agricultural tasks. Despite the severe sanctions imposed by church and

---

[72]Quoted in Ernest Martin, *Les Exiles acadiens en France au xviiie siècle et leur établissement en Poitou* (Paris, 1936), pp. 85–86. For indirect evidence of the improvement in the position of the French peasant in Canada, arguing from population theory, see John T. Krause, "Some Implications of Recent Work in Historical Demography," *Comparative Studies in Society and History*, 1 (1958-59), 164-88.

[73]A. L. Burt, "The Frontier in the History of New France," Canadian Historical Association, *Annual Report . . . 1940* (Toronto, 1940), 96; Renaud, *Origines économiques*, p. 370; Filteau, *Naissance d'une nation*, vol. 1, p. 152.

[74]Frégault, *Civilisation*, pp. 69, 165.

[75]Burt, "Frontier," pp. 96-97; "Inventaire des documents concernant l'église du Canada sous le régime français," *Rapport de l'archiviste . . . de Québec pour 1940–41* (Quebec, 1941), 402; Roy, ed., *Ordonnances*, vol. 1, pp. 213, 70-74, 177-78; Têtu and Gagnon, *Mandements*, vol. 1, pp. 47, 160-61, 275-81, 491-92. See also, Filteau, *Naissance d'une nation*, vol. 1, pp. 163; "Inventaire des documents concernant l'église," *Rapport de l'archiviste de Québec, 1939–40* (Quebec, 1940), 205, 218, 245; ibid., *Rapport de l'archiviste de Québec, 1941–42* (Quebec, 1942), 182, 251, 261, 273; *Supplement to Report Concerning Canadian Archives for 1899*, 362; *Report Concerning Canadian Archives for 1904*, app. K, 140-41; Ordinances of Tracy and Talon, August 23, September 24, 1667, FOM, ser. F³, III, fols. 349-52; Arrêt de Conseil Supérieur de Québec, November 18, 1705, ibid., VIII, fols. 390-91; Requests of habitants to reduce tithes, ibid., CXLII, fols. 56, 69-71; Ordinance forbidding insults to the clergy, October 23, 1730, ibid., XI, fol. 343; "Requête des habitants du Canada," FOM, ser. C¹¹E, II, fol. 18; Duchesneau to Seignelay, November 13, 1680, FOM, ser. C¹¹A, V, fols. 177-79.

state, increasing numbers of people, "excited by the bad example of the *coureurs de bois* and by the profits that they had made," left the field for the forest in search of furs. In the year 1680 approximately one-third of the adult male population had escaped the discipline of society by entering the fur trade. At no time does the proportion of the adult male labor force engaged in trapping and hunting seem to have been less than one-quarter or one-fifth.[76] Not only did they deplete an already inadequate labor force, but they infected those who remained with the example of their rebelliousness. "We weare Cesars, being nobody to contradict us," said Pierre Radisson, greatest of all the *coureurs de bois*.[77] If his was a self-image too elevated for the many to aspire to, they felt themselves at least to be captains of their own fate. "The genius of the people of New England," Minister Maurepas wrote to Beauharnois in 1728, "is to work hard at cultivating the land and to establish new settlements one after the other. . . . The inhabitants of New France think differently. They would like always to move forward without getting tangled up in interior settlements, because they gain more and are more independent when they are more remote."[78] "One part of our youth is continually rambling and roving about," wrote Father Charlevoix, "and . . . it infects them with a habit of libertinism, of which they never entirely get rid; at least, it gives them a distaste for labour, it exhausts their strength, they become incapable of the least constraint, and when they are no longer able to undergo the fatigues of travelling . . . they remain without the least resource, and are no longer good for anything. Hence it comes to pass, that arts have been a long time neglected, and great quantity of good land remains still uncultivated, and the country is but very indifferently peopled."[79]

Litigious, independent, insubordinate, the habitants joined the seigniors in making a mockery of the behavior defined for them. No longer were they willing to act as instruments of those who planned the system; they acted now out of concern for their own survival or improvement. At times, as we have seen, they deliberately violated the norms of their society; at times, they violated them unwittingly because, under conditions of rapid change, it became problematic as to how the norms were to be applied. But the society was turned upside down when its sworn defenders themselves subverted it. "Profit, my dear Vergor, by your place," wrote Intendant François Bigot to Louis Du Pont du Cham-

---

[76] Instructions of the King to Governor Louis Hector de Callières, May 25, 1699, in *Collection de manuscrits*, vol. 2, p. 323; Langlois, *Population canadienne-française*, pp. 81–84, 246; Filteau, *Naissance d'une nation*, vol. 2, pp. 128–31; Frégault, *Civilisation*, pp. 91–95. "I desire you to use all the authority of your office to put an end to hunting and to punish in accordance with the full rigor of my ordinances all those who are captured while hunting. . . ." Louis XIV to Duchesneau, June 2, 1680, FOM, ser. C¹¹A, V, fol. 209.

[77] Quoted in Creighton, *Canada*, p. 82.

[78] Quoted in Frégault, *Civilisation*, p. 118.

[79] Quoted in Clark, *Social Development*, p. 47. See also, "Mémoire attribué à Raudot," FOM, ser. C¹¹A, CXXII, fols. 82–83. A similar development took place in Louisiana. Marcel Giraud, *Histoire de la Louisiane française*, vol. 1 (Paris, 1953), pp. 136–38, 207, 213–14, 265–66.

bon, Sieur de Vergor, commandant of Fort Beauséjour; "trim, lop off; all power is in your hands; do it quickly so that you may be able to come and join me in France and buy an estate near mine." Instead of enforcing the laws against illegal fur traders, the intendants permitted them to carry on and they cut themselves in on the profits. They traded in flat violation of the orders they received from Paris. "Trading is prohibited to persons in office," wrote the President of the Navy Board. "They are placed there only to protect it, not to carry on even the most legitimate, and for the strongest reasons should abstain from dealing in concessions and monopolies that they ought to prevent with all their power. . . . What is certain is, that . . . it can only be regarded as criminal on the part of all those who have taken part in it or those who have favored it or even fostered it, and above all for persons employed in the service. . . ."[80]

The circle was complete when what had once been regarded as deviance came later to be recognized as the norm. "I believe," wrote Denonville to Seignelay, "that Monseigneur should not determine to cease to give letters of nobility but that it would be well to give them only to those who will . . . enter into whatever commerce makes a noble in this country." In 1685 the Canadian noblesse—which had been created as the apex of the seigniorial system—was allowed without derogation of rank "to engage in commerce by land as well as by sea, to buy and sell goods wholesale as well as retail." Never did the French nobility obtain such blanket permission to trade, and such permission as they did obtain came later than in Canada.[81]

The medicine, however, only worsened the disease. Trade "serves but to . . . reduce the number of people in the houses; to deprive wives of their husbands, fathers and mothers of the aid of their children . . . ; to Expose those who undertake such journeys to a thousand dangers for both their Bodies and their souls. It also causes them to incur very many expenses, partly necessary, partly Useless, and partly Criminal; it accustoms them not to work. . . . It Takes them away from all the holy places. . . . So long as all the young men devote themselves to no other occupation . . . There can be no hope that the Colony will Ever become flourishing . . . for it will always lose thereby What would most enrich it—I mean the labor of all the young men."[82] Church might mourn and anathematize and King complain and legislate, but the trend could not be reversed. Instead of docility, disobedience was the rule; instead of agriculture, trade; instead of remaining on the land, the people flocked to the cities; instead of simplicity and austerity, the extremes of grinding

[80]Quoted in Wrong, New France, vol. 2, p. 827; Report Concerning Canadian Archives for 1905, vol. 1, pt. 6, pp. 289-90. See also, Delanglez, Frontenac, pp. 200-207; Garneau, Canada, vol. 1, pp. 546-47; Clark, Social Development, p. 64.

[81]Quoted in Clark, Social Development, p. 72; Royal Decree, Versailles, May 1, 1685, NAF, 9328, fol. 75; Marc Szeftel, "La Règle de vie examplaire des nobles et l'évolution sociale de la France de l'ancien régime," Revue de l'Institut de Sociologie, 16 (1936), 607-8. See also A. Couillard-Després, La Noblesse de France et du Canada (Montreal, 1916).

[82]Father Étienne Carheil to De Callières, August 30, 1702, quoted in Clark, Social Development, p. 55.

poverty and the glitter and tinsel "d'un fort bon ton." Canada had become "a tableau of abuses, and not a body of rules."[83]

So disrupted had the society become, then, and so profitless to its sponsors, that only the merchants of the seaport towns of France objected when Canada was lost to the British. On February 10, 1763, the very day the Treaty of Paris was signed, Voltaire wrote Étienne François, Duc de Choiseul: "Permit me to compliment you. I am like the public; I like peace better than Canada and I think that France can be happy without Quebec."[84]

IV

The French government was faced with the twofold problem of maintaining order and stability in Canada and of motivating its subjects to perform the tasks given them. It sought to assign each man a status, the behavior of which was defined and regulated; when men behave according to prescription, each can act toward the other with the certainty that his own behavior will be understood and with the expectation that the other's responses will be the appropriate ones. At the same time, however, the government was faced with the necessity of recruiting a labor force, and the means it used involved offering such a variety of concessions and incentives that the position of the labor force in the society that was actually created was utterly different from its position in the society that had been contemplated. The government of France, like the General Court of the Virginia Company of London, was fully conscious of its problems, but—again like the Virginia Company—the solution it adopted for the problem of motivation made it impossible to solve the problem of order. Rigor and severe discipline, the distinguishing characteristics of the first social order in Canada as in Virginia, broke down in the face of the need to recruit a *voluntary* labor force. By her own actions, France created in Canada a social basis for disobedience, a society in which deviance became the only means of survival and of taking advantage of such opportunities as existed.

In a sense, a drama was taking place on the North American continent that had been played out before in Europe. At various times in late medieval and early modern Europe, especially in periods of considerable stress, the seigniors had to offer concessions to their tenants, even to the

---

[83] At no time during the French occupation did the number of people living in the cities of Quebec, Montreal, and Three Rivers fall below 20 percent, and for most of the period it was substantially more, despite the existence of severe penalties against those who left the land to migrate to the towns. The figures may be computed from *Censuses of Canada, 1655 to 1871*, vol. 4, pp. 2–67; the regulations may be found in FOM, ser. F³, IX, fols. 24, 42; Frégault, *Civilisation*, pp. 217–19; Filteau, *Naissance d'une nation*, vol. 1, pp. 42–43; Henripin, *Population canadienne*, 9. The quotations are from Montcalm, in Salone, *Colonisation*, p. 435, and *Considérations sur l'état présent du Canada, d'après un manuscrit aux archives du Bureau de la Marine à Paris*, NAF, 9273, fol. 384Vᵉ. For a somewhat different explanation of the retardation of Canadian agriculture, which emphasizes the "peasant outlook" of the people, see Jean Elizabeth Lunn, "Agriculture and War in Canada, 1740-1760," *Can. Hist. Rev.*, 16 (1935), 125–36.

[84] M. Devèze, *Histoire de la colonisation française en Amérique et aux Indes au xviiiᵉ siècle* (Paris: Centre de Documentation Universitaire: n.d.), pp. 78–79.

point of enfranchisement, to prevent, by their emigration to "free" lands, the loss of their labor force. In 1439 the Hospitaliers de la Commanderie de Bure enfranchised their serfs of Thoisy: "all the 'houses and barns which are at the said Thoisy have been burned and destroyed . . . and no one wants to live . . . in the town. . . . in this way everyone withdraws and goes to live in free places.' " In 1628, when the Sire de Montureux-les-Gray, in Comté, freed his serfs, he did not conceal his hope that the "enfranchised village will be 'better inhabited and populated,' and 'consequently,' that the seigniorial rights 'would produce greater revenue.' "

"Misery was sometimes the creator of liberty," says Marc Bloch.[85] So it undoubtedly was in Europe; in North America, the need to recruit a voluntary labor force was the mother of liberty.

---

[85]The quotations are from Bloch, *Caractères originaux*, vol. 1, pp. 113-14. For similar conditions in Germany, see Thompson, "East German Colonization," p. 140; Barraclough, *Modern Germany*, pp. 276-77. See also, F. L. Carsten, *The Origins of Prussia* (Oxford, 1954), pp. 38, 40, 68, 80, 83; G. F. Knapp, *Die Bauernbefreiung und der Ursprung der Landarbeiter in den älteren Theilen Preussens* (Leipzig, 1887).

7

GOVERNMENT AND PRIVATE INTERESTS IN NEW FRANCE*

J. F. Bosher

One of the long-standing assumptions of Canadian history has been that the government of New France (and of the French Empire), since it was hierarchic and autocratic, was also reasonably efficient—at least by standards of the time and in comparison with government in the English colonies to the south. The government of New France was created in the Golden Age of absolutism under the "Sun King," Louis XIV. As its basis, French absolutism emphasized centralization of power, with a hierarchical structure of authority which led to the top—to the king himself. In terms of government in French North America, power descended from the monarch to the minister of marine to the representatives of the crown in the colony: the governor and the intendant. No representative body of the inhabitants existed to interfere with the making of swift decisions for New France. Yet, despite the theoretical efficiency of this administrative system, in actual practice government in New France was nowhere near as systematic as one might expect. Problems of communication between the mother country and the colony and disagreements between the governor and the intendant were responsible for some of the difficulty, but it went far deeper than these obvious factors. French absolutism may have been centralized, but it was not necessarily rational. Louis XIV's state was not a modern one in the sense that government officials were expected to rule in the public interest, and keep their private business out of affairs of state. Indeed, as Professor J. F. Bosher suggests in the following article, the French state had not yet succeeded in clearly identifying precisely what was a public interest. This failure of definition was as true

---

Canadian Public Administration, 10 (1967), 244-57.

in New France as in the mother country. How accurate is it to speak of "corruption" on the part of French colonial officials? What were the standards prevalent at the time? What effect did these standards have upon political practice and economic development in New France?

SUGGESTIONS FOR FURTHER READING

W. J. Eccles, *Frontenac, The Courtier Governor* (Toronto: McClelland and Stewart, 1959); *The Government of New France* (Ottawa: Canadian Historical Association, 1965).

Guy Frégault, *François Bigot, Administrateur Français* (Montréal: L'Institut, 1948).

Gustav Lanctôt, *A History of Canada*, 3 vols. (Cambridge: Harvard University Press, 1963-1965).

Yves F. Zoltuany, *The Government of New France: Royal, Clerical, or Class Rule?* (Scarborough, Ont.: Prentice-Hall of Canada, Ltd., 1971).

J.M.B.

W riting soon after Confederation, Francis Parkman described the government of New France in a concluding chapter entitled, "Canadian Absolutism, 1663-1763,"[1] as monarchical despotism," "stiff-handed authority," "essentially military," "absolute authority"; he wrote of "an ignorant population . . . trained to subjection and dependence" and of the "perpetual intervention of government." Under such a regime the colony could only fail. "If she had prospered it would have been sheer miracle." In Parkman's judgment, what the Canadians needed most in order to succeed in their colonial ventures was freedom from government intervention.

Today, nearly a century later, the best historians hold a contrary opinion. Guy Frégault has concluded a learned series of articles with the idea that New France depended for its prosperity and its economic development upon the efforts and expenditures of the colonial government. Describing colonial development as a joint venture of "the couple State-Society," he suggests that society judged New France to be an "entreprise déficitaire" and left it to the reluctant care of the state.[2] New France suffered from too little government, not too much. Pointing towards the same conclusion, Jean Hamelin has argued that the Canadian merchants wasted many opportunities, and were prevented from playing an important role in economic life as much by their own poverty, selfishness, and short-sightedness as by government interference.[3]

---

[1]Francis Parkman, *The Old Régime in Canada*, 2 vols. (1874), (Toronto, 1899), vol. 2, chap. 24, p. 197 ff.

[2]Guy Frégault, "Essai sur les finances canadiennes, 1700-1750," *R.d'H.A.F. (Revue d'Histoire de l'Amérique francaise)* published in four parts, 1958-59 vol. 12, pp. 307-23 and 459-85; vol. 13, pp. 30-45 and 157-83. The reference is to vol. 13, p. 181.

[3]Jean Hamelin, *Economie et Société en Nouvelle-France* (Cahiers de l'Institut d'Histoire de l'Université Laval, Les Presses de l'université Laval, 1960), pp. 133-37.

Neither of these writers has much praise for French care of the colony's development, but they believe that such development as occurred depended upon that care, such as it was, and they would probably agree with Fernand Ouellet, who writes,

> French mercantilism, because of its rigidity, gave only feeble encouragement to the expansion of New France; but not all the weaknesses of the economy of the Saint Lawrence Valley may be ascribed to colonialism. Some of them were inherent in the Canadian geographical context and others, just as fundamental, came from the very mentality of the colonists. The initiatives taken by the metropolis to stimulate economic progress, and sometimes to allow Canadians a greater participation in large-scale trade, met with little response among the population.[4]

Even more explicitly, Harold Innis wrote, "local industries, especially the tanneries and the grist mills, flourished, and important industries such as naval construction eventually succeeded, but because of government support and not in spite of it."[5] Mason Wade shares the same opinion.[6] In some contrary general statements, Gustave Lanctôt, for his part, adopts the Parkmanian view that a lack of scope for initiative, as well as a lack of capital, prevented the development in Canada of a true bourgeoisie which might have controlled and directed the country's trade and commerce,[7] but nearly all that he writes about the details of economic growth—except for a few industries such as lumber, weaving, and beaver hats—seems to show that it necessarily depended upon government initiative and financial encouragement. Indeed, like other historians, Lanctôt attributes much of the material progress of New France to the efforts of French officials, especially the Intendants, Talon and Hocquart. More positively, William Eccles declares that "without the military forces, the capital, the direction, talent and administrative ability provided by the Crown, little could have been achieved."[8]

Canadian historians have thus formed a judgment of absolutist government intervention in the economic life of New France, but they have not yet appraised the effects of individualism and personal or private enterprise upon the government. If we ask to what extent private interests encroached upon the general interest and upon the public domain, we shall find no answers. If we wish to know how far the royal administration of New France was proof against individual desires for personal enrichment and how far it was a prey to them, we can discover only scattered information and conflicting views. Intrusions of personal and group interests in the royal administration have been called "corruption" when they were illegitimate or illegal—as in the case of Bigot's *grande société*. When they were legal and legitimate, they have been uneasily ignored or else regarded as evidence of low moral standards in the *an-*

---

[4]Fernand Ouellet, *Histoire économique et sociale du Québec, 1760-1850, Structures et conjonctures* (Montréal and Paris, 1966), p. 14.

[5]Harold Innis, a review of Joseph-Noël Fauteux, *Essai sur l'industrie au Canada*, 2 vols. (Quebec, 1927), in the *Canadian Historical Review*, vol. 9, pp. 259-60.

[6]Mason Wade, *The French Canadians, 1760-1945* (London, 1955), p. 32.

[7]Gustave Lanctôt, *A History of Canada*, vol. 3 (Toronto, 1965), pp. 119, 129.

[8]W. J. Eccles, *Canada under Louis XIV, 1663-1701* (Toronto, 1964), p. 251.

cien régime. What, for example, is the historian to think about the great Talon's extensive private investments in industry and trade, or about Bigot's open pride in having outfitted corsaires himself in order to capture English ships and sell them at a profit in France?[9] In books about New France we find uncertain views on "corruption" and its context. Historians are aware that the royal administration was somehow not like our own of the 20th century or even that of the 19th, but they have contented themselves with elementary studies of its structure and with dark hints about the decadence of the *ancien régime* (as in Frégault's writings) or brave declarations about the virtue and benefits of the regime (as in Eccles' works). Most writers have only assumed, without investigating, that there was a public domain clearly separable from the ordinary realms of private life, a set of public officials clearly separable from private citizens, state functions as distinct from private activities, and public finances clearly marked off from private wealth. There is, nevertheless, considerable evidence of a broad no-man's-land between the two spheres, that of the royal state and that of the rest of society. In other words, there is evidence that state officials, finances, property, and functions were confused at many points with private ones. These things need careful study. The sociology of the royal administration has yet to be written.

To take an example, now, of the prevailing uncertainty on this subject, William Eccles has brilliantly exposed the rampant private interests of Frontenac and of the army officers in New France. "Of all the royal officials in New France," he writes, "very few were not accused of having abused their authority to mend, maintain or add to their private fortunes. Yet if the moral climate of the age did not absolutely condemn such conduct, the minister most certainly did; and, judging by the complaints which the minister received concerning Frontenac's malfeasance, so did many people in New France."[10] Quite apart from a near contradiction in this statement (that the minister and many other people condemned Frontenac's malfeasance but "the moral climate of the age" did not), we find Eccles otherwise unsure of his conclusions on this subject. He expresses an apparently contradictory opinion in a more recent work: "Until the closing years of the French regime, when Bigot and his clique made a mockery of established institutions, Canada was provided by the Crown with an efficient administrative system and officials of a relatively high degree of competence and probity."[11] The word "relatively" seems to betray uncertainty because we are not told what the honesty of the colonial government was relative to; but in any case the author's own work on Frontenac's regime appears to make the later generalization rather dubious. Mason Wade, too, comes to a different conclusion: ". . . long before the days of the infamous Intendant Bigot,

---

[9]Eccles, *Canada,* p. 56: ". . . here would have been less economic activity in the colony without [Talon's] investment of capital." Cf. Frégault, *Bigot,* vol. 1, pp. 200–201 where Bigot's enterprises are related in a typically sarcastic tone.

[10]W. J. Eccles, *Frontenac the Courtier Governor* (Toronto, 1959), pp. 98, 216–18.

[11]W. J. Eccles, *The Government of New France* (pamphlet of the Canadian Historical Association, Ottawa, 1965), p. 17.

official graft represented a drain on the colony's finances."[12] To cite a third authority, Guy Frégault concludes his study of Bigot with a judgment more stern and sweeping than either Eccles or Wade makes. "In short," he writes, "the French government did not want Canada; its agents only came here to make their fortunes. *Toul est là*. . . . Bigot was a man of his time. . . . The last intendant of Canada participated in the degradation of his century."[13] Other examples could be adduced to show the confused state of opinion on this subject.

There is no difficulty in finding evidence of royal officials working in their own private interests. A rapid search through printed books alone reveals that not only Bigot and Frontenac but many other governors and intendants engaged in money-making enterprises. Among the governors with interests in the fur trade, we find Hector, Chevalier de Callières, Philippe Rigaud, Marquis de Vaudreuil, La Jonquière, François-Marie Perrot, and Joseph-Antoine Lefebvre, Sieur de la Barre.[14] Vaudreuil also did such things as investing 1,000 crowns of his own money in an expedition to raid the Hudson's Bay Company post at Fort Albany, with the hope of personal profit.[15] De la Barre, like Frontenac, used his official powers to forbid others from trading in order to increase his own profits. Directly under the governors, the army officers in the colony took their cue from their commander-in-chief and involved themselves in fur trading and in keeping the pay of their men, whenever possible, and obliging the men to go out and work for a living.[16] As for the intendants, we find Jacques de Meulles (1682-86), Jean-Richard de Champigny (1686-1702), Francois de Beauharnois (1702-5), who was actually recalled from his post because of "commercial involvements," Michel Bégon (1712-26), and even the great Jean Talon (1665-68, 1670-72) all using their power to exploit the fur trade for their personal profit.[17] Bégon appears to have worked systematically at a whole range of Bigot-like enterprises, speculating in the supply trades and in agricultural products.[18] Gilles Hocquart (1731-48) invested personally in Cugnet's company which took a lease on the ironworks of Saint-Maurice.[19] Even a visiting official from the Ministry of Marine, Armand Laporte de Lalanne, managed to get the lease of a trading post while he was in New

---

[12]Mason Wade, *French Canadians*, p. 34.

[13]Guy Frégault, *François Bigot, administrateur français*, vol. 2 (Montréal, 1948), pp. 394-95.

[14]Adam Shortt, ed., *Documents Relating to Canadian Currency, Exchange and Finance during the French Period*, 2 vols. with continuous pagination (Ottawa, 1925), pp. 111 n., 129 n.; Lanctôt, *A History of Canada*, vol. 2, pp. 86, 159, vol. 3, pp. 19, 81; *Dictionary of Canadian Biography*, vol. 1 (1965), pp. 540 and 230, concerning R.-L. Closse; G. M. Wrong, *The Rise and Fall of New France* (New York, 1928), pp. 497, 652, 881.

[15]Lanctôt, *A History of Canada*, vol. 2, p. 159.

[16]Shortt, *Documents Relating to . . .* , pp. 735 and 790-91; Eccles, *Frontenac*, pp. 216 and 340.

[17]Eccles, *Frontenac*, p. 10; Eccles, *Canada*, pp. 56, 210; Lanctôt, *A History of Canada*, vol. 2, pp. 99, 151; vol. 3, pp. 13, 22.

[18]Rosario Bilodeau, "Liberte économique et politique des Canàdiens sous le régime français," *R.d'H.A.F.* 1956, vol. 9, p. 61.

[19]Shortt, *Documents Relating to . . .* , p. 635.

France in 1741.[20] Not unnaturally, as we move down the scale of civil employees we find more and more who, like the sub-délégué, Nicolas-Gaspard Boucault, engaged in extensive fishing and trading enterprises, or, like the Treasurer General's agent, Nicolas Lanoullier de Boisclerc, invested in anything from floating tide-mills at Québec, for which he secured a monopoly privilege, to the postal services of the colony.[21] Lanoullier was arrested in 1730 for squandering royal funds on his own private projects. Another Treasurer General's agent, Jacques Imbert (1750–59) quietly made a fortune in the Bigot era and escaped detection. When another agent, Jacques Petit de Verneuil, died, 27,900 *livres* were found to be missing.[22] These are only some of the better known examples. It seems likely that a careful investigation would show the great majority of government officials to have used their power or positions for promoting their own private money-making ventures.

The problem is not in discovering such evidence but in drawing general conclusions about it. It may be true to conclude, as so many have done, that private enterprise in government administration ("corruption") was commonplace and generally tolerated in the *ancien régime,* but this is a dubious, tautological conclusion. It usually implies a moral judgment on the times. Vaudreuil had "weaknesses which were those of the age," writes Gustave Lanctôt in a typical explanation.[23] This paper is intended to suggest that a more satisfactory explanation might be found in answer to a sociological question: What sort of an administrative system was it which tolerated the intrusion of personal or private interests on such a large scale? The worth of this question will, I hope, become apparent in the following brief remarks concerning the financial part of the administration.

There was an ambiguity in the royal financial administration of New France, indeed of the entire French kingdom. The system was almost as much a private enterprise as a public function. Of the two principal operations in making payments, one, the *ordonnancement* or authorization, was a public function performed by or in the name of the king, and the other, the *comptabilité,* or responsibility for payment, was in practice largely a private enterprise. The intendant, usually said to have been responsible for the finances of the colony, was in fact only an *ordonnateur,* not a *comptable.* When he issued an *ordonnance* for payment of a salary or a bill for goods and services the payment was thereby authorized but the funds not actually paid nor even provided for. The same was true of *ordonnances* authorized by the Royal Councils. For purposes of illustration, it is not inaccurate to describe an *ordonnance* as

[20]Ibid., p. 699 n. This was a brother of the *premier commis,* Bernaud de la Porte, who directed the affairs of New France in the Marine Department at Versailles during most of Bigot's period of office (P. G. Roy, *Bigot et sa Bande et l'Affaire du Canada* [Levis, 1950], p. 315).

[21]Ibid., pp. 357 and 621.

[22]Ibid., pp. 885 n. and 175.

[23]Lanctôt, *A History of Canada,* vol. 3, p. 19.

a sort of cheque on the royal account managed by a *comptable* who, in the case of New France, would be one of the two Trésoriers Généraux de la Marine or his agent at Quebec.[24] The *comptabilité* was managed by the Treasurer's agent as part of a semi-private banking system largely beyond the Intendant's control and only remotely within the control of the Royal Councils. The Intendant of New France knew what was in the agent's *caisse*, as a rule, and sent working accounts back to France.[25] This colonial circumstance tends to conceal the fact that the part of the Canadian "budget" provided by the Ministry of the Marine suffered from the same ambiguity as the part provided by the monopoly company of the Domain d'Occidant:[26] both parts of the government finances depended upon the management of groups of businessmen in whose affairs the ministers and officials did not ordinarily meddle and over whom the Crown in practice exercised merely the loose control of a very powerful client.

The Canadian agents of the Treasurers General were not, strictly speaking, royal officials, and a typical royal document refers to them as "leur commis"; that is, the *commis* of the Treasurers General.[27] They were normally appointed and paid by the Treasurers General, and the Intendant interfered in their appointment or payment only in the emergency that the Treasurers General failed to send instructions or funds.[28] The agents were personally responsible for their accounts, which were private rather than public. When, for example, the agent Thomas-Jacques Taschereau died in 1749, his widow and eight children were responsible for the unfinished accounts. "I do not know any person whom the widow can employ to straighten out his accounts," wrote Bigot. "Therefore the Treasurer General would do well to send someone, if they wish to see the matter concluded. Monsieur Bréard (the Marine Department Controller) will certainly guide whoever does this work, but there must still be someone who takes charge and who is accountable."[29] The agents kept their records like personal business records at their own residences. When in 1734 a large fire in Montreal burned the house of the agent, de Béry, his papers were all destroyed and there was no way of determining how much money had been lost or what was the state of his accounts.[30] Unless there was a scandal leading to arrest and investiga-

---

[24]From 1749 to 1771 there were also two Treasurers General for the colonies.

[25]Because of their special importance in the financial system of the *ancien régime*, the terms *caisse*, meaning till or chest, as in "community chest," and *comptable*, meaning a *caisse*-holding officer accountable to a Chamber of Accounts, are better left in French, as technical terms. As for the Intendants' accounts, these were not the final, legal accounts required by the Chamber of Accounts, but the rougher and more incomplete *état-au-vrai* sent to the Royal Council of Finance as a kind of report on the implementation of the budget or *état-du-roi* sent to the Intendant earlier.

[26]Frégault, "Essai," *R.d'H.A.F.*, vol. 12, p. 315.

[27]Shortt, *Documents Relating to . . .* , p. 928.

[28]For instance, in 1710 the Intendant was obliged to call on a clerk, Duplessis, to perform the duties of the agent who had gone to France partly in order to render accounts to his employer, the Treasurer General, Barthélémy de Vanolles. See Shortt, *Documents Relating to . . .* , p. 205.

[29]Ibid., p. 787.

[30]Ibid., pp. 635–37.

tion, the exact financial situation of an agent could seldom be determined until his death. Only when Petit de Verneuil died was it discovered that funds were missing. The agent Lanoullier de Boisclerc ran up a debit of some 180,000 *livres* before being arrested and charged. His fraud was then detected by the Treasurer General in France, it appears, not by the Intendant in Canada.[31]

The Treasurers General themselves held no revocable commissions, such as the Intendants held, but instead they purchased offices which, in effect, established them as profit-making entrepreneurs in government finance. When, for example, Louis-Barthélémy Mouffle de Géorville acquired the office of *Trésorier général de la Marine* in 1743, to manage Marine Department finances for even-numbered years, it was at the price of 800,000 *livres*, which he borrowed largely from Aymard-Felicien Boffin, Marquis de la Somme (or Saône), as his official *soumission* to the Chamber of Accounts recorded.[32] A semi-private financier holding a royal account, Mouffle de Géorville was responsible to the Chamber of Accounts for the management of that royal account alone. In practice he was responsible neither for what he did with royal funds between the time they were deposited in his *caisse* and the time they were required again, nor for the part of his business which consisted in borrowing funds on the credit of his prestigious office and investing at a profit in any financial, commercial, or industrial venture that seemed promising. Thus, it was not until he died on January 20, 1764, leaving accounts unfinished for the years 1756 and later, that the Chamber of Accounts was able to investigate his affairs and to discover debts to the Crown which they finally estimated at 1,659,000 *livres*.[33] According to the usual practice, the official *Contrôleur des Restes* endeavoured at intervals to recover this sum from Mouffle de Géorville's estate, but had to compete in the courts with two other claimants to the estate—the principal heiress, Françoise-Louise, a sister married to Louis-Toussaint Duraget de Champlionin, Gouverneur de Vassey, and the principal creditor, Boffin, Marques de la Somme. Like all such cases, it went on for a very long time and the Crown had still not recovered the lost funds as late as 1783.[34] Meanwhile, the vacant office had been sold to Claude-Pierre-Maximilien Radix de Sainte-Foy, who had raised the 800,000 *livres* through members of his family, and who in 1781 was to get into financial difficulties in his turn.[35]

Mouffle de Géorville, like all the Treasurers General who managed the royal funds for the colony of New France (or indeed any other purpose), carried on private business as well as royal business and, to use the expression of the time, "nourished his *caisse*" with private as well as

[31]Frégault, "Essai," *R.d'H.A.F.*, vol. 13, p. 34; Shortt, *Documents Relating to . . .* , p. 357 n.
[32]A. N. (Archives nationales, Paris), P. 2742, *Plumitif de la Chambre*, entry for May 30, 1783.
[33]A. N., F⁴ 2680.
[34]A. N., P. 2742, entry for May 30, 1783; P. 2829, *Journal de la Chambre*, entry for November 18, 1772.
[35]Herbert Lüthy, *La Banque protestante en France*, vol. 2 (Paris, 1961), pp. 689 n., 375.

royal funds.[36] Even the royal funds did not come from the royal treasury (whatever that term may mean). They came from the *caisses* of various other *comptables* who performed similar services on the receiving side of the system, the Receivers General and the like. "The Treasury was empty"—that phrase, so common to historians and memorialists alike, is very misleading to us in the 20th century who think inevitably of a consolidated revenue fund like that of the present Receiver General of Canada. Nothing of the kind was to be found in France until the French Revolution. In the modern sense, then, there was no treasury to be empty, but only a variety of related *caisses* including those of the two Treasurers General of the Marine, the one kept by their agent at Quebec, the ones kept by the Farm of the Domain, those of the two Keepers of the Royal Treasury, and so on. During the *ancien régime* all attempts to centralize the system proved vain.

We have the observations on this system of one of the sub-treasurers of the Marine at Rochefort who knew Bréard, the Controller at Quebec, and who was involved in Bigot's scheme to invade Louisbourg in 1746.[37] This was Simon-Joseph-Louis Bonvallet Desbrosses (1742–1800). Basing his views on many years of direct personal experience, he declared that Treasurers, Receivers, and other *comptables* could become rich or go bankrupt according to the fortunes of their business activities, which the Crown could know almost nothing about, much less control. The trouble derived, in his view, from three conditions: first, the casual arrangement by which a *comptable* received immense sums and could in practice dispose of them arbitrarily, especially for short periods; second, the ease with which a *comptable* could borrow large amounts of money because of the public funds at his disposal; third, "the certainty, almost physical and moral, which he enjoyed of never having to make good the deficiencies in his accounts (produire soi-même l'épurement de ses comptes)."[38] Even though the Royal Council of Finance laid down the annual amounts of money which each Treasurer or Receiver was to receive and spend, its proper sources, and its destinations, and even though there were often *Contrôleurs* whose business was to verify receipts and expenditures, nothing prevented the Treasurer or Receiver from using royal funds in one form or another for their own private financial ventures. "It is even a verifiable fact that the use of these same funds is the origin of those immense losses which are discovered when whoever has caused them finds himself without the means for making them good."[39] New France was a victim of the *caisse* system which Bonvallet Desbrosses criticized so sweepingly, for New France depended to a great

---

[36]The private, personal basis of "public" credit at the time is clearly shown in German-Louis Martin and Marcel Besançon, *L'Histoire du Crédit en France sous le règne de Louis XIV*, vol. 1, "Le Crédit public" (Paris, 1913).

[37]Frégault, *Bigot*, vol. 1, pp. 244, 249. From December 1769, when he quit the service, Bonvallet was occupied in preparing a book which he published in 1789, *Moyens de simplifier la perception et la comptabilité des deniers royaux*, in 4°, 116 pp. (Bib. nat. Lb39 7248). Some of his papers and biographical notes are in A.N., F⁷ 5846 and T 1270–71.

[38]Bonvallet, *Moyens de simplifier la perception* . . . , p. 2.

[39]Ibid., p. 4.

extent upon Treasurers General whose personal failures could affect the financial system. Perhaps the best example is Pierre-Nicolas Gaudion, Treasurer General of the Marine in 1715, obliged to stop receiving bills of exchange drawn on him at Quebec and eventually arrested by the courts and saved from total ruin only by the intervention of the Royal Council. True, he pleaded that since 1708 the government had not provided the funds necessary to meet the demands on him and this claim was no doubt well founded.[40] The point is not that Gaudion was a bad treasurer, however, but that he was a typical treasurer in a bad system. Neither the debts nor the revenues received nor the obligations were ever consolidated, but remained fragmentary because of the system of private *caisses*. Thus, in time of stress or economic recession, individual treasurers could fail and fall because they were not mutually sustaining, not part of an articulated financial organization. Gaudion failed but did not fall only because he was sustained by a watchful Royal Council which took the unusual step of suspending legal judgments against him and holding his creditors at bay. The uncertain operations of this system, half private and half public, were an important aspect of those financial crises in which both Frenchmen and Canadians lost heavily at the end of the War of Spanish Succession and again at the end of the Seven Years War.

In view of this system, the various paper credit instruments issued in the colony can hardly be identified as public funds. The bills of exchange (*lettres de change*) were drawn on the Treasurer General of the Marine by his agent in Quebec and only countersigned by the Intendant. "I never knew," wrote the Minister of the Marine, Pontchartrain, to the Intendant, Raudot, "that the agents of the Treasurers of the Marine charge 1 percent on the bills of exchange *which they draw on their masters*. You have been very wrong to suffer this, and you must warn them that His Majesty will have them punished if they continue this abuse."[41] The *quittances d'appointments, acquits,* and *ordonnances* were orders on the agent of the Treasurers General, issued much like cheques by the Intendant or the Governor in payment of salaries and bills for supplies, etc.[42] Their value depended ultimately on the honouring of them by the Treasurer General. True, an ordinance of March 18, 1733, made them legal tender, but they still rested for their value upon the bills of exchange drawn on the Treasurer General.[43] Michel Bégon wrote of some of this paper to the Minister: "It is the agents of the Treasurers General in this country who have been entrusted with all this money, in accordance with the receipt on the margins of all the official minutes of the issues that have taken place, and who alone should render accounts of it. . . ."[44]

Even the famous card money—what Parkman called "card rubbish"—did not altogether depend for its value upon the fiat of the Intendant acting for the Crown. The Intendants beginning with de Meulles

---

[40]Shortt, *Documents Relating to* . . . , pp. 307–11.
[41]Ibid., p. 180 (italics mine); also the frontispiece, photograph of a bill of exchange.
[42]Unlike cheques, however, they often changed hands at a discount (italics mine).
[43]Shortt, *Documents Relating to* . . . , pp. 383 n. and 635–39.
[44]Ibid., p. 539.

published *ordonnances* to give the cards currency, and the Governors put their official seal on them; yet the signature of the Treasurer's agent on the cards shows that, in the words of the Intendant, Bochart de Champigny (1686-1702), "card notes have been made, signed and paraphed by the Sieur Verneuil, agent of Monsieur de Lubert, Treasurer General of the Marine. . . ."[45] De Meulles originally issued the cards on his own initiative and credit—"par mon credit and par mon adresse"— but his pledge therein was to redeem the cards whenever the ships should arrive at Quebec with the funds from France, that is, to redeem the cards with whatever funds arrived.[46] But the arrival of those funds depended not only upon the royal order but also upon the capacity of the state's banker, the Treasurer General, to pay. As Guy Frégault has put it:

> The card money was henceforth secured on the bills redeemable in Paris. This should, nevertheless, not make us lose sight of the fact that it rep- resented a debt of the metropolitan state to the Canadian people. At bottom, therefore, its soundness rested on the solvency of the French government. Specifically, the card money played its role on two conditions: that every year the intendant disposed of enough bills of exchange to redeem the cards presented to him; and *that the Treasurers General of the Marine in Paris honoured the bills of exchange* that Quebec sent them.[47]

Government dependence upon a private financial enterprise becomes stark and clear in the records of crises when the Treasurers General could not pay. At a difficult time in the long and expensive War of Spanish Succession, for example, the Royal Council recognized that the Canadian Intendants and Governors had issued card money "hoping from one year to the other that the Treasurers General of the Marine would remit the funds appropriated—which they have not been able to do up to the present. As they [the Treasurers] are not in a position to meet them, and as this money has fallen into such discredit that it has greatly increased the price of goods and supplies in Canada, which causes con- siderable detriment to trade to the colony, it would appear that there is no other expedient to remedy this than to have this money converted into debentures [*rentes*] on the Hotel de Ville and on the provinces of the kingdom." As the Crown wrote to the governor and intendant, "there is no ground for hoping that the Treasurers will be in a position to remit the funds necessary to retire all that [card] money."[48] During the next few months, the Royal Council arranged for the cards to be converted into bills of exchange drawn on one of the Treasurers General of the Marine, Pierre-Nicolas Gaudion, by his agent at Quebec, only to find that Gaud- ion was soon unable to cash these bills or meet his other financial obli- gations; he was consequently arrested for debt. Contrary to its usual practice, the Council intervened in the case to protect the Treasurer from the judicial pursuit of the various interested courts, and Gaudion made

---

[45]Ibid., illus. and doc. pp. 80-81. "Parapher" was to make an elaborate personal mark together with one's signature, as an extra precaution against forgery.

[46]Ibid., pp. 69-75.

[47]Frégault, "Essai," *R.d'H.A.F.*, vol. 12, p. 470 (italics mine).

[48]Shortt, *Documents Relating to . . .* , pp. 239-41, letter of June 25, 1713.

use of this reprieve to try to put his affairs in order. In 1720, we find the Royal Council asking Gaudion about the Canada bills:

> . . . the Council desires you to inform it as to what you have done to procure the funds necessary for the payment of these bills, and at the same time to indicate the amount which remains to be paid of these, as well as of those which have been drawn in preceding years, whether you have funds for the purpose and within what time they have been promised to you.[49]

It is clear that even in the minds of the royal councillors themselves, the Canada bills were entirely in the hands of the Treasurer General, who acted as a sort of banker. The financial administration of New France was thus, in part, dependent upon private enterprise.

Private enterprise was not confined to the financial administration, however, and it might be shown that other aspects of the government exhibited the same confusion of public and private. For example, the administration as a whole was contained within a social system that continually interfered with it. Patronage, clientage, the use of public power to advance relations and friends, have not been unknown even in 20th-century Canada, but they have been regarded as evils to be discouraged. In the aristocratic society of the Bourbon monarchy, they were not abuses at all. The King was the greatest patron, setting the pattern for the rest of society by dispensing the highest places, honours, and pensions according to his own pleasure or the pleasure of the royal family, or of an influential group or individual at court. Lower in the social scale, anyone with influence could be a king to those beneath him. If the Marquis de Puysieulx and the Maréchal d'Estrées had a relation, François Bigot, who got into difficulties while serving as the Intendant of New France, it was only normal that they should use their influence at Versailles on his behalf. If François Bigot chose to assist the careers of Jacques-Michel Bréard and Jean-Victor de la Marre, Controllers of the Marine Department, it was only to be expected that they would remain his loyal "clients" so long as the relationship brought mutual benefit. If Varin made the acquaintance of a royal storekeeper, Jean-Baptiste Martel,[50] and threw opportunities for profit into his path, then in the 18th century their relationship might appear very different from the relationship of Bigot and his protectors, but it was nevertheless an example of the same kind of social interference in public administration.

How should the Martels, the Varins, and the Bigots have done otherwise? The King and his nobles intervened continually in the working of the pre-revolutionary administration, just as the operation of the pre-Newtonian universe was continually affected by the intervention of God and his angels. People importuned the high and mighty, just as they prayed to the company of Heaven, for grace and favour. As a matter of normal procedure, recruiting and promotion were based upon the "protection" or "favour" which candidates enjoyed, not upon any impersonal "merit" or "ability" such as our Civil Service Commissions endeavour to

---

[49]Ibid., p. 471.
[50]Roy, *Bigot et sa Bande et l'Affaire du Canada*, p. 67 ff.

discover. Appointment was a result of social competition; and promotion, even as a reward for faithful service, was fundamentally a personal act of patronage, a sign of grace and favour rather than a measure of ability or other merit. As a basic feature of the monarchy rank and place were fundamentally social, whether administrative, military, or ecclesiastical, and the most rapid and profitable advancement lay open to those who could marshal the most support. Rank and place, once gained, opened further avenues to personal advancement and profit.

The intrusion of social and personal pressures in the administration was closely bound up with the indiscriminate plunder of the royal purse and of private wealth. The struggle for advancement could not be separated from the struggle for enrichment. As John Law, a very close observer of the Regency, put it,

> . . . The interest of the State was neither considered nor perceived by anyone, because of the ancient habit which each person had contracted of seeking to enrich himself at the King's expense. The ministers sought to enrich themselves at the people's expense by financial operations which impoverished the State, and which had gathered up wealth for a small number of private persons, while the people, the nobility, the various funds, trade and industry were exhausted.[51]

That could have been written of the entire *ancien régime*, in both France and New France, if it were amended to explain that not only ministers but most people with power used it to enrich themselves. There was nothing unusual in the progress of Jacques de la Fontaine de Belcour, secretary to Governor Beauharnais from 1726, who was granted through his patron the exclusive privilege of catching seals and porpoise on a part of the north shore of the Saint Lawrence, and by 1736 had risen to become a member of the Superior Council at Quebec.[52] Wealth, public power, and social progress were all one currency. It was left for the French Revolution to draw distinctions between the state and the nation, the executive and the legislature, the administration and politics, and to endeavour to protect the administration from outside pressure and interference.

Another aspect of government that made it prey to private interests was the faculty of the higher authorities for recognizing individual honesty and dishonesty, ability and inability, coupled with their rudimentary notion of the collective efficiency of an organization. On the whole, they judged individuals but not organizations. The machinelike qualities of an organization were as yet hardly perceived, so that in practice the government does not seem to have arranged or re-arranged duties and men in order to increase their collective power or efficiency. The Secretaries of State for the Marine Department, who governed New France, apparently unaware of the mechanical advantages of complex articulation, seldom tried to deploy personnel in such a way as to prevent corrup-

---

[51]John Law, "Histoire des Finances pendant la Regence," *Œuvres complètes*, ed. Paul Harsin, 3 vols. (Paris, 1934), vol. 3, p. 316.

[52]Shortt, *Documents Relating to . . .* , p. 639 n.

tion. Versailles knew for many years—since Rouillé's time, at the latest[53]—that Bigot was using the power of his office to maintain a private monopoly of the fur and supply trades, but it appears to have been unable to prevent him from doing so by anything short of the ultimate discharge which waited upon a slow accumulation of incriminating evidence. Dishonesty among *comptables,* too, might eventually be punished, but the administration was not set up to prevent their dishonesty. In the system of finances, each *comptable* was individually responsible for the funds entrusted to him, and there was no collective central control over funds. To set up a collective or organized system would require a revolution, as John Law and Jacques Necker discovered to their cost. In the meantime, a faithless servant might be punished for his dishonest acts, but by then the evil had already been done. The damage might be avenged by law but it could not be prevented by supervision. This failing was fundamental, not incidental, to the administration of the *ancien régime.*[54]

To conclude, the Parkmanian image of the French colonial government, as a leviathan hampering the development of private enterprise, no longer appears in the writings of our best historians. The converse might now be shown—or so I believe—because there is evidence that rampant private enterprise prevented the proper functioning of the government. Biographical studies have discovered innumerable private interests trespassing on what we consider to be the preserves of the state; but to interpret these discoveries in terms other than the language of moral judgment will require studies of the institutions of government. Certainly the division of government and society was vague and complex. Certainly the financial administration was arranged in such a way that it would inevitably fall prey to private interests.

---

[53]Frégault, *Bigot,* vol. 2, p. 83.

[54]Many private and monopoly companies under the *ancien régime* had similar difficulties and failed while individuals in them became rich. See, for instance, R. Bilodeau, op. cit., p. 65; J. Hamelin, op. cit., pp. 127-37; Marcel Giraud, *Histoire de la Louisiane francaise,* vol. 2 (Paris, 1958), pp. 67-70. Or, considering not enrichment but role, we have Jean Gloria of whom André Vachon writes, "Although he was an employee of the Communauté des Habitants, he nevertheless had his own business . . . ," *Dictionary of Canadian Biography,* vol. 1 (1965), p. 339.

8

THE NATURE, COMPOSITION AND FUNCTIONS OF THE CANADIAN BOURGEOISIE, 1729–1748*

Cameron Nish

One of the most important weapons in the historian's arsenal is hindsight. Unlike contemporary participants in the events of society, the historian has the advantage of knowing where it will all lead, what is going to happen. This enables him to give a form to developments, to assign priorities, and to be critical of decisions made. But hindsight also has its disadvantages. It can lead the historian to formulate questions which are less natural to the society being studied than to the society of the historian, and more critically, it can lead to a tendency to read the present back into the past. Perhaps nowhere has this latter tendency been more prevalent in Canadian historical study than in the period of French Canada. A strong sense of historical past is one of the primary components of the French-Canadian identity, but this presentist use of the past has many pitfalls, both obvious and subtle, for objective analysis. In the following article, Professor Cameron Nish deals with one aspect of the history of New France—its social structure and particularly the presence or absence of a mercantile middle class. Cameron Nish is a member of the Department of History of Sir George Williams University. He is, as well, Executive and Research Director of the Centre de re-cherche in histoire, économique du Canada françois, and Director of the Centre d'Étude du Quebec. As Professor Nish points out, most of the controversy over this question has arisen from the fact that French Canada lacked a viable middle class after the British Conquest. Seeking to explain this, some historians have argued that development of a bourgeoisie was arrested (or aborted) by the Conquest, and others that no such class existed in post-Conquest Quebec because there had been none

---

*Canadian Historical Association *Report* (1966), 14-28.

in pre-Conquest New France. In any case, the very question has been conditioned and produced by later developments. In place of either of these approaches, Professor Nish pleads for an examination of early French Canada on its own merits, free from historical hindsight. How does he deal with the problem of defining class structure? To what extent does he see New France as an overseas extension of the mother country, and to what extent does he argue for North American uniqueness? Is he himself influenced by hindsight? If not, does something else replace it?

SUGGESTIONS FOR FURTHER READING

Guy Frégault, *Canadian Society in the French Regime* (Ottawa: Canadian Historical Association, 1964).

Michel Brunet, *French Canada and the Early Decades of British Rule, 1760–1791* (Ottawa: Canadian Historical Association, 1963).

Jean Hamelin, *Economie et Société en Nouvelle-France* (Québec: Presses universitaires Laval, 1960).

H. A. Innis, ed., *Select Documents in Canadian Economic History, 1497-1783* (Toronto: University Press, 1929).

J.M.B.

T his study of the social structures of New France in the years 1729 to 1748 has as its object the study of New France, and not Québec after the conquest. The latter aspect of the subject, though, has aroused some controversy, one might even say polemic, and this necessitates a brief exposition as a prelude. Historiographical barricades have been erected between the history departments of the Université de Montréal and l'Université Laval. Across these barricades, cobblestones containing more or less historical evidence have been verbally tossed. The Montréal school, basing itself on the ideas of Maurice Séguin,[1] has claimed that there existed a bourgeoisie in New France prior to 1760. This claim has Michel Brunet as its most verbal exponent,[2] although the historical data for his contentions has been based primarily on the researches of Guy Frégault.[3] Another figure in the pro-bourgeoisie

[1]None of Séguin's writings reveal clearly the basic axioms of his thought. His lectures, and the writings of his disciples, i.e., Brunet, are the best means of acquaintance.

[2]See, in particular, his "Les Canadiens après la Conquête: Les débuts de la résistance passive," *Revue d'Histoire de l'Amérique Française*, 12, no. 2, (septembre 1958) 170-207; "The British Conquest: Canadian Social Scientists and the Fate of the *Canadiens*," *Canadian Historical Review*, 40, no. 2 (June 1959), 93-107; "Premières réactions des vaincus de 1760 devant leurs vainqueurs" and "La Conquéte anglaise et la déchéance de la bourgeoisie canadienne (1760-1793)" in *La Présence Anglaise et les Canadiens* (Montréal: Beauchemin, 1958), pp. 37-48 and 49-112; *French Canada and The Early Decades of British Rule, 1760-1791* (Ottawa: Canadian Historical Association, 1963; 16 pp.).

[3]Guy Frégault, "Le régime seigneurial et l'expansion de la colonisation dans le bassin du Saint-Laurent au XVIIIe siècle," *Canadian Historical Association Report* (1944), 61-73; "La Colonisation du Canada au XVIIIe siècle," *Cahiers de l'Académie Canadienne-Française*, vol. 2: *Histoire* (Montréal: n.p., 1957), pp. 53-81; "Essai sur les finances canadiennes (1700-1750)," *Revue d'Histoire de l'Amerique Française*, 13, no. 3 (juin 1959), 30-44, no. 2 (septembre 1959), 157-82; "La Compagnie de la colonie," *Revue de l'Université d'Ottawa*, 30 (1960), 5-29, 127-49; *La Guerre de la Conquéte* (Montréal: Fides, 1955, 514 pp.); *Canadian Society During The French Regime* (Ottawa: Canadian Historical Association, 1956, 16 pp.).

hypothesis is Philippe Garigue, a sociologist, and the Dean of the Social Science Faculty at the Université de Montréal.[4] He bases his conclusions on the works of Brunet and Frégault. The historians who have most strongly challenged the *Conquest Hypothesis School*[5] have taught at l'Université Laval: Jean Hamelin[6] and Fernand Ouellet,[7] with an assist from Hubert Guindon, a member of the Department of Sociology of Sir George Williams University.[8] Recently, the subject and controversy has been the object of two interesting historiographical essays,[9] and, at this Association's meeting in 1964, a paper by Alfred Dubuc considered the problem of social stratification in New France and Québec.[10]

An odd feature of this controversy over the nature of *Canadien* society during the French Régime is that neither of the two most renowned controversialists, Ouellet and Brunet, are specialists in the pre-1760 period of Canadian history. In the controversy, Hamelin-Ouellet form one tandem; Frégault-Brunet the other. The latter team contends that "La Nouvelle-France eut sa bourgeoisie. Celle-ci occupait les postes de commande dans le commerce, dans l'industrie, dans l'armée et dans l'administration."[11] The Hamelin-Ouellet pair respond that the *hypothesis is*

---

[4]Philippe Garigue, "Change and Continuity in Rural French-Canada," *Etudes sur le Canada Français* (Montréal: Faculté des Sciences Sociales, Economiques et Politiques, Université de Montréal, 1958), pp. 17–28; "The Social Evolution of Quebec: A Reply," *Canadian Journal of Economics and Political Science*, 27, no. 2 (May 1961), 257–60; *L'Option Politique du Canada Français; Une Interpretation de la Survivance Nationale* (Montréal: Editions du Lévrier, 1963, 175 pp.).

[5]Séguin, Brunet, and Frégault, all at one time members of the Department of History of l'Université de Montréal, propound either a "black" interpretation of French Canada, or, more commonly, a "Conquest hypothesis" which they, and their students, accept as a law. See also Cameron Nish, *The French Canadians, 1759–1766, Conquered? Half-Conquered? Or Liberated?* (Toronto: Copp Clark Publishing Co., 1966, 148 pp.).

[6]Jean Hamelin, *Economie et Société en Nouvelle-France* (Québec: Presses Universitaires Laval, 1960, 137 pp.). M. Hamelin is still a member of the Institut d'Histoire of l'Université Laval. His conclusion is that there was no *grande bourgeoisie* in New France. It should be noted, however, that he seems at times to completely deny the existence of a bourgeoisie in the colony. Professor Hamelin's work is by far the most important study of the economic and social structures of New France. As he himself admits, much further research is necessary to clarify some of the problems he raises.

[7]Fernand Ouellet, "M. Brunet et le problème de la Conquête," *Bulletin des recherches historiques* 62 (1956), 92–101; "Les Fondements historiques de l'option séparatiste dans le Québec," *Canadian Historical Review*, 43, no. 3, (September 1962), 185–203; "Le Nationalisme canadien-français: de ses origines à l'insurrection de 1837," *Canadian Historical Review*, 45, no. 4 (December 1964), 277–92. M. Ouellet's massive thesis, presented at l'Université Laval in 1965, investigates the relations between economic and social and political structures in Quebec between 1760 and 1850. It was published in 1966, by Fides.

[8]Hubert Guindon's "The Social Evolution of Quebec Reconsidered," in *Canadian Journal of Economics and Political Science*, 26, no. 4 (November 1960), 533–51, is a criticism of the findings, and sociological methodology of Philippe Garigue.

[9]S. R. Mealing, "The Concept of Social Class and the Interpretation of Canadian History," *Canadian Historical Review*, 46, no. 3 (September 1965), 201–18; Serge Gagnon, "Pour une conscience historique de la Révolution Québecoise." *Cité Libre*, 16, no. 83 (1966), 4–16. Also, the students of the Institut d'Histoire of l'Université Laval, in November 1965, held a *colloque* on "La Bourgeoisie canadienne-française: ses fondements historiques." The participants were Robert Mandrou, Cameron Nish, Alfred Dubuc, and Fernand Dumont. See, for a brief summary, André Garon, José Igartua, and Jacques Mathieu, "La Bourgeoisie canadienne-française et ses fondements historiques," *Recherches sociographiques*, 6, no. 3 (1965), 305–10.

[10]Alfred Dubuc. "Problems in the Study of the Stratification of the Canadian Society from 1760 to 1840," *Canadian Historical Association Report* (1965), 13–29.

[11]Brunet, "Déchéance," p. 50.

". . . séduisante, mais correspond-elle à l'exacte réalité? Il est permis de poser la question car l-hypothèse a été lancée sans qu'aucune recherche exhaustive ne vienne l'étayer."[12] Little is to be gained by further surveying in depth the positions of past writers on the subject;[13] it is more useful to recognize their contributions as a point of departure with, however, one necessary comment. Past writings on the social structures of New France have not had as a primary object the study of New France, but rather the effects of the conquest on the French Canadians. This tendency is most obvious in Brunet and Ouellet,[14] but is shared as well by Hamelin, Garigue, Frégault, and Dubuc.[15]

Social analysis, even in historical literature, presumes an accepted system of classification. The historian's concept of social classes exist both implicitly and explicitly before his researches.[16] In some cases, this classificatory system may also involve psychological[17] and theological-economic covering laws.[18] This tendency, perhaps inevitable in socio-logical-historical inquiries, makes it imperative to state clearly the frames of reference which guided the present study. The word *bourgeois* has Marxian connotations, but the present essay, apart from emphasizing economic matters, does not use a Marxian system of social classes. Little is to be gained by applying the criterion of class struggle as an analytic tool in studies of the French Régime in Canada.[19] Nor can we use what may be called the traditional sociological-historical classificatory tools:[20] Weber's distinction between a property class and an acquisitive class, with the associated "protestant ethic";[21] Henri Sée's modified Estates concept[22] and Mosca's qualified Estatism,[23] are useful, but not definitive as analytic concepts for a study of the social structures of New

---

[12]Hamelin, p. 127.

[13]See Cameron Nish, "Une bourgeoisie coloniale en Nouvelle-France: Une hypothèse de travail," *L'Actualité Economique*, 39 (juillet-septembre 1963), 240-65. Also, *La Bourgeoisie Canadienne, 1729-1748* (published in 1963, by Fides).

[14]Brunet, "Premières réactions," pp. 37-48; Ouellet, "M. Brunet," pp. 95-96. Also the third volume of Ouellet's thesis: his conclusion, 150 pp.

[15]Hamelin, pp. 132-37; Garigue, *Option*, pp. 15, 27-32, 37-43; Frégault, *Conquéte*, pp. 429-54; Dubuc, p. 29.

[16]For evidence of this tendency see the works of Hamelin, Ouellet, Frégault, Brunet, and Dubuc noted above. And, Stanley Ryerson's *The Founding of Canada, Beginning to 1815* (Toronto: Progress Books, 1960, 340 pp.).

[17]Ouellet, "M. Brunet," pp. 95-96.

[18]Dubuc, pp. 15-16; Ouellet, "M. Brunet," p. 96.

[19]Ryerson's views (*Founding of Canada*) on the conquest, are an example, pp. 199-206. See also W. J. Eccles, *The Government of New France* (Ottawa: Canadian Historical Association, 1965), pp. 7-11, for a counter to class and structure conflicts in New France.

[20]For examples of these, see A. R. M. Lower, *Colony to Nation* (Toronto: Longmans, Green, 1946), pp. 62-69, D. G. Creighton, *The Empire of the St. Lawrence* (Toronto: Macmillan Company of Canada, 1956), pp. 17-24.

[21]Max Weber, *The Theory of Social and Economic Organization*, trans. A. R. Henderson and T. Parsons, rev. ed. (London: William Hodge & Co., 1947), p. 390, and his *The Protestant Ethic and the Spirit of Capitalism*, trans. T. Parsons (New York: Charles Scribner's Sons, 1953, 292 pp.).

[22]Henri Sée, *La France économique et sociale au 18ᵉ siècle*, 6ᵉ éd. (Paris: Armand Colin, 1958), p. 7.

[23]Gaetano Mosca, *The Ruling Class*, trans. H. D. Kahn, revised by A. Livingston (New York: McGraw-Hill, 1939), p. 377.

France. Neither dictionary nor encyclopedic definitions help very much. All accept, as a criterion of social classification for the Old Régime, the classic Estates, that is, First, Second and Third.[24] Recent studies, such as those by the Barbers,[25] Ashton and Hayek,[26] have raised doubts as to the validity of past terms of reference of social analysis of 17th- and 18th-century Europe. This, as we shall see, is also the case in the analysis of American societies.

To reject past systems of classification, however, does not obviate the need for categories. A knowledge of types of activities generally associated with bourgeois activity is needed, and from these activities a definition of a *colonial bourgeoisie* was formulated as a work hypothesis. The historical parentage of this hypothesis was found in the rich lode of American historical literature, specially the works of Labaree,[27] Harrington,[28] East,[29] Schlesinger senior,[30] Diamond,[31] the recent works of Stuart Bruchey,[32] and, most particularly, the many fine studies of Carl Bridenbaugh.[33] These studies of nascent societies, nascent economics, and nascent political systems indicated that the social structures of Colonial America resembled those of the Mother Country, but were not duplicates of them.[34] From this idea a point of departure was established for

---

[24]J. B. Lacorne de Saint-Palaye, *Dictionnaire historique de l'ancien françois ou Glossaire de la langue françoise depuis son origine jusqu'au siècle de Louis XIV*, vol. 3 (Niort: L. Favre, n.d.), p. 86; Carl Brinkman, "Bourgeoisie," *Encyclopedia of the Social Sciences*, vol. 1, pp. 654-55; *Encyclopedia Britannica*, 1962 ed., vol. 5, pp. 968-69; *Dictionnaire Encyclopédique Quillet*, p. 103.

[25]Elinor and Bernard Barber, eds., *European Social Classes: Stability and Change* (New York: Macmillan Co., 1965, 145 pp.); Elinor Barber, *The Bourgeoisie in 18th Century France* (Princeton: Princeton University Press, 1955, 165 pp.).

[26]See their essays in *Capitalism and the Historians*, ed. F. A. Hayek (Chicago: University of Chicago Press, 1954), pp. 33-63, 64-92.

[27]L. W. Labaree, *Conservatism in Early America* (Ithaca, N.Y.: Cornell University Press, 1959, 182 pp.).

[28]Virginia D. Harrington, *The New York Merchant on the Eve of the American Revolution* (New York: Columbia University Press, 1935, 389 pp.).

[29]Robert East, "The Business Entrepreneur in a Changing Colonial Economy, 1763-1795," *Journal of Economic History: The Tasks of Economic History*, supplement 6 (1946), 16-27.

[30]A. M. Schlesinger, Sr., *The Colonial Merchant and the American Revolution, 1763-1766*, new printing (New York: Frederick Ungar, 1957, 647 pp.).

[31]Sigmund Diamond, "Old Patterns and New Societies: Virginia and French Canada in the Seventeenth Century," in *Sociology and History*, ed. W. J. Cahnman and A. Boskoff (London: Collier-Macmillan, 1964), pp. 170-90.

[32]Stuart Bruchey, *The Roots of American Economic Growth, 1607-1861: An Essay in Social Causation* (New York: Harper & Row, 1964, 234 pp.); *The Colonial Merchant: Sources and Readings* (New York: Harcourt, Brace & World, 1966, 199 pp.).

[33]Carl and Jessica Bridenbaugh, *Rebels and Gentlemen: Philadelphia in the Age of Franklin* (New York: Oxford University Press, 1962, 393 pp.); Carl Bridenbaugh, *Cities in the Wilderness: Urban Life in America, 1625-1742* (New York: Capricorn Books, 1964, 500 pp.); *Cities in Revolt: Urban Life in America, 1743-1776* (New York: Capricorn Books, 1964, 434 pp.); and, especially, *Myths & Realities: Societies of the Colonial South* (New York: Atheneum, 1963, 208 pp.).

[34]Robert Mandrou, in his talk at the *Colloque* on the Canadian bourgeoisie, on November 13, 1965, at l'Université Laval, insisted on social resemblances between France and New France, but also differences. In his opinion, the social structures of France became more rigid in the 1670s and 1680s, after the rise of the middle class to the ranks of the *nobilité de la robe*. In effect, the new aristocracy attempted to protect its status by closing the class to new members. *Dérogeance* was not a factor in New France. See Nish, "Une bourgeoisie coloniale," p. 248.

the present study: to look for differences between the French metropolitan and colonial societies in the Americas. Another equally essential tenet was that concerning the differentiation of classes by exclusive function, that is, noble, landed proprietor, administrator, merchant, etc. This analytic tool may be partially valid for the study of European societies. However, it is a useless concept for studies of colonial societies.[35] Further, to look for resemblances between colonial societies regardless of the metropolis. All those became hypotheses, to be sustained or rejected depending on the evidence.

There is general agreement on some of the activities of individuals classified as belonging to a bourgeois group: they are urban based, have property, a relatively high income, are acquisitive, are professionals, engage in industrial and commercial endeavors, and are relatively well educated. Jacques LeClerc adds, correctly, that a bourgeois class is difficult to define because it is "... une classe de fait et non de loi ..."[36] These eight words became the basic criterion of the present study: what a man does will be the basis for including him in a class. Specifically, these actions must indicate a control of the material, political and economic resources of the society. The control of these sources of power by the colonial bourgeoisie of New France had as an end the enrichment of the individual, and the group to which he belonged. The means by which it is proposed to examine and to prove the presence of such a class in New France will be, first, to examine an individual, François-Etienne Cugnet; second, an institution, the Superior Council; and third, the so-called seigneurial class.

François-Etienne Cugnet came to New France in 1719 as the representative of the *fermier* of the Domaine d'Occident, the holder of the tax farm of Canada.[37] He was the *Directeur et receveur.*[38] This placed him in the administrative class. In 1730 he was appointed to the Superior Council;[39] in 1733 he was named *premier conseiller.*[40] He was thus a member of what may be called a judicial class. By profession, he was a

---

[35]Frégault, in *Society*, p. 14, was on the verge of realizing this idea. See, for similar types of social analysis, Harrington, p. 10, Labaree, pp. 2-3.

[36]Jacques LeClerc, *Leçons de Droit naturel*, vol. 4: *Les Droits et Devoirs individuels*, troisieme éd. (Namur: Ad. Wesmael-Charlier, 1955), pp. 224-25.

[37]On the Domaine d'Occident, see Cameron Nish, "Documents relatifs à l'histoire économique du régime français: Les budgets de la Nouvelle-France," *L'Actualité économique*, vol. 40, n° 3 (octobre-décembre 1964), pp. 633-35.

[38]"François-Etienne Cugnet au nom et comme fondé de procuration de Me Ayma (*sic*) Lambert adjudicataire des fermes unies de France et du Domaine d'Occident...," P.A.C., C 11 A, vol. 40, pp. 305-7. For early activities of Cugnet, see also Marine Leland, "François-Joseph Cugnet (1720-1789)," *La Revue de l'Université Laval*, vol. 16, no. 1, pp. 3-13, no. 2, 129-39, no. 3, 205-14, no. 5, 411-20; Alfred Gascon, *L'Œuvre de François-Joseph Cugnet. Etude historique* (Ottawa: Université d'Ottawa, these de maîtrise, 1941), pp. 2-11. F.-J. Cugnet was François-Etienne's son.

[39]P.-G. Roy, "Les Consillers au Conseil Souverain de la Nouvelle-France," *Mémoire de la Société Royale du Canada*, Série 3, tome 9 (1915), p. 181. On the Superior Council, see also Raymond du Bois Cahall, *The Sovereign Council of New France: A Study in Canadian Constitutional Law* (New York: Columbia University Press, 1915, 274 pp.); J. Delalande, *Le Conseil Souverain de la Nouvelle-France* (Québec: Ls.-A. Proulx, 1927, 358 pp.); Eccles, *The Government of New France*; Gustave Lanctôt, *L'Administration de la Nouvelle-France* (Paris: Librarie Ancienne Honoré Champion, 1929, 169 pp.).

[40]Roy, "Conseillers," p. 181.

lawyer.[41] As one of the members of the Compagnie des Forges de Saint-Maurice, he controlled the seigneurie of Saint-Maurice, and was granted that of Saint-Etienne as a personal holding.[42] As well, he owned several lots in the city of Québec valued at 8,000, 2,900 and 7,000 *livres*.[43] These land holdings permit Cugnet's classification as a member of the seigneurial class.

In 1732 the Domaine d'Occident was taken over by the state.[44] One part of this domain, the Tadoussac trade, was leased to Cugnet for a period of nine years at an annual rental of 4,500 *livres*.[45] According to Cugnet he lost so much money that he insisted on retaining the lease for a further nine years.[46] The Tadoussac trade involved furs, fishing, and the manufacturing of fish oil.[47] After his bankruptcy in 1742 he was granted the trade monopoly of three hinterland posts.[48] Cugnet also grew tobacco,[49] manufactured glue[50] and, with the aid of a state subsidy, attempted to domesticate the Illinois cattle.[51] He was also a shipowner.[52]

By far his most important enterprise was the Saint-Maurice Forges. He was an early partner of Poulin de Francheville, the first monopolist, in a company formed in 1733.[53] This company, apart from Francheville and Cugnet, included Bricault de Valmur, the intendant Hocquart's secretary, and Ignace Gamelin, a member of the fur trade group,[54] Montréal

[41]R.P. L. Le Jeune, *Dictionnaire général. . .* , vol. 1 (Ottawa: Université d'Ottawa, 1931), p. 453; A. Shortt, ed., *Documents Relating to Canadian Currency, Exchange and Finance During the French Period*, vol. 2 (Ottawa: King's Printer, 1925), p. 543n. There are misprints, and factual errors in Shortt's biographical note.

[42]"Société entre les intéressés en l'établissement des forges des Saint-Maurice, 16 octobre 1736," P.A.C., C 11 A, vol. 110, pp. 241-51; "Acte de concession . . . au sieur François-Etienne Cugnet . . . du terrain, 15 avril 1737," P.-G. Roy, *Inventaire des concessions en fief et seigneurie; Fois et hommages et aveux et dénombrements. . .* , vol. 5, pp. 45-47. [Hereafter Roy, *Seigneurie.*]

[43]P.A.C., *Documents relatifs à la province de Québec: A: Documents généraux: Registre des aveux, dénombrements et déclarations*, vol. 6, pp. 58-65, 66-70.

[44]"Beauharnois et Hocquart au Ministre, Québec, 1ᵉʳ octobre 1733," P.A.C., C 11 A, vol. 59-1, p. 61.

[45]"Beauharnois et Hocquart au Ministre, Québec, le 16 8'bre 1746," P.A.C., C 11 A, vol. 85, p. 90.

[46]"Cugnet A Monseigneur le Comte de Maurepas, Ministre et Secrétaire d'Etat, Canada 1746," P.A.C., C 11 A, vol. 94, pt. 2, ff. 6-7; "A Monseigneur le Comte de Maurepas, Ministre et Secrétaire d'Etat, 20 octobre 1747," P.A.C. E, *Dossiers personnels, François Etienne Cugnet*, carton 101, pp. 33-41.

[47]"Scellés et Inventaire des effets du Sr. François Etienne Cugnet, Québec, 28, 29, 30 août et le 1ᵉʳ et 3 septembre 1742," P.A.C., C 11 A, vol. 114-1, ff. 144-204.

[48]"A Monseigneur le Comte de Maurepas, Ministre et Secrétaire d'Etat, 20 octobre 1747," P.A.C., E, *Dossiers personnels, François Etienne Cugnet*, carton 101, pp. 33-41.

[49]"Mémoire Tabacs du Canada, 1737," P.A.C., M.G. 1/24, vol. 9, pièce 303, pp. 474-78.

[50]"Hocquart au Ministre, 28 octobre 1741," cited in J.-N. Fauteux, *Essai sur l'industrie au Canada sous le Régime français*, vol. 2 (Québec: Ls.-S. Proulx, 1927), pp. 494-95.

[51]"Maurepas à Beauharnois et Hocquart, Marly, 8 avril 1733," P.A.C., B, vol. 57, f. 620: and "Maurepas à Beauharnois et Hocquart, Marly, 24 mars 1733," P.A.C., B, vol. 58, f. 408.

[52]"Etat de mes Effets actyfs et Passifs, Québec, 21, 22, 26, 27 août 1742," P.A.C., C 11 A. vol. 114-1, f. 216.

[53]"Cession au Roy pour la sécurité du Sieur Francheville du privilège de l'exploitation des mines de fer du 28 8'bre 1735," P.A.C., C 11 A., vol. 110, tome 1, pp. 93-101.

[54]P.-G. Roy, *Inventaire des greffes des notaires*, vol. 16, Guillet de Chaumont, pp. 156-57, and "LaVérendrye à Gamelin, 23 février 1735," P.A.C., *LaVérendrye*, and "Copie de Morare

merchant,[55] and related to the Boucher and La Vérendrye families.[56] After Francheville's death in late 1733,[57] the company was carried on by his widow and brother.[58] Between 1735 and 1737 Cugnet took over the enterprise in association with Gamelin, Thomas Jacques Taschereau, the representative of the Marine treasury in New France, and a member of the Superior Council, and two forge masters, Olivier Vézain and Jacques Simonnet.[59] The enterprise was the recipient of 10,000, 100,000 and 83,642 *livres* in subsidies from the state,[60] plus some sums that Cugnet, as Hocquart gently put it, was obliged to borrow from the funds of the Domaine entrusted to his care.[61] The company went bankrupt in 1741–42.[62]

The recital of Cugnet's little affairs is not yet at an end, but a brief summary of the activities of this most ubiquitous individual indicates that he was the equivalent of a member of the civil service establishment; a judicial administrator; a merchant, fur trader, glue manufacturer, tobacco grower, involved in the fishing trade, and in the production of iron. He was an entrepreneur. His activities indicate bourgeois activities. His total revenues are difficult to determine, and this for two reasons: his personal papers have not, as yet, been found; and, he always lost money, if we are to believe his writings.[63] However, some of his

---

accordé au S. Lamarque et Compagnie contre le Sr de la Verendrye, Montréal 22 juin 1742," P.A.C., C 11 A., vol. 77, p. 162.

[55]See the sales of Gamelin to the state, "Bordereau . . . 1740," and "Bordereau . . . 1741," P.A.C., C 11 A., vol. 113-2, f. 116 and vol. 114-1, f. 287.

[56]On the importance of marital relations in New France, see Cameron Nish, "La bourgeoisie et les mariages, 1729–1748," *Revue de l'histoire de l'Amérique française*, 19, no. 4 (mars 1966), pp. 585–605. On Gamelin, specifically, p. 588.

[57]Shortt, *Currency,* has Francheville dying in 1734; the senior administrators of the colony also err in saying 1734, "Beauharnois et Hocquart au Ministre, Canada, 28 septembre 1734," P.A.C., C 11 A, vol. 110-2, p. 163. Gamelin, in a "Mémoire au Ministre, Québec, 9e octobre mil sept cent quarante et un," claims that Francheville died in November 1733. In this he is supported by an "Obligation de la Veuve Francheville, décembre 1733," P.A.C., C 11 A, vol. 110-2, pp. 179–81, in which she assumes her late husband's obligations to the French state.

[58]"Cession au Roy pour la sécurité du Sieur Francheville . . . 23 8'bre 1735," P.A.C., C 11 A. vol. 110-1, p. 93.

[59]"Ofires et soumission par les Sieurs Cugnet, Olivier de Vezain et Gamelin de se charger de l'Etablissement des forges de Saint Maurice et de l'exploitation . . ." P.A.C., C 11 A. vol. 110-1, pp. 102-8, and, "Société entre les intéressés en l'établissement des forges des Saint Maurice, 16 octobre 1736," P.A.C., C 11 A, vol. 110-1, pp. 241-51.

[60]"Arrét qui révoque le privilège accordé aux Srs Cugnet, Gamelin, Taschereau, Olivier de Vezain et Simonet pour l'exploitation des mines de fer de St Maurice et réunit au domaine l'établissement fait dans cet endroit ainsi que les effets qui en dépendent, Versailles, 1 mai 1743," P.A.C. F3, *Moreau St. Mery*, vol. 13, pt. 1, 1741-1749, ff. 70–73.

[61]"Hocquart au Ministre, Canada, 23 octobre 1743," P.A.C., C 11 A, vol. 80, pp. 27–34.

[62]On the bankruptcy of the Saint Maurice Forges, see Cameron Nish, "La banqueroute de François-Etienne Cugnet, 1742, 1: Les biens de Cugnet; 2: Cugnet et l'Etat; 3: Cugnet et les Forges de Saint-Maurice," *L'Actualité économique*, vol. 41, no. 1, pp. 146-202; no. 2, pp. 345-78; no. 3, pp. 762-810. In future numbers of the same periodical, two more selections of documents will be presented.

[63]See "Memoire du Cugnet, Quebec le vingt quatre octobre 1743," P.A.C., E, *Dossiers personnels, François Etienne Cugnet*, carton 101, pp. 9-26; "Cugnet A Monseigneur le Comte de Maurepas, Ministre et Secrétaire d'Etat, Canada, 1746," P.A.C., C 11 A, vol. 94, pt. 2, ff. 6-7; "Cugnet au Ministre, A Québec le 20 octobre 1748," P.A.C., E, *Dossiers personnels, François Etienne Cugnet*, carton 101, pp. 28-30.

revenues may be determined. His salary as *Directeur* of the Domaine was 3,000 *livres* a year;[64] as a councillor, and first councillor, he received 600 *livres* annually.[65] As administrator of the Domaine, he was provided with an office conveniently located in his own house, for which he charged the state an annual rental of 2,000 *livres*.[66] These are his known revenues. It is possible that he lost money in all of his business enterprises, but to do so he must have reversed the business adage of maximizing profits and minimizing losses to maximizing losses and minimizing profits.

Let us, however, restrict ourselves to the meaning of a guaranteed income of 5,600 *livres* per year. A *livre* contained 20 *sols*.[67] A pound of bread was valued, in 1741–42, at 2 *sols,* and a pound of beef at 4 *sols*.[68] A high annual wage for an artisan in New France was 600 *livres* per year.[69] A *minot* of wheat, sufficient to feed one person for one month, sold for 3 to 4 *livres*.[70] Cugnet's money assets, in 1742,[71] were valued at approximately 20 times those of a Montauban merchant-bourgeois, Paul Sol.[72] To these known revenues one must presume additional ones from his many enterprises.

Another means of determining social classification, and social relationships in New France, still using Cugnet as a point of departure, is by an analysis of marital relations. Cugnet's wife was the sister of Henry DuSautoy,[73] also an employee of the Domaine.[74] Louise-Charlotte, Cug-

---

[64]"Mémoire concernant le Regie (du Domaine d'Occident par Bigot), 4 juin 1749," P.A.C., C 11 A, vol. 121-2, f. 39.

[65]"Mémoire du Roy aux Srs . . . Beauharnois et . . . Hocquart, Versailles, 27 avril 1734," P.A.C., B, vol. 61-1, f. 538 and "Depenses du Canada, Domaine d'Occident, 1729," P.A.C., F 1, vol. 28, f. 52.

[66]"Bigot au Ministre, Québec, 28 octobre 1752," P.A.C., C 11 A, vol. 98, pp. 220-22.

[67]For value of currency, and equivalents see Cameron Nish "Appendix F," *The French Regime* (Toronto: Prentice-Hall of Canada, 1965), pp. 159-60.

[68]"Etat général de la Dépense faite pour l'Exploitation des forges de St Maurice depuis le 1ᵉʳ octobre 1741 jusqu'au 1ᵉʳ août 1742," P.A.C., C 11 A, vol. 111-2, pp. 354-444. The writer is presently analysing prices and wages in New France in the period 1713-48. The study, as yet incomplete, supports, generally speaking, these figures, and others quoted below.

[69]This wage was determined on the basis of 700 wage entries in study mentioned in note 68. The sources are "Bordereau . . . 1736," "Bordereau . . . 1739," "Bordereau . . . 1740," "Bordereau . . . 1741," "Bordereau . . . 1743," P.A.C., C 11 A, vol. 114-1, ff. 19, 20, 29, 31, 51, 52, 55, 58, 122, 123, 125, 294-96; vol. 114-2, pp. 34, 386-89; vol. 115-1, p. 37.

[70]"Lettre du conseil au gouvernement général, 11 juillet 1729," in P.-G. Roy's *Inventaire des jugements et délibérations du Conseil supérieur de la Nouvelle France de 1717 à 1760,* vol. 2 (Québec: l'Eclaireur, 1933-34), p. 56. See also Elizabeth Jean Lunn, *Economic Development in New France, 1713-1760* (Montréal: McGill University, unpublished Ph.D. thesis, 1942), p. 448.

[71]Compare his "Etat" cited in footnote 52 with the money assets of Sol in Ligou and Garison's "La Bourgeoisie reformée Montalbanaise à la fin de l'Ancien Régime," *Revue d'histoire économique et sociale,* vol. 33 (1955), pp. 377-404.

[72]See note 71.

[73]"Etat de la Dépense de la Direction du Domaine d'occident à Québec . . . mil sept cent quarante sept," P.A.C., D 2 D, carton 1. See also "Mémoire de M. Dupuy, Intendant de la Nouvelle-France, sur les troubles arrivés à Québec en 1727 et 1728 apres la mort de Mgr de Saint-Vallier, Evêque de Québec," *Rapport de l'archiviste de la province de Québec* (1920-21), p. 98. See also Nish, "Marriages," p. 590.

[74]"Mémoire concernant le Regie, 4 juin 1752," P.A.C., C 11 A, vol. 121-2, f. 39.

net's daughter, married Liénard de Beaujeu, sieur de Villemonble.[75] He was a fur trade post commandant, seigneur, and a military administrator.[76] Beaujeu's sister was married to Jean Victor Varin de la Marre, the representative of the intendant at Montréal.[77] Beaujeu's brother was married to the daughter of François Foucault, the *garde-magasin* of the King's stores at Québec, as well as a member of the Superior Council.[78] Cugnet's son, François-Joseph, married the offspring of another merchant, seigneur, councillor, Jacques de Belcour, sieur de Lafontaine.[79] This tangle of marital relations had roots in every important social, political, and economic institution in New France.

One final word before leaving Cugnet: he was convinced that he would die a poor man, yet his estate was large enough to pay off all of his creditors and leave his wife in bourgeois comfort.[80]

The activities of Cugnet led us to touch upon the Superior Council of which he was a member. Further investigation of this political-judicial body will permit insights into the nature of the social structures of New France. One of Cugnet's partners, Thomas-Jacques Taschereau, is a typical example of an individual classed as bourgeois in the present study. He began his career as an intendant's secretary.[81] In 1732 he was appointed representative of the Marine treasury in New France, and in 1735 was made a member of the Superior Council.[82] In addition to his administrative posts, he engaged in commerce, and was a seigneur.[83] By marriage he was related to the representative of the Company of the West Indies, de la Gorgentière.[84] The latter's sister was to marry the Marquis de Vaudreuil, and another of his daughters wed Vaudreuil's brother, François Pierre de Rigaud.[85] By his activities, posts, and marriages, Taschereau made a mockery of the Estates concept.

François Foucault is a further illustration. He was *garde-magasin* at Québec,[86] and this was the most important post in the King's stores. At the same time he was a member of the Superior Council.[87] He was a

---

[75]Nish, "Marriages," p. 587.

[76]This information is drawn from the forthcoming *La Bourgeoisie Canadienne*, cited above.

[77]Le Jeune, vol. 1, p. 137, and "Hocquart au Ministre, 16 octobre 1733," P.A.C., C 11 A, vol. 120-1, ff. 39-40.

[78]Nish, "Marriages," p. 593, and "Bordereau . . . 1736," "Bordereau . . . 1741," P.A.C., C 11 A, vols. 114-1, ff. 27, 119, and 114-2, f. 382.

[79]Nish, "Marriages," p. 590.

[80]Madame Rocbert Bégon à son fils, LaRochelle, 1ᵉʳ octobre 1752," *Rapport de l'archiviste de la province de Québec, 1934-35*, pp. 177-78, and "Bigot au Ministre, Québec, 28 octobre 1752," P.A.C., C 11 A, vol. 98, p. 222.

[81]Shortt, *Currency*, vol. 2, p. 635n.

[82]Roy, "Conseillers," p. 181.

[83]Roy, *Seigneurie*, vol. 5, p. 1.

[84]Nish, "Marriages," pp. 594-95.

[85]Nish, "Marriages," p. 595, and Guy Frégault, *Le grand marquis* (Montréal: Fides, 1952), p. 105.

[86]See footnote 78.

[87]Roy, "Conseillers," p. 181.

seigneur.[88] Through extended marital relations he was connected with individuals involved in all of the important economic and political endeavors in the colony. These illustrations may be expanded by a consideration of the 16 individuals analysed in this period,[89] but let us use but one more: Eustche Chartier de Lotbinière. He had been, before the death of his wife, the representative of the Company of the West Indies in New France,[90] a member of the Superior Council,[91] seigneur,[92] and a supplier of timbers to the state.[93] After the demise of his spouse he "got religion" and, as a protégé of the bishop, St. Vallier,[94] was made a member of the Chapter of Quebec shortly after his ordination.[95] In time, he was to become Dean of the Chapter.[96] While a cleric, he retained his seat on the Superior Council, and engaged in commerce.[97] He drew salaries for all of his posts.[98] Discretion dictates that there be no analysis of his marital relations.

This brief survey of the members of the Council indicates, again, the multiple functions of the members of an institution in the colonial society of New France. Again, activities and marital links served to blend the class lines between the Cugnets, Taschereaus, Gorgendières, Vaudreuils, Foucaults, and the Lotbinières. To date, the evidence indicates, at the very least, that the First, Second, and Third estates are not very satisfactory categories of social analysis in Canada before 1760. Let us approach the matter from another usually accepted classification: the seigneurial class.

Munro classified the seigneurs as *gentilhommes* and claimed that they lived on their lands.[99] Of them he wrote:[100]

> In a word, those who were the natural leaders of the colonial population were deficient in the prime qualities of economic leadership.

---

[88]Roy, *Seigneurie,* vol. 4, pp. 245–46.

[89]See Nish, "Marriages," pp. 593–94. The 16 men who were members of the Superior Council in the period under study were analysed in my *La Bourgeoisie Canadienne,* chap. 8.

[90]Shortt, *Currency,* vol. 1, pp. 521–23n. See also P.A.C., C 11 A, vol. 40, for memoirs written by de Lotbinière as representative of the company of the West Indies.

[91]Roy, "Conseillers," p. 181.

[92]Roy, *Seigneurie,* vol. 3, p. 76.

[93]"Ordonnance . . . au sujet d'un marché pour scier deux mille planches au moulin de M. de Lotbinière, 9 mars 1743," cited by P.-G. Roy, *Inventaire des ordonnances des intendants de la Nouvelle-France,* vol. 3 (Beauceville: l'Eclaireur, 1919), p. 37.

[94]Le Jeune, vol. 2, pp. 172–73.

[95]Mgr. Henri Têtu. "Le Chapitre de la Cathédrale de Québec et ses Délégués en France. Lettres des Chanoines Pierre Hazeur de l'Orme et Jean-Marie de la Corne, 1723-1773," *Bulletin des recherches historiques,* vol. 13, pp. 225–26.

[96]"Hazeur de l'Orme à son frère, 21 mars 1737," cited by Têtu, *Bulletin des recherches historiques,* vol. 14, p. 72.

[97]Roy, "Conseillers," p. 181.

[98]"Ministre à M. le Coadjuteur, Compiègne, 29 avril 1732," P.A.C., B, vol. 52-1, f. 680 and "Bordereau . . . 1737," "Bordereau . . . 1739," P.A.C., C 11 A, vol. 114-1, ff. 18, 126–27.

[99]W. B. Munro, *Documents Relating to the Seigneurial Tenure in Canada,* 1598-1854 (Toronto: The Champlain Society, 1908), p. xxi.

[100]Munro, p. xlviii.

E. R. Adair claimed that the seigneurs, as a class, had a decided failure. He wrote:[101]

> But the relative unimportance of the seigneur was not due solely to the fact that he was often of little better birth than his tenant farmers, or that he lacked the feudal prestige of leading his tenants to war, or of administering justice in his own courts, or that the "capitaine" was more in the government's confidence than he was, his economic position was just as important a factor.

Sigmund Diamond, a sociologist and historian at Columbia University, writes of the seigneurs as an impoverished class, and uses, as have some other commentators, a psychological approach based on an implicit "protestant ethic."[102] More recently, Marcel Trudel's revisions of the seigneurial class, and system, corrected many erroneous views, but his revisions are in effect a defense of the system rather than a radical inquiry.[103]

A clue to the nature of the seigneurial system and class in New France is provided in Maurice Dobb's *The Development of Capitalism.* "The bourgeoisie," he writes, "may acquire a particular sort of property when this happens to be exceptionally cheap (in extreme cases acquiring it by duress for nothing) and realize this property at some later period, when the market value of this property is relatively high . . ."[104] The seigneurial system in New France was not a means to nobility,[105] nor did it tie up capital in relatively non-productive agricultural pursuits. In the period under consideration a substantial market for agricultural products was opened up by the establishment of Louisbourg.[106] Sales to the states for this bastion indicate a monopoly in the hands of a favoured group.[107] Agricultural production rose three times as fast as population.[108] As well, and this is a neglected aspect of the seigneurial system in the colony, a fair amount of land speculation was taking place. This is evident not merely from land sales,[109] but in sales of seigneuries as well. An extreme example of the latter is to be seen with reference to the holdings of Terrebonne. In 1718, Louis Lecomte Dupré sold the lands for 5,268 *livres* to François-Marie Bouat; two years later, Bouat sold the holding to the abbé

---

[101]E. R. Adair, "The French-Canadian Seigneurie," *Canadian Historical Review,* 35, no. 3 (September 1954), 196.

[102]Sigmund Diamond, "An Experiment in 'Feudalism': French Canada in the Seventeenth Century," Bobbs-Merrill Reprint Series in History, H. 56, pp. 14, 23.

[103]Marcel Trudel, *The Seigneurial Regime* (Ottawa: Canadian Historical Association, 1960, 18 pp.).

[104]Maurice Dobb, *Studies in the Development of Capitalism* (New York: International Publishers, 1947), p. 179.

[105]Rosario Bilodeau, *Liberté économique et politique des Canadiens sous le Régime français* (Montréal: Université de Montréal, thèse de Ph.D. non publiée, 1956), p. 184.

[106]See "Censuses of Canada, 1720 and 1734" and "Trade Statistics of New France, 1728–1756," in Nish, *The French Regime,* pp. 121 and 124.

[107]See chap. 4 in Nish, *La Bourgeoisie Canadienne,* cited above.

[108]This conclusion is based on an analysis of the Censuses of New France contained in the 4th volume of the census report of Canada of 1870.

[109]The *Inventaires des greffes des notaires,* and the Roy work on seigneurial documents list many land sales by censitaires, and by seigneurs.

Louis Lepage for 10,000 *livres;* in 1745 the cleric sold them to Louis de Chapt, sieur de la Corne, for 60,000 *livres.*[110] This, while an extreme case, is not unique. Other sales of holdings were made for 6,000, 8,010, 10,000, 12,000 and 20,000 *livres.*[111]

Past scholars have emphasized the poverty, poor production, and small returns of seigneuries. This has led to a distortion of both the system, and the class of men who controlled it. A more accurate view requires an analysis of two aspects of the system: (1) what were the revenues? and (2) who were the seigneurs? The revenues were not high, but it must be remembered that these revenues, for the seigneur, were one part of his total income. Even this part, as we shall see, was relatively high, when compared to an average annual income, and the cost of living. The seigneur also was engaged in commerce, the administration and the fur trade.

Trudel, in his pamphlet, writes that the seigneurial burdens sat lightly on the shoulders, and pocketbooks, of the *censitaire.* As an example, he evaluates wheat at 4 *livres* the *minot;* a day's corvée at 2 *livres.* These, with the *cens et rentes,* resulted in an average annual due of $65.30.[112] Translating 18th-century monetary terms into 20th-century equivalences is extremely dangerous. Let us place his figures within the context of the times. A *minot* of wheat, it will be remembered, was sufficient to feed one person for one month. The value of a day's corvée was 40 *sols,* and the seigneur was entitled to three days a year per tenant. Capons, which Trudel does not mention, were valued at 10 *sols* each.[113] If the seigneur had a mill, he was entitled to a share of the wheat milled; an oven produced the same result. The landowner also had the right to the *droit de péche,* and the *droit de commune.* Translated into economic terms these rights, which formed but part of a seigneur's income, were substantial. Concessions to five tenants by François-Antoine Pécaudy produced a return of wheat sufficient to feed one person for 15 months.[114] The monetary returns of these five concessions were, if we use M. Trudel's equivalence, $160 per year.[115] Expressed in terms of the 18th century, this sum represented one-quarter of a high annual wage. The

---

[110]Fauteux, vol. 2, pp. 283–84, 301; see also Roy, *Seigneurie,* vol. 3, pp. 116–117, vol. 4, p. 233.

[111]P.A.C., C 11 G, Domaine D'Occident, vol. 11, pp. 121-32, vol. 9, pp. 1-10; "Acte de vente de la moitié de la Seigneurie de Verchères, Montréal, 2 juillet 1745," P.A.C., vol. 83, pp. 93–99; P.A.C., C 11 G, vol. pp. 12-15; "Acte de vente de la seigneurie et baronnie de Portneuf . . . 12 octobre 1742," P.A.C., *Greffes,* Panet, p. 10; "Contrat d'acquisition de la Malbaye, Québec, 29 septembre 1733," P.A.C., C 11 A, vol. 12102, p. 255.

[112]Trudel, p. 13.

[113]"Concession par Dame Charlotte Denis Veuve de Claude de Ramezay à Jean Baptiste St-Martin, Montréal, 9 janvier 1733," and "Concession à des Montmarque, Montréal, 7 mars 1733," P.A.C. *Sorel.*

[114]"Concession à Benoit, Joseph Berbard; François Sansousy, J. Bte. Felix, François Benoist, 19 mars 1736," *Sorel: Documents légaux.*

[115]Trudel, p. 13.

annual revenues of the seigneuries of Terrebonne, apart from sales of timbers and wheat, were about 10 percent of the original investment.[116] The lands of Portneuf, upon which there never was established a seigneurial domain, returned two-thirds of an annual wage;[117] those of Simblim, one-half,[118] and Jean-Baptiste Couillard, a seigneur and judicial administrator, from his half-interest in *la Riviere du Sud,* received 1,336 capons annually. This, expressed in money, equalled 547 *livres.*[119] Obviously, the terms low, high, small, or great are relative. Relatively, then, the seigneuries returned a fair income.

And now let us examine who owned the seigneuries. First, let us get rid of one myth very quickly: the seigneurs examined in the period 1729 to 1748 did not live on their lands. Rather, they were absentee landlords who lived in the cities of Montreal, Three-Rivers, and Quebec.[120] Further, they were a group not merely noted for landholding, but for involvement in all of the important economic and political endeavors in the colony as well. Without exception, the members of the Superior Council in the period under consideration were granted seigneuries.[121] The more notable merchants of Quebec, Three-Rivers, and Montreal, the Cugnets, Daines, Pomereaus, Rocberts, de Tonnancours, etc.,[122] held and were granted further lands.[123] The commandants of the fur trade posts of the hinterland owned seigneuries;[124] the upper echelon of the civil and military administration owned seigneuries.[125] It is this mixture of the powers of politics and economics which explains the slow application of the Arrêt de Marly against the seigneur, and its rapid application against the *censitaire.*[126] We now know who owned the lands. It is no longer permissible to classify them as a class, at least as a seigneurial class. A new and more accurate designation is required.

---

[116]"Fief de Terrebonne et des Plaine, 20 mars 1736," P.A.C., *Aveux et dénombrements,* vol. 5, pp. 99–128.

[117]"Terrier du fief et Baronnie de Portneuf à M. Eustache Lambert, Ecuer, sieur Dumont, lieutenant dans les troupes du détachement de la marine entretenues pour le service du Roy en ce páys . . . Sur lequel fief et Baronnie il n'y a encore aucun domaine d'établie ni même de principal manoir ni moulin banal . . . 2 avril 1742," P.A.C., *Greffes,* vol. 3, Dulaurent, pp. 5–132.

[118]"Fief de Simblin, 26 juin 1736," P.A.C., *Aveux et dénombrements,* vol. 5, pp. 131–44.

[119]"Rivière du sud, 10 avril 1732," P.A.C., *Aveux et dénombrements,* vol. 4, pp. 148–72.

[120]Cited in tabular form in my *La Bourgeoisie Canadienne.* The data was gathered by an analysis of the censuses of Montréal, 1731, and Québec, 1744, and comparing the results with the information available in Roy, *Seigneurie.*

[121]The same procedure was followed in an analysis of the members of the Superior Council: the 1744 Québec census was correlated to the Roy work.

[122]Many names have not been mentioned in the present study. Detail will be found in the work cited in footnote 120.

[123]See Nish, *La Bourgeoisie Canadienne,* chap. 7.

[124]See Nish, *La Bourgeoisie Canadienne,* chaps. 4 and 7.

[125]See Nish, *La Bourgeoisie Canadienne,* chaps. 7 to 10.

[126]The Arrêts de Marly were passed in 1711. They were applied quickly against the tenant farmers. See Munro, p. lxxxii. The seigneurs did not have the Arrêt which effected them registered in the Superior Council. Eventually, in 1741, 30 years after it was issued, it was applied against the seigneurs.

A hypothesis, a tentative definition of a colonial bourgeoisie was offered early in this study. This ". . . supposition provisionally adopted to explain certain facts and to guide in the investigation of others,"[127] has permitted us, through our examination of the individual Cugnet, the institution of the Superior Council, and the so-called seigneurial class, to determine how the nature, composition and functions of a class in the society of New France may and may not be defined. Contemporary witnesses do not appear to be always very accurate. Charlevoix[128] and Hocquart,[129] for example, both used the prevalent European system of classification. The mixture of functions and activities was remarked upon by one man only, to the best of my knowledge. The man was the chevalier de La Pause. His insight was but a partial one, and garbled. In his "Dissertation sur le gouvernement," he wrote:[130]

> The government of Canada is composed of four orders which are: the Church, the military, the traders or merchants, and the militia which is made up of the artisans and the habitants. The third order is the administrators of justice in the Sovereign (sic) Council, and the traders; it is from the latter that the former are chosen, and one can say that this order is about the same as the second because of the involvement of the military in commerce, (and the) alliances (between them).

This partial insight is correct. The men characterized as nobles or aristocrats or, to use the term of the times, *gentilhommes*, did not belong exclusively to a Second Estate. Some members of the clergy, Lepage and de Lotbière, cannot be neatly fitted into the First Estate. Cugnet and Taschereau, to name but two, cannot be described as members of a Third Estate. Nor can we use the terms military class, merchant class, judicial class, or seigneurial class, for they were all these at the same time.

One of the terms favored to designate this group, this class, is *colonial bourgeoisie*. Whatever class designation is used, the word bourgeois must appear. Carl Bridenbaugh has suggested another term, *"bourgeois aristocracy"*[131] which is the most acceptable definition yet encountered. The use of these two appellations, however, is still not quite satisfactory. A word, a French word, is needed to characterize, as accurately as possible, the functions of those called bourgeois. With all due apologies to Molière, the phrase suggested is *bourgeois-gentilhomme*. In New France, this man, and these men, were not the bumbling pretentious fools of the play, barely able to speak a civilized French, and understanding little the use of cutlery. The merchants, administrators, post commandants, and seigneurs were, for their times, well educated. They lived well, according to contemporary testimony. Their libraries were

---

[127]*Webster's New Collegiate Dictionary.*

[128]"Charlevoix on the Canadians," Nish, *The French Regime*, pp. 131–32.

[129]"Mémoire on the Canadians attributed to Hocquart," Nish, *The French Regime*, pp. 132–34.

[130]Chevalier de la Pause, "Dissertation sur le gouvernement," *Rapport de l'archiviste de la province de Québec, 1933–34*, pp. 207–8.

[131]Bridenbaugh, *Myth and Realities*, p. 13.

surprisingly large. It is usually agreed that they drank too much. The words *bourgeois* and *gentilhomme* were used to describe them, but never hyphenated. Rather, the words were separated by a comma: "bourgeois, gentilhomme."[132] It is to this class that the Cugnets, Vaudreuils, de la Gorgendières, Taschereaus, and the others noted in this study belonged, *les bourgeois-gentilhommes de la Nouvelle-France*.

---

[132]This is the description of Ignace Aubert in the Québec census of 1744.

9

ANGLO-FRENCH RIVALRY IN THE FUR TRADE DURING THE 18TH CENTURY*

E. R. Adair

The fur trade was one of the fundamental, perhaps *the* fundamental, factor in the history of New France. It was always the principle staple commodity and export produced by the colony; it was the source of most revenue and of most political dissension. Many colonial officials bewailed the colony's dependence, indeed overdependence, on the trade, but from Jean Talon on, they uniformly failed in any attempts to diversify New France's economy. Behind the colony's extraordinary feats of transcontinental exploration and geographical expansion lurked omnipresently the quest for new sources of better quality furs. Certainly, an understanding of the mechanics and dynamics of the fur trade is crucial in studying the internal development of New France. But the French were not the only Europeans interested in and drawn by the profits to be made from furs, and competition between the French and the English for control of this critical commodity was a basic factor behind the great imperial conflict for possession of the North American continent waged by the two European powers and their colonies for nearly a century. In the following article, Professor E. R. Adair analyzes in depth the components of this Anglo-French rivalry, with particular reference to the 18th century. What relative disadvantages and advantages did New France have in its struggle with the English for furs? Were the disadvantages more a product of failure on the part of French-Canadians or the mother country? On balance, was New France in an advantageous or disadvantageous position in the competition? Finally, how are the relative positions of the competitors related to the great imperial struggle and its ultimate outcome?

---

*Culture, 7 (1947), 434–55.

SUGGESTIONS FOR FURTHER READING

J. B. Brebner, *The Explorers of North America, 1492-1806* (Cleveland: World Publishing Co., 1964).

H. A. Innis, *The Fur Trade in Canada* (Toronto: University of Toronto Press, 1930).

E. E. Rich, *The Fur Trade and the Northwest to 1857* (Toronto: McClelland and Stewart, 1967).

Thomas Elliot Norton, *The Fur Trade in Colonial New York 1686-1776* (Madison: University of Wisconsin Press, 1974).

J.M.B.

I n an age that is deeply concerned in the struggle between free enterprise and government control it is all too easy to see the ultimate victory of the English over their French rivals in the American fur trade, as a victory for the rugged individual fur trader and fur merchant of the English colonies over the state aided and state controlled French-Canadian, who brought down the furs from the "pays d'en haut" and then was forced to sell them to a monopolistic company who marketed them in France. Some historians will go even farther: on the one hand they see all the profits of the fur trade going to France because the company paid too little in Canada and reduced the market in France by asking too much, while at the same time the all-demanding fur trade strangled the development of industry and agriculture in the colony; on the other hand Professor Innis,[1] and following him Professor Long,[2] see in the French-Canadian fur trade and its rivalry with the English colonies a fundamental cause of the paternalism and centralisation that have been regarded as so typical a feature of French government in America.

To what extent are these conclusions supported by the facts?[3] Let us consider first the position of the Campagnie des Indes and its so-called monopoly—so-called because its existence and extent is much confused by a loose use of words. Most historians, including Professor Innis in his standard history of the *Fur Trade in Canada,* employ the words "fur" and "beaver" almost as though they were synonymous or, if that is too extreme a statement, certainly as though all other furs were of such little importance, that a description of the beaver trade is all that is necessary to provide an account of the whole fur trade of New France. This is far from being the case: in addition to beaver there were exported to France deerskin or buckskin, marten, lynx, wildcat, bear skin, fox, mink, otter, seal, and a variety of other furs, and these formed a by no means negligible part of the whole export trade. In the ten years from 1718 to 1727 furs to the value of 6,680,889 livres were received at La Rochelle, and of this

---

[1]H. A. Innis, *The Fur Trade in Canada* (1930), p. 117.

[2]M. H. Long, *A History of the Canadian People,* vol. 1, p. 230.

[3]I am indebted for the sources of the statistics used in this article to a Ph.D. thesis by Miss A. J. E. Lunn in typescript in the library of McGill University.

sum furs other than beaver accounted for 2,990,283 livres or 44.8 percent of the total amount; in the ten years from 1728 to 1737 of the 11,206,981 livres' worth of furs imported through La Rochelle, 5,894,273 livres' worth or 52.6 percent were other furs; the ten years' figures that we possess between 1738 and 1750[4] show that 12,107,487 livres' worth of furs were imported, of which 8,610,832 livres or 71.1 percent were paid for furs other than beaver; and in the final ten years from 1751 to 1761[5] out of a total of 12,512,159 livres' worth of furs brought into La Rochelle, other furs amounted to 8,644,621 livres or 69.1 percent. So that in this period, between 1713 and 1761, beaver imported into La Rochelle constituted only about 40 percent of the total importation of furs from New France.

This is important, because it was solely for beaver skins that the Compagnie des Indes had the monopoly of purchase in New France and sale in La Rochelle; other furs could be disposed of in any way that the fur traders and merchants desired. Montreal merchants sometimes sold these furs to merchants in Quebec, and sometimes sent them direct to France; sometimes they brought them to Quebec themselves, sometimes they employed an agent there to supervise the shipment. French agents resident in Quebec bought these furs for firms in La Rochelle, Quebec merchants entered into partnership with La Rochelle merchants for the purchase of such furs; the captain of a ship trading to France bought furs for the La Rochelle merchants who owned or had an interest in his ship; occasionally the Canadian merchant despatched his furs to an agent at La Rochelle, who sold them there on commission. Whether the insurance and freight were paid by the Canadian merchant or by the French merchant was really immaterial: it formed part of the increased cost when the furs were sold at La Rochelle. And all this trade was outside the Company's monopoly. The greater part of the rivalry in the fur trade between the French and the English was, therefore, in no sense a contest between a company monopoly and free enterprise.

Nor is this the whole story. There is a tendency to ignore in this connection the English trade through Hudson Bay,[6] and this provided a very considerable portion of the English supply of beaver skins and proved a very serious competitor to the French. In 1739 the Hudson's Bay Company sent to England 69,911 lbs. of beaver; in the same year New France sent to La Rochelle 131,000 lbs. It is true that there was a decline in the late forties; in 1747 Hudson Bay sent only 39,505 lbs. as against over 100,000 lbs. to La Rochelle, but this decline was not permanent.[7] In order to complete the picture it should be added that the furs of every sort from Hudson Bay probably amounted in the fifties to at least one-third of the value of all the furs imported from America into England. And this very large trade through Hudson Bay was certainly not a product of free

---

[4]The accounts for 1742, 1743, and 1745 appear to be missing.

[5]The accounts for 1755 are not available.

[6]Professor Innis, however, gives an admirable account of the activities of the Hudson's Bay Company in his *Fur Trade in Canada*, pp. 123–51.

[7]Innis, *Fur Trade in Canada*, p. 144.

enterprise; it was a most rigid monopoly, much more far reaching than that of the Compagnie des Indes, for not only were the furs carried to England and sold there by the Hudson's Bay Company, but all the trading with the Indians in Canada was done solely by the servants of the Company and for its profit. Anglo-French rivalry in the fur trade can certainly not be stated in the simple terms of a contest between English free-traders and a French company monopoly.

Inevitably one is tempted to probe further and ask whether this limited monopoly by the French company was after all so bad an arrangement, whether its restrictiveness really weakened the French trade in beaver skins and so can be counted as one of the causes that led the English to ultimate victory in the struggle for furs.

During the latter part of the 17th century the trade with France in beaver had been a monopoly which was always coming to grief because the fur traders secured far more beaver than the monopolists could sell on the La Rochelle market. The obvious solution was to reduce the price paid at Quebec and so discourage this overproduction. When this was done, however, it had raised so vigorous an opposition in New France, that in 1700 the government agreed to permit the colonial merchants to form their own company—the Compagnie du Canada—and to market the beaver skins themselves. Having obtained this monopoly with the cry that beaver prices must be maintained, the new company soon found itself in a worse position than its predecessor: it had a great store of beaver that it could not sell and a large debt that it could not pay. Therefore in 1706 it sold out to a small group of French merchants, who were prepared to face the situation on a purely business basis. They were to hold the monopoly until 1717; they would not buy any castor gras[8] at all until 1712 and then only 30,000 lbs. per annum from 1712 to 1717, and that at 40 sous the pound; the purchase of castor sec was to be limited to 80,000 lbs. a year at 30 sous a pound. These measures sound reasonable, but actually they overshot the mark, for the new holders of the monopoly did not take into account the serious deterioration of the mass of castor gras that they had in storage. Therefore by 1714 they were asking for all the castor gras they could get, and in 1715 they were raising the price they offered for it in Quebec to 60 sous the pound. All this had had an extremely bad effect upon the Indians: they had long been encouraged to turn their castor sec into castor gras; then the fur traders told them they did not want any more castor gras, only a few years later to demand castor gras when actually the Indians had very little on hand. This was not only disruptive of the trade, but it drove the Indians into opening up relations with the English who would buy any sort of fur at practically the same price, and it encouraged the coureurs-de-bois to develop a brisk smuggling business with Albany. Moreover, at Montreal and Quebec the financial situation was becoming chaotic, because as a result of mis-

---

[8]Castor gras was the beaver skins that had been made into coats and worn by the Indians; this caused the long guard-hairs to wear off and fall out, and matted together the short hairs with a mixture of grease and dirt; the result was found more suitable for making beaver-felt hats than the beaver skin or castor sec that came straight from the beaver's back.

management combined with these economic difficulties, the holders of the monopoly were going bankrupt and the belief that they would honour the bills of exchange they had given the colonial merchants was rapidly being destroyed. The cause for all this was indicated very precisely in a contemporary memorandum on the subject: "The beaver trade in France and Europe is limited to a certain consumption beyond which there is no sale and the beaver remains a pure loss to those charged with the conduct of the trade. . . . The interests of the Canadians consist in being able to sell yearly the greatest amount possible . . . but it is not sufficient for Canadians to have the desire to sell, it is necessary that they should find at the same time people who wish to purchase and to pay and this does not appear to be possible."[9] And the situation was made all the worse by changing fashions which decreed a beaver hat of smaller size, and by the partial use of substitutes such as rabbit fur and "laine de vigogne" or wool derived from the Peruvian llama; while in the foreign markets to which France had been accustomed to export her surplus beaver, English competition was becoming increasingly severe.

The five years that followed 1717 did nothing to make the trade any more secure. In 1717 the Compagnie d'Occident took over the beaver monopoly from its bankrupt holders, agreeing to buy all good skins that were offered and to pay 60 sous a pound for castor gras and 34 sous for castor sec. This did not satisfy the fur merchants at all, and they protested that the rising cost of trade goods and supplies made double these prices for beaver necessary; if that could not be granted, the trade should be made free. As a result the government freed the trade in 1720, imposing instead an import duty on beaver skins. Again there was protest and again the government tried to satisfy everyone: it regranted the monopoly to the Compagnie des Indes, the successor of the Compagnie d'Occident. There were at first further violent protests, but after the French government had consulted all available authorities, the monopoly was made final in 1722, though an increase in fur prices was granted in order to placate the merchants: castor gras was to bring 80 sous a pound, and castor sec 40 sous. This Company retained the monopoly right down to 1760 and under their control the fur trade entered upon a period of relative calm and stability.

The Company took all the beaver skins that were offered; therefore it cannot be said to have limited the trade in order to keep up the prices in its own interest. Moreover the price paid to the merchants of New France appears to have been a fair one, based upon a consideration of the advice offered by the various parties concerned and maintained under the careful supervision of the government. This supervision was not a mere form, since the government was certainly anxious to see New France as prosperous as possible, for the royal ministers knew from sad experience that if the colony was in financial distress, the mother country would in some way or other have to make up the deficit; moreover they were especially anxious that the prices the traders could afford to pay for furs should not be too low, for fear lest the Indians might fall under the politi-

---

[9]Quoted by Innis, *Fur Trade in Canada*, p. 73.

cal as well as the trading influence of the English. Therefore in 1738 and
again in 1746 the Company adjusted their prices to meet the requests of
the colonial merchants. In 1738 a flat rate of 55 sous per pound for all
good beaver, whether it were castor gras or castor sec, was established,
partly because grading the furs was proving so difficult and was, in
addition, creating discontent among the Indians, and partly in order to
try and counteract the much higher price paid for castor sec by the English. In 1746 the increase to 80 sous for castor gras and 75 sous for
castor sec was in recognition of the higher prices that had to be paid for
trade goods in consequence of the war between England and France;
though there was a slight reduction in the payments for beaver when the
war came to an end, the higher prices soon had to be restored.

As far as one can judge, the profits made by the Company do not seem
to have been large; there was no bleeding of the Canadian merchant. The
spread between the price of beaver at Quebec and that at La Rochelle
averaged about 30 sous a pound. When it is remembered that the cost of
freightage, packing, and insurance came to about 10 sous a pound, when
to that is added the payment of about 4 percent of its annual receipts that
the Company was bound to make to supplement the salaries of the Governor-General, the Intendant, and the Governor of Montreal, when there
is the further addition of the salaries of its own employees, and the expense of losses incurred by shipwreck or capture at sea, by defects or
deterioration in transit or in storage, it will be seen that it is improbable
that the Company made on an average more than 10 sous profit on a
pound of beaver skins.[10] That higher prices were not charged in France
must not of course be laid to the benevolence of the Company, but to the
vigilance exercised by the influential gild of Paris hatmakers and to the
increasing competition from English traders that faced French exports of
beaver skins to the Netherlands and Russia. In the long run, therefore,
the Company seems to have made no more than a fair profit; above all it
kept prices stable and succeeded in selling all the beaver that New
France cared to produce, the old problem of overproduction being met in
part by more skilful business methods in the home market and in part by
expanding the export trade. And this stability was undoubtedly helped by
the fact that the Company's credit in Quebec was almost always good;
the bills that they gave for the beaver were payable in six months and
could be cashed on sight at the modest discount of ½ percent per month
to the date when they matured. These were definitely better terms than
previous holders of the monopoly had granted and they were regularly
adhered to.

So it seems that, on the whole, the record of the Company was a good
one. It guaranteed regularity and certainty of payment, free from price
fluctuations, for all the furs that New France wanted to sell, and this was
of vital importance not only because it kept the Indians reasonably satisfied, but also because, as beaver was a very important export, any inter-

---

[10]The whole question is naturally complicated and difficult to answer with any exactness;
for a further discussion see L. H. Gipson, *The British Empire before the American Revolution*, vol. 5, pp. 58–60.

ruption in that export meant that Canada could not buy from France the goods she needed for her own consumption, as well as for the Indian trade. This does not of course prove that the beaver trade might not have been managed even better had the monopoly been replaced by free sale, but all the evidence points to the contrary. Any increase in prices asked for beaver in France would have been fought vigorously, and almost certainly successfully, by the gild of hatmakers who were the chief buyers; such an increase would, moreover, have seriously decreased the export trade. Therefore free competition could not have raised the prices paid at Quebec, unless the French government agreed to abandon all export duties on beaver, and all the evidence goes to show that this was not likely to happen. Against this it may be pointed out that the English paid the Indians higher prices for beaver than the French did and that consequently there was a considerable smuggling trade with the English merchants in Albany. This is true, but it was the result of physical and economic conditions over which the French had no control, and which would have persisted whether there was a monopoly or not. It is therefore possible to conclude that such victory as the English fur traders gained in the Anglo-French rivalry was not one of free enterprise over monopoly, and was not the result of a selfish, restrictive policy by the French Company; that Canadian profits were not reduced by the fact that beaver skins had to be sold through the Company, and that the Company was not strangling the Canadian fur trade. Why then could the English afford to pay higher prices and why did the English appear to be winning in the race for furs? If the monopoly did no serious harm why did Canadians want to smuggle furs down to the English at Albany?

The question of the smuggling trade can be easily disposed of. Furs were taken to Albany because they commanded a better price and a quicker turnover than they did at Quebec; as there is no evidence that the price at Quebec would have been higher under a system of free competitive buying, the smuggling would have gone on whether the monopoly were abolished or not. Moreover, selling in Albany had another advantage of considerable value, for there the French-Canadians could buy English woollen cloth or strouds, which the Indians liked far better than anything manufacturers in France could provide.[11] Here again this effort to secure English strouds would have gone on, whether there was a Company monopoly or free trade in beaver; in fact, in attempting to secure a legal supply of English cloth for the Indian trade, the Company proved more successful than did private merchants, when they were given permission to import English goods into France and so into New France. Therefore the existence of the smuggling trade to Albany in beaver in no way proves that the Company's monopoly was restricting the prosperity of the colony.

But, if the Company's monopoly was not unfair to the colony, what were the reasons why the English could afford to pay a better price for

---

[11]For a fuller discussion see Miss Jean Lunn, *The Illegal Fur Trade out of New France, 1713-60*, in the *Report of the Canadian Historical Assoc. 1939*, pp. 65-68.

beaver and why did they ultimately win the battle for the fur trade? In trying to answer these questions there should be considered, first of all, the payments demanded by the government for the privilege of trading up country with the Indians for furs. The French posts that were established in the 18th century can be divided into three classes. First there were the King's posts along Lake Erie, Lake Ontario, and the headwaters of the Ohio, of which the oldest and most important were Fort Frontenac (1604) and Fort Niagara (1725); here the trading was done by a royal official with goods from the King's stores, and it was often carried on at a loss, because English competition and the need to keep the Indians' friendship forced up the prices of beaver and other furs. Then there were the posts that were leased to merchants or fur traders, who secured a monopoly of the fur trade there in return for a down payment or an annual rent; the lease was often for three years and the payment might be considerable: in 1743, for example, Temiscamingue was leased for 5,600 livres and La Baye for 8,100.[12] Naturally the traders who paid these rents, having no competition from other Frenchmen, and wanting to make profits as rapidly as possible, drove down the prices paid to Indians for their furs. Sometimes the commandant of the small garrison was allowed to do the trading, either in return for a payment or for an undertaking to meet the cost of maintaining the post; for instance, in 1701 Cadillac, the commandant at the new post of Detroit, was given the right to exclusive trade there in return for meeting the cost of provisioning and paying the garrison and the upkeep of the mission, while in 1752 the posts of La Mer d'Ouest were leased to the commandant, Chevalier de Niverville, for 8,000 livres a year.[13] The third type of post was one where the trade was open to all fur traders who had bought congés or were the agents of merchants who had bought congés, permitting them to go up country. The cost of each congé was about 500 or 600 livres and, after a period of considerable vacillation, the congé system became the normal one for most posts from 1726 to 1742. In the latter year it was decided to confine the use of congés to Detroit and Michilimackinac and lease the trade of each of the other posts to the highest bidder. The outbreak of war interfered with the working of this scheme and in 1748 La Galissonnière proposed that congés should once more be issued and applied to all posts except five, these being ones at which the Indians had not complained of high prices; this was adopted in 1749–50, but before the end of the French régime, most of the posts were being leased out to merchants or commandants as had been the case before 1748.

It is of course obvious that the rent of a post or the price of a congé constituted a tax on the fur trade and therefore lowered the price that the trader could profitably offer for the furs he was buying. This was seen quite clearly by contemporaries: M. de Noyan, writing in 1730, says: "The post of Detroit brought in to the officer in command there eight or ten thousand livres' income every year; each boat pays him five or six

---

[12]Innis, *Fur Trade in Canada*, p. 111.
[13]Gipson, *British Empire*, vol. 5, pp. 46, 55.

hundred francs[14] to obtain permission to go and trade, and the number of boats amounted to 18 or 20 a year. The voyageurs, who are obliged to lay down this sum, sell their goods—in order to recoup themselves—at very dear prices to the settlers at the place. The latter sell them again to the savages, who are the victims of this trading."[15] But there is another side to this picture. A large number of coureurs-de-bois went up country to get furs without paying a sou for a congé or the rent of a post. How many went every year there is no means of telling, but they were numerous enough to be a constant nuisance to the authorities, and not only did they secure a good deal of fur, but they must have provided considerable competition, if the legal traders dropped the price of fur too low or raised that of trade goods too high. Moreover there were always the English to keep prices up to the mark; this fact the government recognised by often selling trade goods at a loss in the King's posts that were most exposed to this competition; while in other posts, where the influence of English prices could be felt, though to a smaller degree, they saw to it that the trade was shared by several holders of congés, hoping that competition among them would keep prices at a reasonable level. It was usually only where there was no fear of foreign competition that the trading monopoly was regularly leased to a single merchant or to the commandant.

Finally it must be considered what use was made of the money coming from the sale of congés and post monopolies. Some of it, it is true, was spent on wholly extraneous objects: in 1728 Beauharnois devoted 6,250 livres received from the sale of congés to provide for the completion of a wall around Montreal; the rest went to the relief of the poor. But much of the money derived in this way and from the leasing of monopolies was spent on the upkeep of the posts themselves; sometimes the monopoly would be granted simply on condition that the post should be properly maintained. If the King's posts are included, it is probable that the cost of maintenance to the Crown was greater than the money that this tax on the fur trade actually produced. And such posts were undoubtedly necessary; even the fur traders of Pennsylvania, though they operated comparatively close to home, established posts for fur-collecting and warehousing in the upper Ohio valley. To the French fur trader, operating a thousand miles or more from Montreal, and often in the midst of Indian tribes of doubtful friendship, such posts were of vital importance, not only for protection, not only for storage and as revictualling stations, but to maintain French prestige among the Indians, without which, so delicate at times was the balance, the French-Canadian fur Empire might have been lost. If the importance of posts, adequately maintained, needs any further proof, the whole system adopted by the English Hudson's Bay Company in the 17th and early 18th centuries provides overwhelming evidence, for the well protected trading post was the real heart of all their activities. And even the rugged individualists from the English colonies to the south found free competition at times irksome. In 1749 Benjamin

---

[14]I.e., livres. Here the right to sell congés had been granted to the commandant of the post, a privilege for which he of course paid the government.

[15]Quoted by Gipson, British Empire, vol. 5, p. 46.

Stoddard suggested the establishment of a trading company at Oswego because "I am certain that if some such Scheme does not go on that the Trade of this Place will be soon ruined, for their [sic] is such a Number of Traders here and such Vile Steps taken to undermine each other in his trade that it consequently can't hold Long; and the little low means used in the Trade to hurt each other must give even the Savages a Damn'd mean Opinion of us; especially our Honesty."[16] While in the same year that very successful fur trader George Croghan, speaking from Pennsylvania, wrote "No people Carries on the Indians Trade in So Regular a manner as the French. I wish with all My hart the Government of this Province wol'd Take Some Method to Regulate the Indian Trade."[17]

And it was not only posts that the French government provided in return for this tax on the fur trade: every year a sum of at least 22,000 livres was used for the purchase of presents for the Indians, some being distributed at the various posts, the rest at the annual pow-wow held at Montreal in the spring, at which the Governor met the chiefs of tribes from the west. If one reads the bitter complaints from English traders of the stinginess with which the New York and Pennsylvania assemblies doled out money for Indian presents, the real value to the French fur trade of what the French government was doing, can be fully realised.

Taking it all in all, it is very doubtful if the French system of regulating the up-country fur trade and the tax thus levied, really had much influence upon the prices that the fur traders paid the Indians; if the government had retired from the business altogether and left the trade completely free, it seems probable that the fur traders would have spent nearly, if not quite, as much in providing the facilities that they needed, and as a result the price paid to the Indians for their furs would have been about the same.

A much more potent disadvantage from which the French fur traders suffered, when compared with the English, is to be found in the quality and price of the goods they had to offer the Indians. Trade goods consisted mainly of woollen cloth, gunpowder, muskets, kettles, tobacco, and brandy or rum. In gunpowder and muskets the French apparently held their own; in regard to each of the other commodities, they were at a serious disadvantage. The Indians found English cloth considerably cheaper than that made in France and in addition they much preferred the quality and appearance of the English strouds and scarlets. At the beginning of the 18th century (1707) a memorandum states "The chief cause [for Indian's trading with the English] is that they do not find with us certain red and blue cloths, an ell and a quarter wide, or they are forced to purchase them more dearly than from the English." And the same was true at the end of the French régime: about 1758 another memorandum states "Scarlets from England are an indispensable necessity for the beaver trade in Canada. To get these scarlets, which they have up to the present tried in vain to imitate in France, the Com-

---

[16]J. Sullivan, ed., *The Papers of Sir William Johnson*, vol. 1, p. 236, *Benjamin Stoddard to Col. W. Johnson*, Oswego, July 16, 1749.

[17]Quoted by A. T. Volwiler, *George Croghan and the Westward Movement*, pp. 67-68.

pany is obliged to bring them from England to Holland and from Holland to France on neutral boats."[18] In 1715 New France received 216 pieces of cloth made in Montpellier in imitation of the English strouds, but they did not sell; the price was too high, they were not as strongly woven as English cloth and above all they did not possess the same details of colouring: the Indians insisted on "blue cloth with a white band as broad as the little finger close to the edge or in the case of scarlets a black band,"[19] and strong colours were essential. Several more shipments were sent from France and proved just as unsatisfactory. Then there was a pause, but the same policy was tried again from 1731 to 1737, with just the same failure; a final attempt was made by La Galissonnière and Bigot in 1748–49 and again the French cloth proved unsatisfactory; some specimen pieces sent out were condemned as "frightful," the scarlet cloth being brown and unpressed, while the blue was rejected as inferior in quality and colour to the English stroud.[20] Therefore from the very beginning the Company was driven to the only alternative, the importation of English-made woollen cloth; 300 pieces were imported and sold in 1715, but the cost of transportation raised their price by about 65 percent, and therefore in Montreal they had to be sold for 50 percent more than strouds illegally smuggled in from Albany. Yet every year from 1722 to 1731 the Compagnie des Indes sent out to New France English cloth for sale to the Indians; they succeeded in gradually reducing their price, so that it could compete fairly well with the cloth smuggled in from Albany; but the Indians still had to pay more than if they had bought it direct from the English. After a disastrous interval from 1731 to 1738, the Company returned to its policy of supplying English strouds, and during the last years of peace that New France enjoyed, they were sending out over 1,000 cloths annually.

There is therefore no doubt at all that the French were at a serious disadvantage in this exchange of woollen cloth for furs: not only were they obliged to import legally or illegally the manufactures of their rivals, the English, but they were forced to sell the cloth at high prices because of the greater cost of transportation via France to New France, the often unfavorable rate of exchange and, in time of war, the serious losses in transit.

"The English have the better of us in the quality of merchandise in two important articles. The first is kettles, the second is cloth."[21] So wrote La Galissonnière and Bigot in October 1748. The trouble was that the French kettles were badly made and too heavy, for they were iron ones; what the Indians wanted were copper ones that would stand rough usage and could be easily carried from place to place. The English seem to have provided yellow copper kettles that were light, durable, and came in various sizes; they also sold good ones of brass and tin.[22] The problem

---

[18]Both passages quoted in Innis, *Fur Trade in Canada*, pp. 79, 87.

[19]Innis, *Fur Trade in Canada*, p. 80.

[20]La Jonquière and Bigot to the Minister, October 1, 1749, in *Documents relating to the Colonial History of the State of New York*, vol. 10, p. 200.

[21]Quoted in Innis, *Fur Trade in Canada*, p. 85.

[22]A. T. Volwiler, *George Croghan and the Westward Movement*, p. 30; Gipson, *British Empire*, vol. 5, p. 63.

of catching the Indian's eye with a shining kettle, however, seems to have been much less serious than that of setting his stomach on fire with the more violent forms of alcohol: to do this the English pinned their faith on rum and the French on brandy. It is possible that brandy was a little more potent, especially as the French traders diluted it with less water than the English added to their rum. But from the French point of view, the trouble was that it cost more, again on account of the distance that it had to be carried, and because for a good many years its legal sale to the Indians was forbidden on pain of refusal of absolution by the Catholic Church. Throughout this whole period the Church steadfastly set its face against the sale of any liquor to Indians and, as the Indians drank merely to get drunk and then went almost insane, there is no doubt the Church was right. But the fur traders pointed out that not only was brandy the cheapest currency with which to buy furs, but that, if the Indians did not get it, they would transfer their trade to the English and drink their rum, upon the sale of which no restrictions were laid. The government recognised the validity of this argument and no doubt felt that, as great quantities of brandy were going to be sold anyway, it were better that it be disposed of legally, so that its sale could be properly controlled.

Except for the years 1716 to 1718, the sale of brandy to Indians outside of towns was strictly forbidden during the early part of the 18th century. Then the foundation of Oswego by the English in 1725-26 brought matters to a head, for at this post, placed close to the main French-Indian trade-routes, unlimited rum could be obtained; therefore reluctantly the French government permitted the sale of brandy up country, though in limited quantities. As a counter-blow, the Bishop of Quebec forbade any man to be given absolution who had provided an Indian with brandy, legally or illegally. This clerical mandate had very considerable effect, so much indeed that Beauharnois and Hocquart suggested that the decline in the French fur trade in the middle 30s was due to the fact that the Indians from the west passed by Detroit, Niagara and Frontenac and traded for rum at Oswego;[23] indeed by 1749 Oswego was taking in more fur than these three French posts put together, though cheaper prices for goods had as much to do with this, as did generous supplies of liquor.[24] Nor were Indian chiefs unaware of the evils of this type of trade. At the Treaty of Carlisle in 1753 they complained to the English "The Rum ruins us . . . . when these Whisky-traders come, they bring thirty or forty Cags and put them down before us, and make us drink; and get all the Skins that should go to pay the Debts we have contracted for Goods bought of the Fair Traders, and by this Means we not only ruin ourselves but them too. These wicked Whisky-Sellers, when they have got the Indians in Liquor, make them sell the very Cloaths from their Backs."[25] Even the sedate commissioners at the Albany Congress in 1754 agreed that the Indians "at Oswego and other licensed places . . . . are almost continuously drunk and, at least, imagine that in their drink they have

[23]N.Y. *Col. Docs.*, vol. 9, pp. 1024, 1049.

[24]Gipson, *British Empire*, vol. 5, pp. 91-92.

[25]Quoted by Gipson, *British Empire*, vol. 4, p. 168, from *Indian Treaties Printed by Benjamin Franklin* (ed. J. P. Boyd), p. 130.

been abused and imposed upon in their trading."[26] Under conditions such as these, the temptation to take brandy up country, legally or illegally, proved overpowering to a great many French traders. Even when the lay authorities were anxious to enforce the law, they could do very little. It is quite impossible to guess how much brandy was sold to the Indians, but there was undoubtedly enough to diminish very considerably any disadvantage from which the French trade suffered, though the fact that the supply was intermittent may have inclined the Indians to seek English posts where a constant stream flowed to assuage their devouring thirst.

Another factor that produced differences in price between French and English traders was that of distance and therefore of cost of transportation. By the beginning of the 18th century the day was long past when the Indians brought furs down to the fair at Montreal; the Hurons as middlemen had been driven off by the Iroquois, and the Ottawas had replaced them, getting "their peltries" as Duchesneau wrote in 1681, "in the North, from the people of the interior . . . . and in the South."[27] But the Ottawas also suffered from the Iroquois and, in addition, good hunting-grounds for fur-bearing animals became more distant; therefore Frenchmen had to penetrate the interior in ever increasing numbers. This meant that trade goods had to be carried farther, that furs cost more to bring back to Montreal, that more food had to be supplied and more wages paid to voyageurs and canoemen. If the price of furs at La Rochelle was fairly firmly established, all this had one inevitable result, that trade goods would cost more to the Indian and that he would get less for his furs.

South of the Great Lakes the French met the competition of the Pennsylvania fur traders who were spreading over the Ohio valley, for the New Yorkers were mostly content with the good business they were still carrying on with the Iroquois middlemen at Albany and Oswego, with the western Indians whom rum and cheaper prices attracted to Oswego[28] instead of to Detroit, and with the smuggling trade between Albany and Montreal. A good deal has been written about the advantages the French enjoyed in possessing such continuous water routes through to the Great Lakes. This did not always work out so well in actual practice: because of the portages that rapids made necessary, it took the French anything from 20 to 40 days to go from Montreal to Niagara, whereas the Pennsylvania traders could reach the upper Ohio in 20 days.[29] This meant greater transportation costs for the French. And added to this the beaver skins they were getting from the area south of the Great Lakes were not of first class quality; in this warmer climate the beaver did not develop that thick, closely grown fur that he had farther north. Still there seemed to be plenty of fur to be gained there and the French were not prepared to abandon the Ohio valley to the English without a struggle.

---

[26]Quoted by Gipson, *British Empire*, vol. 5, p. 118.

[27]*N.Y. Col. Docs.*, vol. 9, pp. 160–61.

[28]In 1749, 147 canoes came to Oswego from 11 western tribes; in that year Oswego bought fur to the value of £21,406 or over 500,000 livres (*N.Y. Col. Docs.*, vol. 6, p. 538).

[29]Volwiler, *George Croghan*, p. 43.

But it was the northern fur that really paid dividends; and here the French in the 18th century were faced by the Hudson's Bay Company, who had regained their posts by the Treaty of Utrecht in 1713; and there is no doubt that the English had definite advantages. Denonville wrote in 1685 "If not expelled thence they [the Hudson's Bay Company] will get all the castor gras from an infinite number of nations at the North which are being discovered every day; they will attract the greatest portion of the peltries that reach us at Montreal through the Outaouacs and Assinibois and other neighbouring tribes, for these will derive a double advantage from going in search of the English at Port Nelson—they will not have so far to go, and will find goods at a much lower rate than with us."[30] In the following year (1686), the French authorities indicated very clearly the reason for this difficulty: "All the commerce of the Bay in a word is of no value except as it could be carried on by sea, since it saves the infinite expense of carrying provisions and merchandise by land. But our merchants are in no position to compete with the English in this way, since they [the English] have good sea-going boats well armed and well equipped. It is much to be feared that our company could not be successful in saving the best furs of Canada since certainly the greater part of the castor gras comes from the north and besides the fur there is very much finer.[31]

But the French, notwithstanding the difficulties and costs of transportation overland did not despair. There were two courses open to them. They took the easier one during the last decade of the 17th century and captured Forts Albany, Moose, and Nelson (York Fort) belonging to the Hudson's Bay Company; but at the end of the war of the Spanish Succession, France, as the defeated country, had to return these posts to England. Therefore the French had a more vigorous recourse to their second alternative, that of taking their goods to the Indians' very door. French competition among the Indians who traded with the Hudson's Bay Company's southern posts on James Bay, Fort Albany, and Fort Moose, was not so difficult, and they were able to bring their prices close enough to those of the English to force the latter to offer the Indian rather better terms there than they gave him at the northern posts of Fort York and Fort Churchill.[32] In competing however with these posts on the west shore of Hudson Bay, the French recognised that the long overland haul would make the prices of their trade goods higher and of the furs they bought lower than those offered by the English, but they took the advice M. de Clerambaut d'Aigremont gave M. de Pontchartrain in 1710: "When these Indians will be obliged to go to a great distance to get their necessaries, they will always go to the cheapest market; whereas, were they to obtain their supplies at their door, they would take them, whatever the price may be."[33]

So the French began the establishment of that series of trading posts that was finally to take them to the foot of the Rockies. The first three of

[30]Memoir of M. Denonville on the State of Canada, November 12, 1685 printed in *N.Y. Col. Docs.*, vol. 9, p. 286.

[31]Quoted in Innis, *Fur Trade in Canada*, p. 46.

[32]Innis, *Fur Trade in Canada*, pp. 145, 147.

[33]*N.Y. Col. Docs.*, vol. 9, p. 853.

these posts were suggested as early as 1717 because they "would prevent many Indians from carrying their furs to Hudson Bay."[34] As the French pushed westward they began to secure the furs that the Assiniboines and the Crees had been carrying to Fort York; they did their utmost to cultivate the Indians' friendship and trust, and soon they had tapped the resources of tribes still farther west, for whom the Assiniboines and the Crees had been acting as middlemen. Of course the enormous distances that the trade goods had to be brought overland made them more expensive and therefore lower prices were offered for furs, but La Vérendrye, the greatest explorer of them all, summed up the situation in a speech he made to the Cree and Nonsoni Indians at Fort St. Charles[35] on May 9, 1734: "When you deal with them [the English at Hudson Bay] you have to do it as if you were their enemies: they give you no credit; they do not allow you inside their fort; you cannot choose the merchandise you want, but are obliged to take what they give you through a window, good or bad. . . . It is true that our traders sell some things a little dearer, but they take all [the furs] you have; they reject nothing, you run no risk, and you have not the trouble of carrying your stuff a long distance."[36] As a result of this policy, the French not only met the competition of the Hudson's Bay Company, but between 1738 and 1748 they seriously reduced the quantity of fur the Company's factors were able to send to England.[37] This was probably the reason why the Company sent Anthony Hendry in 1754 into the Blackfeet country, to try and persuade the Indians once more to bring their furs down to Fort York; French competition was getting too dangerous to be ignored.

Therefore around the Great Lakes and to the south of them the French were definitely hampered by increased prices that resulted from increased costs of transportation and from increased possibilities of the deterioration of the furs on their long journey to Quebec and La Rochelle. In the most valuable area, however, the north and the north-west, the French had found the right solution to the problem and were more than holding their own.

But the final disadvantage from which the French-Canadian fur traders suffered they could do nothing about: the English controlled the sea and, as wars were not infrequent, interruption of the French communications with France and the consequent shortage of trade goods might have disastrous results. The English were able to maintain a fairly even flow of manufactures across the Atlantic for themselves, but French posts were starved of goods, or at best found prices rising beyond reason, and consequently the Indians who knew little about naval power were discontented and ready to carry their furs to the English traders. In June 1745 Beauharnois writes "The scarcity, as well as the high price, of goods is the cause of this falling off in the trade which may be also looked

---

[34]P. Margry, *Memoires et Documents*, vol. 6, p. 502. Memorandum of the Conseil de la Marine. February 3, 1717.

[35]St. Charles on the Lake of the Woods had been established in 1733.

[36]L. J. Burpee, ed., *Journals and Letters of . . . La Vérendrye* (Champlain Soc.), pp. 183–84.

[37]Innis, *Fur Trade in Canada*, p. 144.

upon as entirely lost for next year; should our ships not arrive in safety, it is to be feared that even this year the Indians will be disgusted on account of the few goods sent up to Niagara and other posts, and thereby be induced to take sides with the English in order to obtain their necessaries."[38] A few months later he writes again "I offered licenses for nothing—especially to Detroit, in order that there should be abundance of goods at the post—only ten went up this year."[39] The French experienced these same difficulties during the Seven Years' War. The Compagnie des Indes lost their total shipment of 1,200 strouds in 1755, they lost 300 pieces of scarlet cloth out of 1,160 in 1756, 370 out of 660 in 1757; and increases in freight rates and insurance across the Atlantic raised the price from 50 percent to 100 percent.[40] On one occasion Johnson is said to have given free presents of captured French brandy to the Indians and to have had free clothes made for them out of captured French cloth: a delightful experience for the Indians and a smashing blow at French prestige. Here there is no question about the considerable advantage enjoyed by the English over their rivals.

To balance the more acceptable goods and the higher prices, whatever might be their cause, there were two factors of some considerable importance that told on the side of the French. In the first place the French fur trade was undoubtedly aided by the missionary efforts of the French religious orders, especially the Jesuits, though exactly how great their aid was it is impossible to say. They often served to keep Indian tribes friendly or, especially in the early days, to secure such friendship even before the traders arrived. They strove to keep the peace among the various tribes and thus give the Indians more time for hunting and trading in furs. And they did a good deal to spread an intangible feeling that the French came to the Indians as something more than mere money-grubbing or land-hungry traders. This indicates the second great advantage that the French enjoyed. There seems almost general agreement that the French were usually more honest and more understanding than the English, that they did not entirely ignore the interests and the point of view of the Indian, that they tried to learn at least one or two of his many dialects. In 1746 Robson, a servant of the Hudson's Bay Company records that "The French by kind offers and liberality in dealing, which we think of no consequence, have obtained so much influence over almost all the natives, that many of them are actually turned factors for the French at our settlements for heavy goods."[41] Anthony Hendry, another Hudson's Bay man, reports in the journal of his journey to the country of the Blackfeet in 1754 "The French talk Several Languages to perfection: they have the advantage of us in every shape; and if they had Brazile tobacco, which they have not, would entirely cut off our Trade."[42]

---

[38]*N.Y. Col. Docs.*, vol. 10, p. 2.

[39]*N.Y. Col. Docs.*, vol. 10, p. 21.

[40]Memorandum quoted by Innis, *Fur Trade in Canada*, p. 87.

[41]That is heavy trade goods that cost the French so much to transport. This passage is quoted by Innis, *Fur Trade in Canada*, p. 98.

[42]Quoted by Burpee in his introduction to *Journals and Letters of . . . La Vérendrye*, p. 39. Brazil tobacco was a strong dark tobacco much esteemed by the Indians.

Richard Peters, Secretary of Pennsylvania, wrote to Thomas Penn in 1753 "The chiefs of the Six Nations . . . give way to those who sollicit best, & in this respect the French, by their situation, frequent journeys & address, infinitely surpass the English."[43] And Governor Dinwiddie of Virginia writing to Governor Hamilton of Pennsylvania in the same year makes the difference even clearer when he says, no doubt with some exaggeration, "The Indian traders, in general, seem to be a set of abandoned wretches," while the Pennsylvania assembly speaks even more strongly in 1754: "Our Indian trade [is] carried on (some few excepted) by the vilest of our own Inhabitants and Convicts imported from Great Britain and Ireland."[44] Moreover to the Indians the French had one outstanding merit: they did not drive the Indian westward because they wanted his land. Alarm was at once felt by the tribes who saw the appearance of the agents of the Ohio Company and its rivals in the upper Ohio valley, and that alarm soon turned to hostility; as early as 1749 George Croghan was writing with bad spelling but good sense "The Indians Dos nott Like to hear of there Lands being Setled over Allegany Mountain."[45] Can it be wondered if they began to seek refuge in an alliance with the French?

Therefore, while it may be admitted that the French were handicapped by the higher prices and inferior quality of their trade goods, by the scarcities that war produced, and the interruptions that the Church provoked in the sale of brandy, it must also be admitted that they had some substantial advantages. And they were by no means being beaten in the race for furs: in the north and north-west they were more than holding their own against the Hudson's Bay Company: a substantial part of New York's fur trade was a smuggling trade from Montreal of which French-Canadians reaped part of the profit. Of course it is true that in the forties the English traders had advanced rapidly in the Ohio valley; they had not only penetrated to the line of the Wabash-Maumee rivers where the French had long defended their interests by Forts Miami, Ouiatenon, and Vincennes, but their influence was being strongly felt farther westward in the Illinois country. Here it might seem that the English were winning, certainly they were carrying considerable quantities of furs back to Pennsylvania, and by the conference with the Indian tribes at Logstown in August 1748 it looked as though at least the whole of the upper Ohio valley had been secured by the English for their exclusive trade.

But in the 50s the situation was drastically reversed: the French determined to drive out these trespassers once and for all, and their plans met with complete success. The first blow was delivered in June 1752 by a band of Chippewa Indians, led by the Frenchman Charles-Michel Langlade, who suddenly captured Pickawillany, a village of the Miami or Twightwee Indians and an important fort and advanced post of English trade; their chieftain, called by the French La Demoiselle, and by the

---

[43]Quoted by Gipson, *British Empire*, vol. 5, p. 107.

[44]Both passages quoted by Volwiler, *George Croghan*, p. 43.

[45]Quoted by Volwiler, *George Croghan*, p. 68.

English Old Briton, was boiled and eaten. Both of these events were disastrous for the English: there was no friendly chieftain with enough ability to take Old Briton's place, and the Ohio Indians at once began to lose confidence in the English and to veer towards a French alliance. This tendency was made more pronounced by the failure of the English to recover their losses; the Governor of Pennsylvania made it clear to George Croghan, whose interests were most concerned, that he could do nothing to help "by reason of the principles of the people here [in Philadelphia] who have the disposition of the public money."[46] During the following year the great fur business established by the Pennsylvania merchants completely collapsed and traders such as George Croghan and William Trent went bankrupt, while Indian friendship to the English vanished. At Duquesne's command, the French established Fort Presqu'-Isle and Fort Le Bœuf and linked them by a waggon road; they occupied Venango; and in 1754 the English surrendered their half-finished post at the Forks of the Ohio to the French under Contrecœur and saw it replaced by the French Fort Duquesne; Virginia made that rather futile protest under George Washington that ended at Fort Necessity. The Pennsylvania traders alone estimated their losses at £18,000 and their fur trade west of the Alleghenies was at an end: "There has not been an Indian between Weningo and the Pict Country hunting this Summer, by reason of the French," John Fraser had written in August 1753.[47]

The French were completely successful as the result of their military organisation, their strategically placed posts, their unified command and disciplined action, the freedom of their leaders from hesitating and often parsimonious popular control, and the possession of a uniform Indian policy that took some account of the Indians' feelings and desires. And the English colonies were not going to do anything about it that would be likely to produce results. A lot of nonsense has been written about the importance of the greater population that the English colonies possessed, sometimes it is almost implied that the Ohio valley was reserved by Divine Providence for exploitation by the English, Irish, and Scotch settlers. In fact the efficiency and unity of French organisation were completely victorious. The New York authorities were not very interested in protecting a trade in which New Yorkers were not immediately concerned and the assembly stated that the building of a fort by the French at French Creek "may, but does not by any Evidence or Information, appear to us to be an Invasion, of any of his Majesty's Colonies";[48] therefore they would do nothing. The Quaker government of Pennsylvania was opposed to war on religious grounds, and opposed to spending any money on personal and political grounds; as late as 1755 Governor Morris of Pennsylvania had to write to General Braddock "I am, Sir,

---

[46] Gipson, *British Empire*, vol. 4, p. 256.

[47] Volwiler, *George Croghan*, pp. 41, 47.

[48] Quoted by Max Savelle in *An American Attitude towards External Affairs* (*American Historical Review*, vol. 52, no. 4, July 1947, p. 659); the fort on French Creek was Fort Le Bœuf.

almost ashamed to tell you that . . . . when their *All* is invaded they refuse to contribute to the necessary Defence of their Country, either by
establishing a Militia or furnishing Men, Money, or Provision."[49] Virginia
was prepared to do something because its investments and land schemes
were at stake, but it was not ready to do very much. When Horatio
Sharpe, Governor of Maryland, in March 1754 denounced the French
occupation of the Allegheny valley as "flagrant Acts of Hostility," the
Maryland assembly replied very coolly: "we humbly conceive that the
Situation . . . of our Neighbours of Virginia, with regard to any Violence
or Outrage, threatened or perpetrated against them, by the French, does
not require our immediate aid or Assistance . . . and therefore, we do not
think it necessary to do any Thing in the Matter at present."[50] Not one
colonial assembly accepted the Plan of Union drawn up by their own
commissioners at the Albany Congress in 1754. As a result, notwithstanding repeated exhortations from England, there was going to be
no united action by the colonies to recover the Ohio valley, in fact there
was going to be little or no action at all: and there was going to be no
unified control or consistent policy in regard to the colonies' relations
with the Indian tribes along their western frontier. Even the injured fur
traders could not agree among themselves: there had, for example, been
bitter hostility between the Pennsylvania traders and the fur trading
agents of the Ohio Company of Virginia. As a result of all this, English
prestige with the Indians was so low that even the Six Nations could no
longer be relied upon.

Finally the English government decided that if anything was to be
done, it would have to be done by England; their urging, their advice,
their attempts to avoid wounding the sensitive feelings of the selfish and
obstinate colonial assemblies had been in vain. The assemblies might
have been ready to defend the colonies from actual invasion, but it is
improbable that the French were planning anything of that sort; they
merely wanted control of the Ohio valley and the alliance of the Ohio
Indians, and this they had obtained; the rivalry for the fur-trade had been
won by France. The English government determined to reverse this decision. Their victory was won by English regulars sent out from England,
by the English fleet that broke communications between France and
New France; and, when the English colonies provided men and supplies
of any value, it was only after Pitt had undertaken that their cost would
be repaid to the colonies out of the English Treasury. The Anglo-French
rivalry for the fur trade in the 18th century was not won by the superiority of free enterprise over government regulation, the defeat of the
French was not evidence of the deadening influence of paternalism; the
rivalry was not decided by the higher prices the French charged, by the
inferiority of some of their trade goods, or by the overwhelming population of the English colonies. This rivalry was brought to a final end by the
military and naval power of England, a power France could not match in
America, partly because she was fully engaged in a great European war,

---

[49]Quoted by Gipson, *British Empire*, vol. 6, pp. 68–69.
[50]Max Savelle, *An American Attitude*, p. 657.

and partly because she could not control the Atlantic. It has been said that the fur trade drew men away from industrial development in New France, but there is not the slightest evidence that French-Canadians ever had any interest at all in industrial development, even when every inducement for it was offered by the mother country. It is certain that the fur trade took men from agriculture, but they were men who found the drab routine of the farmer dull and profitless, for the fur trade served as the safety valve for all that was violent and adventurous in French-Canadian life. Moreover it did not produce paternalism and a highly organised system of administration, for those were to be found in New France from the beginning of the colony, because they were the regular techniques of government known to the 17th-century French, and when New France emerged from company control, it was very naturally governed like any other French province. The fur trade was, however, the life-blood of New France; with it New France was an Empire, without it, a mere unimportant agricultural colony on the shores of the St. Lawrence. Control of the great hinterland that lay to the west of the Alleghenies and around the Great Lakes was vital to the people of New France, if this flow of profitable fur was to continue through their ports. It is ironic that while the adjacent English colonies were apathetically squabbling over other matters, the English government, 3,000 miles away, realised this fact and realised the importance of winning over the Indians by the maintenance of English prestige. They finally took action, even though it resulted in involving England in the Seven Years' War, and the Anglo-French rivalry for the fur trade was dramatically ended in England's favour.

10

THE GROWTH OF MONTREAL IN THE 18TH CENTURY*

Louise Dechêne

One of the most interesting developments in Canadian historical research and writing in recent years has been the growth of historical demography. At first glance, the careful recovery of the characteristics of past populations seems a rather dull and prosaic business, and so it once was. Historical demographers have been active in Canada for a long time. But the new demographers are not, as were the old ones, statisticians. They are instead social historians, employing their techniques of demographic analysis not as ends in themselves, but as tools for understanding the lives and environments of people who often left few traces in history except records of such mundane matters as their birth, occupation, place of residence, and death. Modern historical demography first flourished in France, particularly among scholars studying medieval peasant populations, and not surprisingly, both its techniques and frame of analysis are extremely well suited to the study of New France, where the private papers of articulate *Canadiens* are few and far between.

In the following article, Professor Louise Dechêne illustrates the range of rich insights that historical demography can provide for our understanding of the past. Her concern is with the question of what a study of its population patterns can tell us about 18th-century Montreal, particularly in terms of its relationships with the rural hinterland and the European metropolis. How do Dechêne's conclusions fit with the general picture of New France advanced by Diamond, and the discussion of the

---

*This article was presented as a paper at the colloquium "Historical Urbanization in North America" held at York University in January 1973, and was published as "La croissance de Montréal au XVIIIe siècle," in *Revue d'Histoire de l'Amérique Française*, 27 (1973), 163–79. This revised translation is by the author.

bourgeoisie by Nish? Was Montreal an urban community? To what extent can this analysis be said to belong within the so-called metropolitan school of Canadian history?

SUGGESTIONS FOR FURTHER READING

Louise Dechêne, *Habitants et marchands de Montréal au XVIIe siècle* (Paris: Plon, 1974).

Guy Frégault, *La Civilisation de la Nouvelle-France 1713-1744* (Montréal: Fides, 1969).

Marcel Trudel, *La population du Canada en 1663* (Montréal, Fides, 1973).

J.M.B.

I n the middle of the 18th century some 20 percent of the Canadian population lived in towns. This proportion, a high one for the times, suggests at first glance that Quebec and Montreal attracted colonists and grew faster than the rural areas. A few contemporary comments have tended to strengthen this impression.[1] The urban-rural population ratio can be, however, a very deceptive indicator in a colonial context. Trade normally precedes agriculture in a colony and the proportion of urban dwellers decreases as settlement progresses, until it ultimately stabilizes at around 10 percent, an equilibrium point in pre-industrial economies. Because of the slow pace of immigration into New France, the urban proportion of the population declined much more slowly there than in other colonies; thus the ratio of urban to rural population is not very significant.

There is an evident need for a closer study of the demographic evolution of both Quebec and Montreal in the colonial period. This is particularly true for Quebec, the more important of the two towns, which one would expect to show some signs of urban dynamism. This dynamism was clearly absent in the inland post that was Montreal. Despite serious deficiencies in the census, I have attempted through the use of a variety of sources to measure the growth of population in Montreal. Even if my conclusions cannot be extended to other towns, Montreal serves as an example of the sort of inertia that characterizes an economy based on a single staple over a long period.

The figures shown in Table 1 are necessarily approximate. Only 2 of the 23 census returns of the Canadian population made in the 18th century (those of 1707 and 1754), separated the population of Montreal from that of the *banlieue*, an agricultural area included in the same parish. By using the enumerations of dwellings made in 1697, 1731, 1741, and 1781 it is possible to estimate the size of this rural population—a fairly stable group that hovered at a little under 1,000—and subtract it from the fig-

---

[1]See Guy Frégault, *La Civilisation de la Nouvelle-France 1713-1744* (Montreal, 1969), p. 168, and "La Nouvelle-France, territoire et population," in *Le XVIIIe siècle canadien, Etudes* (Montréal, 1968), pp. 48-49; Louis Trottier, "La genèse du réseau urbain du Québec," in *L'urbanisation de la société canadienne-française* (Québec, 1968), p. 23.

TABLE 1

Estimates of the Population of Montreal and Comparative Growth Rates

	Towns and Suburbs				Parish	
Year	Houses	Households	Population	Percent Annual Growth Rate	Population	Percent Annual Growth Rate
1697	152	—	(1,150)[a]	—	(13,200)[b]	—
1707	—	204	1,327	1.4	17,615	2.9
1731	400	—	(2,980)[c]	3.4	(34,850)[c]	2.9
1739	—	—	(3,450)[d]	1.7	43,264	2.7
1741	457	591	(3,575)	—	—	—
1754	—	—	4,000	0.8	55,000	1.6
1781	659	—	5,300	—	—	—
1784	—	—	(5,500)[e]	1.0	113,012	2.5
1831	3,774	—	27,297	3.5	553,134	3.4

Notes:

a. On the basis of seven persons per house, a ratio derived from the 1731 figures. Personnel of religious orders have been added to this figure.

b. Average based on the census returns of 1695 and 1698.

c. Average based on the census returns of 1730 and 1732.

d. Enumerated population of the Parish of Notre-Dame, less 900, the estimated minimum population of the nonurban portion of the parish.

e. The total population of the parish was 6,479. According to the seigneurial enumeration of 1781, there were 120 rural households. Our estimates of the urban population in 1781 and 1784 are maximum figures corresponding to a ratio of eight persons per house, a density that is already a little high for the period. John Hare found a ratio of 7.2 persons in Quebec in 1795 and, at the end of the 19th century, there were no more than eight persons per house in a working class section of Montreal. See "La population de la ville de Québec, 1795–1805", Histoire sociale/Social History, 7 (May 1974), 23–47, and H. B. Ames, The City Below the Hill (Toronto, 1972).

Sources: Livre des tenanciers de Montréal, 1697, Arch. St-Sulpice; recensements du Canada, AC,Gl, 460–1; 1871 Census of Canada, 1V; dénombrement seigneurial de 1731, RAPQ (1941–1942); perquisition de 1741, Transactions of the Royal Society of Canada (TRSC), 111, XV (1921); C. Perrault, Montréal en 1781; recensement de 1784 in W. Kingsford, The History of Canada, 7:204; 1831 Census, Journals of the Legislative Assembly of Lower Canada, 41, app. Oo.

ure given for the parish as a whole, leaving only the population of the town and suburbs.

The compilation of census data published in 1871, used as the basis for the 1931 monograph on the urban and rural composition of the Canadian population and for other more recent works, consistently overestimated the population of Montreal. For example, the town is credited with a population of 18,000 in 1790.[2] The figures presented here have been arrived at through the utilization of all available quantitative data, carefully cross-checked. They are, I believe, much closer to reality. Through the 18th century, after as well as before the Conquest, Montreal grew at a very sluggish pace. What follows is a brief analysis of the nature and implications of this slow development.[3]

URBAN LAND USE

In 1648 an area of 92 acres was reserved for urban occupation and shortly afterwards surrounded by a pallisade. The people who founded

[2]1871 Census of Canada, IV; 1931 Census of Canada, Monograph 6, "Rural and Urban Composition of the Canadian Population," by S. A. Cudmore and H. G. Caldwell.

[3]This article does not deal with other aspects of Montreal's history, such as institutions and political and social organizations, which are partly discussed in the following works: W. H. Atherton, Montreal 1535–1914 (Montréal, 1914); C. Bertrand, Histoire de Montréal

and lived in Montreal never called this area anything except *ville;* they felt from the beginning that they were creating a town. Even though the contemporary reality—some fields and a handful of inhabitants clustered around a warehouse—hardly fits any modern definition of the word, this article also uses the term *ville,* or town.

Until about 1665–70, Montreal was a *comptoir,* a centre for exchanges between people from two different civilizations, set in an expanding agricultural area. The operation of the fur trade involved the participation—certainly on very unequal terms, but participation all the same—of the entire population, which by the end of this period amounted to about 200 *habitants.*[4] The area designated for the town was also the site of the first agriculture, carried out on parcels of land ranging in size from a few hundred square feet to two and three acres. Afterward the fields began to overflow into the surrounding *côtes.*[5] Agricultural and commercial activities were at first closely related. Settlers who obtained land around the town normally lived within the pallisaded area, finding there both protection and easy profits. The latter were in turns applied, with varying degrees of enthusiasm, to clearing their land. At the same time, with the incentive offered by high agricultural prices, most of the fur traders and craftsmen employed indentured labourers to improve their own land.

Initially, the development of an urban concentration was a response to the requirements of defence. By its nature, the fur trade could operate from little more than a warehouse with a very small agricultural base. It would in fact have been to the advantage of the traders to disperse. Had it not been for the military threat constantly hanging over the colony, a more extensive network of trading posts would have been established very quickly. As it was, posts were established above the rapids, at Lachine, Châteauguay, on lake des Deux-Montagnes, as soon as the danger of Iroquois attacks receded.

Montreal's growth was stimulated by the disruption of this initial commercial structure. The recession in the European fur market reducing profit margins, the attempts on the part of Quebec merchants to combine the import trade with fur trading, a part of the business which was eluding them, were among the factors that launched the Canadiens in a century-long march toward the source of the furs.[6] The spread of trading posts within the settled area that had begun was thwarted when the Indians stopped bringing down their furs. It was at this time that the remarkable advantages of Montreal's location came into full play.[7] The

(Montréal, 1935-42); J. I. Cooper, *Montreal, A Brief History* (Montreal, 1969); R. Rumilly, *Histoire de Montréal* (Montréal, 1970), I–II; E. R. Adair, "The Evolution of Montreal under the French Regime," *CHAR* (1942); and others, among which the contributions of O. Maurault and E.-Z. Massicotte must be mentioned.

[4]In this early period the term *habitant* designated free individuals holding titles of property in the colony and thus did not include servants or soldiers. The census of 1666 enumerated 659 persons on the island of Montreal, of whom 141 were habitants, heads of households.

[5]The *côte* was the elementary unit of rural settlement. See R. C. Harris, *The Seigneural System in Early Canada: A Geographical Study* (Québec and Madison, Wis., 1967).

[6]H. A. Innis, *The Fur Trade in Canada: An Introduction to Canadian Economic History* (Toronto, 1956).

[7]Raoul Blanchard, *L'Ouest du Canada français. Montréal et sa région* (Montréal, 1953).

town was in effect reborn around a new predominant function: the transshipment of trade articles and furs between Quebec and the interior of the continent. It became the point where both furs and goods changed hands. The new function brought with it some spatial reorganization. The fields in the urban area were parcelled out to accommodate craftsmen and professionals of the trade. The rising land values encouraged many habitants to sell their urban plots and drove out many tenants and squatters. Being from now on excluded from commercial activities, settlers moved out of the town and scattered over the *côtes*.

This new specialization nonetheless produced only a limited degree of urban concentration. It was Montreal's other functions—religious, military, administrative, and as a service centre to the rural community—which sustained its growth. Even so, its population increase remained lower than that of the colony as a whole until the end of the 17th century. There was a period of illusory growth in the last decade, when the town temporarily became a place of refuge. Ruined or frightened by the Anglo-Iroquois raids, settlers from the island and from the seigneuries on the south shore sought safety in the urban enclosure, where they found ample space for the construction of temporary shelters. A list of properties drawn up at the end of this period shows that, despite its 152 houses, Montreal was still a very primitive settlement.

The town experienced its most vigorous period of development in the first quarter of the 18th century. At this time it attracted a substantial proportion of demobilized soldiers[8] and also a number of Canadiens. The latter, however, were not drawn from the rural areas, but were, for the most part, traders, craftsmen, and labourers from Quebec and Trois-Rivières.[9] These arrivals cannot be associated with any expansion of trade. On the contrary, the movement occurred in the midst of a crisis of overproduction and declining beaver prices, and during the very slow recovery that followed. The period did see, however, the beginning of a number of public projects, including the construction of a stone wall around the town. A further factor was the speculation that accompanied the currency crisis and gave rise to an unprecedented interest in real estate investment between 1710 and 1720.[10] The infusion of new blood was of particular benefit to the building trades, and at this point one begins to witness the appearance of specifically urban trades, such as wigmaking or gardening.

The first detailed picture of Montreal dates from 1731. The urban enclosure then held 379 houses, of which 56 percent were wooden and single-storied, similar in appearance to rural dwellings. The rest were of stone, and about one-quarter of all houses had two stories. Families with modest income usually lived in one room or two, including the workshop, unless the latter had been set up in a lean-to; only one room was heated

---

[8]The island of Montreal received more than 400 demobilized soldiers between 1697 and 1715. A most important inflow of immigrants, part of which benefits the urban area.

[9]Based on the marriage registers giving the husband's place of origin: Register of the Parish of Notre Dame.

[10]The crisis was catastrophic for the administration, but not for the merchants or the colony as a whole. Jean Hamelin draws a grim picture of it in *Economie et Société en Nouvelle-France* (Québec, 1960), pp. 37–46.

by the fireplace. At a higher income level, the house would be of stone, larger (about 50 by 30 feet), and a great deal more comfortable, with its two chimneys and two or three rooms per floor. Merchants' houses normally included a storage room on the first floor and the shop on the ground floor, while grain and furs were kept in the attic. Very rarely was a separate building used for the trading activities. Four or five rooms remained for the use of the family, which on the basis of 5.5 persons per family plus two servants makes an average of 1.5 person per room, about twice the space available to the common people.[11]

Montreal had five convents and five churches and chapels. Public buildings and private buildings of a commercial or industrial nature included two schools, a law court, a prison, barracks, a *canoterie*, a brewery, and seven warehouses. The walls with their gates and bastions were not yet completed by 1731. Two main thoroughfares, about 24 feet wide, ran parallel to the river, cut at right angles by a dozen narrower streets. This grid pattern was broken by short lanes at the water's edge and on the hill. The market place was bordered by the houses of the principal inhabitants. Here and there were large empty spaces, formed by convent properties and by those belonging to the parish or to the Crown. Their presence, however, did not retard possible housing construction, as is evidenced by the existence of 166 gardens in the town. The unpaved streets were dirty or muddy; and, because the town was small and the surrounding roads rarely passable, the bourgeois did not own carriages and stables were rare. Behind most houses was a shed sheltering a few domestic animals, particularly pigs.[12] To the west of the Récollets' gate stood the suburb of Saint-Joseph, which included 21 houses, two warehouses, and the buildings of the Hôpital Général.

Another enumeration made ten years later gives us an idea of the slow pace of the town's development. Even allowing for a fire that destroyed 46 buildings,[13] it is still surprising to find only 387 houses inside the walls, meaning an average of 5.4 new buildings erected every year in the decade 1731–41. The town seems to have been frozen in its tracks. The three suburbs, to the west, north, and east, had a total of 70 houses. Of the 591 heads of households in the town and its suburbs, some 70 percent owned their dwellings. The large number of rental agreements in the notarial archives added to the presence of 176 tenant households on this 1741 enumeration suggests at first sight some degree of concentration of property. This would be an indicator of urban development, but closer examination reveals the absence of such concentration. Twenty-eight individuals or corporate bodies owned two houses,[14] while 33 owners

----

[11]In the French towns of this period the average ratio appears to have been one room per family of 4.5 people: F. Braudel and E. Labrousse, *Histoire économique et sociale de la France, 1660–1789* (Paris, 1970), p. 49.

[12]See the police ordinances concerning uncleanliness, pigs running at large, or fire hazards in the judiciary records of Montreal. These are characteristics common to many 18th-century towns.

[13]The fire of 1734, the second in the town's history. That of 1721 had destroyed about 150 houses, which were quickly rebuilt: M. Mondoux, *L'Hôtel-Dieu premier hôpital de Montréal . . .* (Montréal, 1942), pp. 271–72 and 289.

[14]The concentration of property was perhaps slightly higher than it appears, as people sometimes built small houses on rented lots which were easily dismantled when their leases were not renewed.

shared their house with tenants. In all, 66 houses harboured two families or more. The population density within the walls remained at the low figure of 38.8 people per acre. The list of trades, although very incomplete, does show a little island of merchants and other notables clustered in the centre of the town. Moving outwards, we find shopkeepers and officers living next door to craftsmen and unidentified individuals, presumably of very modest status. Saint-Jacques Street was the only one given over principally to craft workers.[15] In short, the impression left by this enumeration is one of rather drab and uniform standard of living.

TABLE 2
Distribution of Houses in the Town
and the Suburbs

Years	Town	Suburbs	Total
1731	379	21	400
1741	387	70	457
1781	307	352	659

The seigneurial enumeration of 1781 provides an interesting case of urban reorganization. In 1765, the town had been again partially destroyed by fire and it emerged substantially changed after the reconstruction that followed. By 1781, there were only 307 houses inside the walls, about 20 percent less than in 1741. But the houses were now larger, with two and three stories and almost all built of stone. Most of the yards boasted masonry outbuildings, often stables, and those raised storage rooms called *voûtes en plafonds* by the enumerator. The lots, larger than before, still included gardens and were generally enclosed by a wall. Montreal no longer looked like a large village, with rich and poor living side by side. It had been transformed to serve as a business and residential centre for the bourgeoisie.[16] The small craftsmen and the labourers had been pushed outside the walls. To some extent this change was facilitated by the fire, but there were other factors in play: newfound prosperity, rising property values, increasing rents, more unequal income distribution, and so on. More research is needed to reconstitute the mechanism behind this premature segregation.[17] While deconcentration is a normal stage in the process of urbanization, it clearly took place in Montreal in the absence of any demographic pressure, as is evident from the slow development of the suburbs.

---

[15]On all our lists the inhabitants are very poorly identified, sometimes solely by surname. The work of E.-Z. Massicotte on the enumeration of 1741 was of great assistance on this question: TRSC, III, XV (1921), pp. 1-61.

[16]There were only 45 proprietors of British or American origin. The remainder, about 82 percent, were Canadiens, the majority of them belonging to families living in the town for two or three generations.

[17]In Boston, a town which developed very rapidly, the poor already had been resettled on the outskirts in 1774: S. B. Warner, "A Scaffolding for Urban History," in A. M. Wakestein, ed., The Urbanization of America, An Historical Anthology (Boston, 1970), p. 60. On these same problems, at a more advanced stage of urban growth, see L. F. Schnore and P. R. Knight, "Residence and Social Structure, Boston in the Ante Bellum Period," in S. Thernstrom and R. Sennett, eds., Nineteenth-Century Cities, Essays in the New Urban History (New Haven, 1969), pp. 247-56.

The census returns of 1831 have been used as a terminal point in the table of population estimates, but the major transformations that occurred in Lower Canada in the first quarter of the 19th century are beyond the scope of this article.[18] The respective influence of economic progress and of the massive immigration that began after 1815 upon this accelerated urban growth remains to be determined.

THE DEMOGRAPHIC PATTERN

Much of the data necessary to relate the real increase of the population of Montreal to its vital statistics and to the demographic evolution of the whole colony is still lacking. It might be useful, however, to point to some of the methodological difficulties involved in finding and using such data. In 1731, almost a quarter of the population included in the parish of Notre-Dame was rural, making it very difficult to deal separately with the demographic behaviour in the urban area. Setting this problem aside, it would still be pointless to try to calculate crude birth and death rates on the basis of such a small population, subject as it was to the effects of migratory phenomena and resultant short-term variations in the age distribution. Satisfactory results could be obtained only by reconstituting families over a long time. Meanwhile, simple counts in the parish registers might suggest general trends. Counts of this kind for the five parishes on the island of Montreal, in the period prior to 1715, seem to indicate that there was yet no fundamental differences between the urban and the rural demographic patterns. Seasonal variations of marriages and births, for example, were the same, and so was the crude ratio established between these marriages and births.[19] If we exclude soldiers—who were, in any case, never enumerated with the civilian population—epidemics seem to have been no more deadly in the urban parish. These observations are possibly valid for the 18th century as well, because there was little change during this period in the general conditions, such as population density and way of life.

It might be thus possible to use our knowledge of the colonial demographic data to grasp the pattern of population growth in the urban area, but this general data is far from complete. There are no immigration statistics for New France. The estimate of net immigration—about 10,000 people spread unevenly over the period 1608–1760—is based on the difference between real increase, as taken from the census returns, and the natural increase, as recorded in the parish registers. The whole problem of emigration remains obscure. We do not know how many Canadiens went to the west, to Louisiana, nor how many newcomers left the colony after a short stay. Departures for France were fairly common among the officers and the merchants and may have been even more so

---

[18]See Fernand Ouellet, *Histoire économique et sociale du Québec, 1760–1850* (Montréal, 1966), and the numerous articles by Jean-Pierre Wallot and Gilles Paquet on the period 1790–1815.

[19]This ratio is about five to one in both Notre-Dame and the rural parishes. The rhythm of life, as it appears from the seasonal variations, was strongly conditioned by nature, even in the town.

among the common immigrants. For example, depending on the period and the method of recruitment, between 25 and 50 percent of the indentured labourers who came to Montreal in the 17th century returned to France.[20] This two-way migration was certainly more noticeable in the towns than in the rural areas.

Another problem concerns the quality of the statistics from the parish registers. Thanks to the work of Jacques Henripin, we know the nuptiality and fertility rates of the colonial population; but, as yet, we are very uncertain as to the crude mortality rate.[21] The under-registration of burials in the early period has already been well documented by Hubert Charbonneau and his colleagues,[22] and Montreal, apparently, is no exception. For example, the infant mortality rates derived from Montreal's registered burials vary between 10 and 18 percent at the end of the 17th century, when one would expect them to be closer to the 24.6 percent that Henripin arrived at through a careful analysis.[23] It follows that the crude mortality rate before 1740, supposedly under 30 percent, becomes highly suspect. Consequently, an annual rate of natural increase as high as 3 percent, which supposedly prevailed throughout the 18th century, also is very questionable.[24]

What is certain is that, except for a short period, Montreal's rate of growth was much lower than the rest of the colony. It is equally certain that an urban annual rate of real increase of 0.8 to 1.0 percent remained well short of the town's natural increase, even if we adjust the latter to allow for a higher urban mortality and a slightly lower birth rate. Had no immigrants arrived in the town after 1731—which is certainly not the case[25]—it is an inescapable fact that Montreal was undergoing a more or less continuous *loss* of population. While there are still few demographic studies on the French towns of the *ancien Régime,* it seems to be generally accepted that their growth was normally slower than that of the relatively prosperous rural communities.[26] Their lower birth rates com-

---

[20]This is still a very positive balance if we compare it, for example, to Maryland, where only 7 percent of the indentured labourers who came between 1670 and 1689 remained in the colony: A. E. Smith, *Colonists in Bondage,* pp. 298–99.

[21]Jacques Henripin, *La population canadienne au début du XVIIIe siècle, Nuptialité, fécondité, mortalité infantile* (Paris, 1954).

[22]H. Charbonneau, J. Légaré, and Y. Lavoie, "Recensements et registres paroissiaux du Canada durant la période 1665–1668: étude critique", 25, 1 *Population,* (January-February 1970), 97–124.

[23]Henripin, *La population canadienne . . . ,* pp. 103–7.

[24]J. Henripin, *Tendances et facteurs de la fécondité au Canada* (Ottawa, 1968), pp. 5–8. The crude mortality rate per decade would vary from 24 to 25 per thousand between 1700 and 1740, and from 32 to 34 per thousand between 1740 and 1790. It did not fall below 27 per thousand until after 1840. But the proportion of young children—the most vulnerable group—was as high in 1700 as in 1800. It is impossible to explain this supposed increase in mortality. It is easier to assume that the burials were more faithfully registered as the century progressed.

[25]There was an important movement of immigrants into the colony between 1740 and 1760: P. E. Renaud, *Les origines économiques du Canada, L'oeuvre de la France* (Paris, 1928).

[26]This was generally the case for small and medium sized towns but not in the large ports, such as Nantes, Bordeaux, and Marseille: P. Goubert, "Révolution démographique au XVIIIe siécle," in F. Braudel and E. Labrousse, *Histoire économique et sociale,* 72–74.

bined with higher mortality rates produced chronic population deficits, which were not always completely offset by an inflow from the countryside. Montreal's case, however, was quite different, for it certainly showed a surplus of baptisms over burials; but the town was continuously losing part of that surplus. It seems thus unlikely that Montreal could have exerted any pull on the rural settlements.

THE URBAN FUNCTIONS

Slow urban growth can be linked to the colony's economic situation and specifically to the role of the town in this economy. Montreal performed a number of functions, and to give any precise idea of the relative importance of each one would require complete information on the distribution of occupations. My sources unfortunately do not permit that sort of precision. However, on the basis of a general familiarity with this society, based on such relevant material as notarial and judicial records and various tax rolls, I can set out a rough inventory of urban activities around 1731.

The fur trade had been the main incentive behind the creation of Montreal; but once the basic commercial organization had been established, the trade ceased to be a factor of urban growth. After 1731, the pace of development slowed, while the volume of fur exports continued to increase. Fur warehousing and trading expeditions employed relatively little labour. The trade maintained about 30 merchants, while another 20 gained a precarious livelihood from the local market and irregular fur trading ventures. The *voyageurs* were the successors of the more successful *coureurs de bois*. Formerly of rural origin, they gradually attached themselves to the merchants and moved up the social ladder, establishing their families in the town. The group tended to close ranks; the numbers involved did not increase and new members were recruited from within the group or from elements above it. There were perhaps 70 families of *voyageurs* in Montreal in 1731 and by that time a number of them were beginning to move out permanently toward Detroit, Michilimackinac, and other western posts. Each year the merchants and *voyageurs* hired between 250 and 300 of the colony's young men for the seasonal expeditions into the interior. Town-dwellers were proportionally better represented among these *engagés*," but the supply of labourers considerably exceeded the demand. Besides, not every man had the strength to paddle to Lake Superior and to portage with heavy packs. Probably no more than a third of the youth in the town succeeded in getting such jobs. It was this group that displayed the strongest tendency to emigrate. Another 50 individuals—innkeepers, tavern-keepers, teamsters, bakers, and butchers—derived an important part of their clientele from the fur trade. The latter also supported, in a very meagre fashion, a large number of seamstresses, who worked on the putting-out system, making clothes to be used as trade articles. But there again, the merchants' orders were inadequate to support the available feminine labour. In all, about one-third of the work force gained an unequal subsistence from the staple trade.

There were no manufactures in Montreal. Few workshops employed more than two or three apprentices, even if we include the sawmills and tanneries operating at the outskirts of town. About 50 craftsmen produced for the local market, urban, and rural, and there were also gunsmiths, blacksmiths, coopers, and joiners who derived a portion of their income from the fur trade. Complete separation of merchant capital from craft production was the rule; the worker owned his tools and raw material and sold the finished article directly to consumers. Bonds of dependence between producers and merchants occasionally arose from the indebtedness of the former, but the merchants never made use of their advantage to transform production and to establish a permanent capital-labour relationship.[27] During this period, the urban market was scarcely growing and, at the same time, the town craftsmen's rural clientele tended to diminish as elementary rural centers sprang up here and there in the backcountry. Once a son had taken over the shop from his father, chances were that his brothers had to fall back on non-skilled trades for a living.[28]

The building trades employed about half of the town's skilled labour as well as a number of navvies. In 1731, however, half of the houses were simple frame structures, which the owners built themselves, and the pace of construction of more elaborate dwellings was slow. Construction of churches and convents, along with public works projects,[29] created better job opportunities, but even these works were interrupted for at least five months of the year. There was thus a situation of chronic unemployment in Montreal, to which the new generations of townsmen, and those immigrants who had momentarily been drawn to the town, responded by emigrating or settling on farms.

Religious, military, administrative, and domestic services probably employed some two-fifths of the work force. Montreal had few administrative jobs to offer; but here, as in all the French towns of the *ancien Régime*, there was a steady expansion in the personnel of religious orders.[30] Convent life in Montreal was a specifically feminine phenomenon that absorbed women of the upper class, an obvious consequence of the emigration of their male counterparts. The missionary impulse had also been a factor of colonial urban foundation in the 17th century. It brought with it important capital inflow,[31] and the sort of determination and per-

[27]These observations are based on an analysis of the accounts and inventories of Montreal merchants at the beginning of the century. On this question see Maurice Dobb, *Studies in the Development of Capitalism* (New York, 1947).

[28]The shortage of Canadian tradesmen was a consequence and not a cause of economic stagnation. Similarly, Montreal long had to go to Quebec to find skilled workers for its large construction projects, precisely because the demand was too irregular to maintain them permanently in the town. See Pierre Harvey, "Stagnation économique en Nouvelle-France", *l'Actualité économique*, 37: 537–48; also J. Mathieu, *La construction navale royale à Québec, 1739–1759* (Québec, 1971).

[29]Tradesmen were needed to direct the construction projects but in the case of churches or fortifications, *corvées* or statute labour supplied much of the unskilled labour needed.

[30]About 100 nuns and 30 to 40 clerics.

[31]French capital and a part of the colonial budget that these pious founders managed to

severence that religious activity involves. The Church was a source of stability during the colony's difficult early years. As time progressed, however, the religious personnel tended to increase more rapidly than did the services it provided.[32]

Montreal was a garrison town. The size of the military population varied according to the period; in 1731 there may have been 200 soldiers quartered in barracks or billeted on the townsfolk.[33] The local consumer market benefitted, no doubt, from their presence, but these soldiers also competed with civilians for part-time employment. Working at lower wages than the latter, they upset the local job market from the end of the 17th century.[34] While the enlisted men were recruited in France, by the 18th century the majority of their officers were Canadiens. About 40 officers had their homes in Montreal, including the Government's general staff and officers who left their families in the town while they served in remote outposts. A majority of them were closely associated with the fur trade and could legitimately be included among the trade's personnel.

Domestic service was an important outlet for a town labour force in pre-industrial times. So it was in Montreal—at least if the situation in 1731 is somewhat similar to that presented by the census of 1784. By this time, servants (presumably including apprentices) formed about one-fifth of the total urban population. The group included 142 slaves, 129 children under 15 years of age, and 913 adults, with males and females about equally represented.[35] These figures illustrate what was by then a familiar situation: under-employment. For, in a period when the practice of putting children into domestic service was everywhere customary, few Montreal children seem to have been parted from their families.[36] Apparently, the bourgeois usually employed adults because the latter were willing to work for very modest wages. The Indian slaves who appeared at the beginning of the 18th century were also inexpensive, but their life

---

draw in Montreal: L. Gérin, *Aux sources de notre histoire; les conditions économiques et sociales de la colonisation en Nouvelle-France* (Montréal, 1946), pp. 162-91.

[32]There is a contrast between the large number of nuns and regulars and the difficulty in finding priests for the rural parishes.

[33]The soldiers, recruited in France, were not included in the census and therefore do not appear in our estimates. In peacetime they could obtain a discharge to settle in the colony. Many preferred to complete their service and return to France: Mémoires de R. d'Auteuil, Archives des Colonies, C11A:34; E. Salone, *La Colonisation de la Nouvelle-France. Etude sur les origines de la nation canadienne-française*, (reprint, 1969), pp. 339-42.

[34]This was tolerated by the administration and encouraged by the captains who kept their soldiers' pay whenever the latter found employment. I would agree with W. J. Eccles that the soldiers "provided a sorely needed pool of labour" in the early days of the colony, when settlers were few and as yet had no grown children for work on the farms or in the shops. See Eccles, "The Social, Economic and Political Significance of the Military Establishment in New France," *CHR* (March 1971), 5-6. But this was no longer valid at a later period, when soldiers competed with an abundant reserve of unskilled labourers.

[35]W. Kingsford, *op. cit.*, 7:204. These figures must be related to the total population of the parish: 6,474 persons.

[36]In 1689, in the American colonial town of Bristol one child in five was in domestic service. In Montreal in 1784, the figure was only one in 14. See John Demos, *A Little Commonwealth, Family Life in Plymouth Colony* (New York, 1970), pp. 69-74.

expectancy was so short that there was little advantage in substituting them for the abundant local manpower.[37] Such was the distribution of occupations in Montreal for at least a century. The production sector stood in last place.

It is always difficult to determine the nature of the relations between town and countryside, and only a few aspects of the question are dealt with here. Montreal was not in the centre of an agricultural region: it stood on the fringe of the settled seigneurial area, still to a large extent the hinterland of Quebec. Early in the 18th century Canada began to export wheat, but the grain moved directly to port of embarkation without passing through Montreal, so that this tentative orientation to external markets had no effect on the town's development. Only with the opening of lands further upstream, with the settlement of Upper Canada, would Montreal become a transfer point for agricultural products. Until then it maintained a rather tenuous relation with its narrow farm belt, which met the small urban demand and the needs of the western trade. Because external demand had long been non-existent and remained weak and capricious, because of the adverse evolution of the terms of trade resulting from this whole context,[38] the countryside tended to shun unfavourable exchanges, to rely heavily upon itself. But if the peasants rarely prospered, neither did they starve, so that this town did not serve as an asylum for the rural poor. It would be pointless to speculate on the economic diversification prompted by the formation of a large labour pool that might have resulted had a less generous policy been followed towards the settlers.[39] Any increase of their overall burden could only further contract the domestic market. With external circumstances and demographic conditions remaining constant, it is hard to visualize any economic advantages in a heavier taxation of rural production. It could only have spread destitution, without stimulating enterprise.

Merchant capital in New France had no incentive to transform mortgages into rural ownership and to accumulate rents. Town people did not normally invest in the agriculture beyond the limit of one farm, and that only for family needs, not as a means of drawing income. The pattern emerging from these transfers of capital and labour between town and countryside seems, on balance, to run counter to the traditional model.[40] Montreal, for instance, contributed to the growth of the rural population, for, even if the excess urban workers could not easily transform themselves into peasants and generally opt for emigration, one

---

[37]See Marcel Trudel, L'esclavage au Canada français. Histoire et conditions de l'esclavage (Québec, 1960).

[38]Based on the movement of the prices of grain and imported goods from 1650 to 1730. The high agricultural prices at the beginning of the period gave way to a long-term depreciation.

[39]L. R. MacDonald, "France and New France: The Internal Contradictions," CHR (June 1971), 121-43. The Marxist model of the transition from merchant to industrial capitalism is not pertinent in the case of an 18th-century colonial outpost such as New France. It would be more suitable to use another Marxist concept, that of a primitive accumulation through the expansion of far away markets and regional disequilibrium.

[40]G. Friedmann, Villes et Campagnes (Paris, 1953); M. Vénard, Bourgeois et paysans au XVIIe siècle. Recherches sur le rôle des bourgeois parisiens dans la vie agricole au sud de Paris (Paris, 1957), and other studies.

must consider all the town's girls who married discharged soldiers and moved to the land.[41] Furthermore, Montreal did not provide part-time employment for the rural population, if one excepts the hiring for the western trade, an activity incompatible with farming. Making poor use of the ties resulting from the settlers initial indebtedness, Montreal merchants had little interest in agriculture. The economic dichotomy is certainly not absolute; interactions did take place, but they were not sufficiently important either to dislocate or to consolidate the rural society.

My conclusions are not too far removed from the findings of those who, having reflected upon the weakness of New France, stressed the importance of adverse geographic and demographic conditions, two realities that persisted after 1760. The nature of the initial staple was only a secondary element.[42] The distribution of commercial profits and the social dispersion of capital were derivative from the general historical context and do not explain the failure to diversify the economy. The specific conditions of the development may have, in the long run, forged certain patterns of behaviour, but it goes without saying that psychological factors are not an independent variable.

The accumulation of capital that took place in Montreal was only remotely connected with the regional system of production; this accounts for the continued rigidity of the town's economy.[43] Later on, external factors were to lead Montreal merchants into new speculative ventures. Although also based on monopoly and privilege, these ventures succeeded in establishing closer ties between the distribution centre and its territorial base, which was by then enlarged and more populous. The pace of capital formation was hastened. But another century was already well underway before profits from such trade had dwindled sufficiently to compel the merchants to invest in production.[44] Then Montreal entered another age.

---

[41] Of 716 marriages contracted between 1680 and 1715 in the parish of Notre Dame, 95 percent of the brides and 47 percent of the grooms were Canadian by birth.

[42] M. H. Watkins, "A Staple Theory of Economic Growth," in W. T. Easterbrook and Watkins, eds., Approaches to Canadian Economic History, pp. 49–74; P. Harvey, art. cit.

[43] A point of clarification not in the original article might be relevant here. The lack of integration between the mercantile and the productive sectors described above is not unusual in a precapitalist context, especially in a colony that derives its profits from commodities produced by the Indians rather than by the white colonists. But one should keep in mind that such disarticulation is a local economic phenomenon only, observable with respect to the relationship—or lack of relationship—between the mercantile and productive sectors within the colony itself. On an imperial scale, the disarticulation vanishes. The settlements played crucially important strategic and military roles in furthering imperial objectives. There is no real dualism, but a complex all-integrating pattern of development.

[44] For an excellent discussion and illustration of these problems, see Pierre Vilar, La Catalogue dans l'Espagne moderne. Recherches sur les fondements économiques des structures nationales (Paris, 1962).

11

THE EXPULSION OF THE ACADIANS*

C. Bruce Fergusson

Like all national histories, that of Canada has its share of myths and legends, distortions over time of historical fact, usually by romanticism and sentimentality. One of the supreme bases for legend is tragedy, and the more disastrous the better. In the hands of the legend-makers, emphasis is placed on human suffering and on the victimization of those who undergo it. In a sense, the legend itself becomes a part of history, since it becomes a "fact" for those who accept it uncritically. But, while historians can and should devote a good deal of attention to the factors which underlie the perpetuation of national myths and symbols, this should not blind them to the fact that legend remains a distortion of historical reality. The British expulsion of the French Acadians from Nova Scotia in 1755 is certainly one of the most durable and tragic of Canadian legends. The high priest of the Acadian myth was the American poet Henry Wadsworth Longfellow in his epic poem, *Evangeline*, but Longfellow did not create the legend and it has not died even today, when his poem remains unread. Nevertheless, if historians are to understand the reality of the Acadian tragedy, they must get behind the sentimentality. The Acadian expulsion was the largest forcible migration of Europeans carried out in North America in its early history. It was also the first confrontation by the British with the problems involved in ruling the French population in North America. For these reasons, the expulsion is an important historical matter in its own right, quite apart from the aura of pathos which has surrounded the event in subsequent years. Dr. C. Bruce Fergusson in the following article attempts to cut through fiction and romance to outline the issues as they existed for the contemporary participants. He does not deny the tragedy, but he seeks a different con-

---

Dalhousie Review, 35 (1955), 127–35.

text from that of the personal suffering of those affected. What context does he offer as an alternative? What explanations does he give for the British decision to move the Acadians? If one must apportion blame, who was "responsible" for the expulsion? What alternatives were available to the British government? What lessons could the British have learned from their problems with the Acadians? And finally, what was the real tragedy of the expulsion of the Acadians?

SUGGESTIONS FOR FURTHER READING

J. B. Brebner, *New England's Outpost: Acadia before the Conquest of Canada* (New York: Columbia University Press, 1927).

Andrew H. Clark, *Acadia: The Geography of Early Nova Scotia to 1760* (Madison: University of Wisconsin Press, 1968).

Naomi Griffiths, *The Acadians: Creation of a People* (Toronto: McGraw-Hill Ryerson, 1973).

J.M.B.

S ome observers have said that Germany's annexation of Alsace-Lorraine was worse than a crime—it was a blunder; others have seemed to say that the expulsion of the Acadians was not a blunder but rather a crime. However that may be, history caught up with the Acadians in 1755, when six thousand or more of them were uprooted from their beloved lands in Nova Scotia, placed on board ships and deported to British colonies to the south. Ninety-two years later, moreover, in a blend of fact and fancy, Longfellow caught them up in the unforgettable lines of the poem *Evangeline*. Since that time, it seems, the warp of fact and the woof of imagination have been so interwoven by poetic licence in a memorable mosaic of sentimentality and suffering, that it is difficult to separate fact from fancy and to get at the sober truth of the matter. Yet even the most aloof observer must feel sympathy for any group of people who experience the testing of exile from their accustomed place, no matter whose the responsibility for the exile, and no matter whether that forced expatriation was deserved or undeserved. That being the case, the heart goes out to the Acadians of 1755, without any need for the head to appreciate anything of the circumstances, or for any question to be asked of the why or the wherefore. But the two hundredth anniversary of that event should provide the occasion for real attempts to understand what actually happened in 1755, and why and how it took place.

Was the expulsion of the Acadians a misfortune or was it a disaster? Were they the undeserved victims of misfortune, or did they reap disaster from their own folly? These are the salient questions which should be borne in mind whenever consideration is given to the fate of the Acadians in the year 1755. Their story, it is clear, is an admirable illustration of the relative strength of the ties that bind, and of the forces that influence, a people, as well as a supreme example of how a dramatic and colourful episode in the history of any people may be readily translated into the misty realm of romance, so that careful attention is needed for an adequate realization and a proper understanding. The story of the Acadians may be regarded as a tale that is told. But its versions differ, some of them are marred or distorted by emotion or bias, by artificial colouring or by unfounded judgments, and new appraisals are sometimes needed.

Centre or core of the Acadian problem was the oath of allegiance. One important factor was the fact that between the final capture of Port Royal by the British in 1710 and the fateful year 1755 most of the Acadians were unwilling to take the unconditional oath of allegiance. They refused to take the unqualified oath, insisted that they should not be required to take up arms in the event of war, and advanced the rather fantastic claim that they should be regarded as "French Neutrals."

Clearly the Acadian demand was an extraordinary one. It was the accepted conception then as now that the obligations incumbent upon those living within the bounds of the authority of a state included the taking of the oath of allegiance to that state. That was the case when New Sweden was obliged to submit to the New Netherlands in 1655, with those Swedes who desired to remain on the Delaware being expected to give an oath of unqualified allegiance to the new authority. That was also the case when the New Netherlands was obliged to submit to the English in 1664, and the Dutch about the Hudson and elsewhere were expected to do the same, if they remained beyond the period of a year. It was likewise the case, so far as France was concerned, when Frontenac received instructions respecting the expedition against New York, in the event of its capture, in 1689; and when the Duke d'Anville received instructions relating to his formidable but ill-fated expedition of 1746. Furthermore, this rule of broad international application was applied not only to the French in Canada after 1763, but also to those of Louisiana after 1803 when that territory became part of the United States, and to the Mexicans of northern Mexico after its cession to the United States in 1847.

Until the war was officially brought to a close by the Treaty of Utrecht in 1713 the situation was rather unsettled, with the articles of capitulation agreed upon at the surrender of Port Royal applying only to those within three miles of the fort and with the other Acadians anxious and uncertain about what the future held in store for them. One of the articles of capitulation provided that the inhabitants within the *banlieue*, an area having a radius of a cannon shot or three miles from the fort, should remain upon their estates, with their corn, cattle and furniture, for two years, if they were not desirous of leaving before the expiration of that time, they taking the oaths of allegiance to Her Britannic Majesty. In accordance with the terms of this article, the inhabitants within the *banlieue*—57 heads of families—did take such oaths by the end of the third week of January 1711, and that, in itself, seemed to portend auspiciously. But the war had not yet ended, French agents were active and the Acadians outside the *banlieue*, not being included in the articles of capitulation, were in a state of uneasiness and uncertainty. These Acadians applied to the British Governor for protection and offered to take the oath of allegiance. But the Governor who told them that by the arbitrament of war they had become prisoners, and who had collected a tribute from them, could give them no terms until Her Majesty's more particular orders were received. As a result of uncertainty over their situation the Acadians outside the *banlieue* became uneasy, tried to keep the Indians hostile to the English and attempted to stir up the Acadians within the *banlieue* who had already taken the oath of allegiance. Further apprehension was also caused by the hostile designs of the Indians and the French from Canada, as well as by the influence of the French missionary priests. That this apprehension was justified is clear from the fact that a party of 65 Englishmen which was sent in two flat boats and a whaleboat in June 1711 for the purpose of encouraging friendly Acadians in supplying wood and timber for the garrison was ambushed by a war party of French and Indians and all but one of them were killed or captured. Soon even those Acadians within the *banlieue* who had taken the oath of allegiance joined their compatriots in blockading the fort at Annapolis Royal, and the English were not only threatened with assault but with being one and all put to the sword.

The Treaty of Utrecht brought the war to an end. By it such of the Acadians as might choose to leave Acadia or Nova Scotia were free to do so within the space of a year,[1] taking with them their personal effects; while a letter of Queen Anne permitted such emigrants to sell their lands and houses. Those who remained in Nova Scotia were guaranteed freedom of worship under certain conditions. These were that they should accept the sovereignty of the British Crown, and that they and their pastors should keep within the limits of British law.

Now two roads lay before the Acadians, and it was a momentous question for themselves and for the local British authorities which one of them they would choose: whether they would remove themselves to French territory within the year stipulated in the Treaty of Utrecht, or remain in Nova Scotia and become British subjects. The one course meant their continuance as French nationals but their abandonment of their lands in Nova Scotia; the other meant the retention of their lands, the taking the oath of allegiance to the British monarch, and the relinquishment of their French citizenship. Neither of these alternatives was their choice. Instead they tried for many years to combine what they wished of the two alternatives and eventually found themselves in an untenable position.

The best time to have settled the question of the oath was immediately after the Treaty of Utrecht. Then the Acadians numbered fewer than two thousand and, if the interests of security, as well as international propriety, demanded that they take the oath or leave Nova Scotia and they persisted in refusing to do the one or the other, their deportation then

---

[1]There have been different views as to the beginning and the end of the "year" of this Treaty, and some have held the untenable one that it was still in effect at the time of the founding of Halifax.

would neither have been as formidable nor regarded with so much disfavour as 42 years later when they had increased to five or six times that
number. The reason why the question was not then settled was that the
Acadians themselves were loath to leave their fertile meadow-lands in
Nova Scotia, whence they drew subsistence by means of cattle raising
and farming, for uncleared and unknown or less fertile lands elsewhere,
where much hard work would be needed, and the British authorities in
Nova Scotia had neither the forces nor the resources to press the question to an issue. Other factors also supported the tendency to let matters
drift; including the anxiety of the French authorities to maintain good
relations with the British at a time when they were involved in difficulties with Spain.

Time and again the Acadians were given the opportunity to take the
oath of allegiance. But the French authorities, who found that the Acadians were in the main reluctant to remove to Cape Breton Island, soon
saw and seized advantages in the situation and employed French agents
and French missionaries for the purpose of keeping the Acadians faithful
to King Louis. This was indeed an anomalous state of affairs: the "year"
of the Treaty of Utrecht soon passed; most of the Acadians remained in
Nova Scotia; French missionaries, who were French agents as well as
Roman Catholic priests, strove to keep the Acadians attached to both
their religion and the French interest, and, on occasion, openly avowed
that their object was to keep the Acadians faithful to the French
monarch; none of these missionaries was ever molested by the British
authorities, except when detected in practices alien to his proper functions and injurious to the government; freedom of worship continued to
be accorded to the Acadians, notwithstanding the fact that most of them
persisted in refusing to take the oath of allegiance, the condition on
which they had acquired that privilege; and the British government, in
spite of the concern of the British authorities in Nova Scotia, did nothing
effective either to have the French missionaries in that colony give a
pledge that they would do nothing contrary to the interests of Great Britain or to have them replaced by other priests to be named by the Pope at
the request of the British government.

The chief reasons for this anomalous state of affairs were the feeble-
ness of British authority in Nova Scotia, the neglect and the apathy of the
British ministers and the fact that the Acadians leaned so heavily on
their French spiritual and temporal advisers. For a while, it is true, the
imperium in imperio which existed was such that the inner power
seemed to wax and strengthen every day while the outer relatively pined
and dwindled. But the time was to come when the British ministers
would waken from their lethargy, bestir themselves and, warned by the
signs of the times, send troops and settlers into the Province at the 11th
hour. Then it was that the Acadians were to find how deplorable their
position really was. Perhaps the only thing that could have averted the
danger of Acadian hostilities or revolt and have made unnecessary the
harsh measures to which such conduct afterwards gave rise was for
the British ministry to have sent out a force sufficient both to protect the

inhabitants against French terrorism and to leave no doubt that the King of England was master of Nova Scotia in fact as well as in name. But such did not take place until after long delay and until the problem had attained greater proportions. In the meantime, although those Acadians who remained in Nova Scotia had been transferred by France to the British Crown by the Treaty of Utrecht, French officers on occasion denounced them as rebels and threatened them with death if they did not fight at their bidding against Great Britain, and British officers threatened them with expulsion if they did not remain loyal to King George. These were the horns of the dilemma for the Acadians; and while for a time they avoided both they were ultimately confronted with the necessity for a decision they had tried to avoid.

French policy after 1713 reveals that France was unwilling to reconcile herself to the loss of Acadia, although it had with its ancient limits been ceded to Great Britain by the Treaty of Utrecht. Nor was France to neglect Nova Scotia or Acadia, even if for years Great Britain was to do so. On Isle Royale the French not only built up a mighty base at Louisbourg, as the watchdog and protector of the Gulf and the approaches to Quebec, and as the base and the guardian for the fishery, but also established there a Governor who was charged with the management of Acadian affairs, and who had zealous and efficient agents among the Acadians in the missionary priests, who were sent into Nova Scotia by the Bishop of Quebec, or in a few cases by their immediate ecclesiastical superiors in Isle Royale, and whose services in keeping the Acadians in the French interest were recognized and acknowledged by French political leaders and officials. At first the French authorities endeavoured to induce the Acadians to migrate to Isle Royale, where the growing power of the fortress at Louisbourg was a symbol that France was preparing to contest the supremacy of the continent with Great Britain, and sent envoys into Nova Scotia, with the permission of the local British officials, to visit the Acadian settlements and to tell the Acadians what inducements they were prepared to give them to remove. A few of the Acadians did go to Isle Royale, and nearly all of them in the emotion of the moment signed declarations of their willingness to migrate to French territory, but it was soon seen that this mood quickly changed and that the Acadians in the main had no inclination to leave their homes. At the same time the British authorities, realizing the value of settlers in Nova Scotia, hopeful of having the Acadians become loyal British subjects, and having no desire to see them migrate to Isle Royale where they would greatly add to the numbers and the strength of a potential enemy near at hand, were almost as anxious to keep the Acadians in Nova Scotia as they were 40 years later to get them out of it. Soon, moreover, the French authorities realized that the Acadians were of greater benefit to France by remaining in Nova Scotia, whence they could furnish Isle Royale with much-needed supplies, where religion and patriotism might be combined or confused in keeping them in the French interest, and where in time of war they might be a source of strength for French invaders aiming at the recapture of old Acadia or a fifth column which would be a decisive factor in any test of strength. If the Acadians had really wished to emigrate, the British Governor could have done little to stop them for his authority hardly extended beyond gunshot of his fort at Annapolis Royal and all the Acadians except those of Annapolis and its immediate neighbourhood were free to go or stay at will.

While most of the Acadians maintained a careful neutrality in times of trouble, and Mascarene himself declared that their refusal to fight for the French besiegers was one reason for the success of his defence of Annapolis on one occasion, French designs involved the Acadians and some of them were implicated in hostile acts against the British in Nova Scotia. During the 1720s French authorities not only strove to foment trouble between the Indians and the English but they joined the Indians in a raid on Canso. On the outbreak of the War of the Austrian Succession, the French from Isle Royale seized Canso before the British on this side of the Atlantic were aware of the outbreak of hostilities. They then attacked Annapolis. In this attack Duvivier, the French commander, expected help from the Acadians who were French in blood, faith and inclination; and the latter, who would not join him openly lest the attack should fail, did what they could without committing themselves and made 150 scaling ladders for the besiegers. To this seizure of Canso and this attack on Annapolis a contemporary French writer attributes the dire calamity which soon befell the French. When the capture of Louisbourg in 1745 by New Englanders with the aid of a British naval squadron was followed by French plans to retake it, reconquer old Acadia, burn Boston and lay waste to the other seaboard towns, French officials counted on aid from the Acadians for their designs. The result was the assembling of a vast armada, comprising nearly half the French navy, and carrying 3,150 veteran troops, under the Duc d'Anville, in 1746. This formidable expedition set out from France, and Ramesay, with a large body of Canadians, was sent to Acadia to cooperate with d'Anville's force. News of this design and the appearance at Chebucto of part of d'Anville's ill-fated fleet caused great excitement among the Acadians, who undoubtedly expected that they would soon again come under the Crown of France. Fifty of them went on board the French ships at Chebucto to pilot them to the attack on Annapolis. To their dismay, however, they found that no such attack would then be made. Early in the next year, when Coulon de Villiers and his men in the depth of the winter led his men from Beaubassin to Grand Pré, where in the dead of night they attacked Colonel Arthur Noble and his force, who were quartered in Acadian houses, and killed many of them in their beds, a number of Acadians acted as guides for Coulon's band and assisted them in other ways. With the restoration of Louisbourg to France, the British Government founded Halifax as a counterpoise to it and commenced their first real attempt at settling Nova Scotia. By the time of the eve of the Seven Years' War it was clear that a showdown would soon be reached with respect to North America. In 1755 Braddock was defeated on the Monongahela and Beauséjour was captured by New England troops. At the siege of Beauséjour about 300 Acadians aided the French.

The developments of the 1740s, with French attacks on Canso and Annapolis, the d'Anville expedition, the massacre at Grand Pré, and other French designs, as well as the capture of Louisbourg and its restoration and the founding of Halifax, meant a heightened interest and an increased activity in Nova Scotia. New efforts to have the Acadians take the oath of allegiance to the British monarch had no better result than previous ones. British activity at the Isthmus of Chignecto, with a view to protecting the peninsula from French encroachments, were followed by two matters of very special significance. One, in 1750, was the first forcible removal of the Acadians: resolved that the Acadians at Beaubassin should be preserved from the contaminating influence of the British, Le Loutre, who had been unable to prevent the British from reaching that village, went forward with his Indians and set fire to it, in order to force its inhabitants to go to territory claimed by the French near Beauséjour, a short distance away. This was the beginning of the dispersal of the Acadians. Besides these, through great pressure from the French they migrated in such numbers that by 1752 2,000 of them were to be found in Ile St. Jean (Prince Edward Island), and about 700 in Isle Royale (Cape Breton Island). The other, in 1751, was an interesting commentary on the attitude of the French authorities towards the Acadian claim to neutrality which those authorities had encouraged while the Acadians remained under British sovereignty: this was the order of Governor La Jonquière that all Acadian refugees near Beauséjour who did not take the oath of allegiance to the French monarch and enlist in the militia companies would be branded as rebels and chased from the lands which they occupied.

Subsequently, just after the capture of Beauséjour in 1755, while the New England troops, who had achieved that victory, were still in Nova Scotia, the British ships of the line still lay in Halifax harbour, Governor Lawrence of Nova Scotia and his council at Halifax decided that the safety of the colony required that the Acadians should take the oath of allegiance, which they had so often refused to do, or be deported from the Province. They again refused, and they were thereupon deported to British colonies. In the circumstances, and particularly after the attacks on Annapolis Royal in 1744 and 1745 and the deeds done at Grand Pré in 1747, it seems both unfair and inappropriate to attempt to pin the chief responsibility for this decision on either Lawrence of Nova Scotia or Shirley of Massachusetts.

Lack of space prevents an account of the hardships experienced by those Acadians who were expelled or a description of the efforts made by the British authorities to keep families and people from the same community together. Suffice it to say that it might appear that the expulsion was unnecessary, for if the old situation had persisted for but another few years until the French menace on the continent had been eradicated the problem would no longer have existed, or if the Acadians could have taken the oath of allegiance prior to 1755, as those who remained in the Province and those who returned to it afterwards did, those harsh deeds would not have been done. Not many years after 1755, at any rate, probably about 2,000 of the exiled Acadians returned to Nova Scotia, where, along with a like number who escaped the expulsion, they received grants of land, took the oath of allegiance, and assumed their full place in the life of the Province. On the two hundredth anniversary of that catastrophe which emerged from the vicissitudes of war and threats of war, all Nova Scotians of every racial origin rejoice with those of Acadian descent in marking the great achievements of the last two centuries.

part three

The Consolidation of British Hegemony, 1760–1820

12

CHURCH AND STATE IN MARITIME CANADA, 1749–1807*

J. M. Bumsted

Not until well into the 19th century did the notion of a state-supported church die in British North America. The British government, like most of Europe, assumed the validity and intrinsic usefulness of a religious institution which was intimately connected with the civil authority. It was felt that this was necessary to insure the loyalty of the population, to support the state ("No bishop, no King" was the way James I had put it), and to exercise an element of social control over the people which the civil government alone could not accomplish. After the American Revolution, the necessity of a state church (Anglicanism in British North America) appeared even more important to Britain. Much of the antimonarchical democratic sentiment in the rebellious colonies was seen coming from dissenters to Anglicanism, and religious dissent became almost by definition equated with political opposition by the British government. The Church of England in the American colonies had been weakened by the absence of bishops, and one of Britain's early priorities after 1783 was the establishment of an American bishopric.

Although the British ideal was for all American subjects to be communicants of the Church of England, for a variety of historical reasons this was impossible. In both Quebec and the Maritimes, the bulk of the population was not Anglican in sentiment. The early history of church-state relations in the Maritimes offers an interesting example of the continuing difficulties which the ideal of "one state, one church" faced in a multidenominational area, as I attempt to point out in the following article. What factors prevented implementation of the ideal? Did they remain constant or did they change perceptibly over time? In religious

*Canadian Historical Association Historical Papers (1968), pp. 41-58.

terms, did the considerable Loyalist migration significantly improve the situation for the British authorities? What effect did its connections with the government have on the Anglican Church in the Maritimes? Would Anglicanism have been better off on its own?

SUGGESTIONS FOR FURTHER READING

M. W. Armstrong, *The Great Awakening in Nova Scotia, 1776–1809* (Hartford, Conn.: American Society for Church History, 1948).

J. B. Brebner, *The Neutral Yankees of Nova Scotia* (New York: Columbia University Press, 1937).

J. M. Bumsted, *Henry Alline, 1748–1784* (Toronto: University of Toronto Press, 1971).

J. S. Moir, ed., *Church and State in Canada, 1627–1867* (Toronto: McClelland and Stewart, 1967).

Gordon Stewart and George Rawlyk, *A People Highly Favoured of God: The Nova Scotia Yankees and the American Revolution* (Toronto: Macmillan of Canada, 1972).

J.M.B.

T he last half of the 18th century was a critical period in the formation of Maritime Canada, a time of initial organization, settlement, and expansion. By the early years of the 19th century, many of the basic patterns of development and conflict had been set. The Maritime provinces were founded in an era in which religion was still considered a matter of critical importance, the state assuming that an established church was an essential component of the well-being of the body politic, and the church in turn depending upon state support. Since the state was not a neutral observer in religious matters, an understanding of the connections between it and religion is particularly crucial, for a good many of the significant issues in the area were inextricably interwoven in the relationship.

In Maritime Canada the years from 1749 to 1807 constituted a period of Anglican Church supremacy. From 1749—when the appointment of Governor Edward Cornwallis signalled the creation of a full-British colony in Nova Scotia—to 1807—the last year in which Bishop Charles Inglis retained full personal direction of the Church of England—Anglicanism was not only the established faith in Nova Scotia and the provinces of Prince Edward Island, Cape Breton, and New Brunswick subsequently created from it, but it had succeeded in maintaining its position of dominance despite a relative failure to maintain popular support among the inhabitants. A good deal of confusion has persisted over the legal position of the Anglican Church in the Maritime provinces. But at the initial creation of each of them, Crown instructions to the governors directed provision for glebe lands for the Church of England, insisted on the reading of the Book of Common Prayer "as by law established," and in a variety of other clauses indicated the privileged and established position of the Church of England.[1] Such instructions were not considered incompatible with a direction to the governors to permit "a liberty of conscience to all persons so they be contented with a quiet and peaceable enjoyment of the same, not giving offense or scandal to the government."[2] A grant of liberty of conscience to all did not mean that the Anglican Church could not and did not have a special status. Whether governor's instructions embodied the fundamental constitution of a colony or province was never entirely clear, since imperial law was itself never clear (had it been, there might have been no American Revolution).[3] But the legal establishment of the Church of England did not rest solely on such instructions, since enabling legislation to this end was passed by the legislature of every province by the beginning of the 19th century. Nova Scotia's first statute of establishment came in 1758, New Brunswick's in 1786, Cape Breton's in 1791, and Prince Edward Island's in 1802.[4] Beyond instructions and legislation, the Church of England enjoyed an officially privileged position through its intimate connection with the sources of money and power in both England and America.

Despite the undisputable fact that Anglicanism was by law established, the Church of England enjoyed no position of absolute exclusiveness in any Maritime province. Indeed, Bishop Inglis considered the establishment only "nominal," because the legal provisions were not sufficiently favourable to the Church.[5] Not only was liberty of conscience granted to dissenters (with occasional exceptions, particularly regarding Roman Catholics), but it was coupled with the accepted principle that dissenters would not be directly taxed for the support of the established church.[6] Government did aid the Church out of public revenue, but except in educational matters this was usually done within the province

---

[1]For a compilation of pre-revolutionary instructions, see Leonard W. Labaree, ed., *Royal Instructions to British Governors, 1670-1776*, 2 vols. (New York and London, 1935), especially vol. 2, pp. 482-512 ("Religion and Morals"). The 1769 instructions to Governor Walter Patterson of the Island of St. John are fairly typical of the entire period under discussion in this paper and are reprinted in their entirety in Frank MacKinnon, *The Government of Prince Edward Island* (Toronto, 1951), pp. 319-43, particularly 339-41. Instructions are to be found scattered throughout the Public Record Office Colonial Office Series, and are collected in the State Papers Series at the Public Archives of Canada, Ottawa. Only minor alterations were required with the appointment of a resident bishop replacing the Bishop of London in 1787; see, for example, the 1787 instructions to Governor Thomas Carleton in C. O. 189/2, 224-30.

[2]The 1769 instructions to Governor Patterson were the only set for a Maritime province which specifically excluded "Papists" from the grant of liberty of conscience.

[3]Leonard W. Labaree, *Royal Government in America: A Study of the British Colonial System before 1783* (New Haven, 1930), pp. 1-18; J. E. Read, "The Early Provincial Constitutions," *Canadian Bar Review*, 26 (1948), 520-32.

[4]C. O. 219/5, 48-50; C. O. 190/2, 15-16; C. O. 219/1, 101-2; C. O. 228/3, 40. I have examined the C. O. series in microfilm copies at the Public Archives of Canada.

[5]Charles Inglis to Governor Sir John Wentworth, April 14, 1800, "Memoirs of Bishop Inglis, Nova Scotia. Brief Notes of Memoirs of the Public and Various Other Transactions. Taken to assist my memory, and begun January 1775" (typescript, Public Archives of Canada [hereafter referred to as "Inglis Memoirs"]), vol. 3, p. 45.

[6]This reservation was written into the Nova Scotia Act of 1758, and Prince Edward Island passed a special act to this effect in 1790 (C. O. 228/2, 92). The acts of Cape Breton and New Brunswick did not contain such a provision, but there is no evidence that direct ecclesiastical taxes were ever collected from dissenters in those provinces.

only by the granting of glebe lands from the public domain. Glebes were only potential revenue and they were small; no large clergy reserves existed anywhere in the Maritimes to cause public outcry.[7] Dissenters fought, occasionally with success, for grants of glebe land for their clergymen and even for a share of the glebe set aside for the "orthodox" (i.e., Anglican) minister.[8] Anglican clergymen could be paid out of the British government's civil list, which was a sort of indirect taxation.[9] But in the Maritimes, dissenters were never faced with the collection of distinct ecclesiastical taxes which went to the established church, as was the case elsewhere in North America.[10]

The relative mildness of the establishment in the Maritimes was a product of Anglican Church weakness in the early years. Politicians successfully exploited the church for the advantage of the state, and refused to permit it to become oppressive upon those who were not its adherents. But as time went on, the establishment strengthened, and a number of points of friction emerged between the Church of England and dissenters. Its legal position, therefore, not only greatly influenced the development of Anglicanism but created political tensions and problems for the state and had repercussions for religious dissent both Protestant and Catholic.

Relationships between church and state hardly remained static and unchanging in the years 1749 to 1807. The process of settlement alone was sufficient to produce continual flux and alteration, but this was heightened and exaggerated by the great upheaval within the British Empire which dominated many of these years. Three distinct periods in the relationship of church and state in the Maritimes between 1749 and 1807 can be distinguished. The first, from 1749 to 1775, was an Erastian period in which religion and clergymen served fundamentally as servants of the state. Anglican missionaries especially were directed by the politicians for what were essentially political ends. Religion may have been cynically used by the state for its own purposes, but curiously this was a time of minimum religious friction. The second period, from 1775 to 1787, was a transitional period of some confusion, during which large numbers of Loyalist Anglican ministers and communicants flooded into the area. Their arrival, the shock waves of the catastrophe which had produced them, the creation of new provinces in their wake, and a rapid growth of evangelical pietism quite apart from political developments all combined to produce an extraordinarily changed and complex religious picture by 1787, when Charles Inglis arrived in Halifax as the first Anglican bishop of British North America. The third period, from 1787 to

---

[7]One of the recurring themes of the correspondence of missionaries to the Society for the Propagation of the Gospel, and that of Bishop Inglis, was the inadequacy in size and revenue of glebe provisions. See, for instance, "Inglis Memoirs," vol. 2, p. 151.

[8]For example, see John Eagleson to William Morice, January 16, 1775, in Transcripts of Papers of the Society for the Gospel in Foreign Parts, B. 25 (Nova Scotia, 1760-1786), 550-51, in Public Archives of Canada. Further reference to these documents will be SPGFP, B. 25.

[9]Parliament also made grants for the building of Anglican churches in British North America.

[10]Especially in Virginia, Massachusetts, and Connecticut.

1807, was the Inglis years. The bishop successfully resolved many of the most pressing problems which had grown up since the beginning of the Revolution, and he strengthened (or so it seemed) the political position of the Church everywhere. The new strength proved the Church's undoing, however, for it was not matched by corresponding gains in popular support. In 1750 the Church had been a political asset to the state; by 1800 there was increasing evidence that it was becoming a political liability. Inglis fought valiantly to prevent this from becoming apparent and as of 1807 appeared in large measure to have been successful. But his victories were illusory, and the weaknesses of the Church of England would ultimately overwhelm it, at least in terms of its established status.

In the years before 1775 the relationship between the Church of England and the state can quite properly be described as Erastian. All Anglican clergymen in the Maritimes were missionaries of the Society for the Propagation of the Gospel, all schoolmasters were supported by the SPG.[11] Their ecclesiastical superiors were 3,000 miles away. Besides administering to Anglican communicants, the SPG missionaries were charged with converting dissenters, both Protestant and Catholic, and Indians. From the point of view of the SPG, these activities had many spiritual justifications. But the SPG to some extent, the missionaries themselves to a considerable degree, and the government of Nova Scotia almost entirely, saw the missionaries' activities in political terms. Adherence to the Church of England was considered one of the means of assuring loyalty to the British Crown and Constitution. Those Protestant dissenters predominately from New England were to be converted as part of the overall government plan of undercutting New England principles of republicanism and democracy.[12] Protestant dissenters from Europe, especially the Lunenberg Germans, were to be converted and educated to assimilate them into British America and to prevent further ethnic divisions beyond those already present with the Acadians, who were never totally removed from the colony.[13] The French and other Catholics were to be converted to assimilate them and to assure their loyalty, particularly important since Catholics were held to maintain allegiance to a foreign power (not only the Pope, but before 1763 the Bishop of Quebec and all he represented).[14] Missionary activity among the In-

---

[11]The generalizations in the following paragraph are based largely on SPGFP, B. 25. For a more detailed analysis of the early church in Nova Scotia, see C. E. Thomas, "The First Half Century of the Work of the S.P.G. in Nova Scotia," *Nova Scotia Historical Society Collections*, 34 (1963), 1–31; Reginald V. Harris, *The Church of St. Paul in Halifax, Nova Scotia, 1749-1949* (Toronto, 1949), pp. 21–35.

[12]The overall plan is discussed in D. C. Harvey, "The Struggle for the New England Form of Township Government in Nova Scotia," *Canadian Historical Association Annual Report* (1933), pp. 15–22, and John B. Brebner, *The Neutral Yankees of Nova Scotia* (New York, 1937), pp. 211–17.

[13]The definitive work on the Germans is Winthrop P. Bell, *The "Foreign Protestants" and the Settlement of Nova Scotia* (Toronto, 1961).

[14]The governor's instructions in Nova Scotia from 1749–64 stressed conversion and denied authority to the Bishop of Quebec. Labaree, *Royal Instructions*, vol. 2, pp. 498–99; see also William Tutty to SPG, September 29, 1749, "Letters and Other Papers Relating to the Early History of the Church of England in Nova Scotia," *Nova Scotia Historical Society Collections*, 7 (1889), 97–104.

dians was, before final peace with France, designed to counter French influence among the savages and later to assure continuing amicable relations with the red men.[15]

The Erastian nature of the Church relationship in Nova Scotia was considerably enhanced in 1769 by the establishment in the province of a committee of corresponding members of the SPG which was charged with making regulations, reports, and recommendations regarding missions in the area. As the men on the spot, the committee was bound to have an extraordinary influence on both the missionaries and the SPG, and it exercised for several years what amounted to supervisory functions over the Society's activities in the Maritimes. The members of the committee were "His Excellency, the governor, Chief Justice Belcher, and Mr. Sec'y Bulkeley."[16] Holding the chairmanship of the corresponding committee contributed significantly to the governor's claims to being "Head of the Church" in Nova Scotia, an assertion charged against several governors, particularly Legge and Parr.

Although the SPG missionaries were not numerous and always considered themselves grossly undersupported financially, they were on the whole better off than their competitors. This was their greatest asset in their missionary activities. New settlers, in process of establishing themselves and attempting to eke out a marginal living from the soil and sea, were in no position to support clergymen from their own limited resources. Only the SPG missionaries, paid by the Society in England, were assured of a regular income, and they could promise new communities that their religious service would be at no cost to the settlers.[17] As Joseph Bennett wrote to the Society in 1765 while reporting the ordination in New England of two dissenting ministers for service in Nova Scotia:

> I am Certain though the two Clergymen I mentioned shou'd Come down from New England they will not stay as the people are not as yet in a capacity to pay them, and wou'd much rather attend a Church minister who wou'd be no Expence to them than a Dissenter whom they must Support.[18]

Bennett's analysis was echoed by most other missionaries and was substantiated by the dissenters of Cornwallis, who in 1769 petitioned the New England Puritan churches for financial assistance for their minister, arguing:

> For As there is Now A Church in Building in this town And A Church minister provided free of any Expense to all proselites. . . . If we now part with our Minister . . . we of Concequence In A Few years Shall all be

---

[15]Labaree, *Royal Instructions*, vol. 2, pp. 505–506. This major SPG missionary to the Indians was Thomas Wood, who succeeded his friend Father Pierre Maillard as missionary to the Micmac Indians; see Thomas, "The First Half Century," 13–15, and Rev. Angus A. Johnston, *A History of the Catholic Church in Eastern Nova Scotia*, vol. 1 (Antigonish, 1960), pp. 63–76.

[16]SPGFP, B. 25, 377–82.

[17]See, for example, Joseph Bennett to SPG, July 28, 1763, SPGFP, B. 25, 87–88.

[18]Joseph Bennett to SPG, June 14, 1765, SPGFP, B. 25, 167.

Churchmen or Nothing (i.e.) in point of Religion, as it Seams we Shall be in no Condition to Recettle Another Minister.[19]

Most dissenting congregations failed to support their own ministers, and by the Revolution all but a handful had left, most returning to New England.[20] This was a matter of some importance, for Puritan ministers were staunch supporters of the rebels and their absence certainly aided in keeping Nova Scotia quiet during the critical years.[21]

The relative weakness of the dissenters before 1775 assured that there would be no open campaign against the Church of England in Nova Scotia, although most dissenters were not in principle opposed to a church establishment, and the only sect with a firm anti-establishment tradition (the Separate Baptists) had lost all its clergymen by 1771.[22] No trouble could be expected on the Island of St. John, which had no resident Anglican clergyman to oppose before 1777.[23] In Nova Scotia Protestant dissenters regularly appealed to the government for financial assistance, occasionally with success. The dissenters' church in Halifax was given land by the government and assisted from public funds in the building of its meetinghouse.[24] Other ministers received land from the government and many assumed the use of the glebe lands in their communities.[25]

Beyond the difficulties faced by all denominations in the Maritimes, the Roman Catholics operated under the additional handicap of legal disabilities. The same act which established the Church of England in Nova Scotia required "Popist priests" to depart the province by March 25, 1759, on pain of perpetual imprisonment.[26] Communicants suffered under civil restrictions, being forbidden from sitting in the Assembly, after 1758 from holding land, and after 1766 from teaching school.[27] Although Nova Scotia's restrictions were a matter not of imperial policy but rather of legislative enactment, governor's instructions in 1769 for the Island of St. John specifically excluded "Papists" from the grant of liberty of conscience.[28] Priests did remain after their technical exclusion,

---

[19]S. A. Green, ed., "Letters from Congregational Churches in Early Nova Scotia," *Massachusetts Historical Society Collections*, 2nd ser., 4 (1888), 68–69.

[20]Maurice W. Armstrong, *The Great Awakening in Nova Scotia, 1776-1809* (Hartford, 1948), pp. 38–55.

[21]Armstrong, *The Great Awakening*, pp. 55–56. The Massachusetts Loyalist, Peter Oliver, called the Congregational clergy of New England the "Black Regiment," and credited them with a lion's share of stirring rebellion in that area; Douglass Adair and John A. Schutz, eds., *Peter Oliver's Origin & Progress of the American Revolution* (San Mateo, Cal., 1961), pp. 44–45.

[22]G. E. Levy, *The Baptists of the Maritime Provinces, 1753-1946* (Saint John, 1946), pp. 10–14; Armstrong, *The Great Awakening*, p. 60.

[23]A. B. Warburton, *A History of Prince Edward Island* (Saint John, 1923), pp. 385–89.

[24]Walter C. Murray, "History of St. Matthew's Church, Halifax, N.S.," *Nova Scotia Historical Society Collections*, 16 (1912), 137–170, especially 151–55.

[25]Armstrong, *The Great Awakening*, pp. 49–50.

[26]C. O. 219/5, 50.

[27]Johnston, *A History of the Catholic Church*, vol. 1, pp. 77–85.

[28]MacKinnon, *Government of Prince Edward Island*, p. 339.

but they did so at the sufferance of the government, and like their parishioners were in no position to criticize it. Before Catholics could begin to battle the Church of England, they had to gain legal recognition, and this was not accomplished before the Revolution.

Despite the relative absence of actual conflict arising out of church-state relationships in the Maritimes, portents of future trouble were certainly present. On March 26, 1775, a young Nova Scotian named Henry Alline discovered his "call to preach the gospel."[29] He would be the instrument of the awakening of a native Protestant dissent in the area which was much more potentially dangerous to the Church of England than dissent in its New England Puritan form could ever have been. Within the Church itself there was the beginning of resentment at being used a pawn by the state. A stronger and more numerous clergy would not take kindly to this and would object to the governor's pretensions as "Head of the Church." Indeed, unchallenged Erastianism was about dead in Nova Scotia. On June 30, 1775, the corresponding committee of the SPG recommended that "for the best service of the Established Church in this Province, in avoiding all Controversy with the Inhabitants of different persuasions, and provoking them to disgust and Animosities by continuing Missionaries however highly worthy," all SPG missionaries would be recalled to Halifax.[30] A month later the committee met to note that "by the Intervention of too powerful a Cause," its intention to avoid conflict and controversy with dissenters was frustrated, and unless supported by the Society the committee could be of no further use.[31] The SPG did not support it, and the committee, although not formally dissolved until 1777, ceased to function on the eve of the war.

The next dozen years saw extraordinary changes in the religious situation in the Maritimes. From the standpoint of the Anglican Church, the great event was the enormous Loyalist immigration to the area, which brought dozens of ministers (mostly former SPG missionaries from the rebellious colonies) and large numbers of potential communicants. Most of the new clergymen were tenaciously committed to a strong Church of England connection with the state, and their coming should have significantly strengthened the position of the Church. But except in the newly created province of New Brunswick, where the legal position of the Church was firmly assured by strong legislation, Anglicanism failed to demonstrate appreciable immediate benefits from the Loyalist migration.

A number of factors combined to prevent the expectable gains by the Church of England. The coming of the Loyalists, while adding greatly to the number of missionaries in the Maritimes—especially in Nova Scotia—created certain difficulties as well. Although the new clergymen were staunch supporters of the Crown, the Church of England, and the church-state connection, it is doubtful whether all of the immigrants shared the minister's interpretation of church establishment. Most of the Loyalists were not upper-class Tories—as were their clergymen—and

---

[29]Henry Alline, The Life and Journal of the Rev. Mr. Henry Alline (Boston, 1806), p. 36.

[30]SPGFP, B. 25, 575–576.

[31]SPGFP, B. 25, 577–578.

were probably not communicants of the Church of England.[32] The average Loyalist, having previously abandoned his worldly possessions and currently engaged in a life-and-death struggle to make a go of his new situation, was doubtless out of sympathy with a clergy which thought itself entitled to "a large, decent house, well furnished," and a family "elegantly dressed, without attempting to rival people of fashion."[33] The immigrants' lack of resources, the problems of settlement, the bleakness of much of the country, and the lack of sympathy with—perhaps even resentment against—the demands of the Anglican missionaries, all combined to prevent the clerics from gaining much if any financial support from their parishioners. Most were forced to rely on the government and the SPG for financial assistance, but by 1784 Thomas Wood noted: "I see the Societys funds are nearly exhausted, & the replenishing them will be precarious. I have reason indeed to dread our whole fabric is tottering."[34]

The plain reality was that, for existing resources, too many missionaries were all loudly demanding a support in keeping with their stations. The result was an unbecoming and divisive scrambling for places and emoluments, in which the immigrant clergymen fought the pre-revolutionary missionaries and the government which had long been in alliance with them. The old missionaries naturally resented the demands, complaints, and presumptions of the newcomers, and the newly arrived in turn despised the old hands. Mather Byles wrote in 1779 that he had been promised a post at Halifax, but was "violently opposed, and rather roughly treated, by Mr. Bennett, who resolutely claims it as being what he pleases to call his 'Birth-Right,' he being the Senior Missionary of Nova Scotia."[35] On the whole, the government supported the older missionaries, leading Byles to comment that "Sycophants are not wanting to compliment a Governor, who acts entirely under their Influence, with the absurd Title of 'Head of the Church'."[36] The Loyalists turned to the SPG for support, and Byles for several years served as a clearinghouse for Loyalist correspondence with the SPG "to the no small Mortification of some who think themselves equally entitled to their Confidence."[37] This was hardly a wise move on the part of the SPG, for Byles had an extraordinarily high opinion of his own abilities and a malicious tongue and pen. He quickly fell out with kindly Jonathan Breynton, long-time rector of St. Paul's of Halifax (whom he called "Dr. Be-

---

[32]The old myths about the Loyalists dies hard, and more detailed studies such as that of Esther C. Wright, *The Loyalists of New Brunswick* (Fredericton, 1955) are needed. Miss Wright demonstrates quite convincingly that the New Brunswick Loyalists represented a cross-section of the population of colonial America rather than its upper classes. No detailed statistical work on religious affiliation has been done, but the reports of the SPG missionaries, the Bishop of Nova Scotia, and the writings of dissenting evangelists would seem to indicate that large numbers of Loyalists were not committed communicants of the Church of England.

[33]William S. Bartlet, *The Frontier Missionary: A Memoir of the Life of the Rev. Jacob Bailey, A.M.* (Boston, 1853), p. 218.

[34]Thomas Wood to SPG, January 29, 1784, SPGFP, "C" Series (A-167), Box 2, p. 6 (Public Archives of Canada).

[35]SPGFP, B. 25, 686.

[36]SPGFP, B. 25, 758.

[37]"Copies of Letters and Diaries of Rev. Mather Byles, D.D. jr., a United Empire Loyalist who came to Halifax, N.S. in 1776 . . ." (Public Archives of Canada), vol. 1, p. 9.

nevolente Muckworm") and before long with almost everyone else in the province.[38] He was ultimately transferred to an unsuspecting parish in New Brunswick.

Infighting was hardly confined to battle lines pitting Loyalists versus veteran Nova Scotia missionaries. Competition among the Loyalists themselves was intense, each clergyman attempting to pull any strings available to him to gain sufficient patronage "to support himself with decency and to practice hospitality."[39] Some went to the government, and their competitors turned to the "Protection of their Venerable Patrons," the SPG, the only agency "that act upon the true principles of loyalty, and from where one may expect justice."[40] This was bound to lead to conflict between the Society and the government over the direction of the activities of the Church, particularly when the immigrant missionaries charged that the governor had adopted "extravagent Sentiments" of his ecclesiastical power, "his being 'Head of the Church'; 'the best Judge of the Situation of Affairs'; his having . . . all Benefices absolutely and entirely in his Gift."[41] Such conflict, which had long been simmering in Nova Scotia, reached its peak in the Shelburne glebe case.

Soon after the settlement of Port Roseway (or Shelburne) in 1783, the community found itself with two competing Anglican clergymen, both claiming to be the authorized minister.[42] One, the Reverend George Panton, had apparently been invited by a number of the leaders of the Port Roseway venture. The other, Dr. William Walter, claimed his invitation from a sizeable number of the settlers. Both gentlemen had their supporters and both appealed to the SPG and the governor for backing. While Walter was in England in 1784 on business which included pressing the claims of Loyalists missionaries in general and his own in particular, the governor divided the township into three parishes and inducted Panton into what his opponents considered to be the best living of the three.[43] In England, Walter had complained to the SPG of "the State of the Chhes . . . while under the Care of a Gentleman who is totally regardless of their Interest."[44] He returned to Nova Scotia with what he considered to be support from the Society only to discover that behind his back he had been outmanoeuvred by the governor. Outraged and encouraged by his brother-in-law (who happened to be Mather Byles), Walter protested vociferously, denying the governor's authority to locate parishes and to induct ministers until one was presented to him by the parishioners. By questioning the governor's authority and insisting "on the Privilege and Right of the Parishioners by Law to chuse their own minister," Walter opened himself to all sorts of attack.[45] His enemies

---

[38]"Copies of Letters and Diaries of Rev. Mather Byles," p. 32.

[39]Jacob Bailey to SPG, October 14, 1782, SPGFP, B. 25, 754.

[40]J. W. Weeks to SPG, November 1780, SPGFP, "C" Series (A–167), Box 2, p. 25.

[41]Mather Byles to SPG, May 7, 1782, SPGFP, B. 25, 745.

[42]The following paragraph is based on the SPG papers, especially SPGFP, B. 25, 771–900. The only published discussion of the case is [W. O. Raymond] "The Founding of the Church of England in Shelburne," *New Brunswick Historical Society Collections*, 3 (no. 8), 278–93.

[43]William Walter to SPG, November 5, 1784, SPGFP, B. 25, 781–82.

[44]William Walter to SPG, January 17, 1784, SPGFP, B. 25, 771.

[45]William Walter to SPG, December 9, 1784, SPGFP, B. 25, 809. Early in 1785, Governor

doubted the validity of the appointment of a Church of England minister which relied on "the Votes and Subscriptions of a Number of Persons, neither Communicants nor professed Members of the Church," since this had a "dangerous Tendency, as Opening an Avenue for a Majority of *Sectaries* to introduce Clergyman of Obvious Principles equally dangerous to the Church and Government."[46] This was little more than New England Congregationalism! The dispute continued for some months, until Panton (who apparently never sought the controversy) retired in hopes that Walter would do likewise. He did not, and two competing parishes survived in Shelburne for a number of years.[47] In the end, the SPG failed to support Walter. The secretary of the Society called him "ungrateful" and wrote that it was thought he "had more sense than to oppose the Governor."[48] But the questions regarding authority and patronage which had been raised in Shelburne were important ones which would have to be resolved, as would the unseemly scramble for positions among the missionaries. The best solution was undoubtedly the appointment of a resident bishop, and such a step was under discussion in England beginning in 1784.

While the establishment was engaged in internal struggle, it had little time to devote to countering the growing influence of evangelical Protestantism, which had begun its development with the itinerant preaching of Henry Alline.[49] The "New Lights" had no particular respect for learning and ecclesiastical authority; what mattered to them was an individual's conversion, usually produced in waves of local revival by enthusiastic, itinerant preachers like Alline. The evangelicals typically ministered to no settled church and travelled widely the length and breadth of the land encouraging people to demand, "What must I do to be saved?" Religious zealots themselves, such men cared little for money or creature comforts, and they made few financial demands on their adherents. Ideally suited for a newly settled country, they made extraordinary gains. While the Anglicans prided themselves that (as Jacob Bailey put it) "though always obliged to officiate twice and often three times a week, besides distant excursions, yet I never appear without shaving and clean linen," the New Lights preached dozens of times weekly under any and all conditions of personal hardship and disadvantage.[50] Alline died in 1784, but his converts preached on and proliferated, and were joined in

---

Parr protested to the SPG that Walter's disposition towards the authority of Government countenanced a spirit of popular opposition, and added, "I consider the matter of some importance to the future Prosperity of the Church in this Province." SPGFP, Box 25, 297.

[46]Vestry of St. Patrick's Parish to Governor John Parr, December 15, 1784, SPGFP, B. 25, 823.

[47]Raymond, "The Founding of the Church in Shelburne," pp. 290-93.

[48]William Morice to Jonathan Breynton, February 25, 1785, SPGFP, "C" Series (A-167), Box 2, p. 11. Morice added that "as a private person I have a regard for him [Walter], but the public step he has taken is not approved here, & he has no authority from hence."

[49]For the growth of evangelical pietism during the Revolution, see Armstrong, *The Great Awakening*, pp. 61-87.

[50]Jacob Bailey to Samuel Peters, April 29, 1785, reprinted in Bartlet, *Frontier Missionary*, p. 206. Also compare Bailey's "particulars . . . for a clergyman in Nova Scotia" (Bartlet, p. 218) with Joshua Marsden's questions to be asked of a Methodist missionary "when entering upon his mission" (Joshua Marsden, *The Narrative of a Mission, to Nova Scotia, New Brunswick, and the Somers Islands*, 2nd ed. [London, 1827], p. 24).

the mid 1780s by Methodist missionaries from the United States and Britain.[51]

Fortunately for the church-state establishment, the message preached by the New Lights and evangelicals, while enthusiastic, anti-authoritarian, and potentially levelling, was so exclusively spiritual and pietistic that it was no immediate threat to the status quo. Most of the evangelicals agreed with the Methodist William Black who asked rhetorically, "What have the ministers of Christ to do with the adminis-tration of civil government? Christ's kingdom is not of this world. We are neither magistrates nor legislators."[52] Although the revival in the Maritimes has been seen as an extension of the Great Awakening of 1740 in New England, this was not really the case.[53] The growth of evangeli-cal pietism in the Maritimes began as a completely indigenous develop-ment which owed something to broad 18th-century currents, but was not directly influenced by New England revivalism. This was a boon to the establishment, for the Separates and Separate Baptists (the New Eng-land equivalents of Alline and his followers) had developed a rather sophisticated doctrine of the separation of church and state, which they employed in attempts to overthrow the Puritan standing churches of New England and the Church of England in Virginia.[54] During the rev-olutionary period, the government could not afford to alienate dissenters, and the New Lights—who never bothered the government and may have redirected potential political discontent into religious channels—were left pretty much alone, opposed only by a few Congregational ministers.[55]

During the uncertainty of the revolutionary years the Catholics made gains, too. In 1784 the previous disabilities on adherents of the "popish Religion" were repealed in favor of a rather demeaning but not impossi-ble oath of allegiance.[56] That same year a church was erected in Halifax, and in 1786 Catholics were, in Nova Scotia, granted the right to school and schoolmasters.[57]

From the standpoint of the Church of England, the situation in the years 1775 to 1787 was not entirely one of unrelieved gloom. The first missionaries to the Islands of St. John and Cape Breton took up their

---

[51]Goldwin S. French, *Parsons and Politics: The rôle of the Wesleyan Methodists in Upper Canada and the Maritimes from 1780 to 1855* (Toronto, 1962), pp. 29–36; Armstrong, *The Great Awakening*, pp. 119–29.

[52]Matthew Richey, *A Memoir of the Late William Black, Wesleyan Minister* (Halifax, 1839), p. 310. The Baptists used the same text—"Christ's kingdom is not of this world"—to argue for separation of church and state in New England! See William G. McLoughlin, "The Balkcom Case (1782) and the Pietistic Theory of Separation of Church and State," *William and Mary Quarterly*, 3rd ser., 24 (1967), 270.

[53]Armstrong, *The Great Awakening in Nova Scotia* and S. D. Clark, *Church and Sect in Canada* (Toronto, 1948), pp. 3–44, both see the Nova Scotia revival as an extension of New England's.

[54]McLoughlin, "The Balkcom Case," pp. 267–83; C. C. Goen, *Revivalism and Separatism in New England* (New Haven, 1962); Wesley F. Gewehr, *The Great Awakening in Virginia, 1740–1790* (Durham, 1930).

[55]Maurice W. Armstrong, "Neutrality and Religion in Revolutionary Nova Scotia," *The New England Quarterly*, 19 (1946), 50–62.

[56]C. O. 219/17, 75–78.

[57]Johnston, *A History of the Catholic Church*, vol. 1, pp. 101–105; Rev. John E. Burns, "The Development of Roman Catholic Church Government in Halifax from 1760 to 1853," *Nova Scotia Historical Society Collections*, 23 (1936), 89–95.

posts at this time (Theophilus DesBrisay at Charlottetown, 1777, and Ranna Cossitt at Sydney, 1785).[58] This was an obviously essential preliminary to the meaningful establishment of the Church in these provinces. New Brunswick's early legal enactments regarding church-state relationships were also heartening. The New Brunswick assembly produced a reasonably straight-forward act of establishment for the Church in 1786, which included a provision for the licensing by the governor of every clergyman intending to officiate in the province.[59] By "giving a restraining power over unsettled and itinerant preachers," Governor Carleton argued, the law "must also help to secure its [the Province's] political quiet."[60] It would certainly hamper the expansion of the evangelists. Finally, discussion of the appointment of an Anglican bishop for British North America, which had begun in 1784, had by 1786 progressed to a point where it was certain that such a post would be created. On August 12, 1787, Charles Inglis was consecrated as Bishop, an event which clearly would mean a new era in both religious affairs and church-state relationships.

Inglis stepped ashore at Halifax on October 15, 1787, to begin a lengthy term as Bishop of Nova Scotia, his diocese at its inception encompassing all the Maritimes (including Newfoundland), plus Quebec.[61] Probably more biographical studies have been done of Charles Inglis than of any of his contemporaries in British North America, and most of them have been particularly laudatory of his role as builder of the Anglican Church in Maritime Canada.[62] Yet there exists a good deal of evidence to suggest that, by and large, his activities were more disfunctional to the Church than constructive. In a brief space, only a sketchy outline of the relative failure of Inglis as Bishop can be offered.

Inglis saw his immediate task as one of strengthening the position of the Church of England, and he moved at once in this direction. One of his first achievements was legislative support for a public grammar school which he called the "first step" toward "the establishment of a College, without which, Church matters must be in an imperfect state."[63] He also desired "the proper establishment of the Church in this province by an act of the Legislature," but realizing the difficulties of this, settled for pressure to increase glebes and to remove from the governors of Nova Scotia and New Brunswick their control over ecclesiastical patronage.[64] He argued that the parish had the right of selection and presentation of a clergyman to the governor, and the governor only a formal power of

[58]"The Reverend Ranna Cossitt, 1744-1815, First Rector of Saint George's, Sydney," *Canadian Church Historical Society Journal,* 5 (September 1963); Warburton, *History of Prince Edward Island,* pp. 389-90.

[59]C. O. 190/2, 15-16.

[60]An "observation" in Carleton's handwriting on the manuscript copy of the act; C. O. 190/2, 15.

[61]Reginald V. Harris, *Charles Inglis: Missionary, Loyalist, Bishop (1734-1816)* (Toronto, 1937), pp. 74-75.

[62]In his bibliography, Harris lists ten "principle sketches and biographies"; Harris, *Charles Inglis,* p. 182. Since that time (1937) very little has appeared. Almost without exception, biographies of Inglis have been by denominational historians, usually clergymen.

[63]"Inglis Memoirs," vol. 1, p. 46.

[64]"Inglis Memoirs," vol. 1, pp. 46, 31-170, *passim.*

induction. These were not "the rights of the people" as advocated by William Walter, for Inglis emphasized that "the elections will not be popular" since parish "in the law . . . meant the Church Wardens and Vestry."[65] Inglis won these and other points, and succeeded in asserting his episcopal authority over the church and the government.

Had the Bishop been satisfied with such victories, all might have been well. But Inglis insisted on implementing in any way possible his basic Loyalist-Tory philosophy: "the principles of the Church of England [are] the best security for the attachment of these provinces to the parent-state of its constitution."[66] At the beginning, Inglis counselled the need for "time, patience and zeal, our exertions tempered with caution and prudence."[67] But he soon forgot his own advice. This was not surprising, for Inglis had a long record of public controversy. While in New York, he had published pamphlets on theological questions and had debated in print with Alexander Hamilton and Thomas Paine.[68] He had won his bishopric only after a rather nasty exchange of pamphlets with one of his chief competitors.[69] In the Maritimes, his pugnacity led him to produce issues with dissenters where none had existed before. He opposed the New Brunswick marriage act of 1787, and forced one which put marriages entirely in the control of the Anglican clergy and the governor.[70] This led the Methodist leader William Black, about as unpolitical a pietist as was conceivable, to circulate petitions for repeal.[71] He argued a narrow interpretation of the Nova Scotia marriage acts, succeeded in persuading a reluctant governor not to grant licenses indiscriminately, and insisted on taking a Baptist minister to court in 1801 for performing marriages without a license. The result was legal victory for the dissenter; it was, he wrote afterwards, "still doubtful whether the issue of the marriages would legally inherit," but added ruefully that this "was but a feeble restraint on such as had little or nothing to leave to their children."[72]

Inglis's narrow denominational conception of an institution of higher learning and his opposition to efforts by other denominations to establish educational facilities turned the question of higher education into a running sore for the Church and the government. There is no evidence that he advocated liberalization of the rules of King's College, although he acquiesced in the decision of the Archbishop of Canterbury to insist upon

---

[65]"Inglis Memoirs," vol. 1, p. 84.

[66]"Inglis Memoirs," vol. 1, p. 60.

[67]"Inglis Memoirs," vol. 1, p. 35.

[68]A complete bibliography of Inglis' published works is in Harris, *Charles Inglis*, pp. 148–50. Inglis's answer to Hamilton appeared in the *New York Gazette* in 1774; his reply to Paine was published at Philadelphia in 1776 as *The True Interest of America Impartially Stated.* . . .

[69]For the pamphlet war with his competitor, Dr. Samuel Peters, see Harris, *Charles Inglis*, pp. 63–68.

[70]"Inglis Memoirs," vol. 1, pp. 171–78. The 1791 act finally passed is in C. O. 190/2, 225–227. For a discussion of the New Brunswick marriage act and its meaning, see W. Stewart MacNutt, *New Brunswick, A History: 1784–1867* (Toronto, 1963), pp. 91–93.

[71]MacNutt, *New Brunswick*, p. 104.

[72]"Inglis Memoirs," vol. 3, pp. 44–60, especially p. 60. For discussion of the court case, see Isaiah W. Wilson, *History of Digby County* (Halifax, 1900), pp. 112–113.

subscription to the 39 Articles only at graduation rather than matriculation.[73] This was "necessary and prudent," as "three fourths of the inhabitants are Dissenters, and against these, the statute as it first stood
virtually shut the door of the Seminary."[74] With the college closed to
dissenters, moreover, Inglis could no longer have continued to argue, as
he did in objecting to Catholic attempts to establish a school in Halifax:
"Our seminaries are as open to them as to any other inhabitants and no
tests are required at the admission of scholars that would interfere with
their particular tenets."[75]

By the turn of the century, Inglis clearly felt himself on the defensive,
arguing that "an Innovation acts like a wedge; only introduce it once,
and by a little perseverence and force, it will find its way and rend everything before it."[76] Within his own Church, he became increasingly
reactionary, influenced by the French Revolution and the gains of levelling enthusiasts closer to home. Although he had earlier supported
ministerial presentation by the parish, he thought "in these times of
Democratic rage and delusion" it was best to leave presentation and
selection in the hands of the governor.[77] This decision ultimately produced the great schism in St. Paul's of Halifax which benefited only the
Baptists.[78] He opposed open pews on a variety of grounds, but largely
because they were too democratic.[79]

The charges of foreign influence and levelling tendencies were ones
which he levelled broadside at all he considered to be threats. In 1793 he
contented himself with disparaging the evangelicals, but by 1800 he
considered they were "engaged in the general plan of a total revolution in
religion and civil government. . . . And it is a certain fact, that 'The
Rights of Man,' 'The Age of Reason,' 'Volney on the Ruine of Empires,' 'A

---

[73]In the first history of King's College, T. B. Akins wrote of Inglis's opposition to the college
statutes adopted by the board of governors in 1803 and indicated that Inglis had opposed a
number of reactionary statutes, including the one requiring subscription to the 39 articles
upon matriculation. *A Brief Account of the Origin, Endowment and Progress of the University of King's College* (Halifax, 1865), pp. 17-20. Later historians of the college have been
more circumspect, but still give the impression that Inglis was liberal in his attitude toward
the statutes. As his letterbook and memoirs make quite clear, however, his opposition to the
statutes of 1803 was grounded in belief that the Church of England was not given sufficient
preference. He did not object to the rule requiring subscription to the 39 articles upon matriculation, although he was willing to accept the amendment to graduation when it was
made. "Inglis Memoirs," vol. 3, especially 83-98.

[74]"Inglis Memoirs," vol. 3, p. 173.

[75]"Inglis Memoirs," vol. 3, p. 62.

[76]"Inglis Memoirs," vol. 3, p. 46.

[77]"Inglis Memoirs," vol. 2, p. 102.

[78]The documents relating to the dispute and schism, which ultimately led the party supporting presentation by the parish to join the Granville Street Baptist Church in Halifax, are
reprinted in George W. Hill, "History of St. Paul's Church," *Nova Scotia Historical Society
Collections*, 3 (1883), 13-69.

[79]"I never knew an instance before this," wrote Inglis, "in Europe or America, where the
pews were thus held in common, and where men—perhaps of the worst characters—might
come and set themselves down by the most religious and respectable characters in the parish.
This must ultimately tend to produce disorder and confusion in the church and check the
spirit of true devotion and piety . . . the greatest disorder must be the consequence, if this
mode be continued, when the country becomes populous." Wright, *Loyalists of New
Brunswick*, pp. 237-38.

False Representation of the French Revolution' with scandalous invectives against all the crowned heads in Europe, and against the British Administration in particular, have been secretly handed about by professed New-lights."[80] He entered into public controversy with the Roman Catholic Vicar General Edmund Burke largely because Burke was a proponent of democracy and "other dangerous tenets, which are inconsistent with our constitution in Church and State; which have often deluged our country with blood, and must produce incalculable mischief in this young Community."[81]

Perhaps attack was preventative defense and had some effect in resisting the danger from dissenters, which Inglis admitted numbered three-fourths of his diocese. But the failure of the dissenters to produce an open and concerted offense against the "constitution in Church and State" was less because of Inglis's activities than because of their own weaknesses. In the first place, the dissenters were badly divided denominationally. Protestants and Catholics distrusted one another. The Presbyterians were split into feuding factions. Among the evangelical sects, the Methodists, New Lights, and Baptists objected more to each other's theology than to the Anglican establishment, which was seldom a competitor outside the larger communities.[82] The evangelicals, potentially the largest and most aggressive force in the Maritimes, remained out of political activities, partly because of their pietistic orientation and partly because of the American connections many of their missionaries retained. By the early 19th century, however, evangelical Protestantism was losing its American ties, constructing formal organizations, and becoming more concerned with affairs of this world.[83]

In 1807, when Inglis suffered a severe illness and turned more and more of the direction of the Church over to others—particularly his son John—the dissenters had not yet evidenced any sort of united front against the Church. Nevertheless, the weaknesses in the Anglican establishment were fairly obvious. Inglis had not succeeded, in the last analysis, in strengthening the Church of England in the Maritimes. It was not so much a failure to take an active hand in ecclesiastical affairs outside Nova Scotia, although it was true he did not. Church-state relations in Prince Edward Island and Cape Breton—where dissenters clearly predominated—were probably better off for his lack of attention, and New Brunswick managed quite well without much interference. Where Inglis did press his hard line, it created enemies and issues. Not satisfied to have a quietly privileged and favoured church, Inglis advocated what amounted to a policy of "thorough." He did not gain terribly

---

[80]Richey, *William Black*, pp. 298-99; I. E. Bill, *Fifty Years with the Baptist Ministers and Churches of the Maritime Provinces* (Saint John, 1880), p. 191.

[81]"Inglis Memoirs," vol. 3, p. 132.

[82]Many examples of this evangelical disagreement are given in Richey, *William Black*, Marsden, *Narrative of a Mission*, and the autobiography of Joseph Crandall, diary of Joseph Dimock, and journal of Edward Manning (manuscripts at Maritime Baptist Historical Collection, Acadia University Library, Wolfville, Nova Scotia).

[83]French, *Parsons and Politics*, p. 54; Levy, *Baptists*, pp. 69-85; Armstrong, *The Great Awakening*, pp. 131-38.

much by this, but he succeeded in publicizing the special status of the Church of England, and by attempting to employ the state for the ends of the church (although it must be admitted he never saw any distinction between the two), he politicized the establishment unnecessarily. One of the major grievances of the "liberal" opposition in the Maritimes would be the religious policy of those in power.

The emphasized connection—even unity—between the Church of England and the state would not have been so potentially disastrous had not Inglis also failed to construct a Church with a firm and broad popular support. This failure was attributable to a variety of factors which are in much need of further study.[84] Inglis was not entirely to blame for the inability of the Church to escape from its financial reliance on government grants and SPG support. But he must be charged with the failure of the Church of England in the Maritimes to learn anything at all from the successes of the evangelicals. To expect open alliance with the Methodists—which some Methodists favored, at least in the 1790s— would be too much.[85] To expect the Church to adopt an evangelically oriented message might also be chimeric, although this did happen in Britain. But Inglis could have insisted that his clergymen travel more widely and make themselves more accessible to the people, both socially and geographically. He could have, in a word, demanded that his clerics act more like the missionaries they continued to claim to be.

The Church of England was in no immediate danger of disestablishment when Inglis went into semi-retirement in 1807, but by its failure to gain, by its inability to capitalize on half a century of opportunity and privilege, it had already forfeited a large measure of its justification for established status. A good many battles would be necessary over the next half century before Church and state would be separated, but by the beginning of the 19th century Inglis had put the Church on the defensive, and the ultimate outcome could never be in doubt.

---

[84]The best available analysis is in S. D. Clark, *Church and Sect*, especially pp. 64–83.
[85]"Inglis Memoirs," vol. 1, pp. 105–7.

13

FRENCH-CANADIAN NATIONALISM AND THE AMERICAN REVOLUTION*

Hilda Neatby

With the treaty of Paris in 1763, the British acquired New France, a colony of some 60,000 inhabitants whose way of life was quite unlike that of the remainder of British North America. This is not to say that French America and British America did not, underneath obvious differences, have a good deal in common. But French Canada was Roman Catholic, French-speaking, and accustomed to both a legal and a political tradition quite alien to British experience. The acquisition of New France (now renamed Quebec) therefore posed a considerable challenge to British statesmen and colonial officials because of its very "foreignness." The British had some experience in dealing with an alien French population in North America, but the Acadian situation could hardly serve as a positive example. Unfortunately for both Britain and Quebec, as Professor Hilda Neatby points out in the following article, British statesmanship had to deal with French Canada simultaneously with a major colonial crisis in North America—a crisis which had to some extent been brought on by the very conquest of France's American colonies. Quebec could not be dealt with in a vacuum, and British policy there was greatly conditioned by events to the south over which there was no control. But it would be a great mistake to assume that British policy towards Quebec was nothing more than a defensive response to American events. The ends which Britain sought—stability, order, loyalty— were partly a product of external pressures but also what any imperial power governing an alien province would desire. Even if the ends were not entirely Britain's to choose, the means to achieve them were open.

---

*Centennial Review, 10 (1966), 505-22.

What were the means selected by Britain to achieve the desired results? Did they mark a continuation of pre-British developments in the province or were they a new departure? Was British policy liberal or reactionary? What was French-Canadian response to the American Revolution, and why? Have French-Canadian nationalists any legitimate reason for asserting that Quebec's subsequent difficulties and developments were largely a result of British policy?

SUGGESTIONS FOR FURTHER READING

A. L. Burt, *The Old Province of Quebec* (Minneapolis: University of Minnesota Press, 1933).

M. Brunet, *La Présence Anglaise et les Canadians* (Montreal: Beauchemin, 1958).

H. Neatby, *Quebec: The Revolutionary Age, 1760-1791* (Toronto: McClelland and Stewart, 1966).

J.M.B.

I

The bitterness that has attended recent demonstrations of separatism in Quebec, and the present ambiguous situation of the Canadian federal union, give to the preparations for celebrating Canada's centennial year an air of doubt and hesitation which is, perhaps, all too characteristic of the Canadian people. The events of the past few years do, indeed, give rise to many questions.

In view of the passionate historicism of Quebec and the famous motto, *notre maître le passé,* one must ask, has separatism, although requiring two centuries to come to fruition, been from the beginning inherent in the Canadian situation? Did the national spirit have to mature through the romanticism of the early 19th century and the chauvinism of its later decades to the bitter era of 20th-century totalitarianism before the people of Quebec could become convinced that they must have this form of fulfilment? Or was it rather that the latent determination of the people had to wait until the revelation of great mining resources and other wealth made possible a viable Laurentian state? Or, has the accumulation of pin pricks from Anglo-Saxondom (and other alien cultures) in the other Canadian provinces and in the United States grown at last unbearable? Or are the people of Quebec inspired by the examples of the innumerable small and relatively primitive communities now claiming national status? Or are they receiving inspiration from France, their old mother country? Is France, having parted in bitterness from her 19th-century empire, turning nostalgically to the dream of a cultural and political union with the now splendid offspring of her most splendid century?

Any or all of these theories may find some support, but easy references to nationalism leave too much unexplained. It may be useful to the historian to examine once more with particular care the evidence available of the beginnings of the uneasy association between the ancient Canadians and the encroaching Anglo-Saxons during the first generation of British rule. This examination has often been made before by exponents of the classic theory of nationalism, ready to assume with serene dogmatism that any injury to the national spirit must be bad and any concession to it good. Today we have a clearer picture of the dangers and disadvantages of extreme nationalism. At the same time it is recognized in its modern form as a phenomenon which appeared clearly only at the beginning of the 19th century. There is, therefore, less inclination to apportion praise and blame to 18th-century rulers on the basis of their attitude to a supposed Canadian national spirit.

It has also been made clear by a number of scholars, French and English Canadian, that the old legend of Canadian nationalism provoked and inspired by love of France and by British tyranny, sanctioned as this legend was in some degree by the great Garneau, is without much foundation. It would indeed be difficult to think of any community, conquered after a long struggle and a struggle not unattended with events of peculiar barbarity, that has on the whole been treated with greater humanity and toleration. That the motives for such treatment on the part of the British conquerors were not solely benevolent does not alter the fact. It does, however, make it important to look into the roots of that tradition of resentment against Britain which is as ancient as it is tenacious.

From the very beginning the effect of British rule in Quebec was to stimulate, strengthen, and at the same time irritate the newly acquired St. Lawrence community into an increasingly intransigent nationalism which, without any particular malice or ill-will, almost inevitably found its expression in a generalized animosity toward Great Britain and British traditions. This animosity has, however, proved quite consistent with an admiration of individuals, ideas, and institutions in spite of their British origin.

Nothing was further from the minds of the aristocratic oligarchy which became responsible for the security and well-being of the new possession than to provoke or encourage nationalism of any kind. As has already been suggested, no one in those days thought much about "nationalism" as a moral force. The great Metternich who spent so much energy deploring it as a novel and most immoral phenomenon was not to be born for another decade. The basic problem of government in Quebec was seen in quite different terms. Canadians were looked at as individuals and not as an entity. As individuals no one wished to disturb them in their property or their customs; no one wished to harry them because of their religion. It was, however, a fact that they were now part of the dominions of the British Crown; this implied a certain framework of government, and a part of that framework was the established Church of England, the moral and spiritual aspect of the state. Moreover it was hoped and expected that the country, three-quarters empty, would soon be filled by English or American immigrants. Purely from motives of simplicity and convenience it was taken for granted that a policy of gentle and steady transformation to a more or less British way of life, and especially to the Protestant Church of England, could be effected without harshness and with due regard for civil rights. This attitude was assumed without much question by almost everyone, including the first governor, James Murray, who was sincerely devoted to "my Canadians" and who took, as he said, for his guide, "the dictates of clemency."

Anyone is free to speculate on the possible results of such a policy if it had been steadily and skilfully pursued. No one can now positively prove that it could not have had the desired results. At the same time with an attitude assumed so instinctively and unthinkingly, the British were most unlikely to pursue the corresponding policy with any particular steadiness and skill. As it happened the policy was never really tried at all, partly because of the normal indifference and lethargy of British statesmen of that period in relation to all but the most pressing colonial problems, but chiefly because their attention was diverted by a truly pressing colonial problem, the alarming activity and enthusiasm of the colonists to the south. It is true of all periods of our history, but particularly of this one, that the historian who looks at Canada out of its continental context must be misled. During the first quarter of a century of British rule in Canada, the province of Quebec was only one, and one of the less important, of the American group. It had indeed been conquered and retained largely because of its nuisance value. France on the St. Lawrence was a constant and expensive menace to New York and Boston. After the conquest it was natural that British policy in Quebec should be largely influenced by the total American situation.

Just as the French Revolution was to have a peculiarly unhappy effect on Britain by checking and diverting the necessary adjustments of an aristocratic and rural community to the rising urban and industrial society of the late 18th and early 19th centuries, so the immediate impact of the American Revolution, coming directly after the British conquest, was to embarrass and distort the necessary adjustments of the St. Lawrence community in coming to terms with a new age. This missionary and fur-trading colony, which has carried even into the 20th century a most misleading reputation for "quaintness" and simplicity, was not cut off from the ideas and aspirations of the age of enlightenment. If some of the seigneurs made themselves occasionally ridiculous in their aping of the manners and costumes of Versailles, and if the rigidity of church and state had gone so far as to discourage the establishment even of a printing press in the Colony, there were yet members of the clergy and laity who secured and read the latest books from France—and, as the event proved, there were many perfectly capable of grasping what the Americans meant by "liberty." Conservative on the whole, the community was far from being intellectually stagnant. Had peace reigned in North America it is possible that Canadians might have made their own gradual and easy adjustments to the ways of their American neighbours, now in theory their friends, and even to the pressures of the British government. It is not certain that there was such religious fervour or such devoted loyalty to French culture and traditions as to have preserved a distinct community in the face of the steady attrition of an alien government and of alien influences from the south, so long as there was no active persecution.

II

It was the violent impact of the American Revolution involving as it did a new war between Britain and France which not only rendered impossible any steady and gentle policy of anglicization, but produced a type of British government which had a strong and perhaps a lasting effect on a people just awakening to political self-consciousness; a people exposed to a flood of radical ideas on church and state from the English-speaking merchants and traders who had entered the colony, and from the repeated communications that came up to them from the south.

The situation in the southern colonies, the threat and then the fact of the invasion of 1775, the impact of the ensuing war, and the operation of the peace resulted in a British policy which first divided from each other, and from the mass of the people, the literate classes in Canada who should have been the leaders of society, and then flung them once more into an uneasy unity based less on mutual affection than on a common resentment against both arbitrary government from above and against the interlopers from the south who had done so much to teach them the evils of arbitrary government. The historian of Quebec finds this curious process going on with an air of inevitability because it derived not from the internal situation of the colony but from external forces. British ministers and British governors alike were in a sense merely the instruments of a policy dictated to them by circumstances over which they had no control. This is not to say that no other policy might have been followed. It does seem clear, however, that every step of the policy can find some logical justification in considerations which at the time seemed paramount.

The first and most important instrument of destiny was Guy Carleton who took over the administration of Quebec in 1766 and succeeded James Murray as governor in 1768. Carleton on this occasion remained four years in Quebec, after which he returned to Britain to offer advice to the government on necessary legislation for defining the law and the constitution of the colony. The Quebec Act passed in 1774 was the result of his efforts.

Endless debate on the merits and demerits of this act has turned generally on what Canadians "wanted" at the time, and on what they could justly claim from their conquerors. Unfortunately, there was no French Canadian press in the province, and no newspaper of any kind except the official *Quebec Gazette*. Only a small proportion of the population could read or write, and of the body of contemporary written material that probably survives only a part has been found or is available to the historian. It is therefore exceedingly difficult to be certain what Canadians "wanted," to know what they were thinking, to know the extent to which there was any coherent body of ideas in the colony. The fragmentary evidence that exists is tantalizing in the extreme. There is, however, evidence to suggest that at least some Canadians immediately after the conquest, or perhaps before, had imbibed enough of the modern ideas of France and of their neighbours, the American colonies, to be critical of their own society and government. They were possibly also critical of the church, largely controlled as it was by Frenchmen rather than by the native-born Canadians who constituted the bulk of the parish priests. There is clear evidence that Canadian-born church leaders before the arrival of Carleton were trying to rally and unite all classes in the colony for the protection of their religious liberties, urging them to set aside both fear of the British and the resentment of each other which was based on differences of social rank. The purpose of the church leaders seems to have been to secure for the Canadians protection for their own customs and religion by a kind of extra-territoriality centered on the existing Court of Common Pleas which already by law and custom was considered a special "Canadian Court."

It was apparently Carleton who turned what was intended to be a modest community effort under the joint leadership of clergy, seigneurs, and merchants into a much more grandiose scheme which was to exalt both the seigneurs and the hierarchy of the church, while at the same time keeping each group somewhat separate from the other, and dependent on the favour of the governor. Carleton's plan, in his view, was in accordance with justice and humanity. His purpose, frankly stated, was the defence of the undeniably vulnerable province of Quebec against attack by France, and the possible use of the province as a basis for operations against the potentially rebellious colonies to the south.

Carleton's scheme, as he said himself, was to be based on the quality that he admired in the former government of the French colony, "subordination from the highest to the lowest." He did not, however, envisage the triple control of governor, intendant, and bishop which had existed before 1760. He, himself, as governor and commander-in-chief would unite the functions of the former governor and the intendant; and following the British principle that the head of the state was also the head of the church, the bishop, representing the hierarchy of the church, would take his directions from Carleton. Carleton seems thus to have envisaged two hierarchies, each operating under himself, one in the church, the other in the secular aspect of society.

Carleton's plan for the church worked well from his point of view. He was fortunate, and probably the Canadian church was fortunate, in the bishop who had been appointed at Murray's request, Jean-Olivier Briand. Briand was a truly devout man, a Frenchman, who was dedicated to preserving the integrity of the Canadian church. He seems to have seen the total problem very clearly from the beginning. The church must cut off its official connection with France and indicate complete loyalty to the British throne. It must, however, preserve its spiritual integrity by maintaining the absolutely essential links with Rome. In order to do this without arousing the suspicion of the British authorities, churchmen must be absolutely loyal and accommodating to the state in all matters except in those where conscience forbade. Briand's motto and one which he offered to his parish priests was "be ye wise as serpents and harmless as doves." Although a loyal Frenchman with warm affection for his own people, he sedulously laid aside all patriotic emotions with the single purpose of preserving the church in the community. He, therefore, submitted both to Murray and to Carleton, and was indeed able to boast that, following the tactful Ultramontanism to which circumstances compelled him, he had more control in his church after the conquest than he would have had if it had remained an integral part of the Gallican church of France. At the same time, neither he nor his successors were able to do what good sense and tact would normally have dictated in the organization of the church. Carleton supported the bishop's authority but he would not allow it to be shared. Any suggestion that the church become a self-governing body was firmly suppressed. The Quebec chapter which Briand greatly wished to revive ceased to exist. A later suggestion of a representative synod of priests was firmly rejected by the governor. The bishop was left free to govern his church without much interference from the governor, but only if he kept all power within his own hands. Briand succeeded in the task but not without difficulty as his letters abundantly show.

If Carleton was able to achieve without much difficulty his authoritarian ideals in the church, he was much less successful when he turned to the secular matters. He looked for leaders through whom he might govern and he thought he had found them in the seigneurs, the equivalent as he supposed of the nobility of France. Most seigneurs, however, were of relatively humble origins and few had wealth corresponding to the rank that they would have liked to claim. They had been sustained by military service and by the patronage of the French king.

Carleton convinced himself that the Canadians, who had indeed fought with great effect alongside of regular French regiments during the recent war, could be created, through the leadership of the seigneurs, into a formidable force for defensive or offensive operations. To conciliate the seigneurs, therefore, he set aside plans which since 1766 had found favour with the British authorities for confirming Canadian customs of land tenure, inheritance, alienation, and wills within a general British legal framework. Instead, the whole of Canadian law relating to property and civil rights was, following his recommendations, confirmed by the Quebec Act. This was intended to conciliate the seigneurs by restoring the framework of the society of which, they claimed, they had been the leaders.

The seigneurs did not, indeed, consider the concessions of the Quebec Act adequate. They had already demanded a recognition of their rights to *haute, moyenne et basse justice* (long since practically fallen into disuse) and Carleton's special adviser from among the group also argued strongly for the general retention of the entire French criminal law. Carleton probably got as much for the seigneurs as he could, although later he regretted that he had not revived more French law. He compensated as far as possible for any deficiencies by his policy in administering the Quebec Act. He encouraged the seigneurs to believe that what had been granted them was a kind of permanent guarantee of their ancient way of life—"a charter for the nation," the nation which the seigneurs maintained that they represented.

The result was division and bitterness among Canadians. There is no evidence at all that Carleton wished to divide and rule. He did, undoubtedly, wish to isolate the Canadians as a community both from the colonies to the south and from, as he thought, disloyal American and British merchants who were living in the towns of Quebec and Montreal. He hoped and expected that his policy would unite Canadians under the seigneurs. Instead he accentuated the social divisions which already existed in Canadian society, and which it had been the effort of the church to overcome in the interests of religion. Etienne Montgolfier, the vicar general and head of the seminary in Montreal, wrote quite frankly to Bishop Briand that Carleton's seigneurial adviser was unsatisfactory. He asked if the church should not provide funds for sending over a layman who would present their ideas more appropriately. Briand's reply was cautious and tactful: "to do nothing but leave all to the wisdom and benevolence of the governor." Montgolfier was not alone in his views. Although, the evidence is tantalizingly fragmentary, it seems clear that, even before the passing of the Quebec Act, Carleton's obvious patronage of the seigneurs was arousing some irritation and scorn on the part of the better educated and more sophisticated merchants in the towns. This irritation was increased when, in 1775, on the Quebec Act coming into operation, it was found that not a single merchant was among the seven new Roman Catholic appointments to the Council and that the seigneurial pretensions had also been flattered in the Canadians appointed to the Court of Common Pleas. Both judges and councillors were invited to associate themselves with Carleton and his chosen advisers in maintaining, contrary to the views of the British Government, Canadian laws as an inviolable charter.

There is good evidence that neither merchants nor church in the colony wanted quite so complete an ossification of law in a changing community. Some Canadians even protested that they had been promised "English law" and an Assembly and that they wanted an Assembly if only for the adequate protection of such customs as they did wish to keep unchanged. As for the church it firmly refused to support the seigneurial archaism, which at a later date strove to exclude religious communities from the operation of Habeas Corpus.

III

At best then Carleton's scheme for doing justice to the Canadians, and at the same time making the province fully defensible against attack from the American colonies or from France, would have had the effect of introducing an arbitrary form of government, alien to the British tradition, without the excuse that it fully satisfied the Canadian community. Its vindication must then have rested on its success. Unfortunately for Carleton, on the secular side it was a complete failure.

It was soon abundantly clear to everyone in the province that the governor's hope of using seigneurial influence and leadership to exploit the military potential of Canadians, was based on pure illusion. When, in 1775, Americans invaded the province, the bulk of the habitants absolutely refused to take up arms against the invaders. They were, it was reported, already disgusted and alarmed at the renewed and even novel pretensions of the seigneurs. They were attracted by American talk of liberty, and still more by American offers of pay. The influence of the church kept most passive, but not a few engaged themselves to the enemy for 40 *piastres* a month, unhappily for them paid in promises only.

In 50 parishes in the lower part of the province affected by the invasion, almost all the captains of militia compromised themselves by cooperating with the enemy. These men had been trusted agents of the government under the French regime. The British neglect of them in favour of the seigneur and the church perhaps inclined them to listen to American persuasions more readily than they might otherwise have done. Whether or not this is so, the anger of the seigneurs against the recalcitrant habitants and the resentment of the habitants against the seigneurs who as the agents of the governments endeavoured to force them into military service was yet another element of division in the community.

Throughout the war this situation was made even worse by the policy of the government toward the habitants. If the habitants would not fight in the war it was decreed that they must at least perform the various *corvée* duties to which they had been subject under the French regime. The confirmation of much of the former Canadian civil law by the Quebec Act gave an air of appropriateness to the ordinance of the council which seemed to authorize arbitrary and often onerous demands for transport duty by land and by water. English members of the council protested that Canadians were often hardly used and that the ordinances should define their obligations and rights with much greater clarity. It was the little group of seigneurs in council who throughout the war steadily supported Carleton and his successor Haldimand in subjecting the habitant to the often arbitrary claims of the troops, including the German troops used to garrison the province. Five years after the war was over a representative of the radical Canadian merchant group in Montreal asked how the seigneurs could dare to represent themselves as leaders of the country and protectors of the people: "[These] famous protectors took very good care not to join their voices to those of the oppressed when the Germans, sent to defend the colony, came into it as if it were a conquered country. . . ."

No such unhappy effects attended Carleton's patronage of the church. It seems certain that Briand found both parishioners and parish priests rebellious and insubordinate at times. He was undoubtedly aided in his endeavor to maintain ecclesiastical discipline by the knowledge that he had the full support of the governor. Nevertheless he was too astute a person and had too great respect for the dignity of the church and the priesthood to let himself appear as a mere agent of the governor. He was fully aware that, surrounded as the church was with protestant communities, his authority must be spiritual and spiritual only, and he acted accordingly. It can, therefore, be said that far from being divisive Carleton's policy here by enabling the church to continue did preserve the greatest unifying influence in French Canada.

At the same time the patronage of the government cost something, and Carleton's kindness might easily have proved to be the kiss of death. The influence of the seigneurs having failed, the church had to use its authority to the utmost to keep the habitants at least neutral in the war against the Americans. Here it had considerable although not complete success. Much more difficult, however, was the situation of the church after France joined the American Colonies against Britain. Briand steadfastly maintained loyalty to the British government, and insisted that all who had taken the oath of allegiance must do likewise. He, himself, however, acknowledged that during the American invasion most people hoped the Americans would win. At a later date he mentioned his extreme unpopularity during the war when he continued to preach loyalty while a large if unknown proportion of the population were eagerly watching the river for the approach of the hoped for invasion fleet from France. There is evidence that at this time many of Briand's priests joined their flocks in hoping for the return of the French.

This unpopularity, however, earned by loyalty to the British government was passing. The American invaders retreated and the French invaders did not arrive. Much more serious for the church was the anxious solicitude of Governor Haldimand, who succeeded Carleton in 1778, over the shortage of priests to man the Canadian parishes. Briand, himself, had been acutely anxious over this difficulty from the beginning of the period. His solution was the importation of carefully selected priests from France, men whose loyalty and good behaviour he would guarantee. If this could not be done during the war Briand hoped, at least, that it might be done at the conclusion of the peace.

Haldimand rejected this scheme out of hand and pressed one of his own for importing French-speaking priests from Savoy. Briand, aware of a certain feeling even between French-born and Canadian priests could not consider such a scheme without anger and dismay. Fortunately for him it came to nothing for various reasons.

The problem of recruitment for the church remained. Educated priests were badly needed, especially for the seminaries. If Canadians would accept only priests from France, Britain absolutely refused to admit "subjects of the House of Bourbon." The seigneurial party did not support the wishes of church in this matter, but the rather radical Canadian merchants of the towns did. Representatives from Montreal went over to London in 1783 on the conclusion of the peace to beg for permission to bring in priests from France. Their mission was a total failure. After two years' fruitless lobbying with the British government they came back convinced that their only remedy was to join with the English in demanding an elected assembly in order to give weight to the general wishes of their people. This democratic conclusion to a clerical quest was vehemently opposed by the seigneurs. The leading clergy appear to have been divided between those resigned to a respectable obscurantism, leaving the Canadian church to be poorly nourished from its own intellectual resources, without help from abroad, and others who were prepared to support the radical Canadian merchants.

The radical group found support from the American Loyalists and between them they devised a new scheme for maintaining intellectual life in church and state. Although most of the Americans went to new settlements up river and along Lake Ontario, a small but influential group of educated men did remain in the lower province. The leader of these, William Smith, lately a lawyer and Chief Justice of New York, now Chief Justice of Quebec, had an intense but undogmatic interest in religion, a keen interest in education, and an extreme dislike of a state church. He had also sincere admiration for French culture. Out of his association with Canada's radicals, secular and clerical, there came the first and, as it proved, premature scheme for a nonsectarian Canadian university. According to the plan it was to be supported from the estates of the dying order of the Jesuits, and from such other endowments as could be secured. Who took the initiative in this scheme is not certain. It was warmly supported by Smith, by Bailly, the coadjutor to the Bishop, and by a number of Canadians in Quebec and Montreal, including a Montreal lawyer, Simon Sanguinet, who bequeathed what was reputed to be a considerable estate to the new university. According to the proposed constitution the university was to be attached to no church, and would teach only secular subjects. Theological instruction would be given by the various denominations. The new university would thus provide a recruiting ground for servants of church and state.

Smith undoubtedly intended his scheme to be the means of promoting cultural unity among all classes of Canadians and their English fellow subjects. He was encouraged by the support of the prominent churchman and friend of Carleton, Bailly, as well as of the radical merchant group. Even if one assumes that this was a workable scheme at this date, however, there is no doubt that Smith dismissed too lightly the clerical opposition which to him would seem merely obscurantist. Briand had retired in 1784. The new bishop, Charles-Francois Hubert, opposed the plan firmly and carried the church with him. It is not quite clear how much Hubert dreaded the evils of ignorance. He certainly reckoned them less than the perils of atheism, and to him a secular university could lead only in that direction. Not, it seems, without a certain struggle, he retained the support of the body of his clergy and the plan accordingly collapsed.

IV

It seems certain then, that during the later part of the 18th century Canadian society had become sharply divided. If none of the divisions originated with the Conquest all were accentuated by it. The seigneurs who, for all their prominence as loyal councillors and subjects of the British king, had no real power, were used as props by the government. To have given even those who were fully qualified responsible state positions during the period in which France might by the fortune of war re-enter her former colony would have been at once imprudent for the state, and unfair to the seigneurs. They were, however, encouraged to pose as representatives of *la nation* while the habitants disliked them, the merchants scorned them, and even the church had to note their failure to use any of their influence in her support.

British policy, then apparently dictated by the kindest motives, had an unhappy effect on the community. After having, during the early years of the peace, governed the habitants with a mildness that they had grown to accept as a natural right, the British in the crisis of war suddenly attempted to reimpose the authority of the seigneurs in a new form, along with the burdensome and often oppressive *corvées* of the French regime. The land-owning class of the seigneurs which, with increasing agricultural prosperity, might possibly have achieved real social influence, was thus alienated from the habitants. At the same time, the merchants of the towns were treated with a steady neglect which left them resentful of the seigneurs, suspicious of the government, and only restrained from associating themselves with their English-speaking competitors against the government by the somewhat narrow national and religious views of the English. The church, it was true, had been treated with a generosity unexampled at that time, except in the one thing needed—permission to draw on the spiritual and intellectual resources of France, resources essential to normal healthy growth, and unattainable elsewhere. As a result, by the end of the period, while revolutionary and anticlerical ideas were flowing in from the United States and France and circulating freely, the church was hard put to it to find any clergy qualified by natural gifts or training to exercise adequate moral leadership.

In every group in the Canadian community, therefore, there was frustration and irritation. At the end of the war the socially divided Canadians may have been more irritated with each other than with Great Britain. This situation, however, was not to last. Although there were genuine movements of unity and sympathy between Canadian radicals and English loyalists in the lower province, fundamental antipathies were not long in developing. It could hardly have been otherwise. The loyalists, some of them at least, had lost much in position, property, and friends. It was inevitable that they should place an exaggerated importance on the convictions which had inspired their sacrifices. It is perhaps not too much to say that in such people even opinions become sacred and convictions may be cherished with undue fervour. Quebec was invaded by men who equated religion with protestantism, civilization with representative institutions, and culture with general literacy, newspapers, and public libraries. Chief Justice Smith could admire Quebec's handsome buildings (and its beautiful ladies); and, even while deploring the general illiteracy, could remind American loyalists that as inhabitants of Quebec they, with the Canadians, were the heirs of the two greatest civilizations of the modern world. His fellow loyalists were not convinced. Some perhaps could not forget that, but for French intervention in the recent war, they might not have been exiles. Too many indulged in criticism, ranging from solemn warnings against violations of "the sabbath" to scornful references to ignorance, superstition, and despotism. They thus contrived to alienate many Canadians whose views on politics were not far from their own, and whose religion was anything but fanatic.

Thus the bad manners and bad humour of the loyalists and ultimately their insistence on more than their rights forced Canadians who were genuinely divided in their social, political, and religious views into a defensive unity which ultimately became intransigent. The church did help to maintain some healthy community life, but the church itself, in its failure to recruit French clergy, represented a fresh source of irritation and frustration directly attributable to British policy, although not to British ill-will. It is no wonder that the intoxicating sense of nationalism released by the French Revolution took on in Canada an especially tenacious form, expressing itself in a fashion peculiarly hostile to the British who had conquered and divided them, and to the continuing Britishness even of the Americans who appeared to be engulfing them.

14

THE LOYALIST TRADITION IN CANADA*

David V. J. Bell

Beginning almost from the outbreak of hostilities in 1775 and particularly after the signing of the Treaty of Paris in 1783, large numbers of political refugees flocked from the rebellious American colonies to Nova Scotia and Quebec. Perhaps 25,000 came to the Maritimes, most of them settling in what in 1784 became New Brunswick; another 12–15,000 settled in Quebec, particularly in the western part of the province along Lake Ontario. Most of the principal political leaders, merchants, and landholders exiled by the American Revolution went to England and the West Indies, and Quebec and Nova Scotia received what amounted to a cross section of a predominantly middle-class American population, largely farmers and artisans, with only a sprinkling of intellectuals and former officeholders.

The immediate impact of these refugees—or Loyalists, as they were called—was and is indisputable. The population of what remained of British North America was significantly increased; settlement patterns were shifted; and in Quebec the overwhelming French-Canadian numerical predominance upon which British policy had been based was altered. The results were the new provinces of New Brunswick and Upper Canada, and a legislative assembly for Lower Canada. The Loyalist influx determined that British North America would remain British—and American, for most of the new immigrants were thoroughly Americanized and had no personal experience with an Old World environment.

But if the short-run effect of the Loyalist migration has been subject to little debate among historians, the question of the long-range impact is a

---

*Journal of Canadian Studies, 5 (May 1970), 22–33.

different matter entirely. Many Canadians—and a few Americans—have been fascinated by comparative analysis of the development of the nations of Canada and the United States, "children of a common mother," particularly in light of the divisions created by what amounted to a civil war in the American colonies and the presence of a French-speaking population in Canada. Much of the discussion hinges around the psychological differences between Canadians and Americans, aspects developed by David Bell in the following article. What are the main differences Bell identifies between Canadians and Americans? To what factors does he attribute these differences? Are there additional factors which might be added?

SUGGESTIONS FOR FURTHER READING

Wallace Brown, *The Good Americans: The Loyalists in the American Revolution* (New York: Morrow, 1969).

L. F. S. Upton, *The Loyal Whig: William Smith of New York and Quebec* (Toronto: University of Toronto Press, 1969).

Esther C. Wright, *The Loyalists of New Brunswick* (1955).

J.M.B.

NATION AND NON-NATION†

*To forget and—I will venture to say—to get one's history
wrong, are essential factors in the making of a nation.‡*
— *Ernest Renan*

*In speaking of men who have left their impress upon their
age, something, I own, is due to the dignity of history; but
something, too, is due to the dignity of truth.*
— *Lorenzo Sabine*

In its most important aspects, a nation is a psychological entity. To be sure, nations usually require certain minimal objective conditions of geography, economics, communications, etc. But nationalism is a

†This essay is adapted from Chapter 8 of "Nation and Non-Nation: A new Analysis of the Loyalists and the American Revolution." (Unpublished Ph.D. dissertation, Harvard University, 1969.) Work on revision was facilitated by a research grant from the Ford Foundation Fund, administered through the Political Development Studies Group and the International Programs of Michigan State University. Special thanks are due to Editor Nancy Hammond of the Social Science Research Bureau, Michigan State University, for assistance in preparing this manuscript. For its shortcomings and errors, I am alone responsible.

‡"What is a nation?" in Alfred Zimmern, ed., *Modern Political Doctrines* (London: Oxford University Press, 1939), p. 190. Quoted in Dankwart Rustow, *A World of Nations* (Washington: Brookings Institution, 1967).

state of mind. Non-nationalism, therefore, is also a state of mind. And a non-nation is a psychological non-entity.

The American Revolution produced not one country but two: a nation and a non-nation. By virtue of the Revolution, the nation (the United States) acquired a set of national symbols, a gallery of heroes, and a national identity that featured, among other things, an ideologically-based definition of citizenship.[1]

Like all 'internal wars', the Revolution had losers as well as victors. The Loyalists, as the losers were called, were not exterminated (as were many of the losers of the French Revolution); nor were they reintegrated into the community (as were the Southerners after the American Civil War); instead, they were expelled. Most of them migrated north and became the founders of the English-speaking component of the non-nation—modern Canada. With them they brought broken dreams, a distorted image of their experience, and a profound sense of indignation bordering on rage.

No competent study of (English) Canadian history and culture overlooks the Loyalists; several interpretations ascribe to the Loyalist experience crucial significance; yet few students have personally taken the time or effort to examine the Loyalists in depth. Instead they have relied on secondary—or even tertiary—sources that are often more myth than fact.[2]

In the past few decades, some students of Canadian history have advanced the argument that the Loyalists were "organic" anti-liberal conservatives, "tinged with toryism," "counter-revolutionary" elitists.[3] For some, this argument has buttressed their belief in a delicate Canadian national identity, presently disintegrating under pressure from the "American Empire." Indeed, one writer has offered a lament not in despair or cynicism but in pain and regret at the passing of "Canadian" culture.[4]

A few have argued against the "tory" interpretation, but their approach has too greatly *underplayed* the importance of the Loyalist experience.[5] Moreover, both views—the "tory" and the "liberal"—rely too heavily on left-right (i.e., conservative–liberal) distinctions of more use in studying European than New World politics.

---

[1]In America, citizenship (in the sense of membership in the national community) came to signify fidelity to the Revolution and the Ideals for which it was (supposedly) fought. These Ideals embodied many of the principles of English liberal thought, especially as presented in the works of John Locke. They eventually coalesced into what Gunnar Myrdal denoted 'The American Creed'.

[2]See "Nation and Non-Nation: A new Analysis of the Loyalists and the American Revolution." Unpublished Ph.D. dissertation, Harvard University, 1969 (passim) for a critical review.

[3]See John Conway, "What is Canada?" *Atlantic Monthly* (November 1964), pp. 100–105; Gad Horowitz, "Conservatism, Liberalism, Socialism," *Canadian Journal of Economics and Political Science* (May 1966); S. M. Lipset, *Revolution and Counter-Revolution* (New York: Basic Books, 1968).

[4]George Grant, *Lament For a Nation* (Toronto: McClelland & Stewart, 1965). See also this *Journal*, May 1969.

[5]See Kenneth McRae, "The Structure of Canadian History," in Louis Hartz, *The Founding of New Societies* (New York: Harcourt, Brace & World, 1964).

There were some important differences in outlook between Loyalists and Revolutionaries, but they did not correspond to the categories denoted by "conservative" and "liberal." To the contrary, a careful analysis of the prerevolutionary debate between Whigs and Tories reveals that both groups *shared* liberal (Lockeian) assumptions about the nature of sovereignty, good government, the right of resistance, etc.[6] The debate did not juxtapose one ideology with another; instead it featured the conflict of two views of the existing situation derived from identical premises. Briefly, the Whigs (i.e., Revolutionaries) argued that British policy after 1763 constituted a conspiracy to enslave the 13 colonies, and thus justified—indeed demanded—revolution. The Tories, on the other hand, maintained that British policy, though reprehensible, was merely stupid rather than tyrannical. And the resort to violence was unjustified "rebellion" (literally, *re-bellare*), which to Locke meant the brutal act of forcing men into the state of war, "the greatest Crime a man is capable of."[7]

Thus, the Loyalists resembled fairly closely the persecutors from whom they fled. This fact deprived them of the luxury of unambiguous hatred of their own former adversaries. Rather, their attitude was one of ambivalence: the Loyalists found themselves hating America, but loving and envying it as well. As a result, the Loyalists were deprived of the opportunity of erecting their values—which were virtually identical to those of the Americans—into a national identity.

THE LOYALISTS—IRONY, PATHOS, AND IDENTITY CRISIS

For the Canadian Loyalist, the Revolution produced irony; for the English Loyalist (i.e., who returned to England rather than going to Canada), it produced pathos. Both of them, however, shared this much in common: a profound identity crisis stemming from the expulsion.

In the course of the Revolution, violent rhetoric was used by both sides. Whigs and Tories accused one another of heinous, satanic inspiration. (Revolutionary propaganda is always hyperbolic, but the American Revolution was extreme in this regard, a consequence of the fact that both sides in the debate shared the same principles; and these principles predetermined that a debate on the question of revolution would be supercharged with emotion—it was an all-or-nothing question that involved the most basic and crucial values of the ideology.) Each side, therefore, hurled at its opponent the most powerful pejoratives it could find.

These 'names', contrary to the nursery ditty, had tremendous potential to hurt. To be called a name is one thing. To have it stick, to be forced to live with it, is quite another. When a revolution is over, the revolutionary forgets entirely the names he was called. The vituperation poured out by

[6]See Bell, "Nation and Non-Nation," chap. 4.

[7]John Locke, *Two Treatises of Government*, ed., Peter Laslett (New York: New American Library, 1965), p. 467.

the Tories, therefore, became largely irrelevant. Who reads Peter Oliver's acidic portraits of the men who later emerged as the hallowed 'Founding Fathers'? Who even remembers that he wrote it? The answer is no one (an American edition of the work did not appear until 1961!). The successful antagonist celebrates his victory. The wounds of propaganda warfare heal quickly. After all, he is the winner, triumphant and confident.[8]

What happens to the loser is another story entirely. He can never forget the names he was called—the epithets of revolutionary propaganda are, for him, reinforced in the most vivid way imaginable—exclusion from the new society. The hyperbolic distortions of political warfare become operant maxims for the post-revolutionary 'solution'. The Loyalist was violently expelled, he was told, because he did not belong; he was 'un-American'. The Loyalist simply could not understand this. America was his home. The principles of John Locke were his principles. He knew no others.[9] There is much room for sympathy with the Loyalist on this account. He had good reason to be baffled. He was expelled as a *political* exile, but on the basis of a false excuse: that he was also an *ideological* one.

This in turn involved him in an identity crisis that is at once poignant and profound. When the Loyalist asked 'Who am I?' his experience of expulsion precluded his giving the only conceivable answer—I am an American. An American in the sense not only of living in America, but also in the ideological sense of subscribing to the principles of John Locke. When the Loyalist refused to support the Revolution, he did not intend to sacrifice his home, his beliefs, and his hard-won identity.

Robbed of his identity, the Canadian Loyalist invented a new one. It is never a totally adequate substitute, of course. How can it be, when he must continuously deny its very essence, liberalism? "The typical Canadian," an Englishman observed a hundred years ago, "tells you that he is not, but he *is* a Yankee—a Yankee in the sense in which we use the term at home, as synonymous with everything that smacks of democracy. . ."[10] The Loyalist in Canada will always be faced with the paradox

---

[8]There is ideological justification for his brazen self-confidence: Locke explicitly states that the victor in armed combat is *ipso facto* 'right': the success of a revolution is sufficient—indeed the only—demonstration of its morality.

[9]Cf. The following Loyalist poem, written shortly before the Revolution broke out:

> Great shade of Locke, immortal Sage . . .
> Look down with pity, from the Skies!
> Behold a vain, deluded Race,
> Thy venerable Name, disgrace;
> As Casuists Pale, as Savage rude,
> With Glosses weak, with Comments crude,
> Pervert thy fair, Instructive Page.
> To sanctify, licentious Rage;
> To form some wild idea Plan,
> And break the Laws of God, and Man.

(*The Patriots of North America: A Sketch* (New York, 1775) pp. 21, 22.)

[10]G. T. Borrett, "The Levelling Principle in Canadian Life," in *Letters From Canada and the United States* (1865). Reprinted in G. M. Craig, ed., *Early Travellers in the Canadas* (Toronto: Macmillan, 1955), p. 279.

of being 'anti-American Yankee'. But he has a way out of his dilemma: he creates a myth that helps him survive—*he insists that he is British.*[11]

This is a myth that thrives on isolation. The Loyalist builds an American society and calls it by British names. So long as the Loyalist never goes to Britain, never sees the 'pure form' of which his image is such an imperfect copy, his myth can continue unchallenged.

The Loyalist in England was not permitted this luxury. In England the Loyalist sees himself as he really is—a confirmed American. The solution adopted by the Canadian Loyalist (i.e., invention of the myth of Britishness and 'Loyalism for its own sake') is not available to him. He cannot act to alleviate his pain. The Loyalist in England suffers excruciating torture. He pines his life away wishing for his homeland. He packs his bag, in anticipation of the return voyage he will never make.[12] His situation is a classic instance of historical pathos. "Pathos is that element in an historic situation which elicits pity, but neither deserves admiration nor warrants contrition. Pathos arises from fortuitous cross-purposes and confusions in life for which no reason can be given, or guilt ascribed. . . ."[13]

Contrast the pathos of the English Loyalist with the irony of his Canadian counterpart: "Irony consists of apparently fortuitous incongruities in life which are discovered, upon closer examination, to be not merely fortuitous. . . . The ironic situation is distinguished from a pathetic one by the fact that *the person involved bears some responsibility for it.*"[14] The Canadian Loyalist has acted, albeit unconsciously, and therefore "bears some responsibility" for his action (i.e., the invention of the myth of the 'British' Canadian). The English Loyalist, by contrast, is prevented from acting by the accident of history—he is in Britain. "While a pathetic . . . situation is not dissolved when a person becomes conscious of his involvement in it, an ironic situation must dissolve, if men or nations are made aware of their complicity in it."[15] We may make at least some Canadians "aware" of this irony by exposing the myth which has created it.

THE MANY FACETS OF THE LOYALIST MYTH

National sentiments rely heavily on mythical interpretations of the past. The nationalist believes that his is a "chosen" people, that his ancestors were divinely inspired, and hence that his nation is in a sense sacred. To this extent nationalism—and, therefore, non-nationalism as

---

[11]The combination of pro-British and anti-American sentiment was aptly noted by A. G. Bradley: "The U. E. Loyalist . . . through his passion for the British connection was fired by the trials he had endured on its behalf, was no more likely to sit down quietly under the most benignant [sic] despotism than his old rebel friends and neighbors in Virginia and Massachusetts. His peculiar experiences had made him a somewhat strange mixture of political sentiment. He is, in short, a unique figure in history. So far as I know you may look in vain elsewhere for a truculently anti-republican democrat." *The Making of Canada* (London: Constable, 1908), p. 168.

[12]For a full account, see Mary Beth Norton's unpublished Ph.D. dissertation, Harvard University, 1969.

[13]Reinhold Niebuhr, *The Irony of American History* (New York: Charles Scribner's Sons, 1952), pref., p. vii.

[14]Ibid., p. vii (emphasis added).

[15]Ibid.

well—is a kind of civil religion. And the myths of the nation resemble the myths of the church: both celebrate the virtues of an earlier glorious age.[16]

The loyalist experience provided the one element of glory in English Canada's history. All other achievements were subordinated and adapted to the idea of loyalism, which has functioned as the founding and integrating myth of the new society. Thus the War of 1812 allowed Canadians to engage in effusive demonstrations of loyalty to Britain and the crown.[17] (The contrast between myth and fact on this score is extraordinary!) The defeat of Mackenzie's rebellion in 1837 was, so the story goes, a patent case of the rejection of violence as a means of constitutional change. Confederation fulfilled a dream for a united group of *British* North American Colonies, still enjoying good relations with the Mother Country. The Boer War and the "Great World War" each provided the opportunity for further demonstrating loyalty and devotion to Britain, and a splendid example for other members of the Empire to follow.

The consequences of the powerful 'other-worldly' (i.e., New to Old) orientation included a failure to articulate a truly national identity that placed the focus of loyalty within Canada. Thus, Canadian independence was achieved not in a heroic act of defiance but on a complacent note of collaboration with the mother country. (Indeed, how could it be otherwise when the British connection is exalted as the "umbilical cord" through which "the life blood has flowed into the province"?[18]) Instead of a bold Declaration of Independence, Canada produced the *British* North America Act, and even it was passed not in Ottawa but in Westminster. Instead of the ringing "We the people of the (United States). . . ," Canadian 'national' ideals are supposedly enshrined in a document that begins "Whereas. . . ." The Canadian was so eager to affirm his Britishness that until 1947 he was content to be known not as a Canadian citizen but as a "British subject" (and even today the appellation is retained as an alternative denomination). Until the middle of the 1960s, the country's semi-official flags were the Red Ensign and the Union Jack, her national anthem "God Save the Queen"!

The failure to 'repatriate' symbols of identity (until it has perhaps become too late) has left a legacy of problems for national unity. It has, for example, contributed to the present-day disenchantment of French

---

[16]As Dankwart Rustow points out, national mythology "reflects the search for symbols of confidence that is an integral part of early modernization and insecure nationalism." *A World of Nations* (Washington: Brookings Institution, 1967), p. 44. See also the brief discussion of "political myth," "that is to say, the myth of myths dealing with the foundation and origin of a particular political order," in Carl J. Friedrich, *Man and His Government* (New York: McGraw-Hill, 1963), p. 96.

[17]As William Foster, a loyalist descendent, put it in 1871, "We need not ransack foreign romance for valorous deeds. . . . [In 1812,] a call to arms ran throughout the country, echoing from lake to river, and piercing the inmost recesses of the forest. How the eyes of the old refugee loyalists must have flashed as the rusty flintlock was taken from the rack above the fireplace. . . . How must the pulses of the young men have throbbed as they grasped the trusty rifle. . . ." Quoted in Carl Berger, "The Vision of Grandeur." Unpublished Ph.D. dissertation, University of Toronto, 1966, p. 167 (cf. also p. 163).

[18]A statement made more than a decade after confederation by William Canniff, another loyalist descendent. Quoted in ibid., p. 140. Elsewhere, Berger writes that "The [loyalist] tradition flourished [in the late 19th century] because it provided a useful device by which the arguments of the advocates of Canadian independence could be counteracted . . . " (p. 136).

Canada:[19] the celebration of loyalty has functioned as a reminder of the Conquest—a far from popular event in French Canada's history.

One *persisting* component of the loyalist myth has, therefore, been the notion of loyalty to Britain. Considerably less durable was the loyalist 'interpretation' of the American Rebellion and the Rebels. Essentially, this interpretation amounted to a one-sided repetition of tory propaganda that stressed the evil and pernicious motivations of those who threw off the benign rule of Britain and drove from their homes the brave, honest loyalists. In the 1830s, this view was used in a fairly clever fashion to discredit attempts at political reform as manifestations of 'republican tendencies' (which connoted all sorts of evil things). In the name of self-preservation, the Family Compact (which was not representative of all Loyalists) tried desperately to convince the masses that democracy was synonymous with republicanism and annexation. "[A] suspicion of disloyalty," according to one historian, "was the most potent influence against the reformers in the 'thirties."[20] But the masses were not to be duped into throwing out the baby of reform and democracy along with the bathwater of armed rebellion. Eventually democracy came, though it followed the British pattern of responsible government rather than the American pattern of a constitutional republic.

Thus, the loyalist myth of the American Revolution posed some temporary problems for democratization. But it had another consequence as well: it engendered among some 'liberal' Canadian historians in the present century a powerful countermyth. The Loyalists were identified as reactionary conservatives, universally opposed to change in politics (and by analogy changes in all spheres). According to this interpretation, the Loyalists represented the party of wealth and privilege, selfish tyrants and oppressors. (The similarity between the countermyth and *Whig* revolutionary propaganda is obvious.) The view of the Loyalists as a class-conscious group of would-be aristocrats is nevertheless no more accurate than the view the Loyalists held of the reformers as conspiratorial demagogues. Through a dialectic of mistruths, the true character of both groups has been distorted.

A further component of the loyalist myth is anti-Americanism. Loyalist attitudes to America were not entirely one-sided, however. Indeed, they featured agonizing ambivalence: hatred mixed with envious love; invidiousness tinged with pathetic admiration.

The ambivalent quality of loyalist attitudes was evident even before the Loyalists arrived in Canada. Edward Winslow, later to become prominent in New Brunswick society and politics, epitomized the Loyalist outlook when he recorded this desperate aspiration: "By Heaven, we will be the envy of the American States."[21] Surely this is the most classic

---

[19]Much of the original impetus for a 'repatriated' national identity indeed came from French Canadian, Henri Bourassa, in the early decades of the present century. Had his aspirations been fulfilled, Canada might have averted its present crisis of national identity and national integration. Instead, Bourassa became almost a social outcast, condemned for having transgressed on the sanctity of the British connection.

[20]Aileen Dunham, *Political Unrest in Upper Canada* (Toronto: McClelland & Stewart, 1963), p. 141.

[21]Quoted in William Nelson, *The American Tory* (Boston: Beacon Press, 1961), p. 169.

kind of projection! The Loyalist alleviated his own (repressed) jealousy by confidently ascribing identical emotions to the object of his envy.

Winslow's hollow declaration of superiority has been echoed throughout Canadian history. It has led to an obsessive compulsion to make comparisons between Canada and the United States to demonstrate superior Canadian virtue or achievement. A favorite topic for comparison has been law and order. Countless speeches have been delivered on the theme of Canadian law-abiding virtue as contrasted with American vice and criminal violence. But comparison has also been made on issues other than this one (which at least is important and partially defensible as a mark of virtue): even *census* figures have been used as evidence to demonstrate the fulfillment of Winslow's aspiration![22]

From a psychological point of view, Canada's relationship with the United States bears a number of pathological characteristics. Whether the relationship has, on the whole, been beneficial or debilitating is difficult to establish. It has certainly been neither normal nor irrelevant. That the United States would play a crucial role—not only economically and politically, but psychologically as well—in the development of Canada[23] was in large part a function of the Loyalist migration.

In addition to these emotional and psychological effects (loyalty to Britain and anti-Americanism), the loyalist tradition in Canada has contributed to some enduring differences, which we shall now examine, between the United States and Canada, differences in political structure and political culture. It is here that the positive benefits of the loyalist tradition can be found.

LEGITIMACY, DEMOCRACY, AND RESPONSIBLE GOVERNMENT

The American Revolution, like all revolutions, involved a crisis of legitimacy. The policies pursued by Britain after 1763 were adamantly opposed, in part because important groups in the 13 colonies no longer regarded them as acceptable or legitimate. By what standards were these policies judged? This question impels us to examine in general detail the bases of legitimacy.

Legitimacy: Substantive versus Procedural

Broadly speaking, there are two main ways of establishing legitimacy. As early as the time of Plato, what I will call substantive legitimacy was developed as a doctrine, which later dominated Western political thought and practices for hundreds of years. Briefly, substantive legitimacy accords acceptance to a ruler not on the basis of how he is chosen, nor on the basis of how he arrives at or implements his decisions, but rather on

---

[22]See, for example, the New Brunswick Census of 1851, where this extraordinary statement appears: "Comparing the ratio of increase in the population of New Brunswick with that of the four northern and adjoining States of the Union, *it appears that the ratio for the Province exceeds theirs by nearly 2 percent*" (p. 40, emphasis added.)

[23]It is, for example, peculiarly appropriate to the loyalist tradition that Confederation itself was achieved under the shadow of threatened American invasion.

the basis of the quality of his acts and decisions themselves. Thus, for example, any ruler who 'abuses' power by using it to serve his private ends rather than the 'public good' is a 'tyrant' (i.e., an illegitimate ruler). The idea of 'public good', moreover, is fixed, static, and (given proper education) discernible, like the other 'pure forms', truth, beauty, justice, etc.

Notions of substantive legitimacy can be traced through medieval thought (Aquinas argued that the ruler's action must accord with "natural law" as interpreted by the Church) and even down to and beyond Machiavelli's political theory. Perhaps the 'purest' exponent of substantive legitimacy, Machiavelli openly counseled the use of "evil means" to achieve power that would then be legitimized by the performance of "good deeds." (In a sense Machiavelli was not the antithesis but the fulfillment of Plato in this regard.)

English liberal thought as embodied in the writings of John Locke also adopted a substantive view of legitimacy. The ruler's prerogative to be obeyed was operative so long as he did not abuse power repeatedly and with a "general design" of "enslaving" the People. Likewise Hobbes explicitly asserts that the "sovereign," regardless of how he acquired power—i.e., by convention or by conquest—is legitimate so long as he acts to maintain order and the protection of the members of society.

The first significant deviation from substantive legitimacy theory toward a concept of 'procedural' legitimacy occurred in the writings of Jean Jacques Rousseau.[24] For the doctrine that a ruler's actions are legitimate so long as they are not 'tyrannical' in substance, Rousseau substituted the idea of the "general will": acts of the sovereign derive their legitimacy from the way in which the decision to perform the act was reached. In other words, "the people" do not delegate power to representatives (or other agents) who are then sovereign within certain predetermined substantive limits; rather, the people retain sovereignty and agree to legitimize only those actions arrived at through the *procedure* of the general will.[25]

In a sense, Rousseau merely took Locke's idea of 'popular sovereignty' to its logical conclusion and converted it from a negative concept (in

---

[24]The following interpretation of Rousseau rests on the argument presented in the first part of the *Social Contract*. I acknowledge that his discussion of the 'great legislator' and the importance of 'civic virtue' pose problems for the interpretation. In view of these problems, a perhaps even better case could be made for nominating Montesquieu as the first 'pure proceduralist': his concept of separation of powers relied solely on institutional procedures to prevent tyranny. Rousseau has been preferred, however, because, *his* concept of procedural legitimacy stressed participation, the importance of which will be elucidated below.

[25]Detailed examination of the later developments in the twin concepts of procedural and substantive legitimacy is beyond the scope of the present discussion, but a brief overview is of general interest. In 'liberal' theory, procedural legitimacy was engrafted onto the notion of substantive legitimacy to form a dual basis of legitimacy—rulers must be chosen by constitutional procedures (usually election) but then must perform only actions themselves regarded as 'constitutional'. Later (except in the United States) this second (substantive) constraint on the actions of procedurally legitimate rulers was relaxed. (For a critique of this development, see B. de Jouvenel, *Sovereignty*, tr. J. F. Huntington [Chicago: University of Chicago Press, 1957], passim.) Marxist theory, however, rejected almost entirely the notion of procedural legitimacy in favor of a purely substantive view of legitimacy in many ways reminiscent of Machiavelli and Plato.

which the People could *withdraw* support from a 'tyrant') to a positive one (in which the People actually participated in decision-making and rulership). But Rousseau's formulation was strenuously resisted in England for more than a century. During this time, however, the notion of Parliamentary sovereignty gradually superseded the earlier notion of mixed sovereignty (i.e., separation of power among House, Lords, and King). This in turn made possible the transition from the medieval notion of substantive legitimacy to a kind of *de facto* Rousseauian procedural legitimacy. Involved in this evolutionary transition were two changes: (a) the concentration of power in the lower house of Parliament, and (b) the democratization of Parliament. Once these changes had taken place, procedural legitimacy almost totally supplanted substantive legitimacy.

American developments paralleled the British pattern, but some interesting differences occurred. For one thing, the change in the doctrine of legitimacy was not evolutionary but revolutionary. Thus, it was accomplished more quickly and dramatically, and yet, as we shall see, less completely than in Britain.

The leaders of the American Revolution opposed British policy on the grounds that the *substance* of the acts made them illegitimate on their face. The Acts, they argued, amounted to a "system of slavery." But the Revolutionaries also developed an embryonic theory of procedural legitimacy manifested in the cry, "No taxation without representation." Thus, notions of *both* substantive and procedural legitimacy played a part in the philosophy of the American Revolution.

The break with British authority accomplished by the successful Declaration of Independence necessitated the development of a new theory of legitimacy to replace the old one that had been destroyed. Strict conformity to the radical 'democratic' Rousseauian model would have dictated that legitimacy be placed on a purely procedural basis. But the Americans were reluctant (for a variety of reasons) to abandon entirely the substantive notion embodied in Lockeian philosophy. They doubted the efficacy of purely procedural (i.e., 'democratic') constraints on rulers, and insisted on prescribing significant substantive limits to the exercise of power. In at least this one sense, therefore, the Founding Fathers demonstrated a profound distrust of democracy. Furthermore, they transmitted to later generations a legacy of substantive limitations on power that in the 20th century have seriously impaired the ability of the American political systems to adapt to rapid change.

Clearly, the Loyalists held to a substantive concept of legitimacy, almost to the exclusion of any procedural notions. Following the Revolution, the Assembly in the British North American colonies (like its predecessor in the 13 colonies) was not an organ for the formulation of the 'general will' but a negative body, whose function was to oppose acts that were considered illegitimate. Since, however, the Loyalists had not broken with the authority of the British crown, they did not face the immediate decision of whether to introduce a procedural concept (i.e., democratic election) in order to enhance the legitimacy of newly created authority. Instead, the transition to procedural legitimacy in Canada occurred gradually. Thus, Canadian developments tended to follow the

British rather than the American pattern, with the result that the shift from substantive to procedural legitimacy, although (indeed, *because!*) slower and later, was in the end more complete and more successful. It took the form, not of the introduction of 'constitutional government,'[26] but of the achievement of 'responsible government' in which the exercise of authority is legitimated not in accordance with substantive principles outlined in a written constitution but through the subordination of the executive and administration to the elected body. This solution (i.e., responsible government), insofar as it permitted a larger ambit for the exercise of power, was more 'modern' than the American practice, which retained the medieval notion of substantive limits embodied in 'higher law' and 'judicial review'.[27]

COMPETENCE, CRATOPHOBIA, AND CRATOPHILIA

One important aspect of what has come to be known as "political culture" is the individual's general orientation toward the political system. For analytic purposes, this orientation can be broken down into two categories: 'input orientation' and 'output orientation'. This distinction underlies the concepts of 'citizen competence' and 'subject competence' developed by Almond and Verba.[28] Citizen competence refers to the individual's sense of effectiveness or 'efficacy' with respect to influencing the input or political side of the system. High citizen competence indicates a strong belief that one's individual wishes 'count' toward the outcome of what the system does. Subject competence, on the other hand, refers to the individual's confidence that the outputs of the system will affect him fairly, that they are legitimate and deserve his compliance. High subject competence, therefore, indicates a willingness to comply with the system's administrative and bureaucratic institutions and personnel.

What impact did the American Revolution have on these aspects of political culture? For the United States, the Revolution, insofar as it mobilized previously isolated groups and heightened political awareness, led to an increase in citizen competence that has persisted to this

---

[26]The British North America Act, in contrast to the American Constitution, contains no substantive limitations on the exercise of power. The 'residual power', for example, is retained not by the people but by the federal government.

[27]Much of the foregoing analysis can be summarized quite concisely in the language of 'systems theory'. Political and social modernization requires a great increase in the 'outputs' of a political system, especially in terms of 'extraction' and 'regulation'. This increase necessitates a new basis of legitimacy for the system as a whole. One way (i.e., the 'liberal democratic') in which this legitimation can be achieved is through increases in the 'support' inputs of the system (i.e., increased political participation) and the introduction of the concept of procedural legitimacy. But increased participation, in turn, places *new* demands on the system, demands which then necessitate further increase in output. Eventually, (except so far as the U.S.) a stage is reached where outputs are presumed to have all originated from 'legitimate' inputs, and vestiges of substantive limitations on power are discarded.

[28]Gabriel Almond and Sidney Verba, *The Civic Culture* (Princeton, N.J.: Princeton University Press, 1963).

day.[29] But the revolutionary tradition was not an unmixed blessing. A further consequence included widespread distrust of many output institutions, especially the bureaucracy, manifested today in the kind of sentiments expressed by George Wallace and his followers. Thus, while citizen competence was increased by the Revolution, subject competence was impaired.[30] Moreover, the Revolution seemed to augment an underlying sense of what might be called 'cratophobia' (literally, 'fear of power') particularly toward a central government that might re-enact a "system of tyranny" like that experienced under the British. In my opinion, cratophobia—and not hostility to nationalism—underlay opposition to ratifying the Constitution in the late 1780s. And residual feelings of cratophobia are responsible for much present-day opposition in the U.S. to governmental activity in the fields of welfare, regulation of the economy, etc.

THE PARADOX OF 'COUNTER-REVOLUTION'

One might expect that the tradition of counter-revolution (such as the Loyalists experienced it) would result in consequences exactly opposite to the experience of revolution. That is, in Canada citizen competence should be decreased, and subject competence increased. The actual result, however, was more subtle and complex. The Loyalists did not become complacent, compliant subjects, uninterested in their rights as citizens. On the contrary, they, too, became vocal in demanding citizen rights (though perhaps less extreme in this regard than their former enemies)—for they, too, had been mobilized by the Revolution; they, too, had developed new political awareness. Despite this similarity with regard to *input* orientation, the Loyalist attitude to the *output* side of the system was quite different from the tradition developed by the Revolutionaries. Some Loyalists (especially the members of the elite) suffered not from cratophobia but from cratophilia.

An interesting contrast can be drawn between the European, American, and Canadian liberal on this score. According to Louis Hartz, the European liberal found himself involved in a painful dilemma, that of "hating [political] power, but loving it also."[31] The American liberal fought the Revolution against "tyranny": so strong was his hatred of tyranny that the dilemma was scarcely perceived—he 'hated' power.[32] The Canadian liberal, on the other hand, fought to defend government. Hence, he had few predilections to despise it. Moreover, it was good to

---

[29]See Sidney Verba and Gabriel Almond, "National Revolution and Political Commitment," in Harry Eckstein, ed., *Internal War* (New York: Free Press, 1964). Note, however, that high citizen competence applies to American whites, not to blacks. The Revolution did little or nothing to mobilize the blacks. In some respects they were worse off after than before the Revolution.

[30]For a fuller discussion, see Bell, op. cit., chap. 5.

[31]Louis Hartz, *The Liberal Tradition in America* (New York: Harcourt, Brace & World, 1955).

[32]See Bernard Bailyn, *The Ideological Origins of the American Revolution* (Cambridge: Belknap Press of Harvard University Press, 1967), chap. 2, "Power and Liberty."

him. If he was a member of the elite, he was welcomed by the governor, especially if he professed to have aristocratic preferences. His loyalism disguised, to the governor, his underlying liberalism.[33] Consequently, the dilemma of the European liberal was also absent in Canada. The Canadian liberal 'loved' power, with a passion equal (but opposite) to that of his American counterpart. Furthermore, the Loyalist masses themselves developed a peculiar fondness for government as a result of favors they received for having defended it. During the Revolution they were encouraged to expect rewards from the government while they were assured that nothing would be asked in return except the present investment of support. Thus, the post-war period in the new settlements found many demands being placed before the British, who responded with reparations of war losses, free grants of land, tools for farming and pioneering, pensions and grants of half-pay, and even (in some instances) food supplies for several years.[34] The following observation fairly accurately applies to a large number of Loyalists: "Government had meant next to nothing to these independent backwoodsmen until they found it a benevolent agent in Canada. . . ."[35]

The tradition of loyalist cratophilia (as contrasted with American cratophobia) accounts for the greater ease with which Canada accepted general 20th-century development associated with the growth of the positive state. Those who interpret this phenomenon in terms of "tory democracy"[36] have mistaken cratophilia for collectivism.

CONCLUSION—NATIONALISM AND NON-NATIONALISM: THE MELTING POT AND THE MOSAIC

The American Revolution had differential effects on the two new communities in Anglo-America. For the new nation (the United States) the Revolution performed several vital nationalizing functions.[37] In some ways it can be seen as a chemical reaction in which colonial society was broken down or 'analyzed' into its component groups, rearranged, and then separated into two parts. One part was then 'synthesized' into a new element; the other part was discarded through the Loyalist migration. ('Revolutionary waste material' would be an apt phrase to describe the 'leftover' [loyalist] groups.) The Revolution therefore laid the groundwork for American nationalism by (a) rapidly mobilizing previ-

---

[33]See Bell, op. cit., chap. 7.

[34]For a catalogue of the assistance given Loyalists by the British government, see the following works: E. C. Wright, *The Loyalists of New Brunswick* (Fredericton, 1955), p. 48; E. A. Cruikshank, ed., *The Settlement of the United Empire Loyalists* (Toronto, 1934) pp. 41 ff. The extent of financial assistance awarded through the "Loyalists Claims Commission" is discussed in D. P. Coke, *Notes on the Royal Commission on Losses and Services of American Loyalists* (H. E. Egerton, ed., 1915).

[35]A. L. Burt, *The Old Province of Quebec* (Minneapolis, 1933), p. 399.

[36]See Gad Horowitz, footnote 3 (passim).

[37]See David V. J. Bell, "Nationalism and the American Revolution," in David Bell, Karl Deutsch, and Seymour Lipset, eds., *Issues in Politics and Government* (Boston: Houghton Mifflin, 1970).

ously isolated groups, (b) providing a powerful precedent and experience for inter-regional cooperation, (c) providing a set of symbols, heroes, and 'values' for a national identity, and (d) eliminating a number of the most resistant minorities.

For the new non-nation (Canada) the Revolution performed obverse functions. The minority groups which, in an attempt to conserve their autonomy and culture refused to support the Revolution, became its victims. They migrated virtually *en masse* to Canada, and thus provided the basis for the cultural mosaic later discovered to be a Canadian phenomenon.[38] Included in the migration were Highland Scots, Pennsylvania Germans (comprising several religious sects: Moravians, Mennonites, Dunkards, and "Reformed"),[39] Huguenots, German Palatinates, Quakers, Indians, and a number of blacks. Canada served as a sort of non-melting pot into which all these disparate ingredients were tossed. Thrown in gratuitously, so to speak, were a number of Hessian troops who had fought as mercenaries for the British.

Such diverse groups would pose problems for any nation to assimilate. But these were all bound together by the experience of the migration. Moreover, they achieved a loose, but lasting, affiliation under "The Crown." In short, they took on a weak (non-) identity that did not prevent the preservation and persistence of their own peculiar cultures—they were all *Loyalists*.

Of course many minorities stayed behind in the new United States, but their fate further corroborates our thesis: they quickly became absorbed in almost every case. Those minority group members who supported the Revolution earned their credentials as "charter members" of the new nation. Those who did *not*, made a conscious effort to get 'lost' in the new society, probably to escape the stigma of suspected toryism.[40]

Unlike the new nationalist identity in the United States, the loyalist identity in no way interfered with the continuation of ethnic culture.[41] The ethnic group survived in Canada while it was being absorbed in the United States. A mosaic pattern appeared in Canada at precisely the point that it began to disappear in America: it was as central an aspect of the "counter-revolution" as the nationalization of leftover minorities was of the Revolution.

However, at least two leftover minorities—the blacks and the Indians—could not get absorbed because they were racial rather than cultural minorities. The life of the Indian in Canada and the United States

---

[38]Cf. John Porter, *The Vertical Mosaic* (Toronto: University of Toronto Press, 1965). The term "mosaic" was not first applied to Canada by Porter, however. It appeared first in the 1930s in the title of a book called *The Canadian Mosaic*.

[39]George E. Reaman, *The Trail of the Black Walnut* (England: McClelland & Stewart, 1957), "Introduction." All of these groups, Reaman writes, "had important things in common: a love of the land, a thorough knowledge of agriculture, and a rugged individualism" (p. xx).

[40]Professor Charles Dunn of Harvard University, a noted Celtic scholar, has remarked on the great difficulty involved in trying to 'locate' North Carolina Highland Scots after the Revolution, in contrast to the relative ease with which members of the same clans can be fully traced in Nova Scotia. (Personal interview, May 1968.)

[41]The comparative ease with which the original minorities assumed the Loyalist identity set a strong precedent for later immigrants. John Diefenbaker, of German and Dutch descent, is more Loyalist than Lester Pearson, a good English son.

contrasts sharply at least in several respects. Joseph Brant is a great hero in Canada. In fact, he was given the supreme loyalist honor of an audience with the King! His counterpart in the United States became a national anti-hero. Indians were regarded as barbaric villains, obstacles to the successful expansion of business, settlement, and 'civilization'. Nationalism has its costs, even in human blood.

In addition to the *structural* problems the migration of minorities posed for nationalism, the ideological inversions that took place in the course of the expulsion presented insurmountable *psychological* problems for the development of 'fragment nationalism' (i.e., the ideological definition of citizenship, which took place in the United States, French Canada, and Australia).[42] In effect, the Loyalist could not erect his ideology (liberalism) into nationalism for the precise reason that the American *had* done so. The memory of being 'un-American' confused the ideological identity of the Loyalist to the point that he became launched into a permanent identity crisis, a never-ending quest for the "elusive" Canadian identity.[43]

A further confusion beset the emotional orientation of the society: it involved *patriotism* (attachment to the soil) versus *loyalism* (attachment to the parent).[44] This confusion led to the retention of symbols of colonial status to serve as symbols of national status. Not only did this confusion inhibit expression of the uniqueness of Canada and the development of Canadian (as opposed to British) identity, but it also accentuated a kind of social and cultural provincialism, manifested in the continuous aspiration, especially among the elite, to be recognized and

---

[42]For further discussion, see Louis Hartz, *The Founding of New Societies*, p. 15.

[43]See the timely essay of Ramsay Cook, "Nationalism in Canada or *Portnoy's Complaint* Revisited." *South Atlantic Quarterly* (Winter 1970).

[44]Indeed, as the following quotation vividly illustrates, loyalism and patriotism have usually been equated, or at least regarded as complementary: "I yield to no one in my love for my native country. The very soil of Canada is dear to me. I love her lakes and forests, her mighty rivers, her broad and fertile fields. I am proud of the past history of my country, of the wonderful progress it has made not only in material prosperity, but in all that contributes to the higher life of a nation; its advancement in education and culture, the fitness our people have displayed for free and constitutional government, and that observance of law and order which is the noblest characteristic of the Anglo-Saxon race. *But all this is entirely consistent with a deep and abiding love and attachment to the Motherland, whose glorious traditions we inherit, and which are the common property of every subject of the empire.* Is there anything servile or unpatriotic in the feeling which makes the pulse beat more quickly and the heart swell, as we recall the glorious deeds of Britain's heroes on land and sea—whether in the old days of Wellington and Nelson, Waterloo and the Nile, or, coming down to our time, to Balaklava, or Inkerman; or but yesterday, as we read of the rush of the Highlanders upon the foe at Tel-El-Kebir? Is there anything servile or unpatriotic in that feeling of reverence and affection for all that is great and noble in the lives and characters and works of the long array of statesmen, philosophers and poets, of men of mark in Church and State, that have made Britain's history the proud and glorious one that it is? Is there anything servile or unpatriotic in that sentiment of deep and chivalrous loyalty to the sovereign which takes out of self and makes men dare to do and die from the highest motives of faith and duty? Sir, are not all those feelings which elevate and ennoble a people? And if it is good for us to recall to-day the loyalty and patriotism, the bravery and endurance of our Loyalist forefathers, shall we abandon the *rich heritage of centuries*, and cut ourselves and our children adrift from the glorious memories and associations which now belong to us Canadians as members of the one great United Empire?" *The Centennial of the Settlement of Upper Canada*, pp. 61–62. Quoted in Berger op. cit., p. 204. (Emphasis added.)

accepted in England. (How many Lord Thompsons are there in Canada's history?)[45]

An additional attribute of Canadian culture is its doctrinaire (but decidedly emotional as opposed to ideological)[46] anti-Americanism. The English Canadian turned to anti-Americanism as if by instinct, unconsciously and intuitively, despite the profound lack of real difference between the two societies in terms of basic values. One could almost argue that the only element uniting Canadians is a strong sense of dislike for the United States—certainly this is one important aspect of so-called Canadian 'nationalism.' At times of national crisis, appeals to this instinct have never (except perhaps as George Grant points out, in 1962) failed to evoke widespread support. (Witness the current obsession with the 'Americanization' of the universities.)

Although the loyalist tradition has been costly in many respects, the prolongation of the colonial tie which it encouraged bestowed unseen advantages. For example, Canadians consequently did maintain interest in the culture and political developments of the mother country. This interest, in turn, allowed and encouraged adoption of the British model of political institutions in preference to the American model the Loyalists unconsciously brought north with them.[47] Viewed in terms of "cybernetic systems theory" and "self-closure," the colonial tie kept open for Canada an entire source of "inputs" of information and new learning from which the United States, by virtue of the Revolution, isolated itself.[48] Thus, Canadian institutions and theory have continued to grow and evolve and to respond to developments in the 19th and 20th centuries; those south of the border have tended to suffer from a degree of "self-closure" that amounts to a kind of political atrophy.

The American Revolution, in short, produced not one country but two: a successful 'nation' (ideologically, symbolically, and structurally)— that later encountered all the difficulties that stem from having made an ideology into nationalism; and, through the migration, a 'non-nation', that confused colonial with national symbols and identity, and today faces possible disintegration as a result. The United States developed what can be termed as 'assimilative' political culture, in which new

---

[45]Cf. Berger, ibid. p. 156: Not the least of the advantages of being a Canadian imperialist came from associating with the aristocrats of England. The United Empire Loyalist descendants who fancied themselves as members of an indigenous Canadian aristocracy were bathed in the reflected glory of their British counterparts who lent their noble names and titles to the Imperial Federation League and other agencies of Imperialism.

[46]Canadians have from time to time offered numerous criticisms of American society, but never, to my knowledge, a good, systematic critique of it. This failure to transcend an emotional 'gut-reaction' to America is a function, I believe, of the affinity of basic values between the two societies.

[47]These institutions were then adapted to a society that was structurally and environmentally very similar to the American. The result was to produce a kind of socio-political laboratory for the study of relationships between environment, social structure, and political institutions. See S. M. Lipset, Agrarian Socialism (New York: Doubleday, Anchor Books, 1968), "Introduction," pp. xi ff.

[48]These concepts are developed by Karl Deutsch, The Nerves of Government (New York: Free Press, 1966), chap. 13. I am grateful to Mr. Deutsch for suggesting to me the concepts of "assimilative" and "accommodative" political cultures.

members became socialized to a set of values remarkably ideological in nature. It developed an 'American creed' and even an 'American way of life', and thus found it useful in a later period to set up, as a matter of course, a House Committee on Un-American Activities: the logical consequence of Americanism is the possibility of un-Americanism.

Canada, on the other hand, evolved what might be called an 'accommodative' political culture. New groups were not expected to assimilate in large part because there was nothing to which they could pledge allegiance, except possibly the vague and abstract notion of 'loyalty to the crown'. Canadianism remained an unidentifiable entity, and the possibility of "un-Canadianism" was therefore precluded. (The very mention of the notion would indeed evince considerable laughter.) This cultural tolerance—and the mosaic it has permitted to exist—is at once Canada's most attractive feature and tragically her fatal weakness.

15

QUEBEC AND THE
FRENCH REVOLUTION OF 1789:
THE MISSIONS OF HENRY MEZIÈRE*†

Mason Wade

That part of British North America which ultimately became Canada was, particularly in the late 18th and early 19th centuries, put in a state of almost continual turmoil by events beyond its borders over which it had no control and in which it had no direct interest. No sooner had the American rebellion been survived than a new international movement was released by revolution in France. In many ways, the French Revolution posed a potentially greater threat to British authority in North America than did the earlier American one, especially in Quebec. French Canada did not find any great enthusiasm for a revolutionary movement sponsored by "Anglais" and devoted to the rights of Englishmen. The French Revolution's slogan of "liberty, equality, fraternity" was coined in France by Frenchmen, and was far more exportable to France's former overseas possessions than was "no taxation without representation." Moreover, the French revolutionary leadership had a compulsion to extend their movement outside their own national boundaries perhaps matched only by that of international Communism. The activities of Citizen Jean Genet in the United States are fairly well known, but his activities in Quebec have received considerably less attention. As Professor Mason Wade illustrates in the following article, French ambition to fish in the troubled waters of Quebec is not a phenomenon confined to the present. What factors in the Quebec situation did the French hope to

*Canadian Historical Review, 31 (1950), 345–368. Reprinted by permission of the author and University of Toronto Press.

†This paper was read by the author on June 7, 1950, at the annual meeting of the Canadian Historical Association, held at the Royal Military College, Kingston, Ontario.

exploit? To what sentiments did they appeal? Why was not the effort more successful? What does the ultimate failure of Henry Mezière tell us about French Canada at the end of the 18th century?

SUGGESTIONS FOR FURTHER READING

S. D. Clark, *Movements of Political Protest in Canada, 1640–1840* (Toronto: University of Toronto Press, 1959).

R. R. Palmer, *The Age of the Democratic Revolution* (Princeton, N.J.: Princeton University Press, 1964).

M. Wade, *The French Canadians, 1760–1945* (London: Macmillan, 1956).

J.M.B.

T here has been a certain tendency in Canadian historical writing for French historians to minimize and English historians to make much of the influence of the French Revolution of 1789 upon Quebec. The tensions of a dual culture make this tendency understandable, but history has not been particularly well served by it. This paper is devoted to a re-examination, chiefly on the basis of the Canadian and French archives, of the efforts of Citizen Genet, first Minister of the French Republic to the United States, to bring the Revolution to Quebec.[1] Space does not permit telling the long and intricate story of subsequent French revolutionary intrigues in Canada, which sought to harvest the seed he had sown.[2]

I

The archives of the Ministère des Affaires étrangères contain numerous plans for the reconquest of Canada after 1763.[3] But in the last days of the *ancien régime* Vergennes' view, that Canada in British hands was a useful counterweight to growing American power, still prevailed. His successor Montmorin soon suffered from the Assembly's tendency to

---

[1]Cf. M. H. Woodfin, "Citizen Genet and His Mission," University of Chicago dissertation, 1928, and H. L. Vernon, "The Impact of the French Revolution on Lower Canada, 1789-95," University of Chicago dissertation, 1950, neither of which has been seen by the present writer, since they have not been published.

[2]The fullest English-Canadian treatment is W. Kingsford, *The History of Canada*, vol. 7 (Toronto, 1894), pp. 354-65, 378-406, 439-55. The fullest French-Canadian treatment, unfortunately undocumented, is B. Sulte, "Les Projets de 1793 à 1810" (*Transactions of the Royal Society of Canada* [1911], 3d series, 5, sec. 1, pp. 19-67). A wealth of references to the MS materials in the Public Archives of Canada is provided by I. Caron, *La Colonisation de la province de Québec*, vol. 2, *Les Cantons de l'est, 1791-1815* (Québec, 1927), pp. 56-85. L. Didier, "Le Citoyen Genet" (*Revue des questions historiques*, 92, [July 1912], 62-90), makes good use of the French Archives. Cf. Paul Mantoux, "Le Comité de Salut public et Genet" (*Revue d'histoire moderne* 13 [1909-10], 5-35).

[3]W. G. Leland, ed., *Guide to the Materials for American History in the Libraries and Archives of Paris*, vol. 2 (Washington, 1943), passim. Appendix A (1065-70) lists the series available in reproduction in the Division of MSS, Library of Congress, to which reference is hereafter made.

gather all power to itself, and the successive internal reorganizations of the first phase of the Revolution left little opportunity for French concern with Canada.[4] But in December 1792, when Genet's instructions were drafted, France foresaw war with Britain and Spain and was anxious to weaken both powers in North America. Therefore it was decided that "Genet should seek to make the principles of the French Revolution spring up in Louisiana, Kentucky, and in the other provinces bordering the United States." He was also supplied with blank letters of marque and officers' commissions, the latter intended for the Indians who were to be induced "to take arms against the enemies of France."[5] He was formally instructed to work for a Franco-American pact, both commercial and political, "to favour in every way the extension of the Empire of Liberty, to guarantee the sovereignty of Peoples, and to punish the Powers which still hold to an exclusive Colonial and commercial system." It was anticipated that the Franco-American alliance would lead to the freeing of Spanish America, the opening of the Mississippi to Kentuckians, Louisiana's separation from Spain, and "perhaps to reuniting the beautiful star of Canada to the American Constellation."[6]

In his secret instructions Genet was authorized to assure Congress that France, in the event of a French war with Britain and of American willingness to conquer Canada and Nova Scotia, would send "a formidable fleet to their shores, and landing forces, the commanders of which will have orders to combine their operations with those of [the American] troops." He was informed that the South was already well disposed, but that he would need "good correspondents at Boston to guide the sentiments of the inhabitants . . . of northern New England." In case of war, the Americans would find many Frenchmen in Louisiana and Canada ready to fight at their side.[7] Yet in all these explosive matters the ardent young Genet was officially warned "to follow scrupulously the established forms for official communications between the Government and foreign agents," keeping to "a measured and circumspect line with regard to internal affairs."[8]

How young Genet's revolutionary zeal led to his repudiation by both the American and French Governments within four months of his arrival at Charleston, South Carolina, on April 8, 1793 is a familiar story which need not be rehearsed here. France had declared war on England on February 1, while he was at sea, and he set eagerly about his mission as

---

[4]F. Masson, *Le Département des Affaires étrangères pendant la Révolution, 1787-1804* (Paris, 1877), chaps. 1-7.

[5]F. J. Turner, ed., "Correspondence of French Ministers, 1791-1797" (*Annual Report of the American Historical Association*, 2 [1903], 201). Three of these commissions were offered in 1794 to General Isaac Clarke, Colonel Matthew Lyon, and Colonel John A. Graham, all connected with Governor Thomas Chittenden of Vermont (Sulte, "Projets," 38). E. P. Link, *Democratic-Republican Societies, 1790-1800* (New York, 1942), p. 144, adds Anthony Haswell, editor of the *Vermont Gazette* (Bennington), to the list, and connects Colonel Udney Hay with the intrigue.

[6]Turner, "Correspondence," pp. 203-4.

[7]M. Minnigerode, *Jefferson, Friend of France, 1793: The Career of Edmond Charles Genet* (New York, 1928), pp. 143, 145-6. This book quotes the Genet Papers in the possession of his granddaughter, as well as those in the Library of Congress, but without references.

[8]Turner, "Correspondence," pp. 210-11.

soon as he landed. Seemingly he concentrated his attention on the Louisiana and Kentucky schemes until his belated presentation of his credentials at Philadelphia on May 18. His triumphal progress northward in the face of the Neutrality Proclamation of April 23 had led to explosions of republican sentiment which led John Adams to refer to "the terrorism aroused by Genet" in his memories of those stormy days when the Philadelphia mob "*threatened to drag* Washington out of his house and effect a revolution in the government, or compel it to declare war in favour of the French Revolution and against England."[9] The populace of New York and Boston was as rabidly republican as that of Philadelphia, and the agitation aroused by Genet was maintained by the Democratic Societies, whose American economic ends and Francophile idealism induced them to further Genet's projects.[10] It was not merely by romantic chance that in July and August Genet was courting the daughter of New York's Governor George Clinton, whom he later married.[11]

Despite the tumultuous round of public welcomes he received at Philadelphia, Genet was writing as early as June 4 to Hauterive, the French consul at New York, "the center of a very great correspondence," to gather information about the objects of his mission, "particularly on the state of affairs in Canada."[12] He was very anxious to know the various parties there, and he did not attempt to conceal that "I should attain the height of my wishes if I should see the possibility of making spring up there the noble sentiments of independence, and of exciting our former brothers to shake off the shameful yoke of the English which our royal government had the poltroonery to let be imposed upon them and from which our regenerated France will ever be ready to emancipate them." Three days later he wrote in similar terms to Dannery, the Boston consul, including the same face-saving assurance that "if we work to overthrow the thrones of all tyrants, we know how to respect religiously the laws of a free People."[13] Dannery was informed that it was urgent to introduce among the Canadians "the ferment of independence" and to take all useful means to that end.

Genet's Canadian plans were already well advanced, as a crossed-out passage in the draft of this same letter indicates:

> One of the best [means] will be, I think, to communicate to them addresses and printed matter of a sort suited to make spring up in their hearts the sacred faith of liberty. I am busy at this moment with the preparation of one of these addresses in English and French; you will have it printed at Boston and your zeal will discover the channels that must be employed to spread it in Canada. A young inhabitant of this country, the C[itizen] who came here to throw himself into my arms will be very useful to fulfil this object; he is

---

[9]C. D. Hazen, *Contemporary American Opinion of the French Revolution* (Baltimore, 1897), p. 186.

[10]Ibid., pp. 164–88; Link, *Societies*, pp. 141–5 and passim; B. Fay, *The Revolutionary Spirit in France and America* (New York, 1927), pp. 326–32.

[11]Turner, "Correspondence," p. 223; Library of Congress, Genet Papers (1793–1801), Delabigarre à Genet, New-York, 9 août 1793.

[12]L.O.C., Genet Papers (1793–1801), Genet à Hauterive, Philadelphie, 4 juin 1793.

[13]Ibid., Genet à Dannery, Philadelphie, 7 juin 1793.

educated, an ardent republican, and knows his country well, which he was
obliged to quit as the result of the inquisition that the English exercise there
and of the aristocratic views of his father. All these considerations have led
me to attach him to your consulate and I am persuaded that you will find
him useful to execute the instructions which I give you today and those that
I shall give in the future relative to the affairs of Canada.

In the letter as sent, Dannery was urged to transmit all news about the
frontier posts, the continued occupation of which had aroused strong
feeling in Vermont. The settlers of Alburg and Swanton were having
frequent brushes with the British garrisons at Pointe au Fer and Dutch-
man's Point, and the Vermont land speculators were in conflict with the
land-jobbers of official Quebec.[14] Dannery was urged to work up Boston
feeling on the question.

Genet's young Canadian was Henri Mezière, who was born at
Montreal on December 6, 1772.[15] His father, Pierre Mezière, a Frenchman who came to Canada in 1753, was a prominent notary and lawyer
at Montreal.[16] According to his own account, young Mezière found that
"a college entrusted to ignorant clerics was the tomb of my youthful
years," though he made a good record there.[17] Leaving the Collège de
Montréal in 1788, he encountered the works of Rousseau, Mably, Montesquieu, and "other *Philosophes* who were friends of mankind and
truth." This heady diet suited him: "I devoured their works, which
taught me to know my duties and my rights; they ripened in me a hatred
of civil and religious despotism. For the first time existence pleased me."
The dawn of the French Revolution completed the work of books in converting Mezière to a new faith. Unable to write himself, he devoted himself to making available to others the gospel of the rights of man by his
work in a printing establishment, which he made "the vehicle of reason." This was the press of Fleury Mesplet, with whom his father had
legal dealings in 1789 as well as earlier, a press which was a centre of
republicanism at this period. But Mezière soon found that the press was

---

[14]*Records of the Governor and Council of the State of Vermont,* vol. 4 (Montpelier, 1870),
pp. 454–70, app. E, "Surveillance of the Northern Frontier by British Troops, 1783 to 1796";
C. Williamson, *Vermont in Quandary: 1763–1825* (Montpelier, 1949), pp. 206–22.

[15]After this paper had been prepared for delivery, M. Jean-Jacques Lefebvre, archivist at
the Montreal Court House, kindly informed me of a study by Aegidius Fauteux, "Henri
Mezière, ou l'odyssée d'un mouton noir," which appeared in *La Patrie* (Montreal), November
18, 1933. It may be consulted at the Bibliothèque Saint-Sulpice, Montreal, in an indexed
collection of Fauteux's "Carnets d'un curieux." I am greatly indebted to Mlle Marguerite
Mercier for a typed copy of the study, which cleared up several moot points in my first draft.
As curator of Saint-Sulpice, Fauteux had an unrivalled knowledge of early Montreal history.

[16]Public Archives of Canada, Fonds Verreau, vol. 4 (carton 17), no. 49, Delisle à Adhémar,
Montréal, 15 janvier 1785; *Bulletin des recherches historiques,* 12 (1906) 248–52; 26 (1920)
182. According to Fauteux, "Henri Mezière," Pierre Mezière was born at Vilotte (Lanares)
and not Dijon, as his son thought. He was a clerk in the offices of the Marine at Montreal in
1755, and was one of the first to obtain authority to practise law after the Conquest. He
married Michelle Archange Campeau in 1760 and had 15 children, of whom Henri was the
second son.

[17]P.A.C., C"E, vol. 11 (Amérique du Nord; Correspondence générale: Canada et États-
Unis, 1651–1791, 1818), pp. 262–64, "H. Mezière, Américain, au citoyen Dalbarade, Ministre
de la Marine, 15 nivoise An 2 [January 4, 1794], Mémoire sur la situation du Canada et des
États-Unis"; printed in *Bulletin des recherches historiques,* 37 (1931) 194–201. Cf. Fauteux,
"Henri Mezière," for Mezière's academic record.

made "uneasy"—probably after Mesplet had printed a pamphlet in 1790 on the militia troubles at Trois-Rivières, with the title of *La Bastille septentrionale, ou trois sujets britanniques opprimés,* and after his *Gazette de Montréal* had printed an account, without naming the place or the participants, of a meeting of young men who had celebrated the Constitutional Act of 1791 with revolutionary toasts.[18] Mezière decided that the Government was at his heels, and took to them. Having felt "a violent desire to go to France" since the beginning of the Revolution, in May 1793, he walked in three weeks to Philadelphia, where he sought employment from Genet in the hope of getting passage to France.

While deciding what use to make of this energetic young zealot, Genet got him to prepare a memorandum entitled "Observations sur l'état actuel du Canada et sur les dispositions Politiques de ses habitants"[19] which Mezière submitted on June 12. He pointed out that the British had only 6,000 men to defend 200 leagues of frontier, and that the fortifications were in the same state as at the time of the Conquest, with the exception of Quebec, which had been strengthened. The militia was a very feeble barrier against invasion, "for besides the jealously which prevails between the Militiamen and their Officers, who are all young fops, it is notorious that the Canadians have no interest in leaving their own occupations to defend the posts, whose retaining concerns only the King, they say. And the Government so much distrusts the revolutionary spirit that it has not yet given arms to the Militiamen, waiting to distribute them when the occasion demands." Mezière thought that the Canadians owed to the French Revolution "the Constitution, a little less arbitrary than their first one, which was given them in 1791." He considered the government thus established "un corps hermaphrodite." He pointed out that the Assembly was made up almost entirely of Canadians, among whom were "trois français nés qui sont des vrais Républicans." He made much of the Assembly's struggle for the French language during the previous winter,[20] and declared that unless the Governor's veto power was ended, "The Canadians would have no reluctance to shake off the yoke of their stupid tyrant."

He saw an "infinity" of other motives for revolt: the summary hangings for "*non-royalisme*" in the year after the cession; the arrest and flogging of "peasants" for not giving way on winter roads with their heavily loaded sleighs to "English officers taking prostitutes for a drive"; the eviction of "peasants" from their homes to make way for Haldimand's *château;* the burden of *corvées;* and the reservation of lucrative offices to Englishmen. He stressed the Canadian desire for revenge

---

[18]R. M. McLachlan, "Fleury Mesplet, the First Printer at Montreal" (*Transactions of the Royal Society of Canada* [1906], 2nd series, 12, sec. 2, pp. 219, 262-64); F. X. Garneau, *Histoire du Canada* (Paris, 1920), vol. 2, p. 426. The toasts included "the abolition of feudalism," "civil and religious liberty," "freedom of the press," "the French and Polish revolutions," and "the repeal of the militia law and of all laws contrary to individual liberty."

[19]L.O. C., France, Archives des Affaires étrangères, Correspondance politique, États-Unis, vol. 37, pt. 6, pp. 419-23.

[20]See T. Chapais, *Histoire du Canada,* vol. 2 (Québec, 1921), pp. 55-82; R. Christie, *A History of the Late Province of Lower Canada,* vol. 1 (Quebec, 1848), pp. 127-35.

as a result of English monopoly of the export and import trades, which had resulted in high prices for Canadians, and explained the welcome given to the Americans in 1775 as due to this disposition of the Canadians. Subsequently the Government had still further embittered the habitants by new acts of oppression: persecution of American partisans and confiscation of the goods of suspected rebels. Among the sufferers he named Cazeau, Ducalvet, Jautard, Mesplet, Lusignan, and "several others still living."

Anticipating the objections that the Canadians' ignorance, their prejudices, and their clergy were obstacles to their freedom, he declared that the townspeople had all the philosophical works; and that they read them, the French gazettes, and the Declaration of the Rights of Man with passionate attention. Patriotic songs had been learned by heart and sung at the opening of a "Club de Patriotes," which in 1792 had numbered more than 200 members. This club had defied the Government by publicly discussing French affairs, which had been forbidden by proclamation.[21] He declared that the priests were despised "as infamous imposters who use the lie in their own interest," and were as little respected as "a herd of hogs." There were not ten of the "self-styled nobles," and their ignorance and poverty aroused pity. Mezière summed up the present mood of French Canada thus:

> Finally I dare to say that the French Revolution has electrified the Canadians, and has done more to enlighten them in a year on natural rights than a century of reading would have done. Even since the French declaration of war against England [February 1, 1793] the Canadians have made such progress in reason that they do not fear to hope publicly that the French will have the best of it. Every day, they assemble in the cities in small groups, telling each other the news, rejoicing when it is favourable to the French, and being cast down (but not despondent) when it is unfavourable.
>
> I swear that the Canadians love the French; that the death of the Tyrant Capet [January 21, 1793] has indisposed only the Priests and the Government, which fear the coming of a Guillotine to Canada. I declare that the Canadians would rather cut themselves to bits than to fire a single shot against Frenchmen who should come to offer them liberty; I go further and say that they show themselves worthy of enjoying liberty by their courage in defending it. There are in the Province of Lower Canada alone 60,000 brave and robust Canadians, in a situation to crush, at the least signal, all the rapacious English, who number not 24,000 men, troops included.

Despite this confident picture, Mezière urged that the way of revolt should first be paved by the circulation of an address among the Canadians. Among the topics he suggested for it were the language question, "the absence of arts and belle lettres due to the homicidal Policy of England," and the "substitution of the sovereignty of their nation to that of George III (and last, I hope)." He warned against circulating such an address before French forces were ready on the borders of Canada, since the ardour that it would inspire might die down if aroused prematurely.

---

[21]Presumably the Royal Proclamation of May 25, 1792, published in the *Quebec Gazette*, August 9, 1792. Text in *Canadian Archives Report* (1921), app. B, pp. 13-14.

Offering to give further details *viva voce* at any time, he concluded with a fine flurry of rhetoric: "If one of those generous sentiments, fruit of the touching interest which France takes in the happiness of Peoples, engages the National Convention to break the shameful fetters in which groan the sons of France, sold by a King, you will reward my patriotic zeal, Citizen Minister, by giving me the opportunity to join their brave liberators, to avenge them or to die in fighting gloriously for Liberty and Equality. I have no other desire than that." In closing he thanked Genet for welcoming him like a brother "when I left my country, with no resource but my courage, to seek in the arms of the French the liberty of which I saw no trace in Canada." The revolutionary zeal of this 21-year-old Montrealer appealed to the equally hotheaded minister, who was only 10 years older, and Genet made Mezière one of his secretaries while planning a mission for him.

The address, *Les Français libres à leurs frères du Canada,* which Genet drafted, probably after the model of Condorcet, in June, and which was printed as an eight-page pamphlet by July, includes some of Mezière's suggestions.[22] The Canadians were urged to follow the American and French example in similar revolutionary rhetoric: "Canadians, it is time to rouse from the lethargic sleep in which you are plunged, arm yourselves, call to your aid your friends the Indians, count on the support of your neighbors and on that of the French . . . you will obtain liberty and independence, which energetic men never demand in vain." The final pages gave a résumé of the advantages to be gained by revolt: Canada would become free and independent; it could ally itself with France and the United States; the Canadians could choose their own rulers; the veto would be abolished; Canadians could hold all offices; *corvées* would be ended; trade would be wholly free; there would be no fur-trade monopoly; seigneurial rights and privileges would be abolished, as would hereditary titles; there would be freedom of religion, with Catholic priests, named by the people as in the early Church, enjoying stipends according to their usefulness; there would be schools in every parish and town, and institutions of higher learning.

Chilled by Washington and rebuffed by Hamilton in his efforts to collect the American war debt, Genet found a warmer welcome from Jefferson and made him his confidant in June, reading to him this address to the Canadians and a similar one destined for Louisiana. The French envoy, drunk on popular acclaim, relied on Jefferson's sympathy with his course until early August, though by the end of June the Secretary of State had already recorded his highly critical view of Genet.[23]

On July 11 Consul Hauterive sought to sober his superior, whom he

---

[22]Full printed text, dated by hand "juin 1793," in L.O.C., Affs. étran., corr. pol., États-Unis, vol. 37, pt. 6, pp. 439–42 v; referred to as printed, ibid., supp., vol. 28, pt. 2, p. 384, Genet à Hauterive, Philadelphie, 14 juillet 1793. Extracts in P.A.C., Q, vol. 69-2 (State Papers, Lower Canada), 224–26; printed in Kingsford, *History,* vol. 7, pp. 387–89 n. R. Flenley, "The French Revolution and Quebec" (R. Flenley, ed., *Essays in Canadian History Presented to George Mackinnon Wrong for His Eightieth Birthday,* Toronto, 1939, p. 56), suggests Condorcet's *La République française aux hommes libres* as Genet's model.

[23]Minnigerode, *Jefferson,* pp. 211–12, 249–53; Turner, "Correspondence," pp. 232 n.

privately considered rash and imprudent, and whose projects in Louisiana and Canada he opposed.[24] Hauterive had doubtless been alarmed by the descent of Mezière, who reported to Genet from New York on July 8 that he had spent the money advanced him in clothing himself from head to foot for the celebrations for the 4th and 14th; and that more money would be needed, though he realized the need for economy, if he were called upon to open a channel of communication with Canada. Mezière urged Genet not to lose sight of the Canadian plan: "To try, as you want to do, to bring liberty to my country, is to wish to make 160,000 souls happy! How touching this idea must be to a feeling heart, to a Republican like yourself." He renewed his declaration of devotion to his country, and promised to be Genet's "active and faithful instrument in all that you are good enough to attempt for its happiness."[25] On July 14 Genet replied to Hauterive that upon reflection he approved the latter's reluctance to employ Mezière in the New York consulate. He, too, had hesitated to employ him, for should the fact become known to English agents, Mezière would be suspected of involvement in French plans and would be unable to return to Montreal.[26]

Genet was doubtless confirmed in his opinion of Hauterive's wisdom when he received a note written from New York on the morrow of Bastille Day: "You sleep, Brutus, and Rome lies in chains! . . . Quotation from Mezière . . . To cure the malady of the South, the Remedy lies in the North. The unfortunate one who has come to you covered with his own blood could go take the waters at Niagara. Such is the opinion of several doctors of this Country. The interest you take in the invalid is shared here. It is on their behalf that I freely give you this recipe. But hasten to apply the remedy."[27] Now Genet had received word of the Cap François race riots of June 21-24, which occurred after General Galbaud and the French fleet become involved with the civil commissioners of San Domingo, and he had reported them to Paris on July 6.[28] The New York land speculators, among whom were many republican political figures and leaders of the Democratic Societies, were concerned at this time with grants in Upper and Lower Canada, as well as with their own Genesee lands.[29] Niagara was one of the chief points of frontier friction and a convenient backdoor to Canada.

Genet's instructions to Mezière are dated only "1793," but were probably drafted in July, after Hauterive had discouraged the plan to attach the young Canadian to the New York consulate. Since Mezière had supplied proofs of his desire to contribute to the emancipation of "our brothers the Canadians," Genet declared:

[24]L.O.C., Affs. étran., Corr. pol., États-Unis, Supp., vol. 28, pt. 2, p. 385, Hauterive à Genet, New-York, 11 juillet 1793; Link, *Societies,* p. 142 n. 78.

[25]L.O.C., Affs. étran., Corr. pol., États-Unis, Supp., vol. 28, pt. 2, pp. 383-83v, Mezière à Genet, New-York, 8 juillet 1793.

[26]Ibid., p. 384, Genet à Hauterive, Philadelphie, 14 juillet 1793.

[27]Ibid., p. 387, H——— à Genet, New-York, 15 juillet 1793.

[28]Turner, "Correspondence," pp. 219, 223, 224-25.

[29]Link, *Societies,* pp. 80 n. 33, 143-44.

I name him agent of the French nation to this people oppressed by the English and I charge him to employ all the means that his zeal shall suggest to make spring up among them the sacred principles of the rights of man. To this end he will go to the frontiers of Canada, establish Correspondence with Canadians whose sentiments correspond to his, and convey to them the address of which I send him a large number of copies and in which I have developed the political views of the Republic with regard to the Canadians. To reimburse Citizen Mezière for his trouble and expense, I put him on a salary of twelve hundred *livres*, from the funds of the legation, which will be paid him either quarterly or every six months.[30]

Supplied by Consul Hauterive with $222, and with a bill of $155 from a Mr. Hale, an Albany merchant, on Colonel Stevens, Mezière went to Cumberland Head on Lake Champlain. His report to Genet, from New York on September 20, tells the story of his proceedings.[31] For $100 he hired as a French agent and courier in Canada Jacques Rous, a Canadian who had emigrated in 1777 and who in 1789 had established an inn on the New York side of the border at the foot of the lake, at the place now known after him as Rouse's Point. Rous had been "particularly recommended by Colonel Hay." This was Udney Hay, a Scottish Albany trader who had been an army commissary during the American Revolution and was now a leading figure of both the New York and the Chittenden County (Vermont) Democratic Societies, a rabidly republican politician and as such an enthusiastic supporter of Genet, and Ira Allen's New York agent for Vermont lands.[32] Mezière found Rous "intelligent, and a friend of Liberty and Equality," and entrusted him with letters to "people in Montreal, whom I believe to be the most discreet and best disposed, in which I sought to convey all the warmth of the Republicanism which reigns in France today, giving them hope of an approaching liberation and urging them from all manner of motives to use their influence to hasten this happy and desirable epoch." To his own compositions he added "several American papers mentioning the repeated Successes of the Great Nation over its enemies, several leaves of the Journal of Gorsas[33] in which the death of the Tyrant Capet is fully justified; the *Rights of Man* by Paine[34] (English and French, 1st, 2nd, & 3rd parts); *Observations* of Mr. Kintoche on the French Revolution; some patriotic songs;

---

[30]L.O.C., Affs. étran., Corr. pol., États-Unis, Supp., vol. 28, pt. 2, pp. 382–382 v, "Instructions pour le Cit. Mezière, agent de la République française auprès des Canadiens." Cf. Mezière's own account of them, P.A.C., C"E, vol. 11, pp. 264–65, Mezière à Dalbarade, 15 nivoise An 2.

[31]L.O.C., Affs. étran., Corr. pol., États-Unis, vol. 38, pt. 3, pp. 235–38 v, Mezière à Genet, New-York, 20 septembre 1793.

[32]Link, *Societies*, p. 143; A. M. Hemengway, *Vermont Historical Gazetteer,* vol. 1 (Burlington, 1868), pp. 942–43.

[33]Antoine-Joseph Gorsas, a Girondist deputy, whose attack on Marat in *Le Courier* led to a raid on his printing establishment in March 1793, and to his flight to Normandy and Britanny. His arrest was ordered in June 1793 when the Gironde fell; and when he returned to Paris in the fall, he was arrested on October 6 and guillotined the next day.

[34]Thomas Paine's heyday in France was from 1791 to 1793, as a member of the Convention and as a republican pamphleteer. *Common Sense* was translated in 1791, a collection of his revolutionary writings in 1792, and the *Théorie et pratique des droits de homme* in the same year. Compromised by his friendship with Brissot and by Robespierre's disapproval of his *L'Age de la raison*, published in 1793, Paine was then imprisoned. B. Fay, *Bibliographie critique des ouvrages français relatifs aux États-Unis, 1770–1800* (Paris, 1925), pp. 74–75.

and finally 350 copies of the address to the Canadians . . . [and] a dozen copies of a Sermon preached on the Fourth of July last by the Minister Miller, Presbyterian,[35] which, being full of sound ideas of liberty, can only have a very happy effect on members of this Sect, very numerous at Montreal."

After going to Montreal with this mixed bag of propaganda for all tastes, Rous reported back to Mezière that the latter's presence on the shores of Lake Champlain was known and that his arrest had been ordered. Rous may possibly have been playing a double game, for he was later the principal agent of John Richardson, magistrate and head of the secret service in Montreal, in ferreting out French emissaries. According to Richardson in 1805, Rous was "personally acquainted with Clinton the Vice-President, and by him considered a good Democrat."[36] It is curious that "Jn. Fontfreyde," who was coroner of Clinton County in 1788, in writing to Genet from "Lake Champlain" on September 25, mentioned meeting Mezière upon his return from Canada at the beginning of the month; found him pleasant, but perhaps too young for his mission; and exclaimed: "to what a man Governor Clinton has sent him!"[37] But in any case Mezière's presence was soon made known to the Canadian officials through official channels.[38]

Rous reported that Mezière's friends in Montreal were afraid to write him, but sent their signatures as "sign of reception of my dispatches." Rous was to supply a verbal report, while Laforgue, a fur-trader expected at Lake Champlain in a week or two, would supply written ones. Mezière's despatches had been circulated, with the exception of the crucial address, which his friends had decided not to make public as yet, "for, as they observed, with a people wholly plunged in the dense shadows of ignorance and slavery, it is not fitting to suddenly cause to shine the Sun of Liberty at noon." It is clear that revolutionary enthusiasm and enlightenment were not as widespread at Montreal as Mezière had indicated to Genet. Even his radical friends were reluctant to risk the redoubled surveillance which foreign correspondence would incur. But Rous reported that public opinion was "forever fixed in favour of the French, and it seems the present war of England against this generous People has caused a new horror of the English government." Whatever means "English Despotism" took to deceive the Canadians on the state of France proved of little avail against their enthusiasm. "Nothing is so common, even in the country, as the cry of *Vivent les François!* 'We hope to see our brothers', the townspeople tell the peasants, and these, as if they feared that what was said was intended to tease them, reply: 'But is it really true that we shall see *Nos bonnes*

---

[35]The Reverend Samuel Miller of the New Presbyterian Church, New York (Link, *Societies*, p. 164).

[36]E. A. Cruikshank, *The Political Adventures of John Henry* (Toronto, 1936), pp. 7–8.

[37]L.O.C., Affs. étran., Corr. pol., États-Unis, Supp., vol. 28, pt. 2, p. 406, Fontfreyde à Genet, Lac Champlain, 25 septembre 1793; R. S. Palmer, *History of Lake Champlain* (Albany, 1866), pp. 169–70.

[38]P.A.C., C, vol. 673 (Relations with the United States, 1790–1815), p. 21, Shoedde to Le Maistre, Ft. Ontario, September 9, 1793; ibid., p. 20, Simcoe to Clarke, York, September 24, 1793, printed in *Canadian Archives Report* (1891), p. 57, note D: "French Republican Designs on Canada," nos. 1, 2.

gens', and tears of regret furrow the cheeks of the old people." The Government's opposition to making French the legislative language should produce "a great commotion" at the next session in December. (Mezière, knowing the value of the language question in fostering unrest, regretted that it had not been included in the address to the Canadians. He suggested that it might be inserted in another address, sent simultaneously with copies of the new French Constitution of June 1793.) Rous's report went on to say that the Canadian press, despite the severe eye of the Government, had not been silent about the good fortune of French arms. Indeed Mesplet had been so active that the Governor had banned his *Gazette* from the post office, after it had printed a discussion of the origin of governments, "which did not flatter that of Canada in the least."

The British troops remained at the same strength as in the spring. No naval force was on hand, since the frigate which had convoyed the summer merchant fleet had been called to Halifax. When Rous left Montreal, two ships were loading grain for Madeira, two were taking on furs for London, and four or five others, staves. All were expected to sail at the beginning of October, and the Canadians hoped that the French fleet at New York would make them change their destination. "Nothing so easy as to attack them at the mouth of the St. Lawrence." Rous closed his verbal report to Mezière by declaring that "the French flag would only have to show itself to free Canada," and the latter expressed firm faith in the statement.

Mezière urged an immediate naval expedition against Quebec. The St. Lawrence would be open until December, while only a month was needed "to complete the affair." During the month required for the fleet's voyage to Canada, "one would redouble the pamphlets, bulletins, and addresses," and Mezière himself would proceed again to the border with the plan to be followed by the Canadians when the French fleet appeared. Since the English fleet could not reach Quebec until spring, there would be plenty of time to prepare the Canadians to defend "the precious treasure that the generous French would have entrusted to them, against all attacks from without." It was important to maintain a sure and constant channel for communications between New York and Montreal. No written despatches were to be hoped for from Montreal, but verbal reports would be nearly as good. Colonel Hay had told him of persons at Albany and "Squeensborough" (Skenesborough), through whose hands letters to Rous might pass. Mezière concluded with the disarming observation: "It may be, Citizen, that I have committed some errors; I am young; but it is impossible that I have lacked zeal or goodwill." He added a summary account: of the $377 he had received, $100 had been paid to Rous, his own expenses had amounted to $147, and "Brochures, papers, etc." to "$30½" leaving $100, which was to be taken as an advance and deduction from salary for clothing and to pay small debts in Canada.

II

While the new Minister of Foreign Affairs, Desforgues, who had come into office with the downfall of the Gironde in June, was writing Genet on

July 30 sharply censuring his course and the American cabinet was preparing to ask his recall, Genet reported home on July 31 that the great ends of his mission must await the meeting of Congress, when the representative of the peoples would avenge the obstructions placed in his path by the executive and "positively electrify America." Meanwhile, he noted with satisfaction, he had "prepared the Revolution of New Orleans and Canada."[39] Confronted in July with the arrival in the Chesapeake of the mutinous French fleet from San Domingo, Genet adopted the idea of using it against the British in the north. He advised the Minister of Foreign Affairs on August 2 that he was sending the naval vessels "to destroy the English fishery at Newfoundland, to capture more than 600 vessels which are to be found there with a 50-gun ship of the line and a frigate; to retake St. Pierre and Miquelon, capture the rich convoy ready to sail from Hudson's Bay, and burn Halifax, which has been left unguarded in order to reinforce the West Indies garrisons. Thence they will bring their booty here, make repairs promptly, embark the corps of French and American volunteers which I am forming in Virginia, and go immediately to take possession of New Orleans, after having made an attack in passing on La Providence [Nassau], the resort of all English pirates."[40] In a letter of August 15, the plan showed some development: after burning Halifax, the fleet was to go up the St. Lawrence to Quebec, "to sound the dispositions of the Canadians, whom my agents excite to insurrection."[41]

Genet arrived in New York on August 7 to reorganize the fleet, which he had ordered there from the Chesapeake late in July. He considered General Galbaud "either a traitor or a fool," and planned to send him home for trial by the Convention. On failing to incite the fleet to further mutiny, Galbaud fled to Canada, but later returned to the States when Dorchester ordered him sent to England.[42] On October 23 Dorchester professed to Dundas his belief that Galbaud's pretended quarrel with Genet had been used to further the latter's intrigues in Canada.[43] This was an early instance of the increasing inability of the Canadian officials to make distinctions as the flood of clerical and royalist émigrés, San Domingo refugees, and French travellers of all descriptions washed up on Canada's shores. On December 24 Genet coldly offered Galbaud passage back to France, "Since the English have scorned in you, as in Dumouriez your friend and patron, the traitor from whose treachery they had profited."[44]

Meanwhile, Genet had succeeded in getting half of the mutinous fleet off on its expedition to the north. The "vast plan," which he thought on August 2 would succeed "because no one could foresee it,"[45] had dwin-

---

[39]Turner, "Correspondence," pp. 228-31, 232, 235.

[40]Ibid., p. 234.

[41]Ibid., pp. 239-40.

[42]Ibid., pp. 225-26, 238; Minnigerode, *Jefferson*, pp. 299, 306-7; L.O.C., Affs. étran., Corr. pol., États-Unis, Supp., vol. 28, pt. 2, p. 429, Fontfreyde à Genet, Plattsburg, 22 janvier 1794.

[43]P.A.C., Q, vol. 66, p. 171, Dorchester to Dundas, Quebec, October 23, 1797; Kingsford, *History*, vol. 7, p. 365.

[44]Minnigerode, *Jefferson*, pp. 307-8.

[45]Turner, "Correspondence," p. 234.

dled somewhat by October 4, when he drafted Admiral Sercey's instructions.[46] The squadron, consisting of two ships of the line and two frigates, which had aboard 300 volunteers from the San Domingo troops, five field-pieces, a company of dragoons, and arms for 300 men, was to destroy the Newfoundland fisheries, retake St. Pierre and Miquelon, "insult Halifax in passing," and demand the surrender of the prisoners taken at the two islands in the Gulf. On its return it was "to sound the dispositions of our former brothers the French of Acadia; make descents on their coasts, not to pillage them, but to spread among them our principles, our Constitution of June 24, 1793, our patriotic songs, the *Bulletin*, and revolutionary addresses that I have drawn up for the Canadians." The squadron was then to return to New York to refit. Genet passed on to Sercey the details of Halifax's defenceless condition, which had been supplied to him on August 26 by the omniscient Colonel Hay.[47]

The admiral was given a free hand to adopt his own means to achieve the ends which Genet set forth, but Mezière was attached to him as political agent: "Since you will often find yourself in the position, during the campaign, to make proclamations, to pursue correspondences, to call upon the enemy to capitulate, to summon them to surrender, or to pay ransom; to send ashore to sound the dispositions of the inhabitants, to raise recruits, or to buy things of which the Squadron may have need, I have attached to you, for the duration of the campaign, in the role of Political Agent, one of my secretaries, the Citizen Mezière, a young Canadian full of intelligence and Patriotism, who has already rendered essential services to the Republic."[48] Two young French officers who had escaped from Halifax were also attached to the squadron, doubtless as guides for any attack on that place. Genet's orders to Mezière to join the fleet at the same salary as before were also dated October 4. The latter reported on the fleet from New York the following day, and on October 9 sent another brief note to Genet from Sandy Hook. The Minister sent a farewell note to his protégé on the 11th.[49]

It was only a few days after Mezière's departure on his second mission that his father wrote from Montreal, warning him to avoid "espionage, treason, &c." A friend, who signed himself "Jon Charles" and wrote a very French English, reported that he had delivered Mezière's letter to his father, and that one William Henry McNeil was planning to disgrace him and cut off his ears if he ever reappeared in Canada. Since there was grave danger of letters being intercepted at St. Johns, "Jon Charles" declared: "I shall rite [*sic*] you Every safe Opportunity, but you must not rite me."[50] The English were reported very suspicious, and "Most downhearted with rapport [*sic*] to their fleet going home." The French were determined that they "some time or other shall have a republican gov-

[46]L.O.C., Affs. étran., Corr. pol., États-Unis, vol. 39, pt. 2, pp. 99–103.
[47]Ibid., p. 110.
[48]Ibid., pp. 102–102 v.
[49]Ibid., Supp., vol. 28, pt. 2, pp. 407–407 v; 408 v–9; 410; 410 v.
[50]Ibid., p. 413, P. Mezière à H. Mezière, Montréal, 24 octobre 1793; pp. 414 v–15, Jon Charles to H. Mezière, Montreal, October 24, 1793.

ernment." "Jon Charles" also reported General Galbaud's escape from Quebec, and added: "I told sum English Gentle men the other day that if the English would drink less porter and Eat less roast Beef and speak More softly they would not be taken in so Often by the french." He suggested that Mezière announce the coming of a French fleet by means of advertisements in the New York gazettes, for which he suggested a crude code. There was "a Mr. McLain in New York a printer that sends papers to Canada." These Montreal letters probably reached Genet by the hand of Laforgue, for on October 24 the Minister wrote Fontfreyde at "Lac Champlain Sarnake [Saranac] N.Y." that he had received his letter of September 24 from Laforgue. With regard to Fontfreyde's criticism of Mezière, Genet observed: "He did not entirely fulfil his mission as I should have liked and I have embarked him on the American Squadron as an interpreter. I should be delighted to find a sincere friend of liberty and independence who would take it upon himself to replace him in bringing to our former brothers of Canada news of their old fatherland." Laforgue and Fontfreyde were to take steps to see that news reached Canada. Genet forwarded some pamphlets on "the present state of our affairs."[51]

The continually mutinous fleet, which had added so much to Genet's cares during the hectic summer, ran true to form. Once at sea, a naval council of war decided that it was impossible to fulfil the essential part of Genet's instructions "without too much exposure of ships and sailors." It would be best, considering the season, merely to attempt to intercept the fur convoy while making sail for France. Not much time was wasted on this face-saving effort, since Mezière found himself at Brest on November 2.[52] In all events the expedition would not have enjoyed the advantage of surprise, for there had been an English spy in the fleet at New York[53] and its aims were known at Halifax in detail before it was at sea. Lieutenant-Governor John Wentworth informed Lieutenant-Governor Carleton of New Brunswick on October 11 that he had word from New York of the expedition. Carleton passed on the word to his brother, Dorchester, from Fredericton on October 21, adding that similar reports had prevailed there during the summer.[54] And Dorchester considered a report from Sandy Hook in Council on October 25, when the question was raised whether the convoy should sail in view of the departure of the French fleet for the St. Lawrence.[55]

III

Though revolutionary France must have been a strange world for the young Montrealer, in whose wake were letters from his father asking for

---

[51]Ibid., p. 416, Genet à Fontfreyde, New-York, 24 octobre 1793.

[52]P.A.C., C"E, vol. 11, pp. 265–66, Mezière à Dalbarade, 15 nivoise An 2.

[53]Didier, "Genet," p. 82 n.

[54]P.A.C., C, vol. 673, pp. 13, 15; printed in *Canadian Archives Report*, 1891, pp. 48–49, Note C: "War with France 1793," nos. 18, 19.

[55]P.A.C., Q, vol. 66, p. 250, Minutes, October 25, 1793.

"signs of life" and from his mother warning that late hours were bad for him,[56] Mezière was not long in finding his feet. He was soon in touch with Jean-Jacques Bréard, the Canadian-born son of one of Bigot's aides who had returned to France in 1760. Bréard, primarily an orator given to declaiming magnificently "Je suis né dans un pays libre" and "J'ai sucé le lait d'une sauvage," often presided over the Convention, of which he had been secretary and of which he became president on February 8, 1793. He was to become president of the Conseil des Anciens under the Directory.[57] Mezière entrusted his credentials from Genet to Bréard, and probably was encouraged by him, as one revolutionary rhetorician to another, to submit to d'Albarède, the Minister of the Marine, his "Mémoire sur la situation du Canada et des États-Unis," which is dated "15 nivoise An 2" (January 4, 1794).[58]

After recounting his own career and referring to his first report to Genet,[59] Mezière urged French intervention in Canada. The idea was not novel at the time, for Létombe, who had left Boston for Paris on September 17 and later served as Consul-General at Philadelphia, had submitted a memorandum on the United States and Canada to the Committee of Public Safety on December 9,[60] while on November 26 Isafien and Talien had urged an attack upon Britain in North America, and had offered suggestions for instigating revolution in Canada and Nova Scotia.[61] The decision to recall Genet in disgrace had been taken on October 11, but one of his most cherished projects had not been abandoned.[62] Mezière discounted the Canadian reaction to Bigot's bungling, and stressed the antimonarchist feeling which existed in Canada, "since a King sold it and a King bought it" in "a horrible traffic of men." He also made much of anti-English feeling, and of Canadian sympathy for the American Revolution. He offered an interesting, if doubtless highly coloured, picture of Canadian feeling about the French Revolution:

> It was as if the French Revolution took place in Canada, and as if the delights that it promised made the Canadians feel more bitterly their separation from this great country. The revolutionary papers reached us then; more than once we watered them with our tears, more than once they were carried in triumph in the clubs and private societies in the bosom of which we sang the dawn of Liberty, its progress, and the struggle against the thick clouds of superstition and tyranny. Such transports alarmed the Government, which had believed, because of the few means of instruction offered

---

[56]L.O.C., Affs. étran., Corr. pol., États-Unis, Supp., vol. 28, pt. 2, p. 419, P. Mezière à H. Mezière, Montréal, 17 novembre 1793; ibid., p. 420, C. Mezière à H. Mezière, Montréal, 17 novembre 1793. These letters were sent by a "Monsr. Quesnel," probably the French-born poet, Joseph Quesnel.

[57]R. LaRoque de Roquebrune, "Les Canadiens dans la Révolution française," 7 *Nova Francia*, (September–October 1931) 258–61).

[58]P.A.C., C"E, vol. 11, pp. 262–71.

[59]L.O.C., Affs. étran., Corr. pol., États-Unis, vol. 37, pp. 419–23 v, Mezière à Genet, Philadelphie, 12 juin 1793; quoted *supra*.

[60]L.O.C., Affs. étran., Mémoires et documents, États-Unis, vol. 15, pp. 124–25 v.

[61]L.O.C., Affs. étran., Corr. pol., Angleterre, vol. 588, pp. 97–98.

[62]Turner, "Correspondence," pp. 287–88.

in Canada, that its inhabitants must be automatons, beings insensitive to their senseless state. They were unaware that the men of all countries are imbued with the germ of liberty. Soon the Canadians rose together to demand a reform. After many disputes England gave them a form of government designed nearly after its own pattern. Thus Canada owed to France in 1791 a small improvement of its lot.

But the Constitutional Act of 1791 had not satisfied the Canadians. They were discontented with the Governor's veto and the status of the French language. They were not only unfortunate, but aware of their misfortune; and they breathed "hatred and vengeance against the English." "But what else can they do, without arms, without leadership, without support? I cannot close this part of my exposé without expressing the firm hope that I possess to see once more Canada, my country, soon liberated from the yoke of its imbecile tyrant. Like other countries, it will owe to the French its independence and its happiness."

There are only glimpses of Mezière's subsequent career in France. In November 1795 he was freed at Brest, after having been mistakenly arrested. He supplied proofs of "his excellent record of patriotism" and carried a pass of the Commissaire de la Marine good on the first ship sailing for North American ports. Presumably he was to take part in Adet's revival of Genet's schemes, after the interlude in which Fauchet had let them drop. In April 1799 he wrote to his sister, Madame [Adrien Régis] Berthelot of Montreal, who had refused to answer his letters, from Bordeaux, where he was "Comossaire du Directoire Executif, près l'administration muncipale du canton de Bordeaux, extra muros." On July 23, 1806, he wrote his "brother," Louis Levesque, from Bordeaux, where he was a customs inspector, weary of the Revolution and concerned about his loss of reputation at home. On September 2, 1807, he wrote from Bordeaux to his brother-in-law Jean Delisle, or "M. [Joseph] Papineau, notaire." He was then clearly homesick for the Canada he had so lightly left in 1793, as he still was in 1814 when Dr. Pierre de Sales Laterrière reported meeting him as prefect of police at Bordeaux, and being indebted to him for the advice to go to England at once, as Napoleon had returned from Elba.[63]

Mezière finally came home after the recurrent alarms in Canada about French emissaries died down with the close of the Napoleonic Wars. He wrote his sister, Madame Douaire de Bondy, on February 1, 1816, from New York, where he was teaching French, of his desire to end his days with her at home. He also wrote an old family friend, Judge Foucher, who obtained permission for his return to Montreal in August. On September 3 Mezière signed a declaration of repentance and future loyalty before Jean-Marie Mondelet, justice of the peace at Montreal. After entering into a brief partnership with Charles-Bernard Pasteur, publisher of Le Spectateur canadien, in 1817, on August 1, 1818

---

[63]P.A.C., Fonds Verreau, vol. 4 (carton 17), nos. 32½, 33, 34, 35; H. R. Casgrain, *Biographies canadiennes* (Montréal, 1897), pp. 224-25. Cf. Fauteux, "Henri Mezière," for the family relationships, and for a sceptical view of Casgrain's account.

Mezière, who described himself as an "anglo-canadien," founded at Montreal a magazine called *L'Abeille canadienne*, which continued publication for six months. Its prospectus declared: "We have had the notion of publishing a periodical, in which, with due respect to Religion, morals, and legitimate authority, we should be able to follow critically and with discernment all that concerns the Sciences, the Arts, and Literature."[64] This older and wiser Mezière, fearing the influence of "certain productions thrown off from the Old World because of the bloody catastrophes which they occasioned,"[65] proposed to establish an intellectual bridge between the Old World and the New that would be literary and orthodox. *L'Abeille* published the writings of Ducis, Delille, Saint-Lambert, Bernardin de Saint-Pierre, La Haye, and Voltaire's criticism and poetry. It would seem that the reformed revolutionary could not wholly renounce his youthful enthusiasm for the *philosophes*.

IV

The movement which Mezière had launched in Canada steadily gathered strength after he was carried off to France by the fleet in October 1793. On November 10 John Stevens, just back from three days at the Vermont General Assembly, reported to Genet that the Vermonters informed him that "the French Inhabitants in the Canadas profess as openly as they Dear Considering the Bondage they are kept in by the British Government Firm Republican Principles." Stevens's son-in-law, a British half-pay officer who spoke French, was ready to quit Canada, since he was "sure the moment a Descent was made by the Republicans of France that the French Inhabitants would Cut the throats of all that they thought to be in the British interest."[66] Fontfreyde reported from Plattsburg on January 22, 1794, that he had disposed in Canada of most of the papers sent by Genet, though Canadians and travellers were forbidden by proclamation to discuss affairs of the day.[67]

On January 28 René Gatier, the Canadian-born son of a French father, who had quit Quebec on January 17 because of his pro-French sentiments, wrote to Genet from New Haverhill. He had heard talk of a French invasion, to which most of the Canadians were favourable. He judged the time ripe, as there were few troops in Quebec.[68] On February 4, another fugitive from Quebec, Dr. Timothée O'Connor, wrote from Philadelphia, asking employment in the French service. He had studied medicine in Paris, gone to Canada in 1781, married a French-Canadian wife, and recently lost the confidence of the clergy and seigneurs because of his revolutionary sentiments. He had made a speech at the Constitutional Club in 1791 warning the Canadians against choosing a

---

[64]Fauteux, "Henri Mezière"; S. Marion, *Les Lettres canadiennes d'autrefois*, 3 (Ottawa, 1942), 21.

[65]M. Trudel, *L'Influence de Voltaire au Canada*, vol. 1, (Montréal, 1945), pp. 115–16.

[66]L.O.C., Affs. étran., Corr. pol., États-Unis, Supp., vol. 28, pt. 2, pp. 417–18 v.

[67]Ibid., p. 429; Dorchester's Proclamation of November 26, 1793, in *Canadian Archives Report* (1921), app. B, pp. 23–24.

[68]L.O.C., Affs. étran., Corr. pol., États-Unis, Supp., vol. 28, pt. 2, p. 430.

majority of English representatives, considering that these clubs were electoral machines for the English merchants. Faced with growing disfavour, he had fled through the woods, guided by two Indians and spending nine nights out in the snow.[69] On February 13 Jacques Rous reported in atrocious French that he had circulated Genet's address in undercover fashion "in all the parishes of Canada." The Government was alarmed by its success, and had got the priests to preach loyalism from the pulpit. This was clearly a reference to Bishop Hubert's strongly loyalist circular letter of the previous November 9, issued at Dorchester's request, which was to be re-read by the curés "as many times as appears necessary to you." Rous declared that Genet was blamed for the unrest in Canada. General "Garbau" had spent ten days with Rous while escaping from Quebec, leading Captain Hope to curse his place.[70]

Despite Genet's replacement on February 22, 1794, by the less aggressive Fauchet, who had strict orders to respect American neutrality and to halt his predecessor's expeditionary projects,[71] the seed planted in Canada by Mezière bore bloody fruit in 1794. It had fallen upon the fertile soil of the habitants' discontent with the new English seigneurs, who sought to increase the old feudal dues, and the French-Canadian unrest under a new and unfamiliar system of government, which imposed further burdens on the people.[72] While the *élite* of seigneurs and clergy were horrified by the guillotining of Louis XVI and by the Terror,[73] the people found the Jacobin gospel of Genet's emissaries appealing.[74] In February Dorchester feared the establishment of "the Party distinction of Aristocrat and Democrat," as a result of "the seditious papers scattered about the country."[75] A copy of Les Français libres, which had been read in at least one instance at a church door to the Sunday gathering of habitants and had become widely known as "Le Catéchisme," came into Attorney-General Monk's hands in January.[76]

The agitation was furthered by American land hunger, which showed a blithe disregard for the disputed boundary.[77] Dorchester himself anticipated an American war, as his speech to the Seven Nations on February 10 made abundantly clear.[78] This utterance, with its threat of Indian warfare on the frontier, roused the Vermonters to warlike mood. In March the Chittenden County Democratic Society replied to Dorchester, declaring that Vermont wanted peace with the Canadians, but if the latter were misled by the British, there would be trouble. The statement

[69]Ibid., p. 431.

[70]Ibid., p. 433; H. Têtu and C. O. Gagnon, *Mandements, lettres pastorales, et circulaires des évéques de Québec,* vol. 2 (Québec, 1888), pp. 471-73.

[71]Turner, "Correspondence," pp. 292, 294.

[72]Sulte, "Projets," p. 34.

[73]P. A. de Gaspé *Mémoires* (Ottawa, 1866), pp. 85-90.

[74]J. E. Roy, *Histoire de la seigneurie de Lauzon,* vol. 3 (Lévis, 1900), p. 268.

[75]P.A.C., Q, vol. 67, p. 77, Dorchester to Dundas, Quebec, February 24, 1794.

[76]Ibid., Q, vol. 69-2, p. 224; Q, vol. 69-1, p. 4.

[77]Williamson, *Vermont,* pp. 201-22.

[78]P.A.C., Q, vol. 67, p. 109; W. R. Manning, *Diplomatic Correspondence of the United States: Canadian Relations, 1784-1860,* vol. 1 (Washington, 1940), p. 411.

was printed in New York through the good offices of Colonel Hay, together with the constitution of the Colchester Society, which Fauchet characterized as containing "the purest and most elementary principles of Democracy."[79] The Vermont press engaged in much twisting of the British lion's tail during the spring, and by the end of May Ira Allen's Alburg militia had virtually besieged the British garrison at Pointe au Fer.[80]

As a menace from without increased, unrest in Quebec grew greater. In April the Montreal *voyageurs* rose and freed their fellow Joseph Léveillé, who was being pilloried for signing one contract after breaking another. Popular feeling ran so high that the authorities were forced to let the matter pass.[81] In May there was a general refusal of the militiamen to choose by the unfamiliar British method of balloting the 2,000 men that Dorchester had ordered out under the new Militia Act against the threat of an American war.[82] At Quebec the men broke ranks "into a Mob, refusing to ballot or be commanded." A private threw up his hat and cried out, "Vivent les François!" while a sergeant encouraged the riot.[83] At nearby Charlesbourg and Beauport a small-scale revolution broke out for a few days, with a mob of 300 men armed with muskets, hunting knives, hayforks, and flails patrolling the roads lest "one come to enlist them."[84] There was another less turbulent assemblage at Côte-des-Neiges near Montreal, on the report that the habitants were to be disarmed and taken from their families to be soldiers.[85] The talk reported in the depositions zealously collected by Monk was frankly revolutionary. Canadians who remained loyal were threatened with having their houses burned, with disembowelling, decapitation, and having their heads carried on a pole.[86]

But with arrests and mild repressive measures under the Alien and Sedition Act passed at the end of May—Dorchester refused to be panicked by Monk's alarmism into using the regulars—and with the evaporation of the expected Vermont invasion and with the failure of a French fleet to appear as anticipated between Pentecost and Corpus Christi in June, the agitation collapsed.[87] Monk won himself nomination to the Executive and Legislative Councils, and appointment as chief justice of the court of King's Bench in Montreal by his zeal in running down inconsequential French sympathizers and in conducting a counter-propaganda campaign with his Loyal Associations. These were supported by the English merchants, the seigneurs, and the clergy without

---

[79]L.O.C., Affs. étran., Corr. pol., États-Unis, vol. 40, pt. 5, p. 263; Link, *Societies,* p. 144.

[80]*Records, Governor and Council of Vermont,* vol. 4, pp. 472, 482-3; Williamson, *Vermont,* pp. 209-10.

[81]P.A.C., Q, vol. 69, pp. 309-14.

[82]Ibid., S, vol. 43, Internal Correspondence, Lower Canada, July-December 1794, p. 14.

[83]Ibid., Q, vol. 71-1, pp. 5-6, Dorchester to Dundas, Quebec, May 25, 1794.

[84]Ibid., Q, vol. 69-2, pp. 256-57; Roy, *Lauzon,* vol. 3, pp. 270-71.

[85]P.A.C., Q, vol. 69-2, pp. 309-11.

[86]Ibid., Q, vol. 69-2, pp. 256-67.

[87]Ibid., Q, vol. 69-2, p. 299; Q, vol. 69-1, pp. 1-2, 19-25, 49; Q, vol. 68, p. 199; L.O.C., Affs. étran., Corr. pol., États-Unis, Supp., vol. 28, pt. 2, pp. 437, 441-43 v.

much backing from the people, despite the fervent tribute of Curé Plessis of Quebec to the blessings of British rule in his sermon of June 29 on the death of Bishop Briand.[88] The negotiations for Jay's Treaty eased the threat from Vermont, but the land speculators of that notoriously wily region had learned that French intrigues could be used to further their own ends.

The recurrent alarms about French emissaries on the Vermont and New York border and French fleets in the Gulf of St. Lawrence, which troubled the Canadian authorities from 1793 onward, had abundant foundation in fact, for Adet revived Genet's schemes in 1796 and France was slow to lose interest in North America. These alarms were not merely the product of the excited imaginations of nervous men, many of whom had lived through one revolution in America and dreaded another in Canada as the old 18th-century order crumbled. But the mistake of these officials was to overestimate French-Canadian enthusiasm for such projects, which was small after 1797, and to confuse a growing French-Canadian nationalism and North American republicanism with loyalty to a France which had perished in the Terror. It is still not sufficiently realized that many of the later "French conspiracies" were largely the work of Yankee and Yorker land speculators, who thus sought to even the odds which favoured the official speculators at Quebec. And the pervasive fear of "French emissaries" blinded the officials to the value of French *émigrés* in bringing about Quebec's cultural divorce from France. Through their notable role in developing the classical colleges and parish schools, the 45 *émigré* priests who were admitted to Canada[89] instilled a horror of the French Revolution which has left a lasting impression on the French-Canadian mind. A *fils de la révolution* in Quebec today is not a Communist, but a spiritual heir of 1789.

---

[88]P.A.C., S, vol. 44, Loyal Association, Addresses, Lower Canada, 1794 (A-R by parishes); S, vol. 45 (S-W); Q, vol. 68, pp. 201-5; Q, vol. 69-2, pp. 324-59; Garneau, *Histoire*, vol. 2, pp. 442-43.

[89]N. E. Dionne, *Les Ecclésiastiques et les royalistes français refugiés au Canada, 1791-1802* (Québec, 1905), p. v.

16

SERMON LITERATURE AND CANADIAN INTELLECTUAL HISTORY*

S. F. Wise

The history of ideas has until recent years received practically no attention from students of the Canadian scene. Perhaps this is to be attributed to a conviction that since Canada has produced no major intellectual figures of international reputation, the subject is not one worth studying. Perhaps too, the relative dominance of politics as a subject for historical analysis has hampered a thorough study of ideational constructs. Certainly it is true, as Professor S. F. Wise points out in the following essay, that most Canadian ideology has been imported from outside Canada. Nevertheless, while a study of internationally renowned and original Canadian thought may be impossible, and to search for uniquely Canadian ideas chimeric, the analysis of the relationship of ideas and ideology to the fabric of Canadian society can be a meaningful and fruitful exercise. Whether or not men use ideology as motivation or as rationale for action taken for more prosaic reasons is essentially immaterial; every society has its assumptions and beliefs, however unoriginal, and men do tend to explain their actions in terms of these. This seems particularly true in terms of those in British North America who sought to preserve a certain "Tory" image of society in the late 18th and early 19th centuries. Understanding the assumptions of men like Charles Inglis in Nova Scotia or John Strachan in Upper Canada is no easy task, but Professor Wise offers some new source material and new insights into the Canadian Tory mind. What are his basic approaches to the problem and his justification for the use of sermon literature? Why are the ideologies of men like Inglis and Strachan so difficult to ascer-

---

*The Bulletin of the Committee on Archives, The United Church of Canada (1965), 3-18.

tain? What vision of society did they have? Was it in any way "Canadian?" How do the sermons assist to explain Tory action on the political, social, and economic level? In what other areas of Canadian history can Wise's approach be extended?

SUGGESTIONS FOR FURTHER READING

W. H. Elgee, *The Social Teachings of the Canadian Churches: Protestant, the Early Period, before 1850* (Toronto: Ryerson Press, 1964).

J. L. H. Henderson, ed., *John Strachan: Documents and Opinions* (Toronto: McClelland and Stewart, 1969).

C. F. Klinck, *Literary History of Canada: Canadian Literature in English* (Toronto: University of Toronto Press, 1965).

J.M.B.

I

C anadian intellectual history must be concerned, almost of necessity, with all kinds of ideas that lie between the formal thought of the philosopher or the political theorist and the world of action, and probably closer to the latter. Since (to understate the matter) no connected history of formal thought in Canada is possible, the Canadian intellectual historian must be concerned primarily with the interrelationship between ideas and actions, and therefore the intellectual commonplaces of an age, its root notions, assumptions, and images, will be of more significance to him than the study of coherent bodies of abstract thought. This sort of interest, of course, applies not merely to Canada but to the history of ideas in other places at other times. The historian who wants to establish the connections between ideas and events during the Civil War period in England is much less interested in the political philosophy of Thomas Hobbes than in ideas, well-worn though they may be, to be found in the ephemeral writings of such politicians and pamphleteers as Hyde, Vane, Lilburne, Prynne, or Milton (the more so in this particular instance, since Hobbes's political behaviour was not even Hobbesian). But it seems necessary to state the nature of a Canadian intellectual history, because there has been so little of it written; perhaps through a conviction that nothing of the kind was possible in the absence of any vigorous tradition of original formal thought.

It is indeed true that the explicit structures of thought from which most Canadian ideas derive lie outside Canada. It can be shown, for example, that the commonplaces of political or social language by which British American Tories of the early 19th century justified their actions to themselves stem directly from such European thinkers, or their popularizers, as Burke, De Lolme, Montesquieu, and Blackstone. No doubt the stock of Canadian ideas is replenished every generation from

European and American sources; and doubtless it should be an important function of the Canadian intellectual historian to perform the sort of operations that will trace Canadian ideas to their ultimate external source. But his major task, surely, is to analyze the manner in which externally-derived ideas have been adapted to a variety of local and regional environments, in such a way that a body of assumptions uniquely Canadian has been built up; and to trace the changing content of such assumptions. What, for example, are the social assumptions implicit in the early 19th-century term "yeoman"? When is "yeoman" replaced by "farmer," and what is the significance of the change? What is the relationship between changing terminology, and hence changing social assumptions, and the actual social process? Do these changes, both intellectual and social, occur at the same time in different parts of Canada? Again, what is the content, at any given time, of such terms as "loyalty," "order," "liberty," "authority"; terms which are merely abbreviations for complex socio-political assumptions? The content of the words "respectability" and "interest" is radically different today from what it was a century and a half ago; the life history of either term would disclose a great deal about the intellectual history of Canada.

There are good grounds for saying that the content of social image terminology, or the constellation of notions inherent in a word like "orders," will vary from region to region in Canada, and not just between French- and English-speaking regions. This may be the result of varying rates of assimilation of externally-derived ideas in different parts of the country, or perhaps because some are not received at all, being "filtered out" because of the nature of local institutions. Before anything convincing can be said about the possibility that life in different regions of Canada is organized around marginally different sets of assumptions, however, much work must be done in charting the history of ideological configurations. This is not to imply that an approach which employs "French and Catholic mind" and "English and Protestant mind" as its two categories is erroneous; but simply that it is inadequate, because it cannot explain Canadian variety and because it implies that the Canadian mind, of either category, is a constant. Useful statements about the Canadian mind, at least in its historical context, are likely only after a series of careful investigations of those source materials in which the dominant assumptions of any one age are chiefly to be found, used in a context which makes their current meaning plain.

In any period, political rhetoric is a good guide to the current scale of public values, and also can provide a measurement of the frequent lag between professed belief and actual behaviour through a comparison of what the politician says with what he does. Newspaper editorials, public and private correspondence, travel books by Canadians (especially about other countries), the literature of criticism in the arts: all these classes of material are of permanent value. Other kinds of material, however, are of more significance in a particular age than in any other. Institutional and corporate advertising, for example, embalms values important in the age of large-scale economic enterprise; and a study of the advertising of the Bank of Montreal, the Steel Company of Canada, or even O'Keefe

Breweries, over a generation, would probably show some remarkable shifts and changes.

The main purpose of this essay is to show, through illustration, the peculiar value of sermon literature as a medium for the expression of conservative ideas in late 18th- and early 19th-century British America. Sermon literature as a source for the history of ideas, though untapped in Canada, has been used extensively elsewhere. Christopher Morris's *Political Thought in England: Tyndale to Hooker* (London, 1953),[1] and William Haller's brilliant study, *The Rise of Puritanism* (New York, 1938), both rely upon the exploitation of a large body of sermons to reconstruct the intellectual movements of early modern England; R. B. Perry's studies of the New England mind draw partly upon sermons. The most casual check of standard bibliographies of Canadian imprints will disclose that large numbers of sermons were published in the 18th and early 19th centuries; while many more manuscript sermons of the time are preserved in libraries and archives. In the Ontario Archives, for example, are several substantial bundles of the sermons of John Strachan, covering approximately 60 years of our history. They have never been used by an historian. Yet his sermons, and those of his contemporaries, are indispensable to an understanding of the conservative mind of the age.

II

Most of the sermons printed in British North America between 1784 and 1820 were those of "churchmen," that is, clergy of the Church of England, the Church of Scotland, and the Congregational churches of Nova Scotia. Each of these churches, in the land of its origin, was an established church and a defender of the established order of things. It is hardly remarkable that the sermons of the colonial clergy of these churches were uniformly conservative in character. It might perhaps be argued that unpublished, rather than published sermons are a more valid source for the dominant ideas of the time, since they were intended only for the minister's congregation. It is true that since printed sermons were frequently those given on such public religious occasions as the opening of the legislature, days of general fast and humiliation, or days of public thanksgiving, they tended to be concerned with such public matters as the relationship between the state and its enemies, the purposes of God in times of war and revolution, or the duties of the citizen; while unpublished sermons, on the whole, seem to be less taken up with such questions. Even so reputedly political a churchman as John Strachan rarely gave an overtly political sermon to his own congregation. Moreover, the language of manuscript sermons is less studied, less formal, and less concerned with creating an impression of classical erudition. Yet there seems to be no substantial difference in the social and political assumptions which can be found running through the two classes of sermons. Whether on public occasions, or in ordinary Sunday

---

[1] See especially the two chapters entitled "The Elizabethan assumptions."

services, the churchman preached social and political conservatism as well as the gospel.

It is the strategic position of the churchmen of the revolutionary age that lends a special importance to the content of their sermons. Accepted as members of the small colonial upper class, and accorded special respect because of their superior education in a society in which the general level was low, the clergy of the Anglican, Presbyterian and Congregational churches (and indeed those of the Catholic church as well) were well-placed to exert a considerable influence upon the political outlook and behaviour of a large part of the colonial population. It has been argued[2] that social rank and education cut the established clergy off from the "people," but this is so only in a restricted sense, because their influence reached well beyond their by no means negligible congregations. In defining the public philosophy and the public morality, the conservative clergy had little competition, and that chiefly from the judges of the high courts, whose jury charges invaded, periodically, the ideological monopoly of the ministers. Legislative debates were not reported at this time, and thus the politician was virtually stifled. The day of the journalist-politician had scarcely dawned. The popular press did not exist. Society was wholly Christian; freethinkers kept their thoughts to themselves. No challenge to the intellectual primacy of the clergy came from such dissenting denominations as the Baptists and the Methodists, who accepted the political and social, if not the ecclesiastical and theological assumptions of the churchmen.

The position of the conservative clergy in the realm of ideas was reinforced by the outbreak of the French Revolution, and by the long wars which were its aftermath. Men knew that the Revolution had brought a new age, and whether they wished it well, or were horrified by it, they followed the shifts and changes of the huge drama with absorbed fascination. Even in the little societies of British North America, a weekly budget of despatches, letters, bulletins, treaties, atrocity stories, and propaganda borrowed by the infant colonial press from newspapers abroad or from the United States kept the reading public informed (a few months in arrears) of the enormous events that were shaking the old order to its foundations. The deadly antagonism between the Revolution and established ideas and institutions meant that everywhere conservatives rallied to attack it. The politician Edmund Burke, in his *Reflections on the Revolution in France*, provided both a defence of British institutions and an eloquent assault upon the Revolution and all its works, and of course his arguments made a deep impression upon British American conservatives as well as those of Great Britain. In the colonies, however, it was the clergy, not the politicians, who bore the chief responsibility for interpreting the meaning of Europe's convulsions to society at large, and because of this, they made a lasting contribution to the nature of Canadian conservatism. It can be seen in that combination of religious and secular elements which gave to colonial toryism one of its most marked characteristics, and perhaps its only real claim to distinctiveness. This

---

[2] S. D. Clark, *Church and Sect in Canada* (Toronto, 1948).

synthesis, worked out during the long crisis of the Revolution, the French wars, and the War of 1812, proved an extraordinarily durable one. Some illustrations of its beginnings follow.

III

That the French Revolution surpassed previous revolutions in scale and in the social depths to which it reached was not questioned, even by the Loyalist clergy of British North America. To Charles Inglis, the Loyalist Bishop of Nova Scotia, it was an event without precedent.

> The state of France at the present day is an occurrence wholly new in the annals of the human race. The history of mankind . . . furnishes no instance . . . of so general a phrenzy seizing a populous and polished nation; a phrenzy that is not confined to any particular description, but diffused through all ranks and orders of people. The high and the low, the peer and peasant, the learned and the ignorant, are equally stimulated to the perpetration of the most atrocious crimes; delighting in slaughter and unbridled cruelty; sporting with the lives and property of mankind; destroying all religion and subordination; openly avowing atheism; and sinking into a total depravation of principles and manners![3]

That it might be possible to equate the revolutions in France and America does not seem to have occurred to Inglis;[4] it was not the degree of violence or the universality of upheaval that made the French Revolution so radical a break from previous experience, but the shock of such an explosion in a nation so "populous and polished." How could so ancient and civilized a people be "suddenly transformed into a race of sanguinary barbarians and ruffians"?[5] Had the French gone spontaneously mad? Or were there deeper causes for this apparent national insanity? Could an explanation be found in the instabilities of the volatile French character, or was the Revolution a product of causes which could operate anywhere, and not exclusively in France?

The sermons of the day were attempts to answer such questions. In them is to be found an anatomy of the Revolution, and of revolutions: the false ideas from which they spring, the nature and the motivation of the men who concoct and spread inflammatory ideas, the vast deception behind the protestations of reformers. It is not really important that these sermons were couched in the terms of traditional thought, despite some flashes of insight or felicities of phrase. What is important is their contribution to the formation of a conservative political ideology. The principles hammered home from the pulpits during the long crisis with France were those which were to condemn a Gourlay, a Mackenzie, or a

---

[3]Charles Inglis, *A Sermon preached in the Parish Church of St. Paul at Halifax, on Friday, April 25, 1794. Being the day appointed by Proclamation for a General Fast and Humiliation in His Majesty's Province of Nova Scotia* (Halifax, 1794), p. 24.

[4]Cf. R. R. Palmer, *Age of the democratic revolution: a political history of Europe and America, 1760-1800* (Princeton, 1959), chap. 7.

[5]Charles Inglis, *Steadfastness in Religion and Loyalty recommended, in a Sermon preached before the Legislature of His Majesty's Province of Nova Scotia; in the Parish Church of St. Paul, at Halifax on Sunday, April 7, 1793* (Halifax, 1793), p. 22n.

Papineau in the years after the end of the wars, and were to endure, in modified form, long beyond the collapse of political Toryism.

According to the Reverend Andrew Brown, incumbent of the Protestant Dissenting Church in Halifax, the seeds of the French Revolution were planted by the free-thinking followers of Lord Herbert of Cherbury. Under the guise of defending the freedom of the press and the right of private judgment, they launched a subtle attack upon organized religion, and by degrees poisoned the arts, science, and philosophy with their sceptical doctrines. In this they had the assistance of the European aristocracy, who, out of a sense of guilt for their historic crimes, sought "a commodious apology for the disorders of their conduct."[6] Aristocratic complicity was crucial:

> Abandoned by the rich and fashionable, the church continued for a season to be a refuge to the poor and afflicted. But in time the lower orders learned to despise, in their hearts, those religious observances which they saw their more enlightened superiors treat with unreserved contempt. Copying their example with perverse ingenuity, they joined in the ridicule poured upon their clergy, and regarded every scandalous story which reflected on the church or the sacred office, as an invaluable piece of history which could not be too carefully recorded. . . . Amidst the indifference and depravity of a degenerate age, Christianity was publicly renounced by many in the upper ranks of life, and a speculative deism, in no respect distinguishable from actual atheism, was substituted in its room.[7]

It was a cardinal principle of Tory social psychology that the example set by the upper orders would always influence decisively the conduct of the mass of mankind. This is why a relatively few aristocratic followers of "Voltaire, Rousseau, Helvetius, D'Alembert, &c." could produce a "nation of Atheists."[8] Once "Reason" was enthroned, the way was clear for the perpetration of the shocking crimes of the Revolution. But this black page of history had a moral utility, could its lesson be understood:

> . . . from the general tenour of the affairs of France since its rulers abjured religion, the least instructed of mankind . . . may be enabled to institute a comparison between the effects of genuine Christianity, and of that sublime Philosophy which was to regenerate the human race. . . . no sooner had the sceptical philosophers usurped the powers of legislation than . . . strife and anarchy prevailed. The worst passions of the worst persons rioted without controul. . . . The prisons were crowded with victims; new modes of trial and execution were invented; and under the direful agency of a murderous tribunal blood flowed in a continual stream.[9]

The bloody events of the Revolution, then, were the natural and inevitable outcome of the abandonment of religion by the ruling classes of France. It was vain and self-deceiving to imagine that the enlightened

---

[6]Andrew Brown, *The Perils of the Time, and the purposes for which they are appointed. A Sermon, preached on the last Sabbath of the Year 1794* (Halifax, 1795), p. 27.

[7]Ibid., p. 28.

[8]Inglis, *Steadfastness in Religion and Loyalty*, pp. 15, 16n.

[9]Brown, *Perils of the Time*, pp. 29–30.

principles of the philosophers had somehow been betrayed by weak men; the atrocities in France were, in fact, "inseparable from the nature of the new principles, and would mark their rule to the world's end."[10]

Here the conservative clergy were on familiar ground: the mutually supporting nature of religion and the state. While admitting that without government, man would long since have exterminated himself, Inglis argued, following Warburton,[11] that religion was necessary to rectify the imperfections of government. Secular laws, which rested upon force, could not reach "the source and spring of our actions," the conscience. Moreover, society cannot work without such "duties of imperfect obligation" as gratitude, hospitality, charity, and so on. Yet social duties, without which the state of society would be "miserable," cannot possibly be legislated. Indeed, society is incapable of sufficiently rewarding its members to ensure its own preservation. Aside from the very few persons who receive rank and emolument from serving the state, society provides for the general mass of citizens only the reward of mere protection, quite insufficient to stimulate preservative civic virtues. As man grows more numerous, new problems arise: the more populous the society, the larger the cities, the wealthier their citizens, then the greater the increase in crime as "the depraved appetites of mankind" are inflamed. A rise in material prosperity and urban population does not mean progress, but merely more inducements to greater crime. A government based upon secular philosophy, no matter how benign, is powerless against the forces of evil and destructiveness latent in society itself. There is only one principle that will bind up the warring elements within peoples, and that is the "superior principle" of religion. Only religion teaches that government is ordained of God, a principle that gives the state an authority that no secular sanction can give it.[12] Only religion renders man conscious of the all-seeing eye of God and of his own ultimate accountability to God. Without instruction in his duty towards God, man inevitably falls victim to the ever-increasing temptations that surround him, and is drawn into enormous crimes. It is therefore "the avenging terrors of Almighty God" which are "the best support of Government."[13]

Brown's argument was similar, if a little less crudely put. Any system, he held, that considered this life as the whole of existence, and thought of death as an everlasting sleep, would hold out only "safety and self-ag-

---

[10]Ibid., p. 30.

[11]Bishop William Warburton, *Alliance of Church and State* (London, 1766).

[12]Inglis, *Steadfastness in Religion and Loyalty*, pp. 9–12. The Rev. John Burns, Presbyterian minister of Stamford, Upper Canada, could find no other way to express this idea than by enunciating the doctrine of the Divine Right of Kings, in words virtually those of James I! "Kings are God's deputies, or vicegerents, here upon earth. They derive their power from him, and are the instruments, which his providence has made choice of, to govern and protect the world." *True Patriotism; a Sermon Preached in the Presbyterian Church in Stamford, Upper Canada, on the 3rd day of June, 1814.* . . . (Montreal, 1814), p. 10. Upper Canada, the nursery of a variety of out-of-the-way political notions during these years, presents no more extraordinary spectacle than this revival of divine-rightism by a spiritual descendant of John Knox and the Melvilles.

[13]Inglis, *Steadfastness in Religion and Loyalty*, pp. 12–13.

grandisement" as the ends of life, and since man is not accountable for his behaviour, the pursuit of these ends "by all means, even the most atrocious," is justified. But when society is Christian, then "the gospel . . . moderates the passions of the rich, and supports the virtue of the poor."[14] These and other arguments concerned with the vital social and political utility of religion were to be vigorously employed by the next generation of clerical and lay conservatives in their defence of the principle of the connection between church and state, or at least the public recognition of the Christian nature of society through financial aid to churches other than the Church of England. To conservatives, the necessity of some connection between organized religion and the state had been triumphantly vindicated by the horrors which irreligion had caused in France, and by the final defeat of France herself. Andrew Brown, in the early years of the Revolution, had been confident that such would be the outcome of the great contest then beginning:

> To all the arguments in (Christianity's) favour which past ages have furnished, will be added those alarming ones derived from the bloody history of the French revolution. . . . Christianity will thus be restored to new credit and influence. The vain babblings of philosophy will be consigned to everlasting perdition. Men will reject with detestation all the modifications of deism, and be solicitous to establish in their country, in their houses, and in their hearts, the genuine doctrines of the Cross of Christ.[15]

Although the first concern of the conservative clergy was to explain the French Revolution in terms of the abandonment of religion for the pernicious ideas of the free-thinkers, they also addressed themselves directly to radical French politics and the dangers French radicalism posed for British North America. Much is said, for example, of the character of the political innovator. Taken together, these remarks form a kind of compendium of the Tory rhetoric against reform, and are an illustration of a conventional pattern of thought that was to have a long life. To the churchmen, society was delicately and precariously balanced, an entity dependent upon the maintenance of an equilibrium between the desire of all its members for security in life and property, and the desire of each for self-aggrandisement. As we have seen, it was the function of religion to "subdue this restlessness and discontent," and to teach man to be "resigned to the will of God, and thankful for his allotment in the state of life where his providence has placed us."[16] The innovator, however, had more than the ordinary share of natural restlessness. He was a person in whom "ambition, self-interest, and humour" were in dangerous combination. "Not content with (his) proper rank in the scale of beings," he schemed to advance himself by stirring up others.[17] His tactics were ever

---

[14]Brown, *Perils of the Time*, p. 31. A representative Catholic development of similar themes in Rev. Edmund Burke, *Letter of Instruction to the Catholic Missionaries of Nova Scotia* (Halifax, 1804).

[15]Brown, *Perils of the Time*, p. 31.

[16]Inglis, *Steadfastness in Religion and Loyalty*, p. 17.

[17]Mather Byles, *The Victory Ascribed to God* . . . (Saint John, N.B., 1798), p. 5.

the same: he called for redress of grievances in the name of patriotism, liberty, and the public welfare; he formed clubs, circulated inflammatory publications, got up petitions, spread rumours, worked up the multitude in the name of some great cause. He was a demagogue, who played upon the baser desires of the artless populace; he was a hypocrite, because "self-interest generally lies at the bottom" of the ringing ideals he professed. Such men rose on the hopes they created in the masses, and "secretly laugh at those who are the dupes of their artifices."[18] In this timeless game, the people were always deluded; indeed, doubly so: first by the deceitful demagogue who used them for his purposes, and second by their own illusion that programmes of reform could have any beneficial effect upon their condition. Just as the state of France demonstrated the horrible consequences of irreligion, so also it showed the absurdity of impracticable schemes of political reformation, launched "under the specious names of *Fraternity, Equality,* and *Liberty.*"[19] Just as the deists had had the arrogant presumption to challenge 18 centuries of Christianity, so the political philosophers had been dreaming dreams of perfection and calling them constitutions, when the teachings of both religion and history showed that the hard lot of man was to submit to his own imperfections and to put up with the institutions he had, which represented, after all, the wisdom of countless generations. How cruel to hoodwink the masses with glittering slogans!

> To meditate the establishment of equality . . . , that splendid delusion of the present age, the vision of the weak, and the pretext of the wicked, is in fact to meditate war against God, and the primary laws of creation. . . . In society inequality is just as natural as in the forest, but productive of much more salutary effects. Without inequality what would become of the necessary distinctions of parent and child, master and scholar, the employer and the employed![20]

Most clergymen were prepared to admit that there were times when political and social changes were necessary and even desirable, and that failure to change could bring upheavals like the French Revolution. But there were some, like Bishop Inglis, who saw no need at all for change in the present state of perfection. For him, religious history had come to a stop with the salutary changes of the Protestant Reformation, and political history with that culmination of the English genius, the Glorious Revolution of 1688:

> But, blessed be God, those times are now past. We enjoy the benefits resulting from those changes; we should be thankful to heaven for them; and look back with reverence to the fortitude and virtues of our ancestors who were instruments, in the hand of Providence, of conferring those signal blessings upon us. For we live in a period, when the Religion of Jesus Christ is professed and taught in its native purity, as contained in holy Scripture. We live

---

[18]Burns, *True Patriotism,* p. 15; Inglis, *Steadfastness in Religion and Loyalty,* pp. 17, 22.
[19]Jacob Mountain, *Sermon Preached at Quebec January 10, 1799 . . . for General Thanksgiving* (Quebec, 1799), p. 29.
[20]Brown, *Perils of the Time,* pp. 34–5.

under the best of Civil Constitutions; where we enjoy as much Liberty as is consistent with a state of Civil Society. . . . In these circumstances, to think the business of changing should still go on, and never stop, must surely proceed from (the) spirit of innovation, . . . or from something worse.[21]

Therefore, enjoined Inglis in the words of a text no longer in fashion, but then much used: "Fear thou the Lord and the King; and meddle not with them that are given to change."

Another important theme of the sermons of this period had to do with the meaning of the great struggle in which Britain and France were engaged. How could the larger purposes of God for man be reconciled with the necessity to justify a British victory? The interpretive framework upon which these sermons were preached was the providential theology, and, like other churchmen before and since, the clergy of the day were gradually drawn to identify the purposes of God with the policies of their own nation. Preaching in the first months of the war, Andrew Brown, "a short-sighted mortal," was wary of divining God's "precise purposes," but remained confident that He "never ordained impiety and anarchy to be perpetual among men."[22] Inglis was less cautious. He declared that "the judgments of God are actually abroad," and announced his conviction that the war against France was a sacred war. Surely it was "a contest in the cause of humanity against violence and blood, of order and government against anarchy and confusion, of right and justice against lawless rapacity, of real liberty against oppression and tyranny, of truth against falsehood, and of God against the most audacious Atheism."[23] Yet both Inglis and Brown asserted that the war was also a sore judgment of God against Britain and her allies for their transgressions, in which godless France was the divine instrument of punishment, just as God had used such pagan idolators as the Egyptians and Babylonians when Israel had strayed from the paths of righteousness. The war was monitory, therefore, and was to be seen as providing opportunity for a purifying repentance. Should the opportunity so presented be wasted, then Britain would be broken like a potter's vessel.[24]

But as the war went on, the emphasis upon British sinfulness became less and less strong, and more and more the clergy, especially the Anglicans, came to equate the aims of God and Great Britain. When Nelson won at Aboukir Bay, Mather Byles in Saint John adduced the victory as proof that the British people were "the favourites of God," and that France was Satan personified as a many-headed nation. Behind Great Britain was "the secret, irresistible scheme of Providence."[25] In a sermon celebrating the same victory, Bishop Mountain at Quebec nodded to conventional theology in acknowledging that God had used France to chastise a sinful world, but professed to see that the British people, having passed through the refiner's fire of adversity, were now "happily for

---

[21] Inglis, *Steadfastness in Religion and Loyalty*, p. 18.
[22] Brown, *Perils of the Time*, p. 19.
[23] Inglis, *Sermon . . . for a General Fast and Humiliation*, p. 31, p. 23.
[24] Ibid., pp. 24–5, Brown, *Perils of the Time*, p. 24.
[25] Byles, *Victory Ascribed to God*, pp. 9, 12.

ourselves, and for the world, made the instruments of chastising the arrogance, humbling the power of France." Who could doubt that "we are engaged against an enemy whom we may, without presumption, consider as much more wicked than ourselves"?[26]

Mountain, and many another minister of the time, fell into the classic error of accommodating Christianity to the current system of values. They persuaded themselves, and many of their hearers, that God was not merely using Britain to defeat atheistic France, but that British victories meant also Divine approval of the social, religious, and political institutions of the mother country.[27] This delusion, always latent in British nationalism, was given special strength by the zeal with which it was preached during the many years' crisis, and was permitted to take firm hold partly because there was nothing that could be called an "intellectual opposition" in colonial society. The notion that God had staged the quarter-century of destruction as a kind of massive lesson to benighted humanity of the superior virtues of the British constitution in church and state (though never stated quite so baldly), became an article of faith with British American Tories. The special religious element in colonial Toryism owed much to the inculcation, during the war years, of a crude providentialism, as did the fact that British American conservatives had no provision in their scheme of things for orderly change, but merely for the orderly acceptance of things as they were.

In the sermons of John Strachan, the "lessons" the conservative clergy thought the French wars had taught can be read plainly. Unlike the other clergy mentioned to this point, Strachan belonged essentially to the postwar period, but his ideas were formed, once for all, before 1815. This fact is of prime importance, because Strachan was teacher, mentor and minister to a whole generation of Tory politicians in Upper Canada, a central figure in the politics of his province for at least 25 years and a dominant influence in his church for many more years than that. His impact upon the Ontario community in its formative stage was very great, in one way or another, and yet it cannot be said that his ideas have ever been adequately analyzed. Plentiful material for such an analysis is to be found in the large body of sermons, printed and in manuscript, that he left behind him. These sermons establish clearly Strachan's intellectual debt to the clergy of the age of revolution, but also demonstrate that he was much more extreme in his conservatism than any of them.

Strachan's mind was rather like a megalithic monument: strong, crude, and simple. It moved in straight lines, was impatient of subtleties and qualifications (though often itself devious and self-deceiving), and was unleavened by what might be variously described as realism, a sense of proportion or merely as a sense of the absurd. To such a mind, providentialism was heady wine, for Strachan pushed the conclusions to be drawn from it farther than did any of his contemporaries. Not for him the modest disclaimers of Brown, or even the more specious qualifications of Mountain. God's intentions could not be doubted; "never have so

---

[26]Mountain, *Sermon . . . for General Thanksgiving*, pp. 15-17.
[27]Ibid., pp. 25-30.

many unquestionable proofs of a superintending Providence appeared in
so short a period."[28] The secular, egalitarian assumptions upon which
the governments of the United States and France were, or had been
based, had been judged and found wanting; "the two great experiments
in America and France to constitute governments productive of virtues
and happiness only . . . have completely failed." The lesson of the war
was that "no great and decided amelioration of the lower classes of society can be reasonably expected: . . . that foolish perfectability with
which they had been deluded can never be realized."[29] On the other
hand, Strachan was not content to depict Britain as an instrument in the
hands of God, used to accomplish his purposes, as had his clerical contemporaries. Just as God had revealed his truth to the Jews, thought
Strachan, so had he in a later day to another nation. "Here, My Brethren," said Strachan, "I allude to the British nation, but not in the spirit
of boasting or ostentation."[30] His victory sermon of 1814, and such other
sermons as the Rebellion sermon of 1838,[31] disclose that his deepest
beliefs were that the British were God's peculiar people, and that their
order in church, state, and society was providentially blessed. Among
God's British, the Upper Canadians occupied a special position. This
"remnant" of a once-great continental empire had been purified and
united through struggle with the United States, the only country in the
world to become the ally of France by free choice. The miraculous survival of tiny Upper Canada was a North American testimony to God's
gracious dealings with those whom he designed specially to prosper.
Strachan's sermon of 1814, preached in the first flush of victory over
Napoleon and in the knowledge that Wellington's veterans were soon to
be launched against the Americans, is an important document. It is a
kind of manifesto of Upper Canadian Toryism, but it contains not a programme so much as an anti-programme; that is, it lays down those
things—the connection between church and state, the relative perfection of the British constitution, the delusiveness of projects of reform and
the suicidal dangers in listening to innovators—which the will of God as
revealed in the verdict of the war had determined to be beyond challenge.
Rid of her invaders, cleansed of her traitors and secure in her beliefs,
Upper Canada would stand as a shining witness in North America.
"Now," said Strachan, "the dawn of the happiest times is rising upon
us."[32]

IV

One of the great difficulties in reconstructing the conservative mind
(of any period) is the fact that the conservative is rarely explicit about his
most cherished beliefs. He assumes certain things to be immutably true

---

[28]John Strachan, *Sermon Preached at York, Upper Canada, on the Third of June, being
the Day Appointed for a General Thanksgiving* (Montreal, 1814), p. 5.

[29]Ibid., pp. 29–30.

[30]Ibid., p. 8.

[31]Ontario Archives, *Strachan Papers*, Sermon on text "And thy judgments are as the light
that goeth forth," Hosea 6:5, delivered December 14, 1838.

[32]Strachan, *Sermon . . . for a General Thanksgiving*, p. 38.

and established, and finds it unnecessary to explain them to his friends, and pointless to explain them to his enemies. When an Upper Canadian Tory ran for election with a strong belief in the British constitution as his only declared platform, neither he nor his sympathetic constituents found such an appeal platitudinous or ludicrously inadequate. Such phrases stood for a whole set of conservative values.

At no time was the Tory less explicit than in explaining his social values. Quite possibly this was because the standard British arguments in justification of the principle of aristocracy seemed irrelevant to the much more democratic societies of North America; more probably it was because the Tory, while retaining his belief in a graded social order, realized that he was unlikely to get a favourable hearing for his views from the community at large. At any rate, any source which supplies an exposition of what the British American conservative meant by a phrase like "due subordination in society" is valuable.

The unpublished sermons of John Strachan contain some of the most illuminating exposition of conservative social thought available, perhaps because the Doctor in his pulpit, speaking to his parishioners, felt a freedom unknown to his pupils, on the hustings, in the legislature, or in the press. As an illustration, there is his sermon on I Timothy 4:8, "But Godliness is profitable unto all things." Strachan's notations show that it was first preached at sea September 24, 1824, and that he delivered it several more times in the 1820s and 1830s. His ostensible purpose was to comment upon the relationship between the enjoyment of the pleasures of this world and the prospect of salvation. Should religion "stalk abroad with all the rigour of Egyptian Taskmasters?"[33] He concluded (predictably enough) that when not carried to excess the pursuit of pleasure, wealth, and honours was natural, proper, and by no means out of keeping with the religious life.

But Strachan's purpose was not primarily to justify temporal happiness, but the existence and necessity of social inequality. His argument was immeasurably old, a kind of historical pastiche of the commonplaces of social conservatism, but with some quirks which are his alone. Just as in the natural world there is an ascending order of creation, and within each species there are both weak and strong individuals, so in human society are men given an infinite variety of capacities:

> One is formed to rule, another to obey. . . . Subordination in the Moral World is manifest and this appearance of nature indicates the intention of its Author. The beauty and advantages of this arrangement are obvious and universally acknowledged. . . . The various relations of individuals and Societies require a mutual exchange of good offices. . . . Hence it would appear that they who labour in the inferior departments of life are not on that account the slaves of their superiors. The Magistrate requires the aid of his people—the Master of his Servant. They are all dependent upon one another, as they subsist by an exchange of good offices. . . . The lowest order enjoys its peculiar comforts and privileges, and contributes equally with the highest to the support and dignity of Society.

---

[33]Ontario Archives, *Strachan Papers*, Sermon on text, "But Godliness is profitable unto all things," I Timothy 4:8, first delivered September 24, 1824. All subsequent quotations are from this sermon.

Not only did the social order correspond to the different levels of ability given to men by God, but men were also allotted "different shares of sensibility," so that the pursuit of happiness became the pursuit of that degree of happiness one is capable of attaining. Because of this, only bitterness can come to the man who aspires to a place above his station. While "efforts to better our condition are laudable," the man who gets above himself will drink deeply of "Chagrin, Melancholy, Envy, Hatred and other wretched passions." Strachan offered as consolation for the inferiority of one's lot the perennial conservative cliché that the mighty of this world ought not to be envied their luxury and pomp; they pay for their splendours many times over with the heavy burden of care that attends high position:

> Let us not be dazzled by the opulence and splendour of the great. The del-
> icacies of his Table would soon pall upon our sense, vitiate our taste, and
> perhaps enervate us by Sickness or disease. We may admire the pomp of his
> public appearance, when his pride, the duties of his station, the applause of
> a surrounding multitude, or the brilliancy of the whole scene may preserve
> an air of superior ease and happiness in his deportment, but let us follow
> him to his retirement during the season of reflexion and we may see him
> oppressed with cares, which neither the most delicate repast nor costly
> apparel nor a multitude of Friends and dependents nor all the glories of a
> crown can alleviate.

Not pausing to explain to his hearers how it was that the share of sensibility awarded the great did not bring them the kind of happiness commensurate with their rank, Strachan rushed on to provide a sovereign remedy for dissatisfaction with one's subordinate position in life (so long as one was not too subordinate). Instead of eating one's heart out with envy of those more fortunate, why not reverse the process?

> You compare your situation with that of your Superiors. This will turn your
> attention to the advantages you want rather than those you possess. . . . But
> compare it to the inferior stations of life, and the effect will be more favour-
> able to your comfort. . . . You do not consider their blessings but plume
> yourselves as enjoying much superior. By thus contrasting your condition
> with those that are worse, you will see how much more unhappy you might
> be and thus derive satisfaction from your superiority. In this way learn to
> contract your desires and you will obtain all the happiness which others so
> anxiously pursue.

Strachan's recommendation is testimony to his sense of social psychology, if not to his grasp of Christian social ethics.

Stripped of its characteristic individual quixotries, this sermon is probably representative of early 19th-century conservative social thought. How relevant its categories were to the social and economic realities of British North America is quite another question. Deeply-held social and political assumptions change when circumstances dictate, when they have clearly ceased to have any connection with the life they purport to explain. Perhaps it was such a change that explains the superscription scrawled upon this sermon by John Strachan in old age: "Read this Sermon on 12 March 1858 and found it very inferior to what I expected."

17

GOD'S CHOSEN PEOPLE: THE ORIGINS OF TORONTO SOCIETY, 1793–1818*

R. J. Burns

For a number of years before the Rebellion of 1837, reformers complained about the oligarchy which ruled the province. William Lyon Mackenzie gave it the label which stuck when he called it "The Family Compact." The existence of a small elite cadre of officeholders—centred about the provincial capital—with their fingers in all sorts of other affairs, was scarcely unique to Upper Canada. Indeed, no British colony in the 18th and early 19th century was without its "Compact," the basis of which was permanent public appointment at the nerve centre of administration. Governors and Lieutenant-Governors might come and go, but the permanent servants of the province who ran its daily affairs remained, regarding such matters as nepotism and the use of public power for private advantage not as corruption, but as part of the legitimate perquisites of officeholding.

Unlike many provincial elites, that of Upper Canada had a philosophy—forged in the American Revolution and validated by the War of 1812—as the previous selection by S. F. Wise has indicated. But to what extent does that philosophy create the group, and to what extent is it a rationalization for an existence predicated upon other factors? In the following study, R. J. Burns attempts to explain the early development of Upper Canadian Toryism in both its ideational and operational sense. To what extent were the reformers correct in regarding the Upper Canadian elite as a tightly-knit family operation? What was the basis of the elite's success? Could any other structure have emerged in early Upper Canada? How important was philosophy in the growth of this elite?

*Canadian Historical Association Historical Papers (1973), 213-228.

SUGGESTIONS FOR FURTHER READING

A. L. Burt, *The United States, Great Britain, and British North America* (Toronto: Ryerson Press, 1940).

G. Craig, *Upper Canada, 1784–1841* (Toronto: McClelland and Stewart, 1963).

D. W. L. Earl, ed., *The Family Compact: Aristocracy or Oligarchy?* (Toronto: Copp Clark, 1967).

J.M.B.

U pper Canada's first Lieutenant-Governor, John Graves Simcoe, attempted to recreate in the new colony an example of the superiority of British government and society, hoping that he could thereby reveal to the citizens of the recently formed United States the errors of republicanism and independence.[1] In his desire to establish as closely as possible the very "image and transcript" of the constitution of Great Britain, he followed the policy of the home government. In drafting the Constitutional Act, Home Secretary William Wyndham Grenville had felt that Canadian society should mirror that of Britain, having at its apex an hereditary aristocracy based upon landed wealth and service to the King.[2] This plan Simcoe failed to execute; his efforts were blocked by Grenville's successor, the Duke of Portland, who feared that the establishment of an hereditary aristocracy would lead Upper Canada down the familiar road to independence and separation.[3] Yet Simcoe did endow his new capital with a group of provincial officials who were able to establish themselves as a distinct social entity. A quarter of a century later these individuals, their offspring and protégés, were the Toronto[4] society and, in their roles as provincial officials, they were soon to become known as the Family Compact. This study deals with the earliest period of Upper Canada; it is an examination of the creation of the initial Toronto society and the gradual accumulation of power within the capital by a few favoured families. The terminal date has been set as 1818, which marks the accession to power of John Strachan and a consequent restructuring of the internal relationship among the town's elite.

Shortly after his arrival in Upper Canada Simcoe was privately ac-

---

[1]For an excellent analysis of Upper Canadian Tory ideology including the term "God's chosen people" see S. F. Wise, "God's Peculiar People" in W. L. Morton, ed., *The Shield of Achilles* (Toronto, 1968), pp. 31–61.

[2]See Lord Chancellor Thurlow to W. W. Grenville, September 1–10, 1789, E. A. Cruikshank, ed., *The Correspondence of Lieut. Governor John Graves Simcoe*, 5 vols. (Toronto, 1923–31) [hereafter *Simcoe Cor.*], vol. 1, pp. 4–5; Grenville to Thurlow, September 12, 1789, ibid., 6–7; Simcoe to Henry Dundas, November 4, 1792, ibid., p. 251; Simcoe to Dundas, November 23, 1792, ibid., p. 265, Simcoe to the Duke of Portland, December 21, 1794, ibid., vol. 3, p. 235; and Simcoe to Portland, February 17, 1795, ibid., vol. 3, p. 302.

[3]The Duke of Portland to Simcoe, May 20, 1795, ibid., vol. 4, pp. 12–14, and Simcoe to Portland, October 30, 1795, ibid., vol. 4, pp. 115–8.

[4]In keeping with his penchant for British place names, Simcoe christened Toronto "York" in 1793; at the city's incorporation in 1834 it was renamed Toronto and will be referred to as such throughout this paper.

cused of having brought enough followers to fill all the new government positions and there was more than a grain of truth in the claim.[5] Some of the new officials, especially those whose duties required a legal training, were imperial appointees.[6] But many of those chosen personally by the Lieutenant-Governor had served under him in the Queen's Rangers during the Revolutionary War. These original officials of the new colony, whether imperial appointees or members of the Queen's Rangers, shared with Simcoe and the home government certain assumptions about the causes and the nature of the recent American Revolution. They believed that a stronger central government combined with an established church and an hereditary aristocracy would forestall a repetition in British North America of the events which had brought about the loss of the 13 colonies. They also saw themselves as constituting one-third of this conservative social matrix—that is, the aristocracy. From their first arrival in Toronto they viewed themselves as the apex of the town's social scale. They were from the beginning God's chosen people and their mission was to perpetuate and spread their values and way of life as an alternative to those evolving in the United States. For much of the 19th century Toronto's development would be affected by their conservative political and social views. Yet in the decade following the official founding of Toronto the initial leading families and their associates numbered at the most 30 families and individuals.[7]

Since Toronto, for at least a decade, existed solely as a centre of government, it is not surprising that the provincial officials immediately came to control every aspect of the town's existence. Not only were there a number of provincial positions in Toronto, but also the town was the district seat of government and thus had local offices available.[8] As well as a centre of government the town quickly became the part-time residence of the colony's elected representatives, the seat of the Court of King's Bench, and the home of the Law Society of Upper Canada.[9] By 1798 no other centre west of Quebec could match Toronto in its opportunities for advancement.

Simcoe also made certain that his subordinates would grow and pros-

[5]Rev. John Stuart to Rt. Rev. Dr. White, Bishop of the Episcopal Church in Philadelphia, July 17, 1792, *Simcoe Cor.*, vol. 1, p. 180.

[6]The first four Chief Justices, William Osgoode (1791-94), John Elmsley (1796-1802), Henry Allcock (1802-05) and Thomas Scott (1806-16), were imperial appointees. The same was true of the first three Attorneys General, John White (1791-1800), Thomas Scott (1800-06) and William Firth (1807-12).

[7]For recent studies of local elites, see M. S. Cross, "The Age of Gentility: The Formation of an Aristocracy in the Ottawa Valley" *Canadian Historical Association Report [CHAR]*, (1967), 105-17, and S. F. Wise, "Tory Factionalism: Kingston Elections and Upper Canadian Politics, 1820-1836" *Ontario History [OH]*, 57 (1965) 205-223.

[8]In July 1801 York officially became the capital of the Home District. F. H. Armstrong, *Handbook of Upper Canadian Chronology and Territorial Legislation* (London, Ont., 1967), p. 163; [hereafter Armstrong]. It had probably been the unofficial district seat since 1798. See Public Archives of Canada [PAC], Hannah Jarvis to Rev. Samuel Peters, July 10, 1798, *Jarvis-Peters Papers*.

[9]The first Assembly met in York in 1797 and continuously as of 1800. Armstrong, p. 26. The Court of King's Bench arrived with Chief Justice John Elmsley in 1798 and the Law Society began meeting there in 1799. W. R. Riddell, *The Bar and Courts of the Province of Upper Canada* (Toronto, 1928), p. 55; [hereafter Riddell, *Bar and Courts*].

per with his capital by apportioning to them the choice waterfront and town lots and, in 100-acre 'park lots', all the land immediately north and west of the original town site, above what was to become Queen Street.[10] This land above Toronto was not at first especially valuable, but it was, in most cases, held for speculation and gave the initial officials a stake in the town's future. It was also to be the basis of the future fortunes of the Macaulay, Elmsley, and Jarvis families, among others.[11]

Beyond the governor's patronage legal training was a key to the door of government office and social mobility. This avenue quickly came to be carefully guarded by Toronto's elite. While it could not bar the entrance of British lawyers into Upper Canada, the Law Society completely controlled local entry into the profession which in turn opened the door to a number of government offices. The Law Society moved to Toronto shortly after its initial creation in Niagara in 1797 and was dominated by Toronto lawyers who were usually associated closely with the town's elite. A non-Toronto Treasurer (the chief officer) was not chosen by the Society's Benchers, or directors, until well after Confederation; the Benchers, too, especially those who attended regularly, were usually members of Toronto society.[12]

While the possession of government office and land at or near Toronto marked one as a leading member of society and while legal training allowed one to advance, there were other prerequisites for aspirants to the town's highest social circle. An espousal of the proper social and political views was essential, as was an acceptable social background. A sound education was necessary to cope with administrative responsibilities. Finally, one required the ear of the Lieutenant-Governor, the ultimate source of provincial patronage. The imperial appointees who were accepted into Toronto society usually possessed the proper combination of attitudes and attributes. Members of the initial leading families worked to instill in their children and protégés the values necessary for acceptance and advancement and they were regularly successful during the period under study.

It should be noted again that government office was virtually the sole occupational basis for advancement in the embryonic social structure of early Toronto.[13] Only one merchant, William Allan, was accepted into the upper echelon of the town's society and he rose, not through commercial

---

[10]Almost all of the 35 park lots were granted to government officials and Queen's Rangers veterans. T. A. Reed, "Memoranda Re. the Crown Grants of Park Lots in the City of Toronto Based on the Records in the Registry Office", MS. compiled in 1926, Toronto Public Library [hereafter TPL].

[11]The Jarvis lot was subdivided and sold by William's eldest son in the 1840s. John Beverley Robinson purchased one half of an original lot in 1825 for £1000 and three years later sold six acres of it for the same amount. Similar profits were realized by others originally granted these lots.

[12]Twelve of the 22 Law Society Benchers chosen before the War of 1812 were residents of Toronto. Riddell, Bar and Courts, p. 73, n. 21. In assessing the role and influence of Toronto residents in provincial organizations situated in the capital one must consider the inadequacy of early Upper Canadian transportation systems. Given the difficulty of travelling, institutions located at York tended to be dominated by residents of the town.

[13]William Warren Baldwin arrived in York in 1802 with a medical degree from Edinburgh and began to practice; yet in order to support his family he found it necessary to turn first to teaching and then to a legal career. In themselves these professions were not capable of

opportunities, but because he combined a sound, even brilliant, business mind with properly conservative social and political beliefs and also because of his selfless devotion to the cause during the War of 1812.[14] As a garrison town, Toronto was the temporary home of many British officers who were generally accepted into the social life of the local elite. While as a group they added to the tone and impressiveness of Toronto's social activities, as individuals they were transients and had little effect upon the long term development of Toronto society. They were, however, looked upon as suitable marriage partners by Toronto society.[15]

Naturally, not all of those originally granted official positions and land in Toronto were members of the town's elite 25 years later. Some officials were promoted out of the colony and some died, while others, unable to cope with the primitive conditions, left for a more sophisticated life in Britain.[16] Still, few of those who remained lost the elite status which had been bestowed upon them at their arrival. Those who chose to stay came to form the core of a social entity which controlled Toronto's development for much of the 19th century. It is frequently stated that the Family Compact was destroyed in the 1840s but in fact some of its members only removed themselves from the public eye. In reality, they remained active at other levels of the province's and the city's life. Even in the 1860s members of the second generation of the initial leading families were still prominent in Toronto's social and economic affairs.[17]

During the first decade after Toronto's founding in 1793 some newcomers were accepted into its upper social stratum with little apparent hesitation.[18] Even Simcoe's original subordinates, though their land grants date from 1793, did not begin to settle permanently in Toronto until three years later. In addition, the last of the government officials did not arrive from the temporary capital of Niagara until 1798 and it was another year before the Assembly and the King's Bench met regularly in Toronto. Still, by 1803 most of the recently created provincial and local government offices were filled and advancement within Toronto society became a much slower and more jealously guarded process.[19]

Once the original officials had been placed, mobility declined to a

---

quickly advancing one—even a gentleman—in Toronto society. In 1806 Baldwin received official acceptance when he received his first government post as Clerk of the Crown and Pleas, an office of the King's Bench.

[14]See M. L. Magill, "William Allan and the War of 1812" *OH*, 64 (1972), 132–41.

[15]A daughter of the prominent ex-Queen's Ranger and Executive Councillor, Æneas Shaw, was engaged to Sir Isaac Brock while one of Surveyor General Thomas Ridout's offspring married a garrison officer.

[16]Upper Canada's first Surveyor General, David William Smith, retired to Britain in 1804 while the first Attorney General, John White, died in a duel in 1800. The first three Chief Justices of Upper Canada, William Osgoode, John Elmsley and Henry Allcock, were each promoted to the Chief Justiceship of Lower Canada.

[17]James Grant Chewett and William Botsford Jarvis, for example, remained influential in Toronto affairs until their deaths in the 1860s.

[18]Thomas Scott arrived in 1801 as Attorney General and remained to become Chief Justice and a highly respected member of Toronto society; he died in the town in 1824.

[19]Between 1791 and 1803 approximately 100 major appointments were made, ranging from Chief Justice through Executive and Legislative Councillors to first clerkships of the various administrative offices. In the following decade roughly 30 replacement appointments were made. In the seven-year period from 1812 to 1818 this number rose slightly, to 40. The data came from Armstrong, passim.

replacement pace. By 1803 most of those who would later compose the Toronto core of the Family Compact had settled in the town and were beginning to consolidate their positions. Whenever possible they brought their own children or protégés into their administrative departments, or, if lawyers, into the legal profession.

In the decade prior to the War of 1812 these original members of Toronto society continued to improve their own positions and to bring their offspring and assorted protégés within the magic social circle. They benefitted from the fact that through much of Toronto's first quarter century of growth the Crown was represented by an Administrator who was, at times, a member of the town's local hierarchy.[20] They also attempted to use their power and experience to influence Lieutenant-Governors but against a strong personality the established families could not advance. In such cases as those of John Small and William Warren Baldwin, their individual influence was on occasion restricted by a refusal to grant them new and more prestigious positions in the local hierarchy. On the other hand, so entrenched was the position of Simcoe's chosen officials that the Lieutenant-Governor could actually do little to lessen their social status.

Outsiders, in the form of imperial appointees, continued to be accepted into Toronto society as long as they integrated into the increasingly rigid social structure developing in the town. Those who refused or were unwilling to accept the role assigned to them quickly found York to have a very cold atmosphere. Of the 30 major appointments made between 1803 and 1812, 9 went to imperial appointees and 18 to members of families established in Toronto in the first decade after its foundings.[21] Of the five positions filled which required legal training, four went to British trained lawyers.[22] As Toronto's initial leading families produced their own competent lawyers they strengthened their monopoly of the local avenues of vertical mobility.[23]

The War of 1812 caused a tremendous change in the nature of social mobility within Toronto. Military careers, especially within the local militia, increased in importance and led, in the postwar period, to advancement in the civil administration. Nevertheless, upward mobility was intensive rather than extensive. Many rose within the hierarchy of Toronto society, but almost invariably the successful individuals were the sons or protégés of previously established families.

An analysis of important appointments made during this seven-year period does not indicate a large increase in opportunities for advancement; 40 such appointments were made as compared with 30 for the previous decade.[24] However, a glance at the recipients of these positions

---

[20]Samuel Smith, for example, was an ex-Queen's Ranger, an original landholder, an Executive Councillor and twice Administrator of the province.

[21]Armstrong, passim.

[22]The positions were those of Chief Justice, Puisne Justice and Attorney General. Armstrong, pp. 109 and 17.

[23]Between 1791 and 1803, 27 individuals were called to the bar of the Law Society of Upper Canada but 21 did so by two special acts of Parliament. 34 Geo. III cap. 4 and 43 Geo. III cap. 3. Proper legal training was not available until the first decade of the 19th century.

[24]Armstrong, passim.

indicates the nature of the change occurring in mobility patterns in Toronto during and shortly after the war. Only 2 of the 40 positions went to imperial appointees while 28 went to members, often second generation members, of the families originally established as Toronto's elite. No doubt the uncertainty caused by war led to a decline in the number of outsiders interested in acquiring a patronage post in Upper Canada; even the Lieutenant-Governor himself spent the war in comfort in London on an extended leave of absence. Though Toronto's leading families were aided by the decline of imperial appointees, it was the continuation of their earlier efforts to influence recruitment into government service and their activities during the war itself which secured their postwar dominance.

The postwar period was one of consolidation of power for Toronto's elite, as members of the second generation, still largely unhindered by imperial competition, began to take up the civil functions for which they had been raised and trained and for which they had fought during the war. By 1818 the small group of the initial families controlled the major judicial and administrative posts in the colony, often competing with each other for preferment. Still, the stage was set for one individual with the proper values, ambition, and leadership ability to grasp the scattered reins of power and turn Toronto society into a province-wide power. That individual was John Strachan. When he gained the ear of the Lieutenant-Governor Toronto society quickly underwent internal personnel changes, as the future bishop forwarded his plans for the colony by advancing his favoured students and protégés.

The above provides a general evolutionary framework which can be tested by examining the rise of individual families possessing the basic criteria for membership in Toronto society. The six families chosen as case studies in this paper were headed by William Jarvis, Thomas Ridout, William Dummer Powell, D'Arcy Boulton, Sr., William Chewett, and William Warren Baldwin. They are representative of elite recruitment experience and as such they seem to support the theory that a picked and chosen group was preferred for advancement.

William Jarvis was in Simcoe's Queen's Rangers, and all but Boulton and Baldwin were provincial officials during Simcoe's tenure as Lieutenant-Governor. Two of them, Thomas Ridout and William Chewett, were high officers in the Surveyor General's office,[25] while William Jarvis was Provincial Secretary and Registrar and William Dummer Powell a Puisne, or Associate, Justice of the Court of King's Bench. Four were settled in the capital by mid-1798. William Warren Baldwin arrived in 1802 and D'Arcy Boulton and his family settled in the capital the following year. These last two became lawyers and judges, the first at the district, the second at the provincial level. All of those present before Simcoe's departure were granted prestigious front town lots in York and a share of the land north of the town. The Boultons and Baldwin acquired such land later. While several lived in ostentatious comfort on their country estates, each used his official income and the attached fees to enjoy a style of life in keeping with his exalted position in

---

[25]Surveyor General and Deputy Surveyor General respectively.

Toronto society. Thus each of the family heads possessed the prerequisites for inclusion in Toronto's original elite.

In the following decade of relatively limited social mobility each attempted to use his official position and his influence with the Lieutenant-Governor to further his own career and those of his children. In varying degrees, every one of these dynastic founders was able to assure positions of prestige and influence to his offspring and protégés.

The efforts made before the war by Surveyor General Thomas Ridout to secure his own advancement and that of his children form perhaps the best example of the nature of mobility within the elite of early Toronto. Ridout had one son, Samuel Smith Ridout, by a first marriage who was a decade older than his half-brothers. Samuel came to Toronto in 1800 and was duly installed as a junior clerk in his father's department. His own unbridled ambition and a later clash with the Lieutenant-Governor, Francis Gore, whose undying enmity he had earned, led to his dismissal.[26] Thomas Ridout came to his son's rescue and brought him back into the Surveyor General's office when he himself was promoted to the headship of the department in 1810.

Thomas Ridout, however, was aware that in fact Samuel's career in York was at a standstill, as long as Gore remained Lieutenant-Governor. Accepting the inevitable, he began to work for the advancement of his younger sons, who were coming of age in the last years before the war. He first prepared them for their future responsibilities in Toronto society by giving them the best education available in Upper Canada. Along with the scions of York's other elite families they attended school at Cornwall under John Strachan. As part of his determined effort to advance his sons, Ridout advised one: "place yourself, if you can, under the Eye of Government and you will not be forgotten. . . ."[27] To this he added: "a situation in a public office will make you known,—and give you the independence of a gentleman. It will give you their society too—"[28] Despite his eldest son's faux pas, Thomas elicited from Gore the promise that he would do what he could for the younger sons as they became of age.[29] Soon his sons were employed as clerks in a number of government offices, one of which was, of course, Ridout's own Surveyor General's department.[30] If he failed in part to forward their careers, it was not for lack of trying; but he was in some degree and temporarily deterred by the

---

[26]Samuel Ridout had become enmeshed in the well-known feud between Gore and Surveyor General Charles Burton Wyatt. Ridout had failed to inform the Lieutenant-Governor that Wyatt was transmitting confidential material to the Home Government. William Halton, Civil Secretary to Gore, to S. S. Ridout, May 28, 1807, Public Archives of Ontario [PAO], *Ridout Papers*. Though Wyatt later successfully sued Gore, the damage had been done to Ridout's career.

[27]*Ridout Papers*, Thomas Ridout to Thomas Gibbs Ridout, July 16, 1811.

[28]Ibid.

[29]*Ridout Papers*, Thomas Ridout to George Ridout, February 18, 1807.

[30]His second son, George, articled under Solicitor General Boulton and worked as a clerk for the Assembly and in the Surveyor General's office as did his third son, Thomas Gibbs Ridout, who was also Deputy Registrar of Deeds for York County. A fourth son, John, was but 13 when war broke out and he remained in Strachan's capable hands.

limited possibilities for advancement. Still, he did bring three of his four oldest sons into the provincial administration in minor capacities.

The other families, too, can be cited to outline both the limited degree of mobility in early Toronto and the efforts made by the initial families to retain control of advancement and recruitment. Justice Powell was the only member of Toronto's elite present in western Quebec prior to Simcoe's arrival. He was accepted by the Lieutenant-Governor because of his knowledge and experience, but he found his plans for personal advancement thwarted by the presence of imperial appointees. He did not become Chief Justice until 1816 after four incumbents had held the post. Yet Powell was equally determined to pass his position in local society on to his children. His second son, William Dummer Powell, Jr., largely because of his father's influence, was one of 16 individuals permitted to practice law in Upper Canada under the authority of a 1794 statute.[31] When another six men were granted similar privileges in 1803, Powell's eldest son, John, was one of them. Two daughters married members of the prominent Shaw and Jarvis families. As was the case with Thomas Ridout, Powell's lack of complete success in forwarding his family's interests was the result of circumstances rather than indifference. Justice Powell did all in his power to ensure the family's future position yet the Powell family was plagued by personal tragedy and few of their plans developed as they wished.[32]

In a similar fashion, but with much more success, D'Arcy Boulton unlocked the doors to advancement in York for his sons. He, too, was one of the "Heaven sent"[33] lawyers of 1803 and, two years later, became Solicitor General. Since the means of obtaining legal training and entrance into the profession after 1797 was to article under a lawyer, after being entered on the books of the Law Society, Boulton made use of his gratuitous advancement into the profession to sponsor three of his four sons.[34]

William Warren Baldwin officially entered Toronto commerce in 1803 in the same manner as D'Arcy Boulton; he, too, was a "Heaven sent" lawyer and although he could hardly begin advancing his own family— his eldest son, Robert, was born in 1804—he did bring a number of pro-

---

[31]34 Geo. III, cap. 4. Many of the petitions and requests sent to the Lieutenant-Governor were forwarded to Attorney General John White for his opinion and since legal training was not a prerequisite, one can only conclude that White was basing these opinions on more personal factors. Some of the requests and White's views are contained in the Wolford Manor (Simcoe) Papers and are used by Riddell in his *Bar and Courts*, pp. 43-4, n. 7. In conclusion Riddell states: "It is not unlikely that most of these appointments were due to White's knowledge of and friendship with the recipients of the Licences. In his Diary, I find him on friendly terms with the following of them: Smith, Macdonnell, Clark, McLean, Gray, Powell, Stewart, Robinson and McKay." *Bar and Courts*, p. 45, n. 12.

[32]Two of Powell's eight children perished in shipwrecks; a third died suddenly, leaving two infant children to be raised by the elder Powells.

[33]The term was used in Toronto to underline the easy manner by which the six new lawyers were granted the right to practice. Riddell, *Bar and Courts*, p. 57.

[34]These were D'Arcy, Jr., Henry John and George Strange Boulton. He also proposed for acceptance such rising stars as John Beverley Robinson, James Buchanan Macaulay, Allan Napier MacNab and George Ridout. *Minutes of Convocation*, Law Society of Upper Canada, Osgoode Hall.

tégés into the profession.[35] Though he never was granted the major offices which Boulton attained, Baldwin did enjoy the prestige and emoluments of a number of local offices. It is possible that his entrance into Toronto society as a protégé of the declining ex-Administrator Peter Russell[36] hampered his quest for upward social mobility and certainly his lack of rapport with Lieutenant-Governor Gore hurt his chances for advancement.[37] Indeed, it seems likely that Baldwin's early connections with his Irish countrymen and relatives, the Russell and Willcocks families,[38] and his inability to influence favourably Francis Gore, were the first factors leading to his later alienation from and opposition to the Family Compact. Though he was never able to find a place at the core of the town's patronage system, he was a gentleman and every part the social equal of any member of Toronto's elite. Once again the Lieutenant-Governor by the refusal of patronage had arrested the advancement of a member of Toronto society but here too the influence of the Crown's representative was not sufficient to remove Baldwin from the established elite..

William Chewett and William Jarvis were also moderately successful in advancing their families in Toronto society in the decade before the war. Though Chewett as Deputy Surveyor General was not able to rise to the head of the office, the position occupied by Thomas Ridout after 1810, he did successfully defend his own position against Ridout's eldest son.[39] He was able to send his own son, James Grant Chewett, to school under Strachan at Cornwall and to bring him into the Surveyor General's office in a junior capacity shortly before the outbreak of war. In a similar fashion Provincial Secretary William Jarvis protected his own interests and advanced those of his children. Though he complained of being held back after Simcoe's departure,[40] he gained the favour of Lieutenant-Governors Hunter and Gore[41] and remained a respected member of Toronto society until his death in 1817. Both of his sons were educated by Strachan and the eldest, Samuel Peters Jarvis, was articled to Attorney General Firth before the war.

Almost invariably the notable, at times even spectacular, examples of

---

[35]They were his nephews, Henry Ricketts Baldwin and Robert Baldwin Sullivan, and Simon Washburn and James Edward Small, son of the Clerk of the Executive Council. Ibid.

[36]Russell had gained the enmity of his peers when, as Administrator, he transmitted Simcoe's orders that the capital be moved from the relatively comfortable Niagara to the wilderness of Toronto Bay.

[37]In 1812 Baldwin was manoeuvering for the position of Solicitor General and his bitterness at being bypassed for the position of Attorney General in favour of the younger John Macdonell precipitated a duel between the two. PAO, *Baldwin Papers*, Baldwin to William Firth, April 22, 1812. Earlier he admitted to a close friend that his relationship with Gore was at best cool and strained. TPL, *Baldwin Papers*, Baldwin to Quetton St. George, December 28, 1809.

[38]He married a Willcocks, a family of minor officials, and protégés and relatives of Russell. When Receiver General Russell's influence began to decline, so too did the Willcocks name disappear from Toronto society.

[39]*Ridout Papers*, Thomas Ridout to Thomas Gibbs Ridout, September 11, 1811, and Memorial of S. S. Ridout to Sir Gordon Drummond, December 9, 1814.

[40]*Jarvis-Peters Papers*, Hannah Jarvis to Rev. Samuel Peters, July 26, 1796, and July 20, 1797.

[41]Ibid., William Jarvis to Rev. Samuel Peters, March 11, 1800.

failure to attain the inner ranks of Toronto society in the period under discussion were outsiders, imperial appointees. The names which come to mind are of course those of Charles Burton Wyatt, William Firth and Robert Thorpe.[42] In each case these individuals were dissatisfied with their allotted roles in Toronto society and were balked when they attempted to inject an element of change. For Thorpe at least, the sojourn in Upper Canada was but an episode in a troubled and none too successful career. For those imperial appointees, such as William Campbell and Thomas Scott, who accepted the conservative ethos of Toronto society and their own role in it, a happy and fulfilling life was possible. For those to whom such restrictions were intolerable, so, too, was life in York. Failure to be accepted or to advance in Toronto society prior to the war was usually the result of a lack of the proper connections or the favour of the Lieutenant-Governor, or a refusal to accept the positions or the value systems of those previously entrenched in power.

Despite the ease with which Lieutenant-Governors were able to impede or forward the careers of individual members of Toronto society, the latter, too, were developing an increasing ability to influence the provincial apex of power and patronage. Simcoe was clearly in control of his officials, but he was succeeded for a three-year period by Peter Russell who was the first of a number of Administrators in the years 1793 to 1818. During his tenure he was faced with growing opposition and discontent among the government officials. These were also of course members of Toronto's elite.[43] When Hunter died suddenly in Quebec City in 1805 he was replaced by Commodore Alexander Grant, an old subordinate of Simcoe and again, a part-time member of Toronto's upper class. Grant in turn was replaced by Francis Gore, an indifferent but headstrong Governor who, as has been noted, tended to intervene in Toronto affairs for personal reasons and who accelerated the already existing tendency to base promotions in government and local society upon personal connections and private interests.

Gore's absence from 1811 to 1815 created a virtual vacuum at the apex of Toronto society as one military Administrator followed another.[44] Toronto's prominent citizens were not slow to take advantage of the situation. When Gore at last retired in 1817 he was replaced for one year by Samuel Smith, who had also been one of Simcoe's original officials and who was a well-entrenched member of Toronto society. Once again provincial and local affairs reverted to the control of the developing Toronto clique. Finally, Lieutenant-Governor Maitland had not been at York many months before he accepted Strachan as his chief advisor. This is not to imply that the original leading families controlled provincial policies during this period. A strong Lieutenant-Governor such as Gore or the later John Colborne could easily sweep aside such pretensions.

---

[42]See G. M. Craig, *Upper Canada: The Formative Years, 1784-1841* (Toronto, 1963), pp. 60-4.

[43]Hunter relied especially upon John Elmsley until his promotion to Lower Canada. See Elmsley to Hunter, November 24, 1800, December 23, 1800, and December 24, 1800. TPL, Elmsley Letterbook.

[44]There were six military Administrators in all.

Nevertheless, for nine years out of the quarter century under study there was no Lieutenant-Governor present to temper the influence of Toronto's elite. While they did not always agree with their fellow members of Toronto society on who should receive government appointments, they tended to choose from local talent.[45]

The trend of limited and gradual social mobility established in the decade after 1803 was rudely shattered by the American declaration of war in June 1812. The moderate influx of imperial appointees halted abruptly with the coming of hostilities and Toronto's original leading families quickly moved to fill provincial offices as they became vacant. The most startling example of internal advancement during this period was that of John Beverley Robinson who was a protégé of Justice Powell and the Reverend John Strachan.[46] Robinson, largely at Powell's urging, was made acting Attorney General in 1812 when the incumbent fell beside Brock at Queenston Heights; Robinson, who had fought at Detroit and Queenston Heights, was but 20 years old at the time of his promotion and had not yet been called to the bar.[47]

The Ridouts also used the opportunities provided by the war to advance themselves. Samuel Smith Ridout was paroled after Toronto's capture and went on to become Sheriff of the Home District and later Registrar of York County. Thomas Gibbs Ridout returned from Britain to enter the Commissary Department at a more than generous £500 *per annum*.[48] Once in a position of authority he sent for a younger brother to act as his private secretary and manoeuvered to bring in yet a second sibling.[49] Shortly after retiring on half pay as Deputy Assistant Commissary General, T. G. Ridout entered the new elite initiated Bank of Upper Canada as Cashier or General Manager. The elder Ridout was so pleased with his sons' successes that he would have been happy to see the war prolonged if it had meant continued advancement for his family.[50]

Both of the sons of Provincial Secretary Jarvis, Samuel Peters Jarvis and William Munson Jarvis, served in the war, the latter fighting at the battles of Queenston Heights and Stoney Creek. The former became Clerk of the Crown in Chancery, the office of the Assembly, in 1817, and

---

[45]In filling the vacancy occasioned by the death of Provincial Secretary William Jarvis in 1817, Administrator Samuel Smith recommended ex-Sheriff Alexander Macdonell, his own brother-in-law. Jarvis's eldest son, Samuel Peters Jarvis, was passed over for the permanent position because, only one month earlier, he had killed John Ridout in a duel. His younger brother, William Munson Jarvis, was appointed Acting Secretary. PAD, *Strachan Papers,* Powell, August 18, 1817, quoted in *Strachan Letter Book,* p. 134.

[46]Both men claimed this honour. W. D. Powell to J. B. Robinson, undated (about 1824), TPL, *W. D. Powell Papers,* Strachan to Jonathan Sewell, Chief Justice of Lower Canada, p. 26, August 1815; Geo. W. Spragge, ed., *The John Strachan Letter Book: 1812–1834* (Toronto, 1946), p. 88 [hereafter *Strachan Letter Book*]; and Strachan to Hon. John Richardson, May 10, 1813, ibid., p. 37.

[47]Robinson was also appointed Solicitor General in 1815 while Sir Frederick P. Robinson, a relative, was Administrator; Robinson was brilliant but he had the help of powerful patrons as well.

[48]*Ridout Papers,* Thomas Gibbs Ridout to Thomas Ridout, January 6, 1814.

[49]Ibid., T. G. Ridout to George Ridout, January 19, 1814.

[50]Ibid., T. Ridout to T. G. Ridout, January 21, 1814.

later Deputy Provincial Secretary and Chief Superintendent of Indian Affairs.[51] The latter left Toronto to become Sheriff of Gore District.[52] Once again conspicuous services enabled second generation members of the initial leading families to move into prestigious and influential government positions and to accept the roles in Toronto society for which their parents had trained and prepared them.

James Grant Chewett, the son of William Chewett, was also paroled after the capture of York and re-entered his father's office. He replaced his father as Deputy Surveyor General upon the latter's death in 1831 and retired when the capital was moved a decade later, becoming Vice-President of the Bank of Upper Canada. In 1856 he became the first President of the new Bank of Toronto.[53]

The war also pushed forward a new figure at York. John Strachan, previously a teacher of Toronto's leading families in Kingston and in Cornwall, won acceptance through his wartime activities just as did the merchant William Allan.[54] When York was captured in 1813 and militia Colonel William Allan arrested, Strachan bravely stood up to the American commander and made certain that the terms of the capitulation were honoured.[55] This wartime leadership coupled with his influence upon the rising second generation of York's initial families[56] and upon the Lieutenant-Governor were to enable him to grasp virtual control of the development of Toronto and even Upper Canada for a full decade.

The postwar period was one of consolidation of power for Toronto's leading families. Strachan's rise to power, finalized shortly after Sir Peregrine Maitland's arrival in 1818, brought about internal status changes within Toronto society, for he rose at the expense of Justice Powell whose power and influence he gradually eclipsed. Strachan's past students, the Boultons, Robinson, the Jarvises, and some of the Ridouts enjoyed the patronage of the Lieutenant-Governor while other Ridouts and the Baldwins and Smalls languished beyond the pale.[57] The criteria for membership in Toronto society did not alter with Strachan's rise to power, but his protégés did tend to advance more quickly. In this way Strachan's appearance marks a turning point in the development of the town's elite.

The final indication that Toronto society had matured into a positon of self-perpetuating power was the blatant and successful rearrangement of provincial offices which occurred at the end of Maitland's fourth

---

[51]Armstrong, pp. 104, 22, 20.

[52]Ibid., p. 162.

[53]*Brown's Toronto General Director, 1856* (Toronto, 1856), p. 227.

[54]Magill, "William Allan" and the War of 1812, *OH*, 64 (1972), 132-41. See Charles W. Humphries, "The Capture of York," *OH*, 51, (1959), 1-21 for a discussion of Strachan's role and its effect upon his future position of leadership in Toronto society.

[55]PAO, *Strachan Papers*, Strachan to Dr. James Brown, April 26, 1813, quoted in Firth, *Town of York*, vol. 1, pp. 294-6.

[56]Strachan by this date had taught members of the Robinson, Ridout, Chewett, Jarvis and Macaulay families.

[57]Strachan also brought some non-Toronto individuals in, such as George Herkimer Markland of Kingston.

month in office. Shortly before leaving Upper Canada Gore had suggested several shifts in offices to follow the promotion of Powell from Puisne to Chief Justice. Gore wanted Boulton, Sr., then Attorney General, to succeed Powell as Puisne Justice and Solicitor General Robinson to become Attorney General. Boulton tried unsuccessfully to have his son, Henry John Boulton, appointed Solicitor General but the Colonial Office refused and there the matter rested until Maitland arrived.[58] Strachan then persuaded the new Lieutenant-Governor to press again for the young Boulton's appointment and Maitland was successful. Members of Toronto's old families now controlled the major judicial and legal posts of the colony. A decade later, at the height of the Compact's power, a similar 'job' would be perpetrated at the district and provincial levels involving four members of the Ridout and Jarvis families and three responsible government positions.[59] These are but two examples of a situation which was developing by 1818 in which son followed father in government office as though by hereditary right. Simcoe's actions of a quarter century before had borne fruit.

By 1818, the eve of Strachan's accession to power, Toronto society was an amorphous entity whose individual members largely controlled access into their own ranks by selected recruitment, usually from the younger members of their own families. Despite the occasional interjection of imperial appointees, they had succeeded, partly through the disruptive effects of the war, not only in maintaining their positions against outside threats but had also, in most cases, passed their offices and their social positions down to their children. By their very success they had proved to themselves their worthiness to occupy the highest stratum of Toronto society. Confident of the wisdom and utility of their political and social views—views which had been forged in the Revolutionary War and tempered in the second conflict with republicanism—they awaited only a leader to spread the word throughout Upper Canada. Truly by 1818 they were, in their own eyes at least, God's chosen people.

---

[58]*Strachan Letter Book*, Strachan to Gore, June 16, 1817, pp. 136, 250, n. 316.

[59]TPL, *Powell Papers*, Samuel Peter Jarvis to his father-in-law W. D. Powell, December 19, 1827.

18

LORD SELKIRK AND THE CANADIAN COURTS*

Gene M. Gressley

The early history of the Canadian West is largely a story of exploration and fur trading, involving great feats of courage and daring by a host of colourful figures. The early rivalry for control of the fur trade between the French and the English was continued in somewhat altered form between 1780 and 1820 by the North West Company (representing to a large extent Canadian-based trading interests, particularly in Montreal) and the Hudson's Bay Company (ultimate control of which was in the hands of British investors). It appeared for a time at the beginning of the 19th century that the North West Company would emerge from the competition as victor, but a new element was added to the conflict in 1811 when Lord Selkirk (a major stockholder in the Hudson's Bay Company) began to establish a colony on the Red River in what is now Manitoba. The North West Company sensed in this action a threat to its position, and opposed the settlement with all the resources at its command. In 1816 the struggle flared into open violence with the so-called "Seven Oaks Massacre," in which 21 colonists were killed. As Gene M. Gressley points out in the following article, the "massacre" shifted the focus of the conflict from the relatively unregulated wilderness into the nerve-centres of government, both in the Canadas and ultimately in Great Britain. Although the final resolution of the fur rivalry—the merger of the Hudson's Bay and North West Companies in 1821—is well-known, the manoeuvering which preceded the settlement is a less familiar but thoroughly fascinating story, particularly in terms of the judicial proceedings in the Canadian courts in 1818. What were the legal issues in 1818? Do they

*North Dakota History, 24 (1957), 89-105.

reflect the realities of the situation in the West? Was the "justice" of the courts impartially promulgated? What does this legal aspect indicate about both the West and the nature of Upper and Lower Canada in 1818?

SUGGESTIONS FOR FURTHER READING

J. M. Gray, *Lord Selkirk of Red River* (East Lansing: Michigan State University Press, 1963).

W. L. Morton, *Manitoba: A History* (Toronto: University of Toronto Press, 1957).

E. E. Rich, *The Fur Trade and the Northwest to 1857* (Toronto: McClelland and Stewart, 1967).

J.M.B.

O n June 12, 1811, the Hudson's Bay Company deeded Thomas Douglas, fifth Earl of Selkirk, 116,000 square miles in what are now parts of Manitoba, North Dakota and Minnesota.[1] Previous to receiving this grant, Selkirk had made extensive preparations for his colonizing venture. Consequently, within a month after his Lordship received the deed, the first ships set sail for York Factory.

The colonists stayed at York Factory during the winter and journeyed to the fork of the Red River and the Assiniboine in the spring of 1812. Immediately a mass of problems confronted them: food was scarce, housing non-existent and the scarcity of agricultural equipment plagued them.[2] In addition to these misfortunes, they were harassed by the half-breeds and North West Company traders. The North West Company based its hostility on three points: one, it resented any move on the part of its competitor to gain control of the lucrative fur trade; two, North West Company (as well as some Hudson's Bay Company) fur traders were united in their enmity toward an agricultural settlement, especially one in the hands of their opponent; three, (perhaps its greatest objection) the

---

[1]Thomas Douglas (1771–1820), fifth Earl of Selkirk, began life at St. Mary's Isle, Scotland. Upon the death of his father and six brothers, Thomas Douglas succeeded to the earldom in 1799. His interest in colonization was not new; in 1803 he secured from the British government grants on Prince Edward Island and Baldoon Farms near Lake St. Clair. On November 24, 1807, Selkirk married Jean Wedderburn-Colvile, she being the sister of Andrew Colvile, one of the principal stockholders in the Hudson's Bay Company. Shortly after his marriage, the Earl began buying stock in the Hudson's Bay Company. He made his stock purchases with the idea of establishing another settlement in the Canadas. When the dispute arose with the North West Company over the Red River Settlement, Lord Selkirk, with his characteristic vigour, took a leading part in the struggle. He died at Pau, France.

[2]Selkirk's emigration agents did not exercise enough selectivity in choosing prospective emigrants. The colonists' lack of agricultural "know-how," coupled with an ignorance of the hardships to expect in the Canadian West, operated to the detriment of the colony. Agents such as Captain de May (who recruited Swiss colonists for the colony in 1820) painted a glowing picture of a Canadian Eden. In the case of the Swiss colonists, many were mechanics and totally unsuited for agricultural pursuits. Mrs. Adams herself, being a Swiss immigrant, describes the Swiss colonists' hardships in the *Minnesota Historical Collections*. Cf. J. F. Williams, ed., "Mrs. Adams' Reminiscences of Red River and Fort Snelling, 1820–1826," *Minnesota Historical Collections*, vol. 6 (St. Paul, 1894), 75–115.

grant threatened to cut off its routes from Fort William to the rich fur-bearing Athabasca country. Coinciding with this was the War of 1812 and the Yankee threat to snip the North West Company's Great Lakes supply route.[3]

Miles Macdonell, Governor of the colony, believed that the Selkirk forces should assert their authority over the Red River region.[4] The Governor struck upon the idea of restricting the pemmican supply.[5] If this restriction were rigidly enforced, not only would the Selkirk authority over the Red River be asserted, but the operations of the North West Company would be crippled. On January 8, 1814, Macdonell read the "Pemmican Proclamation" which in effect put an embargo on all pemmican leaving the Selkirk grant. The "Pemmican War" had begun.[6]

The North West Company's strategy was constructed on the premise that the colonists could be induced to desert the settlement. Money, transportation to Upper Canada, and rumors of dire consequences if the settlers persisted in staying at Red River were offered as enticements to leave.[7] How well the North-westers succeeded is pregnantly demonstrated by the fact that by April 1815 a group of the colonists carried the cannons from Fort Douglas across to the North West Company post of Fort Gibraltar. Three months later the fruition of the North West Company's machinations occurred with the abandonment of the Red River colony. Some of the settlers were transported to Upper Canada, while others chose to huddle together on the Jack River. The "Pemmican War" had ended with the North West Company holding the Red River secure.

---

[3]The North West Company's objections to the Red River Settlement are stated in several contemporary publications. Especially useful are: Alexander Macdonell, *Narrative of Transactions of the Royal Society of Canada*, 6, sec. 2 [Ottawa, 1900], p. 94.) Additional biographical information is given in Henry Edmund Oliver, ed., *The Canadian North-West: River Settlements: 1815-1819*, Great Britain, Parliamentary Papers, House of Commons, no. 584, [hereafter, *Papers Relating to the Red River Settlement*].

[4]Miles Macdonell (1769-1828) was born in New York State. His family was Loyalist in sympathy. On June 6, 1796, Lord Dorchester appointed Macdonell a captain in the Royal Canadian Volunteers. After his term as Governor of the Red River Settlement, he participated in the legal trials. Nicholas Garry, member of the Hudson's Bay Committee in London, on his long trip to the Canadas in 1821, mentioned in his diary of landing at Long Sault, "where Mr. Miles Macdonald is living, now in a deranged state of mind," (Nicholas Garry, "Diary," *Transactions of the Royal Society of Canada*, 6, sec. 2 (Ottawa, 1900), p. 94.) Additional biographical information is given in Henry Edmund Oliver, ed., *The Canadian North-West: Its Early Development and Legislative Record*, vol. 1 (Ottawa, 1914), p. 40, [hereafter, Oliver, *Canadian North-West*].

[5]Governor Macdonell's proclamation posed a real threat to the North West Company in its fight for the fur-bearing regions. Pemmican was necessary to them if they hoped to supply their northern brigades. Not only was the settlement a hindrance to the North West Company's supply routes, but in addition was now stopping their main source of food.

[6]Miles Macdonell wrote Selkirk of his decision to restrict the pemmican supply. However, before there was time for an answer from Selkirk, Macdonell acted. It is reasonably sure that if Macdonell had anticipated an objection on the Earl's part, he would not have continued to pursue this course. A general account of the "Pemmican War" is available in Chester B. Martin, *Lord Selkirk's Work in Canada*, Oxford Historical and Literary Studies, vol. 7 (Oxford, 1916), pp. 64-89, [hereafter, Martin, *Lord Selkirk's Work*].

[7]Selkirk, Thomas Douglas, 5th Earl of, *A Letter to the Earl of Liverpool from the Earl of Selkirk, Accompanied by Correspondence with the Colonial Department in the Years 1817-18-19 on the Subject of the Red River Settlement in North America* (London, 1819), p. 64, [hereafter, Selkirk, *A Letter to the Earl of Liverpool*]. In the language of Simon McGillivray, the colony had "all been knocked on the head."

While the "Pemmican War" was being fought, the Hudson's Bay Company was making another attempt at capturing the Athabasca fur trade. Colin Robertson, ex-North-wester, was chosen as leader of the expedition.[8] Robertson left Montreal in the spring of 1815 and arrived at the Red River only to discover the charred ruins of the settlement. He found the settlers still at the Jack River, and led them back to re-establish the colony. The colonists were full of enthusiasm during the winter of 1815–16: for once food was plentiful. Robertson furnished imaginative leadership and all went well for a time.

The new Governor, Robert Semple, accompanied by the fifth body of settlers, arrived to re-enforce the colony.[9] A quarrel quickly developed between Semple and Robertson, resulting in the departure of the latter on June 11, 1816.[10] Eight days later the worst catastrophe of all befell the settlement. The events surrounding the Seven Oaks massacre are condemned to polemics. Voluminous propaganda—issued by both parties—in many cases served to obscure the issues rather than to clarify them.[11] Was Semple negligent? Did the Canadian officialdom know of a planned attack? Did the North-westers intend to massacre the colonists? Whether the North West Company planned to massacre or not is not ascertainable, but an unavoidable conclusion is that they did plan the destruction of the colony.[12] The massacre of 21 colonists on June 19, 1816, by half-breeds and North-westers climaxed the five-year attack on the colony. The Seven Oaks massacre was a pivotal event in the struggle; many successive incidents largely revolved around it.

While the flashing blades of the Métis were butchering his colonists,

---

[8]Colin Robertson (1779–1842) was employed as a clerk with the North West Company from 1804 to 1809; the last year he was dismissed by John McDonald of Garth. Robertson joined with Selkirk and the Hudson's Bay Company in 1812. That year found him in charge of the Athabasca Department. After the 1821 union, he was made Chief Factor serving at Norway House, Fort Churchill, Island Lake and the Swan River. Robertson retired in 1842. William Stewart Wallace, ed., Documents Relating to the North West Company, Champlain Society Publications, vol. 23 (Toronto, 1934), p. 494, [hereafter, Wallace, Documents].

[9]Robert Semple (1777–1816) was a native of Boston, Massachusetts. His parents were Loyalists during the American Revolution. After the war, Semple went to England, where he was employed by a commercial firm. His duties with this firm caused him to travel widely. Spain, Italy, Asia Minor, Venezuela, Germany and Brazil were among his habitats during those years. He exhibited some literary ability, with six or seven tomes to his credit. The motives behind Semple's actions at Seven Oaks are not clear. Semple was erratic, but well-intentioned; the uncivilized ways of the fur traders bewildered him. E. E. Rich, ed., Colin Robertson's Correspondence Book, September, 1817 to September, 1822, Champlain Society Publications, Hudson's Bay Company Series, vol. 2 (Toronto, 1939), pp. 241–42, [hereafter, Rich, Colin Robertson's Correspondence Book.].

[10]Rich, Colin Robertson's Correspondence Book, p. lxix.

[11]There are a variety of sources on the Seven Oaks massacre available to the historian: John Halkett, Statement Respecting the Earl of Selkirk's Settlement Upon the Red River in North America; Its Destruction in 1815 and 1816 . . . (London, 1817) embodies the Selkirk case, and A Narrative of Occurrences in the Indian Countries of North America, Since the Connexion of the Right Hon. the Earl of Selkirk . . . (Montreal, 1818) provides the North West Company point of view.

[12]The massacre dramatized in England what previously was regarded as mere local squabbling in the Canadas. Rhetoric poured from both sides in attack and defense of the actions at Seven Oaks. Before the dispute ended in 1821, the whole fur trading industry came under searching examination by the Colonial Office. The legal trials, which broke Lord Selkirk's health and bankrupted the North West Company, were in a large part based on this

Selkirk (who had arrived in the Canadas in the fall of 1815) was hiring mercenaries to be stationed at Red River. He secured the services of a De Meuron detachment.[13] The De Meurons and Selkirk left Montreal for the Red River in June 1816. At Sault St. Marie, the Earl received intelligence of the Seven Oaks massacre. Selkirk now altered his route, turning toward Fort William.[14] Once at Fort William, the Earl committed one *faux pas* after another. Acting as Justice of the Peace, he arrested the North West Company partners and sent them to Montreal. Then Selkirk purchased supplies from a senile and inebriated North West partner, Daniel McKenzie, who had no legal right to sell them.[15] Furthermore, Selkirk sent reprisal expeditions out to the surrounding area to seize North West Company posts, impounding their furs. The seizure of Fort William jeopardized the legal and moral position of the entire Selkirk cause. The Seven Oaks massacre was detrimental to the North West Company case and had put them on the defensive. The Earl lost any benefits he might have hoped to accrue from the capture.

On May 1, 1817, the Earl left Fort William for the Red River. Previously, he learned that the military contingent he had sent out under Miles Macdonell had found the survivors of the Seven Oaks massacre. Reaching the Red River, Lord Selkirk applied himself energetically to the managerial tasks connected with the colony.[16]

News of the Seven Oaks massacre and the capture of Fort William tardily jolted the Canadian governmental machinery into grinding action. Governor Sherbrooke resolved to appoint commissioners, whose duty it would be to investigate the actual scenes of the conflict, find witnesses and take their depositions, and make a report to the Montreal

---

massacre or on the consequences of it. Seven Oaks stimulated the Hudson's Bay Company to fight back with amazing vigor, employing many of the same techniques the North-westers had so successfully used.

[13]These regiments were composed mainly of Swiss, Italian and German nationalities. Selkirk offered them a liberal proposition. Each man would be given eight dollars a month from the time he left the Canadas until he arrived at Assiniboia. There he would be given "open land fit for immediate cultivation." If, upon arrival, the soldier decided against settling there, transportation, plus additional wages, would be furnished for the return east.

[14]Selkirk was motivated by several reasons to turn toward Fort William. He had good basis for believing that a large amount of incriminating evidence would be discovered in the North West Company stronghold. By taking Fort William, he hoped either to force the North West Company into a capitulation or to throw the whole controversy into the courts. Furthermore he knew several Hudson's Bay Company men were being held prisoners in Fort William.

[15]Daniel McKenzie (1769?-1832) was born in Scotland. He was employed by the North West Company in 1790. Between the years of 1791 and 1815, McKenzie saw service at Lake Athabasca, Upper Fort des Prairies, Lower Red River, English River and Fond du Lac. McKenzie was made a partner of the North West Company in 1796. He retired from the fur trade in about 1818. In McKenzie's obituary notice, it is stated that he was from Augusta, North Carolina. Wallace, *Documents,* p. 476.

[16]Selkirk's wisdom and generosity made such a marked impression that tales of his accomplishments were current for several generations. For the De Meurons, houses were built next to the fort; this was done to give added protection for the settlement. Lots surveyed by Peter Fidler were assigned. Each family was given the privilege of distilling as much whiskey as it could make use of, this privilege passing on to the descendants. Lots were provided for church and school. The Earl's achievements were not confined to rebuilding the colony. He gained a notable diplomatic victory by establishing friendly relations with the Indians. An epoch-making treaty was signed with five Indian chiefs on July 18, 1817.

government. Accordingly, William Coltman and John Fletcher were appointed.[17] At Red River, Coltman pitched his tent half-way between the two opposing posts and began assembling evidence. From reading his report, the impression is given that, from the very beginning, Coltman was striving for a compromise solution, in spite of all evidence.[18] Disgusted with the councillors, despondent and discouraged with the government at Montreal, Selkirk left for York, via the United States, in September. Selkirk and his entourage traveled on horseback to Pembina. They crossed to Saint Peter's River, floated to Prairie du Chien, and on to Saint Louis. Here, the assemblage split up, the De Meurons traveling down the Mississippi to New Orleans, Selkirk and the rest of his party following the Ohio River route east. Selkirk rushed on up the Ohio River, then to Vincennes and Louisville, reaching Washington on December 16, 1817.[19] Lord Selkirk received a cordial reception at Washington, an interesting commentary, considering the fact that scarcely five years before, the capitol city had been razed by the British. As much as Selkirk enjoyed the American hospitality, he could not prolong his stay. He hurried on to York, arriving there on January 10, 1818. The impending trials with the North West Company had caused Selkirk's alacrity.

The Earl welcomed the trials for the same reason he had welcomed the appointment of commissioners Coltman and Fletcher: an opportunity for justice that had heretofore eluded him. Had he realized the power the ruling classes of Canada held over the courts, his optimism would have diminished. The judicial officials of the Canadas were appointed by the provincial executive.[20] This arrangement did not lend itself to an independent and fair-minded judiciary. Their corruption was notorious; John Mills Jackson, a contemporary observer, wrote that justice

---

[17]William Coltman's birth date is uncertain. He was a merchant when he was appointed in 1812 to the Executive Council of Lower Canada. Coltman died in 1826.

John Fletcher was born in England in 1787. He arrived in the Canadas in 1810 and began practicing law shortly thereafter. In 1823, Fletcher sat on the bench as provincial judge of the Saint Francis district. He died in 1844. Fletcher played a very inactive part in the investigation, spending most of his time among North-wester friends at Fort William.

[18]Commissioner Coltman's report is given in full in the *Papers Relating to the Red River Settlement*, pp. 152–250.

[19]Selkirk's choice of routes was dictated by several reasons. The primary motivation for this course seems to have been Selkirk's mercenaries. The Earl promised transportation back to Lower Canada for those who did not wish to settle at the Red River. Selkirk felt a personal responsibility for the soldiers and wanted to arrange for their transportation at Saint Louis. Second, the Treaty of Ghent was the first stage in choosing the 49th parallel as the boundary between the United States and Canada. If this boundary were selected, a large part of Selkirk's grant would fall inside the United States. Consequently, the Earl wanted to negotiate at Washington in an attempt to confirm his title to this region. Third, Lord Selkirk considered buying cattle and sheep in Kentucky for the Red River Settlement. Fourth, from purely a pleasure viewpoint, the Earl anticipated an enjoyable trip. Fifth, his personal safety was always a matter of concern. Rumor had it that Selkirk's party would be attacked by the North-westers. The Earl probably considered this factor an additional reason for his choice of route; but in view of the De Meuron escort, this concern was not uppermost. Lord Selkirk's letters and notations of the trip have been edited by John Perry Pritchett, "Selkirk's Return from Assiniboia via the United States to the Canadas, 1817-1818," *Mississippi Valley Historical Review*, vol. 32, 1945, pp. 399–418.

[20]In 1791, Pitt determined to solve the problem of two races in the Canadas by geographic means. Lower Canada would be French in orientation, custom, law and tradition. Upper Canada would be more English in domination. Each province was allowed an electoral assembly, with appropriate power of taxation and lawmaking.

. . . could not be expected where judges held their commissions during pleasure, where their salaries were small, and where they were removed at the will of an imperious ruler. The Judges, subject to the control of power, might seek strength for their decisions, permanency in their stations, and every colonial advantage, rather in the influence of the parties engaged in the cause, than in a disinterested uprightness in upholding the law and enforcing the justice of the case to be decided; therefore the juries disregarded the bench, the court was tumultuous, and the stocks publicly broken before the Chief Justice; the community transferred their apprehensions from dependance of the Judges to the Judicature itself, and all respect for or confidence in redress and security from the law was destroyed: the shopkeepers are Justices of Peace; they have means of extortion, and the power of enforcing payments; they are first criminals, then the judges, and the Court of Appeal seems to be so constructed as to prevent an honest verdict from passing into effect. The practice of the Court is unjust, oppressive, and influenced; favorite Attorneys were made Deputy Clerks of the Peace, so that process might be entered and writs obtained most partially. The Crown Lawyer is allowed nearly seven pounds sterling for every criminal prosecution! An inducement to listen to trifling complaints, and prefer frivolous indictments, when, if power was gratified, and independence harrassed, it was a sufficient excuse for an inflated contingent account.[21]

The February 11, 1817, dispatch of Bathurst's added immeasureably to the trouble faced by Selkirk in securing justice from the Canadian courts.[22] The harmful effect of this dispatch on the Earl's legal status is impossible to adjudge. Its effect could be traced without monotonous persistence through the maze of legal decisions. A copy of Bathurst's dispatch accidently fell into Selkirk's hands. His bewilderment at the Canadian government's previous actions cleared, the entire conspiracy being divulged. Henceforth, there would be no enigma when judicial officials so zealously prosecuted Selkirk. Lord Bathurst had provided an excellent weapon for Selkirk's maltreatment. The dispatch, combined with the North West Company's legal juggling, removed legal justice from realization.

With these obstacles in mind, the Earl argued that the trials should be

---

[21]John Mills Jackson, *A View of the Political Situation of the Province of Upper Canada in North America* (London, 1809), pp. 10–12.

[22]While Lord Selkirk was at Fort William, the North-westers attempted to send an expedition across Lake Superior to recapture the Fort. Weather conditions inhibited the main body of the party. However, Dr. Mitchell of Drummond's Island did succeed in reaching Fort William in time to play a decisive role in the struggle. Warrant in hand, Dr. Mitchell arrested Lord Selkirk. Correctly assuming this to be an artifice inspired by the North West Company, Selkirk refused to submit to arrest. News of this refusal was quickly conveyed to Montreal and from there to the British Colonial Office in England. Colonial Secretary Lord Bathurst instructed Governor Sherbrooke to arrest Lord Selkirk and bring him to trial immediately. Bathurst wrote Sherbrooke: "By resisting the execution of the warrant issued against him Lord Selkirk has rendered himself doubly amenable to the law; . . . You will, therefore, without delay, on receipt of this instruction, take care that an indictment be preferred against his Lordship . . . Surrounded as Lord Selkirk appears to be, with a military force, which has once already been employed to defeat the execution of a legal process, it is almost impossible to hope, that he will quietly submit to the execution of any warrants against himself. . . . It is necessary that the officer, to whom its execution is entrusted, should be accompanied by such a civil (or if the necessity of the case should require it, by such a military) force, as may prevent the possibility of resistance . . ." *Papers Relating to the Red River Settlement,* pp. 72–73.

held in England. He notified the Colonial Office of his objections, but these criticisms were largely ignored.[23] The responsibility for convening the trials in Canada did not rest entirely upon the Colonial Office. As early as January 17, 1817, Bathurst had written Governor Sherbrooke on the subject of the trial's location.[24] Three months later Sherbrooke wrote the Colonial Secretary that a report from his committee of the Council believed it to be a practical impossibility to transport the witnesses to England. The reasons appeared to be well based: one, there was the problem of finding witnesses; two, the legal prerogative of forcibly transporting these witnesses was uncertain; and finally, who would pay the expense?[25] While Bathurst disputed the logical conclusions drawn by Sherbrooke's committee, he agreed to hold the trials in the Canadas. In Bathurst's mind, the main determinant against holding the trials in England was the delay in the legal process that would naturally ensue.[26]

The trials were divided into three different categories. The first category contained accusations against Selkirk, instigated by Bathurst's February 11th dispatch. The main subjects in this grouping were Selkirk's resistance to arrest and his actions at Fort William. The second category comprised the North West Company's charges against the Red River settlers. The third category concerned indictments against the North West Company brought by Selkirk.

The court action in the first category opened at Sandwich in April 1818. The Quarter session had just closed, but a special session was called to deal with the North West Company's accusations.[27] Selkirk was charged with the stealing of the North-westers' arms at Fort William.[28] The two witnesses for the plaintiffs, Jasper Vandersluys and John McTavish, North West Company clerks at Fort William, declared the arms were illegally seized. Selkirk in turn proved that he had seized the arms lawfully, on the basis of a search warrant issued by him as a magistrate. His Lordship argued that there were other wide inconsistencies in Vandersluy's testimony, ". . . the court seeing that no reliance was to be placed upon such testimony, set aside the warrant, and discharged the parties from their arrest."[29]

The next main accusation concerned Selkirk's resistance to arrest. It has been noted above how damaging Selkirk's refusal was to his cause. Chief Justice Powell, before the Sandwich trials opened, informed Selkirk,

> . . . that the charge of resistance to legal process was of a peculiar nature; that the law with respect to it was particularly severe; and that the offence was not bailable, even by Chief-Justice, who, in the case of any other crime,

---

[23]Selkirk, *A Letter to the Earl of Liverpool*, pp. 70 ff.
[24]*Papers Relating to the Red River Settlement*, p. 70.
[25]*Papers Relating to the Red River Settlement*, p. 70.
[26]Ibid., pp. 95–96.
[27]Selkirk, *A Letter to the Earl of Liverpool*, p. 96.
[28]*Papers Relating to the Red River Settlement*, p. 265.
[29]Selkirk, *A Letter to the Earl of Liverpool*, p. 116.

could admit a prisoner to bail . . . and he therefore advised Lord Selkirk, and his friends, *to retire within the frontiers of the United States,* where they might remain in safety till they should think it advisable to make their re-appearance on British ground.[30]

The Chief Justice's opinion clearly demonstrates the influence of Bathurst's February 11th dispatch, rather than any sound legal advice.

Lord Selkirk, in March 1818—prior to the Sandwich trials—had appeared in Montreal on the same charge. His appearance at Montreal was in accordance with the bail under which Mr. Coltman had placed him at Red River. At this time, Attorney General Boulton stated that he was unable to prosecute offenses committed in Upper Canada on a recognizance obtained in the Indian territories.[31] The Attorney General then moved that the case be tried before a special court of Oyer and Terminer in Upper Canada. Samuel Gale, Selkirk's attorney, objected strenuously, on the basis that no one court could compel another court to hold proceedings when it was outside the courts' regular jurisdiction. All appeals were in vain. Lord Selkirk was subjected to this type of legal maneuvering time and time again. A court would declare it had no jurisdiction in the matter, a judge would declare himself prejudiced, or the witnesses would not be available; all these machinations were tried with varying degrees of success. Nor was the frustration of legal justice the only fruition of such procrastinating policies. The cost entailed in retailing legal counselors, moving the witnesses across the Canadas, and miscellaneous costs were financially ruinous to both parties.

A month after the Montreal pronouncement, the charge was repeated. The Solicitor General admitted that he was instructed to bound Selkirk over to the next assizes, instead of trying him at the present court.[32] This was a bland admission, and indication that the executive no longer cared to disguise its intrigues against Selkirk. The Earl proposed in his defense that the writ was illegally served upon him; therefore, his resistance to arrest was not illegal. Selkirk's case was weakened by the lack of witnesses. They had been detained at Montreal, and consequently the magistrates ruled that they could not dismiss the charge on his testimony alone. The magistrates differed with the Chief Justice's opinion that the charge of resistance to arrest was non-bailable. The court lowered the bail from 6,000 pounds to 50 pounds on Selkirk and Dr. Allan's bail was reduced to 25 pounds.

The third major charge of assault and false imprisonment was placed on the docket of the next assizes. The Earl's case received better legal treatment in this court than it was to obtain in later court actions. The

---

[30]Ibid., pp. 113-14. The italics are mine.

[31]The Attorney General suffered from a lapse of memory concerning the Canada jurisdiction Act (43 Geo. II, c. 138). This act specifically delegated the courts the authority to try cases that arose from disputes in the Indian territories. For a discussion of this point, see Charles Gordon Davidson, *The North West Company* (Berkeley, 1918), pp. 151-52 [hereafter, Davidson, *North West Company*].

[32]Martin, *Lord Selkirk's Work,* p. 144.

magistrates' attitude probably reflected public opinion. John Beverley Robinson, North West partisan and Attorney General, complained,[33]

> I was prepared to find a feeling existing in his Lordship's favour among the principal inhabitants of the western district, for I was told it had manifested itself in several instances that had been represented to me before I had any personal concern in these prosecutions. It might be very naturally ascribed to the plausible printed publications of his Lordship, which had been circulated with a mischievous industry throughout the western district, and translated into French for the information of those who might be petit jurors, which were evidently written to discredit the testimony of the most material witnesses for the different prosecutions, and which contained, strange as it may seem, copies of all depositions of importance which his Lordship or other magistrates had takes for the prosecution, in charges which men were afterwards to be tried for their lives.[34]

When the next quarter sessions convened at Sandwich, Selkirk was detained in Lower Canada. The court ruled that his bail would be valid until the next session in September. Dr. Allan, however, attended with a retinue of witnesses. Allan was tried on the charge of assault and imprisonment. This same charge was made against Lord Selkirk, who agreed to be tried in the September sessions. A few days before the opening of this September session, the Attorney General directed that the indictment against the Earl, for assault and imprisonment, be quashed. Why the Attorney General suppressed the indictment is still unknown. Perhaps he thought his case was extremely weak; undoubtedly the "Montreal powers" concurred with his decision. Indeed, they may have ordered it! The solution to this problem and many of the other unintelligible acts during the trials would be solved if the decisions of the North West partners at Montreal had been recorded.

Resistance to arrest was the only indictment left on which to prosecute Selkirk. This charge was tried in the September sessions held at Sandwich. Selkirk arrived, accompanied by D'Orsonnens and Dr. Allan. His witnesses had stayed over from the July session at Selkirk's expense. The Attorney General produced a multitude of witnesses in support of the charge; but in spite of their testimony the bill was thrown out by the grand jury. The jury's decision is not surprising, considering the fact that a majority of the witnesses gave conflicting and unreliable testimony.

Attorney General Robinson decided to attempt one more indictment of Selkirk. He lumped several specific charges together in one inclusive bill of indictment. Robinson then presented this bill to the grand jury. In supporting these charges, he paraded before the court 40 witnesses, many of whom were North West Company clerks.[35] The Attorney Gen-

---

[33]John Beverley Robinson, after the death of his father in 1798, was raised by the Rev. John Strachan. After serving in the War of 1812, he was appointed acting Attorney General. He became Solicitor General in 1815, and then Attorney General in 1818. Robinson was closely allied with the North West Company, at one time being employed as their legal adviser. George W. Spragg, ed., The John Strachan Letter Book: 1812–1834 (Toronto, 1946), p. 4.

[34]Papers Relating to the Red River Settlement, p. 265.

[35]Selkirk, A Letter to the Earl of Liverpool, p. 132.

eral even went so far as to suggest that Simon McGillivray, leading
North West Company partner, be admitted to the jury room. McGillivray,
according to Robinson, should be allowed to "examine" the witnesses.[36]
Two members of the jury were North West Company employees, evi-
dencing further intimidation.[37] Robinson examined the "witnesses" over
a three-day period. The court adjourned on Friday, assembling again on
Monday morning. Before there was an opportunity for the grand jury to
report, Chief Justice Powell adjourned the court *sine die*. Chief Justice
Powell's reason for abruptly adjoining the court remains in the realm of
conjecture. His antipathy toward Selkirk was well known. Powell's ruling on the resistance to arrest charge revealed this attitude. Immediately, in propaganda statements, each side accused the other of
sabotaging the proceedings. The *Niles' Weekly Register* reported,

> The controversey was so warm that the court with difficulty preserved order
> by silencing them both. The friends of his lordship are disposed to charge
> the chief justice with furthering the designs of the North West company,
> and intimate that the court was suddenly adjourned to prevent a formal
> rejection of the bill of indictment by the grand jury, and to preclude the
> opportunity of presenting bills against Mr. M'Gillivray and other servants of
> the company. The other side, on the contrary, charged his lordship with
> practising improperly with the grand jury during their sitting, and inti-
> mated that something little different from direct bribery was used to prevent
> a fair investigation of the charges.[38]

Angry, Selkirk wrote to Sir Peregrine Maitland from Montreal,

> In passing through York lately I understood that this matter had been mis-
> represented, and stated as if the grand jury had dispersed of themselves, or
> had refused to act; but your Excellency will find upon investigation, that a
> quorum were actually sitting, and that the Chief Justice broke up the Court
> without even calling them in from the adjoining room. This precipitancy is
> the more extraordinary, as the assizes at Sandwich were fixed, contrary to
> usual custom, to be held the last of the western circuit, expressly because
> the business which was expected to come before the Court was likely to
> occupy a considerable and indefinite length of time; and it was there fore
> thought necessary to hold the Court a period when no other engagement
> could interfere.[39]

The first act of this farce was completed. The second act began at
Montreal in May 1818. The North West Company charged Colin
Robertson, Michael Heden, John Bourke, Louis Nolin and Martin Jordan
with "riotously destroying certain premises composing a fort of the North
West Company."[40] The court resorted to the same deferring tactics
employed in previous trials, and demanded bail from the prisoners, on
the basis that the Court of Oyer and Terminer could not be convened at

---

[36]Ibid., pp. 129–30.

[37]Ibid.

[38]*Niles' Weekly Register*, 3 (1819), New Series, p. 134.

[39]*Papers Relating to the Red River Settlement*, p. 256.

[40]Andrew Amos, *Report of Trials in the Courts of Canada Relative to the Destruction of
the Earl of Selkirk's Settlement on the Red River* (London, 1820), p. 3, [hereafter, Amos,
Report.].

the present time. This the prisoners refused to do, stating that their trials had already been delayed. Furthermore, what was to prevent a postponement of the designated September trials? On their refusal to give bail, the Chief Justice sent them to prison. This flagrant injustice was evidently too much for even the governmental officials, for soon the Attorney General visited the prisoners and proposed that they post bail day by day. Attorney General Robinson also stated that the trial would begin promptly. "After a few minutes consideration," Colin Robertson and his co-defendants were all acquitted by the jury.[41] This was the one significant legal victory for Selkirk's side. The victory was a temporary one, as was soon shown by the final series of trials.

In the midst of the Canadian trials, the Earl decided that he and his family should have a vacation. Accordingly, on September 1, 1818, shortly before the Sandwich trials, Selkirk and his family left Buffalo on a pleasure cruise. The trip had an added attraction, for the boat, "Walk in the Water," on which they embarked, was making its second trip across Lake Erie under steam power. After a very slow trip, "Walk in the Water" docked at Detroit about nine o'clock on Sunday evening, September 6.[42]

Selkirk seemed to have a propensity for getting involved in legal disputes; the boat had no more than docked before the sheriff of Wayne County, Austin Wing, stepped on board and served Selkirk with a writ. James Grant, whose property had been confiscated by one of the Earl's reprisal expeditions sent out from Fort William, was the plaintiff.[43] Selkirk inquired around the frontier town for a good legal counselor. Solomon Sibley, United States Attorney, was recommended to him. Sibley secured two prominent Detroit citizens to post bond for his client. Shortly after his bond was posted, Lord Selkirk left for the Canadian shore, realizing that any further delay in the United States might prove disastrous for his case at Sandwich. Grant claimed that Selkirk had arrested him illegally and had stolen property valued at $50,000.

In court Sibley moved that the writ be quashed, advancing the argument that it was illegal since the writ was served on Sunday. The case was argued before the court between September 28 and October 7, 1818.[44] Six days after the last argument was presented, Judge Woodward handed down his 20-page decision. Judge Woodward buttressed his opinion with arguments from: the Bible, Coke, Blackstone, and Wilberforce. Reaching his decision, the Judge said,

I am, therefore, of opinion according to the most luminous authorities,

---

[41]Amos, *Report,* p. 27.

[42]William L. Jenks, "The Earl of Selkirk in Michigan Courts," *Michigan Magazine of History,* 12 (1928), 662-68.

[43]James Grant's birth date is unknown. He was in charge of Fond du Lac from 1805 to 1813. The year 1816 found him back at Fond du Lac, where he was arrested by Selkirk's men. He retired from the fur trade in 1821, after which time he disappeared from historical records.

[44]William Wirt Blume, ed., *Transactions of the Supreme Court of the Territory of Michigan, 1814-1824,* University of Michigan Publications, Law, vol. 3 (Ann Arbor, 1938), pp. 91-92.

which I can obtain from the best judgment which I can form, that arrest or civil process was not at the common law legal on Sunday.[45]

While this court action did not affect Selkirk's fortunes in the Canadas, it does illustrate the scope of his legal involvement.[46] The Earl was enmeshed in a tight legal web. From the time Selkirk reached York in January 1818 till he left the Canadas for England nine months later, he was either going to a trial or attending one.

The third and final act of this courtroom burlesque that took place was between May and November of 1818. If the litigation surrounding the Sandwich and Robertson trials was confusing, the legal action between Selkirk and the North West Company concerning the North-westers' attacks on the Red River settlement was nothing short of bewildering. Charges and counter-charges were never in more abundance. In this last series of trials the North-westers brought all their influence to bear on the Canadian courts. Selkirk discovered that first one obstacle and then another hindered his prosecution. His counsels were denied participation in the court proceedings. They were not allowed to examine the witnesses.[47] The Crown lawyers would avoid asking any questions which might prove embarrassing to the North West Company case.[48] On the subject of the cross-examination of witnesses, Selkirk wrote to Sherbrooke,

> It will be evident to your Excellency, that the examination of witnesses is so essential a point, that if that be not properly conducted, nothing else can supply the defect. Whatever may be the information which a witness possesses, it will not come out before the jury unless he be properly questioned; and to put the questions properly, especially in a case that depends much upon circumstantial evidence, acquires an intimate knowledge of the facts of the case . . .[49]

Transferring the trials from Lower to Upper Canada was a vexatious subterfuge used to prolong the trials. The expense entailed in moving the witnesses, plus the cost of keeping them during the long periods of delay, eventually bankrupted the Earl. Since some trials were held concurrently in Upper and Lower Canada, it was impossible for Selkirk's witnesses to attend both trials. Many witnesses became restless after the numerous postponements, and some escaped.

Perhaps the worst consequence of this transference policy was the differing legal viewpoint held by Upper and Lower Canada courts. The

---

[45]Henry S. Bartholomew, ed., *Michigan Historical Collections*, vol. 12 (1908), p. 502.

[46]Correspondence between Simon McGillivray and William Woodbridge; Woodbridge's bill for legal services; Woodbridge's opinion in the case of Grant versus Selkirk; James Grant's oath are to be found in the William Woodbridge Papers, Burton Historical Collections, Detroit Public Library.

[47]*Papers Relating to the Red River Settlement*, p. 114.

[48]*Report of the Proceedings Connected with the Disputes Between the Earl of Selkirk and the North-West Company, at the Assizes Held at York in Upper Canada, October, 1818* (Montreal, 1819), pp. 159–176, [hereafter, *Report of the Proceedings . . . Held at York . . . October, 1818*].

[49]*Papers Relating to the Red River Settlement*, p. 113.

court in York (Upper Canada) objected to what they termed the "generality" of the legal instruments given them by Lower Canada's courts. The result of this objection was that the York court refused to try these "general" offenses. Selkirk notified the Attorney General of Lower Canada concerning these objections, but the Attorney General made no effort to change the instruments.[50] In other words, the practical effect created by this muddle was the freeing of many North-westers.

Releasing witnesses on a small bail was another artifice used by the courts to frustrate Selkirk's prosecution. Once released, the prisoners fled into the Canadian wilderness. Cuthbert Grant, the Métis' leader at the Seven Oaks massacre, charged with 13 different counts, was released on a small bail. Halkett objected strenuously to this type of artifice in his letters to Bathurst, but to no avail. Alexander Ross, North West Company trader, relates,

> Expedients were resorted to, and every artifice that could be devised was requisitioned to defeat the ends of justice. The chief outrages that had perpetrated were committed, not by the ruling powers, but by their subordinates, many of whom were, in consequence, hastily got out of the way. The remote posts of the North, as well as the Columbia had benefit of their company. Those who could not be conveniently disposed of in this way were sent off among the Indians for a time, so that when the various indictments were exhibited in the courts of law against individuals no evidence could be found to convict or prove them guilty. This has been, and always will be, the case in a country so remote from civilization and the seat of justice.[51]

Four bills of indictment were found against the North West Company partners and employees at Montreal in March 1818. While the trials took place, as we have noted, between May and November, 1818, this third series of litigation properly begins with the Montreal indictments.

The Montreal proceedings were followed by legal battles in which the North-westers were confronted with a legion of crimes: 42 charges of murder or complicity in murder, 18 of arson, 9 of burglary, 16 of robbery, 9 of stealing boats on a navigable river, 9 of grand larceny, and 7 of malicious shooting.[52] The Selkirk forces managed to secure only one conviction, and any satisfaction at this was gone with the failure to carry out the sentence.

The one conviction involved Charles De Reinhard, a former De Meuron officer.[53] Reinhard and Archibald McLellan,[54] a North West partner, were accused of murdering Owen Keveny, recruiting agent for Lord Selkirk.[55] De Reinhard freely admitted his guilt, and McLellan was

---

[50]Selkirk, A Letter to the Earl of Liverpool, pp. 153–54.

[51]Alexander Ross, The Fur Hunters of the Far West (Chicago, 1924), p. 268.

[52]Amos, Report, pp. 29–388.

[53]De Reinhard was not a member of the De Meuron contingent that Selkirk hired.

[54]Archibald McLellan (?–1820) entered the North West Company's service in 1792. He served at Bas de La Riviere House and Rainy Lake. McLellan became a partner of the North West Company in 1805. From 1810 to 1815, he roamed the Lake Athabasca region. After the Selkirk trials, McLellan retired from the fur trade, dying shortly thereafter. Wallace, Documents, pp. 479–80.

[55]Owen Keveny was appointed a member of Miles Macdonell's council in June 1813. Selkirk had hired him to take charge of the Irish settlers. He believed in rigid and brutal

generally assumed to be guilty.[56] The jury convicted De Reinhard.[57] The judge pronounced the sentence in the ponderous manner of the 19th-century legal style.

> The judgment of the law is, that you Charles De Reinhard, be taken to the gaol of our Lord, the King, for the district of Quebec, and from thence to the place of execution, on Monday now next arriving, being the 8th of this instant June, and there be hanged by the neck till you are dead, and that afterward your body be dissected and anatomized.[58]

The jury, after a ten-minute deliberation, acquitted McLellan,[59] the obvious conclusion being that employment by the North West Company brought with it legal immunity.[60]

The next trials in this series were held at York from October to November, 1818. Paul Brown and Francis Boucher, North-westers who took part in the Seven Oaks affair, were the first to be indicted.[61] The case against them was considerably weakened by the Attorney General's ruling that the legal instruments transferred from Upper Canada were too general; hence, he would not prosecute Brown and Boucher on some of the enumerated charges.[62] Eight days after the trial opened, the jury declared Brown and Boucher not guilty.[63]

The trial of John Siveright, Alexander Mackenzie, Hugh McGillis, John McDonald, John McLaughlin and Simon Fraser, North West Company partners, for accessories to the murder of Robert Semple, followed the pattern established by the Brown-Boucher trial. An insight into contemporary courtroom practice is revealed in Justice Boulton's charge to the jury:

> Gentlemen, I was going to have said that there was not a scrap of scintilla of evidence, except against Mr. McLeod, and that against him you would judge of its weight. I had thought that Mr. McLeod was one of the defend-

---

discipline, accruing a reputation of being a martinet. The Factory superintendent at York, William Auld, recommended him, "Mr. Keveny, arrived at Red River with his whole party safe and sound, in the same high health as when they left Ireland." (Oliver, *Canadian North-West*, p. 51.) The immigrants did not have the same high regard for Mr. Keveny which the York Factory superintendent held. He was despised by most of them. Keveny brought two groups of colonists from Ireland in the years 1813 and 1815. On his last trip inland, he was arrested by Norman McLeod, North West partner and Justice of the Peace, on a charge of cruel treatment to his boatmen (a believable charge). McLeod sent him to Fort William; it was while he was en route that De Reinhard murdered him.

[56]*Report of the Trials of Charles De Reinhard and Archibald M'Lellan, for Murder, at a Court of Oyer and Terminer Held at Quebec, May, 1818* (Montreal, 1818), app. pp. 24-31, [hereafter, *Report of the Trials of Charles De Reinhard and Archibald M'Lellan*].

[57]Ibid., pp. 651-52.

[58]Ibid.

[59]Ibid., p. 159.

[60]A dispute arose over the boundaries in the Charles De Reinhard case, since Keveny was murdered at the falls on the Winnipeg River. Because the court's jurisdiction was disputed, the execution was stayed and De Reinhard died of natural causes.

[61]The trial's record is contained in the *Report of the Proceedings . . . Held at York . . . October, 1818*, pp. 1-300.

[62]Selkirk had seen the possibility of a dispute arising between Upper Canada and Lower Canada courts, but when he brought the problem to the attention of the Attorney General of Lower Canada, the protestations were overlooked.

[63]*Report of the Proceedings . . . Held at York . . . October, 1818*, p. 291.

ants before you, but I find he is not [a remarkable discovery, after hearing testimony for several days!] Against the others then there is not a scrap, not a scintilla of evidence. Not of any thing before the fact, and after the fact only the giving of the usual supply of clothes to their servants. [This giving "of the usual supply of clothes to their servants" was the partners' part-payment to their employees for the Red River Colony's destruction.] You will therefore consider your verdict.[64]

Justice Boulton's "charge" amounted to instructing the jury for an acquittal. The jury complied and the partners were freed.

Following this blueprint there could be no doubt of the outcome of the last trial at York. John Cooper and Hugh Bennerman were charged with "stealing cannon in a dwelling house of the Earl of Selkirk, at Red River, on the 3rd of April 1815." Cooper and Bennerman were settlers who deserted from the colony to the North West Company. The jury reported the automatic verdict of not guilty. Announced on November 3, 1818, this verdict terminated the last scene in this set of trials. Shortly thereafter, Selkirk left for England, via New York.

After the Cooper-Bennerman trial, the exhausted antagonists paused in their running legal fray. The financial burden involved in retaining lawyers, transporting and paying witnesses plus court costs bankrupted both contestants. An end to the dispute now became imperative for the North West Company as well as Hudson's Bay Company. For the North West Company, it had been a Pyrrhic victory. North West Company trader Alexander Ross estimated that the litigation alone cost the North West Company 55,000 pounds.[65] He ruefully remarked, "My loss amounted to 1,400 pounds which left me almost penniless.[66] Lord Selkirk suffered an even heavier loss. Not only had his personal fortune vanished, but his health was undermined as well. In a little over a year he would be dead of tuberculosis.

At the trials' conclusion, self-vindicating statements were broadcast by both sides. John Halkett, Selkirk's brother-in-law and chief publicist, offered his succinct opinion in a letter to Lord Bathurst:

> Throughout the whole of this vexatious postponement of trials—unnecessary transfer of prosecutions,—and arbitrary setting aside of the indictments, which had been regularly found by Grand Juries,—it is but too obvious, that the Law Officers of the Crown in Canada had some very different object in view than to promote the ends of justice.[67]

Rev. John Strachan wrote to Francis Gore, Lieutenant Governor of Upper Canada,[68]

---

[64]*Report of the Proceedings . . . Held at York . . . October, 1818*, pp. 214–15.

[65]Ross, *Fur Hunters*, p. 269.

[66]Ibid., p. 271.

[67]Selkirk, *A Letter to the Earl of Liverpool*, p. 151.

[68]John Strachan (1788–1862) was born in Aberdeen, Scotland; he attended the University of King's College, Aberdeen. After receiving his degree, he became a part-time member of the Divinity faculty at the University of Saint Andrew's. Later he took a proffered post of tutor to Honorable Richard Cartwright's children at Kingston, Upper Canada. Strachan arrived in 1799 at Kingston; in the year 1807 he married the widow of Andrew McGill. The University of Aberdeen bestowed an honorary degree on him. Strachan slowly allied himself with the lead-

The North West Company have had their trials and were all honourably acquitted. It appeared most decidedly that Lor[d] Selkirk's people were the first aggressors and that Poor Semple went out with the avowed purpose of attacking the party by whom he and his people were slain . . .[69]

Cambridge lawyer, Andrew Amos, who compiled the record of the trials, wrote,

> . . . a state of society, of which no British colony has hitherto afforded a parallel:—Private vengeance arrogating the functions of public law;—Murder Justified in a British Court of Judicature, on the plea of exasperation, commencing years before the sanguinary act;—The spirit of monopoly raging in all the terrors of power, in all the force of organization, in all the insolence of impunity.[70]

What was Amos's solution to the dispute?—"the necessity of an interference on part of the Legislature and of the Executive Power of this country.[71] As the conflict had been removed from wilderness to courtroom, now it would go from courtroom to parliament.

---

ing North-westers of Montreal; his marriage strengthened this tie. Hatred for the Americans was a dominant personality trait. During the North West Company's struggle with the Hudson's Bay Company, he was the former's most vocal partisan.

[69]Spragge, *Strachan Letter Book,* p. 182.

[70]Amos, *Report,* p. xxiii.

[71]Ibid., p. xxv.

part four

Expansion and Readjustment, 1820–1860

19

THE LUMBER COMMUNITY OF UPPER CANADA, 1815–1867*

Michael S. Cross

The common impression of the economy of British North America before Confederation is that it was fundamentally agrarian in nature. This may be true if one thinks in terms of farms and factories as the alternative units of production. But a rather large percentage of the population of British North America was engaged in a variety of nonagricultural pursuits, chiefly connected with primary or extractive industries such as fur trading, fishing, and lumbering. Much of the economic viability of British North America came from the profits of these industries. In some provinces, individuals combined part-time farming with work in the primary industries, but in large sections of Upper Canada, lumbering became a full-time occupation and an industry quite separate from agriculture. Its organization was capitalistic and its orientation commercial. This was particularly true in the Ottawa Valley, as Professor Michael S. Cross points out in the following article. The importance of the lumber industry in the backcountry of Upper Canada raises some rather significant questions about the nature of "frontier" society and its implication for the political, economic, and social history of the province. Were there distinct differences between the "life-styles" of those employed in the lumber industry and those who farmed for a living? Were the lumbermen a "proletariat"? Is lumbering really an "industry"? How does all this alter or affect the commonly held interpretations of political and social conflict in the province between 1820 and Confederation?

*Ontario History, 52 (1960), 213–33.

SUGGESTIONS FOR FURTHER READING

F. Landon, *Western Ontario and the American Frontier* (Toronto: McClelland and Stewart, 1967).

A. R. M. Lower, *Great Britain's Woodyard: British America and the Timber Trade, 1763-1867* (Montreal: McGill–Queen's University Press, 1973).

G. N. Tucker, *The Canadian Commercial Revolution, 1845-1851* (New Haven, Conn.: Yale University Press, 1936).

J.M.B.

I n post Confederation Canada, lumbering became a thoroughly respectable industry, the backbone of the nation's economy. It was not always so. In the half-century previous to Confederation, it was "regarded as a distracting influence, an occupation legal, it is true, but not creditable."[1] And there was a great deal of justification for such an opinion. The lumber community, wherever it touched other segments of society, was a socially disturbing factor, both in the behaviour of its employees, and in the fatal lure of its glamour.

Previous to the first decade of the 19th century, lumbering was a relatively unimportant industry in British North America. Some timber had been brought out of the Richelieu country during the French regime, but logging proceeded primarily as an adjunct to agriculture, the forest being cleared as quickly as possible to make way for settlement. In Upper Canada this process was accelerated by economic circumstances, for the only forest product that justified the heavy transport cost to Great Britain, the sole available market, was potash. In destroying the forests, settlers could fulfil a double purpose—clearing for farming, and burning for potash. By 1835 these inducements had sufficed to clear timber all the way from the Lower Canada boundary to Lake Ontario.

Lumbering could not be profitable in the Canadas. Britain drew her timber from the Baltic area, whose shorter transportation routes and cheap labour priced Canada out of the market. The United States, as yet only cautiously pushing towards the Mid-west, found ample timber at home to meet her needs. New Brunswick, situated on the Atlantic sea-lanes, found more opportunity for lumbering, but even there it remained a minor industry, though by 1803 it stood second to agriculture. Lumbering achieved real prominence in British North America thanks to external events. The Napoleonic Wars destroyed the economic balance of northern Europe and threatened the whole British trading system. Sensing the danger, Britain began to withdraw behind tariff barriers.[2] Napoleon's Berlin Decree of 1806 and the answering British orders-in-council created a wall around Europe, all but snuffing out the Baltic

---

[1]A. R. M. Lower, *Settlement and the Forest Frontier in Eastern Canada* (Toronto, 1936), p. 30.

[2]Duty on foreign timber, 1804, 25s a load, 1806, £1.7.2, 1813, £3.5.0. See, D. G. Creighton, *The Empire of the St. Lawrence* (Toronto, 1956), p. 149.

timber supply. Of a sudden, colonial timber became vital and a lumbering boom was on.

Lumbering became a firmly established industry in British North America during the war, and with the end of the Montreal fur trade in 1821, the new staples—timber and wheat—reigned supreme from Rupert's Land to the Atlantic fisheries. It was with a strangling feeling, then, that the great colonial merchants viewed any tampering with the imperial system. The reduction of the foreign timber tariff in 1822, the Huskisson tariff of 1825,[3] these were severe blows to the trading community, and an indication of a changing mood in Britain. The Canadas met the crisis by a reorganization of their trading pattern. Four new banks—the Montreal Bank, the Quebec Bank, the Bank of Canada, and the Bank of Upper Canada—were instituted between 1817 and 1821, to provide financial footing for trade expansion. The Lachine Canal was finished in 1825, and, during 1824 and 1825, William Hamilton Merritt organized his Welland Canal Company with dreams of carrying the St. Lawrence system to the American West.

The Canadas suffered during the depression years of 1826–28. Only a very small proportion of the population, however, was engaged in the staples trade and the better organized business community quickly recovered from the 'slump'. Nevertheless, the merchants were on the alert for any further threats to their business. When Viscount Althorp brought in a budget in 1831 reducing the imperial lumber preference to 35 shillings (from 45), an outcry arose from all the powerful lumber interests at home and abroad. The Quebec Committee of Trade, the Upper Canadian Legislature, the London Lumber Merchants, all combined forces to bring about the defeat of the measure in the Commons, while in New Brunswick the Lieutenant-Governor Sir Howard Douglas dramatically resigned to express his concern.

Thereafter the lumber industry recovered rapidly. New Brunswick, for example, found a large market in the West Indies which, by 1840, accounted for 26 million board feet of lumber annually.[4] Britain was still an enormous and growing market, for railway building was creating a great new demand. The Canadas too found a great new market after 1835 in the United States. New developments in transportation—canals and lake towing—had opened this trade. To a large degree, transportation created the trade in Upper Canada, not vice versa. The newly opened markets gave the Canadas a buffer against the disasters of the 1840s.

The first indication of things to come was in 1842, when the imperial timber preference to the colonies was reduced by 15 shillings a load. Trade was severely curtailed by this legislation.[5] Then the final ruin of

---

[3]The Huskisson tariff levied heavy duties on meat imported from foreign countries into British possessions. This was a blow to the lumber community, which relied upon pork from the United States for provisioning.

[4]A. R. M. Lower, *The North American Assault on the Canadian Forest* (Toronto, 1938), p. 72.

[5]Lumber exports of New Brunswick, 1841—£1,792,824; 1842—£888,426. Lower, *Settlement and the Forest Frontier*, p. 36.

the colonial system in 1848 threw British North America into a frenzy of fear and despair. For the lumber community to find itself once more, a complete reorganization was necessary. In the Canadas the staples merchants vented their fury in the futile Montreal riots and the Annexation Manifesto of 1849, while in New Brunswick they joined the radicals to force Responsible Government on an unhappy executive. But reorganize they did, to live an unhealthy half-life in New Brunswick, to flourish with new vigour in the Canadas.

This, then, was the general picture of the lumber community in British North America. In Upper Canada it had sharper outlines. Lumbering was the lifeblood of that province. By 1849 forest products amounted to some 42 percent of the exports of the Province of Canada, the bulk of which originated in Canada West.[6] With the gleam of profits in his eyes, the lumberman opened the woods of the colony, sweeping up the Ottawa, across the midland areas, from Lake Ontario to Georgian Bay. He left behind him a trail of ruined forests and embittered farmers. He was the architect of a strange new world. "No medieval ravisher could have been more fierce and unscrupulous than the lumberman. His lust of power and wealth have changed the face of the country, built cities and railroads and created a sort of civilization—as impermanent as the material with which it was concerned, wood, but out of destruction perhaps bringing forth certain fruits of abiding worth."[7] For, whatever his many faults, the lumberman was a trailblazer, opening areas inaccessible to the settler, for "Settlers and Colonization invariably follow in the wake of the lumbermen, who may indeed be styled the pioneers of civilization and development."[8]

Except in the Ottawa Valley the social effect of the lumber community on Upper Canada was not severe. Lumbering, in the section that fronted on lakes Ontario and Erie, was restricted to meeting the local demand and it was a definitely minor scale industry. Until about 1835, the American market was closed. Sufficient timber was still available in the woods of upper New York, Pennsylvania and Ohio to supply the needs of the northern United States. And due to the difficulties in transporting logs along the lakes, Quebec, the base for British bound cargoes, was an impractical market. As a result lumbering did not attract investment for large scale production and hence was often carried on in communal fashion, in keeping with the cooperative tradition of a pioneer community. Saw-mills either were owned by the community at large or operated on a share basis, and cut the boards necessary for local use at little cost to the settler. With no drives, no camps, no temptation to linger in the woods, Upper Canada was free from the demoralization which the industry brought to New Brunswick.

Unfortunately, there was a dark side to this rosy scene. Blissfully unaware that a large export market for lumber was soon to open, the farmers of the lake front butchered the finest trees to build their cabins, their

---

[6]Lower, *North American Assault,* p. 130.

[7]Ibid., p. 26.

[8]*The Lumber Trade of the Ottawa Valley, with a Description of Some of the Principal Manufacturing Establishments* (Ottawa, 1871), p. 6.

fences, their pigsties. Norfolk County was a classic example of this waste. Perhaps the finest stand of white pine in North America was ruthlessly levelled to make way for agriculture. Ironically, the soil proved to be sandy and virtually useless, until tobacco was developed there many years afterward.

The demand from the United States for lumber grew steadily after 1835. By this time American settlement had swept past the lakes, destroying the native timber supply on its westward progress. What was left was almost exclusively hardwood, unsuitable for ordinary building purposes. The canal system, erected after 1822, provided easy transportation to the American markets. Furthermore, a large amount of American capital was released at this time, to be used in exploiting the Canadian timber lands. The West Indies trade of New England had dried up, and the slave trade was cut off. The virgin field of Upper Canada received some of this free capital. Indicative of the sudden upsurge of exports to the United States are the shipments from St. Johns, Lower Canada, an outlet to the United States for Upper Canadian lumber. From 1807 to 1826, the only timber recorded as passing through that port was 112 cords of firewood in 1822.[9] But a flurry of canal building—the Lachine in 1825, the Rideau in 1832, the Chambly in 1835—opened a flood of timber through St. Johns. In 1834 the exports reached a value of £2000, in 1839, £3600, and in 1853, £5100.[10]

In 1835, "United States traders came this year into Canada, bought up wheat, flour, provisions and lumber, and paid heavy American duties on their export out of this country."[11] Mills sprang up all along the lake front as lumber poured through the Richelieu Canal and the Oswego feeder to the United States. This American market was radically different in its requirements from the British. Britain was interested almost exclusively in square pine timber or deals.[12] Since these could be made from only the best timber, the square timber trade was extremely wasteful of forest resources.[13] The United States market was less discriminating, taking a wide variety of timber, ranging from spars to firewood. The largest part of the export to the south was in planks and boards, of almost any quality. In 1853 Canadian sawmills churned out £470,187 worth of board and planks for the American market.[14] Unlike square timbering, a simple process of cutting and squaring, the cutting of boards on the export scale required the establishment of large sawmills and elaborate means of transport. Hence the Canadians were forced to organize lumbering on a capitalistic basis unlike the simple square timber trade. The Montreal—or New York—centred company replaced the family unit as the usual group engaged in the trade and the professional lumberman be-

[9]Lower, North American Assault, p. 96.

[10]Ibid., p. 97: Tables of the Trade and Navigation of the Province of Canada for the Year 1853 (Quebec, 1854).

[11]Montreal Gazette, June 11, 1835.

[12]Deals were planks of 3-inch or greater width, cut from the best timber.

[13]As late as 1853, of £1,682,125 worth of forest products exported to Great Britain, £1,223,811 was made up of deals and pine timber. Tables of Trade and Navigation, 1853.

[14]Ibid.

came a familiar figure. The industry, through a more solid economic basis and better organization, was better able to withstand depressions than the square timber trade, but was susceptible to more, if less severe, fluctuations. In the capitalistic complex of Upper Canada, directed from a distant metropolis, the industry rolled on like a machine. Once started in the autumn, the machine could not be stopped, no matter what happened on the market. While Upper Canada never suffered a complete disaster such as occurred in New Brunswick,[15] overproduction was a constant threat.

The lumber merchants and large entrepreneurs were not solely to blame for the fluctuations in supply and hence in prices. Small firms, encouraged by periods of high prices, were lured into the trade. Without solid financial backing, they were all but doomed in a necessarily large scale industry. The Bytown *Gazette,* viewing the depressing export figures for 1841 through 1843,[16] launched into a tirade against small lumberers as the cause of all the problems in the trade. Lumbering had not been injured by the reduction of the British preference, the *Gazette* insisted, but, rather, "The cause is solely from there being no attention paid to proportion the supply to the demand among those engaged in the trade. . . . We have frequently had occasion to remark that the facility with which men possessed of no means could embark in this trade, deterred capitalists from doing so; and . . . the reckless and extravagant method by which it was carried on by such characters . . . deprived the trade of that character for stability without which no branch of commerce can prosper."[17]

Overly-ambitious farmers turned to the trade to make 'easy' cash. As John Langton related in 1844, "The complaints are universal of the difficulty of making a living by farming, and I feel no doubt, after giving it a fair trial, that in the present state of affairs it is not to be done."[18] But timbering, too, had its perils. "The great source of failure among lumberers," Langton decided, "is their sinking their capital in securing a field to work on long before they use it, and otherwise extending their business so much beyond their means as (to) have to get advances from the Montreal and Quebec men, who thus get all the profit."[19] But, in any event, the problem of the farmer-lumberer was not acute in Upper Canada. The difficulties of a drive down the small streams of the province and the virtual impossibility of transporting one's own logs all the way to Quebec discouraged all but the most venturesome farmers. The general pattern remained that of the farmers taking logs from their own property to the local mill, receiving cash or goods from the mill owner who in turn sold the boards to exporters.

Since this was the case, the capitalistically-based lumber industry of

---

[15]See, Lower, *Settlement and the Forest Frontier;* James Hannay, *History of New Brunswick* (St. John, N.B., 1909).

[16]White pine exports, 1841-91, 637 pieces, 1843-41, 811. Bytown *Gazette,* Thursday, September 1, 1843.

[17]Ibid.

[18]W. A. Langton, ed., *Early Days in Upper Canada, Letters of John Langton* (Toronto, 1926), p. 199.

[19]Ibid., p. 202.

Upper Canada was divorced from agriculture, and avoided the moral laxity and blight, the financial instability characteristic of New Brunswick's often unsuccessful combination of agriculture and lumbering. Indeed, the farmer of Upper Canada was generally blissfully unaware of the value of the forests. Caniff Haight, about 1830, found the settlers of the central area of the province "knew but little of what was passing in the world outside, and as a general thing they cared less."[20] Their connection with lumbering was practically non-existent. "Wood, save the large oak and pine timber, was valueless, and was cut down and burned to get it out of the way."[21] Later, in 1846, Sir Richard Bonnycastle of the Royal Engineers had much the same to report. The farmers were still ignorant of the wooden treasure which surrounded them. With almost child-like agrarian glee, Bonnycastle described the ruin of the forests.

> When you have cut down the mighty trees, then comes the logging. Reader, did you ever log? It is precious work! Fancy yourself in a smock-frock, the best of all working dresses, having cut the huge trees into lengths of a few feet, rolling these lengths up into a pile, and ranging the branches and brushwood for convenient combustion; then waiting for a favourable wind, setting fire to all your heaps, and burying yourself in grime and smoke; then rolling up these half-consumed enormous logs, till, after painful toil, you get them to burn to potash . . . but logging, logging—nobody likes logging.[22]

Agriculture was the future of Canada. This became painfully obvious to the government when the colonial system crashed down about their ears. It seems to have been quite clear to the lumber kings, too, as evidenced by their eagerness to escape from the toils of Britain into the arms of a new metropolis, the United States. In 1848, the merchants made their last bid for 'justice' from Great Britain. Their complaints were summed up in a petition to the Earl of Elgin, and signed by "The Lumber Merchants at Bytown." They called his attention to the fact that "since the year 1842 . . . the lumber trade in this province, with the exception of the year 1845, has been in a languishing, depressed, and even a ruinous state; brought about and experienced from the fact that the manufacturers and shippers in this province, cannot compete with those in the Northern Ports of Europe." To aid them, they asked for a reduction in the duties for cutting timber on Crown land, and a new licensing system to prevent defrauding and clashes over timber rights.[23] Receiving no redress, the lumber tycoons rushed to cut away the vestiges of British control with the Annexation Manifesto.[24] It was a futile and a short-lived

---

[20]Caniff Haight, *Country Life in Canada Fifty Years Ago* (Toronto, 1885), p. 104.

[21]Ibid., p. 106.

[22]Sir Richard H. Bonnycastle, *Canada and the Canadians in 1846* (London, 1846), p. 79.

[23]Toronto *Globe*, February 26, 1848.

[24]Among the signers of the Manifesto, we can distinguish David Douglas Young of the lumber firm of G. B. Symes and Co.; Asa Cook of Petite Nation, a large lumber merchant; Joseph Aumond of Bytown; J. G. Irvine of Quebec; Ruggles Wright of Hull; J. Gilmour and John Thomson of Quebec; and Alexander and William McBean, lumbermen. *The Annexation Manifesto of 1849, Reprinted From the Original Pamphlet With the Names of the Signers* (Montreal, 1881); Appendix No. 3 to the Eighth Volume of the Journals of the Legislative Assembly of the Province of Canada, Session 1849, App. PPPP; Appendix No. 2, Session 1844–45, Appendix OO.

gesture of defiance. Sir John Abbott later rationalized that the signers had "no more serious idea of seeking annexation with the United States than a petulent child who strikes his nurse, has of deliberately murdering her."[25] This seems a rather facile explanation. Their emotions brought them to sign the Manifesto, but their intellect told them that the mass of the Canadian people stood against them and, within a year, their purses told them that their fear of ruin was unfounded.

Far from drying up, trade increased steadily from 1849 to 1865. In 1849, $4 million worth of forest products were exported to Britain from the United Province, $1,200,000 to the United States. By 1865, the figures were, to Britain $9 million, to the United States $5 million.[26] Several factors combined to make the predictions of doom unfounded. Reciprocity was one, although some lumberers had complaints of the treaty.[27] A surge in British railway construction and the Crimean War helped keep the London market booming. The population of the United States continued to spiral and the demands of the Civil War expanded trade. But probably most significant for central Upper Canada was the railway development of North America.

By 1854, the Canadas boasted some 790 miles of railway lines, and the lines under construction, when completed, would bring the total mileage to 1,980.[28] Lumbering accounted for a large part of the increase. American capital, as well as Canadian, pushed tracks into the forests, seeking out huge quantities of timber as traffic. Boston, in particular, was making a bold bid to divert the trade of the Ottawa Valley from the river-route to Quebec and Britain into her metropolitan system. The Boston-Ogdensburg line carried rails to the border by 1850. In 1852, Boston interests embarked upon the Bytown and Prescott Railway, with sanguine hopes of carrying 25 million feet of lumber in the first year of operation.[29] Their line was built to a 4' 8½" gauge, to tie in with the railroads of New England, and to prevent the Grand Trunk, using the 5' 6" gauge, from tapping the flow and diverting it to Montreal. The increased ease of transportation, by rail, they felt, would surely lure lumbermen to their system. By barge, it took ten days to carry lumber from Bytown to Lake Champlain. In four days, the railway would have the wood in Massachusetts.[30] However, the Bytown and Prescott Railway was a fiasco, for trans-shipment across the St. Lawrence proved prohibitively expen-

---

[25]Joseph Pope, *Memoirs of the Right Honourable Sir John Alexander Macdonald*, vol. 1 (Ottawa, 1894), p. 71.

[26]Lower, *North American Assault.*

[27]James Little, a lumberman, grumbled, "It is, I am aware, the general opinion of the people of the United States that Canada benefitted largely by the Reciprocity Treaty while in force, but the very reverse is the fact as regards lumber—Canada lost millions by that treaty. It stimulated production among us to such an extent that the same description of lumber which, the year before it took effect, sold in the Buffalo market at from thirteen to fifteen dollars per thousand feet, paying one dollar duty, could not be disposed of in the same market at seven dollars per thousand three years after Reciprocity came into force." Lower, *North American Assault,* p. 146.

[28]James Bruce, 8th Earl of Elgin, *Conditions and Prospects of Canada in 1854,* (Quebec, 1855), p. 17.

[29]Lower, *North American Assault,* p. 110.

[30]Ibid., p. 111.

sive. Besides, the Bytown terminus was poorly placed, requiring extra handling of lumber from the mills to the railway. At any rate, the attempt was premature. Rail costs could not hope to compete with river transportation. Bytown was still basically a square timber and deal town, and the bulky square timber made water by far the most economical route. Montreal and Quebec had won out over Boston.

Railways pushed into all sections of Upper Canada, generally meeting with better success than the Bytown and Prescott. The Trent River district was tapped by the Peterborough and Cobourg Railway, which tied it to the lake schooner system shipping to Oswego and New York. In the pre-railway period, Peterborough had shipped 3 to 4 million feet of lumber a year by water and wagon. In 1854, this leaped to 20 million feet, by railway.

The Midland, the Northern, the Buffalo and Lake Huron railways, all knitted Upper Canada into the American metropolitan pattern. From 1840, lake towing and schooner routes crisscrossed Lake Erie and Lake Ontario. Fed by railways, Kingsville, Port Dover, Oakville, Toronto, Whitby, Cobourg, Port Hope and Kingston, termini of the lake shipping routes, developed into busy trading centres. Oswego was receiving annually 2 million feet of Upper Canadian timber in 1840; a decade later this had soared to 60 million feet. Oakville is a typical example of the fantastic growth stimulated by the new means of communication, 550,501 feet being exported in 1840, and 4,518,500 feet in 1850.[31] By 1853, no less than 51 ports in the Province of Canada were shipping at least 1 million feet of planks and boards each to the United States, with the unlikely centres of Burwell and Belleville leading the parade.[32] The most dramatic correlation of railway and lumbering is that of Simcoe County. A minor producer of lumber in 1850, the area was first tapped in 1853 by the Northern Railway, which pushed through to Collingwood in 1855. By 1861, Simcoe was the leading county in Upper Canada in lumber production.[33] "Whether tapping new areas of pine forests was the primary motive or not, when a railway was actually built, the result inevitably was a rapid growth in the number of sawmills along it and a corresponding increase in shipment of lumber to the lake ports to which the railroad was tributary."[34]

The railway boom represented a dramatic struggle between New York and Montreal for control of the trade of Upper Canada, and the routes to the West. Myriad lines on the north-south axis competed with the Grand Trunk for the riches of Upper Canada. In lumber, throughout the central area, the victory went to the Americans. But, at this time, it was a hollow victory, for the one area they could not drain with their railroads was the Ottawa Valley, the heart of the lumber community in Upper Canada.

The lumberman of legend, mackinaw-clad, hobnail-shod, this was the

---

[31]Ibid., p. 117.

[32]*Tables of the Trade and Navigation of the Province of Canada for the Year 1853* (Quebec, 1854).

[33]Lower, *North American Assault*, p. 119. Simcoe County produced 207,954,000 feet in 1861.

[34]Ibid., p. 118.

lumberjack of the Ottawa; the Spartan life of the camboose, the giant drive, the roistering plague of Quebec, this was the lumber community of the Ottawa. Lumbering in the Ottawa was unlike lumbering anywhere else in British North America. It was an almost completely professional trade, carried on by "a regular labour force which increasingly became differentiated from the rural population and came to constitute rather a part of an urban proletariat."[35] The lumberer was that, nothing else. Perhaps Professor Clark should have coined a new phrase, "rural proletariat." Quebec suffered under the lumberer's celebrating for a few summer weeks, Bytown for a few more in the early autumn. But the woods and the river were his life. His contacts with the outside world were few and tenuous but his relations with the farm population were equally distant. The lumber community of the Ottawa Valley was a world unto itself, proud, vigorous, vicious, recognizing no law but its own.

Lumbering came to the Ottawa Valley in 1804, with the establishment of the Meares and Hamiltons at Hawkesbury. Then, in 1806, from Hull, 'the father of the Ottawa', Philemon Wright, late of Woburn, Massachusetts, floated his first raft to Quebec. Soon the Rideau River was tapped by other Americans, Braddish Billings and William Marr, who sold their timber to Wright on the Ottawa. The Upper Canadian side of the Ottawa River, in Nepean Township, was first settled by Ira Honeywell, yet another emigrant from the United States.

It was not, however, until the canal era that the Valley really found itself. In 1825 the Lachine Canal eased passage along the St. Lawrence. Encouraged with sanguine hopes, Hull (at the time still called Wrightsville), grew from a population of 703 in 1820, to 1,066 in 1828. In addition to three schools, four sawmills and 12 lime-kilns, it now boasted two hotels, two distilleries, and a brewery.[36] Life was merry on the Ottawa in 1828! With the completion of the Rideau Canal in 1832, two great advantages accrued to the Valley. Not only were the timber lands along the Rideau linked into the Ottawa system, but a ready labour force was provided in the workers imported to build the canal. It is estimated that some 2,000 Irish labourers joined the lumber community upon completion of the works.[37] A series of slides along the Ottawa River completed the system, making it a matter of only six weeks to drive from Bytown to Quebec.

American influences entered the Ottawa early. As we have seen, the early settlers were almost exclusively United States born, Wright at Hull, Honeywell in Nepean Township, Billings on the Rideau. It was an age of great stirrings in the United States. As the East filled up, ambitious young men set out seeking greener fields. Hardened in the stern school of frontier America, they were more likely to find what they sought in the wilderness of the Ottawa than were British emigrants. However, at this

---

[35]S. D. Clark, *The Social Development of Canada* (Toronto, 1942), p. 210.

[36]A. H. D. Ross, *Ottawa Past and Present* (Toronto, 1927), pp. 18-19.

[37]Blodwen Davies, *Ottawa* (Toronto, 1954), p. 58.

stage, their nationality made little difference. They could only centre their business on Quebec, not the United States. Direct American contact with the Valley came in 1835. New York had tied Lake Champlain into her system with the Champlain Canal in 1822. Then in 1835 the Richelieu Canal carried the line to the St. Lawrence. Nevertheless, little of the trade was tapped. Square timbering was the most simple and most profitable business for the lumbermen of the Ottawa, and square timber went through Quebec to Great Britain.

During the 1850s, when American railroad and timber interests eagerly turned their eyes to Canada, Bytown received more than its share of this attention. Relying on the square timber trade, Bytown had never become a mill town. But, soon after, Captain Levi Young of Maine built a sawmill on the Canada West side of the river in 1851. Other Americans followed hard on his heels, among them O. H. Ingram, A. H. Baldwin, and the New York syndicate of Harris, Bronson, Perley, and Pattlee, all great names in the development of the lumber trade. In 1854, E. B. Eddy arrived in Bytown and began to build his empire of wood. The trade of the Ottawa was reorganized. The influx of the American capital created a great boom in the lumber community. T. C. Keefer, the great hydraulic engineer, marvelled at the prosperity in 1854. "I speak from experience when I say that I never saw elsewhere money more plentiful and the means of comfort more universally diffused than on the Upper Ottawa."[38]

As the experience of the Bytown and Prescott Railway showed, American railroad interest fared rather more poorly than American mill owners. A more realistic venture, the St. Lawrence and Ottawa Grand Junction Railway confined itself to carrying supplies to the lumber community, and lived a healthy, if unspectacular, existence.

The new mills of the 1850s brought the Valley into the American board trade on a larger scale than previously. And even though sawn lumber continued a secondary industry as the trade in square timber boomed to new heights, its appearance was in the long run significant, in that it provided an alternative market for wood, preventing the Ottawa Valley from facing a crisis such as confronted New Brunswick when the square timber trade collapsed after 1865.

The importance of the lumber trade to the Ottawa Valley is difficult to overstress. Almost everybody in the Valley was connected in some way or another with logging. Even the appearance of Bytown itself spoke of the debt it owed to the forests. "It is, in fact," wrote John Godley in 1844, "half a town and half a wood: the stumps are scattered through the gardens of the houses, and pine-trees through the streets, so that points of view might actually be selected in the middle of the town where you would lose sight of buildings altogether, and might fancy yourself in the primeval forest."[39] Firms like Egan and Company ruled the Valley. In 1855, this financial giant employed 3,800 men in 100 lumbering estab-

---

[38]Lower, *North American Assault*, p. 109.

[39]John Robert Godley, *Letters from America*, vol. 1 (London, 1844), p. 113.

lishments. Seventeen hundred horses, 200 bullocks and 400 double teams were kept on the road for food and forage conveyance. This company also spent some $2 million a year in its operations.[40]

The realization of this dependence upon the timber trade helped make relations between the lumbering and farming communities much easier than elsewhere in British North America. The forest completely dominated the Valley. The drainage basin of the Ottawa is some 8,000 square miles, of which only about one-eighth is arable. Furthermore, unlike Western Upper Canada, which lay directly in the path of agrarian settlement, the Valley was isolated, and offered few enticements to the settler. There the lumberman was the pioneer. The early inhabitants were quick to recognize that the region offered little future for agriculture, and they turned to the riches of the forest.

Yet, as lumbering became a major industry employing thousands of labourers, the demand for supplies became heavy. Despite unfavourable conditions, agriculture was stimulated. Farmers flocked along the paths cut by the timbermen. These were not the typical many-sided farmers of Upper Canada, but rather specialized businessmen, engaged in the work of feeding the lumber camps. The business was a steady and reliable one. Quite frequently, indeed, the lumberers themselves established farmers near their cuttings to produce supplies convenient to hand. Even when the lumbermen moved on, the markets did not immediately dry up. So poor was the soil farther north along the Ottawa that the farmers near the camps could not satisfy the demand. As the industry moved along, the farmers left in the rear would still join in the business. During the late 1840s, farmers of Carleton County still carried oats, hay, pork and butter to the camps, now on the Madawaska and Bonnechere, a trip of one to three weeks.[41]

We can get some idea of the advantage to the farmer of the supply trade by comparing the prices of 1830, when this trade was just beginning to become important, and of 1880, when the camps had moved too far north for individual farmers to continue in the business. Whereas the price of wood increased from $1 to $5 a cord, of butter from 14¢ to 25¢ a pound, and of port wine from 80¢ to $2.75 a gallon in the 50-year interval, flour remained steady at $3 per hundredweight and pork dropped from $15 to $12 a barrel.[42] In other words, prices generally increased substantially between 1830 and 1880, except in those products farmers had sold, in the earlier period, for boom prices, to the lumbermen.

This attitude of cooperation, so strange in the relations of the farming and lumbering communities in British North America, began to break down after 1850. The Valley, within easy reach of the Quebec market, was becoming exhausted. Lumberers were anxious to seize whatever timber remained in the area, since the new sawmills at Bytown could now cut second-grade wood for the United States market. To see the

40Charles Richard Weld, *A Vacation Tour in the United States and Canada* (London, 1855), pp. 101-2.

41Lower, *Forest Frontier*, p. 46.

42Haight, *Country Life in Canada Fifty Years Ago*, p. 107.

farmers burning trees on their property drove the lumbermen to frenzy. They purchased control, for the small Crown Land down-payment, of every available piece of land. When they had stripped the property of its timber, they allowed the option to lapse, considering their deposit well-invested. The farmers were just as anxious for the land. As the best public lands of Upper Canada began to fill up, the Ottawa Valley received an influx of settlers interested only in agriculture. Land control became an open war between the two communities.

With the breaking of the Tory government cliques with their commercial interests in the 1840s, the official attitude changed also. Sir Richard Bonnycastle typified the growing governmental hostility to the lumber trade. Of the Trent River district, where square timbering flourished, he remarked that it would soon be open to settlers but was "now known only to wretched lumbermen."[43] The failure to complete the Trent Canal he regarded as an unmitigated evil. "In short, had the Trent Canal been finished, instead of the miserable timber slides, which now encumber that noble river, another million of inhabitants would, in ten years more, have filled up the forests, which are now only penetrated by the Indians or the seeker after timber."[44]

As the duel of settler and lumberer went on, a harsh reality became obvious to all who would see. The forests of the Ottawa were not inexhaustible. Complaints of the settlers led to the whole question of preservation of the forests and classification of the land being raised by "The Select Committee Appointed to Examine and Report upon the Present System of Management of the Public Lands," set up by the Legislative Assembly of the Province of Canada in 1854. After the breaking of the governmental cliques by the advent of Responsible Government, the exploiters were very definitely on the defensive, as the testimony before this committee shows. Like the Bytown *Gazette*, they pleaded for co-operation between lumberers and agriculturalists. "For our own part, we consider the country so obviously adapted for both pursuits, that its general welfare and individual prosperity would be overlooked were not both attended to. . . . These two classes mutually assist each other and both are deserving the thanks of their country."[45]

James Henry Burke of Bytown was the spokesman of the lumber community before the Select Committee. He too called for co-operation and division of the land into its proper functions. "We go in for keeping a fair line of separation between the lumbering and agricultural region, as nature has laid it down."[46] He defended the existing land grant system (so easily abused by lumbermen), and the domination of large areas by speculators. He ended with a rousing defence of the social position of the lumbermen. "The manufacturer of timber leads the backwoodsman into the interior where that lumbermen opens up for him a market . . . on the

[43]Bonnycastle, *Canada and the Canadians in 1846*, p. 235.

[44]Ibid., p. 236.

[45]Bytown *Gazette*, Thursday, November 2, 1843.

[46]Appendix to the Thirteenth Volume of the Journals of the Legislature of the Province of Canada, Session 1854–1855, Appendix MM, (Quebec, 1855).

lumber trade then the farmer depends, and the settlement of the land upon the inducement given by the local market formed by timber making."[47] The agriculturalist, on the contrary, made no attempt at compromise. They had the votes, the country was theirs and they would have it. William Spragge of the Crown Lands Department held that "the sanctioning or tolerating [of] speculation in the public lands, and the accomplishing their actual settlement, are incompatible, the one with the other."[48] He proposed that a person buying Crown Land should be given only four months to settle that land. And a large percentage of the purchase price should be paid in advance, "to guard against the land being plundered of its timber, and then abandoned."[49]

Such opinions generally prevailed in Canada West. With most of her best land by now occupied or else controlled by speculators, the province found herself in a backwater of immigration. The flow of settlement swept by her to the Mid-western United States. She felt her future was sorely threatened in this by-passing, for her only major industry was lumbering, universally regarded as a transient trade. New lands had to be opened, then, to attract settlers, and they had to be kept from the hands of exploiters. Roads were projected to Lake Nipissing, to the Magnetawan River, interlacing the north to open it for settlement. Unfortunately, the government frequently found that, "The parties most directly interested in the opening of roads appeared to desire them to be made rather for the purpose of getting out timber than for the sake of the soil."[50]

All too little heed was paid to the arguments of John Henry Burke and the lumber community. Their interests were selfish, their behavior often unscrupulous, but their programme of land classification was sound. Unmoved, the government despatched surveyors to the area west of the Ottawa in 1855 and 1856. It was found eminently unsatisfactory for agriculture, and the surveyor, Walter Shanly, urged that it be turned over to lumbering, initially, which would provide an impetus to settlement.[51] But his words went in vain. Officials carried on their mad schemes of settlement, determined to turn all land to agriculture. Without classification of the land, tragedies such as struck the unhappy Germans brought to Renfrew in 1856, were all too prevalent.

The lumberman, perhaps even more than the agriculturalist, was the true pioneer of British North America. He pushed on ahead of the government, ahead of the farmer, opening the hinterland of Canada. But, in doing so, he became introverted. The lumber trade was not one designed to produce the clean-out, all-round, all-Canadian personality. The lumberman spent from September to June in the woods, cutting and hauling the logs. Late June and July were occupied with the drive to Quebec. His

---

[47]Ibid.
[48]Ibid.
[49]Ibid.
[50]Ibid.
[51]Lower, *Forest Frontier*, p. 52.

only contacts with the outside world were during a few weeks in Quebec, spent in a whirl of drinking and wenching. Then the routine started all over again.

Even those not directly concerned with the cutting of timber were isolated. Bytown was a city living almost exclusively for the lumber trade. It was an island in the forest, kept afloat with wooden moorings. Even the lumber merchant, the great entrepreneur of Montreal or Quebec, lived and thought only for the trade. He was constantly alert for any alteration of the routine, an alteration which could spell ruin. Isolated, delicately-balanced, the lumber community was ultra-conservative.

This insularity, rule of habit and routine, and highly sensitive economic balance, manifested itself in the politics of the Ottawa Valley. Few papers in Upper Canada could have been more conservative than the *Gazette,* the voice of Bytown. Sir Francis Bond Head, the arch-rascal to liberal Canadians, carried an aura of divinity for the *Gazette.* When, in 1836, the Reformers attacked Bond Head, the paper rallied to his support. In a very businesslike commercial fashion, we see the *Gazette* asserting that placemen in the Legislature, like the employees of a firm, should owe their loyalty only to their employer.[52] An interesting political thesis! On Bond Head's departure in 1838, the *Gazette* rose to a pitch of loyalty and tearfully waved him adieu. "There are very few of our readers but will deeply regret that our excellent Lieutenant Governor, Sir Francis Bond Head is about to leave us."[53]

The lumber community of Upper Canada was more concerned with the mechanics of the trade than its political and financial ramifications. The politics of the lumber trade remained primarily those of Montreal.[54] The Family Compact, unlike the Chateau Clique, was made up largely of landowners, not merchants. It was a social and political, rather than a commercial, alliance. But the incidental commercial interests of some members of the ruling group did align them with the lumber-kings of Montreal and Bytown and led to clashes, similar to, albeit less frequent than, the merchant-agriculturalist battles of Lower Canada. The public loans for canal building on the St. Lawrence in the 1820s were carried only against severe opposition.

Throughout the years the lumber community had little sympathy with the Reform cause. Their prosperity was firmly anchored upon the status quo. The lumbermen joined in William Lyon Mackenzie's dissatisfaction with the banking system, but for entirely different reasons than that radical. In November 1836, the Ottawa Lumber Association called a meeting in order to demand greater bank capital for business expansion, to be readily available at Bytown. However, far from backing Mackenzie, who wished to curtail banking activity, they supported the bank laws he

[52]Bytown *Gazette*, Thursday, December 15, 1836.

[53]Ibid., Wednesday, January 24, 1838.

[54]See, Mason Wade, *The French Canadians* (Toronto, 1955); Creighton, *Empire of the St. Lawrence.*

attacked. "The excuse the Banks made for not being able to afford the necessary accommodation is the want of capital; and in this view it is but fair that their application to the Legislature should be supported."[55] Mackenzie disturbed the lumber community again with the Seventh Report on Grievances. Its proposals for heavy duties on American grain, flour, and meal, along with other provisions posed the same threat as the Huskisson tariffs of 1825. The free trade area of the lakes was almost as important to the lumber community as the closed trading area of the Empire.

The defeat of Mackenzie was a victory for the trading interests. Having weathered this storm, the lumber community continued to rally to the defence of the profitable British connection. During the administration crisis of 1844, loyalty stirred in hearts throughout the Ottawa Valley. To the Reformers they thundered, "No, Gentlemen; we want no 'responsibility' such as you could offer us. There is more 'responsibility' on Metcalfe's finger, than in your whole body politic."[56]

Even with the collapse of the colonial system, the basic conservatism of the lumber community was little shaken. After it had vented its spleen in the Annexation Manifesto, it drew together once more to salvage what it could from the ruins. Reform, or liberalism, meant retrenchment, slackening of public works. Conservatism, on the contrary, stood for the expansion of business. Agriculture against commerce, the war was still fought out in the arena of politics. Politics meant, pre-eminently, economics. The chief enemy of lumbering was not Baldwin, not Lafontaine, but Hincks, the "Ancient Chiseler," the "Port Sarnia Monkey."[57]

This thinking continued through Confederation. John A. Macdonald captured the imagination of the lumber community with his National Policy. While we obviously cannot draw too much from them, the election returns from lumbering areas demonstrate this feeling. Of eleven major lumber ridings in 1867, eight were carried by the Conservatives. The election of 1871 was even more decisive, ten of the eleven returning Conservatives or Conservative-Independents. Most of these constituencies had an amazing record of Conservative loyalty. Frontenac voted Tory from 1867 through 1891, Glengarry from 1867 to 1894, and Carleton from 1871 through 1914.[58]

Politically, then, lumbering was a stabilizing factor, firmly committed to the status quo. Socially, however, its effect upon the Ottawa Valley was traumatic. The first lumbermen on the Ottawa were French Canadians, apparently reasonably well-behaved and peaceable. "The French *habitans* make the best shanty-men; they are more cheerful and less likely to fight and quarrel, notwithstanding their evil propensities of card-playing and cock-fighting."[59] However, after the completion of the Rideau Canal and the draw of the lumber trade after that time upon the

---

[55]The Bytown *Gazette*, Thursday, November 17, 1836.

[56]Ibid., Thursday, April 4, 1844.

[57]Ibid., Thursday, December 21, 1848.

[58]Jesse Edgar Middleton and Fred Landon, *The Province of Ontario, A History*, vol. 2, (Toronto, 1927), pp. 1323–46.

[59]Samuel Strickland, *Twenty-Seven Years in Canada West*, vol. 2 (London, 1853), p. 285.

flow of immigration, Irish and Scots began to pour into the camps, replacing the French. The clash of racial groups, with employment rivalry
urging them on, convulsed the Valley for a decade. The so-called "Shiners War" was waged between 1837 and 1845 in the woods, along the
slides and in the streets of Bytown. The term, 'Shiner', has been variously described as derived from 'cheneur' or 'oakman', the black silk hats
'shiners', worn by greenhorns arriving in Bytown, or from the newly-
minted half crown coins with which the lumberers were paid. At any
event, it became universally used of the Irish emigrants who flooded the
Valley. Establishing themselves in the area of Bytown known as 'Cork
Town', centered about the picturesque 'Mother McGinty's Tavern', the
Shiners soon made their presence felt. The first recorded disturbance
was on St. Patrick's Day, 1828, when an Englishman, Thomas Ford,
clashed with a group of Irishmen, and was slain for his bravado.

"For nine or ten years these lawless fellows terrorized many peaceable
citizens by such playful antics as going to an enemy's house, stripping
the children of their clothing and making them run through the snow-
drifts, scattering the furniture over a radius of a hundred yards, or blow-
ing up the little home with gunpowder."[60] In 1837, matters came to a
head. Irish immigration into the Valley was then at a peak. With the
bank crisis of that year, a heavy rise in the cost of provisions and the
general financial stability, jobs in the lumber camps were at a premium.
The Irish determined to drive the French Canadians from the woods, and
by 1845 had succeeded in doing so.

Three magistrates at Bytown, G. W. Baker, Daniel O'Connor, and
Daniel Fisher graphically described the situation in a letter to the Provincial Secretary, dated January 28, 1837.

> Bytown being the focus of the lumber trade, is frequented at all seasons by
> a great number of raftsmen, among whom are some desperate characters
> and others easily misled. This season in consequence of the extraordinary
> rise in the price of provisions, many men are out of employ, and others daily
> discharged and arriving here, some of them without any means of visible
> support. The inhabitants are dependant upon the lumber trade and upon
> these men, and cannot, therefore, be prevailed upon to act with energy
> against them.
>
> "Those constables who perform their duties are always marked out for
> punishment; John Perkins was first assaulted, then fired at, and at last an
> attempt was made to burn his house; John Dunn was waylaid at night, most
> severely beaten and kicked and his collar bone broken; John Mead was also
> severely beaten a few evenings since.
>
> "Last week an ox was stolen from the premises of Philemon Wright . . .
>
> "On the night of the 23rd inst. twenty-six sheep were stolen from a Cana-
> dian. . . . There is no clue to identify any of the burglars concerned, but we
> have every reason to suppose that said sheep were taken up the Gatineau
> River to the chantiers where the rioters . . . are employed.
>
> "Numerous wanton assaults are committed in the town and neighbour-
> hood but the delinquents are either unknown or the sufferers afraid to ap-
> pear against them.[61]

---

[60]Ross, *Ottawa Past and Present*, p. 113.
[61]Middleton and Landon, *The Province of Ontario*, p. 917.

The citizens of the town were forced to unite in "The Association of the Preservation of the Public Peace in Bytown," a vigilante group. But even when the Irish had won their 'war', the disturbances did not end. Freed after long months in the bush, violence erupted whenever lumbermen were in Bytown. "Anything short of murder may be committed with impunity; and even murder has been allowed to pass comparatively unnoticed. . . ."[62]

This violent reaction to freedom was accentuated by the strict regimen of shanty life. In the early period of the trade, the shanty was an unruly haven of the 'rugged individual'. John McGregor, during the early 1830s, described a typical camp, with each lumberman enjoying a 'morning': a drink of raw whiskey—before—his breakfast.[63] However, as the timber business became even more professional, employers could not afford to allow drunkenness and misbehavior among their men. The Earl of Elgin, writing in 1854, reported that, "For some years past, intoxicating liquors have been vigorously excluded from almost all of the chantiers (shanties) . . . and . . . the result of the experiment has been entirely satisfactory."[64] Indeed, the programme of rising with the sun, working till dusk in the woods and then wearily falling into a cot, left little time for licentious behavior by the professional lumberman. Joshua Fraser assures us that by 1883 there was "government and discipline in shanty life, just as pronounced and strictly carried out as in the most exemplary and well-regulated village, town or city corporation of the Dominion. . . ."[65]

Small wonder, then, that the lumbermen, released from eight months of Spartan life, reacted like proverbial 'wild Indians'. When the drive began, all bedlam broke loose. Under its constant pressure and danger, nerves became taut. Tension was released in drink. "In the matter of scenting out and appropriating whiskey," the lumberman was "as keen as a weasel, as cunning as a fox, and as unscrupulous as a wolf."[66] And every few miles along the Ottawa were to be found taverns dispensing "rank vitrolized poison, under the name of good-whiskey."[67] As the drive swept by, farms near the river were terrorized. Langton reported of the raftsmen, "It is a hard and dangerous life but they are a light-hearted set of dare-devils and the greatest rascals and thieves withal that ever a peaceable country was tormented with. Hen roosts have quite disappeared from the river side and lambs and little pigs have to be kept under lock and key."[68]

The lumbermen struck Quebec like a cyclone. Having safely delivered their rafts, they received their wages in a lump sum. In the terms of Canada of that time, this was an immense amount of money—perhaps

---

[62]Ottawa *Argus*, Wednesday, January 16, 1850.

[63]John McGregor, *British America*, (London, 1833), vol. 2, p. 494.

[64]Elgin, *Conditions and Prospects*, p. 82.

[65]Joshua Fraser, *Shanty, Forest and River Life in the Backwoods of Canada* (Montreal, 1883), p. 26.

[66]Ibid., p. 112.

[67]Ibid., p. 331.

[68]Langton, *Early Days in Upper Canada*, p. 206.

£30.[69] They squandered it all on "the fiddle, the female, or the fire-water."[70] Writers of the period delighted in describing the summer roisterings of the colourful woodsmen. John McGregor, at Quebec in 1833, viewed the arrival of the lumbermen. "After selling and delivering up their rafts, they pass some weeks in idle indulgence, drinking, smoking and *dashing off* in a long coat, flashy waistcoat and trousers, Wellington or Hessian boots, a handkerchief of many colours round the neck, a watch with a long tinsel chain and numberless brass seals, and an *umbrella*."[71] The Rev. A. W. H. Rose followed the raftsman to the end of his summer. "He . . . buys a gay suit of clothes, seldom forgetting a particularly smart waistcoat, brushes up ad libitum, and 'sets up for a gentleman', too often indulging in a life of low debauchery, till his cash is gone, his health perhaps shaken; he parts with his gay apparel, if it has not been already destroyed in some drunken row, shoulders his axe, and sets off again to the wilderness penniless, if not, moreover, in debt."[72] It is no surprise, then, that they constituted a rural proletariat, returning to the woods year after year; few could afford to do anything else.

Under such conditions, the Ottawa Valley attracted far more than her share of violence and unrest, and even, despite its essential conservatism, of political unrest. On September 17, 1849, Reformers and Tories clashed in Bytown over an address to Lord Elgin on the Rebellion Losses Bill. In the riot, known as "Stormy Monday," one man was slain and 20 more injured. But a brawl could start more easily over an insult, a racial slur, or even a mud splash, than politics. From the mid-1830s, religious disorders troubled the Valley. With the significant increase of the Roman Catholic population, due to Southern Irish immigration, anti-Catholicism became militant. Aggressive Orange Lodges sprang up in every major town, and St. Patrick's Day invariably was marked by violence, to be repaid with interest on July 12.

We thus must disagree with S. D. Clark's generalizations upon the social conditions of Upper Canada. He tells us, "Political unrest was symptomatic of disturbances extending through the entire range of the pioneer society of Upper Canada . . . The failure of the rural inhabitants to secure cultural status combined with their failure to secure political status."[73] He speaks, too, of Upper Canada as an "agrarian frontier."

The social problems of Upper Canada were far from uniform, and most definitely not exclusively those of an agrarian frontier. The Ottawa was a frontier, but a commercial frontier. Clark has not distinguished between the frontier and rural areas in his generalizations. The "agrarian frontier" of which he speaks was rather the middle area of the province, for example, the Home and Midland districts, where discontent was settled in the Rebellion of 1837. In the Rebellion, the two true frontier areas, the Huron Tract, and the Ottawa Valley, were almost com-

---

[69]Godley, *Letters from America*, p. 115.

[70]Bonnycastle, *Canada and the Canadians in 1846*, p. 70.

[71]McGregor, *British America*, p. 496.

[72](A. W. H. Rose) A Pioneer of the Wilderness, *The Emigrant Churchman in Canada*, (London, 1849), p. 3.

[73]Clark, *Social Development of Canada*, p. 215.

pletely quiescent. Commercial prosperity, rather than 'cultural status' or the lack thereof, was the only potent political consideration in the Ottawa frontier.

The Ottawa was a commercial frontier, just as, in the initial stage of their development, most Canadian areas were. Due to geographical immensity and difficulty, the pattern of growth in Canada was fairly uniform: first came the exploiting business pioneers, operating on an itinerant basis; then the government, seeking to encourage settlement and organizing the territory; and, finally, the sedentary settlers, usually agriculturalists. Such has been the pattern throughout the age of the fur trade, the era of the lumber trade, that of the railway, and, today, of the mining and petroleum industries.

As to the question of cultural or social status, this had but little bearing upon the Ottawa Valley. The frontiersman did not seek social status—there was none to be had. There was only nationality and skill. It was only with a degree of affluence, creating a desire for more, that the psychology of which Professor Clark speaks came into play.

By Confederation, however, this picture of the brawling king of the Ottawa was beginning to alter. The lumber community had been the heart, the very life, of the Valley. It opened the area, it fed it, it nurtured its towns and its farms. But by 1867 the ungrateful children were rebelling against their wooden mother. 'Twas ever thus. Inevitably, the Ottawa could not escape the struggle for land control, the war of merchant and farmer which did so much to retard Canada's growth.

Yet, with what we have seen, we must agree with Professor Lower that, "Undoubtedly the forest has been, if not the prime determinant, at any rate a major determinant in North American life."[74] The significance of the lumber community for the life of British North America is difficult to overestimate. In two areas, New Brunswick and the Ottawa Valley, all life rotated about it. It has been estimated that during the Napoleonic Wars, 17 out of every 20 citizens of New Brunswick were dependent upon the lumber trade,[75] while in the Ottawa Valley, by 1864, some 25,000 men were engaged in lumbering.[76] For Lower Canada and central Upper Canada, the difference between subsistence and prosperity was often lumber. In New Brunswick and the Ottawa, the difference was between life and death.

Lumbering created a whole new society; it opened the doors for industry. By 1861, Upper Canada could boast 15 axe and edge-tool factories, 33 plants producing sashes and doors, 41 shingle factories, 11 match factories, and 143 plants described as producing "cabinet ware."[77] All these industries were directly created by the lumber trade. Not only did timbering produce the raw materials which these trades

---

[74]Lower, *North American Assault*, p. 27.

[75]W. S. MacNutt, "The Politics of the Timber Trade in Colonial New Brunswick," *Canadian Historical Review*, 31 (March 1949), 47–65.

[76]Samuel Phillips Day, *English America* (London, 1864), p. 228.

[77]Lower, *North American Assault*, p. 144.

used, but it lured capital into the country, capital which was the lifeblood of the entire economy of British North America.

Politically, the lumber community led the defence of the status quo. It stood against Responsible Government, to protect the colonies' invaluable links with London, and its powerful ties with St. John, Quebec and Toronto. When this world crashed down about it between 1844 and 1849, the lumber community proved the vigour of its frontier background and the cunning of its metropolitan basis. It accepted Responsible Government on its own terms in New Brunswick, and helped found a new, powerful Conservative party in Canada.

Socially, it made its own world. In the timber lands, there was no law but that of the lumber community. Each spring it loosed its unruly mobs on the outside communities, and, drawing life from these demi-savages, the communities could only bear the curse. Legislation could not reform the lumber communities, as New Brunswick found with her ill-fated prohibitory laws of 1856.[78] As in all matters, the lumbermen imposed controls upon themselves only when the interests of business dictated. Their politics and their morals, both were formed in the mold of commerce.

The lumber community does not present an attractive picture. It was avaricious, uncultured, foolhardy, vicious. It was a society organized for only one purpose—material gain. But wherever it went in British North America, it left its mark. The mark was not always a pretty one. Yet, the wealth it produced, the industry it attracted, and the frontiers it opened, make the lumber industry one of the fountainheads of Canadian civilization.

---

[78]In 1856 the New Brunswick Legislature passed a law prohibiting the importation, manufacture or sale of liquor. An election was called on the issue, and the lumber interests, deeming liquor essential in the woods, returned an Assembly which repealed the bill. See, James Hannay, *History of New Brunswick*, vol. 2.

20

THE TRANSFER OF BRITISH IDEAS ON IMPROVED FARMING TO ONTARIO DURING THE FIRST HALF OF THE 19TH CENTURY*

Kenneth Kelly

Despite the economic importance of lumbering, agriculture remained the principal industry in pre-Confederation British North America. Given this fact, the relative absence of serious historical study of agriculture is a bit surprising. Nevertheless, it remains true that we know surprisingly little about how farmers went about their business in the early period. There is, of course, a received view of farming practice, which began in the contemporary literature and has persisted ever since. Early farmers have always had a very bad press. Observer after observer—and historian after historian—have commented on the wanton wastefulness of the farmer, who exploited the land in extensive agriculture with never a care for tomorrow. According to this view, as much land as possible was quickly cleared, hastily planted in a limited number of cash crops, and farmed generally in ways as far removed from the techniques of scientific European agriculture of the period as it was possible to get. The process of the expansion of settlement was equally exploitative. When the newly-cleared land had been worked for a few years—and exhausted—the frontiersman moved on, selling his "worn-out" farm to a recently arrived immigrant. Such criticisms and observations have become part of the standard version of Canadian history, fitting very nicely into conceptions of settler exploitation of non-renewable raw materials which has long been a central theme of the story of our early development. Farmland, forest, and mineral deposit were exhausted as rapidly as the mania for quick profit could manage.

As Kenneth Kelly suggests in the following article, the received pic-

Ontario History, 62 (1971), 103–111.

ture has some obvious weaknesses. It assumes, for instance, that immigrants immediately dropped their own cultural background upon arrival in North America in favour of a new "frontier" mentality. Moreover, there is precious little concrete evidence for such matters as soil exhaustion, which are central to the general interpretation. What is Kelly's overall conclusion? What are the limitations of the sorts of evidence with which he deals? How has the older view been questioned?

SUGGESTIONS FOR FURTHER READING

E. C. Guillet, *The Pioneer Farmer and Backwoodsman,* 2 vols. (Toronto: University of Toronto Press, 1963).

Robert Leslie Jones, *History of Agriculture in Ontario, 1613-1880* (Toronto: University of Toronto Press, 1946).

J. David Wood, ed., *Perspectives on Landscape and Settlement in Nineteenth Century Ontario* (Toronto: McClelland and Stewart Limited, 1975).

J.M.B.

M any areas colonised by European settlers experienced duality in their development. Ready-made or preconceived facets of a way of life—such as settlement forms and patterns, agricultural types, land tenure and survey systems, and forms of social organisation—were introduced from Europe. However, adaptations were made to the conditions in the newly colonised area, the nature of the changes being governed also by the needs and resources of the settlers. This paper† discusses a single aspect of the agricultural development of Ontario through the first half of the 19th century. During this period two streams of agricultural development were in evidence; one based on the introduction of attitudes to farming and land and of farming types from Europe; the other based on adaptations, at the individual farmer level, to local physical and economic conditions. The former constituted a cultural transfer, while the latter was manifest on the land in two farming types virtually unknown in 19th-century northwestern Europe, wheat-fallow-wheat farming and the continuous cropping of a succession of grains. Cultural transfer has been credited with the introduction of a wide range of agricultural types into early 19th-century Ontario. It is hardly an exaggeration to say that, taking the literature as a whole, every ethnic group entering Ontario in significant numbers has supposedly brought with it a distinctive agriculture—or traits of that agriculture— which it practised in its homeland.

However, this paper is concerned with only one broad category of cultural transfer, the introduction into Ontario of ideas about land and agriculture derived from the British agricultural revolution and of the

---

†This study was made possible by a research grant from the National Advisory Committee on Geographical Research.

several types of improved farming[1] developed out of that revolution. The British comprised the largest group of European immigrants entering Ontario during the early 19th century. Most of the early agricultural literature is not truly descriptive or analytical, it is promotional, to encourage British agricultural types. Thus an understanding of the role of the literature as an agent of cultural transfer and as an advocate of improved farming is a prerequisite for the correct interpretation of the materials contained in it. Finally, improved farming may be loosely defined as mixed farming, and mixed farming came to dominate in Ontario during the last quarter of the 19th century. The question therefore arises as to the causal connection between the early promotion and establishment of mixed farming and its ultimate triumph in the province.

The paper develops the hypothesis that British travellers and writers and some British settlers introduced into Ontario the concepts that the soil was subject to rapid exhaustion and that an essential function of agriculture was to build up or at least to maintain soil fertility. These same agencies, using the agricultural literature, introduced various types of essentially British mixed farming as solutions to the problem of maintaining soil productivity. Towards the middle of the 19th century improved farming was advocated increasingly by Ontario writers. These writers, however, based their thinking not on local conditions, but upon European experience and knowledge.

Throughout the first half of the 19th century the agricultural literature heavily criticised and roundly condemned the dominant agriculture, charging that it caused the rapid exhaustion of the soil. Broadly, two types of farming dominated the province. On the plains lands[2] farmers customarily took a succession of different grain crops which some interrupted occasionally with a crop of legumes.[3] More widespread was what was described as continuous wheat cropping but which was in fact wheat-fallow-wheat farming with wheat alternating with a naked summer fallow. According to the agricultural literature both types destroyed the soil. William Dunlop, discussing the Norfolk plains, regarded the crop succession there as deteriorating and believed that it would cause a rapid impoverishment of the soil and, ultimately, land abandonment.[4]

---

[1]Throughout this paper improved farming is used as an alternate term to refer to the various types of mixed farming which developed out of the agricultural revolution of northwestern Europe and which embodied management techniques designed to maintain long-term soil fertility. Similarly, the terms improving farmer and improver are used only to describe a person who believed that the maintenance of soil productivity was an essential function of agriculture, that the dominant grain-based agriculture would rapidly exhaust the soil, and that only variants of northwest European mixed farming could keep the fields of Ontario productive.

[2]Plains lands were savanna-like areas of grassland with scattered groves of trees, most frequently oaks or pines. Plains lands were common along a line running approximately from Brantford to Chatham.

[3]Joseph Pickering, Emigration or No Emigration; being the Narrative of the Author (an English Farmer) from the years 1824-30 (no place or date of publication), pp. 41 and 64; William Dunlop ("A Backwoodsman"), Statistical Sketches of Upper Canada for the Use of Emigrants, 3rd ed. (London, 1833), p. 77; Joseph Abbott, The Emigrant to North America: from the Memoranda of a Settler in Canada (Montreal, 1843), pp. 74-75.

[4]Dunlop, Statistical Sketches, p. 77.

Dunlop, indeed, warned settlers against buying cleared land in any part of Ontario for "from the slovenly mode of farming practised in this country, these farms are often what we emphatically denominated exhausted."[5] It was generally agreed that the soils of Ontario were "very unfairly treated" and that given the continuation of the dominant practices "they must at length be impoverished."[6] The literature contains many similar statements but it is unnecessary to cite them here. James Johnston effectively summarises them in his allegation that "the net result of the work of the farmer on the state of the soil is to bring it by degrees to a state of more or less complete exhaustion."[7] However, an examination of such statements reveals no supporting evidence derived from Ontario in the form of, for example, an observed reduction in crop yields, land abandonment, or a decline in land values. The contention that the soils of Ontario were liable to rapid exhaustion appears to rest upon the decline in productivity of British soils which was arrested by the spread of improved farming. This cannot explain the attitude that exhaustion would be rapid, for surely the loss of soil fertility in Britain took place over many centuries. Be that as it may, agricultural writers urged Ontario farmers to learn from the experience of others and frequently noted with regret that while in Europe soils were being built up in Ontario they were being destroyed. John Lynch of Brampton warned his readers as follows:

> If there is any truth in . . . the experience of other and older countries, the time will come—if this system [heavy grain cropping] be continued—when the present rich and productive land of Canada will not only fail to produce the heavy crop of wheat which it now does, but will become incapable of producing wheat at all to any profitable amount.[8]

The main point of the criticism of the dominant agriculture came to be, then, that it was unlike the improved farming of Britain. The literature frequently warned the would-be immigrant that he would find few signs of the fruits of the agricultural revolution in Ontario. John Galt, for example, writing in the early 1830s observed that the British farmer on arrival in the province would find that "agriculture there is as yet practised in the rudest manner."[9] Nor did the situation change rapidly. As late as 1851 James Johnston could lament that "little knowledge of improved agriculture has hitherto been diffused in Upper Canada; and it is, as yet, among practical men, held in little esteem."[10] This gave rise to the notion that Ontario farmers were slovenly, lazy, and ignorant; in the eyes of many writers only this could explain the farmers' failure to convert to improved agriculture.

---

[5]Ibid., pp. 26–27.

[6]Martin Doyle, *Hints on Emigration to Upper Canada*, 2nd ed. (Dublin, 1832), p. 16.

[7]James F. W. Johnston, *Notes on North America*, vol. 1 (Boston, 1851), p. 358.

[8]John Lynch, "Agriculture and its Advantages as a Pursuit." *Journal and Transactions of the Board of Agriculture of Upper Canada*, 1 (1856), 199.

[9]John Galt, *The Canadas*, 2nd ed. (London, 1836), p. 294.

[10]Johnston, *Notes on North America*, p. 272.

Its advocates promoted improved farming as fulfilling their two basic principles of agriculture. The first principle, quite naturally, was that agriculture should produce food. The second was that it should at least maintain, but preferably increase, the productivity of the soil.[11] Improvers conceived of the second principle as governing the first; they believed that the need to maintain fertility should strongly influence the types and quantities of foods produced. The second principle rested at the beginning of the 19th century only on the experience of older lands, but by the middle of the century also on ideas popular in Europe which had emerged from the new science of soil chemistry. Both experience and scientific experiment indicated that in the course of cropping "soil nutrients are constantly withdrawn by the plant," and it follows then that "means must be adopted to supply them to the soil, and [that] the main part of the Economics of Agriculture is to consider how this supply may be kept up."[12] The imported concept of rapid soil exhaustion, then, which initially was based only on the experience of older lands, was reinforced or confirmed by a fresh wave of ideas imported from Europe, the principles of soil chemistry. This linkage with scientific advances in Europe is frequently masked in the Ontario literature because the improvers preferred to use more homely images when addressing farmers. Professor Watts, for example, urged that the farmer be encouraged to "regard his field as a purse, containing some money to start with," and to remember that "if he takes all out, and puts none in, he will soon see the bottom of his purse."[13] James Farewell of Oshawa in the same vein described the soil as "the treasury of the farmer's wealth" and warned that "the stores that are found therein may be husbanded with care to the wants of man, . . . or they may be wasted and dispersed in a short space of time." The conclusion which he presented to the farmer was that "the production and maintenance of soil fertility are indispensible to successful farming."[14]

It is not surprising, then, that the techniques and types of farming developed in the United Kingdom were promoted as ideals for Ontario. Many writers believed that these ideals could be introduced and established through the immigration of British farmers. Some indeed felt that nothing less than the wholesale replacement of the existing farmers by immigrants from the "better class of farmers" from Britain would be necessary to achieve the improvement of agriculture in Ontario.[15] Others thought that an admixture of good British farmers would be sufficient to attain the desired effect. The author of the *Canadian Agricultural*

---

[11]For a clear statement of these principles see, for example, William Hutton of Belleville, "Agriculture and its Advantages as a Pursuit," *Journal and Transactions of the Board of Agriculture of Upper Canada*, 1 (1856), 89.

[12]W. A. Watts, Professor of Chemistry at Victoria College, "The Economics of Agriculture." *Journal and Transactions of the Board of Agriculture of Upper Canada*, 4 (1859-60), 333.

[13]W. A. Watts, "The Economics of Agriculture," op. cit., p. 336.

[14]James Farewell, "Prize Essay on the Practical Adaption and Money Value of Science to the Canadian Farmer," *Journal and Transactions of the Board of Agriculture of Upper Canada*, 4 (1859-60), 120.

[15]See, for example, William Dunlop, *Statistical Sketches*, p. 105; and A. Lillie, *Canada: physical, economic, and social* (Toronto, 1855), pp. 155-56.

Reader, for example, wrote that the immigration of English and Scottish farmers would "generally bring to bear upon *our* lands that improved system of agriculture without which the farmers of England and Scotland could never live." With the arrival of such settlers their Ontario-born neighbours would learn something of the new farming.[16] It was through such a scattering of British settlers that Shirreff hoped that there would arise "a new generation of farmers with new opinions" which would allow the spread of improved agriculture throughout the province.[17]

However, most improvers felt that such immigration was not sufficient to achieve the rapid upgrading of Ontario's agriculture. They publicised in the Ontario literature the essentials of superior farming. The pivotal role in improved agriculture, as they discussed it, was played by livestock. They argued from the principle that the nutrient cycle should be almost closed in order to maintain soil fertility; the entire crop should be ploughed in each year. Such a course clearly was impracticable, but they believed that the principle could be approached if the farmer would plough back all of the stalks and stubble and especially if he would feed most of his crops to livestock and then apply the manure (liquid as well as solid) to the fields.[18] Under such a system and with the addition of small quantities of artificial fertilisers, soil productivity would at least be maintained. The use of livestock as agents for the return of most plant foods to the soil led the improvers to regard the rotation of crops as mandatory, for a rotation would allow the production of feed and pasture as well as cash crops.[19] They did not believe that a good crop rotation by itself could maintain soil fertility, but did feel that it would slow down the rate of depletion of nutrients.[20]

The Ontario agricultural literature promoted types of British farming as embodying the necessary components of the raising and feeding of livestock on the farm, the production of large quantities of manure, and the rotation of crops. Most writers never looked beyond British agriculture for a source of models for Ontario. John Lynch of Brampton was one of the few who did; in fact he considered the agriculture of parts of continental Europe to be far superior to that practised in Britain. Yet he, too, was content to accept and promote British types of farming as an

[16]Anonymous, *The Canadian Agricultural Reader* (Niagara, 1845), p. 3.

[17]Patrick Shirreff, *A Tour through North America: together with a Comprehensive View of the Canadas and United States as Adapted for Agricultural Emigration* (Edinburgh, 1835), p. 95.

[18]W. A. Watts, "The Economics of Agriculture," op. cit., p. 334. The farm literature of the 1840s and 1850s contains many articles giving advice on collecting, processing, and applying manure.

[19]A crop rotation also was regarded in the literature as a useful device to eliminate weeds. For example, it was noted that some crops, such as wheat, because of the way they had to be cultivated "tend to the production of weeds." Such crops should not be cultivated in succession but instead in rotation with crops "whose culture admits of the destruction of weeds;" that is with smothering crops such as peas and clover or with cleaning crops such as roots. Joseph Hobson of Guelph, "Essay on Practical Agriculture," *Journal and Transactions of the Board of Agriculture of Upper Canada,* 4 (1859–60), 161.

[20]James Farewell, "Prize Essay on the Practical Adaptation and Money Value of Science to the Canadian Farmer," op. cit., p. 125.

ideal for Ontario. In his opinion British agriculture was "sufficiently advanced to be a good school for Canadians to study in." He saw a link with improved agriculture through Britain as particularly appropriate and easy to develop in part because of the common language but especially because the United Kingdom was Ontario's major source of overseas immigrants.[21] Most improvers recommended no specific type of farming to their readers; they simply urged them to adopt "best British practice." Some, however, offered a single model (or a model and an acceptable, temporary variant). The author of the *Canadian Agricultural Reader*, after stressing the need for the *"augmentation* or at least the *preservation* of the natural fertility of the soil"—which was to be achieved only "by alternating crops, and by blending cattle with tillage husbandry"—continued as follows: "as pertinent to this subject, we subjoin some extracts from British Husbandry, pursuaded that the remarks they contain apply to Canada with almost as great force as they do to British Husbandry."[22] He recommended to his readers the British "alternate system of husbandry" which had bestowed high productivity on such inherently inferior soils as those found in Norfolk, England.

William Hutton of Belleville promoted a different variant of mixed farming; he held up the British five-course husbandry as an ideal towards which the Ontario farmer should strive. According to Hutton, this system most frequently employed the following rotation: (1) a drilled crop, either turnips or potatoes; (2) barley; (3) clover for hay; (4) clover for pasture; (5) wheat or beans. But occasionally the clover pasture of the fourth year was replaced by wheat, and oats were grown in the fifth year. Hutton saw that few farmers in Ontario could employ such a rotation because they lacked the "artificial manures, such as bone dust, oil cake, guano, etc. to cultivate so large a proportion of drilled crops" (one-fifth of the cleared area of the farm). Nevertheless, he felt strongly that farmers ought to come as close to it as possible. To allow this he suggested its modification to a six-course system which would, he thought, fit local conditions more closely. He urged on farmers the following rotation: (1) drilled crops of all kinds (if the farmer did not have sufficient manure to put one sixth of his cleared land under drilled crops, he should sow the rest of the sixth with buckwheat to plough under); (2) spring wheat or barley or oats; (3) clover meadow; (4) clover pasture; (5) peas; (6) fall wheat.[23]

These types of agriculture differed radically from that which dominated Ontario during the first half of the 19th century. The improved farming recommended had the following characteristics: it emphasised the raising and feeding of livestock and the use of their manure; it embodied a complex rotation in which feed crops allowed the alteration of recuperating and clearing crops with cash grains; it had a large pasture component; and it represented a fairly intensive use of the land. Early settlers' guides frequently advocated an improved agriculture under the guise of offering advice on adaptation to local conditions.

[21]John Lynch, "Agriculture and its Advantages as a Pursuit," op. cit., p. 197.

[22]*The Canadian Agricultural Reader*, op. cit., pp. 198–99.

[23]William Hutton, "Agriculture and its Advantages as a Pursuit," op. cit., pp. 183–84.

Many of the authors of these guides stressed the importance of (and urged) the sowing down of large areas to pasture and offered advice on the cultivation of feed crops. Francis Evans recommended that settlers take only one crop of wheat from newly cleared land and then sow the field with grasses.[24] Joseph Pickering agreed, specifying that timothy or, better still, red or white clover should be sown.[25] The field was to remain under grass for from five to seven years, to be mowed for hay for the first year or two and subsequently grazed. Under such a system the acreage in grain would remain constant for the first several years while the meadow and pasture category would expand to cover as much as six-sevenths of the cleared land (this proportion would be reduced after the seventh year until it reached 30 or 40 percent). Three justifications were offered for this procedure. Firstly, it would provide winter feed and summer grazing for the livestock. Secondly, it would check the invasion of the cleared land by recolonizing forest plants. Thirdly, it would allow the tree roots to rot out of the soil.[26] The settlers' guides also gave advice on the raising of feed crops and warned of the necessity to produce feed for livestock. In the opinion of Adam Fergusson, for example, the sowing of a feed crop for the cattle should be the farmer's first objective (along with potatoes for himself).[27] William Evans noted that "the settler who will manage judiciously, and cultivate vegetables or green crops, *principally*, for the first two or three years will seldom fail of success. With these vegetables in abundance he can feed pork in sufficient quantities to supply his table constantly."[28] Both Joseph Pickering and John Galt during the 1830s and John Lynch in the 1850s urged the settler to sow oats to feed to livestock at the latest during his second year on the land.[29] Martin Doyle in recommending a short list of crops to the settler emphasised maize ("fine food for pigs and oxen"); pumpkins ("principally used for cattle feeding"); and swedish turnips and mangel wurzels ("most nutritious for all farming stock"). In Doyle's view also the cultivation of artificial grasses —as opposed to the natural grasses of the beaver meadows —was essential."[30]

The value of livestock in building up land was recognised if not greatly stressed. William Evans recommended that the "respectable class of

---

[24]Francis A. Evans, *The Emigrant's Directory and Guide to Obtain Lands and Effect a Settlement in the Canadas* (Dublin, 1833), p. 103.

[25]Joseph Pickering, op. cit., p. 159.

[26]See, for example, William Evans, *A Supplementary Volume to a Treatise on the Theory and Practice of Agriculture, Adapted to the Cultivation and Economy of the Animal and Vegetable Productions of Agriculture in Canada* (Montreal, 1836), p. 152; Frederick Widder, *Information for Intending Emigrants of all Classes to Upper Canada* (Toronto, 1850), p. 4; and John Lynch, "Report on the State of Agriculture Etc. in the County of Grey, 1853," *Journal and Transactions of the Board of Agriculture of Upper Canada* 1 (1856), p. 373. Only the roots of hardwood trees would rot out in the course of six or seven years. In fact the sowing down of newly cleared lands to grass was not a common practice. Widder reported that only settlers with surplus capital could resort to this device.

[27]Adam Fergusson, *Practical Notes made during a Tour in Canada and a Portion of the United States in 1831* (Edinburgh, 1833), p. 353.

[28]William Evans, op. cit., p. 152.

[29]Joseph Pickering, op. cit., p. 159; John Galt, op. cit., appendix, p. lxvi; and John Lynch, "Report on the State of Agriculture Etc. in the County of Grey, 1853," op. cit., p. 373.

[30]Martin Doyle, op. cit., pp. 57-58.

settler" (presumably the financially respectable) should settle on ready-cleared land. He warned that cleared lands may be run down, but observed that "to anyone with the means of purchasing stock, it must be less expensive to restore cleared land to its original fertility" than to clear the forest.[31]

The descriptions of hypothetical farms offered in the early settlers' guides reveal various elements of improved farming. Joseph Pickering, attempting to show that farming could be profitable in Ontario during the late 1820s, set out the financial statement of an hypothetical farm with 70 acres cleared. His figures show the following cropping pattern: 20 acres under wheat (10 of these acres being newly-cleared land); 10 acres of clover; 8 of timothy; and 10 of sheep pasture; 10 acres of peas; 4 of oats; 6 of maize; and 2 of root crops and vegetables. An alternation of recuperating and exhausting crops is suggested for he has ten acres of wheat following peas and the clover following oats. There was no naked fallow on Pickering's imaginary farm. In his statement the clover and timothy were for hay and the peas were fed to livestock. The farm was stocked with 2 yoke of oxen, 1 horse, 6 cows and 6 calves or heifers, 2 sows and 30 store pigs, and 20 sheep.[32] John Galt, explaining why he believed that at least 40 acres were needed to support a family of 11, assumed a large number of livestock and that they would be fed on cultivated feed. He conceded that 40 acres would produce more grain than could be eaten by 11 persons, but continued his argument as follows:

> But how are horses, cows, and oxen to be fed through a tedious winter of nearly six month's continuance? . . . Ten acres of meadow land will be scarcely sufficient to yield hay enough for a pair of horses, two yokes of oxen, half a dozen cows, and fifty sheep. Fifteen acres of pasturage will be no more than adequate to feed fifty sheep through the summer. Five acres will scarcely yield oats enough to feed the horses.[33]

Galt's point was that only ten acres were left to produce food for direct consumption by the family.

These fragments of evidence drawn from the settlers' guides of the early 19th century suggest that their authors promoted rather vaguely defined variants of mixed or improved farming. While some writers, like Pickering, believed that mixed farming would pay, most were unashamedly advocating the practice of a non-commercial mixed farming. They informed their readers that a significant profit could not be made from a small farm regardless of the type of agriculture pursued. William Evans, for example, stated in 1836 that "the circumstances in British America are such at present, and are likely to continue so for a long period, that a respectable, or even comfortable living is not to be obtained from a small farm."[34] Evans, clearly, was discussing the small commercial farm. In effect he was saying that farmers could not make a worthwhile profit even if they devoted most of their lands to cash grains, and

[31] William Evans, op. cit., pp. 133–34.
[32] Joseph Pickering, op. cit., pp. 163–65.
[33] John Galt, op. cit., appendix, p. lxvi.
[34] William Evans, op. cit., p. 135.

that therefore they should at least strive to live well, while at the same time preserving the fertility of their lands, by practising a subsistence form of improved farming.

Most early 19th-century writers, then, believed that farming would not bring high returns in Ontario. However, towards the middle of the century more and more of them recognised that the dominant agriculture (which they condemned) allowed the farmer to accumulate capital rapidly, while improved farming did not pay. John Lynch demonstrates the dilemma faced by the improvers. He assiduously promoted mixed farming, urging the settler while his land still was in good condition to adopt "a more meliorating system of agriculture," for it was "undoubtedly easier and far less expensive to keep land in good condition than to restore it after it is worn out." And yet he saw that improved agriculture would slow down the farmer's rate of capital accumulation through reduced profits. The returns from green crops as late as 1855 did "not appear as quick and certain as wheat growing alone." Wages were high, labourers were scarce, and there was little direct or indirect market for green crops.[35] William Hutton agreed that conversion to improved farming would cause the farmer's income to decline, and yet this did not prevent him from recommending a five- or six-course husbandry. Hutton observed that "the price of beef in general, is so low, that farmers have not much encouragement to grow either turnips or grain for this purpose."[36] Lynch summarised the problem. The average farmer was being urged to give up a "system by which he is rapidly becoming rich," that is an extensive cash grain farming, for an improved agriculture "which has got to be tried, and of which he is only certain that it will not make him so good a return for his outlay." It seemed to Lynch that a considerable decline in the price of wheat was a precondition for "any material improvement in the system of agriculture in Canada."[37]

Although ideas about farming and the land were transferred and improved agriculture was promoted, few mixed farms were established. In part this was because many of the settlers arriving from Britain came from urban areas and consequently were unacquainted with any type of farming, let alone the improved varieties. But the basic reason was that most settlers were undercapitalised and needed to make an immediate and substantial profit from farming. Mixed farming did not pay; there was no significant market for livestock and livestock products. It seems likely that the manifestation of British agricultural ideals on the landscape of Ontario was possible only where the settler had sufficient capital at his disposal to make unnecessary his getting the greatest possible short-term profit from his land. Although much more work on the subject is needed, it would appear highly likely that officers retired on half pay from the British army and navy were the prime agents in the establishment of British types of improved farming in Ontario.

There were indeed two streams in the agricultural development of

---

[35]John Lynch, "Agriculture and its Advantages as a Pursuit," op. cit., pp. 199-200.
[36]William Hutton, "Agriculture and its Advantages as a Pursuit," op. cit., p. 184.
[37]John Lynch, "Agriculture and its Advantages as a Pursuit," op. cit., pp. 199-200.

Ontario during the first half of the 19th century. The stream representing cultural transfer dominated in the literature, and that representing adaptation to local conditions dominated on the land. Until the late 1840s, when it was recommended also as an import-substitution and as a new staple agriculture, the promotion of mixed farming is indicative solely of cultural transfer. The early farm literature promoted mixed farming, and was an important vehicle for the spread of British ideas on agriculture. As a result its treatment of the dominant agriculture was not objective. Often its description verged on the caricature and its explanations were too simplistic, commonly being couched in terms of either the farmer's ignorance and laziness or the compulsive lure of cheap land. The published literature, then, as a basis for description and explanation is suspect; and yet it forms the major source for agricultural studies of the first half of the century. The literature requires careful evaluation and interpretation before it can be used as a component of meaningful analysis. Once it is recognised that the promotion of improved farming permeates these sources, that the advice offered on how to establish a farm was not widely followed, and that most of the farms described in detail are not typical of the province, much can be accomplished.

21

OF POVERTY AND HELPLESSNESS
IN PETITE-NATION*

R. Cole Harris

One of the obvious facts of the history of 19th-century Canada was the extent to which French-Canadians did not share in the expansion of the nation, but instead settled on poorer agricultural lands within Quebec (or Lower Canada or Canada East) or drifted off into the factories and mills of the northern United States, especially in New England. The inability to expand out of the agricultural ghetto of Quebec is one of the historic grievances of French Canada, constantly debated in a series of bitter controversies among Canadian historians. Few doubt the problem; the issue revolves rather around the question of whether it was inherent in the society and institutions established by the French in New France or whether it was a product of the British conquest. Curiously enough, until recent years, few careful studies of French-Canadian society in the critical years of the 19th century have been undertaken; most disputants content to generalize from views of French Canada before 1760 and after 1900. The lack of concrete study has been particularly marked with regard to the situation and development of the rural population of French Canada in the post-Conquest period. What happened to the *habitant* and *censitaire* after 1760? Given the dominance (at least numerically) of a rural peasant population throughout the 19th century, this question seems particularly critical.

In the following article, R. Cole Harris, a historical geographer who has written one of the most detailed studies of the seigneurial system of New France, pursues the institution and its effects into the British

Canadian Historical Review, 52 (1971), 23–50. Reprinted by permission of the author and University of Toronto Press.

period. In a careful analysis of Petite-Nation, a seigneury in the Canadian Shield, Harris outlines the interaction of the inherent weaknesses of French-Canadian institutions of landholding and settlement, the geography of Quebec, and the new conditions of the post-Conquest period. Why is Petite-Nation a particularly intriguing place to study? What sorts of seigneurs were the Papineaus? Does the picture Harris presents accord with the stereotyped view of the French-Canadian peasant? How does Harris explain the lack of dynamism in French-Canadian society?

SUGGESTIONS FOR FURTHER READING

R. Cole Harris, *The Seigneurial System in Early Canada: A Geographical Study* (Madison, Milwaukee, and London: University of Wisconsin Press, 1966).

Fernand Ouellet, *Histoire economique et sociale du Québec, 1760–1850* (Montreal: Fides, 1966).

Marcel Rioux and Yves Martin, *French-Canadian Society*, vol. 1 (Toronto: McClelland and Stewart, 1964).

J.M.B.

During the 350 years of white settlement along the lower St. Lawrence River there have been three major migrations of French-speaking people: the first bringing some 10,000 Frenchmen across the Atlantic before 1760; the second, beginning shortly before 1820, taking French Canadians to the Eastern Townships, to New England, or to the Canadian Shield; and the third, following closely on the second, gradually urbanizing French-Canadian society. Each of these migrations was predominantly a movement of poor people, and each characteristically involved individuals or nuclear families rather than groups or communities. Their results, however, have been vastly different. The first created a modestly prosperous base of agricultural settlement along the lower St. Lawrence. The third has brought French Canadians into the technological orbit of the modern world. But the second, especially when it turned north to the Canadian Shield, led to poverty as acute as that of any Negro sharecropper in the American South, and then, often within a generation or two, to land abandonment and migration to the cities. The magnitude of the third migration was partly a product of the failure of the second, and this failure still echoes through contemporary Quebec.

This paper† deals with the French-Canadian migration to and settlement in the seigneurie of Petite-Nation, a small segment of the Quebec

†This paper has been written with the support of a Fellowship from the J. S. Guggenheim Foundation and a Grant-in-Aid-of-Research from the University of Toronto. The author acknowledges with gratitude the research assistance of Mr. John Punter and Mr. Ian Walker.

rim of the Canadian Shield some forty miles east of Ottawa. It describes the coming of French Canadians to Petite-Nation and their way of life there before approximately 1860, then considers the reasons for the extreme poverty and the institutional weakness which were, perhaps, the dominant characteristics of French-Canadian life in the seigneurie. Although in most general respects the habitant economy and society of Petite-Nation were reproduced throughout the Shield fringe of southern Quebec, there is some justification for a close look at this particular place. It belonged to Louis-Joseph Papineau, the leading French-Canadian nationalist of his day and a man who believed, at least in his later years, that the seigneurial system and a rural life were central to the cultural survival of French Canada; and it can be studied in detail in the voluminous Papineau Papers in the Quebec Provincial Archives. This paper considers the ordinary French-Canadian inhabitants of Petite-Nation, and a subsequent paper will consider its elite.

THE OCCUPATION OF PETITE-NATION

Although the penetration of the Shield for agricultural purposes had begun as early as the 1730s,[1] it gained little momentum until well into the 19th century. By 1820 a great many *rotures* in the older seigneuries had been subdivided until they produced a minimum subsistence living. French-Canadian agriculture, inflexible, uncompetitive, and largely subsistent, was incapable of supporting a growing population. Some of the young French Canadians whom the land could no longer support moved to the local village finding there a way point, a time and a place of transition between the closely knit society of kin and *côte* and a new life among strangers. Others moved directly from the parental roture to a destination outside the St. Lawrence lowland. Whether from farm or village, French Canadians left the parish of their birth as individuals or in nuclear families, those going into the Shield travelling a relatively short distance from the adjacent lowland. Habitants settling in Petite-Nation before 1820 had come from the Island of Montreal, Ile Jésus, and the surrounding mainland seigneuries. Most later settlers came from a scattering of parishes in the lower Ottawa Valley (see Figure 1).[2] A few of the earliest settlers had been brought to Petite-Nation by the seigneur,[3] a few others had scouted out the land and brought some capital to their destination,[4] but the great majority came unassisted and penniless. They had heard that there were jobs and land up the Ottawa Valley, they had

---

[1] In St-Féréol behind the present settlement of Ste-Anne de Beaupré after the Séminaire de Québec had conceded all the land along the côte de Beaupré.

[2] See Michel Chamberland, *Histoire de Montebello, 1815–1928* (Montréal, 1929), chap. 7, for a description of early immigration to Petite-Nation. The data in Figure 1 are derived from the nominal census of 1851. The place of birth of approximately one-half the heads of households in St-André Avellin is given in the census.

[3] Ibid., pp. 58–59.

[4] See, for example, J. Papineau à son fils Benjamin, Ile Jésus, mai 1824, *Rapport de l'Archiviste de la province de Québec* [RAPQ], 1951–52, pp. 194–96; and a letter of February 9, 1826, ibid., p. 231.

FIGURE 1

Place of Birth of Adults in the Parish of Ste-André Avellin, Petite-Nation, 1861

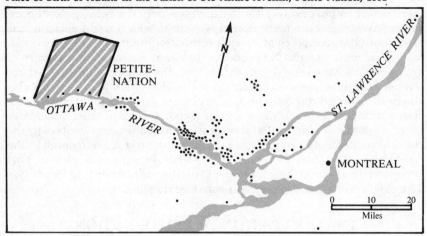

One dot represents one person.

set out with no specific place in mind, had perhaps worked here and there, and arrived, almost by chance, in Petite-Nation.[5]

Petite-Nation was a tract of land approximately 15 miles a side and bounded on the south by the Ottawa River. Barely a tenth of the seigneurie lay in the Ottawa River plain; the rest, in the hilly southern fringe of the Canadian Shield.[6] Only approximately a third of the land was at all suited to agriculture, the rest being too rough, too swampy, or its soils too thin and acidic. The best soils, although they were hardly good even by the standard of those in Quebec, had developed on the marine clays of the lowland or on alluvial material in the north-south valleys in the Shield that once had been glacial spillways. The forest cover of this abrupt, knobby land was a typical segment of the mixed Laurentian forest:[7] white, red, and jack pine, fir, and white spruce predominated in rocky, excessively drained areas; black spruce, cedar, and larch dominated the bogs; and a beech-maple-birch association that included white ash, red oak, poplar, and a few coniferous species was common on more moderate sites. The climate was considerably more severe than at Montreal. Along the Ottawa River the average frost-free period was 125 days and was less than 115 days along the northern border of the seign-

---

[5]This process is described here and there in the Denis-Benjamin Papineau correspondence. See, for example, Denis-Benjamin Papineau à Louis-Joseph Papineau, fév. 1836, Archives de la province de Québec [APQ], Archives Personnelles [AP], P, pp. 5, 29.

[6]The physical geography of Petite-Nation is well surveyed in Paul G. Lajoie, *Etude pédologique des comtés de Hull, Labelle, et Papineau* (Ottawa, 1968), pp. 14–31.

[7]A detailed description of the forest in Petite-Nation before very much of the seigneurie had been cleared is in Joseph Bouchette's Field Book of the Line between the Seigniory of La Petite-Nation and the Augmentation of Grenville, beginning October 1, 1826, APQ, AP, P, pp. 5, 48.

eurie. The climatic limit of wheat cultivation crossed Petite-Nation along the boundary between the Shield and the lowland.

The white settlement of this tract of land began in 1807 or 1808 when Joseph Papineau, then seigneur of Petite-Nation, contracted to cut a small quantity of squared timber,[8] and brought some 20 French-Canadian woodcutters to the seigneurie.[9] Early in 1809 he sold two-fifths of his seigneurie for £7220 to a Boston timber merchant, Robert Fletcher,[10] who in March of that year arrived in Petite-Nation with 160 well-provisioned New Englanders.[11] Within a year Fletcher defaulted on payments, committed suicide,[12] and his portion of the seigneurie reverted to Joseph Papineau. In 1817 when Joseph Papineau sold the entire seigneurie—mills, domain, back *cens et rentes*, and unconceded land—to Louis-Joseph Papineau,[13] his eldest surviving son, there were perhaps 300 people there, a third of them the remnants of Fletcher's New Englanders, and almost all the rest French Canadians. One of the latter was Denis-Benjamin Papineau, younger brother of Louis-Joseph, a resident of Petite-Nation since 1808 and seigneurial agent for his brother until the late 1840s. For some 20 years after Louis-Joseph purchased the seigneurie, only a few settlers trickled into Petite-Nation each year: in 1828 there were 517 people,[14] in 1842 only 1,368.[15] In the 1840s the rate of immigration increased sharply as population pressure in the older settlements dislodged a steadily larger number of French Canadians, and declined again in the 1850s when almost all the cultivable land in Petite-Nation had been taken up. Over 3,000 people lived in the seigneurie in 1851, and some 4,000 a decade later.[16] By this date five-sixths of the population was French Canadian.

Settlers in Petite-Nation, as in all other Canadian seigneuries, acquired a roture (a farm lot or, legally, the final form of land concession within the seigneurial system) which they held from the seigneur. Joseph Papineau had made 40 such concessions before 1817,[17] and by the mid-1850s the rotures shown in Figure 2 had been conceded, most of them by Denis-Benjamin Papineau. The Papineaus adopted without modification the cadastral system of the St. Lawrence lowland, conced-

---

[8]Joseph Papineau à son fils Benjamin, Montréal, 22 juil. 1809, RAPQ, 1951–52, p. 173. Joseph Papineau does not give the date of the contract in this letter, but apparently it was made in the previous year or two.

[9]Chamberland, *Histoire de Montebello*, pp. 58–59.

[10]Vente de partie de la Seigneurie de Petite-Nation par J. Papineau, Ecr. à Robert Fletcher, Ecr., 17 jan. 1809, APQ, AP, P, p. 5.

[11]*La Gazette de Québec*, 9 mars 1809, no 2289.

[12]This account of Fletcher's death is given by Judge Augustin C. Papineau in a short history of Petite-Nation written in 1912. Copy of original manuscript by J. T. Beaudry, October 1819, APQ, QP, P, p. 5.

[13]Vente par Joseph Papineau à Louis-Joseph Papineau, 2 mai 1817, APQ, AP, P, pp. 5, 46. In this case the sale was for £5000.

[14]Lettre de D.-B. Papineau à Mgr Lartigue, Petite-Nation, 25 fév. 1828, APQ, PQ, P, pp. 5, 29; Chamberland, *Histoire de Montebello*, pp. 79–81 gives 512 people in 1825.

[15]Public Archives of Canada [PAC], Nominal census of Petite-Nation, 1842, reel c-729.

[16]Ibid., 1851, reels c-1131 & 1132; 1861, reel c-1304.

[17]Tableau de la Censive de la Petite-Nation, 1818, APQ, AP, P, pp. 5, 48.

ing land in long lots laid out, as far as the interrupted terrain of Petite-Nation permitted, in côtes (or *rangs*) along the Ottawa River and its tributaries.[18] They charged surveying to the *censitaires*, which meant that it was usually inadequately done,[19] and they expected the censitaires to build their own roads.[20]

There is no evidence that the Papineaus withheld rotures from prospective censitaires while Petite-Nation was still a sparsely settled seigneurie. They were well aware, however, that some rotures were better than others and that it was advantageous to establish responsible settlers in new areas. From time to time Louis-Joseph wrote from Montreal to his brother in the seigneurie with instructions about the settlement of specific rotures.[21] By the late 1840s rotures were becoming scarce—almost invariably there were several applications for each new lot available[22]—and Louis-Joseph, who had returned from exile in France and spent much of his time in the seigneurie, granted land more cautiously. His prejudices ran strongly against English-speaking applicants—'foreign squatters . . . infinitely less satisfactory than our Canadians'[23]—partly because they were wont to cut his timber. In 1848 he began withholding formal title to any new roture until the settler had cleared six arpents (1 arpent equals approximately 5/6ths of an acre). Each applicant was informed that until that time he was a tenant, not a censitaire,[24] a procedure that was unheard of during the French regime when seigneurs were required to grant unconceded rotures to any applicant for them.[25] One habitant, wrote Louis-Joseph, "had the insolence to tell me that I was obliged to grant him land."[26] He also required

---

[18]J.-B. N. Papineau, son of Denis-Benjamin, pointed out in 1852 that rotures in Petite-Nation had been laid out "along the course of the Ottawa River or the Petite-Nation River and its tributaries so that the rivers can be used for roads until such time as the censitaires are able to build them." Nominal census of Petite-Nation, 1851, remarks of enumerator on back of page 131, March 6, 1852, reel 1132. See also, Instructions de Denis-Benjamin Papineau sur l'arpentage, 1839, APQ, AP, P, 5, 46.

[19]With inadequate surveying there was always a good deal of confusion about property lines, particularly in the irregular pockets of cultivable land in the Shield for which the cadastral system of long lot and côte was quite ill suited.

[20]During the French regime seigneurs had been expected to build and the censitaires to maintain the roads. The title to Petite-Nation, however, did not specify the seigneur's responsibility to build roads, and there is no indication that the Papineaus built any roads in Petite-Nation other than a few short roads to mills.

[21]Louis-Joseph Papineau à Benjamin Papineau, Montréal, 22 nov. 1829, APQ, AP, P, 5, 5 (folder 153a); and also Joseph Papineau à son fils, Benjamin, Ile Jésus, mai 1824, RAPQ, 1951–52, pp. 194–96.

[22]Louis-Joseph Papineau à Alanson Cooke, Petite-Nation, 22 oct. 1850, APQ, AP, P, 5, 48 (bundle Alanson Cooke).

[23]Louis-Joseph Papineau à Benjamin Papineau, 23 oct. 1848, APQ, AP, P, 5, 5 (folder 185).

[24]Louis-Joseph Papineau à Benjamin Papineau, 11 oct. 1848, ibid. (folder 184).

[25]The legal position in this regard of the seigneur during the French regime is discussed in R. C. Harris, *The Seigneurial System in Early Canada: A Geographical Study* (Madison, Wis., 1966), pp. 106–8.

[26]Louis-Joseph Papineau à Benjamin Papineau, Petite-Nation, 22 oct. 1850, APQ, AP, P, 5, 5 (folder 203). The title deed to the seigneurie of Petite-Nation, unlike most others, did not specify that the seigneur was required to sub-grant land, but it is doubtful that an intendant during the French regime would have permitted Louis-Joseph to grant land as he did.

FIGURE 2
Rotures in Petite-Nation, 1855

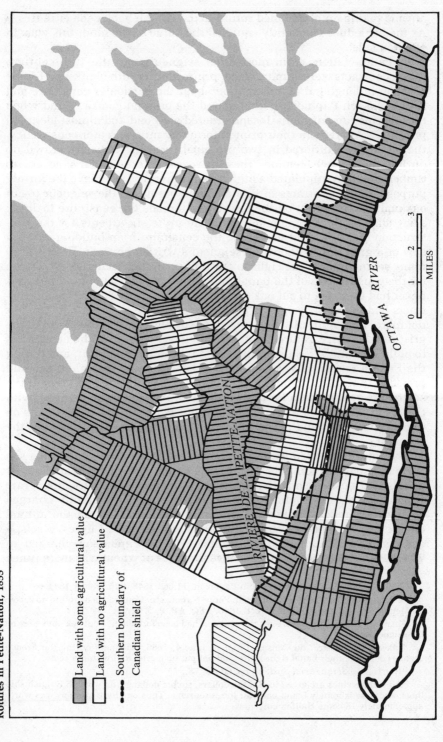

Land with some agricultural value

Land with no agricultural value

Southern boundary of
Canadian shield

RIVIÈRE DE LA PETITE-NATION

OTTAWA RIVER

0   1   2   3
MILES

anyone taking an abandoned roture to pay all the back cens et rentes.[27] As the back dues frequently equalled the value of the land, this was, in effect, a sale.

In Petite-Nation, as in most other seigneuries in the 19th century, roture contracts were standardized, printed forms with blanks left for the addition in longhand of information about the particular censitaire and roture. Joseph Papineau had prepared the original contract, and when these forms ran out Louis-Joseph ordered a second and almost identical printing.[28] Apart from their printed form and much greater consistency, these contracts differed in two principal respects from any drawn up during the French regime: they increased the seigneur's access to timber, and they stipulated a higher cens et rente. To achieve the former purpose, roture contracts in Petite-Nation permitted the seigneur to cut oak and pine for profit on the roture and forbade the censitaire to do so. They allowed the seigneur to confiscate up to six arpents for the construction of a mill, and prevented the censitaire from building either a saw or a grist mill without the seigneur's written consent. Before 1760 many seigneurs had the right to cut timber on their censitaires' rotures for the construction of the banal mill or the seigneurial manor, but they never had the right to cut oak and pine there commercially.[29] Some contracts had given the seigneur power to confiscate an arpent or two, but not more, for a mill. Although the seigneur always had first claim to the grist mill banality, roture contracts had never forbidden the censitaires to build grist mills.[30] Sawmilling had not been a banal right, and during the French regime any censitaire had been allowed to build a sawmill provided that, in so doing, he did not interfere with the operation of the seigneur's grist mill. In Petite-Nation all of this had been changed, with the result that rights to all important forests on conceded as well as on unconceded land, and to the milling of timber, rested entirely with the seigneur.

The rotures granted by Joseph Papineau before 1817 and by his son thereafter paid an annual cens et rente of one *minot* of wheat (1 minot equals 1.07 bushels) and two *livres tournois* for each 30 arpents, a rate which was a third higher than the highest rate consistently charged during the French regime.[31] For a roture in Petite-Nation the annual charge was six and two-thirds minots of wheat plus 13 livres, 6 sols, 8 deniers (approximately \$2.50 Halifax).[32] The Papineaus charged in wheat rather than in capons because the price of wheat was more tuned

[27]Louis-Joseph Papineau à Benjamin Papineau, 11 oct. 1848, ibid. (folder 184).

[28]For an example of a roture contract in Petite-Nation, see: Concession de roture no 2, côte du Moulin . . . à Alanson Cooke, 20 oct. 1846, APQ, AP, P, 5, 51.

[29]In many seigneurial titles, even the seigneur had been forbidden to cut oak anywhere on the seigneurie.

[30]Indeed, by an Arrêt du Conseil d'Etat of June 4, 1686, seigneurs during the French regime could lose their banal right if they did not put up a grist mill within a year.

[31]Harris, *The Seigneurial System*, pp. 63–69, 78.

[32]All dollar values are given in Halifax dollars, such a dollar being worth 5 English shillings, and approximately 5 and one-half livres tournois. Thus one livre tournois was worth approximately 18 cents Halifax currency.

to inflation.[33] In Montreal in the first half of the 19th century, the average price of wheat was between five and six livres a minot, twice the average price a century earlier.[34] In 1813 wheat sold in Petite-Nation at 14 livres ($2.58) a minot, and the cens et rentes for that year were calculated on this basis. These prices could almost quadruple a cens et rente: at two and one-half livres a minot a roture of 200 arpents paid 30 livres ($5.50) a year, at 6 livres a minot it paid just over 53 livres ($9.70), and at 14 livres a minot it paid more than 106 livres ($19.40). Because wheat rarely ripened on Shield lots in Petite-Nation, and was a subsistence crop on lowland farms, cens et rentes were usually paid in the cash equivalent of the minots of wheat owed.[35]

After acquiring land on these terms, a settler usually built a tiny log cabin and cleared a little land. Most of the first cabins were shanties of perhaps 10 to 12 feet long, with a one slope roof, a dirt floor, and a chimney usually made of short green rounds heavily chinked with clay. In a few years a settler might build another, larger cabin, some 14 to 18 feet long, with gable ends, a stone chimney, and a plank floor. Most of these buildings were of *pièce-sur-pièce* construction (squared logs laid horizontally and pegged to vertical timbers at the corners and at intervals along the walls), but some were made of round logs cross-notched at the corners,[36] and a few were frame. By the 1840s a cabin was typically in a clearing of some 10 arpents.[37]

THE HABITANT ECONOMY

The occupations of working men and boys in Petite-Nation in 1851 are given in Table 1. At this date more than 90 percent of the working French-Canadian men in Petite-Nation gave their occupation to the census enumerator as farmer, labourer, or river man. Most of the remainder described themselves as artisans or tradesmen, and only 16, some of

---

[33]Louis-Joseph was fully aware that seigneurs who fixed their charges in money payments were not likely to prosper in the long run from their holdings. He discusses this matter at some length in Tableau statistique des Seigneuries, circa 1851, APQ, AP, P, 5, 55.

[34]A graph of wheat prices during the French regime is in J. Hamelin, *Economie et société en Nouvelle France* (Québec, 1960), p. 61, and a similar graph for the later period is in Fernand Ouellet, *Histoire economique et sociale du Québec, 1760–1850* (Montréal, 1966), p. 603.

[35]In the seigneurial account books the charge for each year was always listed in livres rather than in minots, and depended on the price of wheat in that year. It was not possible for a censitaire to accumulate several years of debt and then, when the price of wheat was low, pay back his seigneur in kind.

[36]Pièce-sur-pièce was the most common form of log construction during the French regime, and was still widespread in the 19th century. Round log construction probably had entered Quebec from New England in the late 18th century and was widely adopted in the Shield by both French Canadians and Irish. French-Canadian and Irish houses in the Shield were often almost indistinguishable, both being essentially simple versions in wood of a Norman house, one brought from the St. Lawrence lowland, the other from southeastern Ireland. The heavily flared eaves, the porches, and the elevated ground storey, all characteristics of the vernacular French-Canadian house of the 19th century, often did not penetrate the Shield, presumably because of the additional work and cost associated with them.

[37]In 1842 the median amount of cleared land per roture was 10 arpents, and by 1861 was 19 arpents (Nominal Census of Petite-Nation, 1842, reel c-729).

TABLE 1
Occupations of Working Males in Petite-Nation, 1851*

	I. All Male Residents*		II. All Heads of Households†	
Occupation	a. French Canadian	b. Others	a. French Canadian	b. Others
Farmer	384	67	344	52
Labourer‡[3]	287	30	46	1
River man§[4]	40	7	2	
Carpenter or joiner	22	2	14	2
Blacksmith	12	4	6	1
Woodcutter	1			
Fisherman	2		2	
Baker	1	1	1	
Mason	4		3	
Sawyer		1		1
Tanner	4		1	
Cooper	6	1	4	1
Tinsmith	1		1	
Painter	1		1	
Carter	1		1	
Saddler	2	1	1	
Miller	2		1	
Shake Maker	3		2	
Sextant	2		2	
Bourgeois		1		1
Innkeeper		2		1
Merchant	7	8	7	6
Doctor	1	1		1
Clerk	5	6	4	1
Priest or minister		2‖		1
Bailiff		1		1
Clerk of the JP		1		1
Clerk of the court	1		1	
Notary	1		1	
Surveyor	1		1	

*This column includes all male residents of Petite-Nation under 70 years of age for whom an occupation is listed in the census.
†This column includes all married men and widowers under 70 years of age for whom an occupation is listed in the census.
‡Including *journaliers* and *engagés*.
§In French, *voyageurs*. Some of this group may have been hired on the river boats, but most must have had some connection with the timber drives.
‖Comprising a Belgian priest as well as a Methodist minister.
Source: Based on the nominal census of Petite-Nation, Nominal Census, 1851, reels C-1131 and C-1132.

them members of the Papineau family, as merchants, clerks, or professionals. Of those describing themselves as farmers, the great majority were heads of households, married men with several offspring. The labourers and river men were largely youths, some of them only 12 or 13 years of age, who still lived on the parental roture, and many of the tradesmen listed in column I-a, Table 1, were boys working with their fathers. Some men gave two occupations—cultivateur et menuisier, négociant et cultivateur—and many of those describing themselves only as farmers must also have worked intermittently in the logging camps.

Although the nominal census indicates that farming was the dominant occupation in Petite-Nation in 1851, agriculture had developed slowly in a rocky seigneurie that had been first settled for its timber. In the first years both Joseph Papineau and Louis-Joseph had sent biscuit and pork from Montreal,[38] and Denis-Benjamin, who doubted that agriculture was climatically possible in Petite-Nation, had imported wheat.[39] Only by the 1820s were the logging camps supplied locally and most settlers self-sufficient in basic foods. Even in 1842, when the first agricultural census was taken in Petite-Nation, virtually all habitant farms were subsistence operations on a few arpents of cleared land. The habitants were not selling produce to the lumber camps, which were supplied almost entirely by a handful of large farms. Table 2 gives examples of both subsistence and commercial farm types. In 1842 there were six large commercial farms in Petite-Nation. One of them (farm 3 below) belonged to Denis-Benjamin Papineau, the other five to English-speaking settlers, among them Alanson Cooke, the sawmill operator, and Stephen Tucker, the timber merchant. Between the commercial and subsistence farm types illustrated in Table 2 there were a few semi-commercial operations, and of these three belonged to French Canadians.

By 1861 there were 25 commercial farms in Petite-Nation, a quarter of them held by French Canadians. Examples 1 and 2 in Table 2 still describe characteristic habitant farms except that by 1861 there were likely to be 15 to 20 cleared arpents and corresponding increases in crop acreage and livestock. Without manuring or adequate crop rotation, seed-yield ratios on the thin soils of Petite-Nation were extremely low, probably not higher than 1:6 for wheat or 1:12 for oats.[40] Livestock were scrub animals that browsed or grazed in the bush for most of the year. Such a farm rarely produced a marketable surplus. With clearing proceeding at an average rate per farm of well under one arpent a year, and with women and children doing much of the farm work, it required no more than a man's part-time attention.

The farmers and farmers' sons who sought off-the-farm employment usually worked in the sawmills or logging camps, thereby providing most of the labour for the Papineaus or the English-speaking timber merchants who controlled the forests. Joseph Papineau and his son Denis-Benjamin had managed the earliest sawmills, but when Louis-Joseph acquired the seigneurie he leased the mill rights in the western half of it to Thomas Mears, a timber merchant from Hawkesbury.[41] Peter McGill,

---

[38]See, for example, lettre de Joseph Papineau à son fils Louis-Joseph, Montréal, 28 fév. 1818, RAPQ, 1951–52, p. 182.

[39]Lettre de Denis-Benjamin Papineau à son oncle Frs. Papineau, Petite-Nation, 29 fév. 1812, APQ, AP, P, 5, 29.

[40]These figures are calculated from data on yields in the Nominal Census of 1861. They assume that French Canadians sowed 1½ minots of grain per arpent. A good deal of land in 1861 was still within a few years of first cultivation. Later without a change in agricultural technology, yields would have been substantially lower.

[41]This lease was arranged sometime before 1822. There is a receipt, dated 1822, for £75 ($300) for lease of the mill in the Papineau Papers (APQ, AP, P, 5, 48).

TABLE 2
Farm Types in Petite-Nation, 1842

| | | | Arpents | | | | | | | | Number of | | | |
| | | | Planted in | | | | | | | | | | | |
	Held	Cleared	Wheat	Barley	Rye	Oats	Peas	Potatoes	Meadow and Pasture	Other	Cattle	Horses	Sheep	Pigs
Subsistence farms														
Farm 1	100	7	2	1		2		1		1	1		1	3
Farm 2	120	7	1	¼	1	2½	1	1		1	1	2		2
Commercial farms														
Farm 3	1,229	320	1			10	3	1	300	5	36	7	57	12
Farm 4	90	40	1					2	37		36	2	18	5

Source: Derived from examples in the nominal census of Petite-Nation, 1842, Nominal Census, 1842, reel C-729.

nephew and heir of the director of the Bank of Montreal, took over the lease in 1834, but the mills were managed by Alanson Cooke, son of one of the early settlers from New England.[42] In 1854 Louis-Joseph sold the mills and timber rights for ten years in the western half of the seigneurie to Gilmour and Company, a firm of Scottish origin then based in Liverpool, and with British North American operations on the St John and Mirimichi rivers as well as the Ottawa. Besides these mills, Asa Cooke, father of Alanson, operated a small mill in the first range;[43] and in the eastern part of the seigneurie another New Englander, Stephen Tucker, held a concession to cut and square timber.[44] A few habitants cut firewood for the steamers on the Ottawa River,[45] and others made potash. There were 14 asheries in Petite-Nation in 1842, eight of them belonging to French Canadians. In 1851 there were 39 asheries, two-thirds of them in the hands of habitants. These were part-time, family operations each producing three to five barrels of ash a year.[46]

The number and the aggregate income of the men employed in the forests and mills of Petite-Nation cannot be determined exactly.[47] Although most of the labourers and some of the farmers listed in Table 1 worked intermittently in forest industries, the census enumerator noted that only 30 to 40 men were employed in Alanson Cooke's mill and another 10 at his father's in 1851, and did not list the number of men cutting or squaring timber.[48] In 1861 Gilmour and Company employed 147 men in Petite-Nation, and Stephen Tucker employed 60.[49] Certainly, during the 1850s there were sawmill jobs for perhaps half the year for not more than 50 to 60 men, jobs in the lumber camps for four or five winter months for not more than another 150 to 200, and jobs in the spring timber drives for perhaps 50.[50] Seeking these jobs were the great majority of able-bodied French Canadians in Petite-Nation. At any given time most of them were unemployed or were engaged in work around the farm that brought almost no cash return. In these conditions wages were extremely low. Mill hands earned $12 to $14 a month in 1861, and wages

[42]Lease from November 1, 1833 . . . between the Hon. L-J. Papineau and the Hon. P. McGill, September 20, 1834, ibid. (bundle Alanson Cooke).

[43]Nominal Census of Petite-Nation, 1851, reel c-1132.

[44]This was a long-standing arrangement, its terms varying over the years. See, for example, D-B. Papineau à Stephen Tucker, 10 fév. 1844, APQ, AP, P, 5, 30.

[45]Joseph Papineau à son fils Louis-Joseph, Montréal, 25 mars 1840, RAPQ, 1951-52, p. 299.

[46]Nominal Census of Petite-Nation, 1851, reels c-1131 and c-1132.

[47]An exact statement would be possible only if the records of all timber concerns operating in Petite-Nation had survived. As it is, there are, apparently, no such records.

[48]Nominal Census of Petite-Nation, 1851. Some of the information given here is listed on the back of folio sheets and is not photographed on microfilm.

[49]Ibid., 1861, reel c-1304. At this date Gilmour and Co. and Stephen Tucker were the only major employers in Petite-Nation, and it can be taken that only just over 200 men worked in forest industries in the seigneurie in 1861.

[50]These figures are my estimates, which probably err on the side of more rather than fewer jobs. In much of the Ottawa Valley the same men were hired to cut and square timber and then to raft it to Quebec. Stephen Tucker may well have hired in this way; if so, the 50 to 60 raftsmen given in these estimates were the same men as 50 to 60 of those estimated to work in the logging camps.

had been even lower.[51] While some French Canadians earned as much as $100 a year in the forest industries, a great many more earned far less. In the 1850s sawmill and forest jobs could not have brought more than $20,000 in cash or credit into the seigneurie each year.[52]

Among the approximately 1,300 people in Petite-Nation in 1842 there were only 12 artisans and tradesmen, 9 of them French Canadians.[53] The two merchants then in the seigneurie were English-speaking. In the next decade the population almost trebled, and the number of artisans and tradesmen increased to the point shown in Table 1. As along the lower St. Lawrence at the same time, the number of tradesmen was essentially a reflection of poverty. With not enough work available in the forests, and little good farm land, several men would turn to carpentry, for example, when there was the opportunity. Of the handful of French-Canadian merchants and professionals in Petite-Nation in 1851, the doctor was a Papineau; the notary, Francis Samuel MacKay, was the son of an immigrant Scot and a French Canadian; the clerk of the lower court was another Papineau; and the eight French-Canadian merchants were small shopkeepers.

Essentially, then, the habitants in Petite-Nation were farmers, loggers, or sawmill hands. Farming was a subsistence activity that attracted few young men who competed for scarce jobs in the forests or mills. When the family depended entirely on farming, as frequently was the case, its annual cash income can rarely have exceeded $25, and often must have been virtually nothing. When the father worked on his roture and one or two unmarried sons had some work in the lumber camps, the family income would likely have been between $50 and $150 a year. In a few cases, as when the father was employed in the sawmill or had a trade, and two or three unmarried sons worked through the winter in the forests, the family income would have exceeded $200. Almost certainly, however, the gross annual income of most habitant families in Petite-Nation was between $50 and $150 a year.

Arriving without capital in Petite-Nation, taking out a roture that only slowly became a subsistence farm, finding intermittent and poorly paid work in the sawmills or logging camps, and facing payments for basic supplies and for land, almost all habitants in Petite-Nation quickly found themselves in debt. By 1822 the holders of 48 rotures in Petite-Nation owed Louis-Joseph over 11,000 livres ($2,017).[54] In 1832 only 10 lots, several of them belonging to the Papineaus, were free of debt, 51 lots each owed more than 500 livres ($92), and 5 owed over 1,000 livres.[55]

---

[51]The 1861 wages are given in the census (Nominal Census of Petite-Nation, 1861, reel c-1304). Wages at Hull, 40 miles away, were $10 a month in 1820 and $12 a month in 1840, and there is no reason for those in Petite-Nation to have been different. See, C. H. Craigie, "The influence of the Timber Trade and Philemon Wright on the Social and Economic Development of Hull Township, 1800-1850" (MA thesis, Carleton University, 1969, p. 94).

[52]My estimate, and probably too generous, based on the wage scale and inventory of jobs given above.

[53]Nominal Census of Petite-Nation, 1842, reel c-729.

[54]Tableau d'arrérages, 1822, APQ, AP, P, 5, 48. In 1825, 46 rotures owed over 20,000 livres (ibid., 1825, APQ, QP, P, 48).

[55]Etat des dettes au 11 nov. 1832, APQ, AP, P, 5, 48. By this date the 73 rotures along the Ottawa River owed approximately 40,000 livres.

Indebtedness had become a chronic condition, most of the habitants owing their seigneur a sum that was approximately equivalent to the value of a man's labour for six months in the sawmill. Many habitants had tried to reduce their debt by subdividing their rotures—as early as 1822 a third of the 66 rotures along the river had been broken up[56]—but after a few years even these fractions were likely to owe several hundred livres. Others attempted to escape from debt by selling their rotures, but the seigneur could exercise his *droit de retrait* in these sales, taking over the roture by paying his former censitaire the difference, if any, between the sale price and the debt.[57]

In the 12 years from 1825 to 1836, Denis-Benjamin Papineau collected just over 19,000 livres ($3,480) from the censitaires in Petite-Nation.[58] As the cens et rentes accumulating during this period amounted to 55,000 livres ($10,080), and the *lods et ventes* to some 20,000 livres ($3,670) he collected each year about a quarter of the annual dues. At least 20,000 livres were also owing for the years before 1825. Louis-Joseph had made several short visits to the seigneurie partly with the hope of collecting more of his debts, but found his censitaires no more able to pay him than his brother. He could sue his debtors but, although he blustered and threatened, in these years he rarely did so. Restraining him was the high cost and inconvenience of court action,[59] the advice of his brother Denis-Benjamin,[60] and undoubtedly, also, Paineau's recognition of the plight of his censitaires.[61]

When Louis-Joseph returned to Canada in 1845 after eight years in exile, he began to manage his seigneurie much more rigorously. He was no longer as involved in politics and had more time for his own affairs, he was more cantankerous, more concerned about his own rights; and he was planning to build an expensive manor house, a project that depended entirely on the collection of debts.[62] In letter after letter Louis-Joseph railed against his brother for allowing "ces animaux" (the censitaires) to fall so heavily into debt,[63] against the high cost of justice,

---

[56]Tableau d'arrérages, 1822, ibid.

[57]There are numerous indications in the documents that the Papineaus exercised this droit de retrait. See, for example, J. Papineau à son fils Benjamin, Montréal, 7 jan. 1825, RAPQ, 1951-52, pp. 198-99.

[58]Comptes entre D-B. Papineau et L-J. Papineau, 1825-37, APQ, AP, P, 5, 48.

[59]At this date there was no court in the Ottawa Valley, and, as a result, minor disputes rarely reached a court. See D-B. Papineau to Philemon Wright, May 14, 1833, PAC, Wright Papers, MG24, D8, vol. 19, p. 8179.

[60]Denis-Benjamin was always an easy-going seigneurial agent, often too much so for his brother's liking. Once, for example, when Louis-Joseph was determined to sue, Denis-Benjamin would go only so far as to tell the censitaires in question that they would be taken to court if their debts were not paid in three years. "Je ne scais si cela conviendra à [Louis-Joseph] Papineau," he told his father, "mais je ne pense qu'a moins de déposseder les habitants l'on puisse exiger d'avantage," (J. Papineau à son fils Louis-Joseph, St Hyacinthe, 27 sépt. 1838, RAPQ, 1951-52, pp. 291-92).

[61]Although he rarely sued, Papineau did expect to be paid, and he pushed his censitaires as hard as he could short of actual eviction. During one brief visit to the seigneurie he wrote to his wife, "je vois que je n'en retirerai rien, il est trop tard, leur grains sont mangés," (Louis-Joseph Papineau à sa femme, Petite-Nation, 9 avril 1828, RAPQ, 1953-54, pp. 247-49).

[62]"Oh il faudrait vivre ici pour reussir à une petite partie des améliorations que je rêve et pour forcer la rentrée des arrérages qui me permettraient de les tenter" (L-J. Papineau à Benjamin Papineau, 23 oct. 1848, APQ, AP, P, 5, 5 (folder 185).

[63]Louis-Joseph Papineau à Benjamin Papineau, Montréal, 6 mai 1848, ibid. (folder 175).

against the sheriff ("maudite invention anglais comme tant d'autres") for pocketing a commission on the sale of rotures. He could also write: "We will threaten court action and we will sue a few people, but in such a new area there is really so much poverty that I feel more repugnance in suing than they do in paying. Lack of foresight, ignorance, the tendency to become indebted to the merchants are the common failings of all the habitants without exception, but a few have acted out of ill will . . . which it is certainly necessary to rectify."[64] When a censitaire lost his roture after court action, it was sold by public auction, usually to the seigneur. As Louis-Joseph pointed out to his brother, "the certainty that the creditor is owed as much as the land is worth and that the debtor has not and never will have other means to pay means that the creditor is in reality the proprietor."[65]

Most habitants in Petite-Nation were also indebted to at least one merchant. At first Denis-Benjamin had acted as merchant, but he was neither particularly astute nor demanding which may explain why, around 1830, the New Englander Stephen Tucker became the principal, and for a time the only, merchant in Petite-Nation. Tucker was a Baptist, a man, according to Denis-Benjamin, "so filled with the missionary spirit that he has promised up to $40.00 to any of our poor Canadians who will agree to join his sect."[66] Some years later he was still described as the most fanatical Protestant in Petite-Nation; nevertheless the Papineaus and a great many habitants bought from him. Of 145 *obligations* (statements of indebtedness) drawn up between 1837 and 1845 in Petite-Nation by the notary André-Benjamin Papineau, 91 recorded debts to the seigneur, and 49 debts to Stephen Tucker.[67] By the mid-1850s Tucker owned 44 rotures,[68] almost all of them confiscated from his debtors.

Stephen Tucker and Louis-Joseph Papineau disliked each other intensely, and in the late forties and fifties when Louis-Joseph lived in the seigneurie, disputes between them were frequent. On one occasion, when the value of many rotures would not cover the debts owed to the two creditors and Tucker complained bitterly about prospective losses, Louis-Joseph who, as seigneur, had prior claim replied icily: "You forget the high credit prices of goods; the interest charges on back accounts,

---

[64]Louis-Joseph Papineau à son fils Amédée, 28 avril 1852, APQ, AP, P, 5, 7 (folder 327).

[65]Louis-Joseph Papineau à Benjamin Papineau, 12 mars 1848, APQ, AP, P, 5, 5 (folder 173). In French law the debts against land were not revealed at the time of its sale, and in this circumstance, bidders were unwilling to pay more than a pittance for rotures sold for the non-payment of dues. The seigneur could acquire them for next to nothing.

[66]Chamberland, *Histoire de Montebello*, p. 165. Denis-Benjamin did not here mention Tucker by name, but other reports about him and the fact he was the only Baptist merchant in Petite-Nation leave no doubt who was being described. There is some indication that his offer was not always rejected. In the nominal census of 1851 Aureole Gravelle and his wife, both French Canadians by birth, are listed as Baptists.

[67]Liste alphabétique des actes reçus par Andre-Benjamin Papineau, notaire à St-Martin . . . transactions en la Seigneurie de La Petite-Nation de 1837 à 1845 inclusivement, APQ, AP, P, 5.

[68]Stephen Tucker to Louis-Joseph Papineau, Papineauville, May 25, 1855, APQ, QP, P, 5, 48; and also, Reciprocal Discharge and acquittance from and to the Honorable Louis-Joseph Papineau and Stephen Tucker, July 14, 1858, APQ, AP, P, 5, 48. Tucker had not been paying the back dues on these rotures and in 1858 he owed approximately £900 on them.

and what you have received from many when I had the right of being paid before you. If you advanced too much with too many, it was your choice."[69] From the habitants' point of view both men were creditors to whom their farms were vulnerable, but Tucker who combined economic and religious coercion and was usually the more insistent must have been the more feared.

THE HABITANT SOCIETY

By the 1820s French-Canadian society in most of the older parishes and seigneuries of the St. Lawrence lowland had sealed itself from outsiders; not only were there few if any non-French Canadians in many parishes, but as time went on there were fewer French Canadians who had not been born in the immediate vicinity. These areas exported many of their young while, with almost no immigration, the people who remained formed an increasingly consanguinous population. Petite-Nation, in contrast, was being settled and it attracted different people: French Canadians from many parishes and seigneuries, New Englanders, Englishmen, Irishmen, and some English-speaking people of Canadian birth. In several cases Catholic Irishmen and French Canadian girls married in Petite-Nation, and the progeny of these matches were assimilated quickly into French-Canadian society.[70] At least three Protestants in Petite-Nation had also married French Canadians.[71] For the most part, however, the two groups kept to themselves socially. In 1842, 47 of the 53 English-speaking families in Petite-Nation had such a family in an adjacent lot, while 205 of 208 French-Canadian families lived next to a French-Canadian household.[72] In 1861 the interior parish in Petite-Nation was overwhelmingly French Canadian (with only 4 Irish by birth and 1,489 Catholics against 45 Protestants), where most English-speaking people lived on the Ottawa Valley plain towards the western corner of the seigneurie (in the parish of Ste-Angélique with 1,007 French Canadians against 545 others). By this date there were three tiny villages in the seigneurie, and only in one of them, Papineauville in the parish of Ste-Angélique, were French- and English-speaking people in Petite-Nation likely to live close together. The habitants encountered the English-speaking settlers as employers, as merchants, as creditors, occasionally as co-workers, but rarely in the ordinary social round of their lives.

The social importance of nuclear family, nearest neighbour, and côte in habitant life in Petite-Nation was not different, as far as can be ascer-

---

[69]L.-J. Papineau to Stephen Tucker, Montebello, May 27, 1858, ibid.

[70]One priest, however, reported that there was "beaucoup d'animosité" between French Canadians and Irish in Petite-Nation (Lettre de M. Bourassa à Mgr Lartigue, 23 mars 1839, cited in Chamberland, *Histoire de Montebello*, p. 174). And, of course, there were many accounts in the Ottawa Valley of strife between rival gangs of French-Canadian and Irish workers.

[71]One of these Protestants was a Lutheran; another, brother of the first, a Universalist; and the third, an Anabaptist.

[72]This information is calculated from the nominal census of 1842.

tained, from that in the older settlements of the St. Lawrence lowland. However, migration into the Shield had weakened drastically the importance of kin group and parish. Not only had settlers in Petite-Nation come as individuals but they had come recently and in relatively large numbers. At mid-century most adults were still immigrants and, because of the speed of settlement, many of their sons had not found land close to the parental roture. Table 3, which compares the kin affiliations in Petite-Nation with those in Lotbinière, a long-settled seigneurie on the south shore of the St. Lawrence some 40 miles east of Quebec City, illustrates the effect of migration on the kin groups. The French Canadians who straggled up the Ottawa Valley had left a web of blood ties which they could not quickly recreate. Habitants in Petite-Nation were far less likely to have a relative as nearest neighbour, or even a relative in the same côte than were habitants in the older seigneuries. Where kin groups existed in Petite-Nation, they rarely extended beyond sibling and parent-child relationships.

TABLE 3
Surnames in the Seigneuries of Petite-Nation and Lotbinière, 1842*

	Petite-Nation	Lotbinière
No. of families	267	458
No. of different surnames	143	126
Percent of families with the most common surname	3	12
Percent of families with one of the ten most common surnames	9	43
Percent of families with unique surname	33	14

*Source: Nominal Censuses of Petite-Nation and Lotbinière, reels c–729 and c–730.

In many ways the parish in Petite-Nation resembled the parishes along the lower St. Lawrence in the late 17th and early 18th centuries.[73] For many years the seigneurie was visited briefly twice a year by a missionary priest who arrived in January on snowshoes and in June by canoe.[74] The first resident priest, an Irishman, was appointed in 1828 and stayed three years, his successor stayed for two years, and in 1833 the parish reverted to the missionary system.[75] In 1835 the Bishop appointed another priest who, in turn, soon begged to be relieved. When in 1838 the Bishop acquiesced, Petite-Nation was left without a resident priest for another four years. In this interval missionaries continued to visit the parish twice a year, but these were short visits, their essential purposes to baptise babies and to say mass for the dead. For the most

---

[73]Resident priests were not established in rural parishes until the 1720s, and before that time parishes were visited intermittently, as in Petite-Nation, by missionary priests.

[74]Copies of all the correspondence between Joseph Raupe, the first missionary priest to visit Petite-Nation, and Joseph Papineau are preserved in the Papineau Papers (APQ, AP, P, 5, 49). Together these letters give a vivid picture of the Ottawa Valley mission in its earliest years.

[75]This intricate history is treated more fully in Chamberland, *Histoire de Montebello*, chaps. 9–11.

part, Catholics in Petite-Nation were left alone, and exposed, as one missionary priest put it, "to fatal communications with methodists and baptists."[76] In 1841 the Bishop established yet another priest, and this man stayed until 1849 when, amidst bitter factional quarrels over the school tax and the location of a new church, he left for a newly-constructed chapel and presbytery in the interior of the seigneurie.[77] The Bishop attempted to placate the feuding parties by dividing Petite-Nation into three parishes,[78] but for several more years the two parishes along the river were visited irregularly by their former curé or by the curé from l'Orignal, a seigneurie 20 miles away.

Priests did not stay in Petite-Nation because their financial support was inadequate. They could not have lived on the tithe (in Canada one-26th of the grain harvest) had it been paid regularly, and agreed to come only after the habitants had subscribed a sum for their maintenance. Yet, whatever the financial arrangements, priests in Petite-Nation were rarely paid. The first complained that he was reduced to "scratching among the stumps"[79] for a living, another that he paid out twice what he received from the habitants and was indebted to the merchant.[80] On one occasion the habitants agreed to tithe in potatoes,[81] but when the new priest arrived in a buggy pulled by two horses, the habitants decided that he was rich and refused to pay either tithe or subscription. The priest explained to his bishop that the buggy was old and had cost only a few dollars. "The mistake," he wrote, "is that I had it varnished, and that gives an appearance of luxury."[82] There were some who doubted that the habitants wanted a priest. One priest noted bitterly that the habitants could support several taverns,[83] and in 1833 the bishop informed Denis-Benjamin that "experience has proved that the habitants could not *or would not* pay even half of what they owed without being forced by law."[84] The priests had attempted to curtail the heavy drinking[85] and some adulterous behaviour, in Petite-Nation, and this may have led to a reaction against them; but in the light of many meetings to petition for a priest, the number of times that funds were subscribed for his support,

---

[76]Lettre de M. Brady, missionaire ambulante à l'évéque, Petite-Nation, 4 nov. 1838; cited in Chamberland, *Histoire de Montebello*, pp. 171–73.

[77]Ibid., p. 188.

[78]Corespondence entre D-B. Papineau et Mgr de Guigues, Evêque de Bytown, 1850–51, APQ, AP, P, 5; see also L-J. Papineau à son fils Amédée, 21 janv., 1851, APQ, AP, P, 5, 7, (folder 299).

[79]Chamberland, *Histoire de Montebello*, p. 135.

[80]M. Brunet à Mgr Lartigue, 1838, cited in ibid., p. 167.

[81]Procès verbal d'une assemblée des habitants de la Paroisse de Notre Dame de Bonsecours, 14 juil. 1844, APQ, AP, P, 5, 46. "Cette assemblée est d'opinion qu'en payant les dîmes de patates en sus des dîmes de tout grain, tel que pourvu par la loi, la subsistance du Curé de cette paroisse serait assurée . . ."

[82]Lettre de M. Mignault à Mgr Guigues, 18 oct. 1854, cited in Chamberland, *Histoire de Montebello*, pp. 218–19.

[83]Ibid., p. 155.

[84]Mgr Lartigue à D-B. Papineau, Montréal, 15 juil. 1833, APQ, AP, P, 5, 28 (folder 1).

[85]There are many references to drunkenness. "Il faut dire," wrote one missionary, "que l'ivrognerie regne en maitresse . . ." (M. Bourassa à Mgr de Telenesse, 10 avril 1839, cited in Chamberland, *Histoire de Montebello*, p. 174).

and the bitter rows over the location of a church, it is clear that most habitants wanted to have a resident priest but that he was a luxury they could hardly afford.

After 1840 a number of civil functions, notably the assessment and collection of taxes and the maintenance of roads and schools, were organized within the parish.[86] These civil functions were open to all parish residents, whatever their religious affiliations (the parish corresponding in this sense to the township in Ontario), and in Petite-Nation most responsible parish positions were held either by members of the Papineau family or by New Englanders. Illiteracy alone disqualified almost all the habitants. New Englanders had established a school in Petite-Nation in 1820, but only two French Canadians (one of them Denis-Benjamin) sent their children to it. The habitants saw no need for formal education, and most of the effort to create schools had to come from outside the seigneurie.[87] The first major initiative in this direction came with the Common School Act of 1841,[88] which provided for the election of five school commissioners in each parish, for the division of parishes into school districts, for an assessment of £50 ($200) on the inhabitants of each district for the building of a school, and for a monthly fee of one shilling and three pence for each child at school. These were heavy charges on a poverty-stricken people who attached no value to formal schooling.[89] Then, when three of the first five school commissioners were English speaking (elected because the New Englanders had attended the organizational meeting in greater number), the priest began preaching that the three English-speaking school commissioners were agents of religious and cultural assimilation.[90] In these circumstances schools were slowly built and then were often closed for want of pupils. The School Act was modified in 1846 to provide more operating revenue from property taxes whether or not parents sent their children to school.[91] Even so, Denis-

---

[86]An ordinance to prescribe and regulate the Election and Appointment of certain officers in the several Parishes and Townships in this Province . . . , December 29, 1840; 4 Vic., c. 3; *Ordinances Passed by the Governor and Special Council of Lower Canada,* 1840 and 1841, pp. 9–16. See also 4 Vic., c. 4.

[87]In 1833 D-B. Papineau and the priest did attempt to raise money for a school. Although they obtained over £40 in subscriptions, the project apparently collapsed (D-B. Papineau à Louis-Joseph Papineau, Petite-Nation, 17 mai 1833, APQ, AP, P, 5, 29).

[88]Ordinances passed by the Governor and Special Council of Lower Canada, 4–5 Vic., c. 18, 1841.

[89]"Le goût de l'Education . . . n'existe pas dans le classe qui en a le plus besoin . . . plusieurs fois des parents ont été assez deraissonables pour retirer leurs enfants de l'Ecole sans aucune juste raison de plainte contre le maître; quelquefois par animosité à cause de quelque châtiment merité infligé aux enfants; quelquefois par pique personnelle contre quelque commissaire ou Syndic; d'autres fois par un motif ignoble de vengeance, qui les portait à fair tout en leur pouvoir pour faire manquer l'Ecole" (D-B. Papineau au Gouverneur General, Petite-Nation, 22 mai 1843, APQ, AP, P, 5, 29). "You, nor no one else not being amidst our rural population could ever conceive the extravagant notions which they entertain respecting that Great Bug Bear "The Tax" [the school tax] and designing Scoundrels are prowling about the Country raising still more the heated minds of the Habitants . . ." (D. M. Armstrong to D-B. Papineau, April 8, 1845, APQ, AP, P, 5, 28 (folder A).

[90]L-J. Papineau à D-B. Papineau, September 26, 1846, Chamberland, *Histoire de Montebello,* pp. 193–94. See also letters from Denis-Benjamin to Monseigneur de Guigues, Evêc ·e de Bytown, December 18, 1850, and 1851 (more specific date not given), APQ, AP, P, 5.

[91]9 Vic., c. 27, 1846.

Benjamin estimated in 1851 that not one French Canadian in 30 in Petite-Nation was literate.[92] The habitants usually became viewers of
ditches and fences, the New Englanders the tax assessors and collectors.[93]

Although the seigneur or his agent was a powerful presence in Petite-Nation, the seigneurie itself was not a social unit. All censitaires had
acquired land from the Papineaus; all paid, or were supposed to pay,
annual charges for their land; almost all were in debt to the seigneur.
This, coupled with Louis-Joseph's fame, his sense of himself as a leader,
his excellent education and meticulous knowledge of Canadian civil law
and, after 1849, his mansion at Montebello which was by far the finest
residence that most habitants in Petite-Nation had ever seen, made him
an awe-inspiring figure in the seigneurie. Louis-Joseph liked to think of
himself as the leader of a flock,[94] but the habitants undoubtedly viewed
him with fear. He was a force in rural life as seigneurs had not been
during the French regime, but not the focus of a rural society. As during
the French regime, seigneurial boundaries were irrelevant to social patterns.

Until Louis-Joseph settled at Montebello, Denis-Benjamin Papineau,
Stephen Tucker, and the two Cookes had been the most powerful men in
the seigneurie. At one time or another each was a justice of the peace. In
1840 Denis-Benjamin was elected unanimously to represent Petite-Nation in the newly formed District Council; four years later he was succeeded by Alanson Cooke. In 1842 Denis-Benjamin was elected to the
Legislative Assembly. His son was parish clerk and, at times, surveyor of
roads in Petite-Nation, and for several years Stephen Tucker was the tax
collector. Several prosperous farmers and merchants, all of them English-speaking, were fringe members of the elite.[95] The position of all this
group rested, finally, on economic power. Denis-Benjamin's authority
depended on his position as seigneurial agent, Tucker's on his role as
employer and creditor, the Cookes' on the many jobs they controlled in
the sawmills. The habitants elected these men to the District Council,
the Legislative Assembly, or to a local parish office because their livelihood, however meagre, was controlled by them. Moreover, the elite were
the only men in the seigneurie who met the property qualification of

---

[92]D-B. Papineau à Mgr de Guigues, evêque de Bytown, 1851, APQ, AP, P, 5.

[93]In 1843, for example, the following men were parish officials in Petite-Nation: parish
clerks: J. B. N. Papineau; assessors: Thomas Schryer, Charles Cummings, and Asa Cooke;
collector: Stephen Tucker; inspector of roads and bridges: Ebenezer Winters; inspector of the
poor: Asa Cooke; commissioners of schools: Mr. Sterkendries (priest), Asa Cooke, Stephen
Tucker, Bazile Charlebois, Charles Beautron; road viewers: Jean Lavoie, Henry Baldwin,
Antoine Gauthier, François Gravelle, Elezear Frappier, Augustin Belile; fence and ditch
viewers: Louis Chalifoux, Edward Thomas, Paul Sabourin, Daniel Baldwin, Antoine Couillard, Louis Beautron (Book of Proceedings of the Civil Corporation of the Seigneurie of Petite-Nation persuant of the Ordinance of the Special Council of the 4th Victoria, c. 3, APQ, AP,
P, 5, 46).

[94]"Et moi aussi je suis chef de colonie" (lettre de L-J. Papineau à Eugène Guillemot,
ex-ministre de France au Brésil, 10 jan. 1855; printed in F. Ouellet, ed., Papineau, Cahiers de
l'Institut d'Histoire, Université Laval, p. 99).

[95]The periods of office of all the elite can best be worked out from the Book of the Civil
Corporation of . . . Petite-Nation . . . , APQ, AP, P, 5, 46.

£300 ($1,200) for such public offices as district councillor or justice of the peace.

PETITE-NATION IN 1860

By 1860 parts of Petite-Nation had been settled for more than 50 years. The Ottawa Valley plain was cleared, long lots were conceded across it, and much of the land was farmed. Farm houses stretched in côtes along the river, and two small villages, Montebello and Papineauville, had taken shape towards opposite ends of this line. In the Shield, the patterns of clearing and settlement were much more irregular, but most of the fertile pockets in the valleys were farmed. In the largest of these valleys, the village of St-André Avellin contained a church, a number of stores, and even a few streets laid out, but still largely unoccupied, at right angles to the main road. North and west from St-André Avellin, where côtes had been settled in the previous two decades, there were still many shanties in tiny clearings amid the bush that was the aftermath of logging. Still farther north, pine and spruce were being cut and floated down the Petite-Nation River to Gilmour and Company's sawmill. In all, some 4,000 people lived in Petite-Nation. Rough as in many respects it was, with stumps in many fields and the slash of recent logging almost everywhere, a settled place had emerged where just over 50 years before there had been only forest.

In this place there were three principal groups of people, and three landscapes associated with their different lives. In the manor he had built in 1848 and 1849 at Montebello lived Louis-Joseph Papineau and as many of his immediate family as he could entice away from Montreal.[96] His was one of the finest country houses in Lower Canada, its main unit 40 by 60 feet and 24 feet high,[97] and its architectural inspiration an amalgam of ideas that Louis-Joseph had brought back from France. The house was sheltered by a row of towering pines, and overlooked a spacious garden to the river. In the village of Montebello just outside the gate to his domain, Louis-Joseph had considerably widened the through road from Montreal to Hull, and had lined the streets with trees, naming each street after its particular tree: rue des cèdres, rue des érables, rue des pins, rue des ormes, rue des sapins.[98] Several miles to the west in the village of Papineauville and its surrounding farms lived Denis-Benjamin Papineau and a group of prosperous New Englanders. Most of their houses were white clapboard in the New England style, or the brick or frame buildings with Italianate trim that were becoming common in Ontario. Their large, well-managed farms produced oats, potatoes, hay, oxen, and meat for the logging camps, and their stores in Papineauville supplied settlers in much of the seigneurie. Throughout most of the rest

---

[96]Louis-Joseph's wife was especially uneasy about leaving Montreal and competent medical attention. In his later years Louis-Joseph often took to task this or that member of the family for not spending more time in the seigneurie where he most loved to be.

[97]L.-J. Papineau à son fils Amédée, 26 juin 1848, APQ, AP, P, 5, 6 (folder 281).

[98]L.-J. Papineau à Mgr Guigues, 29 mars 1856; printed in Chamberland, Histoire de Montebello, pp. 221-22. All these names have since been changed to saints' names.

of the coastal plain and in the cultivable valleys of the Shield were the tiny log houses, the barns, the fields, and the côtes of the French-Canadian habitant. However imperfectly, three traditions had emerged in the human landscape of Petite-Nation: that of the aristocrat,[99] that of the Yankee trader, and that of the habitant community of the lower St. Lawrence.

Underlying and shaping the habitant landscape in Petite-Nation were the two essential characteristics of French-Canadian life in Petite-Nation; its poverty and its weak institutions. The habitants faced the world individually or in nuclear families feebly supported by nearest neighbour or côte. The seigneur was a creditor not a leader, the parish priest was more often absent than not, the kin group was barely forming, and the local government was dominated by those who controlled the habitants' livelihood. Paradoxically, the New Englanders, who valued self-reliance, created more institutional support in Petite-Nation for their way of life than did the habitants, who tended to value community. To conclude this paper it is necessary to consider why this was so.

An explanation for the character of French-Canadian settlement in the Shield lies only partly in 19th-century Quebec, and even less in the physical character of the Canadian Shield or the commercial ascendancy of the English. The same soils on which French Canadians scratched out a living also supported large and prosperous farms. The forests in which the habitants worked for a pittance made the fortunes of others. English-speaking timber merchants exploited the habitants. So did Louis-Joseph Papineau. The Papineau manor at Montebello, Stephen Tucker's 44 rotures confiscated from debtors, and the profits of the Mears, the McGills, and the Gilmours who built and operated the sawmills in Petite-Nation all rested on a poor habitant population. Seigneur and lumberman profited from the situation in Petite-Nation, but neither had created it. Rather, to understand the habitant landscape and society in Petite-Nation is to understand the evolving character of French-Canadian rural society over the previous century and a half.

What apparently had happened was this.[100] The few emigrants who crossed the Atlantic to the lower St. Lawrence in the 17th and early 18th centuries were, for the most part, poor and dispossessed people who had only a toehold in French society before they crossed the Atlantic. Among them were approximately 1,000 girls from Paris poorhouses; 2,000 petty criminals (mostly salt smugglers); over 3,000 ordinary soldiers, most of whom had been pressed into service; and perhaps 4,000 engagés, who came largely from the same group of landless labourers and unemployed as the soldiers. Many of the engagés were young, merely boys according to the intendants, and not very robust. These people came as individuals

---

[99]This characterization of Louis-Joseph hardly does justice to the complex, many-sided character of the man, although in his later years it is probably the single word which fits him best. Louis-Joseph's relationship with Petite-Nation will be looked at much more closely in another paper.

[100]The tentative sketch of the social evolution of habitant Quebec that concludes this paper is based largely on work I have undertaken since the publication of *The Seigneurial System in Early Canada*. It will be given fuller treatment in subsequent essays.

or within the type of temporary social structure—that of a poorhouse, a prison, or an army—in which they had never intended to spend their lives, and which was irrelevant to the settlement of Canada. Along the lower St. Lawrence they found an abundance of land that, when cleared, yielded a higher standard of living than that of most French peasants. They found an opportunity to settle along the river, away from official eyes, and in a setting where their lives could not be controlled. And they found in the untrammelled life of the fur trade contact with largely nomadic Algonkian Indians whose rhetoric, courage, and apparent lack of regime they admired and emulated.

Out of this emerged a habitant population characterized by bravado, insouciance, and a considerable disdain for authority. The habitants lived boisterously, spending their income, enjoying the independence and modest prosperity of their lives in the côtes, and perhaps, too, the Indian girls along the upper Ottawa; a style of life that grew partly out of their French background but probably more out of the opportunities of a new land. They had brought few institutions with them, and needed few in Canada. The Canadian seigneurie was neither a social nor an economic unit, the parish was only slowly emerging as a social unit at the end of the French regime. The village was almost absent; collective open-field agriculture never appeared. The côte did become a loose rural neighbourhood, as time went on neighbours were frequently kin, and, after perhaps the earliest years, the nuclear family was always important. In the background was the colonial government, eager to promote the settlement of the colony, paternalistic, tending to side with the habitants in disputes with the seigneurs. The government could not impose itself on the habitants, but it could offer certain services—inexpensive regional courts, for example, or the right of free appeal to the intendant. In operating hospitals, orphanages, and poorhouses, the religious orders did the same. Such support only increased the independence of the habitants who were not forced to compensate for an oppressive officialdom by a tighter social organization at the local level.

In the century after the Conquest, this way of life had slowly changed. Habitant mobility was constrained by the declining relative importance of the fur trade and, after 1821, by its loss to Hudson Bay; by English-speaking settlement in Upper Canada; and by growing population pressure along the St. Lawrence lowland. Farm land was becoming scarce as the seigneurial lands filled up, the value of land rose, and that of labour gradually fell. Seigneurs found their revenues rising, and close seigneurial management a paying proposition. They kept accounts regularly, insisted on payment of debts, and began to build sizeable manors throughout the lower St. Lawrence. Without an intendant to interfere, they often increased their cens et rentes[101] (indeed, they interpreted the seigneurial system to the English), and as alternative land became

---

[101]Charges in the rate of the cens et rente after 1760 cannot be described simply. In many seigneuries they did not change, and in mány others changes were spasmodic. As yet there is insufficient evidence to support the claim that English or French seigneurs, as a group, adjusted these changes in a certain way.

scarcer, the habitants had no alternative but to accept these charges. A situation which once had favoured the censitaire had turned to favour the seigneur.

At the same time French Canadians were losing control of commerce to more single-minded and better-connected Englishmen, Scots, and New Englanders. A government which had never controlled but had often supported the habitants during the French regime was taken over by an alien people with a different language, religion, and values. This was no longer a government to turn to as the habitants had turned to the courts and the intendant during the French regime. For a time the Conquest connected French Canada to a larger market for its agricultural products, but not to the larger world of social and intellectual change. It shielded French Canadians from the full impact of the French Revolution, for which most of them were thankful, and it filtered the late 18th- and 19th-century world through the eyes of the English-speaking merchant, the colonial administrator, or, especially in the 19th century, the parish priest. The fragment of France which had crossed the Atlantic to settle the côtes of the lower St. Lawrence and become the largely illiterate habitant population of the French regime, had been poorly connected before 1760 to contending French values and ideologies, and the long-term effect of the Conquest had been to prolong its isolation.

In this situation, French-Canadian life had become increasingly rural. Before 1760, 20 to 25 percent of the people along the lower St. Lawrence were townsmen, but by 1815 only 5 percent of the French Canadians. The central business districts and the upper class residential areas of Montreal and Quebec were overwhelmingly English speaking. French-Canadian seigneurs who once had lived in the towns now lived in their seigneuries. In this rural introversion there were two deep ironies. French Canadians were turning to a rural life at a time when, for the ordinary habitant on the ordinary roture, such a life meant subsistence farming, poverty, debt, and eventually, the departure of most of his children. Then, too, many of them gloried in an image of the French regime, of a rural way of life before the coming of the English built around seigneurie, parish, and Coutume de Paris,[102] without understanding that in the vastly different conditions of the French regime these institutions had been extremely weak. Economically and institutionally, the rural core around which French Canada had folded was hollow.

All that could be done was to make the most of what they had. The parish, which slowly had been gaining strength after the decision taken in 1722 to establish resident priests, gradually became more vital after the Conquest, and would have developed more rapidly had there not been a serious shortage of priests.[103] The extended family or kin group enlarged and probably strengthened and, with less rural mobility within

---

[102]The Coutume de Paris had provided a base of civil law throughout most of the French regime, but it was a French law, evolved in conditions far different from those in early Canada, and some of its tenets were irrelevant to Canadian life for many years.

[103]By the 1820s and 1830s, perhaps even earlier, the parish was undoubtedly a strong institution in rural French-Canadian life, and this image of it, as of many aspects of French-Canadian life in the early 19th century, has been projected back to the French regime.

its seigneurial lowlands, the côte and nuclear family may have strengthened as well. The Coutume de Paris, with its emphasis on family rather than on individual rights, and its protective view of landholding that became more relevant to the lower St. Lawrence as the population increased, became an essential prop, in many nationalist minds, of French-Canadian life. The seigneurial system, although neither a social nor an economic unit of habitant life, had become profitable for the seigneurs, most of whom insisted that the survival of French Canada depended on the survival of the system. These institutions, particularly the kin group and the côte, provided a measure of stability, but they did not provide an institutional framework for change, especially as parish priest and seigneur usually defended the status quo. French-Canadian society had achieved some strength in rural isolation, in closely-knit, interrelated communities, and in a retrospective outlook, but had not the ability to cope with change, least of all with the internal problem of population pressure.

When young French Canadians were pushed out of the St. Lawrence lowland, they left in much the condition in which their forebears, a century and a half before, had crossed the Atlantic. They were young, illiterate, often destitute, and, in the sense that they were not part of groups bound by ties of blood and tradition, alone. Immigrants in the late 17th century had found an abundance of agricultural land and a heady outlet in the fur trade. The many more French Canadians who settled in the Shield found a far more meagre agricultural land and lumber camps and sawmills operated by another people. In this setting, they had no defense against what they became, subsistence farmers and underpaid labourers. When their children or grandchildren left for the cities, they, too, left as their predecessors had come to the Shield. The years in the Shield had availed French Canadians nothing but poverty and some lag in the adjustment to changed conditions.

Finally, the tragedy of French-Canadian settlement in Petite-Nation lay perhaps less in poverty than in the habitants' inability to maintain a distinctive way of life. The values of the closely-knit, rural communities of the lower St. Lawrence were neither those of an aristocrat such as Louis-Joseph Papineau, nor of liberals such as Stephen Tucker or Alanson Cooke. The habitants' outlook was more collective than that of the New Englanders, more egalitarian than that of Louis-Joseph Papineau. But communities such as those along the lower St. Lawrence in the 19th century depended on isolation and internal stability. When either is removed they are likely to be undermined, as they were for the habitants in Petite-Nation who stood almost alone to face a changing world.

22

THE REBELLION IN LOWER CANADA, 1837: A NATIONAL-DEMOCRATIC REVOLUTION*

Stanley B. Ryerson

THE ARMED CONFLICT AND THE METROPOLIS INVESTIGATES†

Léandre Bergeron

The major landmark in the history of the Canadas between the War of 1812 and Confederation has always been seen as occurring in 1837, when both Upper and Lower Canada rose in rebellion against their respective local governments. Although loosely connected by chronological contiguity, common complaints, and the correspondence of rebel leaders such as William Lyon Mackenzie and Louis-Joseph Papineau, the two rebellions were quite distinct. The one in Lower Canada was far more complex in its origins and more widespread in its impact and repercussions. While every Canadian historian of the period before Confederation must come to terms with the Rebellions, they obviously pose a particularly fascinating problem for those historians who work from a radical perspective. Rather than presenting one interpretation of the Lower Canadian rebellion, the following selections are taken from the writings of two of Canada's best-known radical historians, both covering roughly

---

*Stanley B. Ryerson, *Unequal Union: Roots of Crisis in the Canadas, 1815-1873* (Toronto: Progress Books, 1973), pp. 69-84.

†Léandre Bergeron, *The History of Quebec: A Patriote's Handbook* (Toronto: New Canada Publications, n.d.), pp. 76-90.

the same time-span. Stanley B. Ryerson offers what may be regarded as an orthodox Marxist interpretation of the events of 1837, while Léandre Bergeron writes from the perspective of a French-Canadian separatist influenced by the emerging "New Left" radical tradition of the 1960s. In what ways are the two interpretations similar? In what ways are they different? Does either selection challenge in any fundamental way the perspective of less "radical" scholarship?

SUGGESTIONS FOR FURTHER READING

Donald Grant Creighton,   *The Empire of the St. Lawrence* (Toronto: MacMillan of Canada, 1956).

Helen Taft Manning,   *The Revolt of French Canada 1800–1835: A Chapter in the History of the British Commonwealth* (Toronto: MacMillan of Canada, 1962).

Joseph Schull,   *Rebellion: Rising in French Canada 1837* (Toronto: MacMillan of Canada, 1971).

J.M.B.

A NATIONAL-DEMOCRATIC REVOLUTION
(Ryerson)

It was in the valley of the Richelieu that the people's movement had reached its highest point; here the forming of the Confederation of the Six Counties foreshadowed the coming into being of a provisional people's government, challenging the imperial power. It was here that Papineau and other leaders had come from Montreal to join the main body of the Patriote forces. So it was against the encampments on the Richelieu that Colborne launched his troops in the first phase of what he planned as a full-scale military campaign. The veteran of Waterloo had 6,000 men under his command. Opposing them were an unprepared, ill-armed Patriote militia; their leaders having foresworn the offensive, they waited, defensively, for the enemy onslaught.

The main body of the Patriote forces had gathered in the villages of St. Denis and St. Charles, situated six miles apart on the Richelieu. Colonel Gore was sent down the St. Lawrence to Sorel, whence his troops were to march south, along the right bank of the Richelieu, against the Patriote force at St. Denis. Simultaneously, Colonel Wetherall crossed over to Chambly, from which point he was to advance, from the opposite direction to Gore, on St. Charles. This converging movement was intended to allow at the same time the "mopping-up" of any Patriote forces which might be encountered en route: notably, at St. Ours, above Sorel on the Richelieu, and at Longueuil, where two arrested Patriotes had been freed by a handful of militiamen, and a detachment of regular cavalry put to flight.

At St. Denis preparations for the defense by some 800 Patriotes led by Dr. Wolfred Nelson were under way. Arriving in the outskirts of the village at about 9 A.M., Gore decided to proceed at once to the attack. Dividing his troops into three detachments, he sent one toward the wood east of the village, another along the river bank to the west, and the main column, with the cannon, along the high road into the centre of the village.

The Patriotes, of whom only about a hundred were armed—with old flint-lock rifles, the rest having nothing but scythes and pitchforks—had barricaded themselves, some in the stone house of the Saint-Germains on the highroad, the rest in neighboring buildings. Those without firearms massed behind the walls of the church, ready to participate in the engagement at the first opportunity. Papineau, meanwhile, had been prevailed upon by Nelson to retire to the safety of St. Hyacinthe.

For six hours the British troops attempted to carry the village by storm: they were met with a withering fire. After attacking in the open, the redcoats entrenched themselves behind fences and wood piles. Three times the troops charged, without success. They were then attacked by a body of Patriotes, a hundred or so in number, who had come to join Nelson from St. Ours and the neighboring villages. Gore's troops began to yield ground; at 3 P.M. he ordered the retreat. The cannon was left in the hands of the Patriotes, as well as a number of prisoners.

Like wildfire, the news spread through the countryside: the Patriotes had put British regulars to rout! Gore had lost 60 casualties, half of them killed, and his fieldpiece. The Patriotes lost 12 killed, 4 wounded.

Meanwhile, Colonel Wetherall was advancing on St. Charles with six companies of infantry, a detachment of cavalry and two pieces of artillery. Here the Patriotes were commanded by T. Storrow Brown, leader of the Fils de la Liberté, one of those for whose arrest a warrant had been issued. With his 200 men (who were as ill-armed as those at St. Denis had been) Brown took up a position in the stone manor house of the seigneur, Debartzch.

Wetherall reached St. Charles on November 25 with a well-equipped and fresh force. At the first discharge of artillery fire, T. S. Brown fled, leaving his men leaderless and occupying an impossible position in the face of an overwhelming enemy. The first return fire of the Patriotes disconcerted the troops; but once the artillery had demolished the improvised fortifications, Wetherall launched his main force in a bayonet charge. In fierce hand-to-hand fighting the Patriotes were overpowered and butchered. A few managed to escape; about 40 were killed, the rest wounded or captured. The troops reported only 3 killed and 18 wounded, likely an underestimate. At Pointe-Olivier a body of Patriotes attempted to attack Wetherall's troops on their return march to Montreal, but were repulsed after a brief skirmish. On November 30 Gore returned to St. Denis and avenged his defeat of the week before: he had every house in the village except two burned to the ground.

Papineau, O'Callaghan, Duvernay and other Patriote leaders, meeting on the U.S. border, decided that so long as the North had not been put down, it was necessary to create a diversion in the South that would prevent Colborne from throwing his whole force against the Patriotes in Two-Mountains. Accordingly, a force of 80 was organized and moved in the direction of St. Césaire, whither Nelson had retreated. At Moore's Corners, close to the frontier, they were met on December 6 by a British force of 400 and, after a brief struggle, dispersed.

As in the Richelieu Valley, the Patriotes northwest of Montreal gathered to defend their leaders threatened with arrest. These were, at St. Benoit, Girouard and Masson; at St. Eustache, Dr. Chénier and the Swiss, Amury Girod.

On November 24 Girod received word of the Patriote victory at St. Denis and a message from Robert Nelson (brother of Wolfred) about the situation in Montreal—that "the town was in a state of panic, that there were no troops there, or few at the most." On the strength of a promise that the forces south of the St. Lawrence would create a diversion, Girod decided in his own words "to move next day on Montreal and to attack it." In this he was overruled by Chénier, Girouard, and other leaders. "They resolved to stay on the defensive," writes Girod; "I repented for the first time that I had placed my confidence in such hesitant men."

On December 5th, Gosford proclaimed martial law in the district of Montreal. Colborne was already concentrating his forces for the expedition to the north. To the beacon-fires of devastated villages set alight by the forces of Gore and Wetherall, were to be added a new chain of fires in Two-Mountains. The object was not merely to defeat the hated "rebels" but to exterminate them. Girouard, writing from Montreal Prison in April 1838 bears witness to the fact:

> It had been decreed by the authorities that the imposing forces which made up the expedition against the Canadians in the county of Two-Mountains were not intended simply to take possession of the so-called revolt or rebellion, but actually, to root out utterly the patriotism in the country, with fire, sword and pillage, among all our brave blue-bonnets . . .

Colborne's strategy in this expedition was essentially a repetition of that employed in the earlier operation south of the St. Lawrence. As his points of concentration he chose Carillon, on the left bank of the Ottawa, and St. Martin, north of Montreal. Thus St. Benoit and St. Eustache would be caught between two fires, in the same manner as had St. Denis and St. Charles.

At St. Martin, Colborne himself took command. His 2,000 men included companies of the 32nd, 83rd, and Royal regiments, accompanied by 70 sleighs laden with munitions and provisions; the Royal Artillery, with seven pieces of cannon; and numerous volunteer detachments—cavalry, carabineers, etc. Another thousand remained to garrison Montreal. With those posted at other points, Colborne thus disposed of well over 6,000 men; and two additional regiments were on their way from England.

Opposing this overwhelming force were 500 men at St. Eustache, less than half of whom had rifles; and a slightly smaller number at St. Benoit. Another 500, who had been with Chénier at St. Eustache, disbanded at the last minute at the urging of the parish priest, Paquin. In contrast, Canon Chartier, the *curé* of St. Benoit, was an enthusiastic Patriote. The priest at St. Charles had given the Patriotes his blessing; Chartier worked actively with the Patriote command, helping to raise barricades and fortifications and encouraging the men.

By December 10, both St. Eustache and St. Benoit were fortified, and the Patriotes proceeded to await the arrival of the enemy. On the morning of the 14th Colborne with his 2,000 men moved out of St. Martin, crossed the river above St. Rose, and advanced on St. Eustache. A small body of volunteers under Globenski, seigneur of St. Eustache, took the shorter route, across Isle Jésus to a point across the river from the village.

The first warning which the Patriotes received was a fusillade, on the morning of the 14th, from across the river. It was Globenski and his volunteers. Chénier with 150 men had started across the ice to the attack when a cannon shot, fired from the shore which they had just left, brought them to a halt. Turning, they saw the main body of Colborne's troops, stretching for two miles along the road which skirts the river bank, their bayonets glistening in the cold December sunlight. The Patriote ranks broke in confusion. Chénier regained the village in haste and began posting his men (estimates of whose number vary from 250 to 400) in the church and the surrounding houses.

Before attempting to enter the village, Colborne subjected it to a heavy artillery bombardment, and at the same time disposed his forces of infantry in a vast semicircle, some three miles long, around the outskirts, and well out of range of Patriote bullets. For a full hour the bombardment of the helpless village continued. At one o'clock in the afternoon an artillery detachment was sent part way up the street facing the church. For another hour the cannonade continued, now concentrated chiefly on the main stronghold—the church itself.

By now, the infantry began to move forward; a part took up a position on the frozen surface of the river; other detachments were moved up towards the first houses at the edge of the village. Thus far, they had scarcely come within range of the fire of the Patriotes. It was now two o'clock, and the troops had not begun an attack.

Finally, under cover of the smoke from a house near the church set on fire by a scouting-detachment, Colborne ordered the advance. The bayonet charge took place as the fire caught three of the houses where the Patriotes were barricaded. Driven forth by the smoke and flames, they fought as they could, against many times their number, fell, or attempted to escape across the ice.

There remained only the Church, which some of Colborne's men managed to enter from the rear and put to the torch.

As the Patriotes made a rush out of the building, one of them, named Forget, was recognized by a captain of the Government volunteers. "What are you doing here, Forget?" exclaimed the officer. "Fighting for my country," came the brief, bitter answer. A few minutes later Forget and his two sons died under the fire of the Government troops. Chénier, too, fell fighting, after leaping from a window of the church.

At four o'clock, the whole village was in flames. As night came on, the disbanded troops gave themselves up to rapine and pillage. Sixty houses were reduced to ashes by the fire; those that remained were ransacked by drunken troops and volunteers. The body of Chénier was taken to the inn, and left lying on the counter for three days. Legend has it that the heart was cut out and exposed to view in the window.

The troops had lost about 30 killed; the Patriotes well over twice that number, and more than a hundred prisoners. Next day, Colborne marched to meet Townshend at St. Benoit. Caught between two armies each of 2,000 men, with no hope of aid from any quarter, the handful of Patriotes there decided to surrender. The only answer to their flag of truce was a repetition of the ravaging fire and pillage with which St. Eustache had been visited. Colborne departed only when the flames reached his own headquarters in the village. St. Benoit was razed to the ground. Girouard, captured shortly afterward, while in prison wrote to a friend about Colborne's sack of St. Benoit:

> It would be impossible for me to describe to you the desolation which his march and the barbarous scenes accompanying it spread through our homes. . . . A considerable number of the inhabitants were assembled in my courtyard, which, as you know, is very large; they were lined up, and two cannon placed in the gateway were aimed at them, while they were told that they would be exterminated in a few minutes. There are no insults and outrages which were not heaped upon them, no threats which were not made, to intimidate them into declaring the hiding-places of those who were called their leaders. Not one would give the least indication. . . . Some officers having learned that Paul Barazeau had guided me to Eboulis, they tortured him to force him to tell my place of retreat. They put a pistol to his throat and several times placed him on a block, threatening to behead him, but the generous Patriot held his ground, and the barbarians' violence was wasted.
>
> Then began scenes of devastation and destruction more atrocious than any seen in a town taken by storm and given over to pillage after a long, hard seige. After completely pillaging the village, the enemy set fire to it and reduced it from one end to the other to a heap of ashes. They then went in different directions, ravaging and burning on their way, carrying their fire as far as the village of Ste. Scholastique.

Colborne earned his title of "the Firebrand" (Vieux Brûlot); when he was named Lord Seaton, there were French Canadians, with bitter memories in their hearts, who pronounced it "Satan."

Early in 1838 the Patriotes who had sought refuge across the border set about organizing an expedition into Lower Canada. Led by Robert Nelson and Dr. Côté (Papineau had withdrawn from participation in the struggle), they received assistance and support from democratic elements in northern New York and Vermont. On February 28, a long procession of sleighs bearing several hundred Patriotes, 1,500 rifles, munitions, and three fieldpieces, crossed Lake Champlain and entered the province. In the face of the onset of heavily superior forces of British soldiery, "Loyalist" (Tory) volunteers and U.S. troops under General Wool (who kept Colborne informed of the Patriote preparations), Nelson's force withdrew across the border, Nelson and Côté being taken prisoner and handed over to the U.S. authorities. The expedition is chiefly memorable for the "Declaration of Independence" issued by Nelson, calling for the establishment in Canada of a "patriotic and responsible government." The declaration, a significant expression of the political and social aims of the Patriote movement, included the following provisions:

> That from this day forward, the people of Lower Canada are absolved from all allegiance to Great Britain, and that the political connexion between that power and Lower Canada is now dissolved.
>
> That a republican form of government is best suited to Lower Canada, which is this day declared to be a republic.
>
> That under the free government of Lower Canada all persons shall enjoy the same rights: the Indians shall no longer be under any civil disqualification, but shall enjoy the same rights as any other citizens of Lower Canada.
>
> That all union between church and state is hereby declared to be dissolved, and every person shall be at liberty freely to exercise such religion or belief as shall be dictated to him by his conscience.
>
> That the feudal or seigneurial tenure of land is hereby abolished as completely as if such tenure had never existed in Canada.
>
> That sentence of death shall no longer be passed or executed, except in cases of murder.
>
> That the liberty and freedom of the press shall exist in all public matters and affairs.
>
> That trial by jury is guaranteed to the people of Lower Canada in its most extended and liberal sense.
>
> That as general and public education is necessary, and due by the Government to the people, an act to provide for the same shall be passed as soon as the circumstances of the country will permit.
>
> To secure the elective franchise, all elections shall be had by ballot.
>
> That the French and English language shall be used in all public affairs.

Despite the failure of the February expedition, Patriote activity went on unabated, with the secret, semi-military organization of the "Frères Chasseurs" (Hunters' Lodges) being built up in Canada and in northern States. It was pledged to "fight to the death for Papineau and Canadian independence." Colborne and the imperial authorities had word of its activities through an informer—the owner of the house in which some of its leaders held their meetings.

All through the summer of 1838 preparations went forward for a rising. "Camps" were organized, at which the men were to gather in the night of November 3–4 at Beauharnois, St. Clément, Chateauguay, Pointe-Olivier, St. Constant, Terrebonne, and the lower Richelieu. In the last-named area, near St. Ours, close to a thousand had gathered. It was planned to move on Chambly, then take Montreal. The main camp was at Napierville, where four to five thousand gathered under the command of Robert Nelson. Here he once again issued the proclamation of Canadian independence. In addition to the old commanders, two French officers, Hindenlang and Touvrey, had joined the leadership of the Patriote force.

In Montreal Colborne (who had now replaced Durham as Governor-General, after the former's brief administration) declared martial law; and proceeded with some six to seven thousand troops and a battery of artillery to march on Napierville.

Here Nelson's 2,000 men had less than 300 rifles amongst them; arms and munitions were expected from across the border, but a "neutrality" proclamation of President Van Buren and the intervention of the American authorities cut off most of the supply. A schooner laden with a couple of hundred rifles, a cannon and ammunition, was sent down Lake Champlain, and anchored off Rouse's Point on the evening of the 5th; but a force of government volunteers having seized the mill at Lacolle, mid-way between the foot of the lake and Napierville, the supplies were intercepted and communications cut off.

At the approach of Colborne's main force, the Patriotes fell back on Odelltown, close to the frontier; but it was in the hands of Tory volunteers. Caught between them and Colborne's force, the Patriotes after a brief engagement were dispersed. The whole county of La Prairie was given over to fire and pillage, and the jails filled.

On Lord Durham's arrival in Lower Canada in May 1838, he had found the jails packed with prisoners. Fearing the effect of public trials, he issued an "Ordinance to provide for the security of Lower Canada," whereby eight Patriote leaders (including Wolfred Nelson and B. Viger) were to be deported to Bermuda; a dozen others of those who were already in the United States (including Papineau, Duvernay, T. S. Brown, Canon Chartier, and Georges-Etienne Cartier) were declared guilty of high treason and condemned to be executed should they re-enter Canada. The rest of the prisoners were set free. On news reaching England of these sentences, passed without trial of the accused, the British Government disallowed the Ordinance; whereupon Durham resigned his post. His place was taken by Colborne who at the first opportunity resorted to court-martials in order to crush opposition.

In Montreal, following the rising of 1837, 501 were imprisoned; at Quebec, five. After the second rising, at the end of 1838, 116 were jailed on charges of treason in Montreal, 18 at Quebec, 19 at Sherbrooke and two at Three Rivers. Of 108 brought to trial by court-martial, nine were acquitted, 27 freed under bond, 58 deported to Australia, and 12 were executed. The 108 who were court-martialled included:

66 farmers	1 each of:	teacher	soldier
6 notaries		miller	"bourgeois"
5 blacksmiths		clerk	
5 merchants		cabinetmaker	
4 innkeepers		seamen	
3 bailiffs	2 shoemakers		
2 doctors	2 carpenters		
2 students	2 waggoners		

These died on the scaffold:

Cardinal, Joseph-Narcisse, of Châteauguay, notary.
Daunais, Amable, of St. Cyprien, farmer.
Decoigne, Pierre Théophile, of Napierville, notary.
DeLorimier, Chevalier, of Montreal, notary.
Duquette, Joseph, of Châteauguay, student.
Hamelin, François Xavier, of St. Philippe, farmer.

Hindenlang, Charles, of Paris, army officer.
Narbonne, Pierre-Rémi, of St. Rémi, bailiff.
Nicolas, François, of St. Athanase, schoolteacher.
Robert, Joseph, of St. Philippe, farmer.
Sanguinet, Ambroise, of St. Philippe, farmer.
Sanguinet, Charles, of St. Philippe, farmer.

Of those executed in Montreal one, Hamelin, was 18 years old; Daunais and Duquette were each 20; Narbonne, 23. Cardinal, who was 30, wrote to his wife on the eve of his execution: "Tomorrow, at the time that I am writing now, my soul will be before its Creator and Judge . . . My only regret, in dying, is that I leave you, dear one, with five unhappy orphans, of whom one is not yet born. . . ."

Another of the 12, Delorimier, wrote before his death his "Political Testament":

> I die without remorse; all that I desired was the good of my country, in insurrection and in independence. . . . For 17 to 18 years I have taken an active part in almost every popular movement, always with conviction and sincerity. My efforts have been for the independence of my compatriots; thus far we have been unfortunate . . .
>
> But the wounds of my country will heal—the peace-loving Canadian will see liberty and happiness born anew on the St. Lawrence . . .
>
> To you, my compatriots, my execution and that of my comrades on the scaffold will be of use. . . .
>
> I have only a few hours to live, and I have sought to divide them between my duty to religion and that due to my compatriots; for them I die on the gallows the infamous death of a murderer, for them I leave behind my young children and my wife, alone, for them I die with the cry on my lips: *Vive la Liberté, Vive l'Indépendance!*

The national-democratic people's uprising in Lower Canada met defeat at the hands of the British soldiery and colonial reaction. Among the main reasons for the defeat were these:

—The armed struggle was only partly organized, and largely spontaneous; despite the fairly marked development of elements of people's power and widespread organization (much more advanced than in Upper Canada), there was no clear plan for the conquest of political power, and the initiative in the struggle was left to the forces of colonial reaction;

—The policy of the defensive, as in every popular uprising, proved fatal: instead of moving on Montreal from the Richelieu and Two-Mountains (the two main bases of Patriote support) and initiating a simultaneous move from within the city, the people's forces allowed themselves to be struck down singly, one after the other, with Montreal serving as Colborne's base for a successful operation on "interior lines";

—The Patriotes failed to launch an action in either of the two urban centres, Montreal or Quebec; in the case of the former, the fact that it was the main centre of English merchant-imperial influence was a determining factor, as was in the latter, the strength of Etienne Parent and the right wing of the people's movement; undoubtedly in both centres (as at Toronto) the still embryonic character of the working class, its lack of organization and political consciousness, deprived the revolution of a major driving force;

—The leaders of the Patriote movement, mainly petty-bourgeois in social composition, in their agitation and program largely evaded the issue of struggle against feudal tenure and did not organize mass struggle in the countryside for its abolition; most of these same leaders, in the military showdown, failed to stand the test—Dr. Chénier, who perished, and Wolfred Nelson's stand at St. Denis, were among the exceptions;

—The right-wing elements—representing, in effect, the bourgeoisie—who feared the mass struggle, went over to the side of reaction, paralyzing the movement in the key Quebec area and dividing it in others;

—While some of the lower clergy sympathized with and in some instances actively helped the insurgents, the upper hierarchy of the Church rendered invaluable aid to the imperial authorities by threatening Patriote supporters with excommunication and by denouncing popular resistance;

—The hopes of substantial assistance on the part of sympathetic U.S. democrats were largely frustrated by the collusion of the American authorities with the British in bringing about the defeat of the rising in 1838.

Each of the foregoing went into the making of the defeat; yet merely to enumerate them as disparate causal factors is not enough. We are left, as Charles Gagnon has pointed out in an important study, with "quite incoherent explanations." They need to be integrated in an overall view: one that sees the risings as a bourgeois-democratic, class, and national revolution, the driving forces of which were insufficiently mature to secure victory. There had been neither a development of a French-Canadian industrial bourgeoisie of any substance, nor an urban-plebeian movement strong enough to combine with the peasant rising. It is within this setting that one must situate the confusion, vacillations, and in many cases cowardice of a petty-bourgeois leadership, and its deficiencies of perspective and organization. A similar inadequacy will be seen in the case of Upper Canada, whose rising in solidarity with the Patriotes was to fail both in its fraternal purpose and its local objectives.

Yet these defeated initiatives of the bourgeois and national revolutions in the two Canadas were not the end but rather the beginning of the process of establishing a capitalist democracy in British North America.

THE ARMED CONFLICT
(Bergeron)

Gosford replaces Aylmer in 1835. His mission is to inquire into the situation in the two Canadas, "to maintain the peace and integrity of the Empire and to act as mediator between the two parties." He got the idea of trying to conciliate the moderate Canayens, by taking them into the government, hoping thereby to neutralize and quietly eliminate the Patriotes. Divide and Rule. And always call on the moderates when the rebels can't be bought.

The 1835 session of the Assembly begins with a call for peace and harmony from Gosford. Papineau has the budget passed for six months only. Nothing can be done: the parties are irreconcilable.

LEGISLATIVE BUILDINGS

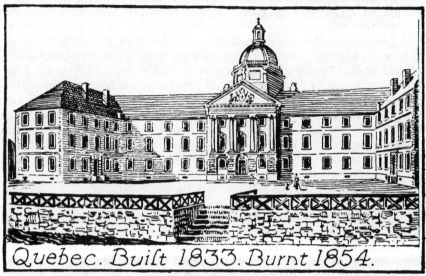

Quebec. Built 1833. Burnt 1854.

But Gosford keeps trying. He dissolves the British Rifle Corps, a gang of armed Englishmen in Montreal who want to defend English 'rights.' They cannot depend on the British army because the mother country is too conciliatory. A contemporary equivalent of this little army is the OAS in Algeria during the Algerian War of 1954-62. The OAS (*Organisation de l'Armée Secrète*) was made up of French colonialists in Algeria determined to keep Algeria French and deny the Algerians their right to independence and sovereignty.

Gosford's tactics of 'moderation' succeed up to a point. The Patriote Bédard and a few others go over to the ranks of Neilson's moderate reformists. Gosford has managed to reduce the Patriotes from a majority position to a single seat when, thanks to a rebel from Upper Canada named Mackenzie, they finally realize that London had instructed Gosford to use these very tactics of conciliation to destroy the Parti Canadien and assimilate the Canayens. The Patriotes come to their senses.

The 1836 special session of the Assembly lasts 12 days and simply confirms the conflict. The Montreal merchants increase their verbal attacks against the Canayens and call for armed confrontation.

The harvest is bad. Unemployment rises. There seems to be no end to the economic depression. England herself badly hurt by the crisis cannot relieve the colonial economy and pacify rebellious feelings.

In 1837, Lord Russel submits his recommendations for the 'solution' to the problem in Canada: no elected legislative council; no executive council responsible to the assembly (control of the budget by the governor if the assembly refuses to pass it); and confirmation of the legal title of the British American Land Company.

Now, the Patriotes get organized. They hold public meetings in the cities and villages. On the Richelieu at St-Ours an assembly of 1,200 adopts 12 resolutions prepared by the Patriotes' Permanent Central Committee, denouncing the British government as an 'oppressor power,' and denouncing the machiavellian tactics[1] used by British colonialism since the conquest. The fifth resolution recognizes the friendship of the United States. The seventh states that the Canayens are tied to the English government by force only. The eighth calls for a boycott of imported products such as tea, tobacco, rum and wine, and asks the people to buy only Canayen products. This same resolution *legalizes* smuggling. The tenth resolution asks all the Canayens to rally "round a single man," Papineau and create the "Papineau Tribute," a kind of tax levied by the Patriotes for the fight against the oppressor.

The Patriotes' newspaper *La Minerve* and the Irish sympathizers' *Vindicator* widely publicize these resolutions. Despite Gosford's prohibition, the popular assemblies of the Patriotes continue to meet. Meanwhile the Governor is busy helping the English party organize meetings which they call 'constitutional assemblies.' The repression begins.

Gosford calls on the Negro-kings to use their influence on the rebellious people. At the consecration of Bishop Bourget, Bishop Lartigue reminds his audience, composed mostly of parish priests, "that it is never permitted to revolt against supreme authority nor to transgress the laws of the country; that we will refuse absolution to anybody who teaches that one can revolt against the government under which we have the good fortune to live, or that it is permitted to violate the laws of the country, in particular those that forbid smuggling."

The Clergy—which has repeatedly told us that it's thanks to them that we have survived—showed again in 1837 that the Church is *against* the people's liberation and *for* colonial domination. During the rebellion, the Clergy's anti-Patriote mouthpiece was its newspaper *L'Ami du peuple*.

In the summer of 1837, Queen Victoria assumed the British throne. The *Te Deum* was sung in all the churches in Quebec but everybody walked out when the parish priests intoned the 'hymn of joy.'

It is now August. Gosford convenes the Assembly to make yet another offer of 'conciliation.' The Patriotes refuse to be drawn in and Gosford dissolves the Assembly.

Some young Patriotes, André Ouimet, Amédée Papineau (Louis-Joseph's son), and Thomas Brown (born in New Brunswick and raised in

---

[1]*Machiavellian tactics:* exploitation of all possible means, regardless of the people's welfare, to attain and maintain power.

the United States) organize a para-military group, the *Fils de la Liberté*. The *Doric Club* is the para-military association of the English.

The Patriotes now push for parallel institutions. The Committee of the Two Mountains decides to elect its own justices of the peace, and an assembly of habitants does so on October 15th. "The Revolution Has Begun!" announces the anti-Patriote newspaper *Le Populaire*. On October 23rd, 5,000 people assemble in St. Charles. But the leader begins to waver: Papineau advises them against taking up arms. He talks about keeping the struggle "constitutional" and limiting the action to boycotting English goods.

Doctor Wolfred Nelson, an English petit-bourgeois gone over to the Patriotes, retorts "the time has come to melt down our tin plates and spoons to make bullets." The popular assembly asks the citizens of the six Richelieu counties to elect their justices of the peace and their military officers. Next day, the delegates call for a meeting of a Convention, that is, of an elected assembly that would draw up a new constitution for Quebec.

In Montreal, the *Fils de la liberté* swear an oath of loyalty to their native land for victory or death. At the same time in another part of the city, Peter McGill is presiding over an anti-Patriote constitutionalist rally.

Bishop Lartigue publishes a pastoral letter that supports Gosford all the way and puts every Catholic on guard against complicity with the "rebels." The letter provokes demonstrations throughout the province. In Montreal, 1,200 Patriotes march in front of St. James Cathedral; in Chambly, Bishop Bourget is booed off the steps of the church. The Patriotes say that the reactionary attitude of the Clergy will hasten the revolution, and they sing the *Marseillaise*. Bishop Lartigue is running scared and offers his resignation to Rome. The Clergy's system of propaganda just goes on preaching loyalty to the British Monarch and respect for the laws—in other words, submission to colonial power.

The newspaper *Le Canadien*, which had formerly supported the Canayen struggle, is getting more and more anti-Patriote. Its owner, Etienne Parent, now defends the bishops' position. *La Minerve* in Montreal is the Patriotes' mouthpiece, as well as *Le Libéral* in Quebec (a bilingual newspaper).

The Patriotes now know precisely who are their enemies: the English merchants, the seigneurs, the Clergy and the *chouayens* (cabbage-head-Canayens), the Canayens who have sold out to the English.

On November 6th, some members of the Doric Club, the English para-military organization, decide to 'nip the rebellion in the bud' and attack the *Fils de la Liberté* as they leave one of their meetings. The *Fils* fight back as well as they can, but they are outnumbered. The English band wins the scuffle and proceeds to ransack the printing office of Doctor O'Callaghan's Irish pro-Patriote newspaper, the *Vindicator*. From there they go on to attack Papineau's house. The armed guards the authorities have patrolling the streets let the Doric Club boys do their thing, while they keep a close watch on the *Fils de la Liberté*.

Gosford writes to London asking for authorization to suspend *habeas corpus*[2] and proclaim martial law.[3] He then calls for reinforcements from the Maritimes and Upper Canada. Regiments of violently anti-Patriote Englishmen volunteer in Montreal, Quebec and the Eastern Townships. The commander-in-chief of this army of repression is Sir John Colborne.

On November 12th, all assemblies and processions are forbidden. On November 16th, warrants are issued for the arrest of 26 Patriotes on the charge of treason. Papineau, O'Callaghan, Desrivières, T. S. Brown and Ovide Perreault escape to the Richelieu. André Ouimet, president of the *Fils de la Liberté*, is thrown in jail. The same day, the Montreal Volunteer Cavalry from St. Jean hunts down the doctor, Davignon, and the notary, Demaray. But it falls into an ambush between Chambly and Longueuil set up by Patriotes under the command of the movement's local leaders, Bonaventure Viger and Dr. Timothée Kimber. The Patriotes fire; the Montreal Volunteer Cavalry flees, abandoning Davignon and Demaray.

This is the first victory for the Patriotes. They organize, regroup, and arm themselves as best they can. In command of the Patriote troops at St. Denis is Dr. Wolfred Nelson; at Montreal, T. S. Brown.

The *chouayens*, the sell-outs, provide Colborne with a good espionage service. He knows the Patriotes' comings and goings well. He sends Lieutenant-Colonel Wetherall with an infantry regiment, a Montreal volunteer cavalry troop and two cannons to join Colonel Gore at St. Denis. Gore has five companies of regulars, a volunteer cavalry troop, and a cannon believed to have come from Sorel.

On the night of November 22nd, Gore veers off the road to avoid St. Ours, which is held by the Patriotes. Thus the surprise attack on St. Denis, planned to take place in the middle of the night, turns into a battle in full daylight between exhausted and frost-bitten soldiers and a village well-prepared for combat. For five hours the fighting is desperate. Young Georges-Etienne Cartier (who later sold out Quebec in Ottawa) is one of the most relentless Patriote fighters. The Patriotes kill 6 soldiers and wound 18 more. Gore retires to Sorel and counts his men: 117 missing—where did they go? The Patriotes count 11 dead and 7 wounded.

Where is Papineau, the 'leader' of the rebellion? He left for St. Hyacinthe with O'Callaghan right at the beginning of the battle. From there they fled to the United States. Papineau was against the armed uprising. When it took place despite his protests, he could not assume the leadership of the revolutionary movement.

But the people understood that power is in the barrel of a gun. The people understood that only an armed revolution could liberate them from Anglo-Saxon colonialism. The habitant logic was simple and powerful: "We are oppressed by a class of English exploiters and by their

---

[2]*Habeas corpus*: a law that prevents prolonged imprisonment of a person without a hearing.

[3]*Martial law*: dictatorial powers that the government uses in times of crisis to systematically repress any revolt. This is the legal justification which the government uses to crush any popular uprising.

puppets, the seigneurs and the Clergy. This class uses the army to maintain its domination over us. Therefore the only way to overthrow the oppressor class is by armed struggle. To arms, Patriotes!"

Papineau did not understand this simple argument. His reasoning was more round-about. Although he realized that the English were an oppressor class, he also believed that the English oppressor would cease being an oppressor if the oppressed made explosive declarations and threatened economic boycott, separation, and annexation to the United States. Papineau did not understand the nature of imperialism. He believed in the English and in a 'gentleman's agreement.' He did not understand that the liberation of a people subjected to economic colonialism can only be accomplished through armed struggle. The fact is, Papineau was bourgeois, and he never changed. He remained a 'gentleman,' a man it is easy to get along with if he is granted a 'gentleman's privileges.' In short, Papineau did not really want a revolution that would bring the habitants to power. He wanted an *evolution* that would give the Canayen petit-bourgeoisie the same rights and privileges that the British and American bourgeoisie had. In fact, he wanted a French Revolution in Quebec, a bourgeois revolution, but without recourse to arms.

Papineau's treason to the cause of the people of Quebec led to a split in the Patriote movement, and weakened it. The leader had run away. How could the struggle go on? It had to be improvised.

While Seigneur Debartzch sought refuge in Montreal, the Patriotes under T. S. Brown fortified his manor at St. Charles. The house was held by 200 men with about 100 guns in bad condition.

Here we must criticize the Patriotes for their lack of military strategy. They thought in terms of well-fortified towns and of pitched battles à la Napoléon. They made their stand in manors (as at St. Charles) or in churches (as in St. Eustache later on) and were perfect targets for the well-armed, well-equipped, well-supplied colonialist army. It would have been better to adopt the guerrilla strategy[4] which had succeeded for the Spanish and the Russians more than 25 years earlier when Napoleon's great, 'invincible' army invaded Spain in 1808 and Russia in 1812. The Patriotes were on home ground; every habitant was a Patriote. They held the countryside. By contrast the English army was in foreign, hostile territory. The Patriotes should have left the villages, faded into the background and systematically harassed the colonialist troops with hard, stinging little jabs to demoralize, decimate and destroy them. One year of guerrilla warfare could have liberated Quebec from British colonialism and imperialism. The strategy of classic warfare was the mistake the Patriotes made.

On November 24th, Wetherall, well-equipped and reinforced, advances on St. Charles. He is preceded by Bonaventure Viger, leading a small group, who slows down the enemy by destroying bridges and attacking reconnaissance squads (Viger seems to be the only Patriote with

---

[4]*Guerrilla:* Spanish word that means 'little war.' It is the strategy of surprise attack and ambush by small armed bands.

any idea of guerrilla warfare, as he demonstrated also on November 16th at Longueuil).

Wetherall burns the village and concentrates on the manor. He sends the classic message to the beseiged Patriotes that if they disperse they will not be molested. Brown replies in kind: he offers the English troops free passage to Sorel if they consent to lay down their arms. Wetherall then attacks the manor with his artillery, and sends in his soldiers, bayonets fixed. They clean out the place in no time. Viger escapes by swimming across the Richelieu.

Brown tries to rally his troops, but it is no use. He flees to St. Denis.

The battle was very unequal: two colonialist soldiers for each Patriote. The score: Patriotes killed, 40; wounded, 30; taken prisoner, 30. Colonialist troops killed, 3; wounded, 18.

Wetherall triumphantly returns to Montreal with his prisoners and the liberty mast of St. Charles.

On December 1st, Gore returns to St. Denis, the site of his defeat. Everything is peaceful. The Patriotes have deserted the village. In the Richelieu he finds the body of an English soldier killed by the Patriotes as he tried to escape from being held prisoner. English fury is suddenly unleashed. The English soldiers desecrate the church, loot and burn the village where, the week before, the habitants had been caring for the wounded the English had abandoned.

The Patriotes taking refuge in the United States have received a warm welcome but only verbal support. On the 6th of December, a troop of 200 Patriotes attempt to rally volunteers and return from American territory. Mailhot and Bouchette are their commanders. But the Missisquoi Volunteers, under Captain Kent, push them back across the border. The wounded Bouchette is taken prisoner, and Wolfred Nelson and Bonaventure Viger are captured and imprisoned in Montreal. During the next few months, the exiled Patriotes in the U.S. split into two factions quite distinct from each other. Papineau speaks of peace and conciliation, but Robert Nelson (Wolfred's brother), Côté, Rodier, Mailhot, Gagnon and Duvernay (founder of the St. Jean-Baptiste Society in 1834) favour armed struggle unto final victory.

It is important to mention the role played during this time by the sell-out Hippolyte Lafontaine. As soon as the conflict became serious he turned against the Patriotes, beseeching Gosford to convene a 'moderate' assembly. When he was refused he left for London to make the same request. A warrant was then issued for his arrest and he fled to Paris. After the repression of the rebellion, this fine gentleman played an important role as a Negro-king.

On December 5th, Gosford decrees martial law. The Patriote leaders now have a price on their heads and the habitants are summoned to surrender their arms. The authorities are counting on the Church to pacify them. The priests need no encouragement. From the pulpit and the confessional come threats of hell for the Patriotes and their sympathizers. The few priests who sympathize with the Patriotes are soon relieved of their duties. Bishop Bourget, co-adjutator to Bishop Lartigue of Montreal, is sympathetic to the Patriotes but doesn't show it.

The Patriotes organize north of Montreal. On November 29th, Jean Chénier, a doctor, and Amury Girod, a Swiss agriculturist and adventurer, lead 200 Patriotes into the Hudson's Bay Company's stores at the Indian mission at Oka and pick up guns, ammunition and a small cannon. They establish their headquarters in a newly-constructed convent at St. Eustache.

The parish priest Paquin, a hard-bitten anti-Patriote, denounces them violently and is put under house arrest by Chénier. However Chartier, the priest from the St. Benoit parish, whole-heartedly supports the Patriotes. Girod musters 1,000 Irish and Canayens, but they are undisciplined and spend their time drinking and quarrelling instead of training.

On December 13th Colborne begins to advance on St. Eustache with three regular regiments and two volunteer cavalry, plus artillery: a total of 2,000 well-equipped men. The next day he arrives at the town where 250 Patriotes have taken refuge in the church, the presbytery, the convent and in the home of an English sympathizer, Scott. Cannons bombard the front of the Church. Soldiers set fire to the back of the church and to the presbytery. The Patriotes jump out the windows and are shot down one after another. The victims include Chénier and 70 other Patriotes. About ten more burn to death in the church. One hundred Patriotes are taken prisoner.

The enemy counts one soldier killed and nine wounded.

Girod flees to St. Benoit and commits suicide four days later. Reverend Chartier escapes to the United States. The colonialist army pillages and sets fire to the village, does the same thing the next day at St. Benoit, meeting no resistance. The army burns all the farms along the way home to Montreal.

THE METROPOLIS INVESTIGATES
(Bergeron)

On February 10, the British Parliament suspends the constitution of Lower Canada and names Lord Durham governor-general and high-commissioner to inquire into the rebellion. The son of a wealthy coal-mine owner, Durham is a leader of the reformist Whigs.[1] He arrives with a royal retinue and straight-away dissolves the special council Colborne had set up when he replaced the sick, discouraged Gosford.

The chouayens and Moderates come out of hiding to pay homage to the new governor. Etienne Parent publishes a laudatory poem by François-Xavier Garneau in Le Canadien.

Durham's first problem: what to do with the Patriotes in jail? A trial with a Canayen jury would acquit them. But, with an English jury, they'd certainly be condemned to death. So he decides to do without a trial. He gets eight of the Patriotes, including Wolfred Nelson, Bouchette, and

---

[1]Whigs: political party with liberal tendencies, made up of the rising industrial English bourgeoisie of the 1830s.

Bonaventure Viger, to write him a letter placing them at his mercy. Then he exiles them to Bermuda. Sixteen other leaders who have fled the country, including Papineau, O'Callaghan, Robert Nelson, Rodier, Brown, Duvernay, Chartier, Gagnon, Cartier, the two John Ryans, Perrault, Demaray, Davignon, and Gauthier, are forbidden to return to Canada. The other prisoners are freed on condition of good conduct.

Durham makes his inquiry and draws up his report. Meanwhile, news reaches England of the measures taken against the political prisoners. The government and the Lords are aroused because they feel that a condemnation without trial is contrary to English tradition. Durham, hearing of this reaction, feels offended, and decides to leave Canada. On November 3, five months after his arrival, he returns to England.

Meanwhile the Patriotes who took refuge in the United States are very active. Robert Nelson had already proclaimed the *Republic of Lower Canada* on February 28, 1838. The document proclaims the independence of Lower Canada (Quebec): separation of church and state; suppression of the tithe; abolition of seigneurial dues; freedom of the press; universal suffrage for all men including the Red man; a secret ballot; nationalization of crown lands and lands of the British American Land Company; election of a constituent assembly; and the use of both languages in public affairs. Robert Nelson is president of the *Provisional Government of Lower Canada*.

Nelson and Côté begin organizing a liberation army called the *Frères Chasseurs* in the bordering American states to prepare for their invasion of Canada. Two hundred thousand persons in Canada and the United States are reported to support this army.

Before his departure, Durham speaks of "elevating the Province of Canada to a profoundly British nature," of "raising Lower Canada's faulty institutions to the level of English civilization and liberty," of "removing all obstacles to the progress of English ventures in that province," and of "dealing with old laws and customs as though they were deeply-rooted abuses." This foretaste of Durham's report provokes violent reactions. Every Canayen can see in it the extinction of his nation. The Moderates at last understand that the extremists are right, and many join the other side. The Clergy, fearing its own extinction if the Canayens are to disappear, revises its position to some extent. But this doesn't prevent the Patriote press from accusing Bishop Lartigue of high treason against the Canayen nation. This gentleman hides away in Quebec for fear of being judged and hanged by a people's court; once again he submits his resignation to Rome.

The Liberation Army foresees an invasion at the beginning of November and is counting on popular uprisings throughout Lower Canada. There are uprisings in Quebec, Sorel, Chambly, and Montreal but only the area south-east of Montreal answers the call. At Beauharnois, 400 men seize the manor of the English merchant Ellice, and 150 men capture the steamboat *Henry Brougham* near Lachine. Then, Chateauguay Patriotes disarm some Scottish loyalists and try to take the Iroquois' arms at Caughnawaga, but they themselves are captured. At St. Charles, St. Denis and St. Ours, Patriotes await in vain the promised arms and their leaders. Finally they disperse.

On November 4, Nelson joins Côté and 3,000 assembled Patriotes at Napierville. The arms at their disposition: 250 guns, some forks and picks and pointed sticks. Côté tries to return to the border to pick up a waiting cargo of arms but a detachment of volunteer loyalists gets in the way.

Four days later, Colborne, who has replaced Durham, advances on Nelson with an army of 6,000 men. Nelson is waiting for him with 1,000 men at Odelltown near the border. But the village garrison gives him a hard time and some of his men mutiny. Next day, Nelson flees across the border as his men withdraw to Napierville, leaving 50 dead and 50 wounded behind them. Later, Colborne's troops pursue the Patriotes into the town and put them to flight.

At the same time, the Glengary Volunteers (Scottish volunteers from Ontario) disperse the Patriotes at Beauharnois and burn the village. The home of every known Patriote is burned.

Colborne has proclaimed martial law on November 4th and suspended *habeas corpus*. By November 9th he can claim 753 prisoners, who are all court-martialled.[2] No Canayen lawyers are permitted to defend them. Ninety-nine are condemned to death. Adam Thom of the *Montreal Herald* demands they be executed immediately. He claims, "it would be ridiculous to feed them all winter only to bring them to the gallows later." Colborne orders the public execution of 12 Patriotes in front of the Montreal Prison at the *Pied-du-Courant* (at the corner of Notre-Dame and DeLormier streets).

The 12 Patriotes publicly executed by Dictator Colborne:

> Joseph-Narcisse Cardinal, 30, notary, member of the Assembly, married, 5 children.
>
> Joseph Duquette, 22, law student, bachelor.
>
> Pierre Théophile Decoigne, 27, notary, married, 2 children.
>
> François-Xavier Hamelin, 23, farmer, militia lieutenant, bachelor.
>
> Jacques Robert, 54, farmer, militia captain, married, 5 children.
>
> Ambroise Sanguinet, 38, farmer, married, 2 children.
>
> Charles Sanguinet, 36, farmer, married, 2 children.
>
> Amable Daunais, 21, farmer, bachelor.
>
> François-Marie Thomas Chevalier de Lorimier, 30, notary, married, 3 children.
>
> Pierre-Rémi de Narbonne, 36, painter and bailiff, married, 2 children.
>
> François Nicolas, 44, teacher.
>
> Charles Hindelang, 29, of French nationality, in the military, bachelor.

Amongst the others sentenced, 58 were deported to Australian penal colonies,[3] 2 were banished from the country and 27 were freed on bail.

The Tories were hollering for more blood. The Canayens denounced Colborne's "blood-thirsty tyranny."

It is to be noted that those whom Colborne executed were not among

---

[2]*Court-martial:* military court which *usually* judges only soldiers and officers guilty of desertion, espionage and other such offences. The judges are military men. There is no jury.

[3]In this period Australia is an English colony used as a concentration camp for criminals and political prisoners of the British Empire.

the leaders of the Rebellion, but simple militants. While the tyrant had been heard to say that executions were necessary 'to set an example,' he did not dare execute the Patriote leaders for fear that popular indignation would turn to violence. By executing rank-and-file Patriotes, he was able to resolve this contradiction.

In February 1839, Papineau left the United States for France where he wrote a *History of the Insurrection of Canada*. He was to return in 1845 and sit in the Canadian Parliament from 1847 to 1854.

Lafontaine, Morin, Cartier and Taché were destined to become prime ministers. Wolfred Nelson would be re-elected to the Canadian Parliament in 1844; T. S. Brown would return to his business and write his memoirs; and Bouchette would become customs collector in Ottawa. Robert Nelson and O'Callaghan remained in the United States.

The Rebellion failed. Many Canayens were discouraged. Some left Quebec for parts of the United States like Massachusetts where industrialization was creating employment, particularly in the textile industry. Half a million Canayens went to the U.S. between the years of 1837 and 1910. Why did they not stay on the farms? There were no farms left. All the arable land in the province had been cleared. The harvests were bad. There was no 'future' in Quebec. For a good number of Canayens the defeat of the Rebellion meant perpetual English colonialism and the domination by the Clergy that went with it. Many chose emigration to the 'States.'

23

WILLIAM LYON MACKENZIE—JACKSONIAN?*

J. E. Rea

The best-known personage in pre-Confederation British North America is unquestionably the fiery newspaper editor and politician, William Lyon Mackenzie. But familiarity and understanding do not necessarily go hand in hand. Indeed, one of the fascinations of Mackenzie for students of early Canadian history is the personal enigma which the man represents. His motivations and the source of his ideas have long been the subject of a good deal of historical debate. Mackenzie was clearly a boat-rocker, but what did this mean in the context of Upper Canada at the time? One continuing theme in the attempt to explain Mackenzie has been to relate him to contemporary events in the United States, particularly "Jacksonian Democracy." His enemies, when they did not dismiss him as a frustrated demagogue, were prone to tar him with the brush of Yankee republicanism. Even those more sympathetic to Mackenzie have emphasized the importance of American influences upon his posture, both in its critical and constructive parts. One of the great dangers in this sort of attribution of "influence" is that it may misinterpret or oversimplify the nature of the source alleged to have been so important. As Professor J. E. Rea argues in the following article, this has clearly been the case with Mackenzie and Jacksonian Democracy, which was a far more complex phenomenon than most Canadian historians have realized. What sort of a picture of Jacksonian Democracy does Rea present? To what extent is Mackenzie a "Jacksonian"? Where else might his "radical" ideas have come from?

---

*Mid-America, 50 (1968), 223-35.

SUGGESTIONS FOR FURTHER READING

James L. Bugg, ed., *Jacksonian Democracy: Myth or Reality?* (New York: Holt, Rinehart and Winston, 1964).

Margaret Fairley, ed., *The Selected Writings of William Lyon Mackenzie* (1960).

William Kilbourn, *The Firebrand* (Toronto: Clarke, Irwin and Co., 1956).

J.M.B.

It has become a cliché of Canadian historiography that the political thought of William Lyon Mackenzie was deeply influenced by the values and objectives of Jacksonian Democracy. As in all clichés there is a kernel of truth in this observation. But unfortunately, it makes no allowance for the varieties and inconsistencies of the Jacksonian faith. It is quite possible to illustrate how several of Mackenzie's political goals bore a close relationship to the aspirations of certain elements of Jackson's party following. Indeed, the extent of his obligation at times would reveal unacknowledged direct borrowing. In a methodological sense, it would be unproductive, however, to catalogue a series of these similarities as a method of demonstrating the degree of influence which was exerted on the development of Mackenzie's ideas. In the first place, the tensions within the Democratic Party were sufficient proof that there was no Jacksonian type; no one representative set of political, economic and social values to which all the party could subscribe.[1] Secondly, Mackenzie's eclecticism would render this method of establishing the origins of his ideas largely conjectural, since it is equally possible to find in his writings the influence of the English utilitarians. When viewed from a distance, however, there is a marked similarity between the *appeal* of Mackenzie and of Andrew Jackson.

Jackson's political projection was essentially moral. He conceived his duty as Chief Magistrate to be the preservation of the simple agrarian values of the "Old Republic." The tension within the party resulted from the fear that this objective could only be gained by sacrificing the benefits of capitalist enterprise. The resolution of this paradox produced no articulated programme, but rather a class appeal identified by moral orientation. The "farmers and mechanics," assured that they were the strength of America, responded gladly to a leader who justified their right to share in the exploitation of a continent.[2] Mackenzie's appeal was more narrowly agrarian but it was couched in rhetoric that was not unlike the Jacksonian message. It was his conviction that:

> The end or object of the "social union" has been defined to be an act of the whole society, or some part of the society, which possesses the power of determining for the whole, fixing certain marks by which the share of the

---

[1]There were three fairly well defined groups included in Jackson's party following. They may be roughly identified as agrarian, entrepreneurial, and urban lower class.

[2]Marvin Meyers, *The Jacksonian Persuasion* (New York, 1960), chap. 1.

good things of this life belonging to each member may be distinguished, and his right to the peaceable enjoyment of that share secured to him.[3]

In Mackenzie's case, the important element of the society was the yeomanry by which he meant, primarily, the farmers of Upper Canada.[4] Like the Jacksonians, Mackenzie did not desire legislated equality but equal rights and protection since "inequality of fortune is not excluded by equality of rights."[5] It is dangerous, however, to push this analogy too far since Mackenzie's ideas were not consistent. It is of more value to examine their development chronologically before judging the effect of the American example.

In his earliest years as a journalist in Upper Canada, Mackenzie was convinced that the province would progress rapidly while maintaining the connection with Britain. His hatred of slavery conditioned his view of everything American. He was not unaware of the political weaknesses of Colonial Government, of course, but his solution for Upper Canada was representation in the British Parliament. While realizing that the loyalty issue was used as a political weapon by the Tories, he had nothing but contempt for the advocates of the American system of government.

> If I am not so brimful of loyalty as some people I find here, I nevertheless have a greater veneration for that constitution which has withstood the shocks of time and the revolutions of ages, than for any of the quack systems of liberty in this western continent, which after telling us that all men are equal allow their votaries to buy and sell justice, and mock the ear with the language of freedom in a capital polluted with negro slavery.[6]

While conceding that the neighboring states were developing more rapidly than Upper Canada, he urged a union of the provinces with Great Britain "as the only measure which can develop our vast and ample resources."[7] It seems startling to read now how Mackenzie urged, as a solution to the unbalanced political arrangement of the province, the establishment of titles, parliamentary taxation and an hereditary aristocracy. There was a sharp logic, however, in his realization that Governor Simcoe's promise of "the image and transcript of the British Constitution" could not be satisfied by half-measures. The reproduction of the British system must be complete in all its details if the connection with the mother country was expected to sustain "in (these) republican and levelling times, the dignity of true nobility."[8]

At this time Mackenzie scoffed at the very idea of independence. In a fiery editorial he asked,

> What is the use of people talking about what they don't understand? How could Upper Canada be independent?—Without an army, without a navy,

---

[3]*Colonial Advocate*, July 15, 1830.

[4]Lillian Gates, "The Decided Policy of William Lyon Mackenzie," *Canadian Historical Review*, 40 (1959), 187.

[5]*Colonial Advocate*, July 15, 1830.

[6]Ibid., April 18, 1825.

[7]Ibid.

[8]*Colonial Advocate*, April 26, 1827; "An open Letter to Lord Dalhousie."

without money or means of defence, without population, without foreign trade or the means of protecting her commerce if she had any; so situated she would have a poor prospect for independence. . . .[9]

He considered the prospect of union with the United States even more distasteful. Its greatest weakness, he felt, was the necessity of the "chief ruler" to seek election, and "liable to be changed at the caprice of the opposition." He criticized the American characteristic of having the legal profession supply the legislators, preferring the English practice of choosing "independent country gentlemen" in whose hands the "liberties of the people are surely far more safe." In the best Tory style Mackenzie defended the primogeniture laws lest "a less valuable class of persons usurp the places of the country gentlemen of education, manly principle and honorable family."[10] To strengthen the government further, Mackenzie contended that the executive and judiciary should "not be placed at the mercy of a majority in the assembly . . . and so oblige the officers of government to court popular favor for daily bread: [this] would place the judges of the land in that slavish state of dependence on the populace which produced so much real evil in Massachusetts and which in the rich state of New York has made cheap justice a byeword."[11]

Even at this point, however, Mackenzie found it necessary to qualify his strictures against the Americans. "It may be fashionable to call the people of Massachusetts rebels, democrats and levellers. But they were Englishmen . . . and resisting as they did the measures of government, they had or thought they had the successful example of England herself as their guide."[12] And he assured his readers that he was "among those who believe it is impolitic (if not unconstitutional) for government to make use of any monies raised by taxation on the people of these colonies without their consent by their representatives. . . ."[13] This seeming ambivalence accurately marks one of the major turning points in Mackenzie's career. Throughout the year—1827—the province was greatly agitated by the debate over the alien question. He became convinced that the reform group in the Assembly were justified in their criticism of the government, and was himself anticipating entering the House. It was characteristic of him that once he had taken the decision, his former opinions would be no severe handicap. There was no sudden about-face, but Mackenzie grew increasingly dubious of the likelihood of efficient, liberal government under the existing arrangement. He speculated on the "possibility that these colonies will be requested by the British ministry, next summer, to assume the management of their own affairs—and this event would (next to our own favorite system) be productive of the greatest possible advantage to the country, for as long as the

---

[9]Ibid., May 7, 1827.
[10]Ibid.
[11]Ibid.
[12]Ibid.
[13]Ibid.

present system is tolerated, so long will the energies of these beautiful countries lie hidden and unknown."[14] Mackenzie was still advocating union with Britain as the best solution. But the significance of this shift in his attitude was that he saw in the ruling group at York a barrier to the development of the province that had to be overcome.

At the same time, he was preparing his readers for another shift in outlook. In commenting upon the career of Dr. Hugh Williamson, the American scientist, Mackenzie advised that

> . . . those who undervalue the people of North America, study their history carefully, and by so doing they will learn their own ignorance of the state of literature and the arts in a country possessed of the spirit of freedom, and blest with the learning and genius of their parent nation, without being burdened by the remains of her feudal system.[15]

Mackenzie was careful to speak of the people of North America not just the United States. But his own values were undergoing a profound change. In the same issue of his paper he reviewed Peter Perry's speech on the jury bill in revealing terms. The Reform leader, ". . . portrayed the happiness and honest unsuspecting candor which is oftenest to be found in the dwelling of the hard-working yeoman. . . ." The agrarian bias of Mackenzie was beginning to quicken. In his campaign for the Assembly in the spring of 1828, he exhibited a very restricted view of the function of a representative. The freeholders of Markham were assured that ". . . where one opinion on political matters was found to subsist, it was probable that the candidate elected would be able to serve his constituents."[16] This apparent willingness to serve as an agent of the constituency rather than a moulder of opinion can probably be consigned to the limbo of most election rhetoric. There was no doubting Mackenzie's position, however, as he recited for his audience the litany of Reform grievances; clergy reserves, the alien law, poor education facilities, relief of religious societies, control of the post office, and to prove his conversion, he now demanded the abolition of primogeniture. Two further demands, local selection of magistrates and the right of the Assembly to impeach judges, indicated the emerging radical strain in Mackenzie's political thought.[17] In another article that same day, he accused the Executive Council of trying to muzzle the press, and the appointed postmasters of tampering with delivery of the *Colonial Advocate*.

But 1828 was also an election year across the border. Mackenzie, in his newspaper office, was able to follow the culmination of the four-year Jacksonian campaign to reverse the electoral decision of 1824. In one of the most vituperative elections in American history Jackson finally gained the White House. A year or two earlier Mackenzie would have delighted in exposing, for the edification of Upper Canada, this example of democracy at its worst. But he was strangely silent throughout the

---

[14]*Colonial Advocate*, January 17, 1828.
[15]Ibid., January 31, 1828.
[16]Ibid., January 25, 1828, was the day of the meeting.
[17]Ibid.

year offering little information on the progress of the American party struggle. Jackson's victory was reported without comment, as was his inaugural address. Mackenzie, who had normally referred to Jackson as simply the "slayer of Ambrister,"[18] decided to see for himself the state of political life to the south. During his tour he sent long dispatches back to the Advocate office, and the balance of his observations was published in book form in 1833.[19] The most striking feature of American government to Mackenzie was its simplicity and frugality. He quoted Benjamin Franklin approvingly, "A virtuous and laborious people may be cheaply governed, determining, as we do, to have no offices of profit, nor any sinecures, or useless appointments, so common in ancient or corrupted states."[20]

In his description of his meeting with the President, Mackenzie emphasized Jackson's simplicity and lack of pomp. The fact that only one youthful attendant was in sight prompted Mackenzie to compare, "this active and useful servant, in my mind's eye, with the hosts of laqueys and bedchamber gentlemen I had seen surrounding the persons and devouring the revenues of European princes. . . ."[21] His desire for frugal government was much encouraged by his tour, since "the officers of the general government are perhaps the most unassuming public functionaries in the world. . . ."[22] His impressions of various state governors also reflected this concern, as his criterion for approbation seemed to be the degree to which the salary of the incumbent "is a burthen to the country." Mackenzie's preoccupation with the costs of maintaining government was both an expression of his increasingly agrarian outlook, and his concern for the political implications of the Upper Canadian practice of voting supply without a rigid accounting. The effect of his trip was to influence Mackenzie more in the development of political attitudes than in remedies. His oversimplified view of the Jacksonian administration tended to reinforce his conviction that public office was a public trust, and that the end of government could be secured to the people only through popular control.

The following year, when the death of George IV brought on another provincial election, Mackenzie made a full statement of his political faith. Employing the journalistic tactics of the time, he addressed an open letter to the Lieutenant-Governor in which he asserted a Lockean conception of government. Assuming that Upper Canada was an extension of the British nation, Mackenzie argued that the inhabitants had acquired three fundamental rights: to choose their own rulers and governors, to cashier them for misconduct, and to frame a government for themselves, suitable to their wants and necessities.[23] In orthodox fashion he appealed to Burke, Fox and the Pitts as supporters of these rights. A

---

[18]*Colonial Advocate*, April 26, 1827.
[19]W. L. Mackenzie, *Sketches of Canada and the United States* (New York, 1833).
[20]Mackenzie, *Sketches*, p. 27.
[21]Ibid.
[22]Ibid., p. 38.
[23]*Colonial Advocate*, July 15, 1830.

distinctly new note, however, was then evident as he accepted "the precise and simple terms 'the greatest happiness to the greatest number' as a definition of the end and object of government."[24] The government of Upper Canada, he claimed, had virtually denied this possibility. He was exhibiting an increasing disillusionment with the ability of the British form of government to provide for "the happiness and improvement of (his) fellow creatures."[25] Mackenzie complained to the Lieutenant-Governor that,

> The visible government of this province . . . may be fairly described as an aristocracy of office-holders, men nearly all above the law, with a monopoly of the paper currency, a monopoly of the places, offices, gifts, grants, territories, sinecures. . . . [Such] powers have been put into the hands of Your Excellency in conjunction with a very small number of other persons, which make you as a body stronger than the rest of the community. Consequently you may take from the community whatever you please. . . .[26]

The implicit assumption of Mackenzie's complaint would appear to be that government had broken its compact with the people. The fact that the government of Upper Canada was established, not by compact, but by Act of Parliament, would scarcely dissuade him. To Mackenzie, this was a question of rights and not of law; and was made more urgent by his view of human nature.

> As every man desires to have for himself as many good things as possible, and as there is not a sufficiency of good things for all, the strong, if left to themselves, would take from the weak as much as they pleased. The weak therefore, who are the greater number, have an interest in conspiring to protect themselves. Hence the creation of rights in favor of all the members of the community, often-times called constitutional rights. . . .[27]

It was obvious that Mackenzie felt the necessary protection was not being provided by the constitution of Upper Canada. The inequality of rights, which he claimed existed in the province, was proof of its defective nature. He recommended that a revision be considered, adopting as a guide the principle of utility, and providing that "the greatest possible happiness of society is attained by ensuring to every man the greatest possible quantity of the produce of his labor."[28]

In his appeal to the people, directed specifically to the "farmers of Upper Canada," the full complexity of Mackenzie's political ideas was revealed. There are three clearly identifiable strains: agrarian, utilitarian and Jacksonian. He urged "the independent cultivators of the soil, [to] watch increasingly over the liberties of your infant country."[29] Since

---

[24]Ibid.
[25]Ibid.
[26]Ibid.

[27]Ibid. It is difficult to establish the origin of this view held by Mackenzie. It may be utilitarian; but it is very like the opinion of James Madison, given expression in the *Federalist*, No. 10. See Clinton Rossiter, *The Federalist Papers* (New York, 1961), pp. 79–80.

[28]*Colonial Advocate*, July 15, 1830.

[29]Ibid., September 9, 1830. Succeeding quotations are also drawn from this election appeal.

agriculture was the "most innocent, happy and important of all human pursuits," Mackenzie did not for a moment believe "that an Assembly of the best and most faithful farmers in the country would have been as easily assailed by the corruptions of a colonial administration. . . ." He warned the electors that their present system of government was inadequate to protect their rights. Even a faithful replica of the British Constitution would no longer be sufficient, since in England, "You will perceive an inequality of the ranks of society, too great for the purposes of producing the greatest quantity of human nourishment, and the greatest sum of human happiness. . . ."[30] The electors of Upper Canada, he argued, must appreciate that successful government is based on a compact which recognizes "the inherent rights of the people as men." The farmer and mechanic should remember that an enlightened people "are the only safe depository of the ultimate powers of society." This appeal was not so much directed toward a plea for a better educated electorate, as to a peculiarly Jacksonian concept; that intuitive wisdom, a product of the agrarian way of life, was equal, if not superior to, acquired knowledge. As Mackenzie put it,

> Many there are of little education, and ordinary acquirements, who yet possess a weight of character, acuteness of observation, industry, and perseverance, which will more than counter-balance the superior acquirements and more imposing appearance of those who would pass for men of wisdom and learning.[31]

The succeeding issue of his paper illustrated the extent to which Mackenzie was becoming indebted to Jacksonian ideas for his political ammunition. He advocated that voters should insist on pledges from members against debt increase and monopolies. Primogeniture and entail must now be abolished, he declared, since "there is a natural aristocracy among men, founded on virtue and talents." He informed his readers that he was now

> . . . a sincere convert to the doctrine of rotation in office . . . —the duties of all public offices are or may be made so simple that men of intelligence may easily fulfill them. If it be true, that few men can enjoy power and not become more or less corrupt . . . many will admit that more is lost by their long continuance in office than is gained by their experience.[32]

The principle of rotation in office was primarily drawn from frontier experience, and presumed a general competence of most men for most jobs. It was not, however, a very prevalent idea in Upper Canada, and in any case, Mackenzie has taken it almost word for word from Jackson's first annual message.[33] Mackenzie's concept of the ideal society was

---

[30]Ibid.

[31]Ibid. An excellent discussion of this idea may be found in John W. Ward, *Andrew Jackson, Symbol for an Age* (New York, 1955), especially chap. 4. Mackenzie's thoughts on the subject are more fully developed in his *Catechism of Education* (New York, 1830), p. 30.

[32]*Colonial Advocate*, September 16, 1830.

[33]See James D. Richardson, ed., *Messages and Papers to the President*, 10 vols. (Washington, 1903), vol. 2, p. 449.

beginning to take shape, however, and it excluded all political, religious or economic interests protected by a privileged position, and assured to all men the fruits of their labor.[34] Their simple needs would be supplied by an honest, frugal and efficient government which responded readily to their wishes. Mackenzie had travelled a long way in two years. His political objectives were already well ahead of the feeling of the Reform party and the province. But the frustrations of the next few years were to drive him toward even more radical solutions.

His repeated expulsions from the Assembly, the defeat of the Reformers in the election of 1832, the decisions on banking policy after his trip to England, and above all, the complete inability of the Reformers to influence the Legislative Council and the Executive turned Mackenzie more and more to elective institutions as the solution to Upper Canada's dilemma. It became his self-appointed task to convince the farmers and mechanics of the province that they were the victims of a conspiracy, contrived by the few to exploit the many.[35] As chairman of a select committee on grievances, set up by the Assembly in 1835, he asserted

> that the Legislative Council, as at present constituted, has utterly failed, and never can be made to answer the ends for which it was created; and the restoration of legislative harmony and good government requires its reconstruction on the elective principle.[36]

He was turning more and more to the example of the United States. The unresponsiveness of the government of Upper Canada, even when there was a Reform majority in the Assembly, had convinced him of the need for change. His impatience for a simple, frugal government dismayed his more moderate followers whom he was asking to choose between radical political reform and the steady economic improvement which was being achieved. His influence in Upper Canada was decreasing steadily as he turned to American precedents. He tended to view Jackson, not as the leader of a party straining in many directions, but ideally. The President was, he claimed,

> not in words only, but in deed and in truth, the friend of the humbler classes against the united rapacity of their more exalted brethren, who, in America, as elsewhere, would willingly concentrate the wealth and power of the republic in a few hands, that it might minister the more securely to the wants of a luxurious and immoral aristocracy.[37]

He was completely unable, however, to imitate Jackson's broad appeal, and maintain a following which could find in his leadership a reasonable solution to the province's political problems. He confessed to John Neilson that, "I am incapable of moderating the spirit of party—I am hot and fiery and age has not tempered as much as I could wish my

[34]*Colonial Advocate,* July 13, 1830. Also Gates, "The Decided Policy of Mackenzie," p. 186.

[35]W. Kilbourn, *The Firebrand* (Toronto, 1956), p. 89.

[36]Upper Canada, House of Assembly, *Seventh Report on Grievances* (York, 1835), p. xxxix.

[37]Mackenzie, *Sketches,* p. 59.

political conduct and opinions."[38] By 1835, he had evidently lost hope of achieving any substantial reform under British institutions. Petitions to England were useless. He informed Neilson, "I have seen enough to convince me that we shall continue to have the very worst possible government in Upper Canada until we get rid of the system which binds us to the earth. I therefore am less loyal than I was. . . ."[39] Mackenzie was not, at this point, considering rebellion, but the election of 1836, which returned a Tory majority, appeared to end all hope of effecting a peaceful revision of the constitution.

Once the necessity for revolutionary change was accepted, however, Mackenzie's political thought shifted to support it. The agrarian element became less prominent than natural rights. The example of the Jacksonians was replaced by the political justification of the American revolution, and the rationale of utilitarianism. The rhetoric remained much the same as it had been during the early 1830s but the underlying assumptions seem to have been borrowed from revolutionary theory. The Declaration of the Reformers of Toronto declared that:

> Government is founded on the authority, and is instituted for the benefit, of a people; when therefore, any Government long and systematically ceases to answer the great ends of its foundation, the people have a natural right given them by their Creator to seek after and establish such institutions as will yield the greatest possible happiness to the greatest number.[40]

The analogy of the Declaration of Independence of the American colonies was continued, as Sir Francis Bond Head, the Lieutenant-Governor, was cast in the role of George III, and the catalogue of his alleged crimes recited, elections debased, increasing debt, unjust taxation, church establishment, denial of public meetings, and so on.[41] Committees of correspondence and vigilance were set up, and non-importation was proposed to enforce their demands. A very new element had also found a place in his political programme. Free trade was held to be an inherent right of the people, and any attempt to restrict their desire to sell in the dearest and buy in the cheapest market was held to be an infringement on their liberties.[42] Mackenzie's new colors were now firmly nailed to the mast. Asserting that "the due influence and purity of all our institutions have been utterly destroyed," the Declaration claimed that the reformers of Upper Canada were now in the same position as "our brother colonists of old."[43] This was, perhaps, the most glaring inconsis-

---

[38]Mackenzie to Nielson, November 23, 1835, cited in R. A. MacKay, "Political Ideas of William Lyon Mackenzie," *Canadian Journal of Economics and Political Science*, 3 (1937), p. 2.

[39]Same to Same, December 28, 1835, cited in Margaret Fairley, ed., *The Selected Writings of William Lyon Mackenzie* (Toronto, 1960), pp. 345–46.

[40]See Charles Lindsey, *The Life and Times of William Lyon Mackenzie*, 2 vols. (Toronto, 1862), vol. 2, app. D, pp. 334–42.

[41]Ibid.

[42]Free trade ideas had been current in England for some time, but not in the terms Mackenzie used. His argument is closer to that of William Leggett, the radical Jacksonian leader of New York. Leggett was, for a long time, the editor of the *New York Evening Post* and the *Plaindealer*, excerpts from which often appeared in Mackenzie's newspapers.

[43]Lindsey, *Life of Mackenzie*, app. D.

tency in Mackenzie's change of front. It was no longer the "Family Compact," or the "local oligarchy" which had to be resisted but the king.

The Draft Constitution drawn up by the reformers was also based on the American example, but more frankly Jacksonian in tone. Its preamble was almost a literal copy of the American document: "We, the people of the State of Upper Canada, in order to establish justice, ensure domestic tranquility, provide for the common defense, promote the general welfare and secure the blessings of civil and religious liberty . . . do establish this Constitution." The body of the document was patterned after the constitution of the state of New York and contained many of its features, bicameral elected legislature, election of militia officers, representation by population in both houses, veto power given to the governor, and other provisions.[44] Specific Jacksonian policies were included, such as the direct election of the chief magistrate, abolition of paper money of small denominations, and hard money was to be the only legal tender in the payment of debts. Some provisions, however, went well beyond anything the Jacksonians would consider. The constitution included the unique provision that all debts contracted by government must be liquidated within 20 years. This was a direct attempt to legislate the agrarian desire for frugality of government and to protect the citizens against an unwise choice of legislators. Furthermore, the reform instrument provided that: "There shall never be created within this state any incorporated trading companies, or incorporated companies with banking powers. Labor is the only means of creating wealth."[45] This was Mackenzie's singular attempt to cope with the problem of monopoly. The Jacksonians solution to this problem was general incorporation laws which would avoid the necessity of individual charters and thus reduce the possibility of legislative corruption. Mackenzie's policy was, in effect, to turn back the clock and deny to the people of Upper Canada the advantages to be gained by new capitalist techniques. This feature of his programme was not only scoffed at in Upper Canada, but would have received the same treatment in the United States.

Mackenzie campaigned for support in his new paper, the *Constitution*. He advised the creation of Political Unions throughout the province, based on the example of the English Radicals. He admitted, as well, that "it is true that a plan such as I have suggested could be easily transferred without change of its structure to military purposes."[46] In several issues that summer he reprinted copious excerpts from Tom Paine's *Common Sense*. The editor felt constrained to explain to his readers that it contained "the most reverential deference for the revelations of Christianity," and was not a product of Paine's deism.[47] Its purpose, he advised his readers, was to serve as "groundwork for the contemplations of the people on the question of government and a written constitution," and directed its message especially to "the farmers, mer-

---

[44]Ibid., app. E, pp. 344–58.
[45]Ibid.
[46]*Constitution*, July 19, 1837.
[47]Ibid., August 9, 1837.

chants and laborers of Upper Canada." It is quite likely, however, that the majority of his readers saw in Paine's work, not a solution to the weaknesses of colonial government, but exactly what it was, a rationalist justification for treason against the King. There was no possibility that any considerable response could be evoked by such an appeal in Upper Canada. Such a plea was completely alien, even to the reform movement in the province. And even from Mackenzie, who had fought for years, not against Britain and the monarchy, but against the local government, it was almost completely uncharacteristic.

Mackenzie, in his career as a journalist and politician in Upper Canada, had covered the full political spectrum. He began as a fervid supporter of British institutions and ended the leader of a rather pathetic rebellion. The changes that took place in his political thought were primarily a result of local, provincial influences. He lacked the depth to create a broad political appeal. His essential concern was the welfare of the farmers of Upper Canada, and agrarianism was the most consistent strain in his thought. He clothed his appeals variously, in the language of the English Radicals and Utilitarians, or in the agrarian aspect of the Jacksonian movement. It would appear, then, that the determining influence was not borrowed abstract theory, but the realities of Upper Canadian political life. There was simply no possibility of Mackenzie gaining his objectives through the existing constitutional arrangements. This forced him to look elsewhere for justification. When Jacksonian Democracy provided the example he sought to advance his agrarian desire for simple, frugal and responsive government he seized upon it. Thus he applauded Jackson's attitude toward universal education and the use of public lands in its support, abolition of imprisonment for debt, separation of church and state, "and his veto message on the Bank question stands forth a splendid and imperishable monument of his hatred to oppression under the form of licensed monopolies."[48] But Mackenzie would never have made a good Jacksonian. He could never comprehend that an essential conviction of that party was not that the economic race should be fixed in favor of the western farmers, but simply that all should have an equal chance at the beginning. The influence of the urban areas was strong in the Jacksonian party, especially the aggressive, entrepreneurial group. Mackenzie would have sought refuge with John Taylor of Caroline, and the "Old Republicans," in their desire to stop the advance of the 19th century.

---

[48]Mackenzie, *Sketches,* p. 59.

24

THE CLERGY RESERVES: "ECONOMICAL MISCHIEFS" OR SECTARIAN ISSUE?*

G. Alan Wilson

Perhaps the hottest single issue in Upper Canada in the first 50 years of the 19th century was the Clergy Reserves. These were the lots—one-seventh of the total ungranted land in the province—set aside by the Constitutional Act of 1791 for "the support and maintenance of a Protestant clergy." The issue was a highly complex one, but basically opposition to the Clergy Reserves sounded two major themes: the question of connection between state and church (the Church of England claimed sole right to revenue from sale of the lands), and the charge that the Reserves were a disfunctional part of the province's land grant scheme, interfering with orderly and equitable settlement. The religious aspect of the question had, of course, political overtones. Since the Church of England relied on its established status and its strong connections with both the imperial government and the provincial government to support its claims, attacks on the religious front became inextricably interwoven with political opposition to the government in power. Opponents of the Reserves were frequently not content to argue against them in terms of religious principle and political hostility, but also complained of them on economic and administrative grounds as well. It is to the latter complaints in particular that Professor G. Alan Wilson turns his attention in the following article, asking whether the criticisms of the Reserves as bad land policy and economic nuisances were really justified in fact. To what conclusions does he come? On what evidence and considerations does he base his arguments? In what way does Wilson's position alter the Clergy Reserves as a political and religious issue in Upper Canada?

*Canadian Historical Review, 42 (1961), 281-99. Reprinted by permission of the author and University of Toronto Press.

SUGGESTIONS FOR FURTHER READING

A. Dunham, *Political Unrest in Upper Canada, 1815-1836* (London: Longmans, Green, 1927).

J. S. Moir, *Church and State in Canada West* (Toronto: University of Toronto Press, 1959).

G. C. Paterson, *Land Settlement in Upper Canada* (Toronto: C. W. James, 1921).

G. Alan Wilson, *The Clergy Reserves of Upper Canada: A Canadian Mortmain* (Toronto: University of Toronto Press, 1967).

J.M.B.

P eople have not been the villains in our accounts of the Canadian past. Like St. George, Canadians have met and conquered mythical or abstracted evils: Manifest Destiny, the Colonial Office, Annexation, the Canadian Shield, the Rockies, and the Clergy Reserves. The Clergy Reserves have been cited as one of the greatest of Canadian rogues. In our treatment of them, moderation and second thoughts have given way before moral certainty, political action, and historical agreement.

> "But everybody said," quoth he,
> "That 'twas a famous victory."

The history of public administration and land endowments seems too prosaic to excite attention or to draw forth any champions but the sober writers of formal dissertations.

The Clergy Reserves have been attacked for their ground plan, their executive direction, their administrative handling, their purpose, and for the protection that they evoked from those so ill-advised as to see some virtue in them. They became a kind of Aunt Sally at which it was considered safe—almost respectable—to throw any sort of abuse. This myth has been perpetuated in the bulk of historical writing, and it almost became written into our economic assumptions[1] despite the successful record of other and similar experiments in land endowment. Durham was most moderate in his day in labelling the Reserves a "grave economical mischief."

In more recent years, R. G. Riddell was the first to undertake the task of investigating the record of these land reserves, together with those of the Crown.[2] He sought to vindicate the principle underlying reserves of land for public purposes. This was a valuable service, but regrettably Riddell did not then carry his investigation the further step of testing this hypothesis in a detailed study. An examination of the surviving records

---

[1]Some qualification of this view, however, has appeared, for example, in W. T. Easterbrook and H. G. J. Aitken, *Canadian Economic History* (Toronto, 1956).

[2]R. G. Riddell, "The Policy of Creating Land Reserves in Canada," in *Essays in Canadian History,* ed. R. Flenley (Toronto, 1939), pp. 296-317.

of the Clergy Corporation of Upper Canada, of private letters and journals, of the papers of the Canada Company, and, above all, of the extensive remains of the records of the Executive Council and Crown Land Office suggests that even in practice the Clergy Reserves have to some extent been judged too harshly.[3] It would be the subject of another study to investigate the purpose of the endowment in the light of contemporary views of the proper relations of Church and state; even here second thoughts might also suggest qualifications of the traditional picture. It is the purpose of this paper to examine some of the ways in which the administration has been attacked, and to enquire to what extent these condemnations were justified.

The Constitutional Act of 1791 established the Clergy Reserves. Charles James Fox, in the Commons, had objected to the suggested proportion of one-seventh of the land as a reservation for the clergy, with a similar amount for the Crown. Pitt ignored the implication that this was an excessive endowment for a pioneer land (if, indeed, this had been in Fox's mind), remarking that he wished to help the clergy into "as respectable a situation as possible."[4] To set aside one-seventh of the land, he asserted, had almost grown into an established custom in England as the proportionate commutation for tithes. A land endowment was best, but if one-seventh proved too much, provision was made in the bill for later revisions. Some Canadian scholars have argued that the creation of the Clergy Reserves was a prime instrument in fashioning a rigid, Anglican-dominated, new British empire, with Pitt as the principal architect. However, Fox's objection to the plan for the Reserves stemmed from his prediction that Upper Canada might soon be swamped with "American sectaries," whereby the Clergy Reserves scheme would "give to dissenters one-seventh part of all the lands in the province."[5] Pitt did not deny this point; he ignored it, thereby betraying no undue desire for an Anglican empire.

The Pitt government gave to the colonial executive the power to determine the administrative structure of the new endowments. Although Simcoe's actual performance was marred by the complexity of the tasks

---

[3] Among these sources is the Minute Book of the Clergy Corporation for Managing the Clergy Reserves of Upper Canada in the Diocesan Archives, Toronto. Important references to the Clergy Reserves and to factors affecting their development occur frequently in the records of the Canada Company, now housed in the Ontario Archives (P.A.O.). The daily petitions respecting Clergy Reserves heard by the Executive Council are among the most useful sources of information on the administration of the endowment. They are found in the records of the Council's activities both as a land board and as an executive authority in general matters, referred to respectively as: Land Book A-U, Land Book, Province of Canada, A-G; and State Book A-M, State Book, Province of Canada, A-O, in Public Archives of Canada (P.A.C.), Ottawa. The daily handling of Reserves business by the administrative officers may be found in a variety of sources in Ottawa and Toronto, chiefly: P.A.C., Record Group 5, A1 (the so-called Upper Canada Sundries); P.A.C., R.G.7, G1, G5, G7, G12, G17c, G20—despatches and minutes relating to details of management; P.A.C., R.G.19, B5 and C7—fiscal records, sheriffs' accounts, Treasury correspondence, and records of commutation; P.A.O., Crown Land Papers (C.L.P.), a vast collection of miscellaneous records—departmental correspondence, surveyors' notes, agents' reports, inspection returns, printed circulars—contained in over 80 shelves, with Clergy Reserves material widely scattered.

[4] *Hansard*, vol. 29 (London, 1817), pp. 112-13.

[5] Ibid., pp. 107-8.

that confronted him, by quarrels with Dorchester, and by interference and indecision in the Colonial Office, he introduced the outlines of the Upper Canada scheme for the Clergy Reserves and instituted the controversial ground plan by which they were to be laid out. In this work, he was ably assisted by his Surveyor General, D. W. Smith.

Whatever the weaknesses of the land administration during Smith's tenure of office, they largely resulted from the overwhelming magnitude of the task, and not from the limitations of his talents or devotion. Smith's was a prodigious task. Despite Nonconformist opposition, Simcoe would have delivered the Clergy Reserves into the hands of an Anglican ecclesiastical corporation.[6] His illness and Smith's objections probably halted this project. Keeping the Reserves in government hands may have complicated the state's commitment to the Church of England, but it provided an opportunity for coordinating the province's land policies. In this task, Smith met with many obstacles.

Within a month of accepting office, in July 1792, he had prepared a report on the best system of laying out the Reserves, conformable to the imperial instructions and the circumstances of the province. This scheme, calling for the reservation of two townships in every seven to be opened up, was not accepted. Simcoe's original land proclamation, based upon Granville's instructions, had stated that the Reserves should "be not severed Tracts each of One Seventh Part of the Township, but such Lots or Farms therein . . . between the other Farms . . . to the Intent that the Lands so to be reserved may be nearly of the like Value with an equal Quantity of the other parts to be granted."[7] This clause still left much doubt as to just how the lots were to be laid out, whether in small or in large fractions of the sevenths set aside for Crown and clergy. If it were his own land, Smith argued, he would lay out the whole country in townships six miles square, reserving every fourth and seventh township. That way, he claimed, the settlers would be least disturbed and the reserved areas brought closer to existing settlements. But Smith was assigned the task of preparing another report, conforming more closely to imperial instructions and, presumably, to the current plans maturing in Lower Canada.

This is not the place to trace the details of this controversy further. Suffice it to say that after several attempts to satisfy local needs and imperial preferences, Smith saw his famous "chequered plan" accepted by the imperial government in the spring of 1794. Significantly, however, Smith was not himself satisfied with this arrangement, and continued until his departure from Canada to urge upon the government further changes in the plan.[8] At least, one of these, which I have called elsewhere the "parcel system," if modified, might have offered greater

---

[6]P.A.C., Q279-1, p. 169.

[7]C.L.P., shelf 77, item 2, Crown and Clergy Reserves Reports, 1794 [1793]-1856, n.p., "[Draft] Report of the Surveyor General respecting such mode of locating the lands intended to be reserved. . . ."

[8]Details of the proposed modifications are treated fully in G. A. Wilson, "The Political and Administrative History of the Upper Canada Clergy Reserves, 1790-1855," unpublished Ph.D. thesis (University of Toronto, 1959), chap. 2.

advantage. Not the least important of Smith's objections was that put forth in a brilliant report of December 25, 1797,[9] in which he sought to persuade Peter Russell's government to integrate the land policies of the new province. He called attention particularly to the dangers inherent in the promiscuous and extravagant granting of Loyalist land rights. The opportunities for the shrewd speculator, the potential conflicts with other land interests (Crown and Clergy Reserves, Crown lands, Indian lands, private holdings), the need for good communication and for more intensified settlement—all were included in this able survey. The Russell government, however, chose to ignore them all, with serious results for the province for the next 50 years. This report and subsequent events ought to have served to place the problems of the Clergy Reserves in realistic proportion to the whole of the land troubles of the province. Perhaps the conflict was irrepressible, but its worst effects might have been mitigated. Moreover, when trouble came, nearly 20 years had passed and other problems had arisen to intensify the conflict.

The first open attacks on the Clergy Reserves were of a special and peculiar nature. The agitations begun by Robert Nichol and Robert Gourlay seem to have been less than spontaneous and popular outbursts. Odious popular comparisons with American land systems emerged later, but these earliest attacks bore the imprint of the professionally injured.

With little industrial or mercantile development before the War of 1812, Upper Canada was still to a large extent dependent on the disposal of lands for the basis of its economy. In that enterprise, the volume of new settlers became the touchstone of prosperity, the pole-star of the speculator. The collapse of the "American" market in immigrants amid postwar hatreds, and the limited British colonization programmes of 1815-16, brought the threat of a major economic depression in 1817.[10] The land speculator found himself saddled with large holdings and little immediate hope of relief. In such circumstances, it is not surprising that the Assembly directed its attention to a full discussion of the land problem.

Naturally, when land played such a vital role in the economy, many prominent men were land dealers. Some members of the Assembly, including Colonel Robert Nichol, were deeply involved in land speculations and in the trade in Loyalist grants. Two legislative councillors, who had vast private holdings in the southwestern part of the province, were William Dickson and Thomas Clark. Dickson alone, among the speculators, persisted in resisting the official regulations limiting immigration from the United States—a significant departure from the stereotype of a Family Compact grip on the province. Moreover, it was a relative of both Dickson and Clark, Robert Nichol, who soon precipitated a crisis over the Clergy Reserves.

Nichol, long a close friend of the Governor and an adornment to York and Niagara society, had suffered badly from the war; by 1817, he was in

[9]C.L.P., Reports, Crown Land Department, 1795-99, pp. 177-211.

[10]Helen Cowan, "British Emigration to British North America, 1783-1837," in *University of Toronto Studies*, 4 (2), 1928, 70-75.

desperate financial straits. Gore and Strachan both charged that Nichol was forced to take the steps he did from his interests in various land deals.[11] Probably he was sufficiently desperate to play the devil's advocate for Dickson and Clark, even if he did not believe that he was acting in the best interests of the Niagara District. It is not true, however, as the myth will have it, that he attacked the Clergy Reserves as the root of all evil. Of 11 resolutions on the evils of the province's land and immigration policies, only two dealt specifically with the Clergy Reserves. The majority were aimed at the situation most deeply affecting the interests of western landholders: the political decision to limit American immigration. It was clear that Nichol and his supporters were not opposed to the Clergy Reserves in principle, for they made no move to do more than to limit this "lavish appropriation." These were criticisms natural to land-jobbers in a part of the province where settlement was reaching the secondary stage of development earlier than in the rest of the country, and where, for unique administrative reasons, there existed larger blocks of Clergy Reserves. When Gore abruptly prorogued the Assembly, he was moved to do so from the fear of the passing of "the most obnoxious . . . part of these Resolutions"[12]—the demand for free American immigration.

It was a fourth disenchanted relative of this growing "family compact" of malcontents who next sought to direct public attention to the evils of the system of public lands. Robert Gourlay, visiting with his relative, Thomas Clark, must have heard the grumblings of Clark, Dickson, and Nichol. Gourlay, however, characteristically fell out with them all, proceeding on his own to assail the government for its land and immigration policies. His two-volume *Statistical Account of Upper Canada* is generally taken to be one of the earliest and most bitter attacks on the Clergy Reserves scheme. Yet, in that respect, it, too, is a much milder document than its reputation suggests.[13] Based on a questionnaire in 31 parts, addressed to the landholders of the province, the *Statistical Account* began with a set of "Sketches" of the province (not written by Gourlay, but included by him in the finished work) that displayed a tone of mild approval of the Clergy Reserves system, "that will eventually furnish a very ample support . . . at moderate rents."[14] Later, in the work, however, Gourlay himself asserted that "no thinking person" could support either Crown or Clergy Reserves.[15] Further, he claimed, his volumes gave the people their first chance to voice their feelings against the Clergy Reserves. In the light of this, it is interesting to review the evidence he presented.

[11]A. G. Doughty and N. Storey, eds., *Documents Relating to the Constitutional History of Canada, 1819-1828* (Ottawa, 1935), 2; for a valuable suggestion pertinent to the whole question of the relation between criticism of the Clergy Reserves and private speculative interests, see J. J. Talman, "The Church of England in Upper Canada, 1791-1840," in *C.H.R.*, 5 (4), December 1934, pp. 369-70.

[12]Q322, Gore to Bathurst, April 7, 1817.

[13]Robert Gourlay, *Statistical Account of Upper Canada*, 2 vols. (London, 1822).

[14]Ibid., vol. 1, Sketch 25, p. 231.

[15]Ibid., "Explanation of the Maps, Plates, etc.," p. xi.

By geographical distribution, Gourlay heard largely from the western parts of the province, and not at all from the Home District. Sixty townships replied, covering 70 townships in fact. Only two questions bore any direct relation to reserved lands: one on the state of the roads, the other calling for suggested improvements. The small proportion of responses naming the Clergy Reserves as a specific abuse is significant. Only 17 townships named them as one cause of hardship, none as the sole source of distress. These 17 linked the Clergy Reserves with all other forms of reserved lands; nearly half the 70, however, reported that the land speculator and the absentee landowner were the primary offenders. Other abuses cited were lack of capital or labourers, the condition of the roads, and the effects of the war. Asked specifically about the roads, only one township out of 70 reporting mentioned the Clergy Reserves as a factor contributing to bad roads.

On the basis of his evidence, then, Gourlay had no reason to single out the Clergy Reserves for special condemnation. His informants did not attack the Clergy Reserves as a weapon of special ecclesiastical privilege; they regarded them primarily as one obstacle to economic advancement, and as part of a much larger problem of the use of wasteland in a community steadily moving into the secondary stage of its development.

None the less, sectarian attacks coincided with these assaults at the end of this decade; before long, the Clergy Reserves were the subject of a widespread attack in which it is difficult to discover either the specific grounds of criticism, or to which of them priority should be given. Nichol, Gourlay, and their associates had done much to stir up a public that had not found cause to attack the Reserves before.

In the years that followed, sectarian interests were not the only ones opposed to the Reserves. It is not unlikely that private speculators were as active behind the scenes as they had been prominent in the Assembly of 1817. Certainly, J. B. Robinson maintained this contention for many years,[16] while other less interested observers gave testimony that "the number of petitions against the Reserves, and number of signers are not in all cases safe data to act upon."[17] It could serve certain interests to preserve the myth that the Reserves were a constant obstacle to the province's advancement. The Canada Company's administrators harboured little love for the Clergy Reserves—a prize they had sought to gain in the original contract establishing the Company. At that time, the Company's friends and officials, with a shrewd sense of the market, had proposed an arrangement from which the Reserves would not have benefited unduly. A spirit of conscious rectitude marked the Company's later negotiations over the Clergy Reserves.[18] It poised ready at any signal to absorb large or small packages of Clergy Reserves at advantageous

[16]P.A.O., Robinson Papers, Robinson to Wilmot Horton, December 24, 1828.

[17]Q379-1, George Biggs to Lord Stanley, July 6, 1833, p. 188.

[18]Canada Company Papers, "Commissioners' Letters and Reports, 1826–1829," 1, Directors to Galt, May 11, 1827; ibid., 2, "Directors to Commissioners," December 6, 28, 1831; ibid., April 5, May 17, 1832.

prices, selling them immediately to strengthen a reputation for not hoarding lands, while the Company's own lands would be withdrawn from sale to fatten and thrive amid a lean market.[19] For this public-spirited concern for the Church's interests and those of the province, the Company was still willing as late as the mid-fifties to accept a commission of 5 to 15 percent. Sir John Colborne spoke many times of the fashionable mode of centring on the Clergy Reserves as "the grievance of the season." Yet, for this recurrence, the Legislative Council was probably as much to blame as the political opportunism of the agitators or the private interest of the speculators. The Clergy Reserves were attacked from all sides, but not least on the grounds that in their operation no steps were taken to adjust the system to the needs of a North American frontier community. This contention, tenable perhaps on the broad grounds of prevailing attitudes to Church-state relations, has been allowed to obscure the substantial administrative adjustments and improvements that were undertaken almost from the start.

The first major overhaul of the machinery of the Reserves was not suggested in the face of public demand, but arose from an imaginative public servant's desire for efficiency and closer control. Prideau Selby, Receiver General, put forth in 1810–11 a ten-point programme with three aims: to establish a Clergy Reserves office; to tighten the controls on rent collections by a system of bondsmen and of regular judicious ejectments for non-payment;[20] and to raise rents in accordance with increased values and the costs of the improved machinery of administration. Selby's plan met with some success: the accounts were improved, rents were raised, and the fees system was reorganized to ensure better administration. The War of 1812, coming so soon after the introduction of Selby's plan, probably halted this first cautious reform. Certainly, the financial trials of the Clergy Reserves administration were increased in the interval and neglect of war. Leases and fiscal control suffered, while the problem of the collection of fees deepened. Some sheriffs reported that no rents could be collected in the troubled state of the province for three years.[21] An urgent need to realize a firm, consistent policy emerged from the strains of war.

While auditing practices were somewhat improved in the latter part of the second decade, new complications soon developed. In April 1819, another reasonable increase in rentals was fixed, but in the Council's desire to appear fair, it once again exempted existing lessees. The result was to institute a third scale of rents—each subdivided into three seven-year periods—for which the sheriffs were responsible in their accounting. The burden of trouble and expense for the civil servant was matched by the confusion in the public mind. Auditing, from the appearance of the surviving records, was now virtually impossible. Other inconsistencies developed from the same motive of seeking to allay criticism by extend-

---

[19]Ibid., "Letters to Directors from [Commissioner] Widder, 1839-1845," December 21, 1844.

[20]State Book E, p. 278 ff.

[21]See, for example, P.A.C., R.G.1, L7, vol. 30, Returns Crown and Clergy Reserves, 1812-1840, Sheriff John Spencer, Newcastle, to William Halton, December 30, 1815.

ing dubious privileges to ungrateful lessees. Sheriffs complained that in their attempt to take direct action against those in arrears, they were stayed by the hand of mercy extended by the Lieutenant-Governor himself. Fortunately, in 1815, an end was brought to the system of absolving applicants from the payment of fees by absorbing these in the rents of the first three years. Henceforth, this drain on the capital fund of the administration was checked. However, the sheriff's 5 percent of collections, surveyor's fees, and all office expenses at York continued to be exacted from the gross income before the capital had been invested in British Consols. Accordingly, substantial sums of investment capital must have been lost through the simple folly of not extracting the fees and expenses from the income earned on the invested gross proceeds.

In 1819, through the vigorous leadership of Dr. Strachan, the Clergy Corporation of Upper Canada was established "for the Superintending, Managing, and Conducting of the Clergy Reserves."[22] While it seemed to be the realization of Simcoe's old plan for ecclesiastical management, the new Corporation was a hybrid. Besides the Anglican clergy of the province, it included on its executive board the Inspector General and Surveyor General, with Stephen Heward, Auditor General of Land Patents, acting as its first secretary.[23] Thus, in the face of growing charges from the Nonconformist public, the government was to some degree committed more openly than ever to support of and co-operation with the Church.

Despite Heward's best efforts in the early years, the Corporation's stewardship was wasteful. The clergy, acting as agents for collections, applications, and mediation, offered the advantages of local administration but failed to realize them. Heward became disillusioned and fell into arrears; his successor, George Markland, was simply inefficient. The executive membership was divisive, compromised the government, proved a sounding-board for John Strachan, and attracted bitter criticism.[24] The confusion in jurisdiction was extraordinary: sheriffs, deputy surveyors, Surveyor General, later Commissioners of Crown Lands, local clergy, Corporation officers, and ecclesiastical, provincial, and imperial officials all shirked or shared the duties of management. By 1830, the government was pursuing a retreat from this bitter failure. Hopes were held that the Clergy Reserves management, firmly undertaken by the new Commissioner of Crown Lands, would at last offer positive benefit and allay criticism.

Meanwhile, these conflicting administrative and political pressures had been affected by two developments in 1826-27. Authorities in

---

[22]State Book G, April 26, 1819, p. 57. For full text of the charter see: C.L.P., 57, 2, Orders in Council of Regulations regarding matters connected with the Department of Crown Lands, vol. 2, n. 11.

[23]P.A.O., U.C. Clergy Corporation Minutes, March 25, 1820.

[24]See, for example, the evidence of a dispute between Strachan and Bishop Mountain over the proper relations of church and state, in which Strachan enlisted the support of the Upper Canada Clergy Corporation, U.C. Clergy Corporation Minutes, November 6, 1823; P.A.C., R.G.5, A1, 63, U.C. Sundries, Mountain to Maitland, December 30, 1823; ibid., 64, Rev. Robert Addison to Maitland, February 13, 1824.

Canada and Great Britain were agreed that the leasing system, as it existed, functioned too slowly and awkwardly to alleviate the pressures of public complaint against the Crown and Clergy Reserves—whatever the justice of these claims. As part of the problem of wastelands, the Reserves might be sold in whole or in part. Three possibilities lay before the administrators of the Clergy Reserves: the Clergy Corporation might be empowered to add sales to their power over leasing; a private corporation might be permitted to buy those not already under lease; or the government might itself sell them. The full pressure of the Clergy Corporation, of John Strachan, of the powerful Society for the Propagation of the Gospel, and of friends of the Church on both sides of the Atlantic set about to frustrate the last two possibilities. Armies of friends and opponents of the Church vied in prayer and clashed in debate over the issue. Religious, administrative, economic, and political motives and criticisms were hopelessly entangled. When the proposed Canada Land Company, a private venture in speculation and colonization, sought to absorb all or a part of the Crown and Clergy Reserves, prayers flew up from all sides that the Company's ambitions would be crowned with success or that the Company should be scattered before the winds of the Church's wrath. The Crown Reserves were sold readily to the Company, but the Clergy Reserves enjoyed the special protection of the British Parliament, where the Church's influence was strong and political perils grave. When the Clergy Reserves emerged intact from the battle with the Canada Company, appearing more than ever to be in the embrace of the Church's friends, cries of shame arose. Purchase of the Crown Reserves released a substantial portion of the government's locked-up lands, but it threw public complaint wholly upon the Clergy Reserves—an undeserved fate in the circumstances. Further, from this battle John Strachan emerged with extravagant claims of his church's right to administer and to enjoy exclusively the fruits of the Reserves.[25]

This agitation—amid other circumstances—prompted public enquiries in Britain and Canada, which drew further attention to the Reserves as instruments of religious privilege, and pointed to their practical mischief. As to the latter charge, the evidence given to the British House of Commons Canada Committee was misleading.[26] Of the 19 witnesses, excepting Wilmot Horton and James Stephen, only two could be said to have had a long and direct association with the affairs of Upper Canada. Questions were often phrased to include both provinces, while responses came from those familiar only with Lower Canada. Large blocks of Clergy Reserves were represented as being the worst impediments to the building of roads, but these were much more common in Lower Canada. In Upper Canada, not even Gourlay's enquiry had brought out this distinction, perhaps for the good reason that the government had often tak-

---

[25] The two most celebrated expressions of this campaign, of course, were Strachan's funeral sermon on the death of Bishop Mountain, and the extraordinarily inept "Ecclesiastical Chart" of the province released by him in England.

[26] This, of course, is the famous "Report from the Select Committee on the Civil Government of Canada." The Canadian Assembly's committee was that led by Marshall Spring Bidwell in 1829.

en steps to open up such areas.[27] No comparable programme had been instituted in Lower Canada, while the Clergy Corporation of Upper Canada had brought pressure to bear upon the government to that end. Significantly, two of the chief witnesses were directors of the newly-formed Canada Company, still smarting from the failure to obtain the Clergy Reserves for their enterprise; their view of the Clergy Reserves would be, to say the least, peculiar. The result was a rather general, almost woolly, approach to the problems of the Clergy Reserves and of religious privilege in Canada. Curiously, it was a Canada Company director, Simon McGillivray, who alone drew the distinction between the Clergy Reserves as "an actual personal grievance . . . operating upon an individual" and the general irritation generated by rival denominational claimants, or by groups seeking large-scale improvements. "The Clergy Reserves," he observed, "take away no man's property, they form an impediment to improvement, but that will be removed by disposing of them." The Canada Committee went on record as condemning the Reserves as leading obstructions to the province's advancement. To correct this situation they favoured sales, while strong recommendations were voiced calling for the use of part of the funds to improve the condition of the unsold balance of Reserves. But lack of direction and persistent inconsistency in imperial land and emigration policies had contributed much in the past to the unsatisfactory state of things in Canada. By neglecting to make this clear, the Committee did an injustice to the administrators in Canada, who groped blindly for principles of their own, and regularly had to take into account new suggestions from Great Britain.

One such suggestion resulted in the second of the important developments of 1826-27. This was the naming by the imperial government of a Commissioner of Crown Lands, whose duties should include sales of Clergy Reserves under a new Sales and Improvement Act of 1827.[28] Peter Robinson, the successful applicant, was not without talents, but the imperial commission and instructions multiplied his duties and confused his responsibilities to such an extent that his personal weaknesses fed on the uncertainty.[29] Neither imperial nor colonial authorities pressed him to effect the limited improvements on vacant Reserves provided for in the 1827 Act. Costly inspections of individual Reserves, frequent delays, and misleading sales statistics marked his administration. These developments, and inept management by the Clergy Corporation, provided a discouraging picture before 1832. In subsequent years, however, the administrative arrangements entered on a steady, if gradual, plane of improvement which did not terminate until the experiment was abandoned in 1854.

During the first four years of the new programme, until the waning

---

[27]The Upper Canada Executive Council failed, when asked by the Clergy Corporation in 1820, to adopt this principle generally and to set aside funds for such a programme. None the less, in practice, the Council was not far off from fulfilling the Corporation's request.

[28]7 & 8 Geo. IV, c. 62.

[29]See, for example, Robinson's commission, cited in J. E. Hodgetts, *Pioneer Public Service; An Administrative History of the United Canadas, 1841-1867* (Toronto, 1955), p. 41.

of the first great tide of immigration in 1832, sales advanced swiftly: 130,000 acres at an average of 13/-5d. an acre.[30] The outcry against "economic obstacles" died down in the rush to buy. Farmers on contiguous lots bought cheerfully to confirm improvements on previously leased lots, or to ensure a good future for their sons. The Canada Company, however, tried to stir up dissension on the grounds that the Clergy sales had pushed its lands off the market,[31] while the imperial government grew alarmed at the threat to sales of ordinary Crown lands.[32] The Clergy Reserves seemed fated to displease somebody at every stage of their history. None the less, sales persisted steadily throughout the thirties, offering eloquent testimony to the demand for the Reserves and ample proof of their ready accessibility. Unfortunately, those who had formerly leased, and who now sought to protect an investment by purchase, proved to be those who had kept up regular payments in the past. Thus, the bulk of the remaining lessees were those with the poorest credit records. Such people came most often into conflict with the vestigial Clergy Corporation Office, run by the government after 1835 but still associated in the public mind with the aggressive church of Archdeacon Strachan. The result was to embitter further the Clergy Reserves controversy.

Despite these serious limitations, individuals and the public at large were coming to have appreciably fewer reasons for complaint. With steadily increasing sales and frequent appeals from land agents for arbitration in private and public disputes arising out of the Reserves, the Council was forced to attend to the Clergy Reserves almost continually on an administrative, no less than on a political and executive, level. The problem was a part of the Council's general crisis over land business, one of the most persistent and crucial in the pre-Rebellion era. The wonder is that the Council attended so thoroughly to Clergy Reserves affairs.

The Council had from the first dealt conscientiously and justly with private problems arising from the Reserves. Although in November 1835 it determined to put to auction unoccupied Clergy Reserves,[33] it continued to entertain appeals from squatters with large improvements who believed themselves to have a just claim to purchase, and from lessees wishing to convert to freehold. In choosing which lots should be auctioned, the Commissioner of Crown Lands was required by the 1827 Act to name those lots that would best relieve the pressure of criticism. Many were chosen on the recommendation of the Deputy Surveyors, who were aware of local needs, but occasionally the Council was appealed to directly by a settler anxious to have the lot of his choice put up for auction at a time when he could best afford to buy.[34]

[30]Q377–1, Colborne to Goderich, January 16, 1833, p. 187.

[31]Canada Company Papers, I,1, a, "Correspondence with His Majesty's Government. . . . ," Price to Hay, October 29, 1829, 88–9.

[32]Q358–3, P. Robinson to Hay, January 22, 1831, 524, and Hay's endorsation in C.O. 42/393, 439.

[33]Land Book R, November 19, 1835, 202–3.

[34]See, for example, petition of Tice, Caistor, Land Book S, October 27, 1836, 236.

Private arrangements for the purchase of the balance of terms of leasehold, or for the alienation of parts of a leased lot, were often left unreported to the authorities. Consequently, the public records might be at variance with the petitioner's memory. Improper descriptions of land and incorrect claims of the original occupants would plague the Council—pertinent details in official records, but often overlooked by uninformed farmers anxious to conclude a bargain. In arranging conversions from leasehold, the Council had to exercise special caution. The slightest irregularity in documentation or claim was passed on from the administrative officers to the Executive Council in special land session. As a general rule, and partly in order to reserve a right of scrutinizing such uncertain claims, the Council refused to acknowledge that conversion was a *legal* right. Conversion was kept in the shadowy world of privilege, or, in the Council's words, "a usage of Government in favour of lessees,"[35] subject to the Council's careful review of all the circumstances of the case. This caution was hailed as a great abuse, breeding uncertainty in the mind of the lessee. Judged by a review of hundreds of similar cases in the Land Books, however, the practice was tedious, thorough, and necessary.

The task of evaluating the lots for private sale and of fixing township averages fell to the Deputy Surveyor. After 1835, the introduction of a 10/-per acre floor price did not ease the burden of conciliar revue. The Council regarded the figure as literally a "floor," permitting lots to be sold at cellar rates as low as 3/-9d.; these it subjected to a special scrutiny, only occasionally rejecting the Surveyor's evaluation as too low. Marginal adjustments in acreage for individual lots were not normally entertained, although occasionally errors in early surveys were later equitably adjusted. Throughout the history of the experiment, one of the continuing cares of Council was to arrange exchanges of Clergy Reserves for those who had located in error or found the lot to their dissatisfaction. Compensation was usually found elsewhere, if the exchange of the suggested lots was deemed impossible.[36] Further examples of individual petitions might be cited, but it must be clear that the opportunities of discrediting the Reserves system by displeasing individual petitioners stretched almost to infinity. No one thought to acknowledge the Council's patience and general success in handling nearly 2,000 land petitions annually—the Clergy Reserves accounting for fully two-thirds of these at times—including one-acre adjustments for unauthorized squatters.

Public interests and those of private business were also given consideration. To prevent the dangers of speculation, large blocks of Reserves were not alienated. Similarly, from the beginning, the administrators

---

[35]See case of L. and M. Hyde, Land Book U, February 27, 1840, 208–9. The application of this principle is best illustrated in this case, where, after losing his lot on the execution of his creditors, the original lessee was ruled to have lost the "favour" of conversion. Thus, the conversion was awarded to the Hydes as occupants at the expiry date.

[36]Examples of these arrangements abound in the records of the Council, but extensive reference here would be impossible.

were careful to protect the proposed routes of public projects: military roads, trunk roads, roads through blocks of Reserves.[37] It is significant that in a survey of every petition affecting the Clergy Reserves that reached the Executive Council between 1791 and 1855, of the surviving records of the Crown Lands Office, and of a sampling of the records of Quarter Sessions for several districts over a wide range of years, fewer than half a dozen requests for the transfer of Reserves as obstructions to roads could be found. All were readily acquiesced in by Council. Canals and other waterways were also given special treatment. Unleased Reserves along the Rideau Canal route, for example, were rigidly excluded from sale during the period of construction lest unforeseen losses should be sustained from flooding, or changes in route be effected.[38] Ironically, by thus protecting new avenues of commerce, the Council may have contributed to the clamour against the "unavailable" Clergy Reserves. From the beginning, first mill sites in any district were not disturbed by Clergy Reserves, for the Reserves were located elsewhere. Second mills might be erected on reserved land, but the owners were protected by relaxed leasing and sales terms. The Council also kept open for the millers any Reserves threatened by flooding from the mill-pond or that might prove useful as wood lots. Similar consideration was given in the case of quarries, some of these being released in the late thirties from the restrictions of the chequered plan.[39]

Little was done about timber-cutting and other depredations on Clergy Reserves, or indeed on any class of public land in the period before the Rebellion. The question was a difficult one, being related to other important aspects of administration, such as the collection of arrears of rent. Outright squatters and timber pirates were not the only offenders; those who paid only the first instalment of rent or purchase price in hopes of extracting the subsequent payments by ruthless timber mining were the largest group responsible for this great waste. In this matter, the folly of lax administration was not confined to the Reserves, but under the system of leasing, the Clergy Reserves were perhaps hardest hit.

The problem of squatting was never adequately settled. Baines, the Clergy Corporation's secretary, reported in 1835 that "the greater proportion of the valuable Clergy Reserves in the Johnstown District and Eastern District [had] been occupied for many years without authority."[40] Such firmness in this matter as came in the thirties was badly conceived and unwisely administered. It arose in the handling of squatters' claims from reservations of rectory lands. The equity demonstrated by the Council in clergy sevenths business broke down in despatching

---

[37]See examples in the cases of the School Reserves, 1809. Land Book F, 224-5, 228; the Mohawk Tract and Long Woods, Land Book K, 472; the Talbot Road, Land Book K, 28; the Penetanguishene Road and Yonge Street, ibid., 340; the road leading to the Huron Tract, Land Book L, 386.

[38]See, for example, petition of Brown et al., Raleigh, Land Book R, June 2, 1826, 440.

[39]Q287-1, Elmsley to Hunter, July 25, 1800, 167. Typical cases may be found in Land Book Q, 332; Land Book S, 368; Land Book U, 252; Land Book T, 192. Concerning quarries, see for example C.L.P., "Letters, Outgong, C.C.L. to Civil Secretary, etc.," Robinson to Rowan, March 12, 1835.

[40]Land Book R, 109.

rectories affairs. Indeed, as Durham observed,[41] endowing the rectories in 1836 changed the nature of the Clergy Reserves conflict: it could no longer continue as a difficult but not impossible situation. Political manipulations had identified the question with the constitutional struggle over executive responsibility. The Rectories Crisis—by seeming to foster Anglican exclusivist claims to the Reserves—intensified this battle, and raised a second constitutional issue, Establishment. The significance of the dispossessions of squatters for the sake of the rectories did not lie in their number, for there were not many; their real importance lay in the impolitic way in which the dispossessions were passed by the Council.[42] The determination of certain Anglican clergy, certain inaccuracies in the land records of the vestigial Clergy Corporation, and the well-calculated Council reports on individual cases as drawn up by John Strachan did little to relieve public distrust.[43] The reputation of the Clergy Reserves was badly soiled by this development.

In the Durham Report, the administration of Upper Canada's Clergy Reserves was not singled out for any special reproof: it shared the general criticisms directed against the land and fiscal business of a public service that was riddled with inconsistencies and faulty arrangements.[44]

During the early Sydenham era, R. B. Sullivan, acting as president of the Committees of Council, played a useful role in furthering reforms in the administration of the Clergy Reserves. Sullivan's qualifications stemmed in part from an able report made earlier while he was still Commissioner of Crown Lands.[45] This report of March 1837 had admitted the limitations of the endowment scheme and had deplored the general error by which the opponents of the Reserves had succeeded in equating one-seventh of the wild lands with one-seventh of the total economy. If this fallacy could not be communicated to the public, then for political reasons he recognized the necessity of selling the remaining sevenths as quickly as possible and of improving the administration in the interests of greater returns.

But Sullivan argued that in fact the Reserves were now proving a positive benefit to the province. He complained that the assumption of the Crown Reserves by the Canada Company had deprived the government of nearly "all its land in the more settled areas of the province." Only the Clergy Reserves remained in those districts that were not simply wilderness. These lands, he noted, were much sought after: they sold well, increased population, and were the means of intensifying settlement. This last point is especially interesting because it is precisely the reverse of the claim made by the Canada Committee a decade earlier. Through the thirties, it seems, the Clergy Reserves had undergone a

---

[41]C. P. Lucas, ed., *Lord Durham's Report on the Affairs of British North America*, 3 vols. (Oxford, 1912), vol. 2, pp. 176–77.

[42]See for example Land Book Q, 332; Land Book S, 368 and 388; Land Book T, 192 and 626.

[43]See, for example, account of Arnot case, in Q387-1, Colborne to Glenelg, September 3, 1835; Land Book R, 142.

[44]Lucas, *Durham's Report*, pp. 103–4.

[45]Q396-4, Sullivan to Joseph, Secretary, March 28, 1837, 577–96.

significant change in their relationship to other lands in the province, and were now emerging as assets in some significant ways. Lessees, Sullivan added, had now become more than ever anxious to buy,

> . . . as the opportunity of selling their improvements to newcomers becomes more frequent and there cannot be anything more desirable than that Emigrants should have an opportunity of purchasing at a moderate rate farms already partially improved or that the tenants who have not had the means of purchasing land unless by the sale of these improvements, should be enabled to raise funds by which they can become independent land-holders in the back settlements.[46]

Thus, the Clergy Reserves had become a means whereby the old order gave way to new, and improved itself in the bargain. Older settlers converted the fruits of their labour to liquid capital before moving on; newcomers with modest means avoided unfamiliar perils and demands in the first frontier. By the thirties, the Clergy Reserves had become a vital factor in the continuum of land settlement in Upper Canada. They offered a source of capital, almost a vital currency, linking the security and ambition of the fresh immigrant with the experience and enterprise of the old pioneer.

Under Sydenham new reforms in the administration of the Reserves were introduced, but they were mixed blessings. Costly errors resulted, and executive discord and political opposition arose. None the less, a useful beginning was made and further reforms followed throughout the forties. For example, in 1837, R. B. Sullivan and W. H. Draper had advocated certain fiscal changes in the Reserve administration.[47] Under the direction of William Morris and Francis Hincks in the forties these reforms were achieved. They resulted in improved handling of the proceeds from Reserves returns invested in England, and later led to the proposal that these investments should be transferred from British Consols to higher-paying Canadian debentures. Glenelg, Grey, Arthur, and Sydenham approved, seeing also the advantage to public works projects in Canada. Lack of faith in Canadian administrative efficiency and solvency united Lord Stanley, James Stephen, the Treasury officials, Strachan, J. B. Robinson, and the S.P.G. The battle raged in official correspondence for nearly a decade, but by 1847, with the firm backing of Bagot and Elgin, the Canadian officials won.[48] Transferring the Reserves fund to Canadian debentures released a large amount of new capital just at the beginning of the speculative fifties. The struggle to achieve this transfer of resources and responsibilities bore a direct relation to the struggle for Responsible Government. Indeed, in these fiscal relations, the Reserves prompted a victory for Canadian responsible administration at a critical time in colonial development.

Meanwhile, during the forties under prodding from John Strachan

---

[46]Ibid., 588.

[47]Q396-4, Sullivan to Joseph, March 28, 1837, 577-96; Q401-1, Draper to Glenelg, June 22, 1837, 220-29.

[48]It would be impossible to list the dozens of pertinent letters. Many can be found in P.A.C., Department of Finance Papers, R.G.19, C7, i; others are scattered through the despatches of the Governors General, R.G.7, G12, vols. 62-5; memos in C.O. 42 are particularly valuable here.

and others, the costs of administering the Reserves were greatly reduced.[49] Salary schedules were effectively trimmed with no reduction in efficiency. The more professionally administered Crown Lands Office relieved the Council of many of the worst burdens of supervision of the Reserves. None the less, the Council remained a conscientious board of appeal, reducing prices set by the land officers to match other competition. Grave "economical mischiefs" and irresponsible administration did not characterize the Clergy Reserves experiment in its last years. Sales were steady, prices reasonable and high, and criticism, other than that on political and sectarian grounds, far reduced.

The announcement in 1848 that limited Clergy funds were available to all denominations was important for two reasons.[50] It suggested that the improved administrative procedures and fiscal arrangements were succeeding—a partial vindication of the endowment in its later years. On the other hand, it rallied the forces of voluntarism to battle for their principles, and the radical reformers to compete for their votes. Bound by law to obtain legislative approval in England for adjustments in the 1840 Clergy Reserves Act, Canadian nationalists, voluntarists, secularizationists, and discontented Reserves beneficiaries found that the winning of Responsible Government emphasized the hiatus existing between Canada's legislative ambition and her competence to settle the Reserves issue.

The decline of the moderates in the ranks of the Reformers, and the ascendancy of the moderates among the Conservatives, paved the way for judicious compromises. The principle of state endowments for religion was nominally repudiated and indirectly maintained through an elaborate system of actuarial compensations to existing incumbents, in the Clergy Reserves Act of 1854. The principle of land endowments was never considered. Ironically, social, political, and constitutional tensions were relieved at a time when the Clergy Reserves system was beginning to fulfil its ancient promise.

Undoubtedly, the Crown and Clergy Reserves assumed too large a proportion of the lands of a frontier province. Conflicts with other land schemes—private and public—were inevitable in view of the widespread speculation in lands. The ground plan of the Reserves might have been improved, but extensive changes in the current practices of private and governmental speculation would have remained necessary. Moreover, imperial interference would have to have been curtailed.

Despite serious and usually successful efforts to accommodate the Clergy Reserves to public needs for better communication and more intensified settlement, the government could not avoid censure or blunders. Private injury was perhaps slight. The worst abuse was certainly the sometimes heavy concentration of reserves in back concessions, to which front reservations had been reassigned to facilitate prior development of the front.

Administrative weaknesses existed, but after 1830 they were being persistently attacked. By that decade, the advent of sales and the further

[49]Land Book, Province of Canada, C, 549.
[50]Canada Gazette, January 29, 1848.

progress of some areas in the secondary stage of their development relieved some of the worst pressures resulting partially from the Reserves and like lands. Indeed, R. B. Sullivan's report of March 1837 suggests that the Reserves had become an effective instrument in furthering new settlement and in improving old.

The chief weakness of the Reserves system as an experiment in land endowment for a public object lay in the purpose to which they were devoted and in the failure to re-examine that purpose responsibly. The Clergy Reserves became, for reasons not connected with their economic value, the symbolic centre of a bitter politico-religious controversy. In several ways, the administration of the Reserves had kept abreast of the movement for Responsible Government, particularly as it affected the public service and administrative improvement. During two-thirds of the period of public controversy, the administration of the Reserves showed signs of steady improvement, even of public usefulness. The last period of their history, following the Sydenham régime, saw the virtual end of all but sectarian and secular arguments against them. These, however, were enough to bring an experiment of some merit to an end.

25

SCHOOL READERS AS AN EDUCATIONAL FORCE (A STUDY OF A CENTURY OF UPPER CANADA)*

William Sherwood Fox

The role of education in the development of the Canadian nation is one which has until recent years been sadly neglected by historians. A variety of explanations can be advanced for this, but one of the chief factors is clearly the emphasis of most educational history upon the development of formal institutions of instruction rather than upon the instruction itself. As a result, we know a good deal about the growth of the concept of public education (and the schools which accompanied it), and much has been written about the founding and progress of institutions of higher learning. But considerably less is known of what was taught in the schools and universities, and how it was taught—particularly before Confederation. Schools are tacitly recognized by almost all historians as a powerful formative influence upon the population; it is clear, for example, that the educational systems of French and English Canada have long assisted in the perpetuation of two different (and frequently mutually exclusive) cultures. It is not schools per se, however, but what one learns or does not learn in them which is so critical. Historians have not focussed much on this aspect, perhaps thinking of intellectual history as the study of the minds of great thinkers rather than as the analysis of the ideology of the people, perhaps afraid of the absence of documentation. The late William Sherwood Fox some years ago explored one set of sources which illuminate the question of what was taught in the schools: the textbooks used there. What conclusions does Fox reach after studying the textbooks? Are there questions which he does not ask? How does the textbook fit into the broader picture of Canadian History?

*Queens Quarterly, 39 (1932), 688–703.

SUGGESTIONS FOR FURTHER READING

C. E. Phillips, *The Development of Education in Canada* (Toronto: W. J. Gage, 1957).

Alison Prentice, *The School Promoters: Education and Social Class in Mid-Nineteenth Century Upper Canada* (Toronto: McClelland and Stewart, 1977).

Alison Prentice and Susan E. Houston, eds., *Family, School and Society in the Nineteenth Century* (Toronto: Oxford University Press, 1975).

J.M.B.

T his paper is the outcome of a casual chat, during which the question was asked, "What are the chief genuinely formative instruments of our formal education?" The reply was just as simple: "Consider the power of McGuffey's Readers in the United States." This led me to reread that part of Mark Sullivan's volumes, *Our Times*, in which the author surveys the United States schools and schoolbooks of the first 75 years of the 19th century. These fascinating pages are indeed a revelation, accounting as they do for the existence of many traits of the American people. The present study, however, is focused mostly upon Ontario, although its lines of vision sometimes stray over the provincial borders, and it deals almost exclusively with Readers rather than with textbooks in general. Nevertheless, it will give at least a partial explanation of the character of the people of Ontario and those of the Western Provinces who have been influenced by Ontario. In other words, it will tell us a good deal about why we are what we are.

In undertaking research in the field of education one must have a clear idea of the real relation between a people and its educational system. The nature of the system is in varying degree a reflection of the nation itself, but when once established it exercises upon the nation certain influences that modify that nation in diverse ways. As of the whole, so it is of the part. In this study we must expect to find that the character of the English-speaking people of Upper Canada determined the type of Readers introduced into the schools, and that after their introduction the Readers in their turn engendered and fostered certain outstanding qualities in the people. The institution of the free school system of North America has brought with it a naïve popular belief that educational machinery is a sort of divine thing which, once installed, will automatically accomplish in fact all that is ideally claimed for it. This belief is the greatest bane of democratic education in all its branches.

A glance at the origins of the succession of Readers used in Upper Canada and, later, in Ontario, is in itself informing. We do not need to go farther back than the beginning of the 19th century. For about 20 years a great many of the schools of the United States and of English-speaking Canada used the same series of Readers—those compiled by the famous grammatical authority of England, Lindley Murray. In 1799 the Murray texts were introduced into the United States and remained in general though not exclusive use until about 1820, when McGuffey began to issue his remarkable Readers. Doubtless these only slowly established their supremacy, for as late as 1835 a Lindley Murray Reader was printed in Toronto from stereotyped plates made in New York. Nevertheless, it serves our purpose to fix 1820 as the beginning of the McGuffey influence. As one would expect, Murray had a longer vogue in Canada than in the United States. Before me are four copies of his best known book, *The English Reader:* one of the 18th edition, printed in York, England, 1824; one edited in Utica, New York, and printed in Toronto in 1833; one printed in Toronto in 1835; one issued in Brockville in 1846. The interesting inscriptions on the fly-leaves of these Readers show that all four copies were used by Canadian pupils in Canadian schools. The dates of their printing are significant when compared with the dates of the series of textbooks that succeeded them.

Recital of the full title of the Lindley Murray Reader and an analysis of its contents enable one to comprehend the nature of the training given in common to the school-children of Canada and the Eastern United States for a quarter of a century. In a paper on "United States Influences in Canadian Education," Sir Robert Falconer points out that in the period under present review the similarities of educational development in the two countries were proportionate to the similarities of stock and social outlook in each section. I am strongly inclined to believe that the contemporaneous use of the Murray Readers in both countries was by far the most potent factor in determining the similarities of social outlook. The fact that the original Readers were produced in England by an Englishman and set forth the accepted English opinions, tastes and practices of the time, is of very great significance. It means that the great-grand-fathers of this generation of Canadian and United States citizens solidly laid the foundations of their intellectual and moral life on the same English standards. The differences between the two national groups were almost wholly differences in politics that had been magnified by the bitterness and hatred of armed strife. The real divergence in manner of thought and attitude toward life began about 1820 with the introduction of the distinctively United States Readers, the McGuffey Series. Several decades later, as we shall see, Canada herself turned away from the path of strictly English education and blazed a new trail for herself by adapting and creating certain new types of textbooks for her schools.

The title page of the Lindley Murray text of 1824 shows the purpose and range of the book:

> The English Reader; or Pieces in Prose and Verse, from the Best Writers; designed to assist young persons to read with propriety and effect; improve their language and sentiments; and to inculcate the most important principles of PIETY AND VIRTUE with a few preliminary observations on the principles of GOOD READING.

The book is divided into two parts, the first consisting of prose pieces, the second, of poetry. The headings of the second section are substantially those of the first.

Chapter 1 offers 15 closely printed pages of "select sentences," each sentence being a proverb, or an aphorism, or a preachment; e.g.,

Diligence, industry, and proper improvement of time, are material duties of the young.

The acquisition of knowledge is one of the most honourable occupations of youth.

Whatever useful or engaging endowments we possess, virtue is requisite, in order to their shining with proper lustre.

The headings of chapters 2 to 9 are: Narrative Pieces, Didactic Pieces, Argumentative Pieces, Descriptive Pieces, Pathetic Pieces, Dialogues, Public Speeches (including translations from the classical languages), and Promiscuous Pieces.

This, then, is that part of the programme of school studies which determined the fundamental social likeness between the two North American peoples. But it was unthinkable that a young nation pulsing with the consciousness of its recent separation from the parent country would long be content to follow the educational example of that distant parent. A new people facing the new problems of a new land needed and demanded its own type of school training for its children. Those who know "the worship of the Union," as Goldwin Smith calls the spirit of the period of Madison, Clay, Webster and Monroe, are not surprised that the introduction of McGuffey's Readers coincides with the admission of Maine into the Union and the establishment of the truce between the slavery and non-slavery States. This worship needed a liturgy to give it uniformity and continuity, and this it was that McGuffey supplied. That his texts retained very much of the content and tone of their English originals was inevitable, but there was enough in them definitely American to make them a distinctly new creation—selections from American authors, descriptions of American scenes, fulsome praise of the Union, glorification of American arms and the achievements of the pioneer, presentation of the old codes of behaviour in American settings. Sullivan thus estimates their influence:

> McGuffey's was the source of America's taste in reading—for many average Americans, the only reading of poetry or classic prose they ever had. Along with that, McGuffey's was the source of that stock of points of view and tastes held in common, which constituted much of America's culture, its codes of morals and conduct, its standards of propriety.
>
> . . . But McGuffey's also taught and accounted for mental attitudes and ethical concepts which differentiated American from other peoples, or were more emphasized in America than elsewhere. In this respect, McGuffey was a kind of American Confucius, the latter, like the former, taking his sayings from the accumulated lore of the race.
>
> . . . At all times and in every respect, McGuffey's Readers had a strong flavour of religion; much of its contents was Puritan and evangelical, none was inconsistent with the religion of Calvin and Knox.

While in the United States the departure from the English model was distinctly nationalistic, in Canada it was quite otherwise. Apparently the reason for the conservatism or caution of the Canadians is that in the judgment of educational leaders the country was not yet ready to take a step in the direction of independence. It is now plain to us that it was far from ready. While the loyalty of the people of Canada could not be questioned, yet their consciousness of attachment to the new land was dim and divided. Like the character in Aristophanes who was enjoined to attempt the ludicrous feat of looking in opposite directions at the same time, too many English-speaking Canadians were keeping one eye on the British Isles and the other upon the land of their domicile. A sentiment of independence, though beginning, was not pronounced; Canadian nationhood was not yet felt. When in 1844 Egerton Ryerson was appointed Superintendent of Education, he turned naturally to one of the old lands to find models for his new schoolbooks. After devoting a year of study to educational methods elsewhere before actually entering upon the active duties of his office, he established a common school system in Ontario that combined features derived from Massachusetts, Prussia and Ireland. Ireland's great contribution was her Readers and the method she had most successfully worked out for harmonizing the educational claims of Catholic and Protestant. Apparently some of the Irish Readers had been used in Montreal a few years before Ryerson's Régime and their usefulness in Canada had been given a good test. At all events, Ryerson secured the formal permission of the Commissioners of National Education in Ireland to reprint their series of Readers in Canada and to authorize their use in Canadian schools.

Before me are copies of these books printed in Canada and ranging in date from 1846 to 1863. *A Sequel to the Second Book of Lessons,* issued in 1859, is one of the most remarkable common school textbooks I have ever seen. As everybody knows, it is very difficult to present real ideas in readable form to boys and girls of the Second and Third Reader stage; yet the author of this little work has been eminently successful in attaining his aim. Balance, sanity, clarity and simplicity are the outstanding marks of his book. Like his predecessors and contemporaries, he has retained current moral religious teachings, but he has added to their effectiveness by delicately reducing the bald and offensive obviousness with which such teachings are usually presented. This sense of restraint is, in the main, characteristic of all the Irish Readers and is in glaring contrast to the method of the McGuffey Series. Possibly we can see in them the origin of a certain moderation which has become one of our Canadian traits. In other respects, also, this little book is notable. The facts that it presents are important, not trivial. Its first 11 pages are devoted to a sound discussion of the principles of education and the national value of schools, all cast in the language of children. The making of this book was a really notable achievement.

The note struck by this Sequel is struck again by the Third and Fourth Readers and apparently with less force. But what a range of instruction they provide! In those days when household libraries of even a dozen books were uncommon, school Readers had to be at once encyclopedias, handbooks of science, literary anthologies, and treatises on ethics, religion, economics, government, and a host of other things. Those who steeped themselves in the contents of these Readers were perhaps better educated than are the masses of our day with its varied but discursive educational ways.

An analysis of the Fourth Reader is illuminating; the text used is that of identical Irish and Canadian editions printed in Canada in 1846 and 1863. Section 1 is devoted to natural history, all the more important departments of which receive some attention. Literary style is provided by selections from Goldsmith, Addison and Milton, while religious lessons are drawn from nature by selections from Paley, Watts and Cowper.

In the 80 pages of Section 2 the geography of almost the whole world is presented—of course, in a most sketchy way. The compiler's purpose seems to be to arouse a spirit of interest in geography and allow the pupil to get the facts for himself afterwards—a sound educational method. Apart from three pages given to Niagara Falls, which is only partly Canadian, Canada is given only 16 lines. The religious and moral lessons organized under Section 3 comprise the whole range of Biblical history and of the doctrines of Christianity. But they are given only 50 pages as against the 80 given to geography.

Section 4, entitled Political Economy and Useful Arts, is what we would call Civics to-day. Through passages from Adam Smith it gave the schoolboy of 80 years ago sound ideas of wages, capital, labour and taxes, and inspired in him a penetrating manner of civic thought for the years of his adult citizenship.

Section 5 is a miscellany of poetry and general information.

An estimate of the book is now possible. Strictly speaking, it is not Canadian at all, but rather cosmopolitan, with strong reminiscences of the British Isles. Its tone is seriously religious and moralistic, but not maudlin. It emphasizes the importance of a wide range of information. Compared with the McGuffey Readers, it exhibits balance, restraint and completeness, and is the very opposite of nationalistic, which seems to account in large part for the fact that Canadians in general have to-day a better 'foreign sense' than the people of the United States. The book is notably deficient in humour and artistic form.

For our purposes it is not necessary to dissect the Fifth Reader of the National School Series. Since relatively few young persons went farther than the Fourth Reader, the Fifth cannot have exerted a widespread influence as a moulder of popular thought and character. At any rate, it was only a more ponderous expansion of its predecessor, marked by even less humour, less literary quality, an equal lack of relationship to Canada, and by a still greater emphasis upon the value of an accumulation of facts. Surely it is not straining the imagination to see in these Readers the source of a number of our present Canadian virtues and deficiencies.

Before we proceed to examine the official series of Ontario Readers that grew out of the Irish Series we shall turn aside to glance at a few other Readers used during the forties elsewhere than in Ontario. With one exception these texts were unauthorized, yet they all cast some light upon the educational views and methods of their time and throw into relief the general superiority of the authorized texts.

The inveterate habit of turning every subject into an instrument of religious instruction is shown in its most reprehensible form in two or three books in particular. In *An English Spelling Book with Reading*

Lessons, published in St. John in 1841, the very first lesson following that upon the letters and syllables reads thus:

> All sin. I sin. You sin. We sin. Sin is bad. Do not sin at all. Sin is not hid. God can see it. Go not in the way of sin. The way of sin is a bad way.

This uninspiring kind of instruction in monosyllabic piety continues without variation for many lessons without omitting a single theological doctrine of importance. Yet one cannot fail to admire an author who by a mere *tour de force* could compress so much into comparatively few lessons consisting solely of words of one syllable. Less successful, but in similar style, is a *Second Book of Lessons* issued in Montreal in 1849. In this the very first lesson of the first section is a sermonette in monosyllables on the Creation, and the first lesson of the second section is another sermonette on the same subject cast in words of greater length and difficulty. The book ends in a terrible warning against falsehood—a warning reinforced by the threat of eternal punishment.

> The Lord delights in them that speak
> The words of truth; but every liar
> Must have his portion in the lake,
> That burns with brimstone and with fire.
> Then let me always watch my lips,
> Lest I be struck to death and hell,
> Since God a book of reckoning keeps
> For every lie that children tell.

A Third Reading Book, dated in 1843 at Montreal, is of the same type as the two foregoing. Quotation from it would add nothing to our interest and information, for the worst has already been said. It is enough to say that such books could not possibly produce, except by accident, anything but prigs and prudes. They must have turned many normal boys and girls against formal religion and the rules of morality by conveying an entirely wrong impression of their meaning and of their place in life. It is now plain why the discerning Ryerson saw the need for new Readers; he had to abate the unwholesome, unnatural influences of these existing texts. Moreover, there was need for him to act quickly, since there was not time for him to prepare a new and thoroughly Canadian Series. With great wisdom he borrowed the Irish texts and patiently used them until Canadian texts could be compiled to replace them.

In 1843 Sherbrooke produced yet another type of Reader. Though as its title page indicates it was "designed for the use of schools in the British Provinces," its composition displays unmistakeable McGuffeyan influences. And no wonder, for Sherbrooke lies only a few miles from the New England border. The book's lack of plan in indiscriminately mixing poetry and prose and stories with moral tags has the flavour of McGuffey. The solemnity with which certain subjects are discussed is in manner both Irish and English. The simple and unquestioning belief in the mechanical effectiveness of education, as revealed in a lesson on that subject, is undoubtedly an importation from New England. The tone of the book is not that of England or of Ireland or of Canada. Indeed, its only claim to be called Canadian is that it bears the imprint of a Canadian press. One notable link it has with McGuffey is its inclusion of that sombre reminder of human mortality:

> Oh, why should the spirit of mortal be proud?
> Like a fast fleeting meteor, a fast-flying cloud—
> A flash of the lightning, a break of the wave,
> He passes from Life to his rest in the grave.

The Sherbrooke Reader is the only Canadian text in which I have found this piece, which, through Abraham Lincoln's partiality, has become the best known piece in the whole McGuffey Series.

The obsession of the early 19th century for using violent methods of rubbing moral instruction into children manifested itself in various forms. In 1844 there appeared in Kingston a small volume known as *A Class Book—Youth's Guard against Crime*. The preface, with its naïve reasoning and assumptions, defies synopsis. As it is not very long it may be quoted in full:

> The author believes that all men were created by their Maker to be useful, in their day and generation, to their fellow-creatures; it is also stated that where there are no Laws there are no transgressions; and it may be enforced safely by every reflecting mind, that the limited knowledge of the existence and bearing of all the Criminal Laws of this Province, amongst the common classes, amounts almost to there being no Laws at all, so far as they have any knowledge of the fact. In proof of my remarks, I have seen Judges and Magistrates compelled to punish offenders whom they believed entirely ignorant of the Law they had violated. It is customary in all the institutions of learning, from the highest to the lowest, to state that it is the object of all concerned to teach useful knowledge,—and what is more useful than to give the community a full understanding of the Criminal Laws of the land, and the consequences of their being violated? I have seen a notice put up on a bridge, stating that a penalty of five shillings would be enforced for crossing the bridge faster than a walk with teams.—Men saw the Law, and therefore did not violate it. If crime is prevented in this case by having a knowledge of the Law, why not in many other cases? Persons knowing the Laws of the Country ought never to violate them, because they also know that they will be punished accordingly.

The most amazing thing about this amazing book is that in its comprehensive recital of the important phases of the Criminal Code it actually gives the juvenile reader a knowledge of crimes that most citizens of adult years have never heard of and are never likely to hear of, even if they live to threescore years and ten. The modern tabloid newspaper cannot begin to offer such a course in crime as is offered by this little book designed to eliminate crime. It was not officially authorized for use in schools, but, as I have come across several copies of it which, according to the inscriptions on their fly-leaves, were used in widely separated places, it must have had no inconsiderable circulation. Assuredly the production of a fanatic, it yet discloses the terrifically serious moral temper of those times. One may see in it one of the faults to the correction and reduction of which Ryerson had to give attention.

Ryerson handled his problem in two ways—first, by means of his

Readers of 1867-68; secondly, through an authorized textbook, *First Lessons in Christian Morals,* published in Toronto in 1871. This book was a treatise on the fundamentals of Christian theology, the practice of Christian living, and formal ethics. For obvious reasons the Consolidated School Act provided that its use be made optional. The objection of parents or guardians exempted their children from studying it. The fact that the time devoted to it came after the close of the regular school day manifestly deprived it of any appeal it might otherwise have had. There is every indication that the book was a failure. For reasons that I cannot detail, but can only feel, I believe that Ryerson prepared the book in order to make a concession to the habitual popular demand of the times that the common school must give explicit training in spiritual matters. I should not be surprised to learn that he really expected this direct method of instruction to fail, and that, with a sound psychology, he pinned his faith upon an indirect method that would touch everybody.

We are now ready to review the Ryerson Readers of the sixties. These are the first authorized Readers which even remotely deserve the name of Canadian, because they were the first designed to instil definitely national ideas into Canadian youth. The genuine need of such organs may be clearly seen in our survey of the earlier textbooks, as well as in the words of leaders of Canadian thought during the period just prior to Confederation. In one of his addresses Thomas D'Arcy McGee said with deep feeling: "When I can hear our young men say as proudly 'our federation' or 'our country' or 'our kingdom' as the young men of other countries do, speaking of their own, then I shall have less apprehension for the result of whatever trials may be in store for us." These words show that at the time they were uttered the idea of Canadian nationality did not exist except in the most germinal form. Ryerson perceived that the common school was the most powerful and promising single agency for fostering the idea.

Of these Readers the Third seems to be the most significant. It opens with a section of "Moral Tales and Anecdotes" which is spun out to the extent of 78 pages. The influence of McGuffey upon it is manifest, for the selection of many of the stories was undoubtedly prompted by their inclusion in the McGuffey Readers. This is an excellent instance of the inevitable effect of propinquity. In these stories some of us will recognize the literary friends of our boyhood—*Brave John Maynard* (the Lake Michigan pilot); *George Washington and the Cherry Tree; The Poor Match Girl; Counting Chickens Before They Are Hatched.* These tales were taken over with their rather maudlin moralizing unaltered, the result being that the first section of the Reader is a strange mixture of United States, Irish and English methods of presenting moral principles to young people. Humour is utterly lacking. The last section, consisting of incidents of history and adventure, gives a great deal of information concerning Canada. An occasional piece glorifying a British or a Canadian victory plays the part that corresponds in kind though not in degree to the accounts of Bunker Hill and Lexington in the United States schoolbooks.

The Fourth Reader continues the good work of fanning the flame of patriotism, but without adding to it the fiery heat of jingoism that emanates from the pages of McGuffey. One of its great merits is that it trained the generation in Ontario that preceded ours to take it for granted that a sincere love of one's country is not necessarily inconsistent with a high regard for the real worth of other countries. Of the 375 pages in the book 312 are devoted to information concerning the geography, the history and the natural history of the six continents; logically, America is given by far the longest section, and most of this deals with Canada. As the Readers advance in the Series the influence of the United States becomes less conspicuous and that of Canada greater.

One notable feature of the Fourth Reader is the preponderance of the secular as compared with the moral and religious. The comparative brevity of this treatment of matters spiritual, however, is more than offset by its sombreness and weight. The pupil has to read a condensed account of Biblical history, expositions of leading theological doctrines (including Christ's Second Coming and the doctrine of the Holy Spirit) and depressing verses on the graver phases of life. Midway in the section are Mrs. Hemans's lugubrious poem, *The Hour of Death,* and its by no means successful antidote, Beattie's *Hope Beyond the Grave.* Any efforts made by the compiler of this section to inspire in the young people *la joie de vivre* are entirely nullified by the gloominess of its closing piece, the saddest poem that Bobbie Burns ever wrote, *Man was Made to Mourn.* Not a few of the older generation have told me that it is by this piece they remember the Fourth Reader and their last day in an Ontario school.

The Fifth Reader of the Series is a stout volume of 528 pages, a veritable library in itself. According to the preface, it was compiled in part to supply "such specimens of the best English authors as are examples of correct style and pure taste, and are suitable for use as Exercises in Reading or Elocution." In no other Reader used up to this time is literary quality considered as it is in this Reader. Moreover, among the pieces it contains one cannot but notice a number written by Canadian authors. Their appearance is an indication that at last an English-Canadian literature has begun and that a conscious and unashamed recognition is being given to it. That D'Arcy McGee was giving expression to a pretty general desire is verified by the presence in this Reader of two patriotic orations, *Canada, the Land of Our Adoption,* by President M'Caul of the University of Toronto; *Canada, the Land of Our Birth,* by Egerton Ryerson himself. But despite the more advanced literary appreciation of this book and its strong nationalistic note, its chief characteristics are in kind those of the Readers that preceded it, namely, emphasis upon the value of information concerning everything under the sun, insistence upon the awful solemnity of life and upon the prime importance of religious and moral living. Its manner of instruction in these matters, however, is in general more palatable than that of its forerunners, in spite of the fact that the author ends his compilation as with two great sighs, the first a very sorrowful one—Mrs. Clive's *The Grave;* the second Pope's laboured effort to be cheerful—*The Dying Christian to his Soul.*

I shall refrain from analyzing the Readers that succeeded this notable Ryerson Series. Those of the eighties adopted the improved features of their immediate predecessors and added a number of new ones, thus becoming the first genuinely Upper Canadian Series of Readers. These were the texts that were used for many years in Manitoba and the North West Territories. They began to develop in Canada the type of national spirit and thought that corresponded broadly to the national feeling inspired in the United States by the McGuffey Readers when in 1820 they broke away from their English models. This means that Canadian national consciousness is at least 60 years younger than the national consciousness of the United States, a fact that will explain many of the differences between the peoples of the two countries. In part it accounts for certain marked differences in the rate of material development, but above all it reveals the causes of present differences in temperament, social thought and habit, outlook upon life, attitude toward the State, ways of approaching the problems of commerce, industry and land settlement. On the other hand, the common use of the Murray Readers in Canada and the United States for a quarter of a century prior to 1820 explains the origin of many points of similarity in the two peoples that cannot be accounted for by propinquity alone.

But the chief result of this study points forward rather than backward. It has brought to me a keen conviction of the paramount power of the common school Reader as a potential shaper of national thought and character. A series of Readers prepared in accordance with a definite plan in a well-organized school system can largely remake the people of a country within a generation or two. The character of the nation will be the character of its Readers, and the character of the Readers will depend upon the character of the men who prepare them. Who the makers of our Readers are becomes, therefore, a matter of great national importance.

26

FRENCH-CANADIAN NATIONALISM AND THE CHALLENGE OF ULTRAMONTANISM*

Jacques Monet, S.J.

The history of the Roman Catholic Church in Quebec is an unusual one which in no way parallels the patterns observable in the religious history of English Canada. Quite powerful in the mid-17th century, the Church in Quebec had seen its position become subordinate to the state long before the British Conquest. In the struggle between the so-called Gallicans (those who supported the monarchy's right to supervise the Church in nonspiritual matters) and the Ultramontanes (those who favoured a Church controlled by the papacy and independent of the national state), the Gallicans won a clear victory. This triumph was considerably vitiated, however, by the British takeover of New France. Searching for support in its efforts to govern an alien population, the new government turned to the Church as one of its logical allies, and the clergy responded favourably. For the next century and more, Quebec Roman Catholicism was one of the firmest supporters of the British government and one of the bulwarks of the status quo in British North America. In return for this support, the government bent over backwards to satisfy the Church, which was able to operate virtually free of state interference. There was no conspiracy on either side, but simply a tacit working agreement, which over the long haul produced strange political alliances in French Canada, one of which is discussed by Professor Jacques Monet, S.J., in the following article. What was the essence of the political divisions in French Canada in the 1840s? Which side is radical and which side is conservative? Are nationalism and ultramontanism compatible?

Canadian Historical Association Historical Papers (1966), 41–55.

SUGGESTIONS FOR FURTHER READING

J. M. S. Careless, *Canada, 1841–1857* (Toronto: McClelland and Stewart, 1967).

Paul G. Cornell, *The Alignment of Political Groups in Canada, 1841–1867* (Toronto: University of Toronto Press, 1962).

Léon Pouliot, *Mgr Bourget et son Temps*, 2 vols. (Montreal: Beauchemin, 1955–56).

J.M.B.

A funny thing happened to French-Canadian nationalism on its away to responsible government. It became ultramontane. At the end of the 1830s French Canada was in ferment. Under British domination for some 75 years, the French had succeeded in surviving, but not in developing by themselves a full, normal, national life. They had kept the essentials: their ancestral land, their French language, their Catholic Faith, their time-honoured and peculiar jurisprudence, and their long family traditions. But they needed a new life. The seigneurial system could no longer hold the growing population, the economy lagged, the problems of education had reached such an impasse that the schools were closed, and the old civil code no longer applied to modern circumstances. Above all, the upward thrust of the growing professional middle class created a serious social situation of which the rebellions of 1837–38 were only one expression. Clearly, if the struggle for national survival were to hold any meaning for the future, French-Canadian nationalists needed new solutions.

They were divided, however. Inspired by the ideology of Louis-Joseph Papineau some considered *la survivance* could be assured only by political isolation in a territory over which French-Canadians would be undisputed masters. Militant idealists, they were led by John Neilson and Denis-Benjamin Viger until Papineau returned to politics in 1847. Others, broader minded and more practical, held to a doctrine of which the Quebec editor Etienne Parent was the clearest exponent, and which Louis-Hippolyte LaFontaine translated into politics. They reasoned that it was the flexibility of the British constitutional system that could best assure not only their acquired rights, but also (by means of self-government) the certain hope of a broadening future for their language, their institutions, and their nationality.

Before achieving responsible government, however, LaFontaine needed to accomplish two things. He had to force the unity of his people in favour of British parliamentary democracy and, along with this, form a united political party with the Upper Canadians. Neither was easy. In the years immediately following the rebellion French Canada's strongest sympathies belonged to the leaders of the Viger-Neilson group, believers neither in responsible government nor in Union with Upper Canada. After the election of 1841, for instance, out of some 29 members elected by French-Canadian ridings, LaFontaine could count on only six or seven to be sympathetic to his views. By 1844, he had succeeded in persuading many more—at least he could then count on some two dozen. But not before the end of the decade could he be certain of victory, for until then Papineau, his followers, and especially his legend remained one of the strongest forces in the country. Still, after a decade of fistfights on electoral platforms, scandals, riots, and racial fury; after a brilliant, dynamic, and flexible partnership with Robert Baldwin, LaFontaine became in 1848 the first Canadian Prime Minister in the modern sense and, by means of the British Constitution, the first French-Canadian to actually express and direct the aspirations of his people.

He had also gradually, and all unwittingly perhaps, presided over the marriage of ultramontanism with the practical politics and the nationalist ideology of his party. At the beginning of the decade, the hierarchy and priests of the Roman Catholic Church in French Canada hardly conceived that practical party politics could be their concern, nor did they think of adding significantly to the nationalist theme. They worked behind the scenes; and, in 1838, for instance, after deciding to oppose the Union, they composed and signed an unpublicized petition which they sent directly to London to be presented to the Queen. But in 1848, during the crisis which consecrated the practice of responsible government, they openly took sides with LaFontaine's party, and allowed their newspapers to give approval to his administration. Likewise, at the time of the rebellions, most of the priests, and especially those among the hierarchy, had officially disassociated themselves from what seemed to be the main preoccupations of the leading French-Canadian nationalists. "Des mauvais sujets . . . prétendus libéraux, attachés à détruire dans nos peuples l'amour de la religion,"[1] Bishop Jacques Lartigue of Montreal called the *Patriotes,* while Archbishop Signay of Quebec tried to explain to his flock that Colborne's devastating march against the rebels had been undertaken "pas à dessein de molester ou maltraiter personne, mais pour protéger les bons et fidèles sujets, pour éclairer ceux des autres qui sont dans l'erreur et qui se sont laissés égarer."[2] Within a decade later, however, they openly wrote and talked of the doctrine that the Catholic Faith and French Canada's nationality depended one upon the other. "Tous les rapports qui nous arrivent des divers points du diocèse," the *Mélanges Religieux* reported on July 7, 1843, about the Saint-Jean-Baptiste day celebrations, "prouvent combien sont vifs et universels les sentiments de religion et de nationalité de nos concitoyens. Partout ces deux sentiments se sont montrés inséparables dans les cœurs: la pompe et les cérémonies religieuses ont accompagné les démonstrations civiles et patriotiques . . . C'est 'parce que nous sommes catholiques que nous sommes une nation dans ce coin de l'Amérique, que nous attirons les regards de toutes les autres contrées, l'intérêt et la sympathie de tous les peuples . . . Qu'on nous dise ce que serait le Canada s'il était peuplé exclusivement d'Anglais et de Protestants?" Of course, much happened between 1838 and 1848 to change the thinking of both nationalists and Catholic clerics.

---

[1]Archives de l'Archevêché de Montréal, Mgr. Lartigue à G. A. Belcourt, 24 avril 1838.
[2]Archives de l'Archevêché de Québec, Mgr. Signay à A. Leclerc, 25 novembre 1837.

One very important thing was the advent of Ignace Bourget. A short time after succeeding to the See of Montreal in 1840, this earnest and authoritarian Bishop made it clear how much he intended to renew the face of Catholicism in French Canada. During his first year—incidentally, after successfully reasserting in an interesting conflict with Poulett Thomson the doctrine of Papal supremacy and of episcopal independence of civil authority—he had organized a great mission throughout his diocese, preached by Bishop Forbin-Janson, one of France's foremost orators. Between September 1840 and December 1841, the French Bishop travelled across Lower Canada, visiting some 60 villages and preaching rousing sermons—two of which Lord Sydenham attended in state at Notre-Dame—before crowds sometimes estimated at 10,000. Bishop Bourget thus initiated close and large-scale religious contacts with France.

Indeed, while Forbin-Janson was still in Canada, the new Bishop of Montreal left on the first of some five voyages to France and Rome, a trip from which he would return carrying with him the reawakened energies of the Catholic revival. While in Europe, he held discussions with a cluster of interesting and influential Catholic ultramontane leaders. At this time, European Ultramontanes—whose intellectual roots reached as far back as the quarrels between Philippe LeBel and Boniface VIII, the pope "beyond the mountains"—had outgrown the traditional belief that the Pope held doctrinal and jurisdictional supremacy over the whole Church. Brought up on DeMaistre's *Du Pape,* a book that urged Papal dominion over temporal rulers in all Church matters, and feverish with romanticism's revival of all things medieval, they urged the subservience of civil government to the papacy, of State to Church. They had not understood that there was a difference between the surrender of all men to God's will, and the obedience of civil society to the Pope. They were mistaken—but they were, perhaps because of this, all the more dogmatic, energetic, aflame with zeal: they directed newspapers, notably Louis Veuillot's *L'Univers,* entertained crucial political polemics over education, censorship, and "secret organizations"; by the 1840s, they had founded hundreds of pious societies for desirable ends, collected a multiplication of relics from the Roman catacombs, covered Europe with imitation Gothic, and filled their churches and parlours with Roman papier-maché statuary.

Bishop Bourget fell under their spell as soon as he arrived. In Paris he had long conversations with the Abbé Desgenettes, curé of the ultramontane cenacle at Notre-Dame-des-Victoires, and the founder of the Archconfraternity of the Most Holy and Immaculate Heart of Mary; he met Théodore de Ratisbonne, a convert from Judaism and the founder of the Daughters of Sion, Jean-Marie de Lamennais, the founder of the Brothers of the Christian Schools, and the most noted of them all, Louis Veuillot, who attended a sermon of Mgr. Bourget's at Notre-Dame-des-Victoires and gave it a rave review in *L'Univers.* At Chartres, he was entertained by the compelling personality of the Abbé, later Cardinal, Louis-Edouard Pie, the future exponent of Papal infallibility at the Vatican Council. In Marseille, he was impressed by Bishop de Mazenod, another staunch defender of the Vatican; and in Rome, he was greeted by Fr. John Roothaan, the General of the Jesuits, with whom he spent eight days in retreat and meditation. Finally, several audiences with the kindly Gregory XVI crowned the series of discussions that made him the most Ultramontane churchman of his generation in Canada.[3]

In Chartres, the Bishop of Montreal also had a long conversation with Bishop Clausel de Montals. The latter was a strong Gallican, but nonetheless the acknowledged champion in the fight for Catholic institutions against the State University. He doubtless recited for his Canadien colleague a long list of the dangers and evils of the *école laïque*. For from that day onwards Mgr. Bourget would battle tirelessly to keep the Church in control of education in Lower Canada. And all Canadian Ultramontanes would follow him in this.

Back in Montreal, Mgr. Bourget began injecting into the Canadien mood the full fever of his Roman creed. With a crusader's singleness of purpose, he arranged for the immigration from France of the Oblate and Jesuit Orders, of the Dames du Sacré-Coeur and the Sisters of the Good Shepherd; he founded two Canadian religious congregations of his own, established the Saint Vincent de Paul Society; carried out an extensive canonical visitation of his diocese, and pressed Rome to establish an ecclesiastical Province that extended within a few years to new dioceses in Toronto, Ottawa, British Columbia, and Oregon, "une vaste chaîne de sièges épiscopaux qui doit s'étendre un jour de la mer jusqu'à la mer: a mari usque ad mare."[4] He also organized a whole series of Parish revivals and religious ceremonies superbly managed to stir the emotion of all classes. At Varennes on July 26, 1842, for example, before a huge crowd of several thousand, surrounded by some 60 priests and in the full pontifical splendour of his office, he presided over the crowning of a holy picture of Saint Anne, according to "le cérémonial usité à Rome pour de semblables solennités." (The end of the day was, perhaps, more Canadien: "Tous ces feux," reported the *Mélanges*, "des salves d'artillerie ou de mousquetterie au milieu du silence d'une nuit profonde, après toutes les cérémonies de la journée, faisaient naître des émotions nouvelles inconnues."[5]) Another time, in November 1843, he presided over a huge demonstration in honour of the transferral to the chapel of the Sisters of Providence of the bones of Saint Januaria, ancient Roman relics which he had negotiated away from the custodian of one of the catacombs. At this service, the golden reliquary was carried by four canons of the cathedral surrounded by eight seminarians bearing incense, and "la foule eut peine à se retirer, tant était grande son émotion."[6] Throughout the 1840s, he ordered many more such occasions. For the blessing of the bells for the new towers of Notre-Dame Church, "on exécuta parfaitement le jeu du *God Save the Queen*—*Dieu sauve notre reine* auquel la

---

[3] I want to thank Fr. Léon Pouliot, author of *Mgr. Bourget et son Temps*, 2 vols., (Montréal, 1955–56) and of *La Réaction Catholique de Montréal* (Montréal, 1942) for pointing out to me the importance of this trip in the formation of Mgr. Bourget's thinking.

[4] *Mélanges Religieux* [henceforth *MR*], 13 mai 1842.

[5] *MR*, 28 juillet 1842.

[6] *MR*, 14 novembre 1843.

bande du régiment fit écho de toute la force de ses instruments."[7] (Yes, the Ultramontanes were also strong royalists. The *Mélanges* often published articles on royalty, one of which began by praising "les principes d'honneur, de devoir, d'ordre, de générosité, de dévouement, qui dérivent de l'idée monarchique."[8]) A not untypical reaction to this type of demonstration was that of the politician Joseph Cauchon who wrote to a colleague about the funeral of Archbishop Signay in October 1850: "Le deuil de l'Eglise était grandiose et solennel à l'extrême. L'installation du nouvel archevêque s'est faite avec une égale solennité. Il y a quelque chose de grand, de sublime dans ce développement des cérémonies soit lugubres soit joyeuses du Catholicisme."[9]

The new Orders naturally aided Mgr. Bourget with his ultramontanism—especially the Jesuits who began in 1843 to lay the foundation of Collège Sainte-Marie, an institution that would train so many energetic young nationalist Catholics. The *Mélanges Religieux* also helped. In this bi-weekly newspaper, the priests from the bishopric published over and over again long articles of praise for the papal states, and copious excerpts from the works of leading ultramontanists: speeches by the Spanish conservative Donoso Cortès, Montalembert's famous oration on the Roman question, Mgr. de Bonald's pastoral letter "contre les erreurs de son temps," and long book reviews such as the one condemning Eugène Sue's salacious *Les Mystères de Paris* for trying to "répandre sur la religion et ses pratiques tout l'odieux possible."[10] They also issued vibrant appeals to Canadian youth to join their movement: "Vous voulez être de votre siècle jeunes amis, vous voulez marcher avec lui? . . . Avez-vous trouvé mieux où reposer votre âme que dans les œuvres immortelles des DeBonald, de Maistre, de Chateaubriand, de Montalembert, du Lamartine *catholique,* de Turquety?"[11] They also gave news of Catholicism throughout the world, concentrating especially on the independence of the Papal States and the University Question in France. "Pour parvenir à remplir leur mission," the *Mélanges* noted on March 31, 1846, "les Éditeurs n'ont rien épargne; ils ont fait venir à grands frais les meilleurs journaux d'Europe, *L'Univers, L'Ami de la Religion, Le Journal des Villes et des Campagnes de France,* le *Tablet* de Londres, le *Freeman's Journal* de New York, le *Cross* d'Halifax, le *Catholic Magazine* de Baltimore, le *Catholic Herald* de Philadelphie, le *Propagateur Catholique* de la Nouvelle-Orléans." In a word, the *Mélanges* opened a window on the Catholic world. And through it there blew in the high winds of ultramontanism, which, for the Canadiens, felt so much like their own aggressive and assertive nationalism.

Through it there also came for the clergy a novel regard for the layman. Since the Restoration in Europe, the Catholic Bishops and priests had achieved some success there in reintegrating the Church into

---

[7]*MR*, 4 juillet 1843.

[8]*MR*, 27 janvier 1843.

[9]*Archives de la Province de Québec* [henceforth *APQ*], Papiers Taché A50. Joseph Cauchon à E.-P. Taché, 9 octobre 1850.

[10]*MR*, 20 novembre 1849.

[11]*MR*, 26 novembre 1842.

educational life and social services. Very often they had done this with the assistance of influential laymen. Through the *Mélanges* publication of articles and speeches by these European ultramontane politicians, the Canadien priests gradually developed a fresh respect for their own lay politicians. They began to think of new ideas on how they could work with them. In fact, with the coming of responsible government the old ways which the priests had grown accustomed to were passing into history forever. The Union had marked the end of the courteous and courtly style which the Bishops and the British governors had so carefully devised over the years to fuse the good of the throne with the good of the altar. Now, effective political power was passing from the hands of Governors-General to those of the Canadien electors. And if the Church was to exercise the influence which the priests felt in conscience it must, then the clergy must begin to deal directly with the politicians and the people.

Besides, they were finding nationalist politicians whom they liked. Indeed, by the middle of the decade, it was becoming obvious how much LaFontaine's followers and the priests seemed made to understand each other. The debate on the Union, during which they had been on opposite sides, was settled. And since then, they had forged new personal friendships. In Quebec, politicians such as René-Édouard Caron, Étienne-Pascal Taché, and especially Joseph-Édouard Cauchon, the editor of the influential *Journal de Québec*, enjoyed frequent hospitality at the Séminaire. Taché and Cauchon were also close correspondents of the Archbishop's secretary, the talented and ubiquitous abbé Charles-Félix Cazeau. In Montreal, LaFontaine's close friend, Augustin-Norbert Morin, also received a cordial welcome at the bishopric, especially from Mgr. Bourget's *Grand-Vicaire*, Mgr. Hyacinthe Hudon. So did other partisans like Lewis Thomas Drummond and Joseph Coursol. Indeed, as these priests and politicians grew to admire each other, a new esteem was also developing between their leaders, between the new Bishop of Montreal and the man who in 1842 had become French Canada's Attorney-General. Despite initial suspicion on both their parts, Bourget and LaFontaine were by temperament made to understand each other. Both were heroes to duty, strong-willed leaders, unyielding in their principles, and expert at manoeuvering within the letter of the law. Especially they had this in common that each one thought in absolute terms that he was in total possession of the truth. Neither could accept from an adversary anything but complete conversion.

Thus it was that slowly within the womb of LaFontaine's party, despite appearances, the pulse of the clerico-nationalist spirit began, faintly, to beat.

*   *   *   *   *

None of these things—Bishop Bourget's trip to Europe and its effects in Montreal, the historical turn in Canadian politics caused by responsible government, the new intimacy between Ultramontanes and nationalists—none could weigh enough to bring the priests officially into LaFontaine's party. But they did prepare the way. Then, in 1846, the public discussion over a new Education Bill and over the funds from the Jesuit Estates revealed to the clergy which politicians were its natural allies and which were not. The Education Bill of 1845, proposed by Denis-Benjamin Papineau, the great tribune's brother, who was Commissioner of Crown Lands in the Viger-Draper administration, did not satisfy the clergy. Although it provided for the Curés being *ex officio* "visitors" to the schools, it did not give them the control they wished. They therefore began a campaign to have the project amended in their favour.

The *Mélanges* took the lead, repeatedly emphasizing the close connection between education and religion. "Nous ne comprenons pas d'éducation sans religion, et conséquemment sans morale," it had written back in November 8, 1842, in words which could easily have been inspired by Bishop Bourgét's conversation with Clausel de Montals, "et nous ne voyons pas ce qui pourrait supplier à son enseignement dans les écoles. Que sera donc l'instruction et l'éducation des enfants sans prières, sans catéchisme, sans instruction religieuse et morale quelconque?" Even as the Bill was being debated, the *Mélanges* kept up the pressure, receiving great assistance from A.-N. Morin, "ce monsieur dont le cœur est droit," as one curé wrote.[12] From his seat on the Opposition benches, with the aid of his colleagues Taché, Drummond, and Cauchon, Morin proposed amendment after amendment to bring about a system which would happily unite clerical authority on the local level with centralized control by the Superintendent at the Education Department. "M. Papineau, auquel j'ai eu le plaisir d'administer quelque dure médecine pour lui faire digérer son Bill d'Éducation, ne veut pas que l'éducation soit religieuse," Cauchon reported to the abbé Cazeau. "J'ai dit, moi votre ouaille, qu'une éducation dépouillée de l'instruction religieuse mènerait à de funestes résultats.[13] Finally, in mid-1846, Denis-Benjamin Papineau bowed to the pressure, and accepted the Morin amendments.

If the Bishops accordingly felt happy about the Act in its final form, they owed it in great part to the support of politicians like Morin and his friends. At the same time, they were receiving support from LaFontaine's friends on another critical issue: the Jesuit Estates.

The problem of these lands which had been granted by a succession of French Kings and nobles to serve as an endowment for education, had definitely passed to the British Crown in 1800 at the death of the last Jesuit. Their revenues were used by the Colonial Office for any number of Government sinecures until 1832 when as a gesture of conciliation it agreed that they be administered by the Lower Canadian Assembly. Then there began another struggle with the Catholic Bishops who claimed that they and not the Assembly were the true heirs of the Jesuits. By 1846 the controversy had reached the floor of the House, and the

---

[12]*APQ*, Fonds de l'Instruction Publique. Lettres reçues. P. Davignon à J.-B. Meilleur, 23 novembre 1843.

[13]Archives de l'Archevêché de Québec, DM H-245. Joseph Cauchon à C.-F. Cazeau, 24 février 1845.

Provincial Government, led by Denis-Benjamin Viger, refused the Bishops' claim. As in the debate over Papineau's Education Bill, LaFontaine and his party supported the priests. LaFontaine, Morin (who had been acting as confidential advisor to the clergy on the question), Drummond, and Taché each delivered an impassioned speech against the "spoliation" of French Canada's heritage; Morin himself proposing that the funds be transferred entirely to the Church. Viger defended the Government's action on the grounds of precedent and Parliamentary supremacy. He won the vote. But in appealing to Parliamentary supremacy, he began a disagreeable discussion which continued in the press for over three months. At the end, it was clear how wide a division had taken place among French-Canadian nationalists: a division as explicit as the opposing doctrines of liberalism and ultramontanism.

While traditionally nationalist papers such as *Le Canadien*, and *L'Aurore des Canadas*, defending Viger, assailed the Church's position, *La Minerve*, *Le Journal de Québec*, and *La Revue Canadienne*, all LaFontaine papers, became like the *Mélanges* defenders of the Faith. In a series of articles probably written by Viger,[14] *L'Aurore* insisted that the Bishops had at most a very tenuous claim to the Jesuit funds which had never, in fact, belonged to them, and which, if the intentions of the donors were to be respected, should be applied to the whole territory of what had been New France. Since they were being spent exclusively in Lower Canada, as the Bishops themselves agreed was correct, then the revenues derived their title from the Imperial decision of 1832 which put them at the disposal of the "volontés réunies des pouvoirs exécutif, législatif, administratif" of the Lower Canadian Assembly, and hence of the Union government which was its heir. When the La Fontaine press generally replied that the taking of the property from the Church in the first place had been a sacrilege, the argument rose to a higher level.[15] Running through precedents that went back to Justinian, La Régale, and the *coutumes* of pre-Revolutionary France, *L'Aurore* retorted that since the Church's possession of property derived from the State's civil law, any change by the government could hardly be a sacrilege. To which, in best scholastic manner, the *Mélanges* retorted that since the Church possessed property by divine and natural right, civil recognition added nothing. And to this *L'Aurore*, in best liberal tradition, asserted that since nature knew only individuals, no corporate body such as the Church could claim existence by natural law.[16]

And so the controversy proceeded. It was one which could not easily be resolved. For while the *Mélanges* was reasserting the doctrine so dear to the 19th century ultramontane that the Church, by natural and divine right, was autonomous with respect to the State, Viger, brimming with the liberal's faith in the individual, denied any natural right to a corporate body. It was an argument that could not be settled for generations;

---

[14]*L'Aurore des Canadas*, 3, 6, 13, 16 juin 1846.

[15]*L'Aurore des Canadas*, 13 juin 1845.

[16]MR, 26 juin 1846; *L'Aurore des Canadas*, 30 juin 1846.

indeed not until both the liberals and the ultramontanes, in the face of other problems, would come to modify their intransigence.

This was not the first difference of opinion that had brought Viger's party and the *Mélanges* into conflict. Back in 1842 they had measured paragraphs against each other over the interpretation of Bishop Lartigue's famous *Mandement* against rebellion in 1837; and at that time also they had been quarrelling from the viewpoint of opposing ultramontane and liberal doctrines.[17] Yet somehow that discussion had not caused any overt split. The 1846 one did—and soon with the re-emergence of Louis-Joseph Papineau into political life, all bridges were broken between his party and the clergy. By 1849, the priests had become one of the great forces on the side of responsible government in Canada.

Having returned from his exile in liberal, anticlerical France, the great rebel found little to encourage him in Canada. He was disgusted by LaFontaine's politics, repelled by the growing power of the priests. Especially he suffered at being forced to witness his people's growing commitment to the British Connection. In the late fall of 1847 he issued what Lord Elgin called "a pretty frank declaration of republicanism,"[18] reviving his dreams of the 1830s for a national republic of French Canada. Around himself he rallied Viger's followers and a group of enthusiastic young separatists who edited the radical newspaper *L'Avenir*. They shared the rebel leader's philosophy: if it only depended on them they would win through the sharpness of their minds what he had not by sharpness of sword.

What struck the ultramontanes about Papineau and *L'Avenir* was of course not so much the attacks against LaFontaine and responsible government. It was their anticlericalism. As things turned out the republicans would hurt their own cause more than they would the Church: on the subject of responsible government, Papineau might conceivably weaken LaFontaine, especially if he concentrated on nationality and the defects of the Union. But by challenging the Church, the *rouges* merely helped to cement the alliance between LaFontaine and the priests.

On March 14, 1849, *L'Avenir* created quite a stir by publishing large extracts from the European liberal press on the Roman revolution which had forced Pius IX into exile and proclaimed Mazzini's republic. The articles were bitter: and the Lower Canadian republicans left little doubt where their own sympathies lay. The *Mélanges* took up the challenge. Through several series of learned front pages, it tried to show "les Messieurs de l'Avenir" how serious were "l'injustice et la faute qu'ils ont commises."[19] But the young editors did not understand. They continued to insult the Pope; and at their Société Saint-Jean-Baptiste banquet that year, they replaced their traditional toast to the Sovereign by a defiant

---

[17]Cf. F. Ouellet, "Le Mandement de Mgr. Lartigue de 1837 et la Réaction libérale," *Bulletin des Recherches historiques*, 58 (1952) 97–104.

[18]Elgin-Grey Papers vol. 1, p. 102. Elgin to Grey, December 24, 1847.

[19]*MR*, 30 mars 1849.

speech on "Rome Régénérée." "Les journaux socialistes et anti-religieux sont sans cesse à vanter les hauts faits de MM. les rouges à Rome," the *Mélanges* complained,[20] adding sadly that "la manie d'aboyer contre la soutane semble être à la mode."[21]

Indeed it was. On July 21, 1849, *L'Avenir* led another attack which would lock the journalists in another discussion for two months: this time on tithing. "La dîme," it pronounced, "est un abus encore bien plus grand que la tenure seigneuriale." Then later, when it began to campaign for the abolition of seigneurial tenure, the radical paper again attacked the Church for its ownership of seigneurial lands. In fact, it averred, one of the very reasons against the system was the amount of revenue which accrued from it to the Séminaire de Québec and other religious institutions.

On September 14, 1849, the *Mélanges* warned the republican youngsters at *L'Avenir:* "Nos adversaires ne doivent pas se dissimuler que par leur conduite et leurs écrits ils se font plus de tort qu'ils nous en font à nous-mêmes." True enough. For as the priests were being attacked by their own political enemies, LaFontaine's publicists naturally came to the clergy's rescue. Thus, all during 1849, the *Journal de Québec, Le Canadien,* and *La Minerve,* defended the Church as if they themselves had been directly concerned.

While the dispute raged about the Pope's temporal sovereignty, for instance, Cauchon's *Journal* featured a serial on the subject by the French Bishop Dupanloup of Orleans, and another series covering several instalments by "Un Canadien Catholique" assailed *L'Avenir* for "la prétention qu'il entretient de catéchiser le clergé sur ses devoirs." So also on the issue of tithing: Cauchon spread an article defending the Church over the front page of three issues in October 1849, and underlined the connection between anticlericalism and the republicans: "Ce sont les aimables procédés du passé, la haine entre le peuple et ses chefs religieux pour assurer le triomphe des doctrines pernicieuses et anti-nationales."[22] When the *rouges* criticized the clergy's role in the schools, Cauchon answered by giving the clergy credit for *la survivance:*

> D'où vient cette haute portée d'intelligence, ce caractère si beau, si noble, si grand de franchise, d'honneur, de grandeur d'âme et de religieuse honnêteté qui distingue nos premiers citoyens et qui contraste si étonnamment avec cette populace de banqueroutiers qui soudoient les incendiaires, les parjures, les voleurs et la lie des villes pour commettre en leur nom, pour eux, et à leur profit des crimes dignes de Vandales? Du clergé national, sorti des rangs du peuple, identifié avec tous ses intérêts, dévoué jusqu'à la mort, initié à tous les progrès des sciences modernes, des arts et du génie, aux tendances des sociétés actuelles.[23]

Finally, when the *rouges* hurled insults, the editor of the *Journal* answered flamboyantly:

---

[20]*MR*, 6 juillet 1849.
[21]*MR*, 21 septembre 1849.
[22]*Journal de Québec*, 2 octobre 1849.
[23]*Journal de Québec*, 2 mars 1850.

Détrôner le Dieu de nos pères et lui substituer l'infâme idole du sen-
sualisme, voilà leur but; vilipender le prêtre, calomnier son enseignement,
couvrir d'un noir venin ses actions les plus louables, voilà leur
moyen . . . Quel but, quelle fin vous proposez-vous en livrant à l'ignominie
le prêtre du Canada, votre concitoyen, votre ami d'enfance, l'ami dévoué de
notre commune patrie! Aurez-vous relevé bien haut la gloire de notre pays
lorsque vous aurez avili aux yeux de l'étranger ses institutions les plus
précieuses, couvert de boue ses hommes les plus éminents dans l'ordre religieux et civil, enseveli sous un noir manteau de calomnies le corps le plus
respectable de la société comme un cadavre sous un drap mortuaire?[24]

Le *Canadien* wrote less lyrically, but like the *Journal*, it, too, came to
the defence of the priests, and struck back at *L'Avenir*. It found that the
republicans' articles "représentent trop de passion et par conséquent une
notable injustice envers les hommes en qui le pays a confiance."[25] And at
the height of the temporal power dispute, it noted how the same republicans who praised Mazzini had also supported those who burned down
the Canadian Parliament buildings, and signed the manifesto demanding Annexation to the United States.

In return, of course, the priests supported LaFontaine. At the time of
Papineau's Manifesto at the end of 1847, during the general election that
swept LaFontaine to the final achievement of responsible government,
reports from different parts of Lower Canada came in to Montreal that
"certains prêtres, méme à Montréal, ont prononcé en chaire des discours
presqu'exclusivement politiques."[26] But more important still than such
electoral advice was the increasing involvement in party politics of the
Mélanges Religieux and its junior associate in Quebec, the weekly *Ami
de la Religion et de la Patrie*. Edited by Jacques Crémazie, *L'Ami* first
appeared in early 1848 under the interesting motto: "Le trône chancelle
quand l'honneur, la religion, la bonne foi ne l'environnent pas." It endorsed La Fontaine's ideas so unequivocally that Cauchon was glad to
recommend it to his party leader for patronage:

Il ne faudra pas oublier quand vous donnez des annonces d'en donner
aussi à l'*Ami de la Religion* . . . qui montre de bonnes dispositions et fait
tout le bien qu'il peut.[27]

As for the *Mélanges*, since mid-1847 it had practically become a LaFon-
taine political sheet. In July 1847, the clergy had handed over the editor-
ship to a 21-year-old law student who was articling in the offices of A.-N.
Morin: Hector Langevin, whose religious orthodoxy they felt well
guaranteed by his two brothers (and frequent correspondents) in
Quebec: Jean, a priest professor at the Séminaire, and Edmond who in
September 1847 became secretary to the Archbishop's *Grand-Vicaire*
Cazeau.

With mentors like Morin, the youthful editor soon threw his paper into

---

[24]*Journal de Québec*, 6 décembre 1849.

[25]*Le Canadien*, 31 mai 1848.

[26]*MR*, 14 décembre 1847.

[27]Public Archives of Canada, MG 24, B-14. LaFontaine Papers. Joseph Cauchon à
LaFontaine, 24 octobre 1849.

the thick of the political fight. In fact he became so involved that at last the priests at the Bishopric felt they had to warn him (they did so several times) to tone down his enthusiasm for LaFontaine. He did not, however. His greatest service was perhaps the publicizing of the clergy's support for LaFontaine at the time of the trouble over Rebellion Losses. At the height of the crisis, on May 5, 1849, he issued the rallying call:

> En présence de cette activité des gens turbulents et ennemies de la Constitution, on se demande ce qu'ont à faire les libéraux [i.e., LaFontaine's supporters] . . . Regardons nos Évêques, regardons nos prêtres, regardons notre clergé; il vient de nous montrer l'exemple en présentant lui même des addresses à Son Excellence Lord Elgin, et en en envoyant d'autres à notre gracieuse souveraine. Après cela hésiterons-nous à agir avec vigueur, promptitude et énergie? Hésiterons-nous à suivre la route que nous trace notre épiscopat, que nous trace notre clergé tout entier?[28]

Half a year later he spelled out his full sentiments in a letter to his brother Edmond:

> Si les rouges avaient l'autorité en mains, prêtres, églises, religion, etc., devraient disparaître de la face du Canada. Le moment est critique. Il faut que le ministère continue à être libéral tel qu'à présent, ou bien on est Américain, et puis alors adieu à notre langue et à notre nationalité.[29]

*   *   *   *   *

Perhaps it was inevitable that during the closing years of the decade the French-Canadian clergy would come to play an increasingly political role. For with responsible government the Canadiens had, for the first time in their long national life, taken over the direction of their own destiny. And as the Catholic Church had long played an important part in fashioning their thought, it was natural for most of those on the political stage to welcome the support of the priests. Yet, would it have happened as effortlessly if Bishop Bourget had not fallen in with the *Veuillotistes*? If LaFontaine and Morin had not supported clerical schools in 1846? If Hector Langevin had not articled in Morin's office? If *L'Avenir* had not attacked the Papal States? Would it have happened at all if Denis-Benjamin Viger had won the election of 1844? If the Papineau legend had persisted? Be that as it may, the *bleu* alliance of priest and politician (since we can now give it its name) radically transformed LaFontaine's party and French-Canadian nationalism.

Except when the rights of the Church were in question, ultramontanes tended to consider politics as secondary. They concentrated rather on Church-State problems, thus gradually moving away from areas of co-operation with Upper Canada—especially at a time when the "voluntary principle" was converting Baldwin's party as ultramontanism was LaFontaine's. Gradually they came to appeal almost exclusively to ideas and feelings which were proper only to French Canada. When he began in the late 1830s LaFontaine aimed at political and economic

---

[28]*MR*, 5 mai 1849.
[29]*APQ*, Collection Chapais, 253. Hector à Edmond Langevin, 25 janvier 1850.

reforms in which both Canadas would share. In his famous *Adresse aux Electeurs de Terrebonne,* he described the problems of French Canada in political and economic terms alone. As the decade moved on, however, under pressure from his opponents and his followers, he found himself becoming more and more involved with ultramontanism and a narrower nationalism. Reluctantly, it seems. Late in 1851, several weeks after his resignation, he recalled to Cauchon, who had bragged about rallying the priests, how he had cautioned him about the faith-and-nationality theme. "Je me rappelle ce que vous m'avex dit," Cauchon admitted, "par rapport à la question nationale. Mais je vous répondais que c'était la seule corde qu'il était possible de faire vibrer avec succès."[30] Later, to another admonition from the former premier, the editor of the *Journal de Québec* admitted that "la question de nationalité était délicate," but protested again that "c'était la corde qui vibrait le mieux. J'espère que vous avez en cela parfaitment compris ma pensée et que vous êtes convaincu que je n'ai pas voulu employer un moyen malhonnête pour atteindre mon but."[31] LaFontaine had wanted to break with Papineau's particularist and republican nationalism. He appealed to a more general, open point of view, founding his hopes on cooperation with Upper Canada and in the British political system. Yet, in the end, he found himself the head of a party which tended to be as particularist as Papineau's (although for different reasons).

His party also turned out to be one which did not understand Parliamentary institutions. The ultramontanes were not rigid republicans like Papineau, but they were rigid Catholics, used to "refuting the errors of our time," with a doctrine which they proudly wanted as "toujours une, toujours sublime, toujours la même."[32] They were accustomed to think in an atmosphere rarified by unchanging principles. Instinctively they reacted in dogmatic terms, pushing ideas to their limits—and students of the absolute make poor parliamentarians. The ultramontanes could not really understand parliamentary practice as LaFontaine and Parent had. They lacked political flair and skill in manœuvring. They could not adapt to the gropings and costs of conciliation. To them, "rights" were an objective reality which could not be negotiated, only acknowledged. "Toleration" could not mean respect for an opposing opinion; at best it was a necessary evil. Applied to theology, their attitude might have had some validity (although not for ecumenism!) but transferred to politics and nationalism—as inevitably it was—it could not but extinguish LaFontaine's hopes for a broadening democracy of the British type.

For years the *bleus* and their Upper Canadian colleagues supported the same men, but as the French party gradually concentrated so dogmatically on Faith and Nationality, there could be no true meeting of minds. Outwardly, LaFontaine's and Parent's wider nationalism seemed to have prevailed: responsible government and British Parliamentary

---

[30]LaFontaine Papers. Joseph Cauchon à LaFontaine, 11 novembre 1851.
[31]Ibid., décembre 1851.
[32]*MR,* 15 décembre 1843.

institutions were secured. Also, a political party uniting Upper and Lower Canadians continued to govern the country for over a generation. But this was external appearance only: in reality, the party from which LaFontaine resigned in 1851 was assiduously becoming less concerned with the larger perspective than with the particular Church-State problems of French Canada; it was becoming decreasingly parliamentarian, increasingly authoritarian.

A funny thing indeed had happened to French-Canadian nationalism on its way to responsible government.

27

JAMES EDWARD FITZGERALD VERSUS THE HUDSON'S BAY COMPANY: THE FOUNDING OF VANCOUVER ISLAND*

J. S. Galbraith

The merger of the North West Company and the Hudson's Bay Company in 1821 eliminated the source of conflict in the Canadian West only momentarily. The two trading companies had been locked in desperate competition, but were both interested in basically the same things: furs and profits. The Selkirk settlement introduced new pressures and tensions into the West, and the pressure of population movement, particularly in the United States, combined with the attractiveness of the Pacific Coast as a region for settlement, made it inevitable that this would soon become a battleground. The nature of the conflict has usually been seen as one between fur trading and settlement. The Hudson's Bay Company has been interpreted as fighting a desperate rear-guard action to prevent colonization in its extensive territory, on the understandable premise that people and fur-bearing animals were incompatible. Certainly it was true that the trade always retreated in the face of population expansion, and that those hostile to Hudson's Bay Company charged regularly and vociferously that it was an intransigent enemy of colonization. Professor J. S. Galbraith challenges this position in the article which follows. What are the basic issues of the 1840s as Galbraith sees them? To what does he attribute the Hudson Bay Company's failure to colonize successfully on Vancouver Island? In what ways were the critics of Hudson's Bay inaccurate? Were there ways in which the critics were quite tellingly correct?

---

*British Columbia Historical Quarterly, 16 (1952), 191–207.

SUGGESTIONS FOR FURTHER READING

J. S. Galbraith, *The Hudson's Bay Company as an Imperial Factor, 1821–1869* (Berkeley: University of California Press, 1957).

A. S. Morton, *History of the Canadian West to 1870–71* (London: T. Nelson, 1939).

Margaret Ormsby, *British Columbia: A History* (Toronto: Macmillan of Canada, 1958).

J.M.B.

D uring the century which has passed since the grant of Vancouver Island to the Hudson's Bay Company on January 13, 1849, the legend has been perpetuated and strengthened that the Company sought control over the Island with the intention of frustrating that colonization which it was pledged to promote. The Company has been cast in the role of the cunning monopolist whose profits from the fur trade were dependent on the exclusion of settlement, Earl Grey as an unconscious dupe or willing accomplice, and James Edward Fitzgerald as an energetic, disinterested advocate of genuine colonization whose plans were frustrated by this powerful combination. The views expressed by Matthew Macfie almost 90 years ago remain generally accepted:—

> It is not generally believed that the company intended to yield literal compliance with the terms of the covenant agreed to between them and the Government. They could have no interest in promoting the colonisation of the island indiscriminately even by British subjects.[1]

This interpretation is based upon two assumptions: that the objective of the Company on Vancouver Island was the maintenance of a fur preserve and that the Company's professions of willingness to promote colonization were insincere. Neither of these assumptions is entirely correct, since each is an over-simplification.

The motivations of the Company in its desire for control over Vancouver Island can be understood only in the context of its general frontier policies. The areas of greatest profit during the period between the amalgamation with the North West Company in 1821 and the surrender of the chartered territory to Canada in 1869 were Rupert's Land and the Mackenzie River district. Could the Company have been certain that it would be permitted to enjoy in tranquillity the fruits of its monopoly in these territories, its zeal for expansion into outlying sections would have been less ardent. After the amalgamation with the North West Company, and particularly after the election of John Henry Pelly as Governor in 1822, the policy was consciously developed of carrying the attack to opposition traders as far as possible from the "heartland" of the Company's power. Trading posts were maintained in Canada, though they provided no prof-

---

[1]Matthew Macfie, *Vancouver Island and British Columbia* (London, 1865), p. 62. One of the first to dissent from the generally accepted view was W. Kaye Lamb, "The Governorship of Richard Blanshard," *British Columbia Historical Quarterly*, 14 (1950), 1–40.

its or even sustained losses, in order to discourage free traders from attempts to cross from Canada over the height of land into Rupert's Land. The Company's posts along Lake Superior and Lake Huron yielded little profit, but were considered necessary to discourage intruders from the United States. To the west of the mountains, the Snake country was hunted long after its immediate economic value had ended to protect more profitable areas of the Oregon country from invasions of American traders.[2]

The chief architects of this policy appear to have been Sir John Henry Pelly and Sir George Simpson, the overseas Governor, but the decision to seek control over Vancouver Island was Pelly's alone. Simpson was convinced as late as September 1848 that the assumption of responsibility for Vancouver Island would produce little, if any, benefit to the Company, that any attempt to colonize Vancouver Island from Great Britain was predestined to failure because of the superior attractions of Oregon and California in soil and climate, and that the Company would incur odium and expense in a useless undertaking.[3] Archibald Barclay, Secretary of the Company, shared this view. He wrote Simpson on October 13, 1848:—

> I quite agree with you as to the estimate of Vancr. Island. It is in my view *worthless* as seat for a colony. It is about the last place in the globe to which (were I going to emigrate) I should select as an abode.[4]

This opposition to involvement in Vancouver Island was shared by Edward Ellice, to whose views on political questions Pelly was usually inclined to defer. So strongly did Ellice oppose the grant to the Company that he was impelled to write his friend Earl Grey, the Secretary of State for Colonies, on September 14, 1848, appealing to Grey to reconsider his decision to issue such authority to the Hudson's Bay Company. Grey's reply that "I do not see what we cd. have done better"[5] did not satisfy Ellice, and he remained hostile to the project throughout the whole term of the Company's responsibility for the colonization of the Island. In a letter to Alexander Grant Dallas on September 14, 1859, Ellice declared:—

> I have always thought the Directors wrong, in accepting the grant of the Island from the Govt. & when that transaction was challenged in Parliament as a great boon to the Company, I stated my opinion that it was a most

---

[2]These statements which the writer hopes to amplify in a forthcoming book, are based upon numerous communications between the Governor and Committee of the Hudson's Bay Company and the Company's North American representatives. See Governor and Committee to Simpson, March 12, 1827, and January 16, 1828, *H.B.C. Archives*, A. 6/21; Simpson to McLoughlin, March 15, 1829, ibid., D. 4/16. The writer acknowledges his obligation to the Governor and Committee of the Hudson's Bay Company for their permission to cite correspondence preserved in their Archives.

[3]This opposition was expressed in Simpson to Pelly, October 3, 1843, confidential, *H.B.C. Archives*, D. 4/70, and in a private letter to Archibald Barclay, September 7, 1848, the contents of which are indicated in Barclay to Simpson, October 13, 1848, private, ibid., D. 5/23. See also Simpson to Governor and Committee, September 18, 1848, and Simpson to Pelly, November 22, 1843, ibid., D. 4/70.

[4]Barclay to Simpson, October 13, 1848, private, *H.B.C. Archives*, D. 5/23.

[5]Grey to Ellice, September 23, 1848, Ellice Papers, National Library of Scotland (microfilm copy in the Public Archives of Canada, reel 35).

rash undertaking on their part, for the exclusive advantage of the public. Ld. Grey was wiser than the opposition who found fault with his policy. . . . There was no chance or hope of Revenue to defray the expense of such an establishment—& very little of emigrants for agricultural settlements & Ld. Grey rightly thought that a large & unnecessary expense might be saved by inducing the H.B. Co. to undertake the temporary administration. Their only object in accepting it, was to protect their own establishments, which might have been exposed in the then state of the Pacific to the danger of plunder or destruction.[6]

The continued opposition of Ellice, the most influential liaison between the Company and the Whig Government, and the initial objections of Simpson, who devoted his life to the interests of the fur trade, suggests that the conventional thesis of the "fur trade conspiracy" should be revised. For the explanation of the involvement of the Hudson's Bay Company in the colonization of Vancouver Island, it is necessary to examine the motivations of the two men—Pelly and Grey—who bear almost exclusive responsibility for the decision.

The first suggestion that the Company might be used as a vehicle for colonization was apparently made not by Pelly, but by Grey. The first communication from Pelly to Grey after the conclusion of the Oregon Treaty was on September 7, 1846. In this letter, Pelly inquired whether the Hudson's Bay Company would be confirmed in the possession of lands around Fort Victoria which they had occupied prior to the ratification of the treaty.[7] Pelly desired the recognition by the British Government of the Company's rights north of the 49th parallel as the United States had done south of the boundary, but Grey's reaction was much more broadly conceived. He saw the prospects of American settlers moving into Vancouver Island, a power vacuum, with no effective authority to control them. Such occupation, he feared, might possibly result in the attachment of Vancouver Island to the United States, which gave ample evidence of an "encroaching spirit." Unlike his Under Secretary of State, James Stephen, Grey believed in the value of the Empire, but his enthusiasm did not extend to support of further levies on the British taxpayer for imperial purposes. The alternative was to assign the responsibility for the government of Vancouver Island to a private association, and the Hudson's Bay Company, with long experience in government of frontier areas and with large capital at its disposal, seemed to him admirably fitted for the task. He therefore asked his subordinates to consult with Pelly to determine "what measure may now safely and properly be adopted with a view to establishing more B[ritis]h settlers in this territory."[8]

After an interview at the Colonial Office on September 23, Pelly evinced a new enthusiasm for colonization under Company auspices,[9] and in ensuing months this conception attained greater magnitude, until

---

[6]Ellice to Dallas, September 14, 1859, ibid., reel 28.

[7]Pelly to Grey, September 7, 1846, *C.O. 305/1*, in the Public Record Office, London.

[8]Note by Grey on Pelly to Grey, September 7, 1846, *C.O. 305/1.*

[9]Hawes to Pelly, October 3, 1846, *C.O. 305/1.*

on March 5, 1847, he made a suggestion of truly imperial proportions that the Company should receive the grant of all British territory north and west of Rupert's Land. Such a proposal was manifestly unacceptable to Stephen, and even Benjamin Hawes and Earl Grey, both of whom were sympathetic to the project of using the Company as the agency of the Crown in Vancouver Island, were apparently taken aback at Pelly's request, which was quickly refused.[10]

The motives which induced Pelly to seek such a colossal grant may be determined from the arguments he later employed to convince a skeptical Sir George Simpson of the advantages to the Company in its control over a colonization scheme. Obviously it was advantageous for Pelly to appeal to Grey on the basis of the Company's ability to advance British colonization, but Pelly also early came to the conclusion that if the Colonial Office did not find in the Company a satisfactory vehicle, it would turn to another joint-stock association to accomplish the objective. The prospect of another company being established with plenary powers in the territory west of the Rockies was a source of deep concern to Pelly. Not only would the fur trade and sales-shop business of the Company in New Caledonia suffer from the presence of a rival enterprise, but Vancouver Island or the Mainland territory in other hands might well serve as a base from which incursions might be made across the mountains into Rupert's Land.[11] This reasoning was compelling enough to convince other members of the London board, and Simpson himself was forced to admit that "it will unquestionably be more advantageous to the fur trade that it should be in the hands of the Company than of strangers."[12] Vancouver Island, then, of little value for the furs it provided, was nevertheless of importance as a protection to the trade, if in control of the Company, or as a threat to the trade in possession of opponents, whether British or American.

It is impossible to determine from available evidence whether or not it was a specific alternative proposal which stimulated Pelly's fears, but it is certain that James Edward Fitzgerald early became to Pelly the major threat to the Hudson's Bay Company's interests. During the spring of 1847 Fitzgerald was introduced to Benjamin Hawes of the Colonial Office by Anthony Panizzi, principal librarian of the British Museum. An introduction by Panizzi was of no small value to one desirous of a hearing, for Panizzi was an intimate friend of the most powerful leaders of the Whig Party. But aside from his association with Panizzi, Fitzgerald's credentials were not overly impressive. His family, though prosperous Irish gentry, were not notably influential, his position in the antiquities department of the British Museum did not suggest intimacy with the business world, and in his initial interview with Hawes, or indeed later,

---

[10]Pelly to Grey, March 5, 1847, and notes thereto, *C.O. 305/1*. The opposition of James Stephen and much of the correspondence between Pelly and the Colonial Office is amply described by Paul Knaplund, "James Stephen on Granting Vancouver Island to the Hudson's Bay Company, 1846–1848," *British Columbia Historical Quarterly*, 9 (1945), 259–271. No effort will be made, therefore, to describe in detail the negotiations during this period.

[11]Pelly to Simpson, October 27, 1848, *H.B.C. Archives*, D. 5/23.

[12]Simpson to Pelly, November 22, 1848, *H.B.C. Archives*, D. 4/70.

he gave no evidence that he was associated with men of sufficient capital to offer any prospects for the success of his schemes. Nevertheless, Hawes was impressed. Fitzgerald had ideas—that they were borrowed from Edward Gibbon Wakefield did not lessen their attraction; he was "very energetic," and his antecedents were "highly respectable."[13] Hawes suggested that he write the Colonial Office a statement of his plans. The resultant letter, on June 8, 1847, was a faithful reproduction of the views of Wakefield on systematic colonization. Fitzgerald proposed that a joint-stock company be formed, to be called the "Company of Colonists of Vancouver's Island." The government of the colony and the management of the company would be vested in shareholders resident in Vancouver Island. The capital of the company and proceeds from the sale of land would be expended in the conveyance to the colony of young married couples. Land would be sold at a "sufficient price" which would ensure a proper balance between land and labour. For each hundred acres of land purchased, six labourers should be sent to the colony.[14] The scheme was not unfavourably received, but Grey and Hawes were not disposed to entertain it seriously until Fitzgerald could demonstrate financial support adequate to support the programme. This evidence Fitzgerald did not, and probably could not, provide. From July 15, 1847, when the Colonial Office made this request,[15] until February 12, 1848, he did not communicate with the Colonial Office, and when he renewed his correspondence, his original plan had been discarded for another with greater commercial prospects.

This change in emphasis was produced by the circulation of the information that important deposits of coal existed on Vancouver Island. Although the directors of the Hudson's Bay Company had been aware before the Oregon Treaty of the availability of this coal, and the Admiralty had expressed interest in its utilization for the steam navy in the Pacific,[16] this knowledge had not been widely shared, and until February 1848, the Colonial Office itself was apparently imperfectly informed.[17]

On January 3, however, Samuel Cunard, having read about these coal deposits in the newspapers, wrote the Admiralty that unless action was taken immediately to protect the coal, Americans in the Oregon territory would be likely to take possession of the coalfields.[18] On February 12 Fitzgerald appeared at the Colonial Office with a new plan, which he elaborated in a letter two days later. He had been informed that the United States Government had negotiated a contract with a New York group headed by William H. Aspinwall for the carriage of mail between

---

[13]Note by Hawes on Fitzgerald to Hawes, June 9, 1847, *C.O. 305/1.*

[14]Fitzgerald to Hawes, June 9, 1847, *C.O. 305/1.* This letter is reprinted in *Report of the Provincial Archives Department of the Province of British Columbia . . . 1913* (Victoria, 1914), pp. V 54–62.

[15]Hawes to Fitzgerald, July 15, 1847, *C.O. 305/1.*

[16]Ogden and Douglas to J. A. Duntze, captain, H.M.S. *Fisgard,* September 7, 1846, *C.O. 305/1.*

[17]See note, Merivale to Hawes, February 16, 1848, on Fitzgerald to Hawes, February 14, 1848, *C.O. 305/1.*

[18]Cunard to H. G. Ward, Admiralty, January 3, 1848, enclosure in Ward to Hawes, February 5, 1848, *C.O. 305/1.*

Panama and the Columbia. To execute this contract, he estimated 20,000 tons of coal would be required annually, and he proposed to form a company to work the coal of Vancouver Island to supply this need, as well as the requirements of the Steam Pacific Navigation Company operating between Valparaiso and Panama. The advantage to the Colonial Office in using such a company as its agent in Vancouver Island, he argued, would be that the working of the coal deposits would require a considerable number of miners and that additional emigrants would be necessary to provide food for the mining community.[19] Again Fitzgerald displayed reluctance to name his associates, and they remained unknown to the Colonial Office, except for one John Shillinglaw of Soho, whose name appeared on the printed version of the plan espoused by Fitzgerald.[20]

The failure of Fitzgerald to produce evidence of substantial financial support is a fact of key importance. The files of the Colonial office entomb many schemes of varying attractions, consigned to oblivion because their projectors could offer no evidence that men of standing in the "City" were willing to invest in the undertaking. What is remarkable about Fitzgerald's proposals is not that they were not accepted; rather, it is that they were given such serious consideration. The communications among the staff of the Colonial Office do not support the view that Grey connived with the Hudson's Bay Company in a corrupt bargain. The primary condition for eligibility as an instrument of colonization on Vancouver Island was capital. The Hudson's Bay Company possessed that capital; Fitzgerald and his friends apparently did not; and no other individuals or groups who possessed this necessary prerequisite presented themselves for consideration. Fitzgerald's effervescent enthusiasm and youthful vitality[21] could not outweigh the resources of capital and experience of the Hudson's Bay Company.

Grey, by mid-February 1848, appears to have decided that the Hudson's Bay Company must be selected as the colonizing agent, but he was so much impressed with Fitzgerald's energy and enthusiasm that he conceived the hope that the young man might be enabled to take an active part in the enterprise through an agreement between Fitzgerald and the Hudson's Bay Company.[22] He therefore moved to reactivate negotiations with the Company, which had been suspended since Pelly's request of March 5, 1847, for a grant of all territory west of the Rocky Mountains.[23]

Pelly's views had not changed during the course of the year. He continued to desire as extensive a grant as possible for the protection of the

---

[19]Fitzgerald to Merivale, February 14, 1848, *C.O. 305/1*. Reprinted in *Report of the Provincial Archives . . . 1913*, pp. V 62–63.

[20]This printed proposal, produced for private circulation, is enclosed in Pelly to Grey, February 24, 1848, and in Fitzgerald to Merivale, February 21, 1848, *C.O. 305/1*. A copy of the proposal is in the *Report of the Provincial Archives . . . 1913*, pp. V 63–64.

[21]Fitzgerald was 29 years of age when he made his first proposal in 1847.

[22]Note by Grey on Fitzgerald to Merivale, February 14, 1848, *C.O. 305/1*.

[23]Hawes to Pelly, February 25, 1848, *H.B.C. Archives*, A. 8/3. Pelly, in a letter to Hawes, February 16, 1848, was the first to renew the correspondence, ibid.

fur trade in the interior of British North America. This objective he did not attempt to conceal, but he expressed the willingness of the Company to accept responsibility for the colonization of Vancouver Island and the extraction of its coal.[24]

Fitzgerald to this time had manifested no antagonism toward the Hudson's Bay Company. Indeed, in his letter to the Colonial Office on June 9, 1847, he had professed to believe that, since Vancouver Island produced little fur, the colonization of the Island by British subjects would form a barrier to American encroachments on the fur trade of the Company in the interior of the continent,[25] a conception completely in harmony with that of Pelly. These early professions of the compatibility of the Company's interests with colonization might be interpreted as being motivated by the desire not to antagonize the Company to the disinterest of his project. But this view is difficult to reconcile with Fitzgerald's later actions. Before February 16, 1848, when the Colonial Office had not yet made a decision on the selection of a colonizing agency, and apparently without any encouragement by the Colonial Office, he visited Pelly at Hudson's Bay House.[26] As Pelly stated, he was "quite hot about coals,"[27] his earlier ardour for the systematic colonization of the Island having cooled. The reason for this abrupt change of emphasis, Fitzgerald contended on June 2, 1848, was that "subsequently to the last conversation" he had had with Hawes and Merivale, Pelly had informed him that the Government had decided to award control of the Island to the Hudson's Bay Company. Fitzgerald stated:—

> Understanding that the matter was settled, I gave up all intention of taking any further part in it, because I did not believe that the Hudson's Bay Comy. could or would, effect the colonization of the Country. In consequence, however, of what passed between a friend of mine and Sir J. H. Pelly, I waited upon that Gentleman. He then offered to make us a grant of all the Coal Mines, upon terms which he specified in detail, and promised at the same time to assist us in procuring the Capital necessary to commence working the mines. I was therefore induced by these liberal promises to take up the Scheme again, and I expected we should be able to sail in the course of the Summer. . . . But on waiting upon Sir J. H. Pelly, in order to bring matters to a final settlement, he informed me that Sir George Simpson had been in communication with Messrs. Aspinwall, the owners of the Steamers destined to run on the N.W. Coast, and had issued orders that the Coal Mines in Vancouver Island should be immediately occupied, with a view to supplying coal to the steamers.[28]

The date of this conversation with Pelly is of some importance. If Pelly was not guilty of wilful misrepresentation, it could not have been before

---

[24]Pelly to Grey, March 4, 1848, *C.O. 305/1* and *H.B.C. Archives*, A. 8/4.

[25]Fitzgerald to Hawes, June 9, 1847, *C.O. 305/1*, reprinted in *Report of the Provincial Archives . . . 1913*, pp. V 54–62.

[26]Pelly to Hawes, February 16, 1848, *H.B.C. Archives*, A. 13/3; Fitzgerald to Merivale. June 2, 1848, *C.O. 305/1*. This latter letter is reproduced in *Report of the Provincial Archives . . . 1913*, pp. V 65–66.

[27]Pelly to Hawes, February 16, 1848, *H.B.C. Archives*, A. 13/3.

[28]Fitzgerald to Merivale, June 2, 1848, *C.O. 305/1*.

March 13, 1848, when the Colonial Office first informed the Company of its willingness to consider the grant of Vancouver Island to the Company.[29] It was almost certainly after February 24, for on that day arrangements were made for an interview between Fitzgerald and Hawes on an unspecified date.[30] But Pelly had described Fitzgerald as "hot about coals" in an interview with him prior to February 16, at which they apparently discussed an agreement by which Fitzgerald would receive aid from the Hudson's Bay Company in working the coal mines.[31]

Reconstruction of available information would seem to indicate that Fitzgerald first approached Pelly before February 16 with a proposal that the Company provide capital for him and his associates in the coal-mining project; Pelly expressed interest in such an arrangement but could not commit the Company without consultation with members of the Committee. Between March 13 and the beginning of April, a second interview was held. This was the meeting described by Fitzgerald in his letter of June 2. Meanwhile, Sir George Simpson at Lachine had received a letter from William H. Aspinwall inquiring as to whether he could buy coal from Vancouver Island for his steamers.[32] Simpson informed Aspinwall that he believed the Hudson's Bay Company could provide the ships with coal deliverable at Fort Victoria,[33] and on March 17, 1848, wrote the Governor and Committee of his correspondence with Aspinwall.[34] Pelly then suspended his negotiations with Fitzgerald; whether or not he was guilty of a breach of faith cannot be determined. But the sequence of events suggests that Fitzgerald ceased to promote his project of systematic colonization after he had read in the newspapers about the existence of coal on Vancouver Island and before the Hudson's Bay Company had been promised control over Vancouver Island, and that he attempted to negotiate an agreement by which the Company would underwrite his coal-mining operations. When these negotiations failed, he, in his wrath, resolved to repay the Company for its repudiation of him by a campaign to demonstrate its incapacity for colonization and to discredit its policies with the British public and with the Government. Before June 2, 1848, Fitzgerald had professed to believe the colonization of Vancouver Island to be compatible with the interests of the fur trade; after June 2 he expressed the conviction that colonization was "opposed to the interests of the H. B. Co. *necessarily.*"[35] The energy which had produced the enthusiasm which had won the admiration of Earl Grey was now concentrated in the vilification of the Hudson's Bay Company.

Fitzgerald's criticisms of the Company, then, were scarcely the conclusions of a detached, unbiased observer, but they were eagerly accepted by those with whose preconceptions about this "evil monopoly"

---

[29]Merivale to Pelly, March 13, 1848, *H.B.C. Archives*, A. 8/4.

[30]Notes by Grey and Hawes on Merivale to Fitzgerald, February 24, 1848, *C.O. 305/1*.

[31]Pelly to Hawes, February 16, 1848, *H.B.C. Archives*, A. 13/3.

[32]Aspinwall to Simpson, March 10, 1848, *H.B.C. Archives*, D. 5/21.

[33]Simpson to Aspinwall, March 17, 1848, *H.B.C. Archives*, D. 4/69.

[34]Simpson to Governor and Committee, March 17, 1848, *H.B.C. Archives*, D. 4/69.

[35]Fitzgerald to Hawes, June 2, 1848, *C.O. 305/1*, and reproduced in *Report of the Provincial Archives . . . 1913*, pp. V 65-66. The italics are Fitzgerald's.

they conformed. Most notable of these opponents was William E. Gladstone, who throughout most of his political career was the *bête noire* of the Hudson's Bay Company. The mind of Gladstone was shuttered and barred against all testimony favourable to the Hudson's Bay Company, but he received information prejudicial to the Company with uncritical enthusiasm. His knowledge of the interior of North America was unimpressive; but the Hudson's Bay Company was a monopoly; and, to him, monopolies were *per se* hostile to the public interest. The disaffected against the Hudson's Bay Company could always receive a sympathetic hearing from Gladstone. Alexander K. Isbister had found in him a champion;[36] and Fitzgerald, after he had been informed by the Colonial Office that an agreement would be consummated with the Hudson's Bay Company,[37] turned in his anger to Gladstone, who utilized Fitzgerald's information in attacks in the House of Commons on the proposed grant to the Company.[38] Also, Fitzgerald published in his own name and through others denunciations of the Company which abounded in vilification and misrepresentation.[39] An article in the *Daily News*, February 17, 1849, unsigned, but bearing the mark of Fitzgerald, contained the accusation that the Colonial Office was guilty of complicity and collusion in a corrupt bargain with a Company which not only was antagonistic to settlement, but guilty of demoralization of the aborigines who had been committed to its care: —

> The Hudson's Bay Company have kept their territories as inaccessible as the Jesuits kept Paraguay, but there all resemblance between the sway of the mercantile and of the priestly monopoly ends. The Jesuits kept their Indians in a state of constant pupilage which unmanned them, but they taught them habits of industry and domestic purity. The agents of the Hudson's Bay Company have discouraged settled habits among their Indians, and communicated to them the worst vices of civilised society without its redeeming qualities.[40]

Grey was highly irritated at the attacks of his opponents, particularly Gladstone, who had "much to answer,"[41] but he was nevertheless forced to modify the terms of the grant to reduce parliamentary criticism. The

[36]For a discussion of Isbister, see J. S. Galbraith, "The Hudson's Bay Company under Fire, 1847–1862," *Canadian Historical Review*, 30 (1949), 322–35.

[37]Fitzgerald received this information at an interview with Merivale early in July, 1848. Note by Merivale on Fitzgerald to Merivale, June 30, 1848, *C.O. 305/1*.

[38]For the Fitzgerald-Gladstone correspondence, see Paul Knaplund, "Letters from James Edward Fitzgerald to W. E. Gladstone Concerning Vancouver Island and the Hudson's Bay Company, 1848–1850," *British Columbia Historical Quarterly*, 13 (1949), 1–21.

[39]See, for example, his *An Examination of the Charter and Proceedings of the Hudson's Bay Company with Reference to the Grant of Vancouver's Island* (London, 1849); also "Vancouver's Island—The New Colony," reprinted from *Colonial Magazine* (August, 1848); "Vancouver's Island, the Hudson's Bay Company, and the Government," reprinted from *Colonial Magazine* (September 1848); and "Vancouver's Island," reprinted from *Colonial Magazine* (October 1848).

[40]Extract from London *Daily News*, February 17, 1849, in *C.O. 305/2*. The association of this article with Fitzgerald is based not only on the language and nature of the argument, but the fact that the author, in his attacks on the validity of the grant of Vancouver Island to the Hudson's Bay Company, had recourse to the experiences of New South Wales, South Australia, and New Zealand, in which Fitzgerald was particularly interested.

[41]Grey to Ellice, September 23, 1848, Ellice papers, ibid., reel 35.

provision was written into the agreement, as a direct result of attacks by Lord Lincoln, Gladstone, and others, that the Hudson's Bay Company would sell land on reasonable terms to all who wished to buy, and that the revenue derived from land sales and receipts from coal and other minerals should, after a deduction of 10 percent for profit to the Company, be applied to the colonization and improvement of Vancouver Island. Also, the provision was made that if, after five years from the date of the grant, the Crown decided that the Company had not sufficiently exerted itself, the grant could be revoked.[42]

There is no basis for suspicion of Grey's intentions. To him, the Hudson's Bay Company was the best-qualified agency for colonization. It possessed knowledge based on experience in Western North America, a disciplined staff of officers and servants, and large resources of capital, and it had already established agricultural and pastoral operations in Oregon and Vancouver Island. Negatively, by its economic power, it could render unprofitable the economic activities of any rival associations or individuals. As to the argument that a fur-trading monopoly was constitutionally unable to advance colonization, Grey and his associates in the Colonial Office could reply that the economic interests of the Company on the Northwest Coast, and in particular in Vancouver Island, were not the same as in the interior areas of North America. In the interior both nature and the interests of the Company conspired against settlement. But in the comparatively mild climate of the Pacific slope and Vancouver Island, the circumstances were "very different":—

> There, the Fur trade must soon be, if it is not already, a very secondary matter. The very natives of that tract are not so much hunters as fishermen and root-diggers. If that region is worth holding, it must not be as a game preserve, but for the purposes of trade, to which its situation so well adapts it, with the neighbouring American country, with its numerous and very commercial population of the South Sea Islands, and eventually to more distant markets.
>
> For these purposes colonization would apparently be to the Hudson's Bay Company an advantage instead of a loss, in the strictest mercantile sense. And the evidence that they so feel it is to be found in the remarkable progress already made in agricultural undertakings, so foreign to the ancient policy, on the Columbia, and in this island itself.[43]

If Grey was not an accomplice, was he a dupe of the Company? A strong case can be made for the contention that both Grey and the Company were victims of precisely the same delusions as James Edward Fitzgerald—that systematic colonization could successfully be undertaken in an area remote from civilization, and that a "sufficient price" could be imposed on sales of land when land could be obtained free or at little cost in the nearby Oregon territory of the United States. Clearly the price of £1 per acre was too high to attract many British settlers to

[42]Hawes to Pelly, September 4, 1848, H.B.C. Archives, A. 8/64. Royal Grant, Letters Patent, January 13, 1849, ibid., A. 37/1.

[43]Confidential print, Vancouver's Island, printed at Foreign Office, March, 1849, apparently for cabinet use, C.O. 305/1. This statement is printed in the Report of the Provincial Archives . . . 1913, pp. V 70-73.

Vancouver Island, and the requirement that five single men or three married couples be transported to the Island for each hundred acres by the purchaser was not attractive to those who possessed capital. The California gold-rush, which drained population from Oregon, also was undoubtedly responsible for loss of actual and potential emigrants to Vancouver Island.

It may also be contended with some basis that the Governor and Committee of the Hudson's Bay Company were sincere in their professions of willingness to colonize. They encouraged Charles Enderby in his desire to establish a whaling-station on the Island because they believed the whaling-ships would provide a market for the produce of the Island.[44] Governor John Henry Pelly displayed interest in the colonization not only in letters to the Colonial Office, but, more significantly, in private letters to his associates in the Company.[45] A prospectus was printed and circulated to stimulate the interest of prospective colonists,[46] and advertisements were placed in English and Scottish metropolitan and provincial newspapers.[47]

It would be an error, however, to conclude that the Hudson's Bay Company was merely the victim of circumstances beyond its control in its failure to colonize Vancouver Island. The Company must assume a share of the responsibility; the unimpressive record of emigration to the Island can be explained in part by the inherent assumptions of the Company and the attitudes of its personnel.

Governor Pelly recognized that if the Company did not consent to act as the chosen instrument of the Government, the responsibility would be assigned to another group of entrepreneurs who might disturb the tranquillity of the nearby fur preserves; for that reason he was willing to assume responsibility for colonization. Other members of the Governing Committee also recognized the danger but reached a different conclusion. At least two of the Committee, Lord Selkirk and Andrew Colvile, sought the grants with the deliberate design to delay the colonization of Vancouver Island. Both desired to exploit its coal mines, since these were a source of profit, but neither desired to assist emigration, which they believed to be incompatible with the interests of a fur-trading company. Selkirk wrote to Pelly on May 27, 1848:—

> I heard incidentally that there are a lot of people who want to go and colonize Vancouvers Island. A man of the name of Fitzgerald who has a place in the British Museum wants to get the command of the expedition & expects the thing to be taken up by the Government. I do not know if there is

---

[44]A. Colvile to Simpson, April 6, 1849, *H.B.C. Archives*, D. 5/25. Enderby first approached Pelly in April 1848 and was informed that the Company, if it received the grant, would look with favour on the use of Vancouver Island by whaling-vessels. The failure of Enderby to carry out this purpose was the result of circumstances unrelated to the Hudson's Bay Company. Enderby to Pelly, August 26, 1848; Pelly to Enderby, September 1, 1848, *H.B.C. Archives*, A. 10/25.

[45]Pelly to Simpson, September 29, 1848, private, *H.B.C. Archives*, D. 5/22; Pelly to Simpson, October 27, 1848, private, ibid., D. 5/23.

[46]Prospectus, "Colonization of Vancouver's Island," copy in Gladstone Papers, British Museum, *Addtl. Mss. 44566.*

[47]John Harthill & Sons to Barclay, September 22, 1849, *H.B.C. Archives*, A. 10/27.

any truth in this story but there is no doubt but there are many people who have got a notion of that country and if they go out they will play the devil.[48]

Selkirk, in order that others would not "play the devil," and in order that the Company could profit from coal sales, supported the grant, but he at no time evinced enthusiasm for emigration of settlers to Vancouver Island. Andrew Colvile held similar views. Colvile, who had served as a member of the Committee since 1810 and as Deputy Governor since 1839, was a man of great influence in the affairs of the Company. From the onset of Pelly's last long illness in 1850 until 1856, when Colvile died, Colvile was unquestionably the dominant force in the Hudson's Bay Company,[49] and his views were therefore of decisive importance in the formulation of policy with regard to Vancouver Island after the grant was made.

The idea of free and unrestricted settlement to any part of the Hudson's Bay Company's area of influence was repugnant to Colvile. Since the Colonial Office had determined to colonize Vancouver Island through private agency, he agreed with Pelly that the Hudson's Bay Company must seek control, but he did not desire to advance the prospects of emigration. The popularity of "systematic colonization" offered a means of solving this apparent dilemma. Colvile was convinced that the imposition of a price on land in the circumstances of Vancouver Island was a certain and severe deterrent to emigration. So long as land was sold for £1 per acre, he informed his confidant Simpson, "you need not be afraid of too many settlers" going to Vancouver Island.[50] With the grant of the Island assigned to it, Colvile believed that the Company could rigidly restrict emigration. Through its subsidiary, the Puget's Sound Agricultural Company, it could produce foodstuffs for its employees and for sale to whalers and coal ships, which might offer a profitable market. The coal mines would provide additional revenue.[51] Such were the views of Andrew Colvile, and the pattern of the Company's emigration programme confirmed his expectations.

Sir George Simpson, who had at first opposed the association of the Company with responsibility for colonization, found comfort in Colvile's arguments. After the grant to the Company was confirmed, he used the full force of his authority to discourage emigration. When James Douglas recommended an initial immigration of 20 families, totalling about 100 persons, Simpson cautioned him against the dangers of too ambitious a programme: —

After reading the description you give of the Southern end of the Island where nearly all the cultivable soil is occupied by the Hudson's Bay and

[48]Selkirk to Pelly, May 27, 1848, *H.B.C. Archives,* A. 10/24.

[49]An abscess in the head which grew steadily more serious from early in 1848 virtually incapacitated Pelly from December 1850 until his death. Pelly to Simpson, May 26, 1848, *H.B.C. Archives,* D. 5/22; same to same, December 6, 1850, private, ibid., D. 5/29; and Colvile to Simpson, December 20, 1850, ibid., D. 5/29. Colvile served as Deputy Governor from 1839 until 1852 and as Governor from 1852 until 1856.

[50]Colvile to Simpson, March 8, 1850, *H.B.C. Archives,* D. 5/27.

[51]Colvile to Simpson, April 6, 1849, *H.B.C. Archives,* D. 5/25.

Puget Sound Companies, I was surprised that you should recommend so large an annual immigration as about 100 Souls—I think it would be safer to regulate the influx of population by the success of the first efforts now making. . . . The great danger to be apprehended in a too rapid settlement of the island is that a year of unfavorable crops might occasion scarcity & that would inevitably lead to the immediate abandonment of the colony by the settlers for the more genial climes in Oregon or California—I think it might be a profitable speculation to lay out town lots as you recommend, the only objection being that in a Country where there is not a sufficient police or military force, it is far more difficult to maintain good order when the people are collected in villages or towns than when scattered as farmers; our experience at Red River Settlement is sufficient to prove the truth of this.[52]

An accusation of deliberate duplicity would probably be unfair to Sir George Simpson, but it would not be unjust to describe his mind as one which forced facts into conformity with the interests of the fur trade and which was prone to exaggerate the difficulties involved in the extension of agriculture to any part of the fur-trade domain. In the guise of solicitude for the welfare of present and prospective settlers, Simpson wished to restrain the influx of free farmers to Vancouver Island.

Simpson was well aware of the provision in the royal grant of January 13, 1849, that if the Company failed within five years to establish a settlement in accordance with the terms of the grant, the Government could revoke the authority;[53] but in the state of the fur trade as Simpson then conceived it, a delay of even five years was advantageous. He was convinced that the encroachment of settlement, particularly from Canada, and the decline in demand for beaver would soon render the fur trade unprofitable, and he expressed the hope that the Company would immediately begin negotiations for the surrender of its chartered rights while they still appeared to be of value.[54] Any measures which might preserve the interests of the fur trade even for a brief period were therefore, he believed, advantageous.

In the point of view represented by Colvile and Simpson, some support can be found for Fitzgerald's contention that the Company was not sincere in its professions of willingness to colonize. Fitzgerald's fault was that, in his wrath at the Company's failure to consummate a bargain with him, he became a receiving-station for all testimony hostile to the Company, that he made no effort to document his facts, and that even in his attacks on the Company's policies on Vancouver Island he overstated his case.

The settlement of Vancouver Island before the discovery of gold in British Columbia was perhaps impossible even for the most enthusiastic

---

[52]Simpson to Douglas, February 20, 1850, private, *H.B.C. Archives*, D. 4/71. In reply Douglas repented his excessive optimism, but pleaded for a more liberal system of land-disposal to encourage settlers. Douglas to Simpson, June 7, 1850, private, *H.B.C. Archives*, D. 5/28.

[53]Letters Patent, January 13, 1849, *H.B.C. Archives*, A. 37/1.

[54]Simpson to Pelly, October 25, 1848, *H.B.C. Archives*, D. 4/70. Simpson continued until his death in 1860 to profess pessimism about the future of the fur trade.

promoters, but the Hudson's Bay Company was a poor instrument for colonization, and it is doubtful whether even at a more favourable time it would have been successful. Though Sir John Henry Pelly was undoubtedly sincere in his expressions of desire to promote British settlement in order to secure the Island against incursions from the United States, the directors of the Company could not be expected to rise above the dictates of the Company's immediate commercial interests, which, at least some conceived, could not be promoted by free colonization. The traditions of the Company were autocratic and paternalistic, repugnant to the free institutions which settlers in a British colony would inevitably demand. At Red River, in the Oregon territory south of the 49th parallel, and on Vancouver Island, the Company attempted to reconcile itself with an agricultural society, and on each occasion it failed. Such failure was probably inherent in the make-up and assumptions of a fur-trade monopoly.

28

THE RELIEF OF THE UNEMPLOYED POOR IN SAINT JOHN, HALIFAX, AND ST. JOHN'S, 1815–1860*

Judith Fingard

British North America experienced a constant influx of immigrants between 1776 and 1867, most of them from the United States and the British Isles. Wave after wave of Loyalists, Scots, Irish, and English came to settle in that part of America which remained firmly British. The colonies, wrote dozens of commentators and immigration promoters, were a "good poor man's country." And indeed they were. The numbers of successful lower-class immigrants were considerable. But the requirements for success were not always explicitly stated, and not always believed. A willingness to work hard was never enough, despite the persistent image of the self-made man. One needed some skill utilizable by the community, a bit of capital, and most of all, continued good health. The cities particularly were the graveyards of those who failed to measure up to the specifications, and the problem of poverty was omnipresent in any urban centre of British North America. The relief of the poor was a major topic of debate.

The complications of relieving the poor in the years before Confederation are analyzed by Judith Fingard in the following article—focussing on three cities of the Atlantic region—but equally applicable to urban areas in the Canadas as well. As Professor Fingard points out, the weaknesses of diagnosis were far exceeded by the limitations of action. Even if contemporaries recognized distinctions between structural and temporary poverty, between structural and temporary unemployment, for example, they were unable, given the constellation of assumptions of the day, to conceive of constructive long-term actions to deal with indigence. What were the causes of poverty? What assumptions did society make

*Acadiensis, 5 (1975), 32–53.
446

about the poor? With what other social questions does poor relief connect?

SUGGESTIONS FOR FURTHER READING

Helen I. Cowan, *British Emigration to British North America, the First Hundred Years* (Toronto: University of Toronto Press, 1961).

W. H. Elgee, *The Social Teachings of the Canadian Churches: Protestant, the Early Period before 1850* (Toronto: Ryerson Press, 1964).

Michael B. Katz, *The People of Hamilton, Canada West: Family and Class in a Mid-Nineteenth Century City* (Cambridge: Harvard University press, 1975).

J.M.B.

As the leading commercial centres in eastern British America, Saint John, Halifax, and St. John's sheltered within their environs a significant proportion of the region's meagre population.[†] This included not only the most comfortable and affluent colonists, but also three categories of poor inhabitants whose problems were never far from the minds of public-spirited citizens. Prominent among the disadvantaged were the permanent or disabled poor—a motley collection that embraced the helpless aged, the physically and mentally infirm, as well as destitute widows and orphans, those unproductive elements in the community without kith or kin to act as providers. The plight of these unfortunates aroused the greatest outward display of local sympathy, though their inescapable presence was largely taken for granted and their welfare sadly neglected. A second group consisted of immigrants who annually swelled the ranks of the poor that infested these major Atlantic ports. These included refugee blacks from the United States, settled near Halifax and Saint John after the War of 1812, who became a special class of permanent poor in town and suburb, as well as the meanest of the urban labourers. Most significant in point of numbers was the incessant flow of poverty-stricken Irish who, on arrival, crowded into the poorhouses of Saint John and Halifax and augmented the paupers of St. John's.[1] Subsequently, as resident labourers, the Irish fre-

---

[†]This essay is a product of a programme of research supported by the Canada Council whose assistance I gratefully acknowledge.

[1]Minutes, November 10, 1847, Saint John Common Clerk, MSJ, Provincial Archives of New Brunswick [hereafter PANB]; Letter from A, *Public Ledger* (St. John's), March 6, 1838.

Residence Indicated for Inmates of Halifax Poorhouse, 1833–1837:

	Halifax*	N.S.	England	Scotland	Ireland	NFLD.	N.B.	U.S.	Other
1833	300	99	94	27	299	17	17	12	32
1834	339	79	80	27	330	27	20	22	41
1835	298	64	77	27	248	10	10	10	47
1836........	280	98	71	23	243	9	12	8	62
1837	350	74	53	25	270	10	20	8	45

*With no orphanage or lying-in-hospital in Halifax more than half of the town inmates were children.

Source: *Journals of the Legislative Assembly, Nova Scotia* [hereafter JLA], 1834–38.

quently re-emerged as members of the third category—the casual poor.[2] Found amongst these casual poor were individuals or families dependent on a hand-to-mouth existence, who became temporarily incapacitated through sickness or misfortune, and the seasonally unemployed, those perennial casualties who formed the most intractable problem for the commercial towns. While the majority of this latter group consisted of common labourers, they were often joined in penury by skilled journeymen thrown out of work or underpaid in wintertime. In St. John's the whole operative class of resident fishermen habitually found themselves idle and destitute for seven months out of 12, a situation which gave the colony "a larger proportion of poor than in other British settlements."[3] Each of these categories—permanent, immigrant, and casual poor—posed its special difficulties for the community, but as constituent elements of society, each was thought by benevolent and judicious townsmen to be entitled to some form of assistance during the period of privation. In the fluid, uncertain conditions of colonial society, prosperous inhabitants were chastened by the possibility "that the calamities which have befallen others may soon overtake ourselves, and that their distressing lot may soon become our own."[4]

When a conjunction of diverse circumstances, including overseas immigration and economic recession, forced urban poverty to the forefront of public attention in the period after the Napoleonic Wars, the towns of the Atlantic colonies, in contrast to those of the Canadas, could draw on a tradition of state poor relief. This government involvement took the forms of locally enacted poor laws providing for municipal assessments in Nova Scotia and New Brunswick and of executive initiative for appropriating colonial revenue in Newfoundland. The methods of dispensing these funds in Saint John, and eventually in St. John's, involved a mixture of both indoor and outdoor relief, whereas in Halifax public assistance was confined to the poorhouse.[5] But the existence of facilities for public relief did not preclude individual involvement in civic welfare measures. Citizens continued to feel that they had a direct role to play both in aiding the poor and in determining the guises that public and voluntary assistance assumed. For one thing, they were well aware that the scale of public relief was inadequate to meet emergencies, a deficiency starkly demonstrated every time fires, crop failures, business recessions, heavy immigration, or ineluctable winter exacted their toll. Haligonians experienced these harsh circumstances in the decade after 1815, when large numbers of poor immigrants and unemployed labourers were thrown on the mercy of a town that had abandoned outdoor

---

[2]Petition of JPs, Saint John, 1839, RLE/839/pe/3, No. 61, PANB.

[3]*Free Press* (Halifax), December 23, 1827.

[4]17th Annual Report of Saint Andrew's Church Female Benevolent Society, *Guardian* (Halifax), January 22, 1847.

[5]In St. John's the piecemeal organization of indoor relief began in 1846 with the erection of the relief sheds or 'Camps,' notorious hovels designed to house the fire victims of that year. These were not replaced until a poorhouse was opened in 1861, followed by the discontinuance of relief for the able-bodied for the first time in 1868.

relief under public auspices and that had, therefore, to rely on voluntary efforts to ward off the threat of starvation and social disorder.[6]

Moreover, goaded by tender consciences and insistent churches, some colonists regarded benevolence as a christian duty. Within a society that prided itself on its christian ethos, the laws of God and humanity dictated that the poor could not be permitted to starve; the sick and aged poor must be cared for. But starvation did occur, and the numerous sick and aged poor in the towns necessitated the erection of institutions to minister to their afflictions. In the absence of this kind of large-scale capital expenditure which city councils or provincial legislatures were reluctant to undertake, privately organized dispensaries and societies for the relief of the indigent sick played a vital role in treating accidents and common illnesses.[7] For the chronically ill, however, circumstances were different. Halifax, for example, possessed no specialized institution for dealing with any category of sick poor until the opening of the lunatic asylum in 1859.[8] The failure "to ameliorate the condition of suffering humanity" offended christians who witnessed ample investment in facilities for transportation and commerce; the neglect of social amelioration seemed to be at odds with mid-Victorian notions of progress.[9]

In these circumstances townspeople responded sympathetically to acute destitution because they considered the existing forms of poor relief outdated and unprogressive. The purely custodial care of destitute lunatics in the temporary asylum established in St. John's in 1846, for example, was said to be inconsistent with the age of improvement.[10] Citizens were particularly outspoken when their local pride was offended. To lag behind other towns in the provision of specialized facilities for the poor seemed unpatriotic as well as undesirable. The example of Saint John, where a lunatic asylum was opened in 1836 and firmly established in a permanent edifice in 1848, was constantly paraded by social critics before the lethargic citizenry of Halifax and St. John's.[11] This call for imitation grew out of a search for self-esteem, since

[6]*Free Press*, February 4, 11, 25, March 4, 1817; G. E. Hart, "The Halifax Poor Man's Friend Society, 1820-27: An Early Social Experiment," *Canadian Historical Review*, 34 (1953), 109-23. The Poor Man's Friend Society (admittedly helped by the legislature) aided as many as one-tenth of Halifax's inhabitants during the winters of the early 1820s. *Annual Reports* of the Halifax Poor Man's Friend Society. Similarly in St. John's the Poor Relief Association of 1867, a voluntary organization, aided one-fifth of the inhabitants during a winter of great distress when government relief was insufficient. *Newfoundlander* (St. John's), May 10, 1867.

[7]*Public Ledger*, March 5, 1847; Editorial, *Times* (St. John's), July 7, 1849; "Death from Starvation!", *Patriot* (St. John's), February 5, 1853; Letter from J. Slayter, M.D., *Acadian Recorder* (Halifax), January 20, 1855; "The Poor," *Morning Journal* (Halifax), December 28, 1855; Editorial, *Newfoundlander*, February 11, 1856; Speech by Dr. Grigor, Legislative Council Debate, March 3, 1857, *Acadian Recorder*, March 7, 1857.

[8]G. Andrews, "The Establishment of Institutional Care in Halifax in the Mid-Nineteenth Century," (honours essay, Dalhousie University, 1974).

[9]Editorial, *Christian Messenger* (Halifax), January 10, 1851; "Lunatic Asylum and General Hospital," *Acadian Recorder*, May 21, 1853.

[10]Letter from Aqua, *Public Ledger*, December 15, 1846.

[11]J. M. Whalen, "Social Welfare in New Brunswick, 1784-1900," *Acadiensis*, vol. 2, no. 1, (Autumn 1972), p. 61; *Sun* (Halifax), January 8, 1851; New Brunswick Lunatic Asylum, ibid., October 15, 1851.

colonial towns aspired to social responsibility and an acknowledgment of their benevolence and modernity.[12]

In an age that witnessed both the heyday of the philanthropic society and in North America the 'discovery of the asylum', the custom of fostering benevolence by means of association also encouraged citizen involvement in directing local poor relief. The bewildering variety of associations, both ephemeral and permanent, that emerged for the social, physical, and moral improvement of the poor fulfilled a basic middle-class instinct for collective efforts as well as for emulating the fashionable course. While few of the large-scale societies and the asylums they sometimes sponsored could exist without some government aid to augment charitable donations, voluntary management provided communities with excellent experience in organization, fund-raising, and social investigation. At the same time, however, voluntary associative benevolence underwent a fragmentation which meant that by mid-century every church and every ethnic and interest group had its own charitable society or charitable function. This occurred despite attempts throughout the period by the most public-spirited citizens to promote the comprehensive, non-partisan relief of the urban poor, on the ground that "we are but a part of one great human family."[13]

Particularly significant was the bifurcation of urban society between Catholics and Protestants, which emerged most graphically in the 1840s, when Irish immigration, the introduction of unfamiliar religious orders, the ravages of epidemics, and the cry of 'papal aggression' led colonial Protestants to resent the indisputable fact that the larger proportion of poor rates and voluntary contributions went towards the relief of poor Catholics. Piqued Protestants did not tire of reminding their Roman Catholic neighbours that nine-tenths of the inmates of the poorhouse in Halifax were Catholics, or that it was the Protestant citizenry in St. John's who supported the Catholic poor.[14] To such an extent did the Catholics constitute the labouring and disabled poor in the towns that the more bigoted Protestants began to pronounce publicly that the Roman Catholics were impoverished because they were Catholics.[15] Not surprisingly, a host of 'separate' charitable societies and institutions resulted. Consequently, vertical divisions in the population of the towns, not only between Catholics and Protestants, but also between Methodists and Anglicans, Irish and native-born, Loyalists and non-loyalists, took precedence over the fledgling regard for the corporate well-being.

Finally, the colonist became concerned about poor relief in his capa-

---

[12]"Benevolent Enterprise," *Morning Post* (Halifax), March 10, 1845; "Fancy Balls versus Hospitals and Asylums," *Presbyterian Witness* (Halifax), March 16,1850; Speech by Dr. Grigor, Legislative Council Debate, March 12, 1851, *Sun*, March 17, 1851; "Public Hospital," *Morning News* (Saint John), October 17, 1856.

[13]Editorial, *Public Ledger*, March 7, 1837; The Poor—God Help Them! Let Man think of them too! Great Suffering in consequence of Scarcity of Fuel," *Morning Post*, March 10, 1846; *Morning News*, July 31, 1846; Address to the Public by the Halifax Poor Man's Friend Society, *Acadian Recorder*, February 19, 1820; Report of Indigent Sick Society, St. John's, *Public Ledger*, May 5, 1840; Appeal of Committee of Ladies' Benevolent Society, Halifax, *Morning Post*, October 7, 1844.

[14]Letter from P. Power's Friend, *Guardian*, March 19, 1847; Editorials, *Public Ledger*, April 18, 1834, December 8, 1835, May 6, 1842.

[15]"Popery in Newfoundland," *Public Ledger*, September 25, 1855.

city as a citizen of a town in which he had a vested interest, and protection of that stake demanded that the community should reflect his own particular values. When he talked therefore about subordinating the relief of the poor to the good of the community, he meant subordinating it to his own purposes. It is these underlying values, shared by contemporaries in three pre-industrial towns of Atlantic Canada, and the various schemes they spawned, that provide the focus of the ensuing discussion. Amongst the townsman's preconceptions, it was his reverence for the family, his regard for the dignity of labour, his preoccupation with good order, and his search for economy which led him to the fundamental conclusion "That the truest charity is to find employment that will give food; and not food without employment."[16]

Those citizens who viewed the relief of the poor within the wider context of the welfare of urban society at large undoubtedly represented the most respectable, dependable, moderately reformist, the middle-class elements in the towns. Whether they paraded as newspaper proprietors, clergymen, assemblymen, or aldermen, they were motivated by a concept of responsibility to the public, the congregation, or the electorate. They expected other men in positions of leadership and authority to take their civic duty as conscientiously as they did themselves. At the base of urban society the leadership they discerned was that of the male head of the organic unit, the family. Since the interests of the family in society received priority over those of the individual, the claims of the poor were likely to elicit a more sympathetic response if they could be fitted into the familial framework. In this respect a special sanctity was accorded the interdependent relationship between the provider and his spouse and offspring. Only sickness and unexpected unemployment were thought to constitute legitimate excuses for the failure of bread-winners to take seriously their duty as providers.[17] Drunkenness, improvidence, low wages, laziness, and fecundity were problems with which the wretched family had to contend alone, though the editor of the *Morning News* wondered whether, in cases of drunkenness as the cause of family poverty, the state should not be vested with the right to intervene and regulate employment and expenditure of wages.[18]

When it came to the vital circumstance of sickness, public health officers recognized that unless the labourer was retained in health, "the family of the victim becomes a charge upon the town for a much longer time" than the duration of his illness.[19] Where sickness of a poor or struggling head of the family led to his death, the citizenry displayed an appropriate concern for the widow and children, as it did for the orphan in the case of double bereavement.[20] Nevertheless, talk about society's responsibilities towards widows and orphans was considerably more

[16]*Free Press*, October 21, 1817.

[17]Editorial, *Public Ledger*, December 9, 1828.

[18]Editorial, *Times* (St. John's), July 29, 1848; Investigator, no. 3, ibid., November 4, 1854; "Drunkenness, Poverty and Suffering," *Morning News*, January 11, 1860.

[19]Board of Health, Saint John, Report for 1858, p. iv, New Brunswick. *JLA* (1857-58), Appendix.

[20]Letter from RP, "Queen's National Fund," *New Brunswick Courier* (Saint John), June 13, 1840; "Bazaar," *Morning News*, November 12, 1855.

energetic than the framing of humane measures to provide for their sustenance. Admittedly, concerted efforts for temporary assistance to widows and orphans sometimes followed severe epidemics or summers of excessive immigration, but attention to the welfare of the fatherless remnant of the family was haphazard and ephemeral.[21] In a society based on commerce, hard physical labour, and male political power, women were utterly expendable. Children, on the other hand, were exploitable as cheap labour. Orphans and foundlings were greatly in demand in the pre-industrial period as apprentices by farmers, house-holders, and craftsmen, apprenticeships secured by indentures that again tended to emphasize the family ambience.[22]

Society showed its greatest concerted anxiety about family welfare when large numbers of heads of families were thrown out of work. While this concern might sometimes extend to female bread-winners, it was the men as labourers and mechanics who commanded the most atten-tion. In those instances where public measures were taken to meet the temporary emergency of seasonal unemployment, preference was given to family men. In fact the work itself, never sufficient to satisfy the demand, was usually confined to heads of families.[23] About 600 of these employed on civic works in Saint John in 1842 received from 1s. to 3s. a day according to the number of their dependents.[24] Coincident with fam-ily considerations, this preoccupation with the labouring poor stemmed from the emphasis placed by the well-to-do on the material progress of the town. As the basis of the socio-economic pyramid, the very fabric of urban society was thought to depend on the labourers' contributions, not only as hewers of wood and drawers of water, but as "the bone and marrow of the country."[25] When 'honest' working men faced starvation, self-interested leaders of society invariably urged the expeditious relief of "that most indispensably useful part of the community," preferably through employment, but if necessary through relief without labour.[26]

---

[21]An example is provided by the Emigrant Orhpan Asylum established in Saint John in 1847. J. M. Whalen, "New Brunswick Poor Law Policy in the Nineteenth Century," (M.A. thesis, University of New Brunswick, 1968), pp. 32, 35–36; also, the Church of England Asylum for Widows and Orphans founded in St. John's after a cholera epidemic, *Times* (St. John's) December 27, 1854, January 20, 1855; *Newfoundland Express* (St. John's), February 20, 1858, February 19, 1859.

[22]Abstract of R. J. Uniacke's Evidence before the Select Committee of the House of Com-mons on Emigration, March 22, 1826, *Novascotian* (Halifax), October 19, 1826. Arranging such places for orphans was the principal aim of the Orphan Benevolent Society of Saint John, which dissolved only after the city's orphanages were well established. *New Brunswick Courier*, August 8, 1840, January 23, 1858.

[23]"Stonebreaking," *Novascotian*, December 20, 1832; Matthew to Mayor, January 3, 1842, and Communication from Chamberlain upon the subject of distress of labouring poor, January 3, 1842, RLE/842/22/2, PANB. The use of the very cheap labour of British soldiers and incarcerated criminals on public works sometimes reduced the opportunities for the unemployed poor. W. Moorsom, *Letters from Nova Scotia; comprising Sketches of a Young Country* (London, 1830), p. 34; Letter from Clerk of the Peace to Commissioners of Streets for Halifax, Special Sessions, September 1837, RG 34, vol. 10, Public Archives of Nova Scotia (hereafter PANS).

[24]"Employment of the Poor," *New Brunswick Courier*, December 4, 1841; "Frightful Extent of Pauperism in the City," ibid., March 5, 1842.

[25]Editorial, *Patriot*, November 9, 1839.

[26]Letter from An Inhabitant of Halifax, *Acadian Recorder*, December 14, 1816; Letter from Beneficus, ibid., February 1, 1817.

Citizens' attitudes towards poor relief were also influenced by the need to distinguish between the honest, deserving, labouring poor and those who were undeserving, profligate, or even criminal. For the public remained anxious that the poor should not endanger the social order of the towns and that relief should preserve a properly balanced relationship between the 'haves' and the 'have-nots.' This determination to ensure that the 'haves' maintained the upper hand goes far to explain the universal abhorrence of mendicancy; begging transferred the initiative to the poor when it ought to remain with their economic betters. Mendicancy was a form of free enterprise, an activity not to be encouraged in the poor who were certain to misuse it. A successful beggar might see in crime his road to further advancement. Beggars were, therefore, not only an expensive nuisance,[27] but a threat to society, whose guardians through their beneficence in furnishing food and clothing might unwittingly admit to their houses imposters or thieves. Such unbecoming and potentially subversive behaviour in the poor might be avoided if the rich took it upon themselves to seek out poor families in their dwellings and investigate their degree of penury and deservedness. The efficacy of social investigation was reiterated as often as hordes of beggars descended on the towns and it became the standard practice of voluntary associations and government agencies.[28]

Despite the need for precautionary measures to safeguard the interests of the town and the welfare of the honest poor, it was often that same apprehension for the good order of society that stimulated citizens to urge generous public relief in times of severest want. In the winter of 1816–17 the first voluntary relief committee in Halifax feared that if the sufferers were "abandoned to the horrors of starvation . . . they may be induced by despair to commit depredations."[29] Thereafter the preference given to civic employment schemes as the most propitious form of assistance pinpointed unemployed labourers as the element in the population most likely to threaten the good order of the city. The spectre of hungry mobs of workers conjured up in the mind of the authorities frightening thoughts of uncontrollable outrage and seething insubordination. Poverty was regarded as an 'evil' which could not be allowed to reach "that stage where it is not stopped by stone walls, or locks, bolts, or bars."[30]

[27]Letter from A Friend to the Deserving Poor, "Beggars," *Acadian Recorder*, March 29, 1834; "Charity," *Novascotian*, December 25, 1844; "Pauperism in Saint John," *Morning News*, November 17, 1847.

[28](Halifax Poor Man's Friend Society) Address to the Public, *Acadian Recorder*, February 19, 1820; (St. John's Dorcas Society) Letter from Clericus, *Public Ledger*, February 5, 1833; (St. John's Indigent Sick Society) ibid., February 27, 1835; *Times* (Halifax), December 20, 1836; (Government relief, St. John's) Resolution of the commissioners for the distribution of £300 for relief of the destitute poor, *Newfoundlander*, February 27, 1840; (St. George's District Visiting Society, Halifax) *Morning Post*, January 27, 1842; (Samaritan Society, Saint John) *New Brunswick Courier*, January 2, 1847, *Morning News*, March 8, 1847; (St. John's Fire Relief Committee) *Public Ledger*, March 30, 1847; (Outdoor relief, St. John's) Speeches by Little and the Speaker, Assembly Debate, March 22, 1853, *Newfoundland Express*, April 2, 1853; (St. Vincent de Paul Society, St. John's) Editorial, *Newfoundlander*, February 9, 1854; Letter from A Clergyman, "How the Poor may be Relieved," ibid., January 28, 1858; (St. Vincent de Paul Society, Saint John) *Morning Freeman* (Saint John), November 22, 1859.

[29]Memorial of the Committee for distributing relief to the labouring poor in Halifax, March 14, 1817, RG 5, series P, vol. 80, PANS.

[30]Letter from Civis, "Feed the Hungry and the Poor—Clothe the Naked," *Morning News*,

Self-interest also demanded economical relief. The search for economy encouraged attempts to eliminate some forms of poverty amongst labourers by the prevention and treatment of diseases and accidents. On its establishment in 1857 the Saint John Public Dispensary for outpatients undertook to diminish the number of inmates accommodated in the tax-supported almshouse. Its managers therefore appealed to the public not solely as a benevolent institution "but a *money saving one to our citizens.*"[31] Similarly, the need for welfare might be reduced by the more rigorous enforcement of the board of health regulations in the city. Otherwise, the health officer argued, "Sickness, debility, death, widowhood and orphanage, connected with pauperism, are expensive contingencies" which the town must sustain.[32] Financial considerations were also paramount in the discussion of the relative merits of indoor and outdoor relief. It was popularly but by no means universally maintained that institutional care was cheaper than outdoor measures. This assumption led to the repeated advocacy of various types of asylums which would offer both centralized and more economical relief. Enthusiasts for the erection of a poorhouse in St. John's claimed that such an institution in Halifax housed more paupers than were then supported in St. John's and did so at less expense.[33] Where outdoor relief was essential, the economy-minded suggested that food, fuel, and clothing should be provided at reduced rates or at cost rather than given away gratuitously to the poor. Not only would the available charitable funds then be less liable to misuse and made to go further, but those suffering from a state of temporary destitution would be retained in their constructive role as colonial consumers.[34] Interest in the poor man as a consumer also afforded a major reason why citizens preferred employment relief to charitable relief in the form of cheap food and old clothes. If he earned subsistence wages, the poor man would still continue to participate in the retail trade of the town at full market prices.[35]

A mindfulness of both economy and order led the benevolent to expect a return on their investment in alms-giving, charitable subscriptions, and poor rates. Gratuitous charity represented the worst sort of investment for an enterprising community. It precluded a productive return on welfare expenditure and did nothing to foster the virtues of thrift and self-reliance amongst the labouring poor, whereas labour extracted from the recipient of relief constituted the ideal recompense, the favoured *quid pro quo.*[36] As a correspondent to the *Acadian Recorder* explained, "every penny given in charity to a healthy person, able to work, is a

---

November 30, 1857; "Employment of the Poor," *Novascotian,* January 5, 1832; Gilbert and Develier to Odell, March 30, 1842, RLE/842/22/2, PANB.

[31]"St. John Public Dispensary," *New Brunswick Courier,* April 4, 1857. Similarly, *Report of the Governors of Halifax Visiting Dispensary for 1860* (Halifax, 1861), p. 6.

[32]Board of Health, Saint John, Report for 1858, p. iv, New Brunswick, *JLA* (1857-58), Appendix.

[33]Speech by Barnes, Assembly Debate, April 8, 1845, *Times* (St. John's), April 12, 1845.

[34]"The Season," *Morning Post,* February 19, 1845.

[35]"Relief of the Poor," *Patriot,* March 30, 1839.

[36]Editorial, *Times* (St. John's), September 29, 1847.

serious injury to society at large, unless that penny produces its own value by some mode of industry."[37] The guarantee that a poor person or family relieved through charity or employment was in fact deserving formed another precautionary, money-saving consideration. Most public relief schemes or welfare services—voluntary or government sponsored—required a means test in the form of a certificate of genuine destitution from a respectable citizen or designated official.[38] Poor youths supplied their *quid pro quo* in another form. All towns and many churches within them organized clothing societies which aimed primarily at sheltering poor children against the inclemency of winter weather. But in return for free clothing, the children were expected to attend Sunday school of catechism classes where proper ideas of christian citizenship were carefully inculcated.[39]

With their interest in economy, good order, and the wider welfare of the town, social commentators of every description urged consistently from the 1810s until the 1860s and beyond that the able-bodied poor should be relieved only in return for an equivalent in labour. Work was seen as the great panacea for the prevailing urban malaise produced by seasonal unemployment, dangerous mendicancy, and exorbitant, gratuitous aid. Effective employment relief would benefit both the poor and the town. For individual recipients, employment would supply what the majority professedly preferred—the means of obtaining the necessaries of life without sacrificing completely their independence by becoming degraded objects of charity.[40] Provision of work would eliminate reliance on charity which was both demoralizing and induced wasteful habits of idleness, intemperance, improvidence, and even worse forms of anti-social behaviour.[41] As far as the town itself was concerned, or more specifically its leading citizens, employment relief was designed to "subserve the Public interest."[42] In the first place, work was favoured as a security measure, the object being to avoid public mischief by keeping the labouring poor busily occupied.[43] Secondly, from the 1840s onwards, when middle-class faith in progress and improvement clearly emerged in

[37]Letter from Agenoria, *Acadian Recorder*, November 29, 1823.

[38]*Morning News*, September 11, 1846; Notice of Commissioners for the Relief of the Poor, *Newfoundland Express*, January 23, 1861.

[39]Catechistical Society, *Cross* (Halifax), August 7, 1847. The Saint John and Portland Ladies' Benevolent Society loaned clothing to the sick poor and if it was returned in good order, the party received a gift of some of the articles. *New Brunswick Courier*, June 22, 1844.

[40]Editorial, *Acadian Recorder*, February 6, 1836; "Relief of the Poor," *Patriot*, March 30, 1839; Letter from Observer, *Newfoundland*, March 9, 1848; Petition of Irish labourers (Halifax) to Sir John Harvey, April 25, 1848, RG 5, series GP, vol. 7, PANS; Speech by Shea, Assembly Debate, December 14, 1848, *Newfoundlander*, December 21, 1848; Speech by Hayward, Assembly Debate, February 10, 1854, *Newfoundland Express*, February 18, 1854; Speech by Surveyor General Hanrahan, Assembly Debate, March 12, 1856, ibid., May 31, 1856.

[41]Letter from Humanus, *New Brunswick Courier*, February 2, 1833; Editorial, *Newfoundlander*, September 30, 1847; Report of Committee of HM Council upon the expenditure on account of paupers in the district of St. John's, *Public Ledger*, July 3, 1849.

[42]"Employment for the Poor," *Morning News*, January 29, 1858; also *New Brunswick Courier*, January 30, 1858.

[43]"Employment of the Poor," and editorial comment, *Novascotian*, January 12, 1831.

debates on social welfare, as it did in the matter of education, relief in the shape of employment was valued as a means by which the poor could contribute significantly to the economy and development of the town and colony. The editor of the *New Brunswick Courier* aptly referred to it as a way "in which the necessities of the labouring poor could be made to dovetail with the general interest of the whole community, so that they might be benefited by receiving work, while those who pay for it might be equally benefited by having it done."[44] As one Halifax paper put it, "the poor might earn a loaf, and at the same time benefit the city."[45] Such a mutually beneficial situation obtained in Saint John in 1842 when the city council spent a grant of £2500 from the executive on the employment of the poor in winter. With the consequent removal of rock from the town squares, "the City was improved and the poor people were relieved at the same time."[46] Similarly in St. John's, the editor of the *Times* applauded the insistence of the governor in 1847 that the able-bodied must work for their relief and favoured the ubiquitous resort in Newfoundland to road works as the method by which the poor could secure their subsistence while "the country at large is benefited."[47]

The public interest would equally be served if such employment reduced the number of those supported by government and voluntary charity. Stephen March, an assemblyman in Newfoundland, was typical of those colonists who believed that poverty was synonymous with unemployment, and therefore that the availability of sufficient work would materially diminish the legislature's staggering appropriation for relief of the poor.[48] In 1829 the editor of the *New Brunswick Courier* claimed that the programme of street building undoubtedly relieved Saint John of potential parish burdens.[49] This interest in economy also motivated those who were less sympathetic towards the poor, and who argued that relief for the able-bodied in the form of compulsory labour would soon send idlers and imposters scurrying to their own resources, or better still, as far as commentators in St. John's were concerned, encourage them to emigrate.[50] A similarly rigorous attitude can be discerned in the workhouse ethic that emerged in the management of the almshouse in Saint John, an institution which, unlike the Halifax poorhouse, catered to the able-bodied as well as to the disabled poor.[51] Anxious to reduce the burden of the poor rate on its citizens, the grand jury of Saint John suggested in its review of the almshouse in 1842 that "even nursing mothers should

---

[44]"Winter Employment for Outdoor Labourers," *New Brunswick Courier*, January 30, 1858.

[45]*Novascotian*, January 11, 1858.

[46]"Employment for the Poor," *Morning News*, January 29, 1858; £500 not used in 1842 was used in 1858, Common Council, ibid., February 19, March 5, 1858; "Employment of the Poor," *New Brunswick Courier*, December 4, 1841.

[47]Editorial, *Times* (St. John's), October 9, 1847.

[48]Speech by March, Assembly Debate, February 3, 1853, *Patriot*, February 12, 1853.

[49]*New Brunswick Courier*, September 19, 1829.

[50]*Newfoundlander*, June 7, 1855.

[51]Letter from an Inhabitant of Halifax, *Acadian Recorder*, December 14, 1816; Letter from An Old Tax Payer, "Poor House," *Morning News*, March 16, 1842.

be required when in health to earn their living."[52] Faced with over-whelming numbers of applicants, the administrators of the almshouse advocated the enforcement of labour to render the institution unattractive to the able-bodied poor. In 1849, the lieutenant-governor of New Brunswick pointed out that "the immediate profit of the work, is not the object of main importance. The able-bodied men, as a class, may earn much less than their maintenance costs the public, but if the knowledge that hard work is required acts so as to deter others from entering the Alms House, a saving to the ratepayers will be effected, and the industry of individuals will be promoted out of its precincts."[53]

Finally, employment relief was singularly attractive to colonial capitalists and ratepayers who relished the existence of a cheap, exploitable labour force. A report of a committee of the Newfoundland legislative council in 1849 clearly delineated how the interests of employers could be served by replacing gratuitous assistance with employment relief. It proposed that the St. John's poor commissioner's office should act as a labour bureau where "artisans and labourers might at the time be had at rates a degree lower than their ordinary rate of wages."[54] In Saint John, a city which in contrast to St. John's was keen to retain its highly mobile labourers, the inhabitants felt a particular urgency to afford employment relief for the seasonally destitute and portrayed with complacent satisfaction those "starving for want of work" as a potentially cheap labour force.[55] For this reason, G. E. Fenety, the civic-conscious editor of the *Morning News*, proposed that the prosecution of public works should be reserved for seasons of scarcity and depression when they would not only benefit the poor by supplying work but the urban authorities would obtain the best return on the expenditure of the citizen's money in the form of useful labour, cheaply done.[56]

The range of proposals for furnishing socially-useful employment for the poor was far greater than the number of schemes actually undertaken. Initially, contemporaries viewed work as a palliative for distress in a very pessimistic light. One sceptical correspondent in Saint John in 1832 urged the citizens to consider whether they had in fact any responsibility in the matter, and if so, whether such a programme of work was feasible. They should determine, the correspondent suggested without expectation of a favourable response, "Either that it is not our duty as members of a Christian community to endeavour to provide for the employment of

---

[52]Grand Jury Presentment, March 1842, RMU, Csj, 1/10, PANB; see also "The Almshouse &c.&c.," *Morning News*, September 27, 1850.

[53]J. R. Partelow, Provincial Secretary, to the Commissioners of the Alms House and Work House, Saint John, *New Brunswick Courier*, September 29, 1849. Work was not consistently provided, see Charges against the Alms House Commissioners, October 1860, RMU, Cjs, 1/15, PANB.

[54]Report of Committee of HM Council upon the expenditure on account of paupers in the district of St. John's, *Public Ledger*, July 3, 1849.

[55]Letter from The Poor Man's Friend, "How to Employ the Poor," *Morning News*, February 19, 1858; "Employment for the Poor," ibid., January 29, 1858; Letter from Citizen, *Morning Freeman*, March 26, 1859.

[56]"A Word in Season—or, a Practical Lesson for the Times," *Morning News*, January 3, 1855; "Work for Labourers," ibid., September 21, 1857.

the poor as well as their relief. Or, that it is an object which we cannot reasonably expect to attain by any united efforts in this place."[57] Part of the trouble was that the people who took it upon themselves to advise the community on this issue tended to be men given to idle talk or theorizing, not practical men of business—newspaper editors, politicians, and bureaucrats rather than merchants, contractors, builders, and entrepreneurs. Moreover, with very few exceptions, the schemes implemented were not placed on a systematic footing, despite the necessity for regularizing employment relief advocated by the amateur political economists of the day. The projects themselves, both in conception and in practice, were of two varieties: heavy outdoor labour and indoor factory work. Public efforts were concentrated chiefly on the former because society was male-oriented and reflected the outlook of a pre-industrial age.

The most widely discussed forms of employment and the jobs most frequently organized can both be subsumed under the general heading of public works. These differed more in time, location, and sponsorship than in form or variety. In Halifax the urgent need for outdoor relief in the years following the Napoleonic Wars forced citizens' committees, in the absence of government measures, to address themselves to the question of providing employment. Much to the disappointment of its energetic proponents and the satisfaction of its critics, the Poor Man's Friend Society in the 1820s failed in its persevering endeavours to find work for the poor, being unable to do more than serve as a labour bureau.[58] Its successors, however, were determined to base their schemes for relieving the labouring poor on employment. Accordingly, a long tradition of outdoor relief for able-bodied men through stone breaking for the metalling or macadamizing of the roads began in the winter of 1830-31 and was revived for the benefit of at least 200 family men according to need over the next three decades.[59] While the sponsorship of this menial, degrading enterprise passed from the voluntary citizens' committees to the city corporation in the 1840s, it continued to be funded largely by private charity with the mayor still appealing to the inhabitants for subscriptions or contributions in stone.

Meanwhile in Saint John and St. John's, stone breaking was also promoted, and requests for financing it, as well as more sophisticated activities like pipe laying and rubbish removal, were often directed to the respective executive governments by hard-pressed civic-leaders.[60] But

---

[57]Letter from Homo, "Employment of the Poor," *New Brunswick Courier*, January 14, 1832.

[58]Editorial, *Free Press*, March 5, 1822; *Acadian Recorder*, February 7, 1824.

[59]"Employment of the Poor," *Novascotian*, January 12, 1831; "Employment of the Poor," *Acadian Recorder*, January 15, December 31, 1831; *Weekly Observer* (Saint John), January 3, 1832; "Employment of the Poor," *Novascotian*, January 12, 1832; "Stone Breaking," ibid., December 20, 1832; "The Employment of the Industrious Poor," ibid., January 3, 1833; "Stonebreaking," ibid., February 21, 1833; *Guardian*, January 4, 1843; *Sun*, February 4, 1848.

[60]Letter from Homo, "Employment of the Poor," *New Brunswick Courier*, January 14, 1832; ibid., February 10, 1838; Editorial, *Public Ledger*, March 23, 1838; Common Council resolutions, *New Brunswick Courier*, November 27, 1841; Letter from Civis, "Feed the Hungry and the Poor—Clothe the Naked," *Morning News*, November 27, 1857; "Winter Employment for Outdoor Labourers," *New Brunswick Courier*, January 30, 1858.

road works remained the ideal form of public works in St. John's and the outports. Initiated principally through the efforts of Sir Thomas Cochrane in the 1820s, road making and repairing became a perennial resort as relief for the able-bodied and for seasonally unemployed fishermen. To such an extent was this enterprise popularly believed to mitigate distress, that until reforms of the late 1860s the road bill came to be associated with other appropriations for eleemosynary aid and therefore considered a little more than a euphemism for a poor relief bill.[61] Indeed, despite approval for the 'dovetailing' nature of this work—that it secured "real value to the country while relieving the necessities of the industrious poor"—the amount of labour provided on the roads was apparently determined by the degree of distress rather than by a comprehensive transportation policy.[62] That some contemporaries were prone to criticize this tendency can be attributed to their preference for a systematic approach to employment relief which would supplant the 'make work' nature of the existing enterprise.

At the opposite extreme to such 'make work' arrangements stood the entirely fortuitous opportunities for employment of the able-bodied poor created by the march of progress in the Atlantic colonies. By the middle of the century skilled and semi-skilled labourers in substantial numbers, sometimes large enough to siphon off the burdensome surplus of the towns, were engaged on railway works in the environs of Saint John and Halifax, on road building for the overseas telegraphic cable in New foundland, and on the construction of a variety of impressive civic buildings, such as the city hospital, provincial lunatic asylum, and city prison in the Halifax area.[63] For the private contractors a pool of unemployed poor supplied cheap labour at the termination of the shipping season; for the public authorities the works saved them the trouble of devising, and more important, financing an alternative employment scheme; for the community, large-scale productive labour meant a positive boon as a result of the exchange of wages for local services. As Fenety pointed out in 1858, railway construction during the depression involved "something like a thousand pounds *distributed*, as it were, among the labouring classes every week, which in turn finds its way into the stores, and thus keeps business moving."[64] But by its nature the work was short term and often interrupted by undercapitalization. Moveover,

[61]Speech by Hogsett, Assembly Debate, March 22, 1853, *Newfoundland Express,* April 2, 1853; Speech by Hayward, Assembly Debate, February 10, 1854, ibid., February 18, 1854; Speech by Hanrahan, Assembly Debate, April 11, 1854, ibid., April 29, 1854; Editorial, *Public Ledger,* August 24, 1855; Speech by Prendergast, Assembly Debate, January 21, 1856, *Newfoundland Express,* January 30, 1856; Speech by Surveyor General Hanrahan, Assembly Debate, March 12, 1856, ibid., May 31, 1856; Editorial, *Newfoundlander,* October 12, 1857.

[62]"State of the Poor—Its Causes," *Newfoundlander,* October 10, 1853. Moreover, by the sixties road money was occasionally granted without a strict adherence to the exaction of labour on the ground that poor men "could not, on their spare diet, be sent four or five miles out of town to work on the roads." Assembly Debate, February 22, 1866, ibid., March 19, 1866.

[63]Speeches by Parsons and Hanrahan, Assembly Debate, April 11, 1854, *Newfoundland Express,* April 29, 1854; "Winter Work for the Industrious," *Morning Chronicle* (Halifax), January 27, 1855; "Remember the Poor," *Morning News,* November 27, 1857; *Morning Journal,* April 28, 1858; *Evening Express* (Halifax), May 26, 1858; "Business and Prospects," *Morning News,* September 29, 1858.

[64]"Ship Building and Saw Mills about St. John—Hard Times—The Way to Relieve Distress," *Morning News,* December 10, 1858.

the climatic limitation imposed on the work when it was most needed meant that rail lines laid on frozen mud near Saint John sank in the spring thaw; that autumnal road building in Newfoundland was inefficient and could not be pursued at all in winter; and that ambitious building operations had to be halted in Halifax when frost attacked new masonry.[65] Unfortunately, such enterprises did not lay the basis of a sustained and systematic employment policy. The jobs tended to terminate with the completion of the railway, the telegraphic communications, or the public buildings concerned.

Those colonists with sufficient foresight to suggest projects, that were neither wholly 'make work', nor fortuitous, nor seasonal in character, appear from the perspective of the 1970s to have had common sense to their credit. Shrewd commentators flourished most noticeably in St. John's, the town amongst the three which suffered most relentlessly from chronic poverty. While the distress of the inhabitants was undoubtedly complicated by the supply system practised by the merchants, contemporaries ascribed it more generally to the predominance of a single economic activity that was seasonal in nature and underdeveloped in scope. In such circumstances alternative forms of employment could be fruitfully designed to meet the demands of the local consumer market or to act as ancillary pursuits to the primary business of the fishery. Several newspaper editors and government reports recommended that both unemployment in winter and one persistent deficiency of supply in the local market might be overcome by setting the ablebodied poor to work in the woods producing lumber on a systematic basis. While many of the seasonally unemployed resorted to the woods on their own initiative, they functioned as independent, small-scale producers without the stimulus of attractive marketing facilities in town. The press suggested several times that the government ought to open a wood yard or depot in St. John's on a cash basis where the poor could be sure of an equitable return for their labour and the sale of all manner of wood and primary wood products on terms advantageous both to themselves and to the public treasury.[66] A perceptive government inquiry in 1856 went a step further by advocating that the poor should be organized in supervised gangs for a more comprehensive and profitable system of employment relief in the woods.[67] Other proposals regarded employment schemes as a means of augmenting the fishery. The government report of 1856 strongly favoured the promotion of shipbuilding through tonnage bounties paid to those shipbuilders who employed a required proportion

[65]"Employment for the Poor," *Morning News*, January 29, 1858; Evidence of James Douglas before the Select Committee appointed to inquire into the Appropriation of Monies voted by the Legislature for the Relief of the Poor, *JLA*, Newfoundland, 1848–49, Appendix, p. 691; *Patriot*, December 27, 1852; Editorial, *Newfoundlander*, October 12, 1857; Speech by Surveyor General Hanrahan, Assembly Debate, March 10, 1858, ibid., March 18, 1858; "The Weather vs. House Building," *Morning Journal*, December 12, 1859.

[66]Editorial, *Public Ledger*, March 29, 1839; "Relief of the Poor," *Patriot*, March 30, 1839; Editorial, *Public Ledger*, September 30, 1853.

[67]Report of Committee of Enquiry into the State of the Poor, March 26, 1856, *Newfoundland Express*, April 23, 1856. Another winter activity which was urged in Saint John and Halifax was the ice trade. *Saint John Herald*, December 10, 1845; *Morning Journal*, January 26, 1857.

of government paupers. Not only was this a labour-intensive industry and directly related to the staple export business of the colony, but it would create many additional jobs in auxiliary areas.[68]

Alternative projects for supplementing the fishery depended on the facilities for indoor work, the other variety of employment advocated in the towns as a means of relief. The forward-looking government report of 1856, for example, claimed that publicly-sponsored factories might offer employment, in lines of work suited to the country—principally the manufacture of nets and seines (imported from Britain at a cost of over £30,000 in 1860),[69] as well as small-scale wooden products such as staves and shingles, the picking of oakum (25 tons of which was imported every year, according to the Public Ledger in 1839),[70] and the production of domestic clothing. That report, however, was published almost 25 years after a factory for the relief of the able-bodied had been established in St. John's, an institution which had served as an inspiration for the government report and a point of departure for many other suggestions that emanated from St. John's. It was a quite unique institution which in terms of longevity, popularity, non-partisanship, and 'dovetailing' was the most successful of the few sustained ventures in the Atlantic towns for employing the labouring poor in this period.

The St. John's factory, a non-resident and therefore non-correctional institutional, was begun in December 1832 by a group of community-conscious women who aimed primarily to teach "carding, spinning, net making" to the children of the poor and to afford useful employment to the indigent of St. John's.[71] Like any new institution, however, the managers of the factory initially encountered difficulties in obtaining appropriate raw materials to be worked into consumer goods and in raising sufficient funds to subsidize its activities.[72] Subscriptions and charity balls raised enough money to finance the construction of a permanent building in 1834, and subsequently financial assistance came from a variety of sources: bazaars, balls, benefit performances by the local theatrical group, public subscription campaigns, and fairly regular aid from the legislature.[73]

Since the factory suffered its share of vicissitudes and never achieved

---

[68]Report of Committee of Enquiry into the State of the Poor, March 26, 1856, Newfoundland Express, April 23, 1856; also, Speech by March, Assembly Debate, December 10, 1860, ibid., December 25, 1860.

[69]Speech by March, Assembly Debate, December 10, 1860, Newfoundland Express, December 25, 1860.

[70]Editorial, Public Ledger, March 29, 1839.

[71]Editorial and Report of the Meeting of Committee of Ladies for establishing a Factory for the purpose of giving useful Employment to the Poor of the Town, Newfoundlander, December 13, 1832.

[72]Public Ledger, February 26, 1833; Newfoundlander, April 18, 1833; Letter from A Friend, Public Ledger, March 28, 1834; Report of St. John's Factory, ibid., November 27, 1835.

[73]St. John's Factory, Newfoundlander, September 4, 1834; ibid., September 18, 1834; St. John's Factory, Public Ledger, January 16, 1835; ibid., February 27, 1835; Report of St. John's Factory, ibid., August 16, 1836; Newfoundlander, March 23, 1837; ibid., June 15, 1837; Assembly Debate, October 1, 1838; Patriot, October 6, 1838; Public Ledger, February 28, 1840, February 28, 1851; Newfoundland Express, October 22, 1853; R. H. Bonnycastle, Newfoundland in 1842 (London, 1842), vol. 2, p. 232.

self-sufficiency, its community-conscious efforts were more noteworthy than its long-term accomplishments. In the first place, the factory undertook to promote industry in place of charity as a means of poor relief. This emphasis, it was popularly believed, would foster all the appropriate virtues and habits in the poor. In a community where dire poverty was endemic and the expense of poor relief crippling, the encouragement of self-reliance, independence, and self-respect amongst the poor was enthusiastically endorsed by the articulate.[74] By supplying work and useful industrial training as well as wages, the managers of the factory hoped "to improve and elevate the mind and feeling of the poor and needy, above relying on eleemosynary aid" from other sources.[75] This was a vital consideration in St. John's where the accustomed rhythm of summer fishing followed by winter distress discernibly undermined the morale and spirit of the working class and disposed them "to lean altogether on public charity for support."[76] The factory also undertook to supply much of its work in the slack commercial season when unemployment was at its height.[77] To those who contributed to its operations, the system pursued by the factory assured the desirable *quid pro quo* in labour. Not only did this ease the qualms of the benevolent about fostering idleness, but it stressed employment as "the panacea for the amelioration" of the condition of the St. John's poor.[78] It was also no mean consideration that the factory might reduce the burden of poor relief on the community since "every shilling earned here is so much withdrawn from the demands on the public which pauperism engenders."[79]

In the second place, the factory endeavoured both to employ those elements in the town population most in need of work and to extend its operations to meet emergencies that arose. Initially the institution catered to the most destitute poor of St. John's, employing some 30 work people.[80] Its normal complement of workers had risen to about 60 by the severe winter of 1837–38.[81] With financial aid from the executive during the famine year of 1847–48, the factory was able to employ between 100 and 150 a day.[82] Within a few years of its foundation experience had shown that indoor employment relief was most eagerly sought by women and children, who constituted two segments of society usually neglected

[74]Speech by Carson, Assembly Debate, March 21, 1835, *Public Ledger*, March 24, 1835; Editorial, *Newfoundlander*, March 28, 1839.

[75]Letter from R. Prowse, *Public Ledger*, February 26, 1847; Report of St. John's Factory, ibid., August 16, 1836.

[76]Annual Report of Committee of Factory, *Public Ledger*, August 3, 1849.

[77]Report of Factory Committee, *Newfoundlander*, August 3, 1837; Report of St. John's Factory, *Times* (St. John's), August 3, 1842.

[78]Editorial, *Newfoundlander*, March 28, 1839.

[79]Report of Committee of St. John's Factory, *Newfoundlander*, September 14, 1843; Annual Report of Committee of Factory, *Public Ledger*, August 3, 1849.

[80]Report of St. John's Factory, *Public Ledger*, November 27, 1835.

[81]Editorial, *Newfoundlander*, July 5, 1838; Report of St. John's Factory Committee, *Public Ledger*, July 27, 1838.

[82]Report of St. John's Factory, *Newfoundlander*, August 10, 1848; *Times* (St. John's), March 23, 1849.

in the pre-industrial period but most in need of work since they comprised the majority of the year-round, as opposed to the seasonally, unemployed.[83] Its essential service as an employer of women and children was noted by the attorney general in 1856 when he asserted that "from the effects of disease and shipwreck" St. John's had more widows and orphans "than in any other city or town of the same size."[84] Priority of employment was given to females of every creed between the ages of 12 and 60. They laboured daily from 10 A.M. to 4 P.M. and were paid on a piece-work rate. Although the actual rate is unknown, contemporaries claimed that workers usually earned between 1s. and 1s.6d. a day, a typical relief wage. One hard-working female was reputed in 1849 to be earning as much as 12s. a week making nets. But on the basis of detailed figures for two months in 1838, the averages of the women and children fell between 3s.6d. per week, starvation wages at best. On the assumption that the adolescents were less productive and paid at a lower rate than the mature women, it is not surprising that commentators declared that it was the "industrious" female who could earn her support at the factory. Advocates of the establishment also proudly boasted that the factory was the agency through which whole families of widows and their children could work together and earn a complete livelihood.[85] One wage packet was clearly inadequate to maintain a family.

Finally, the factory offered specialized training and concentrated on manufactures that were most needed in the community and therefore presumably guaranteed a ready, local market. Two types of manufactures were undertaken: fishing nets for the primary industry of the colony and domestic textiles required by local merchants for sale in their stores. The factory committee was proud of the quality of the nets and publicized them as being superior or at least comparable to the imported commodity.[86] Moreover, the preoccupation with net-making as an activity beneficial to the family and the community at large was frequently celebrated.

> The advantages to the colony by this branch of industry are incalculable—the women and children are taught to make nets for their husbands and fathers, and thus to employ the hitherto unprofitable season of winter—while the fisherman has only to provide the twine instead of the more expensive article, the net or seine, which latter is often beyond his means, and the want of it is not unfrequently a serious hindrance to his getting on in the world.[87]

---

[83]Letter from Malthus, Poor Man's Friend Society, no. 5, "Answer to My Opponents," *Nova Scotian*, February 16, 1825.

[84]Speech by Attorney-General Little, Assembly Debate, April 8, 1856, *Newfoundlander*, April 10, 1856.

[85]Account of persons employed at Factory, *Newfoundlander*, July 5, 1838; Letter from R. Prowse, *Public Ledger*, February 26, 1847; Editorial, *Newfoundlander*, March 11, 1847; "The Factory," *Times* (St. John's), September 8, 1847; ibid., March 23, 1849; Speech by Warren, Assembly Debate, April 8, 1853, *Newfoundland Express*, April 28, 1853; Speech by Prowse, Assembly Debate, April 8, 1856, *Newfoundlander*, April 10, 1856.

[86]Report of St. John's Factory, *Public Ledger*, August 16, 1836; Annual Report of Committee of Factory, ibid., August 3, 1849.

[87]Report of Factory Committee, *Newfoundlander*, August 3, 1837.

Money otherwise sent outside the colony could thereby be kept in circulation, generating employment which would result in "an immense saving" to the colony.[88] At the same time, the training in net-making was thought to promote "an exceedingly useful art" in the economic circumstances of Newfoundland.[89] The needlework, always a supplementary activity, was aimed at producing necessary items of wearing apparel for local consumption. This textile branch, originally of a finishing nature, blossomed into the manufacture of textiles in 1850 when Lieutenant Governor LeMarchant provided several looms for the weaving of homespun, a fabric well suited to ordinary domestic wear and hitherto not produced in the colony. This had the advantage of adding another type of industrial training to the factory's regimen, though the institution's inability to find a qualified weaver in St. John's by 1868 casts doubt on the success of the undertaking.[90]

Despite support from the legislature, endorsement by select committees, and the intermittent interests of governors, official attempts to exploit factory production as an extensive system of poor relief amounted to little more than brief enthusiasm.[91] Whatever their reasons, many prominent citizens were critical both of the management of the factory and of the quality and cost of the nets it produced. Moreover, the retail merchants of St. John's did not absorb all the ready-to-wear clothing made at the factory. If the institution had been designed to employ men in winter rather than women the year round, it might have excited a more lively public concern. It is also possible that prospective workers did not always take advantage of the factory's facilities for voluntary employment. Ultimately, by the 1860s, the management of the institution came to devolve, not on a general committee of citizens as formerly, but on the Catholic St. Vincent de Paul Society, a change that was accompanied by a concentration on purely hibernal operations.[92] Nonetheless, the St. John's factory was the one genuine house of industry in the Atlantic region. In spite of musings about a house of industry as a palliative for poverty. Haligonians did no more than toy with the idea of providing indoor employment relief and seemed unable to devise forms of work that would fit in with the wider interests of the city and thereby appeal to the philanthropy of the townspeople.[93] After public agitation a

---

[88]Report of St. John's Factory, *Newfoundlander*, August 10, 1848.

[89]*Times* (St. John's), March 23, 1849.

[90]Editorial, *Public Ledger*, January 22, 1850; *Times* (St. John's), January 23, 1850; Speech by Emerson, Assembly Debate, March 22, 1850, *Public Ledger*, March 26, 1850. See criticism voiced by Prendergast, Assembly Debate, May 31, 1852, *Newfoundland Express*, June 4, 1852; Report of Proceedings of St. Vincent de Paul Society, *Newfoundlander*, December 22, 1868.

[91]Report of Committee of HM Council upon the expenditure on account of paupers in the district of St. John's, *Public Ledger*, July 3, 1849; Editorial, *Newfoundland Express*, May 3, 1856.

[92]Report of Society of St. Vincent de Paul, *Newfoundlander*, December 20, 1867.

[93]"Proposal for the Establishment of a House of Industry in connexion with an Orphan Asylum," *Nova Scotian*, February 10, 1836; "An Appeal to the Public on behalf of the Establishment of a House of Industry in connexion with Orphan Asylum," ibid., March 28, 1839;

residential house of industry for women and children was opened briefly through voluntary assistance in Saint John in 1834, but it was intended mainly as a self-supporting school of domestic industry which also trained household servants for the city.[94]

Indoor employment, therefore, did not prosper more noticeably than outdoor measures of relief. It is not difficult to discern why employment schemes foundered. For one thing, colonists believed that the conditions which caused unemployment were beyond their control and could neither be anticipated nor rectified in towns whose economies were subject to fluctuating external and international trends.[95] The sudden influxes of immigrants and erratic business depressions made the colonists feel singularly helpless. If leading townsmen felt helpless in the face of such circumstances, they would hardly be capable of helping others to help themselves. Moreover, the launching of extensive schemes for employment required capital, and no agency in the towns appeared willing to sustain a socially useful experiment in the early stages before it could become a self-supporting or even profitable operation. Despite, or perhaps because of, the amazing array of enterprises partially subsidized by government, the provincial legislatures refused to risk their revenues on long-term employment schemes or to favour leading towns at the expense of the other inhabitants in the colony.[96] For their part, the corporations of Saint John and Halifax were not wealthy enough to embark on ambitious projects and were reluctant to resort to unpopular taxation. Nor were colonists agreed how far the various levels of government should involve themselves in manipulation of the labour market. The editor of the *Newfoundland Express,* for example, pointed out that the government report of 1856 on employment for the poor "proceeds upon an assumption which has proved a failure wherever it has been attempted to give practical effect to it—the assumption that the *organization of labour* can be effected by the state."[97]

Left to private capitalists, however, the pauperizing patterns of unemployment were reinforced and exploited because merchants were content to employ town labourers in summer and abandon them to the

---

Letter from One of the Society, "House of Industry, Hints to the Benevolent," *Morning Chronicle,* March 11, 1845; "House of Industry," *Guardian,* March 14, 1845; "House of Industry," *Morning Post,* March 26, 1845; Letter from a Friend to the Poor, "Help for the Poor," *Sun,* January 19, 1846; "The Reclamation of Vagrants," *Morning Journal,* February 22, 1856.

[94]Letter from Homo, "Employment of the Poor," *New Brunswick Courier,* January 14, 1832; Letter from Humanus, "Employment of the Poor," ibid., February 2, 1833; 1st Report of the House of Industry, ibid., July 26, 1834; Petition of Managing Committee of Female House of Industry in City of Saint John, February 2, 1835, RLE/835/pe/4, no. 82, PANB. It also provided home employment relief for women on a piece-work basis. Report of St. John Female House of Industry, *New Brunswick Courier,* January 17, 1835.

[95]Letter from a Sympathizer, "The Present and Former Government," *Morning News,* February 1, 1856.

[96]"Who are the Suffering Poor?", *Morning News,* February 22, 1858.

[97]Editorial, *Newfoundland Express,* April 23, 1856; Speech by Attorney General, Assembly Debate, February 21, 1866, *Newfoundlander,* March 15, 1866; Speech by Receiver General, Assembly Debate, March 6, 1868, ibid., March 11, 1868.

mercy of government, charity, occasional public works, or sharply reduced wages in the private sector during winter.[98] With the notable exception of shipbuilders in Saint John, entrepreneurs were as yet unwilling to invest in industry and thereby ease some of the seasonal fluctuations, and this despite a general conviction by mid-century that sufficient wealth and tradition of prudence existed to sustain "promising and well-considered commercial speculation" in local manufactures.[99] In these circumstances, voluntary, non-profit-making agencies did what they could. Such denominational societies as the St. Vincent de Paul in St. John's and the visiting societies attached to St. Matthew's and St. George's churches in Halifax went unpretentiously about the business of providing essential, if token, indoor work for women and children.[100] But more generally, associations found it easier to dispense discriminating charity without labour and thereby salve their consciences rather than campaign for effective employment relief. In fact society's inability to attack pre-industrial poverty at its source, which was unemployment, led by the 1850s to a marked preoccupation with the symptoms of poverty, especially intemperance, and a corresponding interest in social amelioration as moral rather than economic reform.[101]

---

[98]Speech by Hogsett, Assembly Debate, April 3, 1854, *Newfoundland Express*, April 11, 1854; "Our Trade System," *Newfoundlander*, February 1, 1855; J. Fingard, "The Winter's Tale: The Seasonal Contours of Pre-Industrial Poverty in British North America," Canadian Historical Association, *Historical Papers* (1974), pp. 65–94.

[99]Editorial, *Sun*, December 24, 1853.

[100]St. Vincent de Paul Society, *Newfoundlander*, April 2, 1857; *Newfoundland Express*, December 10, 1861; St. Matthew's Church District Society, *Guardian*, November 15, 1850; St. George's Ladies' Benevolent Society, *Colonial Churchman* (Lunenburg), June 15, 1837; *Morning Post*, January 15, 1842; St. George's District Visiting Society, *Church Times* (Halifax), December 3, 1853.

[101]For example, "Providing for the Poor," *Morning News*, January 18, 1860.

29

JOSEPH HOWE: MILD TORY
TO REFORMING ASSEMBLYMAN*

J. M. Beck

For a rather long time in the 19th century, provincial politics in Nova Scotia was a relatively tame business, with few deep divisions among the politically active and no evidence of party organization. The late 18th-century conflict between newly arrived Loyalists and the pre-revolutionary old guard in Nova Scotia had been pretty well settled by a merger of the two groups, and a sort of gentle Toryism was the prevailing political sentiment in much of the province. Consensus had been assisted by the prosperity of the wartime economy which Nova Scotia enjoyed until after 1815, and while there were a number of potentially divisive issues smouldering the province over such matters as education, religious preference, and internal improvements, none of these became really politicized until the 1830s. One mark of the relative tranquillity of the period before then was the friendship between the later Tory Thomas Haliburton and the later Reformer Joseph Howe. In the following article, J. M. Beck analyses Howe's position at the time he became editor of the *Novascotian* in 1828 and traces his development to a position of potential leadership a few years later. In what ways was Howe a "mild Tory" in the 1820s? What factors led to a change of viewpoint? Did Howe change so much as did conditions and issues in Nova Scotia? How radical was Howe in these formative years? Was the future "reformer" a perceptive critic of his society?

*Dalhousie Review, 44 (1964), 44-56.

SUGGESTIONS FOR FURTHER READING

J. Murray Beck, *Joseph Howe: Voice of Nova Scotia* (Toronto: McClelland and Stewart, 1964).

J. A. Chisholm, *Speeches and Public Letters of Joseph Howe*, 2 vols. (Halifax: Chronicle Publishing Co., 1909).

J. A. Roy, *Joseph Howe: A Study in Achievement and Frustration* (Toronto: Macmillan of Canada, 1935).

J.M.B.

T he Pictou Scribblers . . . have converted me from the error of my ways."[1] In this statement, purported to have been made in 1830, Joseph Howe admitted to a very considerable change in his political thinking early in his adult life. The purpose of this article is to examine this change, particularly as it unfolded between 1828 and 1836.

Who was the young man Howe, who in January 1828, at the age of 24, became sole proprietor and editor of the *Novascotian?* The qualities which distinguished him from other men undoubtedly came from his father. They were, in Principal G. M. Grant's words, "the great heart and open hand . . . , that milk of human kindness . . . which no opposition could permanently sour; his poetic nature which if it inclined him to be visionary at times, was yet at the bottom of his statesmanship; [and] his reverence for the past."[2] To his father, Howe himself attributed his fondness for reading, his familiarity with the Bible, and his "knowledge of old Colonial and American incidents and characteristics."[3] It was his father, too, who led him to believe that the people who governed the Province were able, intelligent, well-intentioned men, and that imperfections in the governmental system were minor.

Having had little formal education, Howe tried to satisfy this thirst for knowledge by reading; yet, when the supply of books failed, he consoled himself that "the world is before me—a library open to all—from which poverty of purse cannot exclude me."[4] In particular, "he welcomed association and collision with highly cultivated minds as a means of trying out what was in himself and making it more fit for use."[5] His self-education proceeded rapidly while he was joint proprietor of the *Acadian* in 1827, and it continued apace after he took over the *Novascotian* in 1828.

To Howe his native province was the best of all possible worlds. It was not, he admitted, a second El Dorado with streets of gold, but what people, he asked, have

> more of the real solid comforts of life—fewer taxes to curtail them—laws which form a more impenetrable bulwark of security—a government which

---

[1] George Patterson, *A History of the County of Pictou* (Pictou, 1916), p. 235.

[2] George Johnson, Manuscript biography of Howe (P.A.C.), p. 11.

[3] Ibid., p. 7.

[4] Extract from a letter to his sister in 1837; in George Johnson Papers (P.A.C.).

[5] J. M. Beck, "Joseph Howe," in *Our Living Tradition* (Ser. 4), p. 4.

sits lighter on the people, or under which they may enjoy more of rational freedom?[6]

Yet Howe was still not satisfied; Nova Scotians, he felt, should work even harder if the province's resources were to be developed to the full. The son of a father whose religion regarded idleness as a sin, Howe himself had developed habits of industry which can only be described as astounding. Hence, when he started to publish his celebrated "Rambles" in the summer of 1828, he showed a profound interest in the qualities of the people. And what he saw did not always please him.

The soil of Kings and Annapolis counties, for example, yielded an abundant harvest with less than ordinary labour. Its farmers ought, therefore, to be moderately independent, but instead they were abnormally encumbered with mortgages. It made Howe's gall rise to see lazy, slow-going fellows spending their afternoons during harvest in the taverns or wasting their evenings in debating about a horse race over a tumbler of brandy. There were better occupations for the evenings. "Let every farmer gather the youngsters about his knees at night, and spreading a volume of some kind before them teach them all he knows himself. . . . Let each man labour as though the character of the Province was his individual concern."[7] But in a new country like Nova Scotia the education of the adult was equally important. Let the farmers establish agricultural societies, which would foster a thorough knowledge of the latest principles of rural economy. Let the mechanics establish Institutes which would follow the practices of their English counterparts. Let the rich, the intelligent, and the influential assist in both these developments.

What is surprising was Howe's lack of interest in the political education of the people. Yet there was a reason. In 1828 he stood for "the Constitution, the *whole* Constitution, and *nothing but* the Constitution."[8] But obviously he had reflected little on the existing form of government. He held that since men were prone to abuse their powers, the opportunity of any group to do evil should be strictly limited. This, he felt, correctly described the state of affairs in Nova Scotia. On the one hand there was the Council of Twelve, the nominees of the Governor, acting both as his advisers and as a second branch of the Legislature. Yet any authority they possessed because they occupied the major public offices and were in daily intercourse with the Governor was more than counterbalanced by the Assembly's being the depository of the people's confidence.

Indeed the Assembly should on no account be given additional power. Had he himself not watched the disgraceful scenes which occurred whenever it divided the road monies? If the existing checks were removed, the expenditures on roads would, he feared, soon devour all the provincial revenue. So when Thomas Chandler Haliburton sought to prevent the Council from approving or rejecting each vote separately,

---

[6]*Novascotian*, January 17, 1828.

[7]Ibid., November 26, 1828.

[8]Ibid., January 2, 1828.

Howe contended that the Council should not be denied the right to defeat outrageous measures for the expenditure of money without threatening the entire Appropriation Act. Thus there is justification for labelling the early Howe as a mild Tory. There is also justification for alleging that the Pictou Scribblers forced him to re-examine his political attitudes.

The District of Pictou—a part of the county of Halifax until 1836—was divided into two uncompromising factions based on the divisions within the Presbyterian Church, namely the Kirk of Scotland and the Secession Church. At this time they were quarrelling over the provision of a permanent legislative grant for Pictou Academy. A newcomer to Pictou, Jotham Blanchard, had recently founded the *Colonial Patriot,* and he and two or three Academy boys had perturbed many Nova Scotians by their writings.

One person perturbed by these Pictou Scribblers had been Joseph Howe. He was outraged when Blanchard published a letter in the *Canadian Spectator* which accused the Nova Scotian Assembly of being servile. To Howe, who had himself witnessed first-class constitutional debates in the Assembly, this was sheer heresy. What he did not appreciate was that the outpourings of a few intellectuals on one or two unconnected issues were relatively unimportant. At this stage he had barely an inkling of the manifold ills which Blanchard perceived were inherent in the governmental structure.

Howe resented even more Blanchard's comments on the servility of the press and particularly his remark that the *Acadian* was "conducted by a man connected with the Post Office, and, of course, tied by a party." Indignantly he challenged Blanchard to quote one servile statement from his columns. Yet the *Novascotian* of 1828 leaves the distinct impression that Howe altogether exaggerated the fearless character of his writings. The reason seems obvious. One who finds the *status quo* eminently satisfactory tends to regard even a small criticism as a highly radical pronouncement. For the moment Howe simply heaped ridicule upon the "windy Patriot" Blanchard and remained smugly satisfied with the conduct of the *Novascotian.* Had he not adopted a firm and liberal tone, and assimilated his paper not to "the wild and reckless blast" but to "the healthful and invigorating breeze"? Had he not cut down his reliance on foreign material and published 500 to 1,000 columns of original material?

Already Howe had become enamoured of the Assembly; he "love[d] to hear the free and thrilling tone of debate ringing in [his] ears, and to mark the clash of minds stirred by astute discussion."[9] Yet the session of 1829 brought little to stir him other than the celebrated Barry affair. John A. Barry was an intransigent Assemblyman who, for refusing to apologize for insulting a fellow Assemblyman, was imprisoned in the County gaol at Halifax. At one stage the Assembly appeared likely to take action against the newspaper editors who were criticizing its conduct. According to Howe, he immediately raised his voice "in a tone of warning and defiance." But on this occasion the criticism levelled at him for

---

[9]*Ibid.,* February 5, 1829.

timidity seems justified. Later, however, when the Halifax mob heaped abuse upon the Assemblymen for imprisoning Barry, he supported them to the hilt.

In July, Howe published the first of his legislative reviews. As an introduction, he inquired into the relations between an editor and his public. From the people an editor got support; they in turn looked to him for counsel. Because he had the people's esteem, he could not be awed by the powerful or the wealthy, nor did he need to fear sudden ebullitions of popular feeling. The reviews which followed demonstrated Howe's complete mastery of the laws passed during the session. But they also provided an inkling of where he would make a determined stand later. On the Act to provide for the Custom House Establishment, he welcomed the British Government's desire to relieve the province from exorbitant fees, and to give it the right to regulate its commerce. Yet he wondered if, in protecting the vested rights of the incumbent customs officials, it had insisted upon an altogether lavish scale of salaries. And did this not diminish the funds available for useful public works, and induce luxurious and baneful habits among the people?

In the same reviews Howe also gave his first general estimate of the Assembly and the Council. These were cold, dispassionate opinions based on largely theoretical grounds. The major flaw he found in the Assembly resulted from "the formidable array of Lawyers by whom its benches [were] lined."[10] No matter how high principled professional men might be, they would occasionally overlook the general interest to further their own interest. As for the Council, Howe refused to "trace more evils than ever sprung from the Box of Pandora, to the defects of [its] constitution."[11] Yet, since public officers and judges constituted a majority of the Council, he considered its structure to be clearly defective. Public officers should at all costs be subject to the scrutiny of both branches of the Legislature. Nevertheless, he was willing to admit that "traces of oppression and bad government [were] no where to be discerned" in Nova Scotia.

Within months, however, Howe's attitude towards the Council had hardened. The reason was the Revenue Dispute of 1830. When the Assembly tried to correct an error in the Revenue Law by adding 4d. a gallon to the duty upon brandy—an amount which both branches of the Legislature had previously accepted—the Council turned down the measure although it meant the defeat of the entire Appropriation Act. Every Assemblyman stood firm in the crisis except Uniacke, Hartshorne, and Barry; in Howe's opinion "they . . . acted like men, . . . and stand justified in the eyes of the people."

Now Howe had to reconsider his previous opinion. Could the power possessed by the Assembly during the few weeks it was in session really counterbalance the patronage and influence of the Council which were daily at work in its support? The Revenue Dispute led Howe to believe that there should be entrusted

---

[10]Ibid., January 28, 1830.
[11]Ibid., January 21, 1830.

as little power to do evil to the Council as to the House, because the great principles of human nature operate as invincibly in one end of a stone building as in the other; making men . . . singularly indulgent to measures which deeply concern themselves.[12]

Subsequently he lost no opportunity to record the ills resulting from the loss of the Appropriation Act. The roads, he pointed out, were becoming so bad through lack of maintenance that trade was being hampered. Everywhere on his "Rambles" he found the Assembly warmly applauded; the Councillors, he said, would find themselves beaten in the constitutional argument by every farmer upon the road.

In the general election which followed Howe advised the electorate to return the old members because of their stand on the Revenue question. None followed more closely than he the campaign in the Township and County of Halifax. The sitting members for the Township, Charles Rufus Fairbanks and Beamish Murdock, had both opposed the Council on the Revenue question. But in contrast with Fairbanks, Murdock had been altogether outspoken in his condemnation. The outcome was his defeat by merchant Stephen DeBlois, the nominee of the Council. Howe duly noted that Murdock lost because he "had to contend with the whole weight . . . of the Government, which was exerted against him through all sorts of channels."[13]

In the County election Howe supported the four sitting members, even Hartshorne, who had defended the Council on the Revenue question. But in this instance the electorate had other ideas. It linked Hartshorne with the three Council nominees, and coupled Jotham Blanchard with the other three sitting members as anti-Council men. Howe himself did not support Blanchard, yet more and more he had begun to respect the Pictonian's opinions and talents. Certainly Blanchard's comments on power were not lost on him:

> Power is of various kinds; there is the power of wealth and the power of office, and when these are combined with executive power and the power of legislation, any one may see that there is a dangerous and unconstitutional combination. . . . Against such a state of things I have contended and shall still contend; for where great powers are coupled with irresponsibility, there can be no security—no good government. Such a government cannot and ought not to exist.[14]

In Halifax itself all the pro-Council candidates secured substantial majorities. But when polling moved to the District of Colchester, matters were quite different. Almost unanimously its voters rejected the Council's candidates. Later the freeholders of Pictou divided fairly evenly on religious grounds, thus ensuring the return of Blanchard and his colleagues.

To Howe the election of 1830 was a glorious victory. He was elated that of 12 new Assemblymen only DeBlois was pledged to support the

---

[12]Ibid., May 27, 1830.

[13]Ibid., September 23, 1830.

[14]Ibid., September 15, 1830.

Council. Yet despite Blanchard's instruction, he was still naïve enough to suppose that an Assembly which had opposed one outrageous act of the Council would be similarly exercised in less extreme cases; he was sanguine enough to believe that the British government would hearken to the people's representatives, whenever they disagreed with the Council; he still considered parties to be nothing more than factions operating in their own and against the public interest; he wanted to belong to only one party, "the party of Nova Scotia."

The year 1831 added little to Howe's political thinking. But it did provide one of those "breathers" which he always welcomed as respites from the consideration of complex problems. While events in Europe especially intrigued him, he found time to expatiate on his first love, his native province. Once he turned vehemently upon William Cobbett, whose *Rural Rides* had given him the idea for his own "Rambles." Cobbett's fault had been to describe Nova Scotia as "heaps of rocks, covered with fir-trees, for the greater part, with a few narrow strips of clear land in the bottoms of the valleys." This was altogether too much for Howe; in his opinion Cobbett's "shameless disregard of truth—his want of fixed principles . . . would have made shipwreck of even a more commanding genius."[15] Howe pointed out that unprecedented fruitfulness presently crowned Nova Scotian agriculture, while commerce had so expanded that every wharf in Halifax from the Lumber Yard to the Dock Yard was being repaired or extended.

By 1832 Howe had established what was to be his normal pattern of publication. Early each year he would exult in the success of the *Novascotian*, especially because "the effusions of our Henrys, Edwins, Albyns, and Alvars, would often have done credit to a London periodical." Just before the Legislature opened he would present his own views on public affairs. During the sessions he would personally report between 150 and 200 columns of debate. By 1834 he could boast that he had written as much manuscript as he could carry and that without it the people would have been "about as incapable of judging the conduct of their Representatives, as if they had assembled in the moon."[16] The session concluded, he was delighted to be "no longer constrained like a Tanner's horse, to one unvarying round. . . ." With zest he would turn to the books, magazines, pamphlets, and newspapers which had been accumulating on his desk. Then, following a short respite, he would review the past session, singling out its shortcomings.

In 1832 the Legislature gave Howe comparatively little to complain about. In fact, he showed as much interest in the courts as in the Legislature. He was utterly contemptuous of the Court of Chancery, "where neither party receives justice [and] where enormous costs accumulate, until the whole cause of action is swallowed up." Against Simon Bradstreet Robie, who as Master of the Rolls presided over the Court of Chancery, he levelled the harshest criticism he had ever accorded any public functionary. Earlier, as Speaker of the Assembly, Robie had de-

---

[15]Ibid., September 28, 1831.
[16]Ibid., April 23, 1834.

nounced petty abuses; yet for seven years he had kept up a body of costly absurdities without making a single effort towards reform. Others, said Howe, might be equally guilty, but unlike Robie, *"they never pretended to be reformers."*[17]

Despite this occasional vehemence, however, the impression left by the *Novascotian* during these years is one of general satisfaction with matters governmental. Howe's suggestion to the Assemblymen before the session of 1833 certainly made no reference to any deep-seated ills. But the session utterly disappointed him, and thereafter a new severity crept into his tone. Much more, he reminded the Assemblymen, had been involved in the election of 1830 than a duty upon brandy. They themselves had begged to be returned to deal with gross defects in the constitution. Admittedly the Council had, of late, been circumspect in dealing with the appropriations and the revenue. But who "would sleep by Vesuvius, merely because some former explosion had for the moment abated its force"?

It was the currency issue, however, which completed Howe's political education. Like no previous issue it laid bare the complex forces at work in Nova Scotian society. For years an important medium of exchange had been the provincial Treasury notes, which had often been redeemable for specie. When the Halifax Banking Company was formed without legislative sanction in 1825, it was looked upon with suspicion. But it conducted its operations circumspectly, and frequently it would redeem its own paper. Nevertheless, Howe had long noted that five of its directors were Councillors and wondered if the public interest would suffer as a result. In 1832 he had welcomed the legislative incorporation of the Bank of Nova Scotia because it would divide the monied influence. But he was annoyed when the Assembly accepted the Council's demand that the new Bank redeem its notes in specie. It perturbed him to see Jotham Blanchard acting in concert with Stephen DeBlois on this matter. Some Assemblymen, he noted, were moved like puppets by wires from the other end of the building.

The new Bank soon had its own innings; it made a run on the old, forcing it to suspend the redemption of its notes. The outcome was a depreciated currency. In 1833 the Assembly tried to force both banks to return to cash payments, but the Council objected. By this time many Assemblymen had returned home, and those who remained eventually accepted what Howe described as a disgraceful solution: they permitted both banks to issue non-redeemable paper. The result was to destroy the little sound currency which remained. In no uncertain terms Howe told the Assembly what the country expected of it. On its return it should forthwith "restore the currency to a just and sound condition, *though [it] should have to sit till mid summer, and even though another year's revenue should be the necessary sacrifice."*[18]

The economic distress was considered at a public meeting in Halifax on January 16, 1834. To a major resolution Stephen DeBlois proposed an

---

[17]Ibid., September 19, 1832.
[18]Ibid., December 11, 1833.

amendment which would have provided an "out" for the Assemblymen who had opposed sound monetary principles. This prompted Howe to deliver his first political address. He willingly admitted that a debased currency was not the only reason for the economic difficulties; certainly "there had been too much of idleness and extravagance in the community"; but the first step towards improvement was a sound currency. So he strongly and successfully opposed DeBlois's "red herring."

The session of 1834 further increased Howe's irritation with the Assembly. The British government had proposed to commute the quit rents in return for a suitable establishment for the public officers and the judges. Howe's own position was unequivocal. Quit rents ought to be commuted unconditionally; Nova Scotia was prepared to do justice to its public servants. But in five days of debates he saw no evidence of "those honest views of *justice* and *economy*, which the *circumstances*, and *feelings*, and *prospects* of the country ought to prompt."[19]

So strongly was he aroused that he embarked almost immediately on a vigorous discussion of the state of the province. In his opinion "gentleman merchants," "gentleman mechanics," and "gentleman farmers" had no place in Nova Scotia. Yet the whole tendency of a garrison society like Halifax was towards habits of idleness. The high salaries of the public officers were equally pernicious; even at the hazard of bankruptcy the industrious classes tended to imitate their style of living. Unfortunately, each village also contained a little knot of traders, lawyers, and public officers, through whom the fashionable follies of the capital were reflected upon the surrounding country where even the most affluent farmer was lucky to clear £100 a year. Yet this was the society upon which the British government sought to impose salaries which were double those of comparable officials in England. Howe told the people that the outcome of this issue depended upon themselves. Until now, he said with satisfaction, he had rarely found them to fail in their duty when they were properly informed. This faith in the ordinary Nova Scotian he was to retain throughout his life.

A more and more belligerent Howe had his worst fears of the prevailing system confirmed early in 1835. For publishing a letter which alleged that during the preceding 30 years "the Magistracy and Police [of Halifax] ha[d], by one stratagem or other, taken from the pockets of the people, in over exactions, fines, etc.-etc., a sum that would exceed in the gross amount £30,000,"[20] he was prosecuted for criminal libel. Through his own unaided efforts he secured an acquittal. "The Press of Nova-Scotia," he proudly proclaimed, "is free." He hoped that, with the light of day permitted to penetrate the municipal institutions, the work of reformation might begin. But that was not to be. The Council appointed a man of such dubious reputation as Custos of the County of Halifax that any prospect of reform was doomed from the beginning.

Hence, when Howe discussed "Halifax and Its Prospects," in August, he painted a thoroughly bleak picture. Look at the faulty structure of the

---

[19]Ibid., March 20, 1834.
[20]Ibid., January 2, 1835.

Council! Look at the oversized judicial establishment! Look at the great string of public officers, who took so much of the revenue that they were "in truth our masters"! Look at the Assembly, in which the lawyers led a time-serving and obedient majority! The only remedy was an energetic and public-spirited Assembly which would bring "the sentiments of the Country . . . to bear upon the rottenness of Denmark." This was not possible unless the people lost their supineness. In future let the free-holders assemble and select candidates on the basis of qualifications and principles; let these candidates be told that if they abandon these principles they will be replaced.

Howe expressed himself in a similar vein to Jotham Blanchard. The letter is interesting because it indicates a reversal in the positions of the two men since 1828. For some time Howe had been expressing doubts about Blanchard's political conduct; "there was good reason," he said, "to suspect you of becoming if not a covert enemy to popular measures at least a very suspicious and languid supporter of the principles you had always professed." Hence he felt relieved to discover that it was the state of Blanchard's health which had deprived him of the energy which the times demanded. No reforms, Howe continued, could be effected "without a majority pledged to the people, and kept in salutary awe of them in the Assembly."[21]

A by-election for the Township of Halifax late in the year permitted Howe to develop these ideas further. In Halifax itself, he pointed out, past elections had often been decided by a few public officers and wealthy merchants over their wine. Howe begged the ordinary voter not to succumb this time to their sinister influence or to their rum and porter. Before the by-election Howe's opponents interpreted his every act as motivated by a desire to get into the Assembly. "I could not go out to shoot a partridge in the woods or catch a Trout in the streams," he said, "without being suspected of canvassing for the next election." For the moment he expressed his satisfaction with the candidature of Hugh Bell, but it had become quite evident that he would not long delay an attempt to get into the Assembly.

As the year 1836 advanced, Howe had good reason for elation. No longer did he feel as if he were addressing strangers. "We sit in our Editorial chair," he said, "as if in the midst of a family." Public opinion, he felt, was finally beginning to act upon the Legislature. Had not the Council commenced printing its Journals? Had not the Assembly resolved that the fees exacted by the Chief Justice were unconstitutional? It also pleased him, as the dissolution of the Assembly became imminent, that election cards were no longer short documents in which the candidates made vague promises to behave well if elected; almost without exception the new-style cards stated the broad principles which would govern the candidates' conduct. Furthermore, in more than one county candidates were proposed at public meetings. It was three such meetings in the Musquodoboit Valley which endorsed Howe as a candi-

---

[21]Howe Papers, vol. 6, Howe to Blanchard, October 26, 1835.

date for the County of Halifax because of "his known political principles."

Thomas Chandler Haliburton had already warned Howe about the perils of going into the Assembly:

> I do think you won't advance your own interest or influence by going there. Why does a Judge's charge have more influence than an Attorney's speech? Because he belongs to *no side*. I fear your paper (always enough on one side of politics) will be thought after your election (for that I take for granted if you offer) a party paper altogether. I fear you will hurt it, and it will hurt you, like a gig that runs over a cow, it kills the animal and breaks the carriage.[22]

But as Howe told his sister,

> conceiving certain improvements to be essential to the welfare of the country of our birth, I ought to strive to get them introduced—and being under great obligations to many thousands who have aided and protected me in my designs, I ought not to shrink from any sacrifice of time and labor to pay the debt.

Furthermore, the Legislature would be "an admirable school" for his own development.

When Howe announced the dissolution of the Assembly on October 27, he reminded his readers that for more than five years he had tried to create "a virtuous and enlightened public sentiment." Now it was their duty to choose well. Those Assemblymen who had invariably followed reform principles should be returned; otherwise let genuinely public meetings propose suitable candidates.[23]

At a meeting endorsing his own candidature on November 9, he admitted that his position as Assemblyman would engross "all the little leisure" which his occupation permitted. Yet he did not wish to grow old and leave the redress of grievances to the next generation. All his efforts to arouse the people would prove useless "unless a majority [was] formed in the Assembly which will follow out a system of rational reform. . . . If suitable materials for combining that majority were more abundant, I should not have ventured out of the ordinary paths of my profession." Some were worried that he might neglect his business; at that he laughed: "one who has been accustomed to labor from boyhood . . . is not very suddenly likely to become negligent of his private affairs." And what if he were defeated? "I shall return to my books—and spend the little leisure which business affords, with the Poets, Philosophers and Historians; who, as they delighted and informed my youth, I trust have a chance to cheer and solace my old age."

For what were he and his friends contending? Simply the free institutions of Britain:

> In England, one vote of the people's representatives turns out a ministry. . . . Here, we may record five hundred votes against our ministry and

---

[22]Haliburton to Howe, November 15, 1835.
[23]*Novascotian*, November 17, 1836.

> yet they sit unmoved. . . . In England the people can breathe the breath of life into their government whenever they please; in this country the government is like an ancient Egyptian, wrapped up in narrow and antique prejudices—dead and inanimate, but yet likely to last forever. . . .
>
> Gentlemen, all we ask for is what exists at home—a system of responsibility to the people.[24]

In these words Howe stated more clearly what he wanted than in any previous utterance.

Howe ended his speech on a note of warning. Let the reformers not split up into parties like their counterparts in England. That could result only in a disastrous wasting of their strength.

In the actual voting Howe was an easy victor. On being declared elected, he gave a pledge that "truth, and open and candid dealing"—his guides of the past—would be his guides in the future. Above all, he would follow the teaching of his recently deceased father; he would respect his fellow creatures and do them good.[25]

The years 1828 to 1836 coincided with the latter part of the so-called intellectual awakening of Nova Scotia. For rousing his countrymen out of their political lethargy no one was more responsible than Howe; by the mid-thirties he was well on his way to becoming the educator in public affairs of his native province. But it would be wrong to regard him as the typical colonial Reformer of the 1830s. Until the mid-thirties he conceived the basic task of Nova Scotians largely in non-political terms. The qualities needed to make Nova Scotia the model colony were industry, frugality, and a thirst for knowledge. Circumstances made him a supporter of the *status quo,* and the label of mild Tory is an apt one.

By 1830 the Pictou Scribblers had forced him to recognize a few political imperfections even in the happy land of Nova Scotia. The conduct of the Council on the Revenue question was something of an eye-opener to him; yet the specific issue was solved so readily that he failed to appreciate the forces which were operating in Nova Scotia. It required a whole series of incidents, starting with the currency issue in 1833, to make him realize that the merchant office clique which controlled the Council could pull sufficient strings to manipulate all the provincial institutions as they pleased. By 1835 he had fully grasped the nature of the power complex in Nova Scotia. He concluded that, although the physical resources of the province and the generally sound qualities of its citizenry assured continued progress, yet the defects of the governmental structure would inevitably slow it down.

What was the remedy? It was to introduce the responsibility of the British system, although not necessarily an exact copy of British institutions. For the moment Howe felt that the setting up of an elective Legislative Council would do the trick; apparently two elective Houses would constitute an adequate check upon the advisers of the Governor and the provincial bureaucracy.

How was this remedy to be achieved? The first step was to elect the

---

[24]Ibid., December 21, 1836.
[25]Ibid.

right type of Assembly. Let the freeholders assemble in public meetings and propose candidates on the basis of the principles they professed. The assumption was that the ordinary Nova Scotian freeholder would speak almost as one for liberal principles and against an entrenched oligarchy. Thus the curious feature about Howe at this stage was his attitude towards political parties. In the manner of Halifax, Bolingbroke, and George Washington, he still regarded them as selfish factions. Somewhat like Charles de Gaulle, he was in 1836 advocating a rally of the Nova Scotian people which would stand entirely above faction. Because there was a scarcity of persons who had the capacity to persuade the reforming Assemblymen to combine for the public good, he was induced to enter the Assembly.

Once there, and face to face with practicality, the untypical reformer saw the basic problem through entirely different spectacles. So when the Durham Report recommended a responsible executive on the British model in 1839, Howe welcomed the proposal. It took somewhat longer for him to agree on the only possible method of effecting this remedy. Not until the breakdown of a coalition with the Tories in 1843 did he accept the absolute necessity of a disciplined Reform Party as the prerequisite to reform. Thus, step by step, he had been induced almost against his will to don all the trappings of the typical colonial reformer of his day.

30

AMERICAN CULTURE AND THE CONCEPT OF MISSION IN 19TH CENTURY ENGLISH CANADA*

Allan Smith

British North America existed to the north of an extremely dynamic, vigorous, and expanding nation, the United States of America. This fact was not easily ignored or forgotten. Men descended from Loyalists remembered the United States in one context. Continual border troubles with the Americans called the United States to mind in another context. One war and the threat of several others were part of the experience of all British North Americans. The United States was a constant threat, but also a continual example. As the Americans found and developed a distinctly national culture in the first half of the 19th century, their neighbours to the north both feared that culture's impact on their own and found it useful for their own purposes. The attitude of British North Americans to the United States was then—as always—one of ambivalence.

In the following article, Allan Smith explores the relationship of American culture to English-speaking Canadians in terms of one of the most powerful ideas of the period, the notion of mission. Although "Manifest Destiny" was a word of later coinage, the Americans always believed in theirs. Surprisingly enough, however, British North Americans also had a sense of mission. How did American culture influence British North America? What distinctions did Canadians make between their culture and that of the Americans? Did British America transform American ideas in a significant way, or merely mimic them in slightly different circumstances?

Canadian Historical Association Historical Papers (1971), 169-182.

SUGGESTIONS FOR FURTHER READING

J. M. S. Careless, *The Union of the Canadas: The Growth of Canadian Institutions 1841-1857* (Toronto: McClelland and Stewart, 1967).

Peter Russell, ed., *Nationalism in Canada* (Toronto: McGraw-Hill, 1966).

S. F. Wise and Robert Craig Brown, *Canada Views the United States: Nineteenth Century Political Attitudes* (Seattle and London: University of Washington Press, 1967).

J.M.B.

I

A society's sense of mission rests upon the belief that it has been charged by God or history with the performance of some great task. Islamic civilization saw itself chosen by God as the instrument by which His plans for mankind, revealed to the prophet Mohammed, would be realized throughout the world. Its violent encounters with the people of Africa, Europe, and the East became triumphal stages in the great *jihad* Allah required it to prosecute. "As for their victories and their battles," wrote the writer of *Al Fakhri* in satisfied contemplation of the wonders wrought by the Prophet's followers, "verily their cavalry reached Africa and the uttermost parts of Khurasan and crossed the Oxus."[1] In time the historical process itself came to be viewed as the agency responsible for issuing the call to action. It was Lenin's conviction that history had selected the peasants and proletariat of Russia, acting in temporary alliance through their soon to be established dictatorship, to "carry the revolutionary conflagration into Europe"[2] and thereby begin the remaking of the world. The peculiar attributes held to be associated with each society's special character, in the view of their beholders admirably equipping the society possessing them for the performance of its task, became proof that that task was indeed its to fulfil. The lightning strength of the Islamic invaders itself seemed to justify their programme: it must be for them to act as they did for had they not been given the capacity? To Lenin, paradoxically, the very backwardness of Russia offered revolutionary socialism its initial opportunity and gave the Russian people the chance to play a great role in history.

A people's understanding of its special character and of the mission whose fulfillment that character validates and makes possible has frequently arisen from the manner in which meaning is attached to its location in space. From antiquity men have supposed that climate and geography did much to make them what they were.[3] A long line of mod-

---

[1] Cited in Christopher Dawson, *The Making of Europe* (New York: Meridian Books, 1958), p. 134. Dawson refers to the "intense religious enthusiasm" of the Moslems which made the Holy War "a supreme act of consecration and self-sacrifice." Ibid., p. 133.

[2] Cited in Leon Trotsky, *Stalin: An Appraisal of the Man and His Influence*, ed. and trans. Charles Malamuth (New York: Harper and Brothers, 1941), p. 424.

[3] J. W. Johnson, "Of Differing Ages and Climes," *Journal of the History of Ideas*, (October–December, 1960), pp. 465–80.

ern thinkers, beginning with Montesquieu, has similarly postulated the existence of links between environment and the character of nations.

A society's location in space may do more than inspire its sense of character and mission. It may also sharpen and refine that sense. To be located in a strange and new land may be to become more fully alive to the responsibilities one bears as the representative of a special and chosen society. In such a land, one functions on behalf of those things for which his order stands in especially challenging and difficult circumstances.

The sense of mission and responsibility held by the Spanish and Portuguese was clearly heightened by the opening of the New World. The discovery of that place, heathenish, yet wealthy and inhabited by God's creatures, made more urgent the business of extending the sway of the culture and civilization whose leading representatives they felt themselves to be.

For 300 years before the rise of creolism and the sense of estrangement from the Old World that accompanied it, they took it as their duty to incorporate the land in which they had been placed into the life of the land from which they had come. What was implied by the spirit in which they undertook the colonizing process, writes one observer, was not "the annexation of terra incognita, but the bringing together of what should rightfully be joined."[4] Another concurs: "The Spaniards who left Spain had not migrated initially in an act of independence; they came to America in the service of the Crown and the Church."[5]

The French of New France shared this perspective. It was theirs, they thought, to extend in the New World the French and Christian civilization whose creatures they were. "I came," wrote Champlain, "to the conclusion that I would be doing very wrong if I did not work to find some means to [introduce New France] to the knowledge of God."[6] And that knowledge was not to be drawn from some new and purer form of the old faith but from the old faith itself. Their activities controlled from the imperial metropolis, clergy, fur traders, and government officials alike functioned as its agents. They moved at the edge of the Empire, sometimes for reasons very much their own, but did not in the end feel themselves divorced from its centre.

Those Englishmen who came to live in America likewise found their sense of mission affected by their removal to a new world. What resulted in their case, however, was different than that yielded by the experience of the continental Europeans. The English in America did not consider that their position in the New World imposed upon them an obligation to hurry its incorporation into the Old. They did not see it as their divinely

---

[4]Richard M. Morse, "The Heritage of Latin America," in Louis Hartz, et al., *The Founding of New Societies: Studies in the History of the United States, Latin America, South Africa, Canada, and Australia* (New York: Harbinger Books, 1964), p. 152.

[5]Germán Arciniegas, *Latin America: A Cultural History* (New York: Alfred A. Knopf, 1967), p. xxv.

[6]Cited in Morris Bishop, *Champlain: The Life of Fortitude* (Carleton Library; Toronto: McClelland and Stewart, 1963), p. 183.

appointed task to function as the agents of the civilization from which they came. They moved instead to escape the confines of that civilization until they might return to it on their own terms. Their task was to create in the free and uncorrupted New World a Christian society untouched by the impure influences of the Old. Theirs would be a society which might act as an inspiration to all of mankind and even, in the course of time, regenerate the civilization whose offspring its makers were. And so, where Champlain strove to introduce the principles of French and Catholic culture into the New World, John Winthrop set himself the task of establishing a new and exemplary form of human society, one that would function, in his famous phrase, "as a city upon a hill."

II

More, clearly, went into the making of the view the English and the Europeans had of themselves in the New World than the stimulus offered by life in that world. However strong and powerful that stimulus might be, it did not act uniformly on those exposed to it. It could not prevent these peoples from extracting a different meaning from the signal circumstance which brought them into contact with it. What determined that this should be so was the fact that each of them was accompanied on its journey across the Atlantic by more than an undifferentiated capacity to react to a fresh new land. Each brought with it a way of seeing the world. In the end it was its highly articulated manner of viewing reality which determined the fashion in which each reacted to the lands of the western hemisphere.[7]

The Spanish and Portuguese were men of the medieval world. They knew no challenge to the unity of Catholic civilization and authority. The English who crossed the Atlantic were products of a different age. With them came new modes of social organization, new economic forces, and a modern spirit. What they brought with them shaped their attitude to the world they left behind. It made them impatient with its traditions and anxious to be active. It made them knowledgeable of communities apart, for in their experience the unity of medieval Christendom was no more and men stood divided from one another. It helped, in the words of a Latin American historian, "to create a dynamic heritage contrasting with the relatively static heritage of the longer established Spanish-

---

[7]For a clear and concise account, by an historian, of the manner in which the cultural environment operates in the shaping of a society's outlook, see David M. Potter, *People of Plenty: Economic Abundance and the American Character*, 9th impression (Chicago: Phoenix Books, 1965), especially part 1, "The Study of National Character," pp. 3–74; for an account by two sociologists of the influence exerted by culture in the formation of ideas, see Peter L. Berger and Thomas Luckmann, *The Social Construction of Reality: A Treatise in the Sociology of Knowledge* (Anchor Books edition; Garden City, N.Y.: Doubleday, 1967); for a brief history of the concept of ideology, see George Lichtheim, "The Concept of Ideology," *History and Theory*, 4 vols. (1965), vol. 2, pp. 164–95. Potter's account is straightforward and uncluttered; Berger and Luckmann argue for a new understanding of the sociology of knowledge; Lichtheim is concerned with what they would consider merely one branch of it; but all make the simple and basic point upon which the argument in this paper turns: the cultural environment in which men live shapes the manner in which they perceive their universe.

American."[8] In short, it distinguished the English in America from their Latin neighbours and made them feel much less closely linked to Europe.

Even more than the shape of their parent cultures was involved in the process by which these people acquired their understanding of their character and role as New World societies. Of great significance was the relationship each bore to that culture. The attitudes enjoined by the relationship themselves became primary components in the world view articulated by each of these peoples.

The English arrived as men alienated from their society. They had left their land in protest. Their goal, as Winthrop reminded his fellows, was to establish a society based on true Christian principle. In that sense it would be a new society, to be distinguished in the most basic of ways from that out of which it had come.[9]

The French and the *peninsulares,* by contrast, did not cross the Atlantic as men estranged from the culture that gave them birth. They came as the agents of a power and civilization whose values they accepted and wished to promote. Only in time, with the ideas of the Enlightenment, the example of revolutionary France and America, the rise of indigenous elites, and the collapse of the Bourbons before them did the societies of Latin America learn to reject the world from which they came.[10] Their French and Catholic neighbours to the north never did reject it. They did not think the chasm that yawned between them and their parent society after the 18th century to be of their making. They considered themselves to have been abandoned by a power which first gave them up and then launched itself upon the path of revolution.

At the centre of their sense of mission through the 19th and into the 20th centuries was the conviction that they must keep alive in the New World the old faith of Catholic Europe. "The mission with which Providence entrusted French Canadians," wrote Mgr. L.-F.-R. Laflèche in

---

[8]Irving A. Leonard, "Introduction," Mariano Picón-Salas, *A Cultural History of Spanish America from Conquest to Independence,* trans. Irving A. Leonard (Berkeley and Los Angeles: University of California Press, 1965), p. x.

[9]For a classic account of the manner in which Winthrop and his colleagues viewed their situation in America, see Perry Miller, "Errand into the Wilderness," in his *Errand into the Wilderness* (Harper Torchbooks: New York: Harper & Row, 1964), pp. 1-15. For a brief yet comprehensive examination of the American concept of mission, see Russel B. Nye, "The American Sense of Mission," in his *This Almost Chosen People: Essays in the History of American Ideas* (Toronto: Macmillan, 1966), pp. 164-207. For a lengthier treatment of the same theme, see Albert K. Weinberg, *Manifest Destiny: A Study of Nationalist Expansion in American History* (Encounter Paperbacks; Chicago: Quadrangle Books, 1963). For a reply to Weinberg, see Frederick Merk, *Manifest Destiny and Mission in American History* (Vintage Books, New York: Random House, 1966). Recent writers, without denying the proposition that Americans felt themselves apart from the Old World, have emphasized the extent of their involvement with that world's culture. See Frank Thistlewaite, *America and the Atlantic Community: Anglo-American Aspects, 1790-1850* (New York: Harper Torchbooks, 1963); Howard Mumford Jones, *O Strange New World, American Culture: The Formative Years* (New York: Viking Press, 1967); Robert Kelley, *The Transatlantic Persuasion: The Liberal-Democratic Mind in the Age of Gladstone* (New York: Alfred A. Knopf, 1969); and Robert O. Mead, *The Atlantic Legacy: Essays in American-European Cultural History* (New York: New York University Press, 1969).

[10]"The independence proclaimed in the *Mayflower* Compact of 1620," writes one observer, "was not formulated in Hispano-Indian America until 1810." Arciniegas, *Latin America.*

1866, "is basically religious in nature: it is, namely, to convert the unfortunate infidel local population to Catholicism, and to expand the Kingdom of God by developing a predominantly Catholic nationality."[11] It was of particular importance to resist the materialist perfectionism implicit in the New World ethic. Central to the Ultramontane persuasion was the notion that the New World could not be seen as a place apart. Men there were not different from other men. They were not above the laws of nature, remade by their sojourn in the New World, and able to set aside the constraints which had made their fellows on the other side of the Atlantic selfish and sinful. Their lives, accordingly, must be regulated by the same truths which had regulated them in the Old World. It was the special duty of French Canada to make clear what those truths were. This did not mean a total rejection of materialism: as Mgr. L.-A. Paquet observed in 1902, concern with material things had its place.[12] What it did indicate was a clear reluctance to commit French Canada to unqualified acceptance of the idea that the New World possessed a special and distinctive character. "We have the privilege," said Mgr. Paquet, "of being entrusted with [the] social priesthood granted only to select peoples. I cannot doubt that this religious and civilizing mission is the true vocation and the special vocation of the French race in America. . . . Our mission is less to handle capital than to stimulate ideas; less to light the furnaces of factories than to maintain and spread the glowing fires of religion and thought, and to help them cast their light into the distance."[13]

III

English Canadians, like other men in the New World, developed a conviction that they had a special mission to fulfil. Like that of their neighbours, their sense of mission owed much to the fact that those who framed it were acutely conscious of their location in space. And it too was modified by the cultural environment in which its makers operated.

The principal and overriding fact shaping the outlook of those Englishmen who first came to the northern part of North America was their reverence for continuity, tradition, and properly constituted authority. The Western world was passing through a great upheaval. That upheaval had sundered the unity of the Empire and introduced dangerous principles of government to men on both sides of the Atlantic. Those who came to British North America, whether as Loyalists or immigrants from Britain, brought with them an outlook at the core of which was a determination that the pernicious and destructive doctrine which rested on those principles must be resisted. Their task was to erect on the North American continent a bulwark against this formidable cancer of the body

---

[11]Mgr. L.-F.-R. Laflèche, *Quelques Considerations sur les rapports de la société civile avec la religion et la famille* (Trois Rivières, 1866), cited in Ramsay Cook, ed., *French Canadian Nationalism: An Anthology* (Toronto: Macmillan of Canada, 1969), p. 98.

[12]Mgr. L.-A. Paquet "Sermon sur la vocation de la race française en Amérique," cited in ibid., p. 158.

[13]Ibid., p. 154.

politic. It was for them to recreate in this territory a society governed by modalities the very image and transcript of those at the heart of the British constitution.

Striking and incontrovertible proof that this was indeed their mission was offered, they thought, by their success in maintaining a precarious existence next to their expanding republican neighbour. British North America had been placed under a severe test in the first years of its existence. Its people had been cajoled and threatened and finally invaded. But they had not yielded nor given up the true faith. For one of them especially there was a deep lesson in British North America's demonstrated capacity to endure. To John Strachan, as S. F. Wise has pointed out, "the miraculous survival of tiny Upper Canada was a North American testimony to God's gracious dealings with those whom he designed especially to prosper."[14] It was a clear and dramatic indication that they were His agents in the New World.

Strachan's sense of his community as an outpost of British civilization and a bastion of the true faith was shared by other British North Americans. Montreal's *Canadian Review and Literary and Historical Journal* noted in 1824 that the special character of the British American provinces derived from the fact that they, "unlike most other appendages of the Empire",[15] were almost wholly inhabited by natives of Great Britain or their descendants. They thus possessed "the same moral and political sentiments"[16] and cherished "the same domestic and national feelings as their fathers and their ancient kindred."[17] Culture in Canada, when at last it developed, would surely function as a branch "of that venerable tree of art and science which has from old spread its fruits and its shelter over so great a portion of the world."[18]

The *Canadian Magazine,* published at York, found British North America in the 1830s in process of becoming a mirror image of European society. It was, in fact,

> Europe, with only one difference—means to gratify a love of reading, and intellectual acquirement—That difficulty is about to be surmounted, and then the resemblance will be complete.[19]

At mid-century the *Anglo-American Magazine* told its readers how appropriate it was

> That we should rejoice over the triumph of civilization, the onward progress of our race, the extension of our language, institutions, tastes, manners, customs and feelings. . . . The genius of Britain presides over the destiny of her offspring—the glory of the Empire enshrouds the prosperity of its Colony—the noble courage and strength of the Lion inspires and protects the

---

[14]S. F. Wise, "Sermon Literature and Canadian Intellectual History," *The Bulletin of the Committee on Archives of the United Church of Canada,* 18 (1965), 15.

[15]"Quebec Literary and Historical Society," *The Canadian Review and Literary and Historical Journal,* no. 1 (July 1824), 3.

[16]Loc. cit.

[17]Loc. cit.

[18]Ibid., 2.

[19]*Canadian Magazine,* I (1) January 1833, 1.

industry of the Beaver—the Oak and the Maple unite their shadow over breasts which beat in unison for the common weal.[20]

British culture and civilization was the *élan vital*. The job of men in the wilderness was to unleash its power as quickly and fully as possible. There must be no compromise between the culture of the Old World and that of the New. The one did not need purification by the clean air of the other. The culture of the Old World might indeed be altered by the atmosphere of the New. But the growth yielded by this process would be strange and abnormal. It was not therefore to be encouraged. What should be encouraged was a reaffirmation of the vitality and relevance of the Old World and its culture.

This view of British North America's character and mission, possible only so long as the cultural milieu which shaped it retained a powerful grip on the Canadian mind, was not to endure. As American culture and ideas flowed northwards into Canada English Canadians came increasingly to form their ideas of what was signified by their location in space in terms of that variant of the New World idea which was most fully articulated in the United States. They came to view themselves not as the agent of an Old World culture charged with civilizing the New, but as men uplifted and restored by their New World environment whose duty it was to regenerate the Old.

No small part in this process was played by the massive and continuing entry of American publications into 19th-century Canada. With them came that vision of life's meaning which reposed at the centre of American culture. It found itself in time positioned to do in Canada what it did in the United States: mediate the experience and shape the understanding of those exposed to it.

The entry of these publications was as visible as its consequences were momentous. William Lyon Mackenzie noted in the early 19th century that "In many parts of Canada, and New Brunswick, the United States journals have an extensive circulation . . . "[21] In the 1850s the traveller Isabella Bishop observed the tendency of Canadians to read American literature: "Cheap American novels", she wrote, "often of a very objectionable tendency, are largely circulated among the lower classes . . . "[22] At Confederation D'Arcy McGee drew attention to the manner in which Boston functioned as the cultural metropolis for Montreal. Take a thousand, he suggested, of our most intelligent citizens, and, while you will find Montreal unknown among them as an intellectual community, half will have been swayed by Boston books and Boston utterances.[23] Twenty years later, in an article entitled "American

---

[20]"The Cities of Canada: Toronto," *Anglo-American Magazine*, I (1) July 1852, 1.

[21]"A Letter to England by Peter Russell," *Colonial Advocate*, April 6, 1826. Cited in Margaret Fairley, ed., *The Selected Writings of William Lyon Mackenzie, 1824–1837* (Toronto: Oxford University Press, 1960), p. 116. "Peter Russell" was a pseudonym used by Mackenzie.

[22]Isabella Bishop, *The Englishwoman in America* (London, 1856), cited in G. M. Craig, ed., *Early Travellers in the Canadas, 1791–1867*. Pioneer Books (Toronto: The Macmillan Company of Canada Ltd., 1955), p. 217.

[23]D'Arcy McGee, "The Mental Outfit of the New Dominion," Montreal *Gazette*, November 5, 1867.

Influence on Canadian Thought," Sara Jeanette Duncan argued that more American than British writers were familiar to Canadians. Canadian writing displayed American characteristics. Persons born in Britain might retain an interest in British literature, but "the mass of Canadians" prefer American writing. In short, she concluded, a "great number of American books and magazines . . . find ready readers here."[24]

The presence of these publications, and of the ideas contained in them, insured that Canadians would not for long see the significance of their location in terms similar to those of the Spanish and French who sought to incorporate the lands to the west into the great civilization from which they had come. They would, like Americans, come to see themselves as men free of the constraints imposed by old world civilization and positioned to build a new community.

IV

Some English Canadians adopted with enthusiasm this view of their society's experience and mission. Rebels, Reformers, and Liberals worked vigorously to have their society recognized as one in all essentials distinct from British and European. Canada's mission was to function fully as a community of the New World. It must throw off the trappings of the Old. Having done this, it might then strive to revitalize those decaying societies on the other side of the Atlantic.

William Lyon Mackenzie pronounced it essential that Canada identify itself with the struggle for liberty being waged in America in the 1830s. Nor was his vision limited to North America. Not only were the people of the New World rising up "in stern and awful majesty." It was not "to this country and continent alone, nor chiefly, [that] this revolution [is] confined. It reaches the old world."[25] The New World, free and unencumbered, was reaching out to inspire those who remained in chains across the Atlantic.

Later commentators shared Mackenzie's conviction that it was the destiny of the New World to liberate the Old by showing it what true democracy and freedom could accomplish. From the New World would radiate outwards across the Atlantic knowledge of the principles upon which society must be founded. The idea of involvement with the Old World was not, then, objectionable; indeed it was to be welcomed, for it would allow the New World to fulfil its destiny. But precisely because it was through involvement with the Old World that the New World fulfil its destiny, that involvement had to be of the right kind. It must advance the principles which had come to be associated with life in the New.

"It is," the essayist and historian J. W. Longely wrote in 1882,

---

[24]Sara Jeanette Duncan, "American Influence on Canadian Thought," *The Week,* IV (32) July 7, 1887, 518.

[25]*The Constitution,* July 26, 1837. Cited in Fairley, *The Selected Writings of William Lyon Mackenzie,* pp. 218–19.

the business and mission of the Western Continent to leaven the Old World with the principles of a more enlarged freedom and a juster equality, not to bend its back to the remnants of a feudalism broken but not destroyed, decaying but not extinct. A king, an hereditary aristocracy, and a State Church, would scarcely be congenial to the ideas of a free-born Canadian, who has always enjoyed a universal freedom as broad as the sky, and has imbibed from infancy a notion of equality which would be irritated and galled by closer relations with a country which still preserves privileged order and worships vested interests.[26]

If some Canadians thought it the destiny of their society to communicate to the Old World knowledge of the proper principles upon which society should rest others thought that it could best fulfil its role in the world by serving as a haven for the oppressed. William Norris of Canada First, in the words of Carl Berger, believed that "the North American environment, assisted by liberal institutions, virtually transformed ignorant Europeans into self-reliant and respectful citizens."[27] Because of this belief, he conceived "the ultimate purpose of an independent Canada to be roughly similar to the mission of the United States."[28] As Norris himself put it, independence would enable

> Canada to fulfil her destiny, to be the asylum for the oppressed and downtrodden peoples of European asylum where under their own vine and fig tree, they can live in the enjoyment of happiness and liberty, perpetuating British institutions down to the most remote generation.[29]

V

The manner in which the thought of these men parallelled that doctrine of the New World's significance articulated in the United States is impressive enough; even more illustrative of the power wielded by the American ethos was the fate met by that sense of Canada's mission held by the most imperially minded of her citizens. These were the men whose ancestors had sacrificed much to keep a united Empire. These were the men who were determined to keep the flame of British and monarchical civilization alight in the New World. These were the British North Americans whose sense of mission most closely resembled that of the French and Spanish. These were men who knew they were in the New World but did not at the beginning agree that this fact alone made them unique and set them apart. Yet in time even they were moved to construct a vision of Canada's destiny which turned on the conception that it was indeed a fresh and vital community with qualities that clearly distinguished it.

---

[26]J. W. Longely, "The Future of Canada," *Rose-Belford's Canadian Monthly*, VIII (2) February 1882, 153-54.

[27]Carl Berger, "The Vision of Grandeur: Studies in the Ideas of Canadian Imperialism, 1867-1914" (unpublished Ph.D. thesis, University of Toronto, 1966), p. 147.

[28]Loc. cit.

[29]William Norris, "The Canadian Question," (Montreal, 1875) cited in loc. cit.

By mid-century they had begun to suggest that the strength of Britain might after all be augmented by the peculiar vapours of the New World. The old country, suggested William Kirby in 1846, had denied itself. Its great land-based traditions had collapsed midst the smokestacks of industrialism. It no longer had the special strength necessary to sustain the principles which had made its civilization worthy and honourable. But those same principles, at the heart of which was a reverence for authority, justice, order and a carefully regulated and hierarchically organized society, might find new life in the uncorrupted soil of the New World.[30]

This was far from an assertion that Britain and its institutions were wholly decadent and corrupt. It did not represent a total commitment to the New World idea. But it did involve a clear suggestion that the things most to be valued in British civilization might be restored by the magic of the New World. And so the idea that Canada was destined to serve as an outpost of British culture was combined with a modest and restrained version of the New World myth to produce a new conception of Canada's role and purpose in the world.

A traveller to British North America in 1849 caught the beginnings of this change. The British North American colonies, wrote James Dixon conventionally enough, "will carry out and perpetuate all that is venerable in our system."[31] But then came the new note: the suggestion that there were special and potent forces operating in the New World. England was now, in fact, Dixon asserted, being planted in "new soil," soil which "will reproduce our nation on a gigantic scale."[32]

By the 1880s G. M. Grant, stressing his country's tie with Britain, could take time to point out that it was very much a community of the New World. "We are," he wrote,

> devoted to the monarchical principle, but any aristocracy, save that of genius, worth, or wealth, is as utterly out of the question with us, as with [Americans].[33]

And in 1899 Colonel George Taylor Denison considered that the days of the British race itself might be numbered "unless the new blood in the Colonies, will leaven the mass."[34]

VI

Canadians, then, found their assessment of what duties they had, and what strength they possessed, affected by a particular vision of what life in the Western hemisphere entailed. They found themselves engaged in

---

[30]William Kirby, *The U.E.: A Tale of Upper Canada* (Niagara, 1859).

[31]James Dixon, D. D., *Personal Narrative of a Tour Through a Part of the United States and Canada: with notices of the history and institutions of Methodism in America* (New York, 1849) cited in Craig, *Early Travellers in the Canadas*, p. 171.

[32]Loc. cit.

[33]G. M. Grant, "Canada's Present Position and Outlook," *Rose-Belford's Canadian Monthly*, V (2) August 1880, 198.

[34]Sir Sandford Fleming Papers, Denison to Fleming, May 6, 1899, cited in Carl Berger, *The Sense of Power: Studies in the Ideas of Canadian Imperialism 1867–1914* (Toronto: University of Toronto Press, 1970) 181.

defining their place and role in the world in terms of what they increasingly held to be Canada's quintessential New World character. They found themselves, in short, subscribing to a view of their national destiny which had much in common with that expensive vision articulated so enthusiastically by the people to their south.

There were, of course, differences. The Canadian, for all that he became convinced of his special power and capability as a creature of the New World, could not forget his link with the Old. He could not rest content with a role which involved him merely in acting as a model and source of inspiration for the rest of mankind. He felt himself linked directly to the Old World. He must act directly upon it. He must use his new strength in support of that from which he had come. And so, argued the *Canadian Monthly* in 1877, Canada's

> ultimate destiny is not annexation to the United States or a precarious independence . . . but to be a free British dependency, at once the grateful scion and the faithful potent ally of the mother-stock.[35]

Canada's tie with Britain and its heritage of British institutions made it inevitable that some of its people should conceive of their society in a manner different from that in which Americans conceived of theirs. Its tie with the Old World, they thought, had prevented it from yielding to materialism and vulgarity. Its vitality was uncorrupted by excess. Yet that vitality, though channelled by Old World restraint, remained a gift of the New. It must be used to uplift and regenerate that which had kept it pure and undefiled.

Nowhere was this argument advanced with greater force than in Sara Jeanette Duncan's turn-of-the-century novel *The Imperialist*. Influenced by Henry James in both style and conceptualization, Duncan used her book to explore the tension between the Old World and the New. She examined one way in which the Empire might be revitalized and the growing American influence in Canadian and imperial affairs limited. For Murchison, the novel's protagonist, the answer lay in closer association of the Empire's different parts. Thus strengthened it might withstand American pressure. Canada, now bearing the brunt of that pressure, would certainly find its position improved.

But imperialism would not merely serve and protect Canadian independence in North America. Britain, Murchison was convinced, was in decline. What would revitalize it was a closer association with Canada. Canada, like the United States, was a community of the New World. It was in fact potentially stronger than the United States for it had not let the potent magic of the New World go to its head. The flow of the vital New World juices through its veins had been regulated by the sense of moderation and restraint acquired from its Old World parent. But they remained the juices of the New World. Canada's destiny lay in a supreme activism directed towards allowing them to course unimpeded to the centre of the Empire.

In Murchison himself was the old made new. On the platform to make his speech to the electors of Elgin, he appeared as "a dramatic figure,

---

[35]*Canadian Monthly*, XII (2) August 1877, 198.

standing for the youth and energy of the old blood . . ."[36] He was the man of the Old World, regenerated by his sojourn in the New. Fresh and vigorous and innocent, he was prepared to use his strength and that of his society to regenerate the land from which he had come.

VII

English Canadians, then, came to view their mission as one befitting a society not merely an extension of, but qualitatively different from, those of the Old World. How, indeed, could it have been otherwise? Their point of view was determined by the cultural matrix within which the elements composing it took form. As the character of that matrix changed, the ideas to which it gave rise changed also. English Canadians came, irresistibly, to form the fundamental myths articulating that which was supposedly basic in their national experience in terms of a vision of reality created by another people.

[36]Sara Jeanette Duncan, *The Imperialist* (New Canadian Library; Toronto: McClelland and Stewart, 1961) 229.

part five

The Coming of Confederation

31

HALIFAX NEWSPAPERS AND THE FEDERAL PRINCIPLE, 1864–1865*†

P. B. Waite

The confederation of British North America was hardly the first act of political unification through constitution making on the continent. It was not even the first confederation. The United States had experimented with a Confederacy under the Articles of Confederation from 1781 to 1789. Not happy with the arrangement, the Americans replaced it with the 1789 Federal Constitution, which allowed for a strong and competent national government at the same time, that it perpetuated state governments. As Alexander Hamilton and James Madison argued so brilliantly in the *Federalist Papers*, this was a federal government rather than a confederation, because the national government was more than simply the sum of its constituent parts—although it took a bloody civil war to decide this finally. British North America had the advantage of both the great American debate over ratification and the resultant history of the United States (then engaged in civil war) when it began to consider its own constitutional arrangements. While the discussion waxed heavy in many areas, it was particularly well argued in the Maritimes, for reasons which Professor P. B. Waite considers in the following article. The Maritimes, particularly Halifax, enjoyed a full-scale discussion not only of the practical issues, but of the theoretical ones as well. What were the great constitutional questions raised by the Halifax newspapers? Do they seem to have done justice to the problems raised by the British North America Act? Just how searching was the debate? Why was the force of opposition to Confederation so weak in the newspapers?

Dalhousie Review, 37 (1957), 72-84.

†This article is an abridgement of a paper read before the Nova Scotia Historical Society.

SUGGESTIONS FOR FURTHER READING

P. B. Waite, *The Life and Times of Confederation* (Toronto: University of Toronto Press, 1961).

P. B. Waite, ed., *Confederation Debates* (Toronto: McClelland and Stewart, 1963).

W. M. Whitelaw, *The Maritimes and Canada before Confederation* (Toronto: Oxford University Press, 1934, 1966).

J.M.B.

Confederation came dramatically to the Maritimes in 1864; in August the Canadian legislators and newspapermen appeared in Saint John and Halifax to smooth the way, with Thomas D'Arcy McGee in the van; in September the leaders of the Canadian Government steamed into Charlottetown to offer their scheme of union. Confederation was, suddenly and inexplicably, alive and breathing. It was a vital issue, forced abruptly upon the attention of the Maritimes, and it was brought at once into the forefront of the public press.

In Canada Confederation was a remedy for genuine difficulties, and it tended to have an elevating and even a tranquillizing effect on political life; but in the Maritimes Confederation was the remedy for no particular evils, and it was an issue to be decided on its merits. It promised practical benefits of course, but it offered few practical solutions for Maritime problems. Confederation raised new problems: it did not solve old ones.

In Nova Scotia these new problems erupted quite suddenly in public debate in August 1864 with the first appearance of the Canadian visitors. The debate thus begun filled the pages of the newspapers. In Halifax four of the major newspapers carried an editorial on Confederation in virtually every issue from that time on for over three years. It is the purpose of this paper to discuss this debate with reference to the ideas about federal government that developed out of it. Although economic issues were important, they were not the first to be considered. Nor perhaps is there much profit in exploring the arithmetic that every Halifax newspaper and politician juggled to suit his own argument. What are interesting—in some ways remarkable—are the constitutional and political views that the Halifax newspapers expounded with intelligence and vivacity. These views were developed between October 1864 and January 1865. By April of 1865 the arguments were already beginning to wear thin from hard use.

It should be borne in mind that the Halifax newspapers were not altogether representative of the feeling in the province as a whole. Halifax City and Halifax County supported Confederation more strongly than any other part of the province.[1] Outside Halifax only one newspaper supported Confederation.[2] So that it is the anti-Confederation papers of

---

[1] The election returns for 1867 confirm this.
[2] The Pictou *Colonial Standard.*

Halifax that are most apt to represent provincial feeling. Yet even these are not fully representative, for the provincial papers, unlike their Halifax cohorts, showed little disposition to venture upon flights of constitutional argument. When they did, they often followed the lead from Halifax that suited them. In this respect Halifax papers acted as a metropolitan press. The *Morning Chronicle* even had a special weekly provincial edition. And a Roman Catholic paper, like the *Evening Express,* exercised a strong influence on its readers.

In 1864 Halifax had 11 newspapers for its population of some 25,000.[3] There was one daily, the *Morning Chronicle,* and seven tri-weeklies. The other three were weeklies of a religious bent, one Baptist, one Methodist, and one Presbyterian. The Roman Catholic paper was a tri-weekly.

In attitudes to federal government, the Halifax newspapers shared certain views with the rest of British North America. The innate dislike of the federal principle, perhaps derived from traditions of responsible government, was heavily reinforced by the American example. The Civil War was ample evidence of the divisive principle that British North Americans believed inherent in federation,[4] and every Civil War battle drove the lesson further home.

But there were also views that were rather more positive than the simple dislike of federation. Not only was federation bad, but legislative union was positively good. Legislative union was generally conceded to be the ideal form of government. If perhaps it was not applicable universally, it was certainly applicable to the union of the provinces in British North America. A constitution for a united British North America ought to approximate this ideal. Legislative union was a surprisingly persuasive ideal and its hold upon Halifax newspaper opinion is astonishing.

It is astonishing because Nova Scotian loyalties to both Nova Scotia and the Empire were very strong. Joseph Howe preferred Empire solidarity to visions of a continental domain. The Empire was tangible; the lines of communication across the accessible ocean were broad and easy, while those across the forest and rock and hills of British North America, behind Nova Scotia so to speak, were tortuous and remote. The idea of Empire ought to have conditioned Nova Scotians to divided responsibilities in government. Government in London, government in Halifax: authority had been divided between them. A federation of British North America would simply substitute a government at Ottawa for that in London. But this transposition was not made. The reason it was not was because there did not seem to be any analogy. A central government of British North America would not, in Nova Scotian eyes, be analogous to the government of Great Britain in the Empire.[5] Rather there was a belief that any central government in British North America would as-

---

[3]There was an ephemeral 12th; it was independent, and called the *Bullfrog.* It appeared for only eight months, between 1864 and 1865. It had only minor influence.

[4]There are some exceptions to this view. It may be said that many French Canadians and many Prince Edward Islanders did not share this prejudice. This whole theme is discussed at length in the writer's Ph.D. thesis for the University of Toronto, *Ideas and Politics in British North America,* 1864–1866 (1954).

[5]Howe made comparisons, but under different circumstances, and he drew different conclusions. See infra, p. 82.

sume all the major functions of government. What would a provincial government have left to do with Great Britain managing foreign affairs and defence, and the government of British North America dealing with all the other major spheres of government activity? Three governments: a bewildering array indeed! Perhaps that is the reason why federation often seemed so ludicrous to the Halifax press. In any case federation never seemed to suggest itself as a way of reconciling provincial loyalties with loyalty to a new and united British North America.

The Halifax newspapers reveal how reluctant people were to think in terms of divided responsibilities. Nowhere in all of British North America was the ideal of legislative union stated so forcibly. Nova Scotia as a whole probably did not want union of any kind; the Halifax papers were not sure; but, generally speaking, it is true to say that if there was going to be a union, they felt it ought to be a legislative union, a union of legislatures, a union that would obliterate provincial boundaries and transcend provincial prejudices. Charles Tupper was called upon to defend the Quebec Resolutions, not because they formed too centralized a constitution, but because the constitution they formed was not centralized enough. It was a federation. But federation, said the Halifax *Citizen,* "is not union. . . ."[6] It has sectional legislatures, and sectional legislatures were only nurseries of sectional feeling.[7] Howe spoke of Confederation as a monstrous creation of seven parliaments, like a seven-headed Hydra, snarling at each other yet unable to separate.

So it is that against Confederation in the Halifax press there appear two arguments, often set forth side by side; first, Nova Scotia does not want union of any kind; second, this Confederation is as weak and ineffective a union as could be imagined and is worse than useless. Time and again recurs this curious double theme, deploring the prospective end of Nova Scotia's independence, and at the same time damning Confederation as a weak and jumbled compromise with a thoroughly bad principle at its heart.

These views are not entirely consistent, and the inconsistencies in them were pointed out time and again by the newspapers supporting Confederation. But it made not the slightest difference. Joseph Howe recognized the inconsistency but avoided any public attempt to reconcile the difficulty. The two views made two excellent sticks to beat Confederation with. Hit Confederation on one side with "Nova Scotia's independence"; then hit it again on the other side with the epithet "federation." And this is just what the opposition did.

When Tupper came back from Quebec he was forced to defend the Quebec Resolutions against the bogey of federation. The whole Confederate press was forced into showing that the Resolutions really framed a legislative union—in all but name. The *Evening Reporter* said that the hue and cry against federation was the reason for its editorial "Federal vs. Legislative Union," in which it attempted to show that the alleged evils in federation were duly guarded against in the Quebec Resolutions.[8]

---

[6]*Citizen,* Saturday, November 19, 1864.
[7]Loc. cit.
[8]*Evening Reporter,* Thursday, December 8, 1864.

Tupper himself defended the Quebec Resolutions in the *British Colonist,* and from the beginning denied that the word "federal" was really applicable to them.

> We have heard of late a great deal of playing upon words in the use of the term "Federation" and other cognate expressions. People are apt to be misled by words which, like these, admit of somewhat varied definition. Consequently we, in discussing this subject, purpose dropping the use of such terms except where it cannot be avoided. When the word "Federation" is used it instantly calls up in some minds the example of the United States as the perfect embodiment of that form of Government; and the tide of anti-republican feeling amongst us at present suggests disagreeable reflections in connection with that term. What the delegates in the Quebec Conference had to provide for was, first, a strong central Government, a sufficiently firm consolidation of the provinces to insure their acting as an undivided and indivisible *unit in all cases where necessary.*[9]

But British North America comprised a vast territory, and had public institutions of some diversity. Some concessions to local government were inevitable. No general government could handle all the local and private bills that would be put forward; the men sitting in the central parliament would neither have sufficient local knowledge nor feel sufficiently the local interest. But, Tupper said,

> these [local] Legislatures will not be Legislatures in the sense in which we have been used to understand the term. They will be essentially Municipal bodies; for, under the proposed Confederation, their functions will be limited and clearly defined. Nova Scotia, for instance, will be a large Municipality under the Central Government; but just as clearly a municipality as the City of Halifax now is under our Provincial Government. . . .[10]

In short the system would, Tupper said, guard against the "absurdity" of having local governments with "sovereign" pretentions.

Having attempted to show that the Quebec Resolutions formed what was in all important essentials a legislative union, Tupper went on to say why legislative union itself had not been adopted. It might be, he said, that legislative union was the best thing in the world. Unfortunately there was one slight objection—unimportant though this objection was to "many of our more sanguine journalists"—it was impossible. Lower Canada would have none of it. Nor was there a practicable way that the objections of Lower Canada could be removed.[11]

In Halifax at this stage, i.e., December 1864, four out of the seven tri-weeklies, and the daily, supported Confederation. The *Evening Reporter* and the *Evening Express,* both Conservative, were supporting Tupper and his *British Colonist.* In addition, the Liberal daily, the *Morning Chronicle,* owned by William Annand and under the editorship of Jonathan McCully, supported Confederation. However in January 1865 McCully and his old colleague Annand parted company on the question of Confederation. Annand continued the *Chronicle,* as an

---

[9]*British Colonist,* Tuesday, November 22, 1864. (Original italics.)
[10]Loc. cit.
[11]*British Colonist,* Saturday, December 3, 1864.

anti-Confederate paper now, and the most formidable one in Nova Scotia. McCully bought out the flagging tri-weekly *Morning Journal* and made it into the *Unionist*.

However, until the split occurred, the *Morning Chronicle* gave Confederation its support, and along the lines suggested by the *British Colonist*. The Quebec Resolutions, so the *Morning Chronicle* said, would establish a truly national state.

> There will be no Upper nor Lower Canada—no Nova Scotia, New Brunswick, P.E. Island or Newfoundland, apart from the whole Federation.[12]

No one province would be injured by policies common to all; for, as the *Chronicle* put it, "the prosperity of one portion will be that of the whole. . . ."[13] As for local government, it was simply a convenience. Surely no sensible man could believe that the central government could manage

> all the roads, bridges, Post Offices, County and Township disputes, with the supervision of all the Revenues and public works from Newfoundland to Red River, not to refer to Columbia or Vancouver. . . .[14]

When McCully was freed from the restrictions of the unenthusiastic Annand, he waxed even more fervent in the *Unionist*. Some people, he said, think Nova Scotia might be swamped in Confederation. Of course it will be swamped. In this Union

> we hope and believe that Nova Scotia, like each and every one of the other Colonies comprised in it, will be effectually swamped; that we shall then hear nothing of local parties; that our public men will not be known as Canadians and New Brunswickers and Nova Scotians, but only as British Americans.[15]

Not all the Confederate press were as sanguine. The *Evening Reporter* said regretfully in October that the French Canadians, despite "a large group who want legislative union"(!) would probably insist on federal union.[16] In the end, however, after some heartburning on this subject, the *Reporter* became reconciled to federal union. It came to believe that local spirit and local institutions ought to be fostered as a check on a powerful central government. In this view the *Reporter* was quite alone among the Confederate newspapers. And even the *Reporter* was not prepared to consider anything so wild and dangerous as actual provincial sovereignty. It pointed to the American Civil War as the example of what would happen if local powers—important though these were—were ever extended beyond the strict limitations imposed on them in the Quebec Resolutions.[17]

---

[12]*Morning Chronicle*, Friday, November 11, 1864.
[13]Loc. cit.
[14]*Morning Chronicle*, Saturday, November 12, 1864.
[15]*Unionist*, Monday, January 23, 1865.
[16]*Evening Reporter*, Thursday, October 28, 1864.
[17]*Evening Reporter*, Thursday, December 8, 1864. See also Saturday, December 17, 1864.

All the Confederate journals would in the end have agreed with the *Evening Express* when it said, "We seek Union because we are, in reality, one people, and ought to be one nationality. . . ."[18] The idea of one national government over all British North America stirred them; every newspaper supporting Confederation took it up, in some cases with great force. On the other hand, concessions to local powers were accepted as unfortunate but probably unavoidable. Nothing more closely like legislative union could have been got; besides, there were some advantages in leaving the central Parliament untrammelled with petty questions of roads, bridges, and other local works.

The opposition, it will be remembered, had two main arguments against Confederation. First, that Nova Scotia did not want union at all; second, if there was to be union, federation would be the worst possible kind. The anti-Confederate press in Halifax had at this time two leading lights: the Liberal-independent *Citizen* and the Conservative *Acadian Recorder*. These were joined in January 1865 by the powerful beacon of the Liberal *Morning Chronicle*.

The Halifax *Citizen* was the foremost supporter of legislative union in the Maritime provinces—probably the foremost of all British North America.[19] Its position was clear even before the Charlottetown Conference, and its opposition to Confederation was almost wholly on the ground that Confederation was, or purported to be, a federal union. Nova Scotians, it said,

> have learned to distrust that combination of union and disunion—that expensive double machinery of government that attempts to neutralize sectional feelings and interests through a general government, while perpetuating these feelings by means of local legislatures. . . .[20]

This theme was sustained with some ability, probably by William Garvie, who was part owner and later was involved in getting up the anti-Confederate petitions of 1866. The main purpose of the *Citizen* in opposing the Quebec Scheme was, so it said, to wait for something better. Federation, it believed, must in its very nature intensify sectionalism, when the whole purpose of union was to abolish sectionalism. Although the Quebec Conference had realized this difficulty, in fact had even attempted to meet it, it had not really dealt with sectionalism effectively enough. The very existence of sectional legislatures was dangerous, for they would be the nuclei around which would crystallize sectional prejudice.

> It makes no matter that it [the Conference] has given these local legislatures very little to do. The Legislatures have to meet, and having met, they will find something to do, if they have to make employment—to elaborate grievances or increase taxes. . . . A sectional legislature under a general

---

[18]A comparable view is that of the Hamilton *Spectator*, but the *Spectator* never carried its views *a outrance* the way the *Citizen* did.

[19]*Evening Express*, Friday, December 9, 1864.

[20]*Citizen*, Tuesday, September 13, 1864.

congress is only a nursery of sectional feeling, a fruitful factory for local jealousies, grievances and deadlocks to progress.[21]

The *British Colonist*, the *Citizen* continued, says legislative union is impossible because of Lower Canada. But need this be so? "Is everything to give place to Lower Canadian sectionalism?"[22] Nova Scotia was in no urgent haste for union; there was no need for her to rush headlong into alliance with Lower Canada, a section which was blind to the very first principle of Union. Nova Scotia could afford to wait until Lower Canada outgrew her prejudices. Nor was the part of Upper Canada in this business altogether blameless. The truth of the matter was, said the *Citizen*, that Confederation simply wiped off the old scores between the Canadas. Upper Canada got her long-awaited "rep. by pop.," Lower Canada the "un-British" system of local autonomy, Nova Scotia and the rest of the Maritimes have been left to pay the piper, economically and politically.[23]

The *Acadian Recorder* preached from a similar text, though it had many more regrets for the lost—and hopeless—project of Maritimes union. Like the *Citizen*, the *Acadian Recorder* said a legislative union could be realized given time, and pressure from Lower Canada for federal union was all the more reason for delay. Had the Quebec Conference brought forth legislative union all would have been well; the *Acadian Recorder* believed that "Acadia is ready and anxious to accept it. . . ."[24]; but the Conference, despite its avowed desire to follow the British model, had in fact diverged from it considerably.

The *Acadian Recorder* thought the division of powers a particularly glaring example of this divergence. Who could ever have believed, it reflected sadly, that North American statesmen trained in British institutions and traditions would "attempt to write the duties and functions of government in a list," as if they were merchants taking stock.[25] Surely the powers of any responsible government were in essence illimitable.[26] No mere inventory of powers, said the *Recorder* scornfully, can ever be complete. What was needed in British North America's new central government was "an unwritten constitution . . . where the central power would be absolute to decide every question as it arose. . . ."[27]

The *Recorder* was prepared to allow local legislatures, but they ought to be "stripped of power," and should consist only of a small single chamber. If the local legislatures were given anything more than this, the game of constitution-making was not worth the candle.[28] Certainly there was no reason for Nova Scotia to throw over her "excellent un-

[21]*Citizen*, Saturday, November 19, 1864.
[22]*Citizen*, Saturday, December 31, 1864; see also Tuesday, November 22, 1864.
[23]*Citizen*, Thursday, November 24, 1864.
[24]*Acadian Recorder*, Monday, October 3, 1864.
[25]*Acadian Recorder*, Friday, November 18, 1864.
[26]Subject only, the *Recorder* admitted, in the case of the North American colonies, to ultimate review under certain conditions by the Crown of Great Britain.
[27]*Acadian Recorder*, Wednesday, January 4, 1865.
[28]*Acadian Recorder*, Friday, January 6, 1865.

written constitution" for the squabbles that would attend a written one.[29] And in this connection, the *Acadian Recorder* argued—shrewdly enough as it turned out—that the power of disallowance in the hands of the central government would continually embroil it in quarrels with the local governments. Such quarrels would be bound to increase sectional jealousies.

Thus the *Citizen* and the *Acadian Recorder* had similar ideas and criticisms, though they elaborated them a little differently. They both agreed that federal government was, in its very nature, dangerous to internal peace. The *Citizen* wanted legislative union, with Nova Scotia split up into municipalities: the *Acadian Recorder* was prepared to concede a small subordinate assembly. The *Citizen* thought local autonomy "un-British." The *Acadian Recorder* saw only folly in giving local governments any really independent power. Both newspapers had their particular penchants; the *Citizen* was critical of the French insistence on federal union, while the *Acadian Recorder* sighed for the lost hope of a united Acadia. Both were convinced it was better to wait than to accept the Quebec scheme.

The *Morning Chronicle* presents a somewhat different picture. This is because its opposition began in January 1865, when the arguments over Confederation had shifted. The preponderant concern of the opposition before mid-December 1864 had been the question of legislative versus federal union. After that time there was a noticeable shift of emphasis. The opposition took up, in Tupper's words, "that peculiar line of argument which is perplexing to all and interesting to none," finance. "Every man of them crammed on arithmetic."[30] But Tupper knew perfectly well how potent the question of finance and taxation was. His letters to Macdonald show plainly that he feared arguments that used the heavy Canadian debt, the Canadian tariff, the whole lurid history of Canadian finance, to say nothing of the "expensive double governments" of federation, to show that Confederation would bleed Nova Scotia white.[31] Tupper therefore resorted to the remarkable expedient of trying to redirect the argument back to what he must have thought were the safer levels of purely constitutional questions. He told the opposition that they had been sidetracked by finance. They should, he said, lay

> more stress . . . on the beauties of legislative Union and the evils of Federation. Something was done in this way, but it was too feebly put forth, and too quickly given up. . . . They have often appeared in newspapers and speeches, but only in an incidental way; or if they have sometimes been presented with vigor, the blow has not been followed up. The opposition turned their backs on such resources as these, and took up Finance.[32]

This statement was simply a red herring. The appeals of the opposition

---

[29]*Acadian Recorder*, Friday, November 18, 1864, and Friday, January 13, 1865.

[30]*British Colonist*, Thursday, January 17, 1865.

[31]Tupper to Macdonald, April 9, 1865: "I knew that it would be excessively easy to excite our people on the question of taxation. . . ." PAC, *Tupper papers.*

[32]*British Colonist*, Thursday, January 17, 1865.

press to legislative union were hardly incidental, any more than the replies of Tupper and his cohorts. But now the issues had shifted.[33] Tupper was trying to divert the pack, now in full cry on the track of finance and taxation. It was in this context that the *Morning Chronicle* published the Botheration Letters.

These first appeared on January 11th, 1865. In them Joseph Howe[34] summed up the anti-confederate arguments, political as well as financial, enlivened them with his vitality, studded them with examples from his lengthy political experience, and appealed boldly and frankly to Nova Scotian patriotism.

Howe saw Confederation as an attempt to repeat in British North America the constitutional disasters that had marked the development of the first and second Empires. Great Britain he said, had found it difficult enough to work an Imperial Parliament in harmony with local legislatures; any British North American Parliament would encounter the same results in dealing with the provincial legislatures if the Quebec plan was to be the Constitution. "Why shall we try over again an experiment which the experience of the Mother Country condemns?"[35]

The only reason for such a wretched experiment as federation was the French Canadians. Here, with an unerring eye, Howe sketched the French position:

> Ever since the Union of the two Provinces, the French Canadians, by sticking together, have controlled the Legislation and the Government of Canada. They will do the same thing in a larger union, and, as the English will split and divide, as they always do, the French members will, in nine cases out of ten, be masters of the situation. But should a chance combination thwart them then they will back their Local Legislature against the United Parliament. . . .[36]

Union was certainly not strength in these circumstances. There was no strength when "new wine was added to the old bottle." Nor was Sampson stronger after Delilah "got him confederated and cut off his hair . . ."[37]

Howe's letters deeply stirred Nova Scotian feeling. When the discussion of Confederation began in Nova Scotia, the delegates to the Conferences and others supporting Confederation controlled the majority of the newspapers; they were familiar with the plans of union and the arguments by which they could be sustained: yet by the end of five months

---

[33]The question of taxation had been brought to the forefront by a series of public meetings in December, known as the Temperance Hall meetings, in which the delegates publicly debated the question of Confederation. They began on December 12th and continued intermittently until December 31st. The best account of them is in R. H. Campbell, *Confederation in Nova Scotia to 1870* (M.A. thesis, Dalhousie University, 1939), pp. 107-19.

[34]Howe published these letters anonymously, for he was still H. M. Fishery Commissioner, but his style was well known, and apparently it was recognized. *Evening Express*, January 2, 1865: "We are not exactly certain who blows the literary bellows of the *Chronicle* now, but judging from the easy style introduced, we have a shrewd suspicion who he is."

[35]Botheration Letter no. 2, *Morning Chronicle*, Friday, January 13, 1865.

[36]Botheration Letter no. 2, *Morning Chronicle*, Friday, January 13, 1865.

[37]Botheration Letter no. 10, *Morning Chronicle*, Wednesday, February 8, 1865.

party alignments had been overturned, "the Botheration Scheme was ventilated in every part of the Province, and so far as Nova Scotia is concerned, may now be considered as dead as Julius Caesar."[38] As these words appeared, in the *Nova Scotian*[39] of Monday, March 6th, the Tilley government in New Brunswick was meeting a resounding defeat at the polls. By that time Confederation was to all appearances just as dead as Howe said it was.

The Halifax newspapers, like many others in British North America, approached Confederation with a viewpoint conditioned by their political inheritance. Responsible government seems to have engendered a genuine reluctance to admit the dual sovereignty implicit in federalism. And the British Empire only suggested to Joseph Howe reasons why federalism should *not* be adopted. One government or another had to be supreme. Apparently both could not be. In these circumstances legislative union had a powerful appeal. Most Halifax papers believed that legislative union was the only kind of union worthy of the name or the trouble of forming. It was the only kind of union that would elevate provincial loyalties to a new and higher order. Howe admitted in 1865 that the idea was an attractive one;[40] the *Citizen* and the *Acadian Recorder* were convinced of its merits. It is clear that the idea of one country united under one system of laws and institutions *a mari usque ad mare* had great emotional force. As the *Sun* remarked in 1866:

> The vision of a vast country stretching across the continent from sea to sea, with but one government and one law had in it something sublime which captivated at first sight.[41]

The irreverent Prince Edward Islanders sometimes called this "the glory argument",[42] but for all that it was a persuasive ideal. Despite the opposition to Confederation, the ideal of legislative union persisted. In 1867, M. I. Wilkins, who was strongly opposed to Confederation, spoke with fervour nevertheless of

> an incorporation of the Colonies . . . to be one flesh and bone, having one head and one heart. Where there would no longer be a Canadian, Nova Scotian or New Brunswicker, but they would all be combined under a common name.[43]

Would Nova Scotia as a whole actually have accepted a legislative union of British North America? Probably not, though it seems possible that

---

[38]*Nova Scotian*, Monday, March 6, 1865.

[39]The *Nova Scotian* was the weekly provincial edition of the *Chronicle*. It has been used when the *Chronicle* has not been available.

[40]"To myself individually it [legislative union] would have the attraction of simplicity, durability and strength." Howe to Cardwell, September 1865. Draft in the *Howe Papers*, PAC. Howe did not however say he would have supported it had it been offered.

[41]Halifax *Sun*, Wednesday, April 11, 1866.

[42]This phrase appears first in the debates of 1865. Prince Edward Island, Legislative Assembly, *the Parliamentary Reporter: debates and proceedings* (1865), p. 61.

[43]M. I. Wilkins, *Confederation examined in the light of reason and common sense* . . . (Halifax; Hall, 1867), p. 8.

Halifax would have. Nearly all Nova Scotians could, however, agree at least with the *Yarmouth Tribune's* verse:

> Our native land! of lands the flower!—
> Blest far beyond our meed
> Safe 'neath the shield of Britain's power,
> No Federation needs.[44]

---

[44]*Yarmouth Tribune,* Wednesday, January 4, 1865.

32

GEOGRAPHICAL CIRCUMSTANCES OF CONFEDERATION*

W. L. Morton

Canada is, of course, the "Big Land," and Canadians are probably more aware of their physical and spatial environment than are most peoples. Almost every textbook in Canadian history opens with a discussion of the land and the climate, and the formal discipline of geography is particularly vital and alive in Canadian schools and universities. Given this sensitiveness to land and weather, it is surprising that Canadian history has not been more dominated by environmental determinism than is actually the case. Most Canadian historians, for example, have never been seduced by the "frontier thesis," although Turner's environmental factors should be equally valid in Canada as in the United States. This refusal to subscribe to oversimplified theories has been good for Canadian history, although there has frequently been a tendency to ignore or play down not only simple determinism but also more complex variants of relationships between man and his environment. As Professor W. L. Morton argues in the following essay, geography played a critical role in Canadian Confederation. He illustrates, moreover, some of the complexities and sophistications of historical interpretation which have been most highly developed by geographers. What factors does Morton consider? What part did these factors play in the creation of Confederation? Does geography explain how the provincial particularism which characterized the pre-Confederation period was overcome? What does?

*Canadian Geographical Journal, 70 (1965), 74–87.

SUGGESTIONS FOR FURTHER READING

C. Martin, *Foundations of Canadian Nationhood* (Toronto: University of Toronto Press, 1955).

W. L. Morton, *The Critical Years: The Union of British North America, 1857–1873* (Toronto: McClelland and Stewart, 1965).

R. G. Trotter, *Canadian Federation: Its Origins and Achievements* (Toronto: J. M. Dent & Sons, 1924).

J.M.B.

G eography, in one sense at least, is man's concept of his environment at any given time. This essay is first an attempt to sketch how the people of British North America understood the geography of the northern half of the continent in the period 1857 to 1871, and what they anticipated might be made of it.

It is at once necessary, in such an attempt, to point out that in the British North American colonies as a whole, from Newfoundland to Vancouver Island, the factors making for regionalism and disunity had long prevailed, as they continued to prevail down to 1867, over the factors making for unity. Each separate colony, and also the two parts of the Canadian Union of 1840, had its own geographical views and preoccupations. It will be best to begin by noting these, in order from east to west.

The Atlantic Provinces of Newfoundland, Nova Scotia, New Brunswick and Prince Edward Island, as we now know them as a group, were maritime rather than continental in their situation and outlook, as they had always been, and as they were to continue to be. Two were more continental in nature than the others. These were New Brunswick, actually a part of the continental mass, if dominated by its Fundy and North Shore ports, and, paradoxically, Prince Edward Island. The latter was an island, of course, and profoundly insular in spirit, an insularity increased by the winter's practical separation from the continent by the ice of Northumberland Strait. But its fertile soil, its preoccupation with agriculture, and its dependence on the markets of the continent for the sale of its produce, tied it to the continent despite its insularity. Nova Scotia, on the contrary, although a peninsula geographically, was an island in spirit, looking to and living in the main by shipping and by fishing. This tie with the Atlantic world was strengthened greatly by the naval base of Halifax, which kept the province orientated to England when all the others since 1846 and the end of the old commercial system had tended more and more towards the continent, its markets and even its customs and institutions. And Newfoundland, until 1834 regarded as a fishery rather than a colony of settlement, had even fewer connections with the continent. It lived by its fishing on the Grand Banks and by sealing along the waste of Labrador and in the Gulf of St. Lawrence. It was more maritime than its Maritime sisters; nothing really attracted it to the rest of British North America, except the passing thought that its sister colonies might perhaps do more for it than England would in dealing with the difficulties of the French Shore, the source of endless difficulty with France, or with those of maintaining order and abating poverty in the outports.

In Canada East (Quebec) the story, except for the fisheries in the Gulf,
was quite different. The settled part of this subdivision of the Canadian
Union, and it was now fully settled, consisted of the St. Lawrence Valley
between the edge, marked by the Laurentian Mountains, of the Precambrian Shield to the northwest, and the end of the Appalachian system, marked by the Notre Dame Mountain to the southeast. This trough,
consisting of forested land of both high and low fertility, had now been
settled and cleared back to, and indeed over, the margin of fertile land at
the foot of each mountain limit. It was a farming country, most of which
had been farmed for several generations, some for over a hundred years.
It had for the most part passed through the inevitable frontier crisis of
passing from staple agriculture—in Canada, wheat-farming—to a more
diversified and more stable economy. A good deal of the lumber industry
of course continued, on sandy lands, on the mountain fringes, and in the
form of furniture making and, at Quebec City, of shipbuilding. But it was
mostly a region of farms and small villages and market towns serving a
population French for the most part, except in the Eastern Townships,
which, however, was now both English and French, with the French
increasing. Land had to be found for farmers' sons. But the great river
that flowed through the midst of this agricultural region was only a scant
part of its economic life. The river served the trade and commerce of the
city of Montreal, largely supplied and stimulated by the western district
of the Union, Canada West, or Upper Canada.

That area, still popularly called Upper Canada in 1857, and Canada
West officially, was Canada above the rapids of the St. Lawrence and
north of the Great Lakes. It was itself made up of a number of interior
regions. It was in its settled parts south of the Ottawa River and the edge
of the Shield divided into two regions. One was the immediate hinterland
of Montreal. This ran as far west as the Trent River and consisted of the
rugged country of the north shore of the St. Lawrence and Lake Ontario—basically, when not actually, Shield country—as far as Whitby—
and the Ottawa valley's southern and western half, itself partly an intrusion into the Shield, and partly modified Shield country in land and
forest. This was "central" Canada, in the usage of the day.

West of it—there was no sharp border—one entered "peninsular"
Ontario, again in the usage of the day. The climate was warmer, the land
not broken by rock and more fertile. It was indeed the area of the orchards and rich wheatlands of Canada, a farmer's elysium. It tended,
moreover, to look to the Erie canal and its parallel railways and the port
of New York, as at least an alternative to the St. Lawrence route and the
port of Montreal. Hence it was regarded as being somewhat "American"
in sympathy; but the habit was one Canadians were prone to, as westerners
were later to reveal in their demand for the Hudson Bay railway as an
alternative to the St. Lawrence outlet for their grain.

These areas of Upper Canada had for the most part been settled for at least a generation, and much longer of course along the great river and the lakes. The first easy returns of frontier farming on virgin soils had ended. The midge, the weevil, and the Hessian fly, in part at least the result of soils exhausted of their virgin constituents, had come to plague the farmer and begin that maturing of agricultural science and practice that was to be so rapid and so fruitful in Ontario in the next generation.

Upper Canada still had its frontier—in the Ottawa valley above Pembroke, in the counties across the edge of the Shield, Lanark, Hastings, Lennox and Addington, Haliburton, Peterborough, and in new counties such as Muskoka. Government in the late fifties, here as in Lower Canada, was cutting colonization roads into these districts, and beginning the policy of free land grants to provide lands for farmers' sons and immigrants who would otherwise go, as many were, to the prairie lands of Illinois, Wisconsin and Minnesota. But the effort and expenditures were misdirected. The acid soils of the Shield yielded, at best, crops of oats and hay for sale to the lumber camps and railway construction gangs. They were incapable of supporting a vigorous and diversified agriculture. Abandoned farmsteads, or worse, shanty farmsteads now the concern of ARDA (the Agricultural Rehabilitation and Development Agency), marked the highwater mark of agricultural settlement in the Canadas.

This Canadian impingement on the Shield was typical of the rural and agricultural Canada that had become dominant, at least socially, in the course of the century up to Confederation. It was, of course, not the only one. Since the Napoleonic wars the great Canadian industry had been the timber trade. Much Canadian wood and wood products, such as potash, had of course come from the clearing of the hardwood forests. But its great pineries stood on the sandy lands of the terraces that paralleled the Lakes and the St. Lawrence, or were the outwash of the Shield. By the late fifties the lumber camps were thrusting up the valleys of the Shield like the Saguenay, the Gatineau, the Mississippi, the Mattawa, the Ottawa itself, both for the square timber for rafting to the timber ships from Britain at Quebec, or for the mills that sent sawn lumber by rail to the booming cities across the border.

This was a natural development, an ever deeper penetration of the Canadian forest of the St. Lawrence Lowlands leading up into the Shield. Rather different was the search for minerals. The splendid reconnaissance geology of William (later Sir William) Logan had revealed the southern edge, and the most dramatic traits, of the Precambrian Shield, the erosion of its primitive mountains, the rugged nature of its terrain. It had also opened up the possibility of mineral finds. A search began that followed the southern edge of the Shield. It had led to some small mining ventures—gold at Madoc, copper at Bruce Mines—and now in the fifties the quest was pushed into Lake Superior itself, as in Allan Macdonell's venture at Michipicoten.

Macdonell had trouble both with the Indians and the Hudson's Bay Company and that fact indicates one factor in the Canadian approach to the Shield and the Northwest. Not only were Canadians profoundly ignorant of both vast areas; they resented, not without some reason, those regions being the preserves of the Hudson's Bay Company. This rivalry between the Company approaching its second centenary and the province of Canada, bursting at the seams of its Laurentian existence, was to be one of the main themes of the narrative of Confederation.

In geographical terms, it was inevitably so. In terms of the Company's own claims, Rupert's Land looked down from the northern height of land upon Laurentian Canada. It indeed quite literally did so, because some of its posts were well south of the watershed it claimed as boundary—the King's Posts on the St. Lawrence, Temiskaming on the headwaters of the Ottawa, Fort Coulonge lower down, Sault Ste. Marie, Michipicoten, Fort William. It is true that, as J. L. Galbraith details in his excellent *The Hudson's Bay Company As An Imperial Factor*, that this overlapping of Canadian and Company territory was ending. The King's Posts were sold to Canada in 1858, duties were collected on goods coming over the watershed to Timiskaming in 1858. Sault Ste. Marie, Michipicoten, Fort William, were all being agitated by incoming Canadian settlers and traders.

This was true even of Red River beyond Fort William. In 1857 George Brown's *Globe* began an agitation for the acquisition of the Northwest by Canada. The *Globe* spoke for the business interests of Toronto, who hoped to win a share of the profitable trade St. Paul already had with Red River. Some notable results followed this agitation. One was the creation of an interest among Upper Canadian farmers in the lands of Red River. Another was the assertion in Canada—not by the Canadian government—of the old French claim to all the Northwest as far as the Rockies. This was followed by the dispatch of the Red River Exploring Expedition which in its second and third years was to make the lands of the Red and the Assiniboine favourably—all too favourably—known. Still another was the movement of Canadian adventurers to Red River, traders like Henry McKenny and John Schultz, farmers like Alexander Mclean at Portage la Prairie, the two newspapermen, late of the *Globe,* William Buckingham and William Coldwell, who founded *The Nor'wester,* the first newspaper in Red River. Henceforth there was to be a "Canadian" party in Red River, a party which attacked the continued, if largely ineffective, monopoly of the Hudson's Bay Company, and which demanded annexation to Canada.

More striking than this guerilla warfare by certain Canadians against the Company was the profound ignorance of the generality of Canadians of the Shield and the Northwest. The ignorance was not absolute, of course, nor was it to continue. But it was general and profound. The extent and nature of the territory beyond the blue rim of the Shield seem not to have been known by Canadians. Canadian lumbermen did indeed exploit the forest resources of the southern Shield, and were developing the technique of lumbering in the winter northern forest. Canadian sportsmen kept alive the use of the canoe and the snowshoe and seasonally penetrated the rivers and woodlands of the southern Shield. But this vast, overhanging wilderness to the north was no part of Canadian consciousness. It was not thought of as a potential asset; it was not thought of as a barrier to the Northwest. As railwayman J. J. Ross's testimony before the Select Committee on the Hudson's Bay Company in 1857 indicates, it was ignored. The water route by the Lakes and the old waterway from Fort William to Fort Garry, improved if necessary, were thought to be a means of turning the Shield. What was alien and incomprehensible was therefore ignored, which perhaps was just as well. Without this wilful disregard of the obvious, so dourly underlined by Alexander Monro in his *The United States and Canada* in 1879, Canada would perhaps never have succeeded in making, to use Wreford Watson's fine perception, a second class route to the Northwest serve in first class fashion its national purpose to expand.

Even less, because they were more remote, was Canadian knowledge and awareness of the northwest territory of the Mackenzie and Yukon river basins, and of the Pacific slope, until the Fraser River gold rush of 1857 caught Canadian as well as world attention. Then, as to Red River, there began a Canadian migration—one is tempted to write infiltration—to the diggings, and the beginnings of Canadian interest and influence. On the whole Canadians went, not as immigrants to settle and possess the country, but as adventurers and professional men—traders, journalists, lawyers—who sought a career beyond crowded Canada, and sought on new frontiers a livelihood they might not be able to win at home.

Even more remote was the Arctic. That had long been an English and a Hudson's Bay Company interest. As such it was a faintly diplomatic, largely sporting interest, and also a means of keeping an idle naval force in training. The search for Franklin was news in Canada as elsewhere, but neither then nor for many years was there to be any popular Canadian interest in the near or the far North. The drive to expand was oriented to the prairies of the Red and Saskatchewan and the ports of the Pacific.

The strength, the demographic necessity, of the need of the Canadas to expand in years of Confederation has never, to the writer's knowledge, been adequately studied or expressed. Yet there can be no doubt of its reality as a geographical factor in the circumstances of Confederation. It was the Canadian counterpart of the need of the tobacco and cotton economy of the South to take in new soil, of the Boer to seek new veldts, of the Australian squatter to claim broad miles of the outback. It was a demographic pressure created by physical limits on the extent of fertile soil, by the exploitative nature of frontier and unskilled agriculture, by domestic traits such as large families and the pursuit of agriculture as almost the only way of life above that of the hired man or the lumberjack for the surplus sons of the Victorian household, whether English or French.

If these characteristics require much study for their clear delineation, the statistical results of this expansive growth are revealed in the crude and simple, but cumulative, first two general censuses of Canada in 1851 and 1861. The population of United Canada in 1851 was 1,842,265; in 1861 it was 2,507,677. The decade was one of phenomenal growth and contained the year of greatest rate of increase of any in Canadian history to 1951, that of 1856. The growth was both by natural increase and by

immigration, with a very high rate of retention of both natives and immigrants. The decade of 1861–71 was by contrast, to show a great falling
off, despite a general prosperity. But it was in the former decade that the
demographic pressure and the outburst of energy that led to Confederation were created.

The increase and retention of population were of course a result of
great material prosperity. The still unexhausted pineries, the ever-wid-
ening wheatfields, the Reciprocity Treaty, the Crimean War, the building
of the Grand Trunk Railway, produced the greatest and perhaps the most
effective boom of Canadian economic history. (Certainly it ranks with
those of 1901–1911 and 1951–1961). It left the Canadas equipped with
the full complement of Victorian productivity, canals, railways, factories, and a banking system to finance the crop year, the lumber drive,
and the factory run.

Government revenues and expenditures responded. In 1851 revenues
were £842,184 5s. 2d. and expenditures were £634,666 6s. 8d.[1]; in 1861
they were $12,655,581.48 and $14,742,834.28 respectively. In fact expenditures rose to levels from which there could be no retreat to former
positions, and government reluctantly carried heavy deficits from 1858
to 1863, much to the scandal of opposition and of the City of London
where Canada did its borrowing. But what the deficits really signified
was that government was committed, however counter to economic
theory, to a creative role in financing of expansion both in territory and in
transport. Politics, particularly the politics of the Liberal-Conservative
Party in power from 1854 to 1862, were positive and in the usage of the
day, nationalist, not negative and cosmopolitan.

The popular forces of expansion could be seen in action then, and may
be traced on a map of historical geography now, may indeed be noted by
the observant tourist. The towns in the valleys of the Shickshock mountains, the villages along the coasts of Gaspé, the settlements in the crev-
ices and on the slopes of the Laurentian Shield, in the counties of the
North Shore of Lower Canada, Haliburton and Muskoka in Upper
Canada, were for the most part founded in the 1850s and 1860s. As the
work of ARDA today reveals, as the abandoned farmsteads still witness,
there were farmsteads made and fields cleared on the margin of agricultural settlement. They could survive, if they survived at all, only in
virtue of virgin soil and local markets, such as lumber camps. When
these transient aids ended, the flush of rural prosperity ended also, in
removal elsewhere, or in accumulating poverty, material and spiritual.

Even in old settled districts a related movement occurred, as the
French, perhaps more frugal and more desperate, moved into the unoccupied land and then took over much of the occupied land of the Eastern
Townships and of the counties of the south and Upper Canada shore of
the Ottawa River. Glengarry and Stormont, Carleton and Renfrew became French and Roman Catholic settlements where they had once been
British and Protestant. The racial constitution of Canada was changing
within the provincial limits laid down in 1791. Lower Canada was

---

[1] In terms of 1861 dollars, approximately $4,090,000 and $3,085,000 respectively.

creating a French Canada—and a French America—beyond Lower Canada. Upper Canada was ceasing to be merely British American, and was becoming French American also.

The currents of the expansion of population were not only overrunning economic and political limits, they were also beginning to flow towards the Northwest. The north shore of Lake Huron and the Island of Manitoulin, in which the treaty of 1862 was to a degree a forerunner of the trouble in Red River in 1869, were being settled. As a result of this infiltration of settlement the District of Algoma, not a county on the traditional model but the predecessor of the Districts of the Northwest Territories, was created in 1858. Canada was organizing its own wilderness frontier, it was preparing to expand into the unorganized, the unknown, Northwest.

This Canadian expansion was not without parallel in the Atlantic Provinces. It is true that for almost a decade—since the outpouring caused by the potato famine in Ireland—those provinces had received relatively little immigration; as a result they were both less expansive than the Canadas, and more native, more American in character. But there was expansion, as is indicated by the appalling poverty of the outports of Newfoundland, the serious revolt of 1861, and the spread of settlement into the French shore. This was part of the northeastern shore and all the western shore of the Island yielded by the treaties of Utrecht and of Paris, 1783, to the French for the purposes of the French fishery. Now Newfoundland settlers, not denied the right to settle by the treaties, were beginning to move into the coast and live there throughout the year. The result was to be a half century of friction both with England and with France.

In the other provinces the best lands and much of the interior had already been settled. Pressure of population was indicated by the migration of groups of people from Nova Scotia and Prince Edward Island in ships built and manned by themselves to New Zealand and Australia. It was indicated also by the eagerness of politicians in both Nova Scotia and New Brunswick to build railways, fully to serve the interest of the trading communities, but especially to begin capital investment that would make work and win votes. Here was the fertile soil from which the project of the Intercolonial Railway kept springing. Such a railway would give the existing railways system; it would create work for population pressing on the margin of exploitable resources; it would win gratitude and votes for the politicians who could claim to have British and Canadian support for so fruitful an enterprise.

If the Canadas and the Atlantic Provinces were, however, to expand a frontier was needed. Such was lacking in the latter, except for Labrador which was not then, as it has become since, a frontier of settlement. For the Canadas, on the other hand, an abounding frontier was available beyond the constricting bulk of the Precambrian Shield. This was the Red River Valley, and the parklands and plains beyond. For a half century and more the belief had been firmly held with some assistance, interested but no doubt reasonably honest, from the officers of the Hudson's Bay Company, that this was a land suitable only for the fur trade. But the acceptance of the Northwest as a frozen wilderness properly to be left as a preserve of fur traders had rapidly been diminishing. The evidence heard before the Select Committee of the Imperial House of Commons on the Hudson's Bay Company in the first half of 1857 had given much ground to the new belief, strongly asserted by the prejudiced *Globe*, informed by anti-company people in Red River, that much if not all of the southern plains of the Northwest were suitable for agriculture.

This assertion, inspired as much by feeling against the great Company as by positive information, was suddenly greatly and in the most substantial manner reinforced by a book of substantial weight. This was the American climatologist, Lorin Blodget's work, *The Climatology of North America*, published in September 1857. Blodget combined the work of Alexander von Humboldt, of Maury, the report of Perry's expedition of 1854 to Japan, the American transcontinental railway surveys and the journals of the fur trade of the Northwest, to advance the thesis that climate was not bound to latitude, and that in particular in North America the isothermal lines ran, not east and west, but sharply northwesterly and southeasterly in summer. The effect of this was to make the great area of the continent west of Red River suitable for agriculture, settlement and railway construction. The *Globe* of Toronto and the journalists of St. Paul at once seized on this scientific support of a proposition they were advancing for other reasons. Science now supported both commercial enterprise and agrarian need.

The same year 1857 saw the launching of two expeditions which, like Blodget's work, gave considerable scientific support to the pragmatic demand that the Northwest should be open to settlement. One was the Red River Exploring Expedition dispatched by the Canadian government to determine the nature of the route to Red River, and the quality of the lands and climate of the Red and Assiniboine rivers. It came to be headed by the Trinity College scientist, Henry Youle Hind. The other was organized by the Royal Geographical Society with financial assistance from the British Government. It was headed by Captain John Palliser, R. A., a one-time hunter on the buffalo plains. He was accompanied by a well-qualified and able staff.

Hind's expedition was a reconnaissance, and suffered from the fact that Hind shared the enthusiasm of the Upper Canadian annexationists. In his report the aspects of the soil and climate favourable to agriculture were exaggerated, the unfavourable diminished, or ignored. The reports of the Palliser expedition were more cautious, more scientific, and more reliable. They warned that the construction of a railway from Fort William to Red River would be difficult and costly. They detected and described the difference between the short grass plains of the southwestern prairies (Palliser's Triangle) and those of the northeastern. They pointed out the importance and uncertainty of a frost-free growing period. The two sets of reports gave grounds both for optimism and caution.

Both had no immediate effect. The depression that began in 1857 was severe and was prolonged by the outbreak of the American Civil War.

There was neither interest nor means for the annexation of the Northwest by Canada. Its achievement depended on the realization of a greater political and economic complex of which Northwest annexation could only be a part.

In the years preceding the Confederation of 1867 there were, then, abundant reasons arising from their geographical circumstances to inspire the movement towards a wider political union. These, when combined with the desire of liberal Victorian England to be rid of the burden of defending British North America against an ever more powerful United States, and with the emergence of a United States capable not only of maintaining the union of the States but after 1865 the dominant power in the Americas, these circumstances produced what may be called the dynamics of Confederation.

The first and most powerful was the separation of the Canadas. Reunited in 1840 to realize the geographical and economic unity of the St. Lawrence River, they were now separated for all local matters to allow a degree of local self-determination that experience had proved to be necessary. Protestant Upper Canada could no longer resist the incorporation of religious orders, nor Catholic Lower Canada vote to extend the educational privileges of the Roman Catholics of Upper Canada.

The next dynamics were two, inseparably related and each embodied in a particular railway enterprise. One was the acquisition of the Northwest, the other was federal union with the Atlantic Provinces. The former required the building of a railway westward, a Pacific railway; the other of a railway eastward, the much debated Intercolonial. Nova Scotia and New Brunswick would not enter Confederation without the Intercolonial, Upper Canada would not support the Intercolonial without the Northwest and the western railway. Thus the ingrained sectionalism of British North America actually operated to promote the geographical expansion which the internal needs of its parts called for.

Next was the need of Pacific ports to ensure traffic to a westward railway. This linked up with British Columbia's desire for a railway to the Atlantic, and with the concept of a transcontinental union to match the United States. Thus the political union envisaged in the movement for Confederation was a geographical unity, each part necessary to this whole, and all designed to make up an economic system as well as a political nationality.

Finally, there was the desire to avoid absorption by the United States. American manifest destiny had seldom really turned northward; access to the Lakes and the St. Lawrence, and the same to the ports of Puget Sound, once achieved, the United States could rest easily with a northern neighbour similar in language and institutions. American policy had only one major design to the north and that was the removal of British military power. This was accomplished by the British withdrawal from the St. Lawrence in 1871. The place of the defending power of Britain, in fact little more than an irritant since the Trent Affair of 1861, was taken by the political union begun in 1867 and largely completed by 1871. The political union of the geographical fragments of British North America, a union that was no conceivable danger to the United States, left that power no cause to intervene in the affairs of a northern neighbour ready and capable of keeping its own house in order.

The geographical effects of Confederation were in accord with the motives realized in Confederation. The withdrawal of British troops from Quebec in 1871, coupled with the grant of free navigation of the St. Lawrence by the Treaty of Washington in the same year, realized practically that geographical unity of North America imposed by the Treaty of Paris in 1763, and ended by the American Revolution in 1783. At the same time the maintenance of the fortress and naval base of Halifax kept Canada still within the orbit of British seapower and attached to the British Empire, political nation though it had become. At the same time the diplomatic unity of the inshore fisheries, when Prince Edward Island came in in 1873, was, except for Newfoundland, effectively though not formally, transferred to the jurisdiction actively concerned with their retention for the people of the Maritime Provinces from New England aggression.

The third geographical effect was the ignoring of the Canadian Shield except as an obstacle between Fort William and Fort Garry. This had two effects. One was that the spirit in which Confederation was conceived was quite unrealistic, as Munro pointed out; it led to such absurdities as the oft repeated claim that Canada was to be a second United States. Second, it meant that the Shield that had yielded much of the produce of the fur trade and timber of Canada in the past, as it was to yield much of the electrical power, woodpulp and minerals of Canada in the future, was set aside for a decade while Canada concentrated on agricultural settlement and production. From this came a certain misdirection of economic policy and of social development, and a certain misplacement of political power. The Shield, not being really habitable to any degree, ought to have been made and kept a federal empire, not without representative democracy where warranted, but controlled from Ottawa with its own department of government.

As it was, the Northwest because of its geography produced new and lasting features of Canadian life. The Canadian militia was given a role to perform from 1869 to 1873, when it was replaced by the North-West Mounted Police. A new Indian regime was created. Governments, provincial and territorial, were established. Land and immigration policies were evolved; a fourth Canada, not Maritime, French, or British, was evolved, to complicate the economic and political balance of the Dominion.

And beyond was a fifth Canada on the Pacific slope. An outlet for the Canada of the St. Lawrence in 1871, it was never to rest until it became an alternate to the great river. It created an internal watershed within Canada, from which the flow westward ever increased and that eastward, relatively that is, steadily decreased. A second and a geographical ambiguity was introduced to go with the English-French one, a continental duality to accompany the racial dualism.

Thus the aspirations of British North America in the decade before

Confederation reached a geographical consummation in the four years that followed. It had expanded and it was united. It had escaped the frustrations of racial friction and provincial lack of means by creating a new combination of the various elements of British American life, economic, political and geographic. For almost a hundred years the new frustrations and limitations of that combination were to try, but never threaten, the work of Confederation. The geographical base and the political structure were in sound accord in the original concept of Confederation and in its development into the present century.

33

ACT OR PACT: ANOTHER LOOK AT CONFEDERATION*

George F. C. Stanley

The nature of Confederation, particularly the British North America Act, has been the subject of considerable debate in Canada in recent years. Whether or not Confederation was initially a compact between certain parties may at first glance appear to be a rather esoteric question, but it is really the nub of the current discussion. The nature of the agreement entered into by the various parties (or provinces) in 1867 becomes inextricably connected with the matter of federal-provincial government relations and with the entire question of the future of Canada. Probably the most critical product of an acceptance of the British North America Act as *compact* is the implication that those who entered into the bargain are entitled to renegotiate the terms of the agreement, and if unable to satisfy themselves through amendment, may abrogate it entirely. Put into concrete terms, "compact theory" is the political-constitutional heart of separatism and provincial rights. In the article which follows, Professor George F. C. Stanley—speaking as a historian—defends the notion of Confederation as compact on historical grounds. Does his interpretation of the sweep of history in the century before Confederation ring true? Is this historical background relevant for understanding the historical issue? How can the compact theory as historical fact be attacked? In the last analysis, does historical "truth" matter here? Does it matter anyplace?

Canadian Historical Association Annual Report (1956), 1-25.

SUGGESTIONS FOR FURTHER READING

J. M. S. Careless, *Brown of the Globe*, 2 vols. (Toronto: Macmillan of Canada, 1959, 1963).

D. G. Creighton, *John A. Macdonald, the Young Politician* (Toronto: Macmillan of Canada, 1952).

L. Groulx, *La Confédération canadienne, ses origines* (Montréal: Devoir, 1918).

J.M.B.

There are probably few Canadian historians, and even fewer political scientists, who have not, at some time or another, taken a second glance at the British North America Act of 1867; few of them, too, who have not lectured to their students upon the facts underlying the federal union of which the Act is the legislative expression, and commented upon the nature and essence of Canadian federalism. It is because of the generality of interest in the British North America Act that I have yielded to the temptation, not to present to you, as my presidential address, a detailed paper upon some narrow aspect of the historical researches which have absorbed my time during the last two or three years, but to offer for your consideration a few general comments upon a subject which has both a wide and a topical interest at the present time. My approach is, of course, that of the historian. I am concerned, not with what our constitution is or ought to be—that I leave to my scientifically political brethren—but with how it became what it is.

To my mind the principal factor—I do not suggest it as the sole factor but as one of the most important—in determining the course of Canadian constitutional development, has been the existence, within Canada, of two competing ethnic, cultural groups. The Earl of Durham, in his famous *Report*, chose to refer to them as "two nations warring in the bosom of a single state."[1] Were he writing in today's idiom, he might have preferred to substitute the word "co-existing" for "warring." Certainly "warring" is too strong and too inaccurate a word to describe what has been simply the political struggle on the part of the English-speaking population for supremacy, and on the part of the French-speaking population for survival. This struggle has dominated the whole story of Canadian politics. It probably accounts for the prepossession of Canadian historians with political and constitutional history. The struggle is one which still continues, and the issues are still the same; supremacy as against survival, or to use the contemporary terms, centralization as against provincial autonomy.

And yet, perhaps, if the word "warring" is unsuitable as a general

---

[1]Sir Reginald Coupland, *The Durham Report, an abridged version with an introduction and notes* (Oxford, 1945), p. 15. For an unabridged edition see that published by Methuen & Co., Ltd., London, (1902); or Sir Charles Lucas, *Lord Durham's Report on the Affairs of British North America*, vol. 2 (Oxford, 1912).

description of Anglo-French relations within the bosom of this country, Canada, at times it has not been without some aptness; for the bitterness and misunderstandings which have frequently accompanied our relations have cut, on occasions, close to the bone. That civil strife in Canada has never degenerated into civil war has been due, in part at least, to the recognition by both peoples of the necessity of some *modus vivendi* and the recognition by each of the rights of the other. The recognition and definition of these rights is the basis of the entente, understanding, pact, compact, call it what you will, which is the foundation of our political unity. Without such an entente there would have been, and would be no Canada as we know it today. Much has been written, both in the French and English languages about this pact; some of it narrow and legalistic; more of it unhistorical; much of it purely polemical. If we attempt to look upon this pact or entente as a legal contract, freely entered into by two parties and intended by them to be legally enforceable in a court of law, our vision will be so limited as to be distorted; for a pact or compact is not a contract in the legal sense. It is a gentleman's agreement, an understanding based upon mutual consent, with a moral rather than a juridical sanction. The Anglo-French understanding which alone has made government possible within the boundaries of the larger Canada has become sanctified by time and continued acceptance, until today it is looked upon by many as a convention of our constitution. It is my immediate purpose, this evening, to trace for you the origin and growth of this convention, and to discuss some of its implications in the development of our constitution.

II

It was the cession of Canada to Great Britain in 1763, that initiated the problem of which our bi-racial pact in Canada became the ultimate solution. It brought within an English, Protestant empire, a French, Catholic colony. How the one could successfully incorporate the other was the question which confronted British statesmen following the Treaty of Paris. Previous experience with Acadia offered little in the way of guidance; the expulsion of the inhabitants of the new colony was neither a humane nor a politically satisfying solution. The easy answer seemed to be assimilation; the King's new subjects might even be induced to abandon their heretical ways before they were swamped by British immigration to Canada. Assimilation was the object and essence of the Proclamation issued on October 7, 1763, over the sign manual of George III.[2] It was also the object of the long commission and letter of instructions issued the first British Governor of Canada, James Murray.[3] But assimilation, particularly a half-hearted assimilation, proved unsuccessful. Its one effect was to stiffen the heart and mind of the French-speaking population, and to give strength and cohesion to its determination to survive as a cultural and as a political group. Ten years of crimi-

---

[2]A. Shortt and A. G. Doughty, *Documents Relating to the Constitutional History of Canada, 1759-1791*, vol. 1 (Ottawa, 1918), pp. 163 ff.

[3]Ibid., pp. 173 ff, 181 ff.

nations and recriminations between the King's old and new subjects resulted in a victory for the latter. In 1774, the Quebec Act[4] definitely removed the anti-French, anti-Catholic bias of earlier policy. It cleared the way for French Canadians to accept government appointments; it guaranteed to the French those civil laws and religious privileges which, to this time, had either been denied, neglected, or merely tolerated. In brief, the Quebec Act placed the French Canadians, the King's new subjects, on a basis of political and religious equality with the English and Anglo-Americans, the so-called old subjects. The Act did not father the French fact in Canada; what it did do was to provide it with a juridical foundation. An English-Canadian historian, Professor A. L. Burt, has written "the Quebec Act embodied a new sovereign principle of the British Empire: the liberty of non-English peoples to be themselves";[5] a French Canadian, Etienne Parent, has called the Act, "a true social contract between us and England . . . the consecration of our natural right."[6] The Quebec Act, it might be noted in passing, was never repealed by the British Parliament; some of its provisions have been nullified by subsequent legislation, but it still stands, honoured by French Canadians as the Magna Charta of their national rights and privileges.

From the standpoint of the French Canadians, the guarantees afforded by the Quebec Act had come none too soon. Within several shot-riddled years, the whole demographic premise upon which the British Government had made the concessions embodied in the Act, that of a continuing predominance of the French-speaking population, had been altered by the coming of the United Empire Loyalists. From one-twentieth of the total population, the English-speaking inhabitants of the old province of Quebec increased, in a few months to one-seventh. Co-existence, or perhaps I should say co-habitation, became more difficult than ever. The constitution of 1774 became an anachronism. It brought neither understanding nor prosperity to the province. It was, in truth, satisfactory neither to the French nor to the English-speaking population; both of whom could unite their voices upon two demands only, political separation from each other and a greater share in the management of their own local affairs. The loyalists had been accustomed to and demanded elective, representative institutions on the British parliamentary model; many French Canadians, imbued with the pro-English ideas of Voltaire and the Encyclopaedists, or perhaps only with those of Pierre du Calvet, likewise demanded the political freedom denied them by the constitution of 1774. Some there were in London who wondered what the effect of the changes would be: some who argued that the establishment of a "separate and local" legislature "under any form or model which can be adopted for the purpose" would lead inevitably "to habitual Notions of a distinct interest," and "to the existence of a virtual independence" and then, "naturally to prepare the way for an entire

---

[4]Ibid., pp. 570 ff; 14 Geo. III, c. 83.

[5]A. L. Burt, *The Old Province of Quebec* (Toronto and Minneapolis, 1933), p. 200.

[6]Quoted in L. Groulx, *Histoire du Canada français depuis la découverte*, vol. 3 (Montréal, 1952), p. 75.

separation, whenever other circumstances shall bring it forward."[7] But the British government believed that it knew what the situation required: the old province of Quebec should be divided into two new, separate and distinct provinces on an ethnic basis, which the Ottawa river as the line of division; and each province should be provided with a new constitution generally assimilated to that of Great Britain, including an elective assembly as well as appointed legislative and executive councils. On June 19, 1791, Canada's second constitution by British parliamentary enactment received the royal assent and became law.[8]

Few British politicians, or Anglo-Canadians for that matter, fully appreciated what impact the Constitutional Act would have upon the problem of reconciling the French and English-speaking inhabitants of the two Canadas. Grenville seems to have had some vague ideas when he wrote to Lord Dorchester, sending him a draft copy of the new constitution, that "a considerable degree of attention is due to the prejudices and habits of the French Inhabitants who compose so large a proportion of the community, and every degree of caution should be used to continue to them the enjoyment of those civil and religious rights which were secured to them by the Capitulation of the Province, or have since been granted by the liberal and enlightened spirit of the British Government."[9] So, too, did William Pitt, when he answered Fox's objections to dividing the old province, that any effort to unite the two peoples within a single political entity governed by a single legislature, would lead only to "a perpetual scene of factious discord."[10] But Grenville, when he wrote about the rights of the French Canadians, was thinking only of how the British Government might distract their attention away from what Frenchmen, and French women, too, were doing and saying in the streets of the Paris of the Revolution. And William Pitt beclouded his argument with Fox by talking airily and unrealistically about how the French Canadians, novices in the art of parliamentary government, would be so impressed with the success attending the working of the new English-type constitution in the neighbouring province, that they would strive to enjoy its fullest benefits by uniting with English-speaking Canada. Race, religion, laws and traditions would, one after the other, be discarded as Lower Canadians sought the Holy Grail of political success and economic prosperity. The very fact of splitting Quebec into two provinces, Upper and Lower Canada, of which Fox (and the English-speaking minority in Lower Canada) had complained, would, in the end,

---

[7]Shortt and Doughty, *Documents*, vol. 2, p. 983; Discussion of Petitions and Counter Petitions re Change in Government in Canada, enclosed if Grenville to Dorchester, October 20, 1789.

[8]Ibid., vol. 2, pp. 1031 ff.

[9]Ibid., p. 988; Grenville to Dorchester, October 20, 1789.

[10]*The Annual Register or a View of the History, Politics and Literature for the Year 1791* (London, 1795), p. 111. Charles James Fox had criticized the proposed division of the old province on the grounds that "the French and English Canadians would be completely distinguished from each other. But he considered such a measure big with mischief; and maintained that the wisest policy would be to form the two descriptions of people into one body, and endeavour to annihilate all national distinctions" (*Annual Register*, 1791, p. 110).

be the means of bringing about ultimate unity. Edmund Burke spoke in a similar vein. It was a strange kind of reasoning. Granting the sincerity of their convictions, one may only conclude that they were ignorant of Canada, that they had misread its history, and that they misunderstood the whole concept of nationality.[11]

Far from encouraging the French to abandon their own consciousness of identity, the effect of the Constitutional Act of 1791 was to give renewed vigour to the idea of French Canadian separateness. It provided the French fact with a geographical as well as a political buttress. If the Quebec Act of 1774 guaranteed the survival of the French Canadians, the Constitutional Act of 1791 guaranteed the survival of French Canada. The Act of 1791 was the logical, if not the inevitable sequel to the Act of 1774. It was, in the words of Canon Groulx, "a renewed consecration of the French fact in Canada."[12]

This is not the place to discuss the internal defects of the Constitution of 1791. They are familiar to every student of our history. And yet I wonder, sometimes, whether there has not been too much inclination on the part of Canadians to treat the Act of 1791 as a kind of constitutional whipping boy; whether in trying to be political scientists, we cease to be historians. Do we not sometimes fall into the error of confusing the regime with its institutions? Do we not, all too frequently, look upon the history of Canada in isolation, forgetting that these years are, at the same time, the years of Conservative ascendancy in Great Britain, the years of the anti-liberal restrictive legislation inspired by the excesses of the French Revolution? It is wholly without significance, when considering the constitutional developments of Canada between 1791 and 1840, to recall that only three weeks before the passage of the Act the same British government which sponsored it issued the first of the decrees against sedition; and that in 1830, only seven years before blood was shed on the banks of the Richelieu, and near Gallows Hill, the Duke of Wellington had cried that he would never bring forward any measure of parliamentary reform, and that "as long as he held any station in the Government of the country, he should always feel it his duty to resist any such measure when proposed by others."[13] I do not mean to imply that the Constitution of 1791 was without fault. I simply suggest that, taking conditions as they were, there could be no answer during these years to the dilemma of how to reconcile imperial centralization and colonial autonomy. There could be no accommodation between a reactionary, metropolitan Toryism and a revolutionary provincial democracy, within the rigid framework of the constitution. Under other circumstances the Constitution of 1791 might have worked moderately well; under the circumstances such as they were, it collapsed in fire and bloodshed.

The immediate sequel to the rebellions in Upper and Lower Canada was the suppression of the ill-fated constitution and the appointment of a

[11]W. P. M. Kennedy, The Constitution of Canada, 1534-1937, an introduction to its development, law and custom (Oxford, 1938), p. 86.

[12]Groulx, Histoire du Canada français, vol. 3, p. 133.

[13]Quoted in J. A. R. Marriott, England Since Waterloo (London, 1936), p. 88.

special commissioner, the Earl of Durham, to inquire into the political situation and make recommendations regarding "the Form and Administration of the Civil Government" to be granted to the two Canadas. In his Report, dated January 31, 1839, Durham exposed the weakness of the previous regime, and recommended the concession of effective self-government to the Canadians. But if Durham favoured self-government (or what is known in our history as responsible government) it was only for a government dominated by English-speaking people. Essentially an Imperialist and a centralizer, Durham was the effective advocate of the supremacy of things English. He toyed with the idea of a federal union of the British North American provinces, but cast it aside when he realized that it would inevitably give the French Canadians of Lower Canada control over their own local affairs; instead, he recommended that Upper and Lower Canada be joined together in an indissoluble union with one government and one legislature. "I believe," he wrote, "that tranquillity can only be restored by subjecting the Province to the vigorous rule of an English majority; and that the only efficacious government would be that formed by a legislative union."[14] It was the old policy of assimilation all over again.

In 1840 the British Parliament performed the marriage ceremony. The two Canadian provinces, dissimilar in numbers, as well as in origin, faith, language and tradition, were united by the Act of Union.[15] The new constitution did not, however, follow strictly to the letter the recommendations which Durham had penned the year before. The union was not a thorough-going, punitive, Anglicizing union such as the Earl had contemplated. The demographic situation would not permit it. The fact was that the English-speaking populations of the two provinces combined did not enjoy what Durham mistakenly believed to be the case, "a clear English majority."[16] A legislative union pure and simple, instead of overwhelming the French Canadians, would have had the opposite result; it would have given them unquestioned control of the legislature of the united province, and this state of affairs, even though it might endure only a few years, was regarded as intolerable. The only way to defeat the French majority would be to crib, cabin and confine it to Lower Canada; and this could best be done by preserving as distinct, political entities the two provinces which it had been proposed to obliterate and by giving each of them equal representation in the new legislature. Since the English-speaking representatives from Upper Canada could always hope to find a few compatriots among the representatives of Lower Canada, together they would outnumber the delegates of French origin. The new constitution was thus, in effect, a vague, unintended, and undefined form of federalism, with the provinces of Upper and Lower Canada continuing in existence under the names of Canada West and Canada East, despite their union in one political entity called

---

[14]Coupland, *The Durham Report*, p. 161.

[15]W. P. M. Kennedy, *Documents of the Canadian Constitution, 1759-1915* (Toronto, 1918), pp. 536-50, 3 & 4 Victoria, c. 35.

[16]Coupland, *The Durham Report*, p. 161.

the Province of Canada. *Nil facit error nominis, cum de corpore constat*, the name does not affect the substance so long as its identity is manifest, is a maxim familiar to every lawyer.

But British policy in the end defeated itself. By denying French Canadians the temporary advantage of representation according to population, the British authorities not only strengthened French determination to hold securely every privilege gained in 1774 and 1791, they unwittingly provided them with the very means of holding these privileges, when as expected, the numbers of the French-speaking population fell below those of their English-speaking rivals. Equality of representation for the two provinces which were the political and geographical expressions of the two racial groups, was a sword which cut both ways.

The federal nature of the new constitution became more and more apparent as the years passed. Voting and acting as a political unity, the French Canadians were too large and too significant a *bloc* to be ignored. Government by one province alone, Canada West, was impossible; the collaboration of Canada East was not only desirable, it was a political necessity. And this collaboration could only be obtained upon French Canada's own terms. Sir Charles Bagot recognized this fact when, in 1842, he finally took Louis LaFontaine, the French Canadian leader, into his ministry along with his English-speaking colleague, Robert Baldwin. Sir Charles wrote to an infuriated Colonial Secretary in London:

> I knew . . . that I could not hope to succeed with the French Canadians as a Race . . . and not as a mere party in the House, unless I could secure the services of men who possessed their confidence, and who would bring to my assistance, not only their own talents, and some votes in the House of Assembly, but the goodwill and attachment of their race, and that I could not obtain such services unless I was willing to place the individuals in a position in my Council which would prevent them from feeling themselves a hopeless minority against a suspicious and adverse majority.[17]

Bagot congratulated himself that he had "satisfied" the French Canadians that the Union was "capable of being administered for their happiness and advantage, and have consequently disarmed their opposition to it". He had, however, done a great deal more. He had established the first of the dual ministries with their premiers and their attorneys-general from both Canada East and Canada West; he had pointed the way to the development of the principle of the double-majority; he had given official sanction to the federal idea implicit in the Act of 1840. The two old provinces of Upper and Lower Canada might have ceased to exist in law, but they did exist in fact and in practice, and continued to exist throughout the whole of the Union period. There was real truth in John A. Macdonald's statement in 1865, "although we now sit in one Parliament, supposed constitutionally to represent the people without regard to sections or localities, yet we know, as a matter of fact, that since the union in 1841, we have had a Federal Union."[18] There was a wide gap between

[17]K. N. Bell and W. P. Morrell, *Select Documents on British Colonial Policy, 1830-1860* (Oxford, 1928), pp. 62-71: Bagot to Stanley, September 26, 1842.

[18]*Parliamentary Debates on the Subject of the Confederation of the British North American Provinces* (Quebec, 1865), p. 30.

intention and reality. In spite of Bagot's precedent, the original idea behind the Union died hard. Metcalfe tried to win French support by appealing not to a race but simply to individuals of French origin. He failed. In the end Lord Elgin gave the *coup de grâce* to Durham's policy of denationalization and assimilation. He reverted to Sir Charles Bagot's policy, and in so doing restored the principle that an Anglo-French entente or understanding was the *sine qua non* of the successful operation of the Canadian political system. It is a principle which has lasted to the present day. Not only did Lord Elgin recall Baldwin and LaFontaine to his ministry, he also set the seal of approval upon the bi-national character of the regime by obtaining from the British authorities the abrogation of Article 41 of the Act of Union declaring English to be the one language of official record. And then, at the opening of the legislative session in January 1849, he read the speech from the throne both in French and in English.[19]

The Union did not, however, enjoy a long or peaceful life. Fundamentally the explanation for its early demise is to be found in the internal contradiction upon which it was based, for it was neither frankly federal nor unequivocally unitary. The union, indeed, managed to survive its 25 harried years only by applying the principles of disunion. The heavy hammer blows which finally brought about its end were those wielded by the French-baiting, Catholic-hating Clear Grits of Canada West and their francophobe journalist leader, George Brown. *No Popery* and *No French Domination* were the constant Grit refrain; to which was added, once Canada West had passed the neighbouring province in population, the more positive and more politically dangerous slogan, *Rep. by Pop.* Representation by population was a denial of the political understanding upon which LaFontaine and Canada East had agreed to colaborate with Baldwin and Canada West in the administration of the United Province. It meant the end of the principle of equality, the collapse of the federal concept, the exposure of Lower Canada to the rule of a hostile, alien majority, the overthrow of the entente which had alone made government possible. As the new slogan gained adherents so, too, did the idea that the premise upon which Anglo-French collaboration was based, namely the mutual acceptance of equality of status, was a vital and fundamental principle of the constitution; that it constituted, if not an unbreakable pact, at least a gentleman's agreement between the two racial groups which went to make up the population. In 1849 LaFontaine had replied to Papineau:

> It is on the basis of the principle of looking upon the Act of Union as a confederation of two provinces . . . that I hereby emphatically declare that never I will consent to one of the sections of the Province having, in this House, a greater number of members than the other, whatever the numbers of its population may be.[20]

Hincks, Cartier and Macdonald all spoke in a similar vein. In April 1861, during one of the periodic debates on representation by population,

[19]Kennedy, *The Constitution of Canada*, p. 257.
[20]Quoted in Groulx, *Histoire du Canada français*, vol. 4, p. 21.

Macdonald uttered what may possibly be the first statement in English of what we today speak of as the Compact theory of Confederation, when he said "The Union was a distinct bargain, a solemn contract."[21] This was no slip of the tongue. In 1865, during the Confederation debates, he again referred to "The Treaty of Union" between Lower and Upper Canadians.[22]

III

There is no need for me to discuss the various factors leading to Confederation—the threat of American imperialism, the fear of the westward expansion of the United States, the necessity for improved railway communications, the political impasse in Canada; all of this is familiar ground to generations of Canadian students. Nor is it necessary for me to chronicle the erratic course of the ambulatory conference of 1864 or to follow its members, bottle by bottle, as they travelled through the Maritimes and Canada, dispensing good will and self-congratulatory speeches to all who were prepared to listen to them. However, I do wish to direct your attention, for a moment, to the fundamental problem which faced the delegates who met at Charlottetown and at Quebec, that of reconciling the conflicting interests of the two racial groups and of the conflicting principles of centralization and provincial autonomy. Broadly speaking—and there are, of course, exceptions to this general statement—the English-speaking representatives, pragmatists, suspicious of ideas and generalizations, preoccupied with economic and political interests and secure in their ever increasing majority over the French Canadians, were disposed to favour a strong central government, if not actually a legislative union; the French Canadians, empiricists, uneasy, apprehensive, and deeply concerned with the survival of their culture, were by religion and by history in favour of a constitution which would, at the very least, secure them such guarantees as they had already extracted from the British government during the hundred years which had gone before. No French Canadian, intent upon preserving his national identity or bettering his political future could ever agree to a legislative union. Only federalism would permit the two, distinct, and separate, cultures to co-exist side by side within the bosom of a single state. Federalism, not a half-way, hesitant, ill-defined, semi-unitary federalism like that which had evolved out of the Act of Union, but an honest, whole-hearted, clearly-stated, precise federalism was the only solution acceptable to the French Canadian leaders. Thus, the one group was, at heart, for unity and fusion; the other for diversity and co-operation; the one was dominated by economic fact and the other, philosophical principle.

---

[21]*The Leader*, Toronto, April 30, 1861. *La Minerve* (April 25, 1861) praised Macdonald for his stand against *Rep. by Pop*: "Soyons francs! est-ce qu'il ne faut pas un grand courage, une grande force d'âme et beaucoup d'honnêteté pour agir ainsi? Mettez donc cette conduite ferme et sincère en parallèle avec la lâche conduite d'un de ses adversaires, et dites où est l'homme d'état, où est l'allié naturel das Bas Canadiens?"

[22]*Confederation Debates*, p. 28.

The fundamental opposition of these two divergent points of view does not, unfortunately, appear in the documentary fragments of the conferences which we possess; it does, however, emerge clearly in a letter written by Sir Arthur Gordon, Lieutenant-Governor of New Brunswick, following his visit to Charlottetown and his conversations with Cartier, Brown and Glat. In a lengthy despatch to the Colonial Office outlining the details of the union scheme as the Canadians had put it up to the Maritimers, Gordon wrote:

> With regard to the important question of the attributes to be assigned to the respective Legislatures and Governments, there was a very great divergence of opinion. The aim of Lower Canada is a local independence as complete as circumstances will permit, and the peculiarities of race, religion and habits which distinguish its people render their desire respectable and natural.[23]

It was at Quebec that the new constitution took form and shape. To the old capital of New France came delegates from the six provinces, the four seaboard provinces of Nova Scotia, Newfoundland, Prince Edward Island and New Brunswick, and the two provinces of Canada, which, if they did not have a juridical basis, had, at least, as I have pointed out, a factual foundation. This gathering at Quebec was the first and only constituent body in the whole of our constitutional history. All previous constitutions had been drafted, considered, and passed, by an outside authority; in 1864 the 33 representatives of the British North American provinces met, with the blessing and approval of the British Government, to do what had hitherto always been done for them.

The constitution which they adopted in the form of 72 Resolutions had already been prepared in draft form before the Canadian delegates had ever disembarked at Charlottetown. In many respects it bore a striking resemblance to an outline plan which had appeared over the name of Joseph Charles Taché in *Le Courrier du Canada* in 1857, and which had been published as a book in the following year.[24] In summary form, what the Quebec Conference decided was that the new union should be federal in character; that its central parliament should comprise two houses, the upper based on representation by provinces, and the lower upon representation by population; that the powers of the central government should be of a general character and those of the provincial legislatures of a local nature. These powers were carefully enumerated, but the legislative residuum was given to the central parliament. The French and English languages were to enjoy equal status in the central parliament and courts and in the legislature and courts of the province of Lower Canada.

---

[23]Public Archives of Canada, New Brunswick, C.O. 189, vol. 9: Gordon to Cardwell, confidential, September 22, 1864. This letter is reproduced, in part, in W. F. O'Connor, *Report pursuant to Resolution of the Senate to the Honourable the Speaker by the Parliamentary Counsel* (Ottawa, 1939), Annex 2, pp. 84–86. Large sections of the original letter were, however, omitted in the printed version. The quotation given here is one of the omitted portions.

[24]J. G. Taché, *Des provinces de l'Amérique du Nord et d'une union fédérale* (Québec, 1858).

Georges Cartier, generally, was satisfied with what had been achieved. He felt that even though he had been obliged to yield much to the demands of Macdonald and Brown and other advocates of a strong central government, he had, nevertheless, succeeded in preserving the rights and privileges of his own people and of the province in which they lived.[25] He had, moreover, succeeded in maintaining the fundamental principle of the entente between the two racial groups in Canada, equality of race, equality of religion, equality of language, equality of laws. Even George Brown, the old francophobe, had gone as far as to admit to the Canadian legislature "whether we ask for parliamentary reform for Canada alone, or in union with the Maritime Provinces, the French Canadians must have their views consulted as well as us [sic]. This scheme can be carried and no scheme can be that has not the support of both sections of the province."[26] The new constitution might not be designed to be the most efficient, but it would, at least, be just.

The next step was as easy as it was logical. Since both races were equal, a decision taken, an agreement arrived at by the equal partners on the fundamental character of the new constitution, could not be changed without the consent of each. It was, in fact a treaty, a compact binding upon both parties. This was a view which scarcely roused a dissenting voice in the Canada of 1865. Not one of the Canadians who fathered the resolutions at Quebec failed to stress the unalterable character of the agreement they had made. Macdonald said, "these resolutions were in the nature of a treaty, and if not adopted in their entirety, the proceedings would have to be commenced *de novo*."[27] McGee, in his high pitched but not unmusical voice, cried:

> And that there may be no doubt about our position in regard to that document, we say, question it you may, reject it you may, or accept it you may, but alter it you may not. (Hear, hear.) It is beyond your power, or our power, to alter it. There is not a sentence—ay, or even a word—you can alter with-

---

[25]"Objection had been taken to the scheme now under consideration, because of the words, 'new nationality.' Now, when we were united together, if union were attained, we would form a political nationality with which neither the national origin, nor the religion of any individual would interfere. It was lamented by some that we had this diversity of races, and hopes were expressed that this distinctive feature would cease. The idea of unity of races was utopian—it was impossible. . . . We could not do away with the distinctions of race. We could not legislate for the disappearance of the French Canadians from American soil, but British and French Canadians alike could appreciate and understand their position relative to each other." (Cartier, February 7, 1865, *Confederation Debates*, p. 60). Subsequently, in answer to the criticisms of A. A. Dorion, Cartier said, "I have always had the interests of Lower Canada at heart and have guarded them more seduously than the hon. member for Hochelaga and his partisans have ever done." (*Confederation Debates*, p. 714). Hector Langevin, the Solicitor-General, took the same view. He said: "We are considering the establishment of a Confederacy—with a Central Parliament and local parliaments. The Central or Federal Parliament will have the control of all measures of a general character. . . , but all matters of local interest, all that relates to the affairs and rights of the different sections of the Confederacy, will be reserved for the control of the local parliaments . . . It will be the duty of the Central Government to see that the country prospers, but it will not be its duty to attack our religion, our institutions, or our nationality, which . . . will be amply protected." (*Confederation Debates*, pp. 367-68. See also pp. 373, 392.)

[26]*Confederation Debates*, p. 87.

[27]Ibid., p. 16. Macdonald repeated this idea several times throughout his speech; see pp. 31-32.

out desiring to throw out the document. . . . On this point, I repeat after all my hon. friends who have already spoken, for one party to alter a treaty is, of course, to destroy it.[28]

Taché, Cartier, MacDougall, Brown, all of them described the Quebec Resolutions as a "treaty" or as a "pact," and argued for adoption without amendment.[29]

It is easy for the lawyer or the political scientist, three generations later, to reply that in 1865 there was no treaty really made at all, that the Compromise of Quebec could not possess the attributes of a treaty or of a legal contract. Nevertheless the historical fact remains that the men who used these terms were the men who drafted the Resolutions; they chose their words with deliberation; many of them were lawyers, they knew what they were saying. They were not, every one of them, trying to becloud the issue before the legislature or to confuse the legislators. I have found no evidence which would lead me to question their sincerity or to believe that they disbelieved their own assertions. In strict law it is probably true that the terms they used to describe the Quebec Resolutions were not all that could be desired in the way of legalistic exactitude; but to my mind these terms adequately expressed the ideas which the Fathers of the Confederate Resolutions wished to convey to their listeners and to posterity, for they spoke to both. The idea of a compact between races was not a new one in 1865; it had already become a vital thing in our history. It influenced both the political thinking and the political vocabulary of the day; and it was already on the way to become a tradition and a convention of our constitution.

The idea of a compact as I have outlined it was essentially, in its origin, a racial concept. But the meeting of the maritime delegates with those of Canada at Charlottetown and at Quebec introduced a new interpretation which has had mighty impact upon the course of our later history, namely, the idea of a compact between the politico-geographic areas which go to make up Canada. Even before the conferences it had become the common practice to identify the racial groups with the areas from which they came. When thinking of French Canadians or of Anglo-Canadians, it was all too simple to speak of them in geographical terms, as Lower Canada and Upper Canada. It was a confusion of mind and speech of which we in our own day and generation are all too frequently guilty. Almost without thought "Quebec" and "French Canadians," or "Ontario" and "Anglo-Canadians," become synonymous terms in the mouths of Canadians of both tongues. It is, of course, a slipshod way of thinking as well as of speaking, for there are French Canadians in Ontario and English Canadians in Quebec; and in many ways it has been unfortunate, for it has limited to Quebec language rights which might, under happier circumstances, have been accorded French Canadians in other parts of the country. That English did not suffer the same fate in

---

[28]Ibid., p. 136.

[29]Ibid., pp. 83, 88, 714, 720. See also chap. 2 in Sir George Ross, *The Senate of Canada, its Constitution Powers and Duties Historically Considered* (Toronto, 1914).

Quebec as did the French tongue in other provinces, was due in part to the effective role of English-speaking Quebeckers, like McGee and Galt, in the drafting of the federative act, as well as to a greater appreciation on the part of French Canadians of the need for toleration. However, the point which I really wish to make is this: once Canadians (as distinct from Maritimers) began to identify provinces with specific linguistic groups, the idea of a pact between races was transformed into the idea of a pact between provinces. And the Compromise of Quebec became a compact between the provinces which participated in the conference. I have no need to labour this point. It emerges in all clarity from a careful reading of the speeches to be found in the Confederation Debates of 1865.

However, the compact idea, was still, in 1865, peculiarly a Canadian one. It was not shared by the delegates of the several Maritime colonies who had journeyed to Quebec. From what I have seen of the debates in the legislatures and the speeches reported in the press of Nova Scotia and New Brunswick, the words so familiar in Canada, words like "pact," "treaty" or "compact" were rarely used in reference to what had been decided upon at Charlottetown or Quebec. There was never any idea in the minds of the Maritime representatives that the Seventy-Two Resolutions were sacrosanct. Thus, when Nova Scotia and New Brunswick resolved in 1866 to renew the negotiations for a federal union with Canada, they sent their representatives to London with full authority to make any changes and to conclude any new arrangement they might see fit. In the case of Nova Scotia, Sir Charles Tupper, an ardent exponent of federation on the basis of the Quebec Scheme, accepted without comment a proposal that the Quebec Resolutions should be abandoned and a new confederate agreement drawn up in conjunction with the other provinces concerned.[30] This distinction between the Canadian and Maritime approaches to the Quebec Resolutions was brought out when the Canadian and Maritime representatives met in conference in London in December 1866. Macdonald, Galt and McDougall, all agreed that the Canadians, at least, were bound to adhere to the details of the Quebec scheme. Jonathan McCully and J. W. Ritchie of Nova Scotia took the view that, as far as they as Nova Scotians were concerned, they were bound by nothing. Said John A. Macdonald in reply, "The Maritime delegates are differently situated from us. Our Legislature passed an address to the Queen praying for an Act of Union, on the basis of the Quebec Resolutions. We replied to enquiries in our last Session of Parliament that we did not feel at liberty ourselves to vary those resolutions."[31] W. P. Howland, another Canadian delegate, added, "We place ourselves in a false position in every departure from the Quebec scheme."[32]

In the end, the terms of the agreement drafted and adopted at the Westminster Palace Hotel in London in December 1866 were substan-

---

[30]*Nova Scotia Parliamentary Debates, 1866. 3rd Session. 23rd Assembly.* See debate April 3, 1866. Quotations from these debates will be found in O'Connor, *Report,* Annex 2, pp. 67-71.

[31]Joseph Pope, *Confederation: being a series of hitherto unpublished documents bearing on the British North America Act* (Toronto, 1895), p. 121.

[32]Ibid., p. 122.

tially those which had previously been discussed and accepted at Quebec. A great deal has, I know, been made of the London Resolutions as a new departure and as an effective denial of the idea of a binding pact having been concluded at Quebec; but a detailed comparison of the two sets of resolutions reveals no really substantial points of difference. The outline is similar; the wording in many instances is unchanged. Such alterations as were made, appear to have been either of a minor nature intended to clarify an ambiguity or inserted to strengthen, rather than to weaken the bi-racial, bi-cultural aspect of the pact. Certainly the people of the day who were most concerned viewed the revised resolutions after this fashion. On January 5th, 1867, the editor of *The Morning Freeman* of St. John, N.B., wrote, "If the Quebec Scheme has been modified in any important particulars they are profoundly ignorant of what the modifications are."[33] Two months later he wrote again while the British North America Bill was before Parliament:

> We ask any reasonable, intelligent man of any party to take up that Bill, compare it with the original Quebec Scheme, and discover, if he can, anything that could possibly have occupied honest, earnest men, for even a week, no matter what the particular objections to the few changes that have been made. . . . Could not all these matters have been settled as well and as much to the satisfaction of the public by letter, at an expense of a few shillings postage . . . as by this large and most costly delegation?[34]

The London Resolutions of 1866 were, in a word, little if anything more than an edited version of the Quebec Resolutions of 1864; the contractual nature of the pact remained unaffected.

The British seemed to like the idea of a provincial compact. Both the Colonial Secretary, Lord Carnarvon and his undersecretary, the Honourable Charles Adderley, accepted it as an accurate description of what was intended and what was achieved. Mr. Adderley, who introduced the Bill based on the resolutions into the British House of Commons, urged upon the members, in words which might have come straight from the mouth of Macdonald or Cartier, that no change or alteration should be made in the terms of the Bill:

> The House may ask what occasion there can be for our interfering in a question of this description. It will, however, I think, be manifest, upon reflection, that, as the arrangement is a matter of mutual concession on the part of the Provinces, there must be some external authority to give sanction to the compact into which they have entered. . . . If, again, federation has in this case specially been a matter of most delicate mutual treaty and compact between the provinces—if it has been a matter of mutual concession and compromise—it is clearly necessary that there should be a third party *ab extra* to give sanction to the treaty made between them. Such seems to me to be the office we have to perform in regard to this Bill.[35]

Lord Carnarvon, in the house of Lords, said:

---

[33]*The Morning Freeman*, Saint John, N.B., January 5, 1867.
[34]Ibid., March 7, 1867.
[35]Quoted in O'Connor, *Report*, Annex 4, p. 149.

the Quebec Resolutions, with some slight changes, form the basis of a measure that I have now the honour to submit to Parliament. To those resolutions all the British provinces in North America were, as I have said, consenting parties, and the measure founded upon them must be accepted as a treaty of union.[36]

Later in the same speech Carnarvon, after pointing out that a legislative union was "impracticable," because of Lower Canada's jealousy and pride in "her ancestral customs and traditions" and her willingness to enter Confederation "only upon the distinct understanding that she retains them," stated emphatically that the terms of the British North America Bill were "of the nature of a treaty of union, every single clause in which had been debated over and over again, and had been submitted to the closest scrutiny, and, in fact each of them represented a compromise between the different interests involved." "There might be alterations where they are not material," he continued, "and do not go to the essence of the measure. . . . But it will be my duty to resist the alteration of anything which is in the nature of a compromise between the Provinces, as an amendment of that nature, if carried, would be fatal to the measure."[37]

The legalist will, of course, reply that the intervention of the Colonial Office and the passing of the Bill as an Act of the British Parliament in effect destroyed the compactual—I prefer to avoid the word "contractual" with its juridical connotation—basis of the historical process of confederation. Perhaps it does, to the lawyer. But to the historian the simple fact remains that the officers of the Colonial Office accepted without question the assessment of the situation given them by the colonial delegates. To them the Bill was in the nature of a colonial treaty, even if such a treaty were not to be found in the classifications usually given in the text books of international law. In consequence they were prepared to leave the colonial delegates alone, to let them make their own arrangements, thresh out their own differences, draft their own agreement. Neither Lord Carnarvon nor the members of his office entered the negotiations or took part in them until the Quebec Resolutions had undergone the revision or editing to which I have referred. When they did, it was at the specific request of the delegates, with the object of acting in an advisory capacity only. Perhaps the British role is best expressed in the suggestion that the Colonial Secretary acted in the capacity of a notary reducing to proper legal terms an understanding already arrived at by the parties concerned. That certainly was the role in which Carnarvon saw himself. The British North America Act was, therefore, not the work of the British authorities, nor the expression of ideas of the British Colonial Office; it was, in essence, simply the recognition in law of the agreement arrived at originally in Quebec and clarified later in London, by the representatives of the provinces of Nova Scotia, New

---

[36]Sir R. Herbert, *Speeches on Canadian Affairs by Henry Howard Molyneux, fourth Earl of Carnarvon* (London, 1902), p. 92.

[37]Ibid., pp. 110, 130.

Brunswick, and Canada with its two divisions, Canada East and Canada West.

The British North America Act passed through its necessary readings in the House of Commons and in the House of Lords without change or alteration; on March 28, 1867, it received the Royal Assent. By royal proclamation it came into effect on the first day of July following. The new constitution was, without question, a statute of the British Parliament, and as such possessed the attributes of an ordinary statute. But it was a statute distinctly unlike any other previously passed by the Parliament at Westminster. The Quebec Act of 1774, the Constitutional Act of 1791, the Act of Union of 1840, all of them had been devised, drafted, and enacted, without reference to the people of the provinces concerned. Individuals and groups of individuals had been consulted, it is true; but the work was done and the responsibility was taken by the Imperial authorities. The British North America Act, however, was, to all intents and purposes, the work of the several self-governing, quasi-sovereign colonies themselves. The Colonial Office did no more than put the words into proper form and the British Parliament no more than give them legislative sanction. The British North America Act was, therefore, to use the words of an early Canadian jurist, "a simple ratification by the Mother Country of the agreement entered into by the provinces, which in confirming its provisions rendered them obligatory by giving them the authority of an Imperial Act."[38]

IV

But the legal supplementing of the interprovincial pact, both by the Canadian and British governments, did not mean that the problems of the coexistence of the two contending races within the bosom of a single state had been solved. Agreement there could be on broad lines of how to divide authority between the central and provincial governments, but disagreement on the details of the division was inherent in the very nature of a federal constitution, and particularly in Canada where federal union in the mouth of a Lower Canadian usually meant "the independence of his Province from English and Protestant influences"[39] and in that of the Upper Canadian, a preference for a strong central govern-

---

[38]Hon. Justice T. J. J. Loranger, *Letters upon the Interpretation of the Federal Constitution known as the British North America Act 1867* (Quebec, 1884), p. 63.

[39]O'Connor, *Report*, Annex 2, p. 83: Gordon to Cardwell, September 12, 1864. After visiting Charlottetown during the meeting of the provincial delegates and receiving daily reports from the New Brunswick delegation, Lieutenant-Governor Gordon wrote to the Colonial Secretary:

A "Federal Union" in the mouth of a Lower Canadian usually means the independence of his Province from English and Protestant influences. In the mouth of an inhabitant of the Maritime Provinces it means the retention of the machinery of the existing local Executive Government, the expenditure within each Province of the revenue raised from it, except a quota to be paid towards Federal expenses, and the preservation of the existing Legislatures in their integrity, with the somewhat cumbrous addition of a central Parliament to which the consideration of some few topics of general interest is to be confided under restraints prompted by a jealous care for the maintenance of Provincial independence.

ment.[40] Ministers and Prime Ministers might pay lip service to the doctrine of a Pact;[41] they might honestly believe in its validity; they could shelve but could not shed their centralizing proclivities. There was never any underhand conspiracy to destroy the Anglo-French entente; but there was an open-handed effort to add to the powers of the central government at the expense of those of the provinces. I need only mention the names of Macdonald, Mowat and Mercier to recall to mind the early trials of strength of the two opposing points of view. Fortunately the arbiter was there, the courts: the controversies which opposing points of view engendered were resolvable by due process of law. The powers of the federal parliament and those of the provincial legislatures had, in 1867, been carefully tabulated. All that was necessary was to apply the tabulation to each specific dispute.

Although Canadian judges were at first disposed to take the view that the British North America Act was something more than a simple British statute,[42] the judges of the Privy Council preferred to base their judgments upon the principle that the courts should always "treat the provisions of the Act . . . by the same methods of construction and exposition which they apply to other statutes."[43] These rules or methods are well known: the meaning of a statute is primarily to be gathered from the words of the statute itself, and not from what the legislature may be supposed to have intended;[44] if the words of a statute are ambiguous, recourse must be had to the context and scheme of the Act;[45] if there are seemingly, conflicting provisions in a statute, the conflicting provisions must be read together and, if possible, a reasonable reconciliation effected;[46] and, the "parliamentary history" of a statute may not be referred to for the purpose of explaining its meaning, although "historical knowledge" of the circumstances surrounding the passing thereof may, on occasions, be used as an aid in construing the statute.[47] This one concession to the historical approach did not, however, mean very much. Rarely, if ever, did references to the Quebec and London Resolutions ever have a controlling or determining effect upon the decisions handed down by the Judicial Committee of the Privy Council. Judges and lawyers are bound by precedent and rule; they cannot shake off the shackles of a rigid legalism to enjoy the freedom of historical speculation.

The remarkable thing is that the courts have, nevertheless, rarely

[40]*Confederation Debates*, p. 29.

[41]See, for instance, statements by Sir Wilfrid Laurier (*House of Commons Debates, Canada*, January 28, 1907, p. 2199); Robert Borden (ibid., January 28, 1907, p. 2199); Ernest Lapointe (ibid., February 18, 1925, pp. 297–300); Arthur Meighen (ibid., February 19, 1925, p. 335) and Richard B. Bennett (ibid., February 24, 1930, p. 24).

[42]See Strong J. in *St. Catharines Milling and Lumber Co.* v. *The Queen* (1887), 13, S.C.R. p. 606. For a criticism of this point of view see W. H. P. Clement, *The Law of the Canadian Constitution* (Toronto, 1916), p. 364; and V. C. Macdonald "Constitutional Interpretation and Extrinsic Evidence," (*The Canadian Bar Review*, 27, [February 1939] p. 2).

[43]*Bank of Toronto* v. *Lambe* (1887), 12 App. Cas., p. 579.

[44]*Brophy* v. *Attorney-General for Manitoba* (1895), A.C., p. 216.

[45]*Attorney-General for Ontario* v. *Attorney-General for Canada* (1912), A.C., p. 583.

[46]*Citizens Insurance Company of Canada*, v. *Parsons* (1881), 7 App. Cas., p. 109.

[47]*Edwards* v. *Attorney-General for Canada* (1930) A.C., p. 134.

misunderstood the meaning of the union. This is, indeed, a tribute to the skill with which the Resolutions of 1866 were transformed into legal parlance by the lawyers of the Colonial Office. And perhaps it is just as well that the lawyers have not been prepared to take readily to the historian's approach; for nothing could be more frustrating to the legal mind than the effort to determine the "intentions" of the Fathers of Confederation. Including, as they did, some Fathers favouring a unitary state and others aiming at a wide degree of provincial autonomy, to try to determine the common denominator of their joint intentions from their speeches and their public statements before and after 1867 would produce only a series of irreconcilable contradictions.[48] The one sure guide as to what the Fathers really agreed to agree upon, was the language of their resolutions, or better still, the language of the British North America Act itself. And in construing this Act in the way they have, the judges probably arrived at a more accurate interpretation than have the multitude of critics who have so emphatically disagreed with them.

There have been many and severe critics of the judgments laid down by the courts. Within the last 20 years in particular it has been the common sport of constitutional lawyers in Canada to criticize, cavil and poke fun at the *dicta* of the judges of the Privy Council and their decisions in Canadian cases. Canadian historians and political scientists have followed the legal party line with condemnations of "the judicial revolution" said to have been accomplished by Lord Watson and Lord Haldane, and the alleged willful nullification of the true intentions of the Fathers of Confederation.[49] The explanation of these attacks on the part of lawyers, professional and lay, court and class-room alike, may be found in the impact of the Great Depression of the 1930s upon the economy of the country and the inability of governments, provincial and federal, to deal with it. It is natural for the human mind to seek simple solutions and to find scapegoats for their ills.[50] If, by the simple process of an Act of Parliament, full employment can be secured and that Act of Parliament is unconstitutional, then change the constitution and the problem is solved. No provincial jurisdiction, no acknowledged right or privilege, no historic pact should be allowed to stand in the way of such an easy solution for the economic problems of the day. Facts, not principles should be the decisive determinants of history. Unfortunately, however, neither the causes nor the solution of the Great Depression were as simple as all

---

[48]See, for instance, the conflicting points of view of Sir John A. Macdonald and Sir Oliver Mowat after Confederation, although both of them had been delegates to the Quebec Conference. It is equally difficult to reconcile some of the statements of men like Galt and Macdonald, who hoped that federal union might develop into a legislative union, and those of Cartier and Langevin who upheld provincial rights, all of whom were "Fathers of Confederation."

[49]The most complete criticism from a legal standpoint is to be found in O'Connor, *Report.* See also N. M. Rogers, "The Compact Theory of Confederation," (*Proceedings of the Canadian Political Science Association* [1931], pp. 205-30) F. R. Scott, *Canada Today, a Study of her National Interests and National Policy* (Toronto, 1938) pp. 75-78; A. R. M. Lower, *Colony to Nation, a History of Canada* (Toronto, 1946) pp. 328-29. For views contrary to those of O'Connor, see V. E. Gray "The O'Connor Report on the British North American Act, 1867," (*The Canadian Bar Review,* 27 [May 1939], pt. 5, pp. 309-37).

[50]L. Richer, *Notre Problème Politique* (Montreal, n.d.), pp. 20-21.

that. The economic crisis of the 1930s was the result of a multiplicity of factors, external as well as internal, and a change in the interpretation of the British North America Act or in the Act itself would have given rise to as many new problems as it might have solved of the old. In any event, it is no part of the task of the judges to try to make the constitution fit the constantly changing facts of economic and political history.

Here is the criticism in its simplest terms. Proceeding from the basic premise that the fundamental intentions of the Fathers of Confederation were to limit strictly the powers of the provincial legislatures and give the central government a real, effective, and dominating position in the federal scheme, the critics of the courts contend that the tabulated or enumerated powers given to the federal parliament by Section 91 are, in fact, not specially allocated powers, but rather illustrations of an overriding general jurisdiction embodied in the well-known words "And it shall be lawful for the Queen, by and with the Advice and Consent of the Senate and the House of Commons, to make Laws for the Peace, Order and Good Government of Canada. . . ."[51] They argue that the enumerated powers which follow later in the wording of the same section are not in addition to this general power, but flow from it and are examples of it. The critics take the view that the courts, by attaching a primacy to the enumerated powers, have altered the balance of Sections 91 and 92, and have, in consequence, distorted the aims and objects of the founding fathers and given greater authority to the provincial legislators than it was ever intended that they should have. The cumulative effect of judicial decisions over the years has been to establish a union in which the sovereign provincial legislatures, in effect, possess a field of jurisdiction so great, and the federal parliament a field so restricted, as to alter the whole purpose of the original federative Act.

It is not for me, at this point, to discuss the syntax of the controversial sections of the British North America Act. As I said at the beginning, my approach is, of necessity, historical. And, the pre-parliamentary history of the Act appears to me to confirm the interpretation of the criticized rather than that of the critics. From the date of the publication of the first practical scheme of confederation, framers of federal constitutions in Canada have followed the procedure, not of enumerating only the subject matters upon which one party to the federation may legislate and giving all the rest (the residuum of powers) to the other, but rather of tabulating or enumerating the legislative powers of *both* parties. The scheme advanced by Joseph Charles Taché in 1857, upon which the later Canadian scheme is sometimes said to have been based, followed this course. Taché allocated to the federal parliament "Commerce, including laws of a purely commercial nature, such as laws relating to banks and other financial institutions, of a general character; moneys, weights and measures; customs duties, including the establishment of a uniform tariff and the collection of the revenues which it produces; large public works and navigation, such as canals, railways, telegraph lines, harbour works, coastal lighthouses; postal service as a whole both inside and

---

[51]O'Connor, *Report,* Annex 1, pp. 18–51.

outside the country; the organization of the militia as a whole; criminal justice including all offences beyond the level of the jurisdiction of police magistrates and justices of the peace." All the rest "dealing with civil laws, education, public welfare, the establishment of public lands, agriculture, police, urban and rural, highways, in fact everything relating to family life in each province, would remain under the exclusive control of the respective government of each province as an inherent right."[52] The draft scheme of 1864, presented by the Canadians to the Maritime delegates at Charlottetown, likewise included a series of enumerated powers to be allocated to the federal and provincial legislatures. According to this scheme the "Federal Legislature" was to be given "the control of—Trade, Currency, Banking, General Taxation, Interest and Usury Laws, Insolvency and Bankruptcy, Weights and Measures, Navigation of Rivers and Lakes, Lighthouses, Sea Fisheries, Patent and Copyright Laws, Telegraphs, Naturalization, Marriage and Divorce, Postal Service, Militia and Defence, Criminal Law, Intercolonial Works." The local legislatures were "to be entrusted with the care of— Education (with the exception of Universities), Inland Fisheries, Control of Public Lands, Immigration, Mines and Minerals, Prisons, Hospitals and Charities, Agriculture, Roads and Bridges, Registration of Titles, Municipal Laws."[53]

When the delegates finally convened at Quebec to settle the details of the federation which they had agreed upon at Charlottetown, these lists of items, were thoroughly discussed between the 21st and 25th of October. The simplest method of proceeding would have been, once it had been decided to concede the residuum of powers to the federal parliament, to define only those powers which would belong exclusively to the provinces. This course was, in fact, suggested. "Enumerate for Local Governments their powers, and give all the rest to General Government, but do not enumerate both," said J. M. Johnston of New Brunswick; William Henry of Nova Scotia echoed this view, "We should not define powers of General Legislature. I would ask Lower Canada not to fight for a shadow. Give a clause to give general powers (except such as given to Local Legislatures) to Federal Legislature. Anything beyond that is hampering the case with difficulties."[54] But the Conference did not agree. From Henry's remark we may infer that Cartier and his colleagues were determined to follow the plan of specifying in detail the powers of *both* the federal parliament and the provincial legislatures. Accordingly, Sections 29 and 43 of the Quebec Resolutions contained an enumeration of the powers of each party to the federation. Section 29 read: "The General Parliament shall have power to make laws for the peace, welfare and good government of the Federated Provinces (saving the sovereignty of England), and especially laws respecting the following subjects," and then listed 37 specific matters upon which the federal parliament would be free to legislate. Section 43 outlined 18 matters over

---

[52] J. C. Taché, *Des provinces de l'Amérique du Nord* . . . , p. 148.
[53] Gordon to Cardwell, confidential, September 22, 1864, (cf. supra, note 23).
[54] Pope, *Confederation Documents*, p. 87.

which the provinces would have exclusive jurisdiction, ending with what may be regarded as a provincial residuum of powers: "generally all matters of a private or local nature, not assigned to the General Parliament."[55] From the evidence afforded by Joseph Pope, it would appear that the delegates at no time seriously attempted to define the scope of the enumerated items or their possible overlapping, beyond George Brown's suggestion that "the courts of each Province should decide what is Local and what General Government jurisdiction, with appeal to the Appeal or Superior Court."[56] The same procedure was followed at London. Sections 28 and 41 of the London Resolutions are almost identical (with one or two small exceptions) with their counterparts in the resolutions of Quebec.

The evolution of these two sets of resolutions through the various drafts of the British North America Bill supports the view that the Fathers intended that primacy should attend the enumerated heads. Section 36 of the first "Rough Draft" of the Bill prepared by the Canadian and Maritime delegates themselves, read simply that "The Parliament shall have power to make laws respecting the following subjects" and then listed 37, one of which was the power to pass laws for "the peace, welfare and good government of the Confederation respecting all matters of a general character, not specially and exclusively herein reserved for the Legislatures [of the provinces]."[57] This was altered in the draft prepared by the Imperial Government's draftsman and dated January 23, 1867, which adopted a wording which, with only insignificant changes, was to be that of Section 91 of the British North America Act.[58] Thus, only in the final stages, after the Imperial authorities had been invited to put the bill into final shape, were the introductory words of Section 91, as we know them, interpolated, apparently for the purpose of lessening the possibility of overlapping jurisdiction. The colonial delegates had believed the enumerated powers to be mutually exclusive; only agriculture and immigration, which had been included among the powers assigned to both federal and provincial legislatures, seemed to provide any real problems, and these were to be obviated by giving federal legislation in respect to these matters precedence over that of the provinces. While there is no documentary evidence directly bearing on this point, it seems more than likely that the British draftsman pointed out the possibility of further overlapping and therefore revised the first draft of the Bill in such a way as to ensure, syntactically, the unquestioned paramountcy of the enumerated federal powers, upon which the delegates, ever since 1864, had placed so much emphasis.

That some of these conclusions may appear to be based upon circumstantial historical evidence is a valid criticism; but historians, no

[55]Copies of the Quebec and London Resolutions will be found in Pope, *Confederation Documents*, pp. 38-52, 98-110; in O'Connor, *Report*, Annex 4, pp. 49-66, and in *British North America Act and Amendments 1867-1948*, (Ottawa, 1948), pp. 39-58.

[56]Pope, *Confederation Documents*, p. 85.

[57]Ibid., pp. 130-32.

[58]Ibid., pp. 152-54.

more than lawyers, are not to be debarred from using circumstantial evidence. The majority of the problems of historical synthesis are really problems of probability.

V

But to return to the question of the Confederative pact. Despite the frequency with which Canadian political leaders have reiterated the existence of the pact, despite the legal support afforded the concept of the pact by the highest court of appeal—as late as the 1930s, the Privy Council referred to the British North America Act as a "contract," a "compact" and a "treaty" founded on the Quebec and London Resolutions[59]—the pact concept was never universally understood or wholly accepted by each and all of the provinces of Canada. Indeed the popularity of the pact idea seems to vary in some provinces in inverse ratio to their fiscal need. The concept of the pact was slow to be accepted in the Maritimes. In the early years after Confederation, there was still strong opposition to the very fact of union, and the pact upon which it was based was never very popular. In 1869 the Saint John *Morning Freeman* criticized the idea of a pact of confederation, denying that there was any continuity between the pre- and post-confederation provinces.[60] From time to time, various provinces have supported the doctrine of the pact, including New Brunswick, Alberta and British Columbia; but their support has not been marked by unanimity or consistency. Only in Ontario and Quebec has the concept remained undiminished in strength and popularity, at least in political circles, if not always in legal and academic. The Ontario-Quebec axis has transcended both time and political parties. The original alliance of Mowat and Mercier, has carried on through that of Whitney and Gouin, Ferguson and Taschereau, and Drew and Duplessis. It has always been the principal buttress of provincial autonomy.

The explanation why the pact idea has remained most vigorous in the two central provinces is to be found in their history. We need only recall the point I have established earlier this evening, the fact that the pact was, in its origin, an entente between the two racial groups of Old Canada, between the two provinces which were each the focus of a distinctive culture. Only in the two provinces of Old Canada did the racial struggle play any real part in our history; only in the two provinces of Old Canada did this struggle have any real meaning. The Maritimers of 1864 were not concerned with racial problems; their interest in federal union was largely financial, in the recovery of a passing age of sea-going prosperity. The western provinces, with the exception of British Columbia, which found its own version of a compact in the terms of union in 1871, were the offspring of the federal loins; their interest in federal union was

---

[59]*Attorney-General for Australia* v. *Colonial Sugar Co.* (1914) A.C., p. 253; *In re the Regulation and Control of Aeronautics in Canada* (1932) A.C., p. 70; *Attorney-General for Canada* v. *Attorney-General for Ontario and others* (1937) A.C., p. 351.

[60]*The Morning Freeman* (Saint John, N.B.), November 25, 1869.

in their maintenance and subsistence. But in Upper and Lower Canada federation was the solution of the politico-racial contest for supremacy and survival, which had marked their joint history since the day Vaudreuil and Amherst signed the Capitulation of Montreal. The concept of a pact of federation was thus peculiarly a Canadian one (I use Canadian in the sense in which it was used in 1864, and in which it is still used in some parts of the Maritimes today); it still remains peculiarly Canadian. Duality of culture as the central feature of the constitutional problem has a meaning and a reality to the people of the two provinces of Old Canada which it cannot have to those of the other provinces. That is why neither Ontario nor Quebec has departed in its provincial policy from the strict interpretation of the federal basis of the constitution, or from the concept of a federative pact. The identification of the racial pact, which was a very real thing in the 1850s and 1860s, with the compromise arrived at by the several provinces in 1864 and 1866, has tended to obscure the racial aspect of the bargain and to deprive it of some of its strength. The Canadian delegates to Quebec and London were thoroughly convinced that their bargain was a treaty or a pact; however, this conviction was always weaker among the Maritimers than among the Canadians, and especially the French Canadians, whose principal concern as a vital minority, has been and must be the survival of their culture and the pact which is the constitutional assurance of that survival.

It is the racial aspect of the pact of Confederation which gives the pact its historicity and confirms its continued usage. If the population of Canada were one in race, language, and religion, our federation would be marked by flexibility; amendment would be a comparatively easy matter where there was agreement upon fundamental issues. Since history has given us a dual culture, with its diversities of race and language, we must maintain a precarious balance between the two groups; and our constitution is rigid and inflexible. That is what I meant, when I said at the outset, that the historic pact of the Union has become, by acceptance and usage, a necessary convention of our constitution. It will continue to be such so long as the minority group retains its numbers and its will to survive.